SOCIAL CAPITAL

Social Capital

An International Research Program

Edited by

NAN LIN AND BONNIE H. ERICKSON

OXFORD
UNIVERSITY PRESS

OXFORD

UNIVERSITY PRESS

Great Clarendon Street, Oxford OX2 6DP

Oxford University Press is a department of the University of Oxford.
It furthers the University's objective of excellence in research, scholarship,
and education by publishing worldwide in

Oxford New York

Auckland Cape Town Dar es Salaam Hong Kong Karachi
Kuala Lumpur Madrid Melbourne Mexico City Nairobi
New Delhi Shanghai Taipei Toronto

With offices in

Argentina Austria Brazil Chile Czech Republic France Greece
Guatemala Hungary Italy Japan Poland Portugal Singapore
South Korea Switzerland Thailand Turkey Ukraine Vietnam

Oxford is a registered trade mark of Oxford University Press
in the UK and in certain other countries

Published in the United States
by Oxford University Press Inc., New York

© The several contributors 2008

The moral rights of the authors have been asserted
Database right Oxford University Press (maker)

First published 2008

British Library Cataloguing in Publication Data

Data available

Library of Congress Cataloging-in-Publication Data

Data available

Typeset by SPI Publisher Services, Pondicherry, India
Printed in Great Britain
on acid-free paper by
Biddles Ltd., King's Lynn, Norfolk

ISBN 978–0–19–923438–7

1 3 5 7 9 10 8 6 4 2

Contents

List of Figures   ix
List of Tables   xi
List of Abbreviations   xvii
List of Contributors   xix

1. Theory, Measurement, and the Research Enterprise on Social Capital   1
   Nan Lin and Bonnie H. Erickson

SECTION I. THE POSITION GENERATOR METHODOLOGY: ITS RELIABILITY, VALIDITY, AND VARIATION

2. Position Generator Measures and Their Relationship to Other Social
   Capital Measures   27
   Martin van der Gaag, Tom A. B. Snijders, and Henk Flap

3. Position Generator and Actual Networks in Everyday Life: An
   Evaluation with Contact Diary   49
   Yang-chih Fu

4. Social, Cultural, and Economic Capital and Job Attainment: The
   Position Generator as a Measure of Cultural and Economic Resources   65
   Henk Flap and Beate Völker

5. The Formation of Social Capital among Chinese Urbanites: Theoretical
   Explanation and Empirical Evidence   81
   Yanjie Bian

SECTION II. MOBILIZATION OF SOCIAL CAPITAL

6. The Invisible Hand of Social Capital: An Exploratory Study   107
   Nan Lin and Dan Ao

7. Social Resources and Their Effect on Occupational Attainment through
   the Life Course   133
   Hester Moerbeek and Henk Flap

8. A Question of Access or Mobilization? Understanding Inefficacious Job
   Referral Networks among the Black Poor   157
   Sandra Susan Smith

SECTION III. SOCIAL CAPITAL, CIVIL ENGAGEMENT, SOCIAL PARTICIPATION, AND TRUST

9. Social Networks of Participants in Voluntary Associations   185
   René Bekkers, Beate Völker, Martin van der Gaag, and Henk Flap

10. The Internet, Social Capital, Civic Engagement, and Gender in Japan   206
    Kakuko Miyata, Ken'ichi Ikeda, and Tetsuro Kobayashi

11. Social Capital of Personnel Managers: Causes and Return of
    Position-Generated Networks and Participation in Voluntary
    Associations   234
    Ray-May Hsung and Yi-Jr Lin

12. It's Not Only Who You Know, It's Also Where They Are: Using the
    Position Generator to Investigate the Structure of Access to Embedded
    Resources   255
    Sandra Enns, Todd Malinick, and Ralph Matthews

13. Gender, Network Capital, Social Capital, and Political Capital: The
    Consequences of Personal Network Diversity for Environmentalists in
    British Columbia   282
    D. B. Tindall and Jeffrey J. Cormier

14. Civic Participation and Social Capital: A Social Network Analysis in
    Two American Counties   308
    Marc Porter Magee

SECTION IV. SOCIAL INSTITUTIONS AND INEQUALITY IN SOCIAL CAPITAL

15. Why Some Occupations Are Better Known Than Others   331
    Bonnie H. Erickson

16. Marriage, Gender, and Social Capital   342
    Gina Lai

17. Access to Social Capital and Status Attainment in the United States:
    Racial/Ethnic and Gender Differences   364
    Jennifer L. Moren Cross and Nan Lin

18. Access to Social Capital and the Structure of Inequality in Ulaanbaatar,
    Mongolia   380
    Catherine A. Johnson

19. Assessing Social Capital and Attainment Dynamics:
    Position Generator Applications in Hungary, 1987–2003   394
    Róbert Angelusz and Róbert Tardos

References   421
Index   446

List of Figures

4.1. The adapted version of the position generator, the cultural and economic resources of 30 occupations in the respondents' network   70

4.2. Average attained economic and cultural status by cultural and economic status of the network (source: Survey of the Social Networks of the Dutch (SSND), $N = 1,007$)   72

4.3. Path diagram of regression models of classic attainment model (SSND, $N = 1,007$)   73

4.4. Path diagram of regression models of occupational status *including status of network with friends and acquaintances* (SSND, $N = 1,007$)   73

4.5. Path diagram of regression models of *economic status* (SSND, $N = 1,007$)   74

4.6. Path diagram of regression models of *cultural status* (SSND, $N = 1,007$)   74

4.7. Path diagram of regression models of *economic status including status of friends and acquaintances* (SSND, $N = 1,007$)   75

4.8. Path diagram of regression models of *cultural status including status of friends and acquaintances* (SSND, $N = 1,007$)   75

5.1. A conceptual model explaining the formation of social capital   85

6.1. Hierarchical cluster analysis on follow-ups   128

6.2. Hierarchical cluster analysis on follow-ups for those who received routine job information that was not about their current jobs   129

10.1. The causes and the consequence of social capital   212

10.2. Path model between social capital and civic engagement (male respondents)   226

10.3. Path model between social capital and civic engagement (male respondents)   227

10.4. Path model between social capital and civic engagement (female respondents)   228

10.5. Path model between social capital and civic engagement (female respondents)   229

11.1. The hierarchical cluster analysis of accessed associations   246

13.1. A synthetic theoretical model explaining political capital   289

13.2. Empirical model explaining political capital   289

15.1. The election survey item   335

17.1. Conceptual diagram of the model   369

List of Tables

2.1. Position generator items, associated occupational prestige and socioeconomic index values, and item responses (SSND 1999–2000; $N = 999$)   31

2.2. Distribution characteristics of social capital measures from position generator items (SSND 1999–2000; $N = 989$–996)   35

2.3. Correlations between social capital measures from position generator items (SSND 1999–2000; $N = 989$–996)   36

2.4. Correlations between social capital measures from position generator items and name generator items (SSND, 1999–2000; $N = 1,004$)   37

2.5. Correlations between social capital measures from position generator items and resource generator items (SSND 1999–2000; $N = 1,004$)   39

2.6. Proposal for parsimonious measurement strategy in social capital studies (basis: SSND 1999–2000)   43

3.1. A profile of informants and their contact diaries   53

3.2. Alters listed in position generator and contact diary—Case 1   55

3.3. Alters listed in position generator and contact diary—Case 2   57

3.4. Alters listed in position generator and contact diary—Case 3   58

3.5. Comparison of tie strength and contact situation among selected PG alters, omitted PG alters, and non-PG alters—Case 1 and Case 3   61

3.6. Logit regression of the alters selected in PG—Case 1 (logit coefficients) dependent variable: selected in PG = 1, omitted from PG = 0   62

3.7. Logit regression of the alters selected in PG—Case 3 (logit coefficients) dependent variable: selected in PG = 1, omitted from PG = 0   63

4.1. Average status attained by network resources (Survey of the Social Networks of the Dutch (SSND), $N = 1,007$)   71

4.2. Regression of child achieved cultural and economic status on status of father, education, and status of network (source, SSND, $N = 1,007$; standardized coefficients)   76

5.1. Dependent variables: social networks and social capital, the 1999 Five-Chinese City Survey ($N = 4,521$)   93

5.2. Descriptive statistics of independent variables ($N = 4,521$)   94

5.3. Regressions predicting social capital and social networks   99

6.1. Sample characteristics   116

6.2. Position generator and social capital capacity indexes   120

6.3. Factor structure of capacity of social capital prior to current job   121

6.4. Regression on social capital capacity   122

6.5. Determination of receipt of routine job information [exp (B): odds ratio]   123

6.6. Analyses for occupational attainment and supervision   124

6.7. Analyses for economic returns (annual income and high wage)   126

6.8. Distribution of follow-ups for those who received routine job information   128

7.1. Access to occupations through social ties   142

7.2. Access to occupations through social ties   142

7.3. Access to occupational categories by father's occupational prestige   143

7.4. Access to occupations through relatives, friends, and acquaintances ($N = 2,362$)   144

7.5. Regression of access variables on father's occupational prestige and respondent's education and on strength of ties variables   145

7.6. Regression of prestige of first and current job on social background variables and social capital variables   146

7.7. Regression of the way a job was found on the number of occupations accessed   148

7.8. Regression of the way a job was found on the number of occupations accessed through friends, acquaintances, and relatives, respectively   149

7.9. Unsuccessful job applications and the way people learned about the job broken down by education, father's education, prestige of first job, age, and sex   151

7.10. Logistic regression of unsuccessful applications on social background and social capital variables   152

7.11. Regression of current job on unsuccessful application, social background variables, and social capital variables   152

8.1. Summary of sample characteristics ($N = 103$)   166

8.2. Position generator variables by neighborhood poverty status   167

8.3. Position generator variables by employment and neighborhood poverty status   169

8.4. Motivation for distrust by reluctance to assist   171

8.5. Orientation to providing job-finding assistance, reputational concerns, and history of being burned by neighborhood poverty status   174

8.6. Position generator variables by (dis)trusting job contacts   176

8.7. Position generator skill level by (dis)trusting job contacts   177

8.8. Position generator variables by orientation to providing job-finding assistance   177

8.9. Position skill level by orientation toward providing assistance   178

9.1. Correlations among indicators of collective and individual social capital   196

9.2. Logistic regression analysis of instrumental membership   199

9.3. Logistic regression analysis of expressive membership   200

9.4. Logistic regression analysis of expressive and instrumental membership by gender   202

10.1. Summary of sample characteristics ($N = 1,002$)   213

10.2. Summary of position-generated variables in the whole sample   214

10.3. Means of diversity of contacts by gender of respondents   215

10.4. Percentages of participation in online communities   217

10.5. Multiple regressions for diversity of contacts   218

10.6. Means of civic engagement, general trust, and generalized reciprocity by gender   220

10.7. Multiple regressions for civic engagement   222

10.8. Multiple regressions for general trust and generalized reciprocity   224

11.1. Summary of sample characteristics ($N = 126$)   241

11.2. Summary of variables on position-generated networks and participation in voluntary associations   244

11.3. Factor structures of access to social capital   247

11.4. Access to social capital by kin   247

11.5. The determinants of social capital variables   248

11.6. The determinants of job prestige and log income   250

12.1. Descriptive statistics for relevant response and predictor variables ($N = 1,763$)   268

12.2. Summary of variables by gender ($N = 1,763$)   269

12.3. Civic participation by gender ($N = 1,763$)   270

12.4. Relationships between membership/social activities and social ties ($N = 1,763$ for all; all correlations calculated using Kendall's $\tau\text{-}b$)   271

12.5. Model predicting weak ties inside the community ($N = 1,763$)   272

12.6. Model predicting weak ties outside the community ($N = 1,763$)   274

13.1. Standardized regression coefficients for model predicting *political participation* using *personal network range* variables as an independent variable   296

13.2. Standardized regression coefficients for model predicting *political participation* using diversity of *occupational ties* as an independent variable to explain political participation: by gender   297

13.3. Standardized regression coefficients for model predicting *political participation* using diversity of *organizational ties* as an independent variable to explain political participation: by gender   298

13.4. Standardized regression coefficients for model predicting *political participation* using diversity of *ties to politicians* as an independent variable to explain political participation: by gender   299

14.1. The community context   316

14.2. Correlations among social network, civic participation, and neighborhood   317

14.3. Regressions of network diversity on participation, with controls   319

14.4. Regressions of network diversity on 12 forms of civic participation listed in order of percentage of respondents' involvement   321

14.5. Regressions of network diversity on 12 forms of civic participation listed in order of percentage of "very familiar" membership — 323

14.6. Correlations among network diversity, civic diversity, and four means of communication — 324

14.7. Regression of network diversity and civic diversity on newspaper, television, telephone, and email, with controls — 325

15.1. The extent to which occupations are known — 336

15.2. Percentage of knowing men, women, or both in occupations — 337

16.1. Sociodemographic characteristics of respondents — 347

16.2. Gender comparison of network integration, network size, and social capital — 350

16.3. Regression analyses of network overlap — 351

16.4. Regression analyses of network size — 353

16.5. Regression analyses of social capital — 354

16.6. Regression analyses of social capital by gender — 357

16.7. Regression analyses of social capital by length of marriage — 358

16.8. Regression analyses of social capital by length of marriage and gender — 359

16.9. Regression analyses of social capital by degree of network overlap — 360

16.10. Regression analyses of social capital by degree of network overlap and gender — 361

17.1. Descriptive statistics for variables used in analysis ($N = 557$) — 374

17.2. Co-racial/ethnic homophily in access to social capital ($N = 557$) — 375

17.3. Structural equation measurement model estimates controlling for age, gender, and race/ethnicity ($N = 557$) — 376

17.4. Unstandardized coefficients from the structural equation model ($N = 557$) — 376

18.1. Occupation categories — 382

18.2. Logistic regression analysis on access to occupations as a function of the gender, education, income, and location of respondents ($N = 312$) — 383

18.3. Comparison of means between men and women and diversity of contacts — 387

18.4. Multiple regressions on effect of age, education, employment, income, marriage, and residence location of respondents on diversity of contacts, by gender of respondents — 389

19.1. Predictors of material attainment—changes in the relative role of social resources from 1987 to 1998 — 403

19.2. Predictors of personal earnings by distinct educational categories, 1987 and 1997–8 — 405

19.3. Predictors of personal earnings by distinct sex and age categories, 1987 and 1997–8 — 406

19.4. Social milieus mapped by patterns of accessed occupations, 1997–8 — 409

19.5. Mean scores of broad occupational categories on the five components/connectedness with milieu-types, 1997–8   411

19.6. Predictors of personal earning—modeling decomposed nexus diversity by total population and broad educational categories, 1997–8   412

List of Abbreviations

AEIC	Association of Edison Illuminating Companies
BC	British Columbia
CBS	Central Bureau of Statistics
CFS	Carmanah Forestry Society
CPI	Consumer Price Index
EPZs	export processing zones
FDI	foreign direct investment
FL	Florida
GDR	German Democratic Republic
GNI	Gross National Income
GSS	general social survey
IQV	index of qualitative variation
IRT	item response theory
ISEI	international socioeconomic index
KMT	Kuomintang Party
MCSUI	Multi-City Study of Urban Inequality
NELA	National Electric Light Association
NORC/GSS	General Social Surveys, National Opinion Research Center
NORS	National Opinion Research Services
OLS	Ordinary Least Squares
PA	Pennsylvania
PG	Position Generator
PMSA	primary metropolitan statistical areas
RCP	Resilient Communities Project
SCWC	Sierra Club of Western Canada
SES	socioeconomic status
SIOPS	Standard International Occupational Prestige Scale
SNA	social network analysis
SP	science park
SSHRC	Social Sciences and Humanities Research Council of Canada
SSND	Survey on the Social Networks of the Dutch
WCWC	Western Canada Wilderness Committee

List of Contributors

Róbert Angelusz is Professor at the Institute for Sociology, Eötvös Loránd University, Budapest; angelusz@ludens.elte.hu

Dan Ao is an Assistant Professor of Sociology at the Chinese University of Hong Kong; danao@duke.edu

René Bekkers is an Assistant Professor at the ICS/Department of Sociology, Utrecht University, the Netherlands, and a Researcher at the Department of Philanthropic Studies, Vrije Universiteit Amsterdam; R.Bekkers@fss.uu.nl

Yanjie Bian is a Professor of Sociology at the Department of Sociology, University of Minnesota; bianx001@umn.edu

Jeffrey J. Cormier is an Assistant Professor in the Department of Sociology, King's College, University of Western Ontario; jcormie4@uwo.ca

Sandra Enns is a doctoral candidate at the Department of Sociology, the University of British Columbia; senns@interchange.ubc.ca

Bonnie H. Erickson is a Professor of Sociology at the Department of Sociology, University of Toronto; ericson@chass.utoronto.ca

Henk Flap is Professor of Sociology at the ICS/Department of Sociology, Utrecht University, the Netherlands; h.flap@fss.uu.nl

Yang-chih Fu is a Research Fellow and Director at the Institute of Sociology, Academia Sinica, Taiwan; fuyc@sinica.edu.tw

Ray-May Hsung is a Professor of Sociology at the Department of Sociology, National Chengchi University, Taiwan; hsung@nccu.edu.tw

Ken'ichi Ikeda is a Professor at the Department of Social Psychology, Graduate School of Humanities and Sociology, the University of Tokyo, Japan; ikeken@l.u-tokyo.ac.jp

Catherine A. Johnson is Assistant Professor, Faculty of Information and Media Studies, University of Western Ontario, Canada; cjohn24@uwo.ca Studies, University of Wisconsin-Milwaukee; Caj3@uwm.edu

Tetsuro Kobayashi is a Research Associate at Information and Society Research Division, National Institute of Informatics, Japan; k-tetsu@parkcity.ne.jp

Gina Lai is an Associate Professor at the Department of Sociology, Hong Kong Baptist University; ginalai@hkbu.edu.hk

Nan Lin is the Oscar L. Tang Professor of Sociology, at the Department of Sociology, Duke University; nanlin@duke.edu

Yi-Jr Lin is a doctoraal candidate at the Department of Sociology, Tunghai University, Taiwan; yijr@seed.net.tw

Marc Porter Magee is the Director of Communications and Research, at Connecticut Coalition for Achievement Now (ConnCAN); marc.magee@conncan.org

Todd Malinick is a doctoral candidate at the Department of Sociology, the University of British Columbia; malinick@interchange.ubc.ca

Ralph Matthews is a Professor of Sociology at the Department of Sociology, the University of British Columbia; ralphm@interchange.ubc.ca

Kakuko Miyata is Professor of Social Psychology, Department of Sociology, Meiji Gakuin University; miyata@soc.meijigakuin.ac.jp

Hester Moerbeek is an Assistant Professor at Wageningen University, the Netherlands; Hester.Moerbeek@wur.nl

Jennifer L. Moren Cross is a Research Associate, Department of Ophthalmology, University of Alabama at Birmingham School of Medicine; jmcross@uab.edu

Sandra Susan Smith is an Assistant Professor of Sociology at the Department of Sociology, University of California, Berkeley; sandra_smith@berkeley.edu

Tom A. B. Snijders is Professor of Statistics in the Social Sciences at the University of Oxford, and also Professor of Statistics and Methodology at the University of Groningen, the Netherlands; tom.snijders@nuffield.ox.ac.uk

Róbert Tardos is Senior Researcher of the Research Group for Communication Studies of the Hungarian Academy of Sciences at Eötvös Loránd University; tardos.robert@ppk.elte.hu

D. B. Tindall is an Associate Professor in the Department of Sociology, the University of British Columbia; tindall@interchange.ubc.ca

Martin van der Gaag is Assistant Professor in social networks analysis at Urije Universiteit Amsterdam, Faculty of Social Sciences, Department of Public Administration and Organizational Science; gaag@xs4all.nl

Beate Völker is an Associate Professor at the ICS/Department of Sociology, Utrecht University, the Netherlands; B.G.M.Volker@fss.uu.nl

1

Theory, Measurement, and the Research Enterprise on Social Capital

Nan Lin and Bonnie H. Erickson

In the past two decades, social capital has gained currency in the social sciences as a paradigm for capturing the contributions of social elements in explaining a wide variety of individual and collective behaviors. It has been used to examine topics ranging from status attainment and social mobility, competitive advantage in economic organizations, and political participation to psychological and physical well-being (see recent reviews in Portes 1998; Lin 1999*b*, 2001*a*; Burt 2000*a*). Its research saliency reflects the recognition by many social scientists that collective and individual actions significantly depend on the social context in which such actions are embedded. It also reflects the sense that, as a type of capital, the term shares an affinity with other forms of capital, such as human capital and cultural capital, which have been formulated to understand the utility of resources in affecting life chances. It seems logical to argue that social elements may constitute capital as well.

However, as research expands into numerous arenas and applications, both the conception and operationalization of social capital have become diverse and multidimensional. There looms an increasing danger that the term will become a handy catch-all, for-all, and cure-all sociological term. This danger may have emanated from conceptual generality in its formative development. For example, Coleman has proposed conceiving of social capital as "these social-structural resources" and consisting of "a variety of different entities having two characteristics in common: They all consist of some aspect of a social structure, and they facilitate certain actions of individuals who are within the structure" (Coleman 1990: 302). As such, any and all elements of the social structure are candidates, and any of them become social capital when they work for a particular outcome in a particular context for a particular actor—a tautological argument. When interpreted liberally, little theory is implicated or needs to be evoked, and falsification becomes impossible (Portes 1998; Lin 2001*a*).

In extending Coleman's definition, Putnam (2000: 19) defines social capital as "connections among individuals—social networks and the norms of reciprocity and trustworthiness that arise from them." While the intention may be to specify social networks as social capital and its anticipated consequences (the norms of reciprocity and trustworthiness), many subsequent empirical studies have blurred these elements as interchangeable or alternative elements and definitions of social capital. Extensive emulation of Putnam's work with civic engagement (e.g. participation of voluntary association) has further added to the confusion. Theoretically, it is not clear how social capital or social networks are associated with civic engagement, trust, or norms of reciprocity. These diverse approaches have led to numerous and often freely construed measures of "social capital" in empirical studies[1] and rendered it impossible to assess the validity of the concept and theory, or reliability and accumulation of empirical findings. Contradictory findings cannot be resolved because of the lack of any uniform theoretical or measurement understandings. Without a clear and firm theoretical basis, a standard measurement, and a collective research enterprise built around these shared understandings of theory and measurement, with contributions from scholars around the world, social capital may eventually suffer the fate of faddish notions in social sciences and die an untimely (or timely) death.

For two decades, a significant number of scholars have subscribed to a common definition of social capital (resources embedded in social networks), employing a standard measurement (the position generator methodology), and conducting original research. Their sustained efforts have consistently demonstrated the utility of the concept of social capital in diverse arenas of research and cultural and societal settings. Their works, all with original data designs and collections, have contributed to the substantiation, development, and expansion of social capital as a viable scientific concept and theory. Much of their work has been scattered in different publication outlets and in different societies and continents. As this collective enterprise has gained in quantity and maturity, it seems appropriate to introduce and present some of the most recent works in a single volume. The present volume serves this role in the critical junction of the theoretical and research developments of social capital. While the space limitation does not do justice to the number of publications available, the volume editors commissioned active scholars in North America, Europe, and East Asia to offer original reports of their own research studies. As such, they showcase the fruition in a consistent theory-measurement-research enterprise and the continued viability of social capital as a guiding concept and theory in social sciences today.

This chapter briefly reviews the core theoretical basis of social capital and the standard measurement shared in these works, and introduces the studies under the themes where the selected works make their contribution.

---

[1] Measures, e.g., have included network features (strength of ties, density), social relations (parent–child, parent–teacher, number of friends or peers, influence of friends or peers), frequency of interactions, perceived relations or support, as well as generalized or interpersonal trust, cohesion, reciprocity, and so forth.

1.1. THE THEORETICAL GROUNDING OF SOCIAL CAPITAL

To gain a better understanding of social capital, it is necessary to get acquainted with the concept of capital and to place it in the context of different theoretical types of capital (Lin 2001*a*). "Capital," first of all, is both a concept and a theory.[2] As a concept, it represents investment and possession of resources of value in a given society. A theory of capital enumerates a mechanism by which such valued resources are produced, reproduced, and accumulated (Lin 2001*b*). For example, in the classical theory of capital, Marx defines capital as part of the surplus value created in a production process (Brewer 1984; Marx [1849] 1933, [1867, 1885, 1894] 1995). He also proposes a theory of capital (Lin 2001*b*)— it entails exploitative relations between holders of the means of production and the labor force. By extracting surplus value from the difference between the production value (wages paid to the laborers) and the marketing and consuming values (prices charged in the trade and consumer markets) in goods and services, the exploiters (i.e. the capitalists) are able to reinvest part of it for further production and reproduction of the goods, and therefore further extract surplus values.

Neocapitalist theories offer a similar definition of capital but different theories, in that they argue that investment and return of capital may apply to the laborers as well. The human capital theory, for example, postulates that investment in certain human resources (skills and knowledge) may also generate economic returns, even for laborers participating in the production market (Johnson 1960; Schultz 1961; Becker [1964] 1993). Thus this process affords the laborers the ability to strike down exploitative relations by investing in skills and knowledge with which they can negotiate for wages above what is necessary for subsistence of survival, and extract surplus value for themselves. Part of the surplus value can then be reinvested into gaining further skills and knowledge; thus capital is reproduced and accumulated. Cultural capital (Bourdieu [1972] 1977; Bourdieu and Passeron 1977), another neocapitalist theory, proposes a theory on the investment in rituals and routines as valued resources or capital. It describes the processes of the production and reproduction of routinized practices and behaviors imposed by the elites on the mass. Through social mechanisms such as education and schooling, the mass is indoctrinated into "mis-recognizing" the elitist practices and behaviors as normative. In this manner, the elites are able to produce and reproduce these routinized behaviors and practices as principles of practices, rewarding themselves and maintaining their advantage from generation to generation. Presumably, the nonelites also receive rewards for their complying practices and behaviors.[3]

---

[2] Applying both definition and theory to a term has been a common practice in the social sciences. It is also true in the cases of classical Marxist theory, human capital, and cultural capital as well as social capital.

[3] Bourdieu focused on the rewards and benefits reaped by the elites in these processes. It is unclear what happens to the nonelites who "mis-recognize" the elitist practices and behaviors as normative

Likewise, social capital theory conceives of capital as valued resources that generate returns to individual and collective actors in a society. A core orientation in the conceptual development in the notion of social capital is that it is capital captured in social relations, and its production is a process by which "surplus value" is generated through investment in social relations (Lin 2001a: 2). Social capital argues for investment in social relations so that resources embedded in these relations become the mechanism with which individual and collective actors gain advantage. There is not or should not be any dispute that social capital *is rooted precisely at the juncture between individuals and their relations and is contained in the meso-level structure or in social networks*. That is, individual actors and their relations form the basis of social capital, and these relations have microconsequences for the individuals as well as macroconsequences for the collectivity. The general premise that social capital is network based is acknowledged by all scholars who have contributed to the discussion (Bourdieu 1980, [1983] 1986; Lin 1982; Coleman 1988, 1990; Flap 1991, 2001; Burt 1992; Putnam 1993a, 1995, 2000; Erickson 1995, 1996b).

However, social capital goes beyond mere structural or network features. The fundamental and consistent definition of social capital focuses on *resources embedded in social relations and social networks*. Lin (1982, 1999a, 2001b) argues that social capital should be defined as resources embedded in social networks or social resources. They are not goods possessed by the individual. Rather, they are resources accessible through one's "direct and indirect ties" (1982: 132). A similar definition was offered by Bourdieu ([1983] 1986); for him it is "the aggregate of the actual or potential resources which are linked to possession of a durable network of more or less institutionalized relationships of mutual acquaintance and recognition" (248). Likewise, Flap (2001) identified three elements of social capital: (*a*) the number of others who are prepared to help, (*b*) the extent to which they are prepared to help (the strength of the tie), and (*c*) what is at the other end of the tie in terms of accessible resources. In this conceptualization, social capital is, first of all, resources, and secondly, linked to relationships. It is resources embedded in social networks.

Through such social relations or through social networks in general, an actor may borrow or capture other actors' resources (e.g. their wealth, power, or reputation). Such resources and relations facilitate information flow, influence flow, rendering of social credentials, and affirmation of self-identity (Lin 2001b: 20–1), which in turn can be used to generate returns in the marketplace. A theory of social capital, therefore, focuses on the production and returns of social capital and explicates how individual and collective actors invest in social relations through which they gain access to diverse and rich resources for expected returns (Lin 1982, 1999b; Burt 1992).

and adopt such practices and behaviors for themselves. My suspicion and derivation from his work is that these complying nonelites would likewise be rewarded, although perhaps to a lesser extent than the elites.

1.2. THEORETICAL DEVELOPMENTS AND EXAMPLES IN THIS VOLUME

1.2.1. Occupational Returns to Social Capital

Of the many possible returns to social capital, getting a good job is one of the most important in a person's life and in research. This was the first return to be studied in this paradigm, and research on it continues to flourish in current work, including several projects reported in this volume. A person with strong social capital has links to others located throughout the occupational hierarchy, increasing the chances that the person knows a person well located to help in gaining a good position. Lin (1999*b*) reviews numerous studies showing that network diversity leads to a more prestigious job, partly because those with diverse networks get job-search help from contacts with higher prestige. Network diversity is also an important job qualification for many upper-level jobs that include extensive networking. Employers often want to hire people with rich networks for such positions in order to appropriate the employee's social capital for the firm, so those with good networks get good jobs even if they do not use a contact (Erickson 2001).

Research in this volume extends past work in several ways. It shows that social capital is linked to occupational attainment in several different kinds of societies: the United States (Moren Cross and Lin; Lin and Ao), the Netherlands (Flap and Völker; Moerbeek and Flap), Hungary (Angelusz and Tardos), and Taiwan (Hsung and Lin). Social capital leads to several kinds of desirable job outcomes, including but not limited to the occupational prestige that was the first kind of return to be examined. Moerbeek and Flap show that social capital leads to occupational prestige in the Netherlands; Angelusz and Tardos show that social capital yields higher income in Hungary; and Moren Cross and Lin show that stronger social capital leads to higher levels of class, supervision, and income in the United States.

Still more important, research in this volume expands our understanding of just how social capital provides occupational gains. Chapters 6, 7, and 8 in Section II provide important insights into how and why social capital is mobilized and why it sometimes cannot be mobilized, insights summarized and discussed in the introduction to this section below.

Societies vary in how resources are distributed in stratification hierarchies, in how social networks connect different parts of hierarchies, and in the cultural and political rules governing how networks may be used to access resources. Thus the details of the processes by which social capital leads to better jobs necessarily vary with the context. Important contributions from past work include Bian's (1997) work showing that strong ties played a stronger role in China when jobs were supposed to be allocated by the state, and the use of private network connections was illegitimate and dangerous, though irresistibly useful. Studies in this volume further advance our understanding of structurally induced variations.

Flap and Völker report on the Netherlands, in which the higher levels of the occupational hierarchy are divided into two structurally distinct sectors, one with occupations richer in cultural capital (average education) and one with occupations richer in economic capital (average income). Network connections are stronger within sectors than between them, and contacts strong in a sector's dominant form of capital have more power and influence within that sector, so doing well in either sector requires good contacts in that sector. The better a person's access to occupations rich in cultural capital, the higher the cultural capital (but not economic capital) of the occupation the person can enter. The better a person's access to occupations rich in economic capital, the higher the economic capital (but not cultural capital) of the person's occupation.

Angelusz and Tardos report on occupational attainments in two different contexts: Hungary before and after transition toward a market economy. As people increasingly sought jobs allocated by private employers instead of the state, personal connections became even more important, and as the private search of occupational advantage became legitimate, weaker ties could be more safely used. Thus the income returns to social capital grew substantially overall. But these income returns did not grow for all. The young, but not the old, got better income for their social capital, and young women made especially large gains in their returns to their social capital. The connections between occupational stratification on the one hand, and gender and life course stratification on the other, altered as older men found their networks, their work experience, their education, and themselves outmoded and unwelcome in the new labor market.

1.2.2. Political Returns to Social Capital: Power and Influence

Not only do those with superior social capital gain greater rewards in the world of work, but they also gain more influential roles in politics and civic life. The more diverse the people one knows, the more different kinds of things they are interested in, well informed about, and like to talk about. Thus the more diverse one's network, the wider the range of one's own cultural repertoire, including interest and information (Erickson 1996). This general principle applies to politics: people with diverse networks are exposed to a variety of political information and points of view, stimulating their own political knowledge and reflection. The more diverse the network, the more likely it is that one or more people in it is a political enthusiast who recruits people for political activities. Thus social capital leads to political activities of various kinds, both in the environmental movement in British Columbia (Tindall and Cormier) and in the rather different social and political context of Japan (Miyata, Ikeda, and Kobayashi).

Diverse networks stimulate a range of interests, many of which people can pursue in voluntary associations. The most common reason for joining an association is being asked by someone one knows, and those with diverse networks are more likely to know association members who can act as recruiters for their groups. Thus social capital goes with higher levels of voluntary association membership and activity in the United States (Magee), Canada (Erickson 2004; Enns, Malinick, and Matthews), the Netherlands (Bekkers, Völker, van der Gaag, and Flap), and Taiwan (Hsung and Lin).

Social capital leads people into more powerful positions in political and associational life, giving them more than average leverage on political and social issues, and contributing to political as well as occupational stratification.

Networks are relevant to politics in other ways besides shaping position in political stratification. Notably, networks provide both political influence and a person's perception of politically relevant aspects of social stratification as represented or misrepresented in the person's social world, and hence networks shape political opinions (e.g. Erickson 2006). While these are important topics, they fall outside this volume's emphasis on social capital as a source of instrumental rewards, so we will not pursue them further here.

1.2.3. Sources of Social Capital

Since social capital is a powerful source of both occupational and political advantage, it is important to know which kinds of people gain more social capital. Alas, social capital winners tend to be people who are in advantaged social locations that systematically provide better chances to enrich networks, so social capital often reproduces and reinforces stratification hierarchies.

Unequal access to social capital begins at birth with important ascribed statuses. One of the most important is family background. Social capital is greater for those with parents in higher stratification positions, such as fathers with higher socioeconomic status (Moerbeek and Flap) and fathers with higher education or income (Flap and Völker). Social capital gains are also shaped by other ascribed social locations, notably gender and race or ethnicity. Women often have less social capital than men, especially in contexts with stronger gender stratification systems. Men have more social capital in Taiwan (Hsung and Lin), Japan (Miyata, Ikeda, and Kobayashi), and several other Asian countries reported elsewhere, but not in British Columbia (Tindall and Cormier) or Canada as a whole (Erickson 2004), nor indeed in most highly developed Western nations. Erickson and Miyata discuss these contextual differences using Japan as an example of a highly gender-stratified nation and Canada as an example of a much less gender-stratified society, showing that the higher level of macrolevel gender stratification leads both to unequal access to social settings and to unequal network gains within most settings. In societies with ethnic or racial variation, groups higher in the ethnic stratification system gain more social capital. Thus whites have more social capital in the United States (Moren Cross and Lin) and in Canada (Erickson 2004).

Education is a series of social settings in which people meet, a valued and attractive form of social status in modern societies, and a powerful way to gain other forms of high status like better jobs, so better education also leads to better social capital. In addition to the many earlier studies documenting this trend, see Bekkers, Völker, van der Gaag, and Flap, Flap and Völker, and Moerbeek and

Flap on the Netherlands; Johnson on Mongolia; Enns, Malinick, and Matthews on British Columbia; and Angelusz and Tardos on Hungary.

Later in the life course, social capital becomes greater for those who work for pay and thus meet people through work (e.g. Enns, Malinick, and Matthews). Social capital gains from work are especially great for those who work in higher-level positions, which typically include much more diversified, in-depth inter-action with people. For example, Bekkers, Völker, van der Gaag, and Flap find that those with higher incomes have higher social capital. The more unequal a stratification system is, the greater the resulting differences in social capital, so Angelusz and Tardos find that wealth had a greater effect on social capital after the free-market transition in Hungary.

Once again the impact of one system of stratification, like work, depends in part on how it is related to others, like gender. Working in Hong Kong, Lai finds that the social capital of wives is more strongly related to their husbands' education or employment than to their own, while the social capital of husbands depends on their own education or employment but not at all on their wives'. This is striking evidence of the greater power of men in both work and family life.

Voluntary associations bring together people who share some kind of common interest, but who can be very different in other respects including their social positions, so research in many contexts routinely finds that voluntary association activity goes with higher social capital. Examples in this volume include Enns, Malinick, and Matthews, who add to the core finding by showing that the location of associational activity shapes the location of social capital.

The rise of modern communication systems has provided another form of inequality that shapes social capital. Social capital is greater for those more active in Internet communities in Japan (Miyata, Ikeda, and Kobayashi), and for more active users of newspapers, telephones, and the Internet in the United States (Magee). While this may seem like a new story, it is just a new version of the same old story of advantage reproduction. Those who use new technologies more, like those who are more active in voluntary associations, are those with higher levels of education and occupation.

1.3. MEASURING SOCIAL CAPITAL WITH THE POSITION GENERATOR

1.3.1. The General Strategy of Position Generators

If social capital is the valuable resources embedded in a person's social network, how can we measure this in a valid and practical way? At first the task may seem overwhelmingly difficult. An average North American knows hundreds of people, far too many to ask about. There are many kinds of potentially useful resources that one's contacts can provide, again far too many resources to ask about directly. But the measurement task becomes surprisingly easy when we remember that most important resources are concentrated in particular parts of social structure. Instead of asking about social relationships with particular people, or people with particular resources, we can ask about social links to social locations in which different kinds of resources are concentrated. Measures of this general kind, designed to assess access to social positions, are called "position generators."

Since work is the master role in modern societies, the role most strongly and broadly associated with other aspects of a person's life and social condition, occupations are the first social locations we should consider (though not the last or only ones, as we discuss below). While occupations differ in many ways, their prestige is one variable strongly linked to resource differences. People in occupations with higher prestige generally have greater amounts of instrumentally useful resources, including income, education, and authority in the workplace. As we go down the ladder of prestige the overall volume of resources may fall but the kind of resources concentrated in an occupation changes to include some useful ones that are relatively rare in high-prestige occupations. For example, occupations with middling prestige include many with a wealth of blue-collar skills. Even the lowest-ranking occupations provide some access to modest but useful resources, such as job opportunities based on employee referrals. Thus the more that a person knows people from all levels of the occupational hierarchy, the more likely it is that the person has access to a wide range of potentially useful resources.

Lin and Dumin (1986) were the first to develop a practical measure using this strategy. They selected a number of occupations ranging from high to low in prestige and asked respondents whether they knew anyone in each of the occupations. Most of the position generators developed later are variations on this original template. Using our 20 years of experience since Lin and Dumin (1986), including work in this volume, what do we know about the performance characteristics and good design principles for this kind of measure?

The most critical consideration is the choice of occupations. The occupations should have prestige levels sampled from the full range in the society, from very high to very low prestige, to sample access to a wide range of resources. At every level of prestige there are multiple occupations. From these candidates, the researcher should choose one with many occupants. If there are very few people in an occupation, few respondents will know any of them, which is bad for the researcher (who wastes a question by getting answers with little or no variation) and bad for the respondent (who feels more like a social loser with every position to which he or she does not have a link). It is also useful to choose occupations from different sectors of the economy, to represent some horizontal as well as vertical differences in occupational resources. It is important to choose occupations with clear, widely understood titles that appear in the society's census. Using census information, one can choose occupations with many incumbents as just recommended. And one can pursue some important research questions, as Erickson does in this volume.

Another important consideration is the nature of the respondent's access to an occupation. Researchers define this by the wording of the start of their question. For example, several projects reported in this volume use some variation on the question "among your relatives, friends or acquaintances, are there any in the following kinds of work?" This asks the respondent to think of a wide range of contacts, from the strongest to the weakest, and so samples all of the potential access throughout the person's network. Sometimes a researcher wants to focus on somewhat stronger ties, because extremely weak ties are not likely to be productive, and so uses a question like "please think of people you know by name and by sight and well enough to talk to." However, the role of ties of varying strength is an important research question that should be investigated, not decided in advance of evidence, by asking respondents to report ties of different kinds. For example, Tindall and Cormier's position generator asks people to report separately on three kinds of ties they may have to an occupation: acquaintance, close friend, and relative.

1.3.2. Measurement Performance

Experience shows that such classic position generators, based on occupational positions, have outstanding performance characteristics. They are highly reliable. For example, Angelusz and Tardos report on Hungarian research in this volume. They found cross-sectional reliability (Cronbach's α) of .83 in two different studies, one in 1987 and one (in a much changed Hungary) in 1997–8. Others (e.g. Erickson 2004) report similar high cross-sectional reliabilities. The 1997–8 Hungarian study was a panel study where the same people were interviewed twice, with a year between interviews. The total number of occupations a person reported links to in 1997 was strongly related to the number reported a year later (with a correlation of .62) despite the passage of a year in a rapidly changing society.

These position generators are also highly practical. Response rates are very high; in fact, almost all respondents answer this question. For example, Tindall and Cormier report a 98.7 percent response rate. The question takes up little time, roughly 2–4 mins of interview time, depending on the number of positions. The position generator works well in any research format. Examples in this volume include face-to-face interviews (e.g. Johnson), telephone interviews (e.g. Moren Cross and Lin), mailed questionnaires (e.g. Erickson), and questionnaires dropped off for self-administration and then picked up by researchers (Miyata, Ikeda, and Kobayashi). With suitable adaptation (which involves issues we discuss below), the classic position generator has proven performance in very different kinds of societies and communities. Examples of varied community and national contexts include small towns in West Coast Canada (Enns, Malinick, and Matthews), the environmental protection movement in British Columbia (Tindall and Cormier), two quite different Florida counties (Magee), poor inner-city neighborhoods in the United States (Smith), export zones in Taiwan (Hsung and Lin), the city Ulaan Baatar in Mongolia (Johnson), Hong Kong (Lai), and large cities in mainland China (Bian). Examples of wider regional studies include a representative section of Japan (Miyata, Ikeda, and Kobayashi). And examples of national samples from different kinds of societies include the United States

(Moren Cross and Lin), Eastern Europe (Angelusz and Tardos), Western Europe (e.g. Flap and Völker), and Canada (Erickson).

Of course, none of this impressive reliability and practicality would matter if the measure were not valid. Fu's innovative and remarkable work is invaluable here. He persuaded noble volunteers to keep detailed records of all their interactions with other people for several months (an arduous task indeed), then gave them a position generator several months later. Every time someone in an occupation on the position generator appeared in a respondent's diary, the respondent reported knowing someone in this occupation when answering the position generator. Thus people do remember the occupations of the people they know, and report them even when they do not know the people well nor see them often. Moreover, people reported knowing 20–40 percent more occupations on the position generator than appear in the diaries, as they should, since we all know people whom we do not encounter for months at a time. Thus the quick and easy position generator reports network contacts as accurately and more completely than the dreadfully onerous but meticulous diary method.

People sometimes wonder whether the position generator taps valid relationships, or relationships that may be weak but have enough content to provide potential access to alter's resources. For example, they wonder whether a respondent may report "knowing" a cashier regularly met at the local store, even though the respondent does not know the cashier's full name and never talks to the cashier about anything of substance. Erickson reassures us on this point: Canadians report knowing a cashier at the same low rates as they report knowing people in other low-prestige occupations.

Besides these valuable forms of direct validation, the position generator has amply demonstrated "construct validity," meaning that it is related to the things it theoretically should be related to if it is a valid measure of social capital. All of the substantive chapters in this book are examples, as is a wealth of earlier research.

1.3.3. Comparing Position Generators to Other Network Measures

Another important methodological consideration is how well the classic position generator works compared to OTHER ways of measuring networks. The diary method is in many ways the "gold standard" because of its detail and accuracy, but as discussed earlier, it is totally impractical for large samples because of its outrageous demands on the respondent's time. Another more feasible and very popular approach is the "name generator." Researchers ask respondents to name particular people to whom they are related in a particular way: the several people they feel closest to (Wellman 1979), the people with whom they discuss important matters (Marsden 1987), the people they can call on for important kinds of social support (Fischer 1982), and so on. Then the respondent answers "name interpreter" questions about the people named: age, gender, education, occupation, ethnicity, and so on. This can provide a rich record of the social locations (and hence resources) in this part of a person's network. Sometimes the respondent also describes the ties among the contacts, such as which ones know each other, to show the social structure of the network as well.

Name generators are invaluable for some research purposes, and appropriately popular, but they do not work for our goals. Theoretically, the critical problem is that name generators are limited to a small number of closer relationships. People can give such detailed reports only on a small number of connections, typically as few as three to five, and never more than a dozen or so, because each description of each connection takes a good deal of time and effort. Close ties are important for some outcomes, especially the more demanding forms of social support, which usually come primarily from closer connections who are motivated and informed enough to help (Wellman and Wortley 1990). In that respect, close ties are an important form of social capital. But our focus is on social capital that provides access to a diverse array of resources and hence yields instrumental profits like getting a good job, becoming more active and influential in civic life, and gaining diversified information. Diverse access to resources is precisely what close ties do not provide, because the closer people are to you, the more they are much like you: similar in social location, in resources, and in whom they know. McPherson, Smith-Lovin and Cook (2001) give a useful review of work on this well-documented "homophily" effect. Because strong ties are so similar, and provide such poor linkage to resources different from the ones a person has herself, weaker ties are routinely stronger in providing instrumental gains (Granovetter 1974; Lin 1982; Burt 1992). Further, the name generator is limited to people connected to the respondent in selected ways, such as being a close friend or being the provider of particular kinds of help. People linked to the respondent in other, unstudied ways are also potential sources of useful resources but their potential contributions remain unknown.

In contrast, the position generator forgoes detailed information about individuals in a network in favor of information about the social locations represented in the network. This allows us to probe the entire network, including ties of every level of strength, and to fully sample the spectrum of resources a network contains.

The final alternative approach we consider is the newly developing "resource generator," which van der Gaag, Snijders, and Flap report on in this volume. They ask whether the respondent knows anyone who has each of 30 resources, including economic resources (e.g. "Do you know anyone who earns over 5,000 florins a month?" [a high income]), information ("Do you know anyone who knows a lot about government regulations?"), skills ("Do you know anyone who can work with a PC?"), and support ("Do you know anyone who can be talked to about important matters?"). The study also included a name generator and a position generator. The number of occupations a person reported access to was rather strongly correlated with the number of resources he or she reported access to, and especially well correlated with resources useful in instrumental action rather than expressive social support, consistent with our claim that the position generator measures access to useful resources associated with positions in an occupational structure. Various measures based on the name generators had little or no relationship with measures based on the position generator, consistent with our claim that name generators measure a special small part of a network and are a poor guide to the network as a whole.

The resource generator has two strong advantages: it measures specific resources of interest directly and it measures access to resources from any part of the network including people who do not have an occupation. However, it demands that the researcher know the useful kinds of resources to ask about, in a specific context, in advance of observing the uses the resources may have. As van der Gaag, Snijders, and Flap point out, the value of potential resources depends on the social context and is quite variable from one social setting to another, in ways not yet well understood. Meanwhile, we know that valuable resources of different kinds tend to concentrate in different layers of stratification hierarchies in every society. Locally valuable resources help people to get into more powerful positions, and powerful positions use power to leverage greater access to these resources. Thus the position generator is a more widely useful way to measure access to all of the resources associated with stratification hierarchies in any setting. Van der Gaag, Snijders, and Flap recommend the position generator for those doing research on instrumental outcomes, while also suggesting supplementing it with some resource generator items when useful resources are well understood.

1.3.3.1. Adapting the Position Generator to Different Social Contexts

Social settings have different occupational structures, with different kinds of associated resources, so researchers usually sample prestige levels and occupations from the specific occupational prestige hierarchy of the community or society being studied. Thus all the position generators in this volume are theoretically equivalent, but no two are the same in their choice of occupations. Some lists include occupations uniquely important in the research context. For her study in Ulaan Baatar, Johnson includes lama, an important religious position in Mongolia though one that no one else in this volume would find it useful to include, as well as small kiosk owner and foreign agency worker. Similarly Bian includes party official, or Communist cadre, a very important position in China. Some lists are largely composed of occupations important in one specific kind of context. Enns, Malinick, and Matthews include occupations consequential in the coastal British Columbian towns they study, towns that are largely resource dependent and that often have large aboriginal populations. They include, for example, mine managers and aboriginal leaders.

Designing unique position generators that are particularly relevant to one's research site has been the norm until lately. However, some of the most hugely successful comparative research projects take a different approach. The World Values Surveys and the International Social Survey Program both insist on using identical items in dozens of very different countries, for the sake of strict and literal comparability. True, the "same" occupation may have a different relative position in a different occupational structure, so that the owner of a tiny kiosk is a more important kind of entrepreneur in Mongolia than is the equivalent (like a hot-dog vendor) in North America. But we can turn this into a researchable question by including the same occupations everywhere, and determining how much societal variation there is in access to the "same" occupation. Probably the best strategy is to build position generators with a common list of occupations, including ones sampled from levels in many societies, from the highly skilled occupations relatively common in more developed societies to the less skilled and more primary sector intensive ones relatively common in less developed societies. To this common list, a researcher could add occupations uniquely relevant in the research context, like lamas in Mongolia. At present Lin and his collaborators are working with just such a fully comparable position generator used in identical surveys in China, Taiwan, and the United States.

1.3.4. Moving beyond Occupations

All social settings have more than one kind of stratification or differentiation. Within any setting, different kinds of subgroups divide up valuable resources in different ways. For example, class and gender differences go with different kinds of information resource differences in the Toronto security industry (Erickson 1996). Men know more about sports and women know more about literature, but men and women are equally well informed about restaurants. Those in different classes are equally well informed about sports, but higher class people know more about restaurants. To more fully map the different kinds of resources to which people have access, we must ask about their access to more different kinds of positions, not just occupations.

Theory suggests we need to examine forms of stratification and differentiation that are especially strong in a setting, because these will be especially well related to resource differences. Gender stratification is important almost everywhere, though different in the degree of inequality, so gender is an important addition to the position generator. Erickson (2004) pioneered this approach in a position generator developed for the Canadian 2000 federal election study. She developed a list of occupations varying in prestige level, and at each prestige level varying in gender dominance. Respondents reported whether they knew a man in each occupation, and whether they knew a woman. Miyata adapted this approach for Japan, in a study partially reported here by Miyata, Ikeda, and Kobayashi.

Woolcock (1998) argues that community economic development and political effectiveness requires good network connections both within the community (so people can organize, cooperate, and pool their own resources) and between the community and the wider society (so community members can access outside resources, which are usually far greater and critical to community success). Thus Enns, Malinick, and Matthews asked their respondents in British Columbia towns whether they knew people in each occupation in their own town and outside their own town.

In multicultural settings, ethnic stratification is important. In ongoing research in Toronto, both Eric Fong and Bonnie H. Erickson extend the classic position generator to include ethnicity, asking whether people know someone in an occupation both inside and outside their own ethnic group (Fong) and whether they know anyone in an occupation in each of several ethnic groups of special interest (Erickson).

Given the useful flexibility of the position generator, the possible extensions are limitless. But given practical limits on the number of questions one can ask, it is not possible to ask about very many different forms of stratification at the same time. So recently Lin and colleagues have initiated another way to add stratification dimensions to a classic position generator. They ask whether the respondent knows someone in an occupation. If so, they ask the respondent to describe that person's characteristics. The advantage of this approach is that one can ask about a contact's location in quite a few kinds of stratification hierarchies. The disadvantage is that we only learn about one contact in each occupation. From the work of Fu, we know this person is very likely to be the contact closest to and most similar to the respondent. Thus Moren Cross and Lin find that respondents describe contacts highly similar to them in race, being of the same race 85–90 percent of the time, a rate similar to that for very close ties. We know that weaker ties are less homophilous, so this finding represents reporting bias. If we asked people to describe all the people they know in an occupation, they would report many more who are less like themselves. Despite the bias, the information is useful, since it describes those contacts that the respondents are most likely to try to mobilize and most likely to mobilize successfully.

1.3.4.1. The Bottom Line: Useful Measures Based on Position Generators

At the end of the day, the purpose of all position generators is to provide useful measures of social capital. In fact, they provide many measures useful for a range of theoretical purposes.

The classic and most widely useful measure is occupational network diversity, or the number of occupations in which the respondent knows someone. Diversity has a number of important payoffs including getting a good job, richer information and cultural resources, a greater sense of control over one's life, and better health (Erickson 2003). Many of the studies reported here use diversity as a key measure of social capital. Some use the term "extensity" instead of diversity. Some researchers also use the prestige of the most prestigious position known, to measure how high a person can reach in the occupational hierarchy, or the range from most to least prestigious, to measure the range of resources accessed. But these measures are very highly related to diversity and based on much less information in most cases. Neither can be calculated if diversity is zero, and range cannot be calculated if diversity is one.

The classic position generator includes occupations of different kinds, so it is often useful to decompose the set of occupations into subsets different in theoretically important ways. Flap and Völker argue that the Dutch occupational structure has a form similar to that theorized for France by Boudieu, that is, higher-prestige occupations are divided into those higher in cultural capital and those higher in economic capital. They divide their position generator occupations into those relatively high in education (a core component of cultural capital) and those relatively high in average income. Contacts with greater cultural capital help people to gain jobs higher in cultural capital, while contacts with greater economic capital lead to jobs with greater economic capital. That is, the two social capital scales represent access to different resources with different kinds of social mobility payoffs.

Cote and Erickson (forthcoming) argue that middle-class and working-class people in Canada today are likely to have very different attitudes towards ethnic or racial minorities and immigrants. Middle-class people are more educated, and more educated people are more tolerant. Further, middle-class people are less at risk of competing with minorities for jobs, because immigrants and minorities face labor market discrimination that often forces them to compete for working-class jobs for which they are overqualified. Thus Cote and Erickson divide their position generator into two scales: diversity of contacts with middle-class positions (which is positively related to tolerance) and diversity of contacts with working-class positions (which is negatively related to tolerance).

Flap and Völker, and Cote and Erickson, define subscales deductively from theoretical arguments. One can also build scales inductively. Angelusz and Tardos use factor analysis to find five subsets of occupations on their position generator and show these have distinctive correlates.

Those who add another form of stratification to the classic occupational position generator develop other relevant measures. Enns, Malinick, and Matthews compute the occupational diversity of ties inside and outside the community, and find that the variety of social activities inside the community predicts local social capital while the diversity of activities outside the community predicts external social capital. Miyata, Ikeda, and Kobayashi, and Erickson (2004) compute the occupational diversity of ties to men and to women, and find distinctive causes and consequences rooted in gender stratification. Many other variations are possible, depending on one's theoretical framework.

1.3.5. The Question of Causality

Most studies of social capital have been cross-sectional so far, which means causal directions are not clear. For example, we usually find that people with better social capital have better jobs. Is that because their social capital helped them to get a better job, or because better jobs give them better opportunities to enrich their networks? The only way to answer such questions definitively is to do longitudinal research, so several of the researchers represented in this volume are currently working on longitudinal studies in Hungary, Japan, Canada, China, Taiwan, the Netherlands, and the United States. Results are eagerly anticipated but not yet available at the time of writing.

But in this volume Moren Cross and Lin report an ingenious way to get some leverage on the causality problem using a cross-sectional survey. Their respondents reported whether they knew someone in an occupation on the position generator, and, if so, how long they had known this person. They also reported how long they had been in their current job. Thus Moren Cross and Lin could identify those contacts held before getting the job and use only those contacts to compute social capital. Obviously the value of this approach depends on how well people remember how long they have known others. We will soon know, since Lin and colleagues are currently doing a three-nation study that includes both the retrospective approach and true longitudinal data.

To conclude this methodological section, we remind the reader that this is also a theoretical section. All of the key developments in position generator methodology are deeply rooted in theories of stratification, social networks, and the various processes that generate forms of social capital and their rewards.

1.3.6. The Research Enterprise

Over the past decade, significant research efforts have been made by many scholars using this definition and theory of social capital and the measurement of the position generator as the starting point of their investigations into the investment and expected returns of social capital. Their pioneering work is characterized by certain distinctive features. For one, most of the research has been conducted with original data designed and collected by the investigators themselves for the specific purposes of the research interests at hand. Thus each reflects innovative and imaginative features, adding to the normative requirements of reproducing earlier findings. Second, studies have been conducted across many societies in the continents of North and South America, in Western and Eastern Europe, and in much of East Asia, under diverse social, cultural, political, and economic regimes. These diverse sites have afforded the examination of possible universal and generalizable features of the theory and the methodology. They also provide opportunities to identify institutional contingency and variations for the theory and the measurement. Third, the studies not only examine the production and returns of social capital within the scope of the proposed theory and measurement but also often explore their conceptual and empirical linkages to other critically different but related concepts and theories (e.g. human capital, cultural capital, economic capital, civic engagement, and trust).

This volume collects invited, original contributions from some of these scholars, which reflect the distinctive characteristics of this ongoing and growing research enterprise. All of the chapters are based on original research carried out by the authors. The reported studies were conducted in the United States, Canada, Japan, Hong Kong, Taiwan, Mongolia, the Netherlands, and Hungary. They carried out rigorous and systematic implementation of the theory (embedded resources, and its production and returns) and methodology (the position generator), to allow for comparisons and verifications. They also touch on significant issues about the nature of social capital and the position generator and its variations, how social capital is mobilized in social actions, the intricate relationships among social capital, civic engagement, social participation and trust, and inequality of social capital in institutional contexts. Together they represent samples of how systematic studies and observations can be carried out with shared understandings of theory and measurement, what critical, conceptual, and theoretical issues can be addressed in empirical studies, and why social capital should be seen as a vital concept and theory in social science research around the globe.

Inevitably, this collection represents only a small portion of ongoing research using the network theory and the position generator methodology to examine the production of and returns to social capital around the world. Nevertheless, the collection hopefully illustrates fruition of a scientific enterprise that adheres to a consistent set of theoretical and methodological principles; extends the theory, measurement, and scope of social capital research; and at the same time demonstrates imagination and innovations in many theoretical and substantive arenas.

In Section 1.4, we briefly introduce the themes (sections) under which the chapters and scholars make their contributions to social capital research.

1.4. THEMATIC INTRODUCTION TO SECTIONS AND CHAPTERS

1.4.1. The Position Generator Methodology: Its Reliability, Validity, and Variation

An important issue in the employment of a standard measurement for a concept is estimating its reliability and validity. In this section scholars explore these characteristics of the position generator with several alternative measurements and estimate the methodology's research validity.

Employing data from a national survey of the Netherlands, van der Gaag, Snijders, and Flap examine three possible instruments of social capital: the position generator, the name generator, and the resource generator. The resource generator, a variation of the position generator, identifies and samples resources deemed useful in daily lives. The study compares determinants of these instruments as well as their returns. They find that the best predictor for the instruments is the size of the social networks, rather than the diversity of the networks. Further, for major issues such as attainment in social stratification and instrumental returns, the position generator is the best instrument. For expressive returns, they recommend both the extensity measure of the position generator and the resource generator. In his chapter, using intensive daily data on all personal contacts from three informants over a period of 3 months in Taiwan, Fu generates their actual personal networks and compares the occupation data from these personal networks with those estimated with the position generator. He concludes that the position generator contains 20–40 percent more occupations than the occupations identified in the personal networks mapped in 3 months and covers more distant ties. When there are multiple possible occupants for an occupation in the position generator, the choice prefers a stronger tie and also depends on the social context in which the informant is linked to the tie.

Flap and Völker explore more specifically the embedded resources represented in the position generator. Using data from the 2000 Survey of the Social Networks of the Dutch, they decompose two different types of resources represented by the accessed positions in the position generator: cultural (education) resources and economic (income) resources. They identify three sources leading to better attained cultural and economic resources: parental, cultural, and economic resources; the cultural and economic resources in the respondents' networks (from the position generator); and education. They conclude that the position generator effectively represents the cultural and economic resources embedded in one's social networks.

Bian assesses the validity of the position generator in specific socially meaningful contexts. Using data from a 1999 five-city survey of China (Changchun, Guangzhou, Shanghai, Tianjin, and Xiamen), he formulates a significant context for the identification of accessed positions in the position generator: people with whom the respondents exchanged visitations during the Spring Festival, an important Chinese cultural context for visiting those people considered significant in one's networks. This approach allows him to uncover the structural positions of these preferred ties. He hypothesizes and confirms that such social ties represent two types of structural linkages: links to advantaged class positions and bridging to important bureaucratic and/or market positions.

In another study, conducted by Angelusz and Tardos in Hungary and presented in Section IV, the authors decompose by factor analysis the accessed occupations in the position generator into five meaningful clusters (managerial/professional, public sphere/cultural intelligentsia, market/service intermediaries, workers/urban manual, and rural/agricultural manual). These clusters afford the opportunity to examine differential contributing factors.

Taken together, these studies, diverse in methodology (extensive national and community surveys and intensive case studies) and in societies, confirm the reliability and validity of the position generator as a meaningful measurement for social capital. They also provide important information about the strong linkage between the measurement and instrumental returns, the internal structure of the embedded resources (cultural and economic dimensions and clustering of positions) in social capital, and the utility of the methodology to examine social capital in culturally meaningful contexts (e.g. the Spring Festival in China).

1.4.2. Mobilization of Social Capital

Mobilization of embedded resources for a particular action is a complementary rather than a substitute measurement of access to embedded resources, as it inevitably focuses on a particular and limited number of ties and their resources used in a particular action. Research typically employs a critical-episode approach to identify the use of social capital. For example, a large body of research examines whether personal contacts are used in job searches and whether the resources that the contacts possess (e.g. socioeconomic characteristics) make a difference in the likelihood of success or the level of attained status. The evidence is that anywhere from one-third to two-thirds of studied samples around the world indicate that contacts are used, but of the others anywhere from one-third up to two-thirds of the respondents mentioned no use of contacts (Granovetter 1974; Marsden and Gorman 2001). Further, it is clear from the literature that mere use of any personal contacts provides no relative advantage in the labor market. However, contact resources (e.g. the contact's power, wealth, or status) that represent mobilized social capital do make a difference (Lin, Ensel, and Vaughn 1981*b*; De Graaf and Flap 1988; Marsden and Hurlbert 1988). That is, among those who use contacts in a job search, those who mobilize contacts with better resources tend to obtain better jobs. This confirms the significance of mobilizing embedded resources in the labor market.

However, this literature has been criticized for several limitations. For one, it tends to focus on successful job searchers; thus questions have been raised as to whether the findings are representative of all job searchers, including searches that have failed. Second, this literature, which relies largely on social surveys, may attribute causal relations (using resource-rich contacts) to yielding better returns (e.g. attained status), since many of the data are provided by cross-sectional surveys. Third, since a significant number of respondents in any job-search surveys indicate no use of personal helpers or contacts, a focus on the limited number of respondents who indicated such mobilization may indeed point to the limitation of the validity of social capital for generating extensive returns, for example in the labor market.

Chapters in Section II address these issues about the mobilization of social capital. Lin and Ao pursue the issue of those who do not indicate any use of personal contacts in job-search studies. Specifically, they examine those who "mobilize" social capital informally—they hear about job opportunities in informal conversations with others without actually seeking jobs. Using data from a national representative survey, specifically designed to study social capital in the United States, they show that this invisible hand is significant in facilitating attainment in the labor market. Further, individuals rich in social capital are also likely to be the ones who benefit from this informal "mobilization."

Moerbeek and Flap, using the Dutch Telepanel Survey held in 1992 and 1993 on a sample of 3,000 households in the Netherlands, explored whether unsuccessful job searches used social capital differently from successful searches. They do not find significant differences, lending some support to the argument that studying successful job searches did not bias the linkage between social capital and attainment. However, they also caution that it is not easy to ascertain how social capital may be mobilized in job searches and suggest that there may be multiple ways in which social capital may be mobilized.

Smith explores the mobilization problem for low-income blacks. She argues that many of them not only access less social capital compared to blacks not living in poverty but also suffer from their contacts rendering less help. Using intensive case studies, her interviews show that many of her subjects were enduring a lack of social capital (capacity of embedded resources in their social networks). Moreover, their helpers exert less effort in their help as compared to those not living in poverty neighborhoods. The in-depth data provide a close-up look at the double jeopardy of those living in poverty areas: less access to social resources and less likely to receive adequate help in job searches.

These studies, again conducted in varied social and cultural contexts, demonstrate that the previously obtained information on the mobilization of social capital in job searchers is valid and did not suffer from the focus on successful searchers or the survey methodology. Further, they also point to new directions in examining other avenues in the process of social capital mobilization, especially in the labor market.

1.4.3. Social Capital, Civil Engagement, Social Participation, and Trust

As mentioned at the start of this chapter, much confusion in social capital research has resulted from the multiple definitions initially discussed by Coleman and pursued by Putnam; namely, social capital is not seen as a network concept, but is also related to civil engagement, social participation, and trust. Most scholars use one or two of these definitions and proceed to assess how it is related to other concepts such as attainment, performance, cohesion, or well-being. Seldom can we find research in the literature reporting on how these concepts are related or even overlapped. Therefore, an important research task is to actually conduct research on their associations. A group of scholars adhering to the network-resource-based concept and the position generator as its measurement have specifically undertaken this important research task.

Section III comprises several studies examining the relationships between social capital, as represented by the position generator, and other related concepts, including social participation, civic engagement, and trust. These scholars use the position generator as the principal measurement of social capital, based on their shared conceptual understanding and consistency of its reliability and validity in numerous studies. However, there is no prejudice in the analyses for possible relationships among the position generator, participation in voluntary associations, or trust as possible measurements for social capital.

Using another national survey in the Netherlands, the 1999–2000 "Creation and Returns of Social Capital" project, Bekkers, Völker, van der Gaag, and Flap assess the relationships among social capital (the position generator), participation in voluntary organizations, trust, and cohesion. They find that participation in voluntary organizations is strongly related to social capital, but not to trust or cohesion. These relations hold for memberships in both instrumental and expressive organizations.

Miyata, Ikeda, and Kobayashi also examined social capital (the diversity of accessed positions in the position generator), participation in online communities, civic engagement (participation in voluntary associations), trust, and reciprocity in a survey of more than 1,000 adults in Yamanashi prefecture, Japan. They find that online communities affect social capital, which in turn affects participation in voluntary associations. But these relationships hold only for men, not for women. Likewise, social capital also affects generalized trust for men, but not for women. Social capital is not significantly related to reciprocity.

Hsung and Lin look at a more specific population (managers in 126 firms in an export processing zone) in Taiwan and examine the relationships among a number of possible measures of social capital, including 6 positions in the position generator, participation in 13 voluntary associations, membership in the personnel management club, and membership in the human resources club. They find significant associations among these measures, again confirming the association between social capital and participation in voluntary associations.

Enns, Malinick, and Matthews also pursue the relationship between social activities and social capital. With survey data from the Resilient Communities Project (RCP) in British Columbia, Canada, they differentiate social capital (the position generator) by whether such accessed positions are inside or outside the community and whether they are strong or weak ties. They find that social activities and social capital are strongly associated, and that these associations exist for both strong and weak ties, and inside as well as outside the community.

Tindall and Cormier use survey data from three samples of environmental organizations in British Columbia to explore the relationship between network diversity (diversity of occupational ties, diversity of voluntary organization memberships, and diversity of ties to politicians) and political participation. They find that network diversity is associated with political participation for all three types of ties for men. For women, however, only diversity of organization memberships is associated with level of political participation.

Magee examines the associations among trust, civic participation, and social capital in a survey of residents in two counties: Dade County in Florida and Allegheny County in Pennsylvania. He finds a significant association between civic participation and social capital, but trust is not related to either social capital or civic participation in Allegheny County. In Dade County, in fact, trust is negatively related to civic participation. Among civic associations, religious organizations are the most pervasive and have significant associations with social capital in both counties.

These studies have not resolved the ultimate cause–effect issues among the concepts, but they offer remarkably consistent findings: that measures derived from the position generator are significantly related to a variety of measures derived from participation in voluntary associations. They also consistently find a lack of (or marginal) relationships between these two measures and measures of trust or reciprocity, suggesting that, at the minimum, these may be indicators of independent concepts. Unless further studies present dissimilar findings, caution must now be exercised to refrain from using trust and reciprocity as measures of social capital. This tentative conclusion does not negate the possible utility of trust and reciprocity as useful concepts, but their conceptualization may need to be theorized independently of social capital.

Also rather consistent in the studies is the finding that gender may be a significant contingent factor in the utility of social capital. Men rather than women seem to have richer and more diverse social capital; part of this may be due to their more extensive or diverse participation in voluntary organizations. This finding suggests that social capital research needs to focus more attention on how social institutions may affect differential social capital, a topic given further and more nuanced attention in Section 1.4.4.

1.4.4. Social Institutions and Inequality in Social Capital

While much of the research attention given by the studies reported in the previous sections focuses on individuals, it is also clear that social capital is unequally distributed in society among different social groups (Lin 2000*a*). Chapters in Section IV explore the contingency of social capital on various social institutions, ranging from gender and marriage to race/ethnicity and social transformations.

The issue of how the position generator reflects the unequal distribution of power and prestige in a society and among different social groups is the focus of Erickson's investigation. Using a national survey in Canada, she uncovers the unequal salience or attention given to sampled occupations with higher prestige scores. Compared to the real composition of the workforce, people know few people in humble jobs and a great many in higher-prestige occupations. Thus much of networking power differentials favors transmission of higher-status interests and perspectives. Among higher-prestige occupations, those with a substantial proportion of women have greater networking power. Where networking power is strongest overall, in higher-prestige occupations, much of that networking power favors transmission of information that reinforces gender stereotypes.

Lai, employing a telephone survey in Hong Kong, examines the effects of gender and marriage on social capital. She hypothesizes that married individuals' network overlap (or network integration) with their spouses would enhance their social capital. This association is confirmed, but she does not find confirming evidence. Rather, she finds that this effect may be contingent on the length of marriage. She finds that network integration enhances social capital only for those who have been married over a significant period.

Moren Cross and Lin pursue the issue of social capital inequality across gender and racial/ethnic boundaries. Employing data from a national survey designed to explore social capital and conducted in a random-digit dialing sampling of urban residents in the United States, they examine whether social capital (e.g. extensity of access to positions in the position generator) is distributed unequally among gender and racial/ethnic groups. Their data confirm that being female or a member of a minority group disadvantages social capital.

Johnson conducted a survey of 320 residents in Ulaanbaatar, Mongolia, probably one of the first social surveys conducted in that community. She assesses the effects of gender, education, income, and location on social capital. Johnson finds that men do somewhat better than women in social capital. But, for both men and women, income is a major determinant of social capital. These preliminary data offer confirming evidence on the contingency of social capital on gender and economic resources. Thus there is evidence that the production of social capital follows familiar patterns in a society recently transformed from a central command system to a market system.

Angelusz and Tardos provide more systematic data from a transforming society—Hungary. Their report provides a review of their long-term efforts since 1987 to study social capital in Hungary with the use of the position generator. They have replicated and modified the instrumentation of the position generator for the Hungarian population. Data collection methods range from intensive case studies to national longitudinal surveys. The rich data and variations in instrumentations allow them to estimate stability and change of factors contributing to the distribution of social capital before and after the collapse of the Communist regime. While cultural and political resources continue to contribute to social capital, wealth has increased its significance in contributing to social capital after the regime change. In turn, the effect of social capital on earnings has increased after the regime change.

These studies provide initial but vital leads about the essential contingency of social capital by different social institutions, ranging from the more microlevel spousal and marital relations to the more macrolevel institutions such as race/ethnicity and social transformations. Effects of gender, marriage, and race/ethnicity on the production of social capital are expected in industrial societies such as Hong Kong and the United States. However, perhaps not surprisingly but reassuringly nevertheless, data from Mongolia and Hungary suggest that economic resources gain significance in contributing to social capital in societies recently transformed from a command economy to a market economy.

Section I

The Position Generator Methodology: Its Reliability, Validity, and Variation

2

Position Generator Measures and Their Relationship to Other Social Capital Measures[1]

Martin van der Gaag, Tom A. B. Snijders, and Henk Flap

2.1. INTRODUCTION

Since the position generator's first use in the 1975 Albany study (Lin and Dumin 1986), it has proven to be not only a consistently constructed but also popular and consistently applied method for the measurement of social capital. The instrument has been especially useful for investigations of the productivity of general individual social capital, such as social capital research about general populations, that do not focus on a particular life domain. The logic and theoretical rigor behind the instrument's operationalization enable the development of a position generator for every society in which occupations, occupational prestiges, and/or job-related socioeconomic indices have been cataloged. These characteristics make the instrument very appealing for comparisons of returns to social capital among populations.

It must be kept in mind, however, that the original idea of operationalization behind the construction of the position generator implies clear theoretical restrictions. Lin (2001b: 45–6) suggested that individual actions accomplished with the help of social capital can be classified into *instrumental* actions (gaining resources) and *expressive* actions (maintaining resources). The operationalization of social resource measurement in position generator measures is traditionally molded in access to higher occupational prestiges and access to diverse networks (see also Section 2.4.2). These are useful abstractions to characterize networks helpful in the accomplishment of instrumental actions: finding a better job, house, and so on. For the investigation of other social capital questions, such measures are less suitable. In expressive actions, expected returns from social capital include the

[1] This research is part of the Research Program 'Creation and returns to Social Capital; Social Capital in education and labor markets' (SCALE), a combined project of the universities of Utrecht (UU), Groningen (RuG), and Amsterdam (UvA), funded by the Dutch Organization for Scientific Research, project number 510-50-204.

reception of personal support and the sharing of sentiments (Lin 2001*b*: 45). Such outcomes are less obviously a result from access to prestige-rich positions; there is no reason to believe that network members in more prestigious occupations are also more directly supportive in expressive actions. Lin (2001*b*: 63) already observed that having only ties of high status does not meet many different life needs; support in the form of practical assistance may come especially from network members in lower positions. Also, the argument that alters in powerful positions are more influential and more likely to provide access to resources in *their* network is less relevant for expressive actions since, for example, socioemotional support from "friends of friends" is generally not useful. Position generator indicators of network diversity that do not refer to occupational prestiges may be more valid for studying expressive actions. It could be argued that more diverse networks give better access to *any* kind of social resource, since they include a wider variety of alters, each with different personal resource collections and different relationships to a focal individual. Yet the expected relationship between diversity in network prestige, occupational diversity, and personal support remains rather indirect.

Because of its focus on accessing network members holding occupational titles, the position generator also ignores access to network members who have positions in society that are traditionally not associated with occupational prestige: homemakers, the unemployed, retired people, and younger people who are still in school. While not having a classifiable occupation, such network members can be valuable social capital for expressive actions; they can all contribute attention, care, accompaniment, love, and various other resources incorporated in their human and cultural capital. The presence of these resources is mostly independent of job title. Therefore, when we aim to measure the social capital of the general population across the general life domain using only the position generator instrument, measurements will result in underestimations of specific parts of social capital.

In this work, we aim to begin answering the question: For which social capital research question is which measurement instrument most useful? We do this by using the position generator as a reference point, and subsequently observe for which questions other models and measures may be more suitable. We will compare position generator measures with indicators constructed from alternative social capital measurement instruments and, in addition, investigate the interrelationships between the various measures that can be calculated from position generator data.

2.2. AVAILABLE INSTRUMENTS

The position generator is a measurement method for the social capital of individuals from a class of models that starts operationalization from specific theoretical choices. The first of these choices is the inclusion of indicators for all three dimensions of social capital that have been established as essential for measurement (Lin 2001*b*; Flap 2002): the presence of alters, the resources of these alters, as well as the availability of these resources to a focal individual. Furthermore, it includes an emphasis on the construction of "access"-type measures that indicate potentially available, positive social resources embedded in personal social networks, but that do not consider their actual use or application in individual actions. Such a separation between studying access and use avoids confounding social capital measurements with individual needs and other contextual variables (Lin 2001*b*; Flap 2002; van der Gaag and Snijders 2004). In its aim to be "content free" (Lin, Fu, and Hsung 2001), the position generator is also one of several social capital measurement instruments designed to cover the "general" life domain of the modern Western individual (see also Lin and Erickson, this volume), without considering specific areas of goal attainment, life domains, or subpopulations.

Other measurement instruments for social capital complying with these choices are versions of the *name generator/interpreter* method and the *resource generator*. The extensive social network inventory performed with the name generator/interpreter is the oldest measurement method for social capital, and has been applied by many researchers. While various types of name generating questions have been tested (e.g. Van Sonderen et al. 1990), the "exchange"-type name generator proposed by McCallister and Fischer (1978) was eventually most widely used, its most famous example being the single "core"-network identifying general social survey (GSS) item "with whom do you talk about personal matters?" (see e.g. Burt 1984; Marsden 1987). For social capital research, the name generator/interpreter can provide detailed social network and social capital information, but its costs may be high (see also Lin and Erickson, this volume), while for many research questions it may also retrieve much superfluous data (van der Gaag and Snijders 2004). The resource generator (Snijders 1999; van der Gaag and Snijders 2005) offers a new development in measuring social capital by using a "checklist": in an interview situation, access is checked against a list of useful and concrete social resources for which exchange is acceptable. This method combines the economy of the position generator with the thoroughness and content validity of the name generator/interpreter method. While its data are concrete and its administration is quick, its construction proves to be challenging and is bound to a specific population (van der Gaag and Snijders 2005).

While position generator, name generator, and resource generator instruments operate from the same theoretical perspective, an overall comparison of their measures shows that each instrument emphasizes different aspects of social capital; in addition, measures from each instrument have distinctive predictive value on specific outcomes of social capital (van der Gaag and Snijders 2003). While these outcomes emphasize that a social capital measurement instrument needs to be carefully chosen, it also tells us that each instrument has its own merits. In this contribution, we will further specify *which* measurement instrument best fits each situation.

2.3. DATA AND METHODS

For the investigation of relationships between three social capital measurement models, we analyze data of the "Survey on the Social Networks of the Dutch" (SSND), which were collected for this purpose in 1999–2000. Specially trained interviewers administered questionnaires in the respondents' homes, with interviews lasting 1 hrs and 50 mins on average (questions of other research projects were also included). The sample (N = 1,004), collected in 40 randomly selected municipalities across the country, consisted of two subsamples of the adult population (ages 18–65) for the Netherlands. In the initial sample, only wage-earning individuals were selected (N = 593); in an additional sample, all who agreed to an interview were included. This resulted in an overrepresentation of wage earners in the sample. The response rate for the combined, final sample is 40 percent (for a more detailed description of the sample, see Völker and Flap 2004).

In the SSND questionnaire, a set of 13 exchange-type name generator/interpreter questions (see Methodological Appendix, Table A.1) was based on many earlier investigations (e.g. Fischer 1982; for a detailed description of all questions and interview procedure, see van der Gaag and Snijders 2003). A 33-item resource generator was newly developed for this purpose (van der Gaag and Snijders 2005; see Methodological Appendix, Table A.2). The set of 30 position generator items central to our investigations (Table 2.1) was based on earlier research in the Netherlands (Boxman, De Graaf, and Flap 1991; Moerbeek 2001) and the former German Democratic Republic (GDR) (Völker 1995; Völker and Flap 1999).

It was assumed that this set of occupations was representative for the Netherlands in 1999. The occupations were coded using the 1992 standard classification for occupations of the Dutch Central Bureau of Statistics (CBS 1993), and linked to Sixma and Ultee's (1984) occupational prestige measures and International Socioeconomic Index (ISEI) measures for socioeconomic status (Bakker et al. 1997; see Table 2.1). These measures have a slightly different interpretation: prestige measures refer more to "social rewards people can expect in human interactions," while socioeconomic indices refer more directly to human resources and economic rewards (Ganzeboom and Treiman 2003; p. 173). Each of the measures therefore focuses on distinct aspects of "access to occupations" as intended by Lin (2001a, 2001b): while prestige measures could be argued to indicate *influence* attached to positions in society, socioeconomic measures may be closer to indications of (social) *resource* collections associated with occupations. Also, because ISEI measures enable better comparisons with other data, in the remainder of this chapter, all position generator measures are based on ISEI measures.[2] However, for reasons of fluidity, we will use the term "prestige" for these indications.

---

[2] Ultee and Sixma prestige and ISEI values for the 30 occupations in the SSND position generator are highly correlated (r = 0.91; $p \leq 0.001$); the same analyses with Ultee and Sixma prestige measures (reported in Van der Gaag 2005: ch. 6) show almost the same results.

Table 2.1. Position generator items, associated occupational prestige and socioeconomic index values, and item responses (SSND 1999–2000; $N = 999$)

Item no.	"Do you know[a] anyone who is a/an…"	Prestige U&S[b]	Prestige ISEI[c]	% "yes"	Relationship if yes (%) Acquaintance	Friend	Family member	Scale[d]
11	Lawyer	86	83	47	40	25	35	h
1	Doctor	84	87	50	41	19	40	h
15	Policymaker	82	70	45	33	28	39	h
3	Engineer	76	68	65	24	21	56	—
17	Information technologist	68	70	66	30	27	42	—
7	Manager	67	69	66	21	27	52	h
6	Director of a company	67	69	71	24	24	52	h
10	Trade union manager	66	65	17	57	20	23	—
14	Scientist	65	71	42	26	28	46	h
4	Higher civil servant	64	61	53	35	21	44	h
9	Estate agent	64	61	31	59	20	21	—
12	Mechanic	63	59	69	23	20	57	—
8	Teacher	62	66	73	23	26	51	h
18	Police officer	54	50	42	53	20	28	—
19	Secretary	52	53	67	32	26	42	—
20	Insurance agent	52	54	40	53	19	28	—
13	Bookkeeper/accountant	52	51	63	37	22	40	—
16	Musician/artist/writer	45	64	54	30	31	39	—
22	Nurse	44	38	75	26	22	52	—
26	Engine driver	44	26	18	41	17	42	l
30	Hairdresser	39	30	48	53	20	27	—
2	Cook	39	30	46	40	24	36	—
23	Farmer	36	43	50	34	17	49	—
21	Foreman	27	25	26	39	18	43	—
25	Postman	26	39	28	57	17	26	—
24	Truck driver	26	34	50	41	17	42	—
27	Sales employee	22	43	62	28	23	50	l
29	Cleaner	20	29	35	52	15	33	l
28	Unskilled laborer	15	26	38	41	17	42	l
5	Construction worker	15	26	66	34	18	48	l
	Average	41	43	50	38	22	41	—

Note: SSND, Survey on the Social Networks of the Dutch; ISEI, International Socioeconomic Index.

[a] As a minimum criterion of "knowing" a person who could give access to each of the 30 occupations, the respondent was asked to imagine that when accidentally met on the street, he or she would know the name of that person and both could start a conversation with each other. Occupations were coded using the standard classification for occupations of the Dutch Central Bureau of Statistics (CBS, 1993).

[b] Sixma and Ultee's (1984) measure for occupational prestige (Bakker et al. 1997).

[c] ISEI measures (Ganzeboom and Treiman 2003).

[d] Inclusion in inductive scale: h = high prestige social capital; l = low prestige social capital (see also Table 2.2).

The general question for the position generator was whether the respondent "knew anyone in each of these occupations." Table 2.1 shows the occupations in order of occupational prestige but in the questionnaire the order was randomized (see column "item no."). As a criterion of "knowing" a person, the respondent was asked to imagine that when accidentally met on the street, he or she would know the first name of that person and both could start a conversation with each other. A second question asked the respondent to identify the person as an acquaintance, a friend, or a family member holding that occupation; the exact interpretation of these roles was left up to the respondent. Responses to the items were coded as 0 (no person at all), 1 (an acquaintance), 2 (a friend), or 3 (a family member). In order to save interview time, only the strongest relation was coded following this increasing order of tie strength, arguing that it would be better to emphasize the availability of social resources via strong ties than their uniqueness via weak ties. Thus, when a respondent mentioned an acquaintance, the person was asked whether he or she also knew a friend or family member; when a friend was mentioned, whether a family member in that position was also known, and when a family member was mentioned as a first response, the interviewer moved to the question about the next occupation. As compared with other position generator studies, this resulted in information implicitly including an assumption of a positive effect of accessing social capital through stronger ties. To avoid this bias, for the calculation of social capital indicators, only dichotomized answers were used: 1 (knowing at least one person, in any relationship) or 0 (no person at all).

2.4. POSITION GENERATOR RESPONSES AND MEASURES

2.4.1. Distribution of Initial Responses

The distribution of initial responses to the position generator items is shown in Table 2.1. Averaged over the 30 occupations, 50 percent of the respondents say they know at least one alter in this occupation, through any relationship. The most popular items (with the most positive responses) are nurse, teacher, mechanic, and director of a company. Occupations that are least often accessed are trade union manager, engine driver, foreman, and postman. There is no relation between the prestige of the occupations and their overall popularity ($r = 0.19$; $p = 0.33$).

On average, 37 percent of the occupations were accessed through acquaintances, 22 percent through friends, and 41 percent through family relationships (see Table 2.1, right columns). For most occupations, "friends" comprised about 20 percent of the relationships that give access to these positions; occupations more often accessed though "acquaintances" were trade union manager, estate agent, police officer, insurance agent, hairdresser, postman, and cleaner. Family members gave access to the most popular occupations: manager, director of a company, teacher, nurse, and sales employee. On average, family relationships gave access to more different occupations (6.39) than did acquaintances (5.19) and friends (3.35).

2.4.2. Indicator Construction

Irrespective of the type of questions used, several morphological notions have been developed to express the beneficiality of social capital. These have been described as social capital *volume* or *extensity, diversity*, and the presence of *specific elements* in social networks (van der Gaag 2005: ch. 3). Position generator, name generator, and resource generator data all enable the calculation of measures based on these ideas (van der Gaag and Snijders 2005).

Since the introduction of the position generator, the construction of social capital indicators from this instrument has remained largely standardized. Three deductive measures, directly derived from Lin's social capital propositions (Lin 2001*b*: 61–3), are also the measures most frequently used. *Highest accessed prestige* is currently the only regularly used social capital measure referring to beneficial effects resulting from the presence of specific elements in social networks. It is based on the hypothesis that accessing network members with high prestige leads to the generation of higher returns (Lin 2001*b*: 62). Two other position generator measures are diversity measures based on the idea proposed by several authors (Granovetter 1973; Flap 1991; Burt 1992; Erickson 1996*b*, 2003; Lin 2001*b*; see also Erickson, this volume) that specific resources and relationships can be located and accessed more succesfully when more differentiation in resources and relationships is present in the network, hence resulting in better social capital. *Range in accessed prestige* is calculated as the difference between highest and lowest accessed prestige, while *number of different positions accessed* is the total number of occupations in which a respondent knows someone.

In addition to these often used measures, we calculated two additional ones. The *average accessed prestige*, a measure introduced by Campbell, Marsden, and Hurlbert (1986), is calculated as the mean of the prestige of all occupations in which the respondent knows someone. *Total accessed prestige* is a social capital volume measure used in earlier studies by Boxman, Flap, and Weesie (1992: 47–8) and Hsung and Hwang (1992*a*); it is calculated as the cumulative prestige of all accessed occupations.

An alternative way to construct measures may be performed in an *inductive* rather than a deductive fashion: multiple sets of domain-specific social capital measures can be constructed by identifying latent traits in social capital data (van der Gaag and Snijders 2004, 2005). Models developed from Item Response Theory (IRT) provide the most suitable methodology to construct such measures, since social capital data typically have an ordinal level of measurement with few categories. Within IRT, a distinction can be made between cumulative and unfolding models (see e.g. van der Linden and Hambleton 1997). For the identification of latent traits in social capital, cumulative models are closest in meaning to the idea of having "more" or "less" access to subcollections of social capital (van der Gaag and Snijders 2005). Therefore, we chose to perform explorative analyses with nonparametric cumulative "Mokken"-scaling analyses (Mokken 1996; Sijtsma and Molenaar 2002), with special software MSP (Molenaar and Sijtsma 2000), for all sets of social capital measurement items in the SSND data. These analyses result in the identification of subscales with a cumulative character (more detailed information about this procedure is provided in the Methodological Appendix to this chapter). This means that on a population level we can expect that respondents who access very unpopular (rare) items in a scale will also access more popular (common) items in the same scale. This will become clear in the results below.

An exploration of SSND position generator data identified two scales. *High prestige social capital* is a scale indicating access to a scientist, policymaker, lawyer, doctor, higher civil servant, manager, director of a company, and teacher. Since the scale is cumulative, respondents who access a scientist (least accessed item) will also access the other positions; similarly, respondents who access a policymaker (second least accessed item) will also access more popular items: lawyer, doctor, manager. *Low prestige social capital* is a cumulative scale indicating access to an engine driver, cleaner, unskilled laborer, hairdresser, sales employee, and construction worker.[3]

2.4.3. Indicator Characteristics

Table 2.2 shows the distribution characteristics of all calculated position generator measures. Clearly, the distribution of some measures seriously deviates from normality, which can be a disadvantage in their use as variables in predictive analyses (Table 2.2, column "skewness"). For the most skewed measures, highest accessed prestige and range in accessed prestige, this is caused by the fact that there are only 30 occupations in the position generator, as a result of which, these measures can show only a limited number of different values. The deductive measures show less variation in scores than do inductive measures (see Table 2.2, column "variation"). Correlations between the measures are almost all positive.

Highest accessed prestige is substantially positively correlated with almost all other measures. Because it is almost uncorrelated with low prestige social capital, these measures clearly refer to a separate, resource-rich, and possibly influential domain within social capital (Table 2.3). This is also shown in the correlations between average accessed prestige and the inductive measures: a higher average accessed prestige means better access to higher prestige social capital but less access to lower prestige occupations. Table 2.3 also shows that average accessed prestige is relatively independent from social capital diversity: it is unrelated to range of accessed prestige and *number of items accessed*. Finally, the measure total accessed prestige is positively correlated with all other measures, and even almost identical to *number of accessed positions*.

---

[3] The position generator items also form a bipolar unfolding scale for the SSND data; the two cumulative scales are reconfigurations of both ends of this scale. For reasons of space, these analyses are not discussed in this chapter.

Table 2.2. Distribution characteristics of social capital measures from position generator items (SSND 1999–2000; N = 989–996)

	Min	Max	Mean	SD	Variation[a]	Skewness	Reliability[b]	Homogeneity[c]
Deductive measures[d]								
Highest accessed prestige	26	87	79.83	9.17	0.11	−1.32	—	—
Range in accessed prestige	0	62	52.14	10.50	0.17	−1.34	—	—
Number of positions accessed	0	30	15.04	5.60	0.19	0.00	.81	.18
Average accessed prestige	15	72	51.67	6.82	0.08	−0.55	—	—
Total accessed prestige	0	1,522	781.40	301.87	0.20	−0.11	—	—
Inductive measures[e]								
High prestige social capital	0	7	4.46	2.29	0.29	−0.19	.74	.34
Low prestige social capital	0	6	2.67	1.63	0.27	0.12	.61	.31

Note: SSND, Survey on the Social Networks of the Dutch.

[a] Standardized distribution defined as standard deviation of rescaled measure (to range 0–1).

[b] Cronbach's α for number of positions accessed, reliability measure ρ (estimated by the MSP scaling programme) for the inductive measures.

[c] Homogeneity measures calculated as Loevinger's *H* (see Methodological Appendix).

[d] Deductive measures calculated using International Socioeconomic Index (ISEI) (Ganzeboom and Treiman 2003).

[e] Inductive measures were constructed using nonparametric cumulative Mokken scaling (see e.g. Sijtsma and Molenaar 2002). High prestige social capital is a cumulative scale indicating access to a scientist, policymaker, lawyer, doctor, higher civil servant, manager, director of a company, and teacher. Low prestige social capital is a cumulative scale indicating access to an engine driver, cleaner, unskilled laborer, hairdresser, sales employee, and construction worker. For construction of these measures, see text and van der Gaag (2005: ch. 6).

2.5. COMPARISON WITH NAME GENERATOR MEASURES

For comparison with position generator measures, several social capital indicators were computed from name generator data (see Table 2.4). Since one name generator question (item 3, see Methodological Appendix Table A.1) referred to negative social relationships, the responses to this question were left out of all calculations.

Network size is a typical measure of social capital volume, counting the total number of people mentioned in response to the 12 items. Seven other measures are indicators of social capital diversity, based on alter or relationship characteristics previously discussed by other authors: gender, education, age, and tie strength (see e.g. Campbell et al. 1986; Campbell and Lee 1991). For gender and education, network diversity measures were calculated as the Standardized Index of Qualitative Variation (IQV) introduced by Mueller and Schuessler (1961) (cf. Agresti and Agresti 1978). For diversity of age and tie strength, network-level standard

Table 2.3. Correlations between social capital measures from position generator items (SSND 1999–2000; $N = 989$–996)

	Highest prestige	Range prestige	No. of positions accessed	Average prestige	Total prestige	High prestige	Low prestige
Deductive measures[a]							
Highest accessed prestige	1	—	—	—	—	—	—
Range in accessed prestige	.87	1	—	—	—	—	—
Number of positions accessed	.51	.64	1	—	—	—	—
Average accessed prestige	.60	.28	.10	1	—	—	—
Total accessed prestige	.62	.67	.97	.33	1	—	—
Inductive measures[b]							
High prestige social capital	.70	.62	.72	.60	.84	1	—
Low prestige social capital	.06	.32	.65	−.49	.47	.13	1

Note: SSND, Survey on the Social Networks of the Dutch.

Pearson correlations, $p \leq .01$ in bold.

[a] Calculation of deductive measures using International Socioeconomic Index (ISEI) (Ganzeboom and Treiman 2003).

[b] Inductive measures were constructed using nonparametric cumulative Mokken scaling (van der Gaag 2005: ch. 6). High prestige social capital is a scale indicating access to a scientist, policymaker, lawyer, doctor, higher civil servant, manager, director of a company, and teacher ($0.33 \leq H_i \leq 0.37$). Low prestige social capital is a cumulative scale indicating access to an engine driver, cleaner, unskilled laborer, hairdresser, sales employee, and construction worker ($0.29 \leq H_i \leq 0.33$).

deviations were calculated. To calculate the measure indicating network diversity of tie strength, a tie strength indicator was first constructed as the unweighted sum of the perceived liking, trust, and intensity of relationships ($a = 0.85$),[4] similar to Boxman (1992: 101–2).

Seen from Burt's perspective on structural holes, a measure of network density should work as an inverse indicator of network diversity: more disconnected networks give access to more diverse relationships (Burt 1992). A density measure was calculated as the fraction of positive relationships between the first mentioned alters to five of the name generator questions (for a more detailed calculation of the density measure, see van der Gaag and Snijders 2003). For the construction of a final network diversity measure, it was assumed that each name generator item also referred to the exchange of specific resources. Therefore, *exchange relationship diversity* was defined as a measure indicating the number of different name generator questions in answer to which at least one alter was mentioned (i.e. the sum score of 12 dichotomized name generator items, see Methodological Appendix, Table A.3). An inductive cumulative scaling analysis (see Section 4.2) resulted in a homogenous, reliable subscale for this measure, indicating access to a diversity of work relationships in specific (i.e. the sum score of work-related name generator items 1, 2a, 2b, 4, and 5; see Methodological Appendix, Tables A.1 and A.3, and van der Gaag 2005: ch. 8).

[4] These relationship attributes were all part of the name interpretation part of the name generator procedure.

Table 2.4. Correlations between social capital measures from position generator items and name generator items (SSND, 1999–2000; $N = 1,004$)

Position generator measures[a]	Name generator[b] measures							Inductive measure[c]
	Deductive measures							
	Network size	IQV of gender	IQV of education	SD age	SD tie strength	Network density	Exchange relationship diversity	Work exchange relationships
Deductive								
Maximum prestige	.20	–.11	–.08	–.07	–.01	–.03	.17	.10
Range in prestige	.21	–.12	–.06	–.05	.00	.00	.17	.11
Number of positions	.25	–.08	**–.09**	–.03	.02	.01	.25	.19
Average prestige	.16	**–.09**	**–.15**	–.06	–.02	–.05	.16	.11
Total prestige	.28	**–.10**	–.11	–.05	.02	–.01	.27	.21
Inductive								
High prestige	.27	**–.12**	–.11	–.08	.02	–.06	.25	.20
Low prestige	.08	.00	.00	.02	.02	.08	.07	.07

Note: SSND, Survey on the Social Networks of the Dutch; IQV, Index of Qualitative Variation.

Pearson correlations, $p \leq .01$ in bold. For calculation methods of individual measures see text.

[a] Position generator measures referring to prestige scores based on International Socioeconomic Index (ISEI) values (Bakker et al. 1997).

[b] The name generator comprises 13 items capturing network exchange relationships across various life domains; for calculations, 12 positive items were used (see Methodological Appendix, Table A.1).

[c] Inductive measures were constructed using nonparametric cumulative Mokken scaling for position generator (van der Gaag 2005: ch. 6) as well as name generator data (van der Gaag 2005: ch. 8).

An overview of all correlations between position generator and name generator measures (Table 2.4) shows that the outcomes of both measurement models have little to do with each other. Higher maxima, ranges, averages, and totals of accessed prestige are positively associated with larger networks; the same is true for the number of different exchange relationships present in the social network. Network density, age, and tie strength composition of networks are almost all unrelated to accessed prestige or slightly negatively correlated: networks with higher prestiges are somewhat less diverse in gender, education, and age composition. By contrast, the inductive measure indicating access to lower prestige occupations has low correlations with all other measures.

2.6. COMPARISON WITH RESOURCE GENERATOR MEASURES

Only one deductive measure was calculated from the resource generator model: the total number of resource items accessed (see Methodological Appendix, Table A.3). Being the sumscore of all items, this measure has characteristics of both a social capital volume and diversity indicator. Several domain-specific social capital measures were constructed in an inductive fashion. Nonparametric cumulative scaling analysis (see Section 4.2) identified four social capital subscales referring to specific resource collections present in social networks: *prestige- and education-related social capital, political and financial skills social capital, personal skills social capital,* and *personal support social capital.* All these scales have medium homogeneity values for *H*, and all except one show sufficient reliability (see Methodological Appendix, Table A.3, and van der Gaag 2005: ch. 7; van der Gaag and Snijders 2005).[5]

Measures from the resource generator model are more in accordance with position generator measures than those from the name generator; overall correlations are positive and of medium size (Table 2.5). Networks in which higher maxima, ranges, averages, and totals of prestige are accessed also give access to more diverse social resources. There is, however, variation in the extent to which such networks give access to various kinds of more domain-specific social capital. Position generator measures are most related to prestige- and education-related resources, and less related to personal skills social capital.

2.7. DISCUSSION

In this study, we investigated the measurement properties of the position generator for a Dutch population sample by constructing several measures from its data, and making internal and external comparisons of their measurement

---

[5] The *reported* four scales are those that showed sufficient reliability. The explorative scaling procedure also identified more fragmented social capital domains, for which additional scales could have been constructed if larger numbers of appropriate items had been included in the instrument.

Table 2.5. Correlations between social capital measures from position generator items and resource generator items (SSND 1999–2000; $N = 1,004$)

Position generator measures	Resource generator measures[a]				
	Deductive measures	Inductive measures[b]			
	No. of items	Prestige and education	Political and financial	Personal skills	Personal support
Deductive					
Maximum prestige	.37	.43	.25	.09	.21
Range in prestige	.38	.40	.25	.03	.23
Number of positions	.46	.44	.34	.06	.27
Average prestige	.28	.39	.20	.13	.13
Total prestige	.50	.51	.37	.08	.29
Inductive[b]					
High prestige	.48	.52	.35	.11	.28
Low prestige	.17	.09	.13	−.03	.12

Note: SSND, Survey on the Social Networks of the Dutch.

Pearson correlations, $p \leq .01$ in bold.

[a] The resource generator comprises 33 items capturing general, acceptable social capital across many possible life domains, worded in concrete resource terms (see Methodological Appendix, Table A.2).

[b] Inductive measures were constructed using nonparametric cumulative Mokken scaling for position generator (van der Gaag 2005: ch. 6) as well as resource name generator data (van der Gaag and Snijders 2004, 2005). Prestige- and education-related social capital included knowing persons who have good contacts with media, own a holiday home abroad, have knowledge of literature, earn $\geq$ Dutch guilders (DFL) 5,000 monthly, have senior high school education, or higher vocational training; political and financial skills social capital included knowing persons who were active in a political party, have knowledge about governmental arrangements, and knowledge about financial matters; personal skills social capital included knowing persons who read professional journals, own a car, speak or write a foreign language, and are able to work with a PC; personal support social capital included knowing persons who can give good references when applying for a job, who can give advice in case of conflicts with family members or at work, and who can help when moving a household.

properties using two alternative measurement instruments. In this discussion, we will focus on two main questions: (*a*) which measures should be considered using the position generator model? and (*b*) which measurement model is most suitable for which research question?

2.7.1. Position Generator Measures

Similar to earlier findings (Lai, Lin, and Leung 1998; Lin et al. 2001), the three "traditional" position generator measures (highest accessed prestige, range in accessed prestige, and *number of positions accessed*) are substantially positively correlated with one another: networks with higher prestiges also show a larger diversity in occupations. When all three position generator measures are used as independent variables in predictive analyses, this can cause multicollinearity problems. We can think of three general solutions to this problem.

The first, as has been proposed and performed by other authors, is by calculating an unrotated principal component over all three measures as a single social capital indicator (see Lin et al. 2001; Lin, this volume). However, when correlations between position generator measures are very high, a second solution could be to simply omit one or two measures from analyses. For example, in our data measuring an upward reach in social capital besides resource diversity in another measure (or vice versa) seems to have limited added value. A third solution is to select a single measure for subsequent analyses. Based on our results, two measures are candidates. Total accessed prestige could be a good choice, since this measure is highly positively correlated with all other position generator measures and summarizes these in a similar way to an unrotated, first principal component. In addition, it can also have the advantage that its distribution does not deviate significantly from normality, which for some analyses and interpretations may be problematic with the measures highest accessed prestige and range in accessed prestige.

The use of a single position generator measure is featured on theoretical grounds in the works of Erickson (1996, 1998, 2001, 2004), where generally only the number of accessed positions is used in analyses. A good practical argument to use this single measure is that it is the simplest for the researcher because it does not involve the choice and application of a socioeconomic index or prestige measure associated with occupations. For the same reason, it is also the most content-free of all position generator measures; it can also be interpreted more generally as access to a diversity of people controlling various resource collections, and is therefore less bound to studies focusing on instrumental action only.

The social capital researcher should be aware, however, that using a single social capital measure a priori can mean a loss of potentially interesting information. After all, high correlations between position generator measures may not be found for every population. In earlier contributions we have emphasized that including opportunities for more specific social capital measurement, and therefore the use of multiple measures, is more than welcome and can lead to more specific predictions (van der Gaag and Snijders 2004). Therefore, when position generator measures *do* correlate highly, a more sophisticated and more informative third option is to choose differently constructed sets of indicators. In our data, a position generator measure relatively independent from other measures is average accessed prestige: it is only moderately correlated with range in accessed prestige and number of positions accessed. This measure could therefore be a valuable addition to the other, more frequently used measures. It could also be considered as a replacement for the measure highest accessed prestige. Its theoretical interpretation is not identical, but close to "the best resource accessed through social ties" (Lin 2001*b*: 62); and for some social capital questions, a reformulation to "*good* resources accessed through social ties" may also be sufficient. For some analyses and interpretations, the average accessed prestige measure also has the advantage that its distribution is less skewed than that of highest accessed prestige. A disadvantage, however, is that other analyses on our data showed that average accessed prestige is also more correlated to sociodemographic variables than are other position generator measures (van der Gaag 2005: ch. 6), and is therefore a less independent social capital indicator.

Other ways to make position generator data more specific and informative for analyses are also available. In this chapter and elsewhere (van der Gaag and Snijders 2004), we have already suggested that dimensional analyses of measurement items, leading to more domain-specific measures in an inductive way, may lead to better predictions of the goal-specificity of social capital. Scaling analyses performed on position generator data showed that multiple domains can be distinguished in accessed occupations. Differential access to each of these domains may be directly linked to access to the specific resource collections of the holders of these occupations. Specific measures for access to each of these domains may therefore be promising social capital indicators. However, in our data, the structure of social capital measured this way is fragmented, and it is difficult to construct reliable, homogenous measurement scales from a limited number of position generator items not specifically designed for such analyses. Völker and Flap (this volume) follow a different approach to this problem, by disaggregating the occupational prestiges of position generator items into separate indicators for specific financial social resources and cultural social resource collections.

When the social capital researcher considers the use of the position generator but is still in the stage of planning data collection, another innovation may also be considered. Erickson (2004) used a position generator with separate questions for knowing men and women in several occupations. Based on the idea that knowing a man or woman in a certain position may give access to different resources, this is also an option to retrieve more specific social capital information from survey questions.

The position generator used in this chapter is also subject to improvement. When respondents are asked to report ties in each of the categories of family, friends, or acquaintances, the widest access to occupations is usually found through acquaintances (Erickson 1996b; Völker and Flap 1999). Also, in the Netherlands, acquaintances are the most diverse and numerous fraction of social networks (van der Gaag 2005: ch. 5, 8). The finding in the present chapter that the widest variation of occupations is accessed through family members must therefore result from the interview methodology used. In retrospect, coding only the strongest relation through which positions are accessed is a design flaw that limits the researcher in options for analyses and hampers the interpretation of results, and should be avoided.

A final advice for future users of the position generator is to include a large enough number of occupations in the instrument. This has the regular advantages of more reliable estimations of measures, but the use of larger numbers of items may also lead to less skewed distributions of some measures (see above). Finally, the suggested dimensional analyses on position generator items are feasible only when larger numbers of items are available: at least 15–20, but preferably more.

2.7.2. Comparison of Measurement Models

We also considered other social capital measurement instruments besides the position generator. An overview of the relationships between social capital measures from different measurement instruments showed that these refer to different aspects of social capital, or—more carefully put—tap different cognitions from respondents, since their mutual correlations are low. Relationships between position generator measures and name generator measures were found to be especially weak.

In the Netherlands, having a social network with more diverse members regarding age, gender, education, and the strength of relationships maintained does not seem to be related to having access to network members with higher prestige. Only having a larger social network is correlated with position generator measures; larger networks contained alters with higher (average) prestige, larger ranges in prestige, and more diversity in occupations, a finding also reported by others (Lin 1999b; Lin et al. 2001). However, some of these findings are also very logical, and hence somewhat trivial: if all relationships present in the population were randomly distributed over networks, larger networks would also show higher maxima and ranges of prestige because they have a larger chance to include relationships with the highest and lowest prestige, respectively. Also, the correlation between social network size and the diversity of potential exchanges with network members is only partly interesting: within a certain range, it is logical that giving a positive answer to more name generator questions leads to more network members listed.

More interesting is that larger networks include a higher average prestige of network members, and that networks including persons with higher prestige and wider ranges in prestige show more diversity in both network exchanges and access to more specific collections of concrete social resources. This is emphasized by the finding that accessing lower prestige social capital shows much lower correlations with access to various resources. Access to prestige- and education-related social capital is most strongly related to position generator measures, which emphasizes that the position generator model (consistent with its purpose) puts more emphasis on measuring resources that figure in the "big issues" in social capital related to instrumental action: unequal distributions in human and financial resources underlying social mobility and inequality (Flap 1991). Measures of personal, instrumental assistance on a practical level show lower correlations with position generator measures, while the lowest correlations are found with personal skills social capital. Since most people in our sample indicated access to these social resources, this implies that access to them is independent from other characteristics of network members: they can easily be found in any network.

To summarize, these findings make the idea that "larger networks are better" somewhat more explicit in terms of actual resources, although an interpretation of the causal order of these associations must remain tentative with the present, cross-sectional data.[6]

---

[6] A second wave of the SSND data collection is under development.

2.8. CONCLUSION: A PROPOSED MEASUREMENT STRATEGY

Since each social capital measurement instrument taps information of different quality within a general population sample, the social capital researcher should carefully select instruments when planning measurements for specific studies. In Table 2.6, we suggest a tentative, parsimonious measurement strategy based on our findings.

The most general questions about whether there is *any* effect of the presence of social networks on an outcome of interest can be answered with any

Table 2.6. Proposal for parsimonious measurement strategy in social capital studies (basis: SSND 1999–2000)

Study emphasis	Multiple measures	Single-measure version
General (including use of less-specific, older data)	Domain-specific measures constructed from available data	PG; number of accessed occupational or alternate positions
		RG or similar data; total number of accessed resources
		NG; network size or number of accessed exchange relationships
Instrumental actions	PG; range and average accessed prestige, number of positions accessed	PG; total accessed prestige
	PG; deconstruction of occupational prestige in social, financial, and cultural resources	PG; unrotated principal component over traditional measures[a]
	RG; domain-specific measures	RG; total number of accessed resources
Expressive actions	RG; domain-specific measures	PG; number of accessed occupational or alternate positions
		RG; total number of accessed resources
Instrumental and expressive actions; goal specificity	RG; domain-specific measures	n.a.
	PG; deconstruction of occupational prestige in social, financial, and cultural resources	
	NG; explicit name interpretation in terms of social resources	
Network structure and specific relationship constituents	NG studies	NG studies

Note: SSND, Survey on the Social Networks of the Dutch; NG = name generator/interpreter combination; PG = position generator; RG = resource generator.

[a] Highest accessed prestige, range in accessed prestige, and number of accessed positions.

instrument. In our results, network size, all position generator measures, and most resource generator measures are all positively correlated. If our findings can be replicated for other populations, such measures should all be able to detect the most basic of social capital effects. This could then also be a confirmation of the use of older datasets, which have often been collected with name generators. However, it should be noted that single social capital indicators cannot detect whether there are either goal-specific or more general "castor oil" effects of social capital (Flap 2002; van der Gaag and Snijders 2004). For the collection of new data for general questions, the position generator may be the most economical choice, since its construction and administration are the easiest of all instruments. Of its derivative measures, number of accessed positions is the most content-free and easiest to construct, and therefore the most useful for general questions.

When studying effects of social capital on *instrumental* action in particular, the use of a position generator and the calculation of multiple, derivative measures is a good choice. Our results showed that its derivative measures are also correlated to the actual presence of available social resources in social networks, but are unrelated to network structure and network relationship heterogeneity. When separate social capital effects are expected from access to network prestige and network diversity, choosing alternatively constructed indicators from the position generator (such as the average accessed prestige) may offer some methodological advantages over traditionally used measures. When a parsimonious, single-measure version is desired, the total accessed prestige measure or an unrotated principal component over various measures are good measurement choices. When new data are going to be collected, versions with gender-specific and/or larger numbers of items are recommended.

For the investigation of *expressive* actions with social capital, the position generator offers limited possibilities. If it is the only instrument available or affordable, the most valid measure is the number of accessed positions, since it does not refer to occupational prestiges. However, even then, underestimations of social capital useful in expressive actions are possible (see Section 2.1). For the investigation of social capital in expressive actions, it may therefore be worthwhile to construct a version of a resource generator, listing various social resources possibly useful in any domain of individual goal attainment. From the resulting data, separate domain-specific measures may then be constructed in a deductive or inductive fashion (see van der Gaag and Snijders 2004). When parsimonious use of variables in analyses is an objective, a single sumscore measure over applicable items may also be used.

Finally, the social capital researcher may want to investigate both "castor oil" and goal-specific effects on outcomes of interest *without* a special interest in either instrumental or expressive actions. This most elaborate social capital question may be performed with either a resource generator or a name generator/interpreter combination; of these, the resource generator is the most economic in use. When general social capital is studied, the construction of both instruments can be a challenge, however, with the danger of incomparability between studies. Conducting an elaborate name generator study with various name interpretation questions that may include information about any social resource also remains an option. Such queries can be customized to provide answers to questions about any social capital dimension: alters, relationships, resources, and the availability of resources. When specific questions about the influence of network structure on social capital outcomes need to be studied, it is also the only measurement option, since it is the only method that identifies network members. However, its costs remain considerable.

APPENDIX 1

Methodological Appendix

The dimensional exploration of name generator, position generator, and resource generator data is performed with nonparametric cumulative "Mokken"-scaling analyses (Mokken 1996; Sijtsma and Molenaar 2002) with special software MSP (Molenaar and Sijtsma 2000). This method aims to find robust and unidimensional scales in sets of items, in a search

Table A.1. The SSND name generator items and responses: percentage of sample who mentioned at least one alter per item, range, mean, and standard deviation of number of alters mentioned per item (SSND 1999–2000; $N = 1,004$)

	"Do you know[a] anyone who ..."	% "yes"	Number of alters mentioned			
			Min	Max	Mean	SD
1	Helped you get your current job	27	0	2	0.3	0.47
2a	Gives advice on problems at work	73	0	8	1.4	1.31
2b	You give advice regarding problems at work	65	0	13	1.7	1.75
3	Disturbs you in doing your job	28	0	5	0.4	0.70
4	You often work with	71	0	7	1.4	0.94
5	Is your boss	68	0	4	0.7	0.54
6	Helped you get this house	28	0	5	0.3	0.51
7	Helps you with small jobs around the house	88	0	6	1.7	1.30
8	Keeps a spare key to your house	81	0	6	1.5	1.20
9	Is your direct neighbor	88	0	6	1.8	0.98
10	You visit socially	94	0	14	3.9	2.09
11	You talk to about important matters	87	0	14	2.4	1.97
12	Is another person important to you	49	0	10	0.9	1.30
	Average	65	—	—	0.9	

Note: SSND, Survey on the Social Networks of the Dutch.

[a] As a criterion of "knowing" a person associated with each of the 13 exchange name generator items, the respondent was asked to imagine that when accidentally met on the street, he or she would know the name of that person and both could start a conversation with each other (see also van der Gaag and Snijders 2003). For calculation of social capital indicators, answers to item 3 were not included.

Table A.2. The SSND resource generator and responses: percentage of sample who mentioned at least one alter per resource item in any relationship, and strongest relationship when known (SSND 1999–2000; $N = 1,004$)

"Do you know[a] anyone who..."	% "yes"	If "yes", access through			
		Acquaintance	Friend	Family member	Scale[b]
1 Can repair a car, bike, etc.	83	16	18	66	—
2 Owns a car	87	0	3	97	g
3 Is handy repairing household equipment	72	12	17	71	—
4 Can speak and write a foreign language	87	4	11	84	g
5 Can work with a personal computer	90	2	9	89	g
6 Can play an instrument	79	10	16	74	—
7 Has knowledge of literature	70	9	23	67	p
8 Has senior high school (VWO) education	87	6	14	81	p
9 Has higher vocational (HBO) education	94	6	13	82	p
10 Reads a professional journal	78	7	13	81	g
11 Is active in a political party	34	34	26	39	e
12 Owns shares for at least DFL 10,000[c]	54	11	21	67	—
13 Works at the town hall	42	44	23	34	—
14 Earns more than DFL 5,000 monthly	76	10	19	71	p
15 Own a holiday home abroad	41	34	26	41	p
16 Is sometimes given the opportunity to hire people	65	21	23	57	e
17 Knows a lot about governmental regulations	69	23	25	52	—
18 Has good contacts with a newspaper, radio, or TV station	32	36	24	41	p
19 Knows about soccer	80	7	16	77	—
20 Has knowledge about financial matters (taxes, subsidies)	81	15	22	64	e
21 Can find a holiday job for a family member	61	29	23	47	—
22 Can give advice concerning a conflict at work	73	22	32	46	s
23 Can help when moving house (packing, lifting)	95	4	17	79	s
24 Can help with small jobs around the house (carpenting, painting)	91	9	20	70	—
25 Can do your shopping when you (and your household members) are ill	96	11	24	64	—

(Cont.)

Table A.2. (*Continued*)

"Do you know[a] anyone who ..."	% "yes"	If "yes", access through			
		Acquaintance	Friend	Family member	Scale[b]
26 Can give medical advice when you are dissatisfied with your doctor	56	20	31	48	—
27 Can borrow a large sum of money for you (DFL 10,000)	60	3	13	84	—
28 Can provide a place to stay for a week if you have to leave your house temporarily	95	2	15	83	—
29 Can give advice concerning a conflict with family members	83	3	33	64	s
30 Can discuss which political party you are going to vote for	65	5	27	68	—
31 Can give advice on matters of law (problems with landlord, boss, or municipality)	64	24	32	44	—
32 Can give a good reference when you are applying for a job	65	37	37	26	s
33 Can babysit for your children	57	12	17	71	—

Note: SSND, Survey on the Social Networks of the Dutch.

[a] As a minimum criterion of "knowing" a person who could give access to each of the 33 resource items, the respondent was asked to imagine that when accidentally met on the street, he or she would know the name of that person and both could start a conversation with each other.

[b] Inclusion in domain-specific social capital subscales: p = prestige- and education-related social capital; e = political and financial skills social capital; g = personal skills social capital; s = personal support social capital (see also Methodological Appendix, Table A.3, and van der Gaag and Snijders 2005).

[c] A Dutch guilder was equal to about half a euro or dollar.

procedure based on patterns of association, in which well-fitting items are added to an initial pair of highly associated items. The criteria for initiation and inclusion of items into scales is based on Loevinger's H-coefficient (Loevinger 1947). The search technique is constructed so that every item can occur in one scale only; ill-fitting items may not be included in any scale during the procedure (a more elaborate explanation of this procedure can be found in van der Gaag and Snijders 2005). In this scaling procedure, there is a trade-off between reliability and homogeneity; we chose to focus on scales with sufficient reliability, resulting in scales with relatively weak homogeneity.

The quality of the identified subscales can be judged as follows. Scale homogeneity (or unidimensionality) is expressed with Loevinger's H, which can reach a maximum value of 1 (perfect homogeneity) but can also reach negative values. Scales with $H \geq 0.4$ are regarded as medium strong scales and those with $H \geq 0.5$ as strong scales (Mokken 1996; see e.g. Table A.3). Within each scale, an item-specific homogeneity value H_i indicates its fit into the scale. The reliability of cumulative scales is expressed with coefficient ρ, which can reach values between 0 and 1; values from about 0.60 are considered sufficiently reliable (Molenaar and Sijtsma 2000).

Table A.3. Scale characteristics of social capital measures from SSND name generator and resource generator items (SSND 1999–2000; N = 1,004)

	Min	Max	Mean	SD	Variation[a]	Skewness	Reliability[b]	Homogeneity[c]
Name generator								
Deductive measure								
Exchange relationship diversity	0	12	8.47	2.51	0.19	−0.66	.68	.29
Inductive measure[d]								
Work exchange relationships	0	6	3.33	1.96	0.16	0.80	.84	.65
Resource generator								
Deductive measure								
No. of items accessed	2	33	23.56	5.54	0.17	−1.01	.84	.23
Inductive measures[e]								
Prestige/education-related social capital	0	6	4.01	1.46	0.24	−0.79	.68	.48
Political and financial skills social capital	0	3	1.84	0.93	0.31	−0.45	.54	.47
Personal skills resources social capital	0	4	3.44	1.01	0.25	−1.96	.70	.48
Personal support social capital	0	4	3.19	1.00	0.25	−1.08	.61	.40

Note: SSND, Survey on the Social Networks of the Dutch.

[a] Standardized distribution defined as standard deviation of rescaled measure (to range 0–1).

[b] Cronbach's α for the deductive measures, reliability measure ρ (estimated by the MSP scaling programme) for the inductive measures.

[c] Homogeneity measures calculated as Loevinger's H (see Methodological Appendix).

[d] Inductive measure constructed using nonparametric cumulative Mokken scaling (see Methodological Appendix). This scale included knowing at least one alter who helped get the current job, gives advice on problems at work, receives advice regarding problems at work, with whom the respondent often works, or is his or her boss (see also Methodological Appendix, Table A.1). For construction of this measure, see text and van der Gaag (2005: ch. 8).

[e] Inductive measures constructed using nonparametric cumulative Mokken scaling (see text). Prestige- and education-related social capital included knowing persons who have good contacts with media, own a holiday home abroad, have knowledge of literature, earn ≥ DFL 5,000 monthly, have senior high school education, or higher vocational training (0.36 ≤ H_i ≤ 0.82); political and financial skills social capital included knowing persons who are active in a political party, have knowledge about governmental arrangements, and knowledge about financial matters (0.44 ≤ H_i ≤ 0.48); personal skills social capital included knowing persons who read professional journals, own a car, speak or write a foreign language, and are able to work with a PC (0.45 ≤ H_i ≤ 0.55); personal support social capital included knowing persons who can give good references when applying for a job, who can give advice in case of conflicts with family members or at work, who can help when moving a household (0.34 ≤ H_i ≤ 0.45; see also Methodological Appendix Table A.2). For construction of these measures, see text and van der Gaag (2005: ch. 7).

3

Position Generator and Actual Networks in Everyday Life: An Evaluation with Contact Diary

Yang-chih Fu

3.1. INTRODUCTION

The position generator methodology, in contrary to name generator and other network proxies, has revealed the segments of personal networks that are relatively extensive, diverse, peripheral, and weakly tied to ego. The methodology helps differentiate individuals' networks, and captures the extensity of networks along the occupational hierarchy that represent effective measures of social capital. It also allows researchers to enhance understanding of a host of larger social issues, such as organization, social stratification, and gender segregation in the labor market (Lin and Dumin 1986; Erickson 1996*b*, 2004; Lin et al. 2001).

Like other social network proxies, however, data produced by the position generator have rarely been evaluated against actual personal network. As a result, it remains uncertain how well these diverse segments delineate what exists exactly in real personal networks. We may get a clearer picture by exploring two questions. First, exactly how deeply and how extensively does the position generator reach in an actual personal network? Second, how do respondents select certain network members over others when they answer probing questions about specific members?

Answers to these questions would enable researchers to confirm how valid their conclusions are, and how much they can infer based on what they learn from the position generator. As is the case with other network proxies, not only does empirical validation increase the merit of survey estimates tremendously, but it also greatly expands the knowledge about personal networks in real life. Lacking genuine and complete information about personal networks, however, researchers have been unable to examine the validity of the position generator in great detail. While such a limit is common to many other network studies, it may hinder the potential of the position generator methodology.

This study evaluates position generator against actual network data. Since it is nearly impossible to collect information about actual personal networks, most empirical studies have relied on survey generators or experimental designs. The data used in this study differ from such generators or designs in a significant way. In 2001, three informants in Taiwan kept records of every single interpersonal contact daily for three to four consecutive months. Each diary contained detailed information about the characteristics of the contact situation, the persons contacted (alters), and the relationships between these alters and the diary keeper (ego). The informants also answered questions in a typical position generator. These answers were then compared against the diary data.

Using such rare actual network data as the baseline data for comparison, this study aims to disclose and verify the advantage of applying position generator in the context of everyday life. The specific goals are thus twofold. First, to show to what extent the network members enlisted in the position generator represent an active contact network in three to four months. Second, to analyze which people are more likely to be selected into the position generator when multiple alters fit into a specific position.

3.2. EVALUATING POSITION GENERATOR AGAINST ACTUAL CONTACT NETWORKS

The position generator asks if certain occupations fit any acquaintances of the respondent. The approach bridges the network generators that focus on a small number of specific alters, such as a name generator, and an overall item that targets at a global network. In general, a similar "global network" approach provides no guidance and sets no limit about whom to include. For example, different studies have asked respondents to name the first 60 people they can think of, or "about how many good friends" they had (cited in McCarty et al., 1997: 313; Marsden 2003: 8). Although this approach typically generates a large number and a broad range of alters, is it also more likely for the respondent to forget to include those alters who have not been in contact for a long time? By situating this global approach in the context of occupational hierarchy, and with specific positions in particular, can the position generator remind the respondent of those distant relatives and friends?

Network generators vary significantly in the kinds of networks they produce. On the one hand, a name generator tends to yield information about core network members who are very close to ego (Burt 1984; Marsden 1987, 1990a). On the other hand, position generator, resource generator, and generators using given names or subpopulations to elicit network members all help reach weaker ties (Snijders 1999; Lin 2001b, 2003a; Killworth et al. 2003; van der Gaag and Snijders 2004, 2005). Different experimental designs also generate various kinds of networks. For example, the small-world studies search for a chain of connections at different removes, while the reverse small-world method targets far more acquaintances within immediate social circles (Milgram 1967, 1969; Killworth and Bernard 1978).

Thus, different proxies often generate very different networks. As a result, research outcomes vary so much that, in both surveys and experiments, what we get highly depends on what we ask (Bernard et al. 1987). Further, the outcomes are subject to various interviewer effects, and vary according to the way we approach the network members (Marsden 2003). Whether it is network generator or experimental design, empirical network studies could benefit greatly from being verified against actual personal networks.

The records of actual contacts denote valid and reliable network data. More importantly, the information about such networks is typically direct and genuine. Instead of relying on proxies or estimates—which incur problems of recalling, interviewer effects, and bias toward strong ties—researchers use contact records to delineate parts or whole of personal networks that actually exist or remain active.

As the basic units of social interaction, such genuine and active contacts demonstrate how actors formulate and maintain personal networks through social actions. While generators and experiments help us explore the network structure by tapping into specific actions, actual contacts reveal the underlying features of personal networks. Without such social actions, it would be difficult or impossible for personal networks to function at all. In other words, it takes social actions or actual contacts to accumulate or mobilize the social resources that are embedded in social networks (Lin 2001*b*). Only with actual contacts do such resources function as a component of social capital.

After asking if the respondent knows someone in a number of occupations, whether each person is male or female, and how each of them is related to ego, a position generator normally runs out of space to further probe about real contacts. Given that the genuine baseline data are available for comparison, then, how well does such an innovative instrument work in revealing social resources that are embedded in actual contacts? How closely does the position generator measure up to its potential for acting as a reliable and valid index of social capital, as evaluated against actual personal network? While such an evaluation is long overdue, it is worth taking a closer look at how precisely the network it helps generate reflects what actually happens in everyday life.

Actual contact records not only serve as direct and legitimate measures of personal networks, they also provide a solid baseline against which one can evaluate network generators. Rather than relying on various stimuli, the contact records avoid clues, aids, and many measurement errors. By comparing those listed in the position generator with whom ego actually contacts within a specific period of time, researchers can better understand the strength and possible limitations of the position generator. Such a direct comparison allows researchers to check in detail how many occupational positions match in both the generator and the actual network. They also help show how many alters in the actual network occupy the same positions that the generator produces, and determine to what extent ego enlists acquaintances in the position generator who have not been in contact in everyday life for a while.

Actual contact records take many forms. Some studies use preexisting appointment calendars to construct network data, others simply ask informants to keep contact diaries. While the appointment calendars are a useful source to examine celebrities' contact networks, the diary approach directly identifies the boundary and content of personal networks in everyday life. In a pioneer study,

27 informants each kept a list of all persons whom she or he met and knew each day for about 100 days. Such contact data have helped distinguish frequencies and patterns of contacts in various occupational groups (de Sola Pool and Kochen 1978: 21–7; Freeman and Thompson 1989: 149).

Although the diary in the pioneer study covers only alters' characteristics (sex, age, occupation, and so on) and limited information about the contacts, the approach shows great potential because it generates rich content, helping to compile a complete profile of personal networks within a specific time period. The diary serves as a tool to elicit network *proxies* or *estimates* when we study long-term personal networks (Freeman and Thompson 1989: 154; Bernard et al. 1990: 180–1; Killworth et al. 1990: 290, italics added). More significantly, the direct and comprehensive contact information embedded in the diary taken within a specific time frame in fact comprises the only available actual and comprehensive personal network (Fu 2007).

With such a comprehensive profile, measures of actual contacts cover ties of all strengths, add valuable information about various network subsets, and even help predict how many alters an individual is able to recall (cf. McCarty et al., 1997). When one evaluates the unique network subsets that the position generator produces, it should thus be fruitful and stimulating to employ these measures of actual contacts as the solid baseline data. Only with such genuine and complete network data can one clearly identify and confirm the advantages and mechanisms of the position generator.

In this evaluation, we first show how extensively the position generator elicits network members from and beyond actual networks in everyday life, recorded in three to four months. We then analyze how ego selects specific alters over others when there are two or more acquaintances in the same position. The analysis follows two major principles of networking: (*a*) homophily and (*b*) strength of tie. Although the position generator may help reach more extensive and diverse segments in personal networks, it is still up to these two principles of social relationship to determine how far it actually extends beyond one's core network (cf. Erickson 2004: 30). Following the arguments and findings in the literature, we expect that those alters selected in the position generator tend to be more similar to ego in sociodemographic background than those who are not selected. Compared with those who are omitted, they should also maintain stronger ties with ego. That is, in general these alters represent a more remote group in ego's personal network. Within that peripheral territory, however, they are still more similar to ego and have closer relationships with ego.

3.3. DATA AND METHODS

This study examines samples taken from a position generator against a comprehensive database of personal networks in everyday life. In early 2001, three informants in Taiwan were instructed to record diary logs, keeping track of all

Table 3.1. A profile of informants and their contact diaries

Characteristics	Case 1	Case 2	Case 3
Sociodemographics			
Gender	Female	Male	Male
Age	Mid-40s	Early-30s	Mid-40s
Years of schooling	14	18	20
Occupation	Freelance survey field-supervisor	Junior college lecturer	Researcher
Residence	Midsize city	Small town	Large city
Diary content			
Days	89	91	119
Total contacts	2,638	1,764	3,354
Contacts with acquaintances	1,962	1,553	2,802
Unique individuals	1,089	539	953
Unique acquaintances (alters)	437	346	451

one-on-one interpersonal contacts in detail for at least 13 consecutive weeks (Fu 2005). The first informant (Case 1, a female freelance survey field-supervisor in her mid-40s, see Table 3.1) recorded 2,638 contacts with 1,089 unique individuals in 89 days. Among these contacts, 1,962 occurred with 437 unique family, friends, and acquaintances. The second informant (Case 2, a 31-year-old male college instructor) recorded 1,764 total contacts with 539 unique individuals in 91 days. Among these, 1,553 contacts were with 346 network members. The third informant (Case 3, a male researcher in his mid-40s) recorded 3,354 contacts with 953 individuals (or 2,802 contacts with 451 network members) in 119 days.

In addition, three months after finishing the diary, each informant completed a module on social networks used in the 1997 Taiwan Social Change Survey, which included a position generator. Like most other versions, this specific position generator posed questions about one acquaintance in each occupational position. If the informants knew more than one acquaintance that fit a certain position, they were instructed to choose the first person they could think of (cf. Lin et al. 2001). In the module, these three informants recorded the name of each acquaintance that occupied the corresponding position. These names were then matched one by one with those recorded in the contact diaries, thus providing a direct comparison between separate data collected by these two research instruments.

The diary used in this study has been expanded to cover all one-on-one interpersonal contacts, recorded in three categories. The first category includes each alter's demographic and socioeconomic characteristics. Two demographic characteristics are used as independent variables in the subsequent analyses: gender and age group (ranging from 1 to 7). Because socioeconomic characteristics (notably education, class, and occupational prestige) vary largely with the occupations listed in the position generator, they are not included in the statistical models. The informants were instructed to use their best knowledge to describe an alter's characteristics. While some characteristics of strangers are difficult to estimate, the problem has been minimized in this study since it only analyzes contacts with acquaintances.

The second category measures the strength of tie between the informant and each contact person. This category covers both objective and subjective measures, such as years of acquaintanceship (from 1 "under 5 year" to 3 "over 20 years"), frequencies of contact both in person and by phone (from 1 "rarely" to 3 "often"), familiarity with the alter (from 1 "not familiar" to 3 "very familiar"), and the importance of the alter to the informant (from 1 "not important" to 3 "very important").

The third category registers the unique situation of each contact. Two contact characteristics represent the major factors that may determine what kinds of contact situations help the informant choose certain alters over others into the position generator. The first variable is the "duration" of contact, ranging from 1 (under 5 min) to 4 (over 2 hr);the second is the "significance" of each contact (from 1 "not significant at all" to 4 "very significant").

Since the informants recorded items in all three categories for every single contact, the strength of tie may have changed over the three to four months. That is, the measures of tie strength between each informant and a specific alter are not necessarily identical among all the contacts with that alter. The subsequent analyses thus remain at the "contact" level, instead of the "tie" or "relationship" level.

3.4. EXTENSITY OF ACCESSED POSITIONS

The most obvious measure extracted from the position generator is the total number of positions that are present in the respondent's acquaintance network, to be termed the "extensity" of accessed positions. Like the total network size or "acquaintance volume," extensity has served as an effective index to distinguish people. It also plays an important role in helping us understand how the individual gets connected to the larger society (Sola Pool and Kochen 1978; cf. Freeman and Thompson 1989; Lin et al. 2001). To evaluate this basic measure, we first check the total number of positions selected in the position generator against the number of positions actually recorded in each diary.

Table 3.2 lists all 15 positions from the position generator used in the survey module (see details in Lin et al. 2001). These positions are listed in the order of prestige scores, from 78 (physician) to 22 (housemaid or cleaning worker, Column 1). Column 2 shows the positions that Case 1 (the female survey field-supervisor) checks in the instrument. In her judgment, there is someone in her acquaintance network whose occupation matches an occupation in the list, with the exception of one position—the lawyer. Thus, the extensity of accessed positions is 14, implying quite a large and diverse personal network for this supervisor.

Column 3 indicates the positions that actually appeared among the informant's contacts in three months. These actual positions add up to 10. At first glance,

Table 3.2. Alters listed in position generator and contact diary—Case 1

Positions	Prestige (1)	Listed in PG (2)	The position appeared in diary (3)	Listed alter contacted in 3 months (4)	No. of alters contacted (5)	Contacts with selected PG alter (6)	Contacts with all PG alters (7)
Physician	78	✓			0	0	0
Lawyer	73				0	0	0
Owner of large firm	70	✓	✓		1	3	3
Assemblyman/woman	69	✓		✓	0	0	0
Manager of large firm	62	✓	✓		5	0	19
High school teacher	60	✓	✓	✓	21	2	58
Division head	55	✓	✓		12	0	56
Reporter	55	✓			0	0	0
Nurse	54	✓	✓	✓	3	23	50
Owner of small firm	48	✓	✓		0	0	0
Policeman/woman	40	✓	✓	✓	7	62	72
Electrician/plumber	34	✓	✓	✓	5	1	9
Truck driver	31	✓	✓		2	0	3
Office workman/guard	26	✓	✓	✓	5	21	32
Housemaid, cleaning worker	22	✓	✓	✓	4	8	11
Total		14	10	7	65	120	313

then, the position generator clearly helps the informant list more positions (14) than what ego has actually encountered within 3 months (10). Although she had no contact with any physician, assemblyman/woman, reporter, or owner of small firm during that period of time, she identified at least one of her acquaintances in each of these four positions.

The gap becomes even wider when we cross-check whether those individuals listed in the position generator also appeared in the diary. As Column 4 shows, only 7 of the 14 acquaintances were actually contacted in three months, 7 others were not in touch. In addition to the four positions mentioned earlier, three more individuals in other positions—manager of large firm, division head, and truck driver—were named in the position generator but absent from the actual contact records. Thus, while the informant listed the names of 14 acquaintances in the position generator, she only made contact with half of these individuals during the diary-keeping period. The other half remained somewhere in the peripheral segments of her personal network that were inactive for at least three months.

Case 2 shows a very similar pattern (Table 3.3). The second informant, the junior college lecturer, named an acquaintance in each of 10 positions in the instrument (Column 2). But in his three-month contact records, only eight matching positions were present (Column 3). Further, among the 10 unique acquaintances, only 5 had actual contact with the lecturer within the three months (Column 4). Coincidentally, this informant made contact with half of the network members generated by the instrument; the other half remained inactive.

Like Case 1, Case 3 also checked 14 positions in the position generator (Column 2, Table 3.4). Out of these positions, 11 appeared in his contact diary. When we check all the names in the diary, 10 alters match those listed in the position generator. Therefore, compared with the other informants, the third informant had actual contact during the period of diary keeping with more alters listed in the generator. Despite the fact that this third diary lasted for one month longer, all of the 10 listed names actually appeared in the first three months in the diary.

Such preliminary comparisons raise one important question: Why does the position generator elicit from one-and-a-half to two times the positions than in the contact records? There may be at least two reasons. First, it is because the informants may have overestimated their acquaintance networks. Second, because 3 months is too short a period of time to track any contacts with some acquaintances. The first reason is implausible, since all informants clearly identified those acquaintances by full names and their relationships. These acquaintances were indeed their network members.

However, another concern is more complicated. The position generator methodology typically uses the global acquaintance network as the reference group, offering no clear guidance about time frame or criteria of acquaintanceship. Without definite boundaries, personal networks are difficult to delineate. This issue in fact applies not just to the position generator, but also to nearly all survey generators and experimental designs. It would be fruitful to phrase the leading question within a more specific time frame or criterion if we are interested

Table 3.3. Alters listed in position generator and contact diary—Case 2

Positions	Prestige (1)	Listed in PG (2)	The position appeared in diary (3)	Listed alter contacted in 3 months (4)	No. of alters contacted (5)	Contacts with selected PG alter (6)	Contacts with all PG alters (7)
Physician	78	✓			0	0	0
Lawyer	73				0	0	0
Owner of large firm	70	✓	✓	✓	1	2	2
Assemblyman/woman	69				0	0	0
Manager of large firm	62				0	0	0
High school teacher	60	✓	✓	✓	9	10	106
Division head	55				0	0	0
Reporter	55	✓	✓	✓	1	1	1
Nurse	54	✓	✓		2	0	3
Owner of small firm	48	✓	✓		0	0	0
Policeman/woman	40	✓	✓		3	0	3
Electrician/plumber	34	✓	✓		2	0	12
Truck driver	31	✓	✓	✓	3	2	4
Office workman/guard	26	✓	✓	✓	1	10	10
Housemaid, cleaning worker	22	✓			0	0	0
Total		10	8	5	22	25	141

Table 3.4. Alters listed in position generator and contact diary—Case 3

Positions	Prestige (1)	Listed in PG (2)	The position appeared in diary (3)	Listed alter contacted in 4 months (4)	No. of alters contacted (5)	Contacts with selected PG alter (6)	Contacts with all PG alters (7)
Physician	78	✓	✓		6	0	17
Lawyer	73	✓			0	0	0
Owner of large firm	70	✓	✓	✓	1	3	3
Assemblyman/woman	69	✓			0	0	0
Manager of large firm	62	✓	✓	✓	8	4	14
High school teacher	60	✓	✓	✓	14	4	73
Division head	55	✓	✓	✓	7	9	20
Reporter	55	✓	✓	✓	8	2	39
Nurse	54	✓	✓	✓	6	4	18
Owner of small firm	48	✓	✓	✓	2	3	5
Policeman/woman	40	✓	✓	✓	3	1	6
Electrician/plumber	34	✓			0	0	0
Truck driver	31				0	0	0
Office workman/guard	26	✓	✓	✓	4	40	63
Housemaid, cleaning worker	22	✓	✓	✓	3	75	80
Total		14	11	10	62	145	338

in unique subsets of networks or special areas. To study personal networks as a whole, however, the global statement still functions more properly.

The second reason sounds more likely. Within three months, the female supervisor kept contact with 437 family members, friends, and other acquaintances. The other two informants contacted 346 and 451 network members, respectively (Table 3.1). A personal network of this size in fact approximates what some empirical studies have estimated (cf. Killworth et al. 1990; McCarty et al. 2001). Nonetheless, according to the contact patterns or the estimates from various network generators, a few inactive network members may have been excluded from these actual contact records.

Judged by extensive and comprehensive contact data in the limited cases, the position generator indeed reaches well into the distant network members. As far as the selected 15 positions are concerned, the extensity of accessed positions stretches significantly deeper than the contact records taken in 3–4 months. Given the tremendous costs and efforts involved in tedious diary keeping, the position generator methodology indeed represents a highly cost-effective design that elicits wide-ranging network resources.

3.5. WHO ARE THE ALTERS SELECTED IN THE POSITION GENERATOR?

The position generator effectively reflects one's range of connections, but it remains unclear who represents the acquaintances listed in the instrument. In order to capture the overall range and cover enough variance in the occupational hierarchy, researchers typically use more than a dozen positions. As a result, it would be necessary to limit the number of acquaintances in each position before examining their demographic and relational characteristics. Like other generators (e.g. the resource generator), the position generator normally elicits information about only one acquaintance for each position. When two or more acquaintances fit one position, the respondent is usually instructed to screen and choose only one. The criterion used to screen varies from study to study, but most studies adopt either the "first" principle (the first such person that you can think of), or the "important" principle (the person who is most important to you). How people screen may largely determine what kinds of network members are being generated. In this study, the informants are asked to list the first individual that comes to mind (cf. Lin et al. 2001: 78).

According to the first contact diary, 65 of 437 acquaintances fit somewhere among the 10 positions (Column 5, Table 3.2). Among them, however, only seven individuals were actually selected in the position generator (hereafter "selected PG alters"). Others (58) were omitted even though they fit the positions (hereafter "omitted PG alters"). While the informant made 120 contacts with 7 selected PG alters, the contacts with all 65 PG alters (both selected and omitted) totaled 313 (Columns 6 and 7).

In the second case, 22 of 346 acquaintances held the positions as listed in the position generator (Column 5, Table 3.3). Of the 22, only 5 counted as "selected PG alters," 17 others were omitted. The informant made 25 contacts with the 5 selected alters, and 141 contacts with all 22 PG alters (Columns 6 and 7).

Case 3 shows a similar pattern with Case 1. Of the third informant's 451 active acquaintances, 62 occupied the 11 occupational positions (Column 5, Table 3.4). He made a total of 338 contacts with these PG alters, of which 145 contacts were with the 10 alters selected. Measured by both position generator and contact diary, then, the first and the third informants possessed much larger networks. In these small and large personal networks, why does ego select some alters over others? To what extent do the "homophily" and "strong ties" principles govern how ego enlists them in the generator?

At first glance, the selected PG alters may not have strong ties to the informant. As indicated in Column 5, Table 3.2, the first informant actually made contact with 5 managers of large firm, 12 division heads, and 2 truck drivers among her acquaintances. However, she selected none of these active network members in the position generator. Similarly, although the second informant actually contacted two nurses, three policemen/women, and two electricians/plumbers, he named someone else to fit in each respective position (Column 5, Table 3.3). To a lesser degree, the third informant had contact with six physicians in 4 months, but he selected another physician (Column 5, Table 3.4). Thus, it appears that when ego thinks of a specific network member out of those who match the same position, the first person that comes to mind may be the one that has been out of contact for at least three months, rather than someone that had recent contact with ego.

However, in all cases, there are still at least half of the selected PG alters who indeed have kept in touch with the informants in 3–4 months. Who are the alters that eventually get into the list? Who are omitted and left behind? How do these two groups of acquaintances differ from each other in the degree of homophily and the strength of tie with the informants? Are the contact situations also different between the two groups? Since only Case 1 and Case 3 provide sufficient number of contacts for analyses, we examine these questions with the contact data from these two cases.

As Table 3.5 shows, homophily appears to work unreliably with the selected PG alters. Compared with either the omitted PG alters or "non-PG alters," more selected PG alters are in the same age group with the first informant, while more have the same gender with the third informant. However, gender homophily is less clear in Case 1, and age homophily does not apply to Case 3. Thus, it is hard to say whether ego selects an acquaintance into the generator based on the homophily principle.

A more consistent pattern emerges with the strength of tie. On average, both informants had known the selected PG alters longer and had been in contact with them more frequently, either in person or by phone. In terms of subjective evaluation, the informants also felt more familiar with these alters and thought they were more important than either omitted PG alters or non-PG alters.

Table 3.5. Comparison of tie strength and contact situation among selected PG alters, omitted PG alters, and non-PG alters—Case 1 and Case 3

Ties/contacts	Case 1			Case 3		
	Selected PG alters	Omitted PG alters	Non-PG alters	Selected PG alters	Omitted PG alters	Non-PG alters
Homophily (0–1)						
Same sex	.57	.41	.67	.70	.48	.53
Same age group	.71	.31	.29	.30	.29	.37
Strength of tie						
N	(7)	(58)	(375)	(10)	(52)	(388)
Years known (1–3)	1.9	1.8	1.5	2.1	1.5	1.6
Frequency of contact						
In person (1–3)	2.1	1.4	1.4	1.7	1.3	1.5
By phone (1–3)	2.1	1.3	1.3	1.0	1.0	1.1
Familiarity (1–3)	2.4	1.9	1.7	2.5	1.7	1.9
Importance (1–3)	1.7	1.3	1.2	2.4	2.0	1.7
Contact situation						
N	(120)	(193)	(1,647)	(145)	(193)	(2,463)
Contacts per person	17.1	3.3	4.4	14.5	3.7	6.3
Duration (1–4)	2.5	2.2	2.4	1.2	1.7	2.0
Significance (1–4)	2.7	2.6	2.4	1.6	2.3	2.7

Such a difference between the groups appears to replicate in contact situations. During the diary keeping, both informants made many more contacts with the selected PG alters than with the others. In each of these contacts, only the first informant tended to spend more time with the selected PG alters, and seemed to indicate that these contacts were more significant to her.

Some of these preliminary findings need to be modified after further analyses. Tables 3.6 and 3.7 list the results of logit regression analyses about what kinds of alters are more likely to get listed in the position generator in Case 1 and Case 3, respectively. In both tables, the unit of analysis is "contact," while the dependent variable is whether or not a contact occurs with a "selected PG alter" or an "omitted PG alter." Models 1 and 2 (as well as Models 3 and 4) share all independent variables except the measures in the frequency of contact, which are alternated either in person or by phone. Moreover, Models 1 and 2 include all alters and contacts. Because the number of contacts with some alters is exceedingly high, however, Models 3 and 4 exclude the most obvious outliers in both cases.

The most obvious finding lies in gender homophily. For both informants, a contact with a selected PG alter is more likely to occur with a person of the same gender. Because both homophily indices are based on demographic characteristics which do not vary by contact, the unit of analysis here coincides with the individual. Thus, in both cases, the informants clearly prefer someone of the same gender when they select from multiple alters that fit an identical position. Age homophily also seems apparent in Case 1 (Models 1 and 2, Table 3.6), but it is largely due to the large number of contacts with the outlier (Models 3 and 4).

Table 3.6. Logit regression of the alters selected in PG—Case 1 (logit coefficients) dependent variable: selected in PG = 1, omitted from PG = 0

Independent variable	Model 1	Model 2	Model 3	Model 4
Homophily				
Same sex [0,1]	2.10 (.57)***	1.59 (.50)**	2.28 (.65)***	2.30 (.69)***
Same age group [0,1]	2.18 (.38)***	2.71 (.35)***	0.53 (.43)	0.38 (.45)
Strength of tie				
Length of acquaintanceship[1–3]	−0.69 (.47)	−1.20 (.40)**	−1.28 (.54)*	−1.30 (.49)**
Frequency of contact				
In person [1–3]	1.69 (.34)***	—	0.67 (.42)	—
By phone [1–3]	—	1.11 (.33)***	—	1.19 (.43)**
Familiarity [1–3]	0.21 (.48)	0.62 (.50)	1.26 (.61)*	1.14 (.58)*
Importance [1–3]	1.17 (.40)**	1.59 (.38)***	−0.49 (.52)	−0.83 (.58)
Contact characteristics				
Duration [1–4]	0.09 (.14)	0.16 (.14)	0.12 (.17)	0.24 (.18)
Significance [1–4]	−0.09 (.23)	−0.07 (.22)	0.24 (.27)	0.18 (.28)
Constants	−7.40 (1.33)***	−6.97 (1.22)***	−5.41 (1.47)***	−5.62 (1.56)***
Pseudo R^2	0.457	0.413	0.369	0.391
N	308	308	236	236

Notes: Numbers in parentheses are standard errors; numbers in brackets after each independent variable indicates range of values. Models 1 and 2 include all alters and contacts; Models 3 and 4 skip the alter contacted most often in the case. "In person" and "by phone" represent two different measures of contact that correlate with each other too highly ($r = 0.71$ in Case 1 and 0.34 in Case 3, both significant at the .001 level) to stay in the same model.
* $p < .05$; ** $p < .01$; *** $p < .001$.

The first informant is much more likely to select someone into the position generator if she makes contact with that person more frequently, or if she thinks that person is more important in her life (Models 1 and 2, Table 3.6). Not counting the contacts with the outlier, however, only the frequency of phone contact helps her select. The effects of both face-to-face contact and importance become insignificant (Models 3 and 4).

Taking the contacts with all PG alters into account, the chance of being selected does not always vary significantly on how long she has known that person, or how familiar she is to the person (Models 1 and 2). But when the outlier is excluded, both factors become significant—she tends to choose those who have come to know her more recently and those with whom she is more familiar (Models 3 and 4).

Holding homophily and tie strength constant, the chance of being selected changes very little regardless of whether the informant and her acquaintance spend more time when they do make contact, and whether the contact is more significant to her. In other words, the contact situation is not a significant factor on how she selects an alter. Regardless of how long each contact lasts or how significant it is, however, gender homophily, the frequency of phone contact, and the familiarity with a person all help assure that the person will come to the informant's mind first.

Table 3.7. Logit regression of the alters selected in PG—Case 3 (logit coefficients) dependent variable: selected in PG = 1, omitted from PG = 0

Independent variable	Model 1	Model 2	Model 3	Model 4
Homophily				
Same sex [0,1]	1.70 (.35)***	1.45 (.36)***	2.61 (.44)***	2.28 (.46)***
Same age group [0,1]	−0.81 (.51)	−1.09 (.49)*	−0.36 (.52)	0.14 (.54)
Strength of tie				
Length of acquaintanceship.[1–3]	−0.50 (.26)	−0.85 (.34)***	0.94 (.34)**	1.47 (.38)***
Frequency of contact				
In person [1–3]	0.92 (.23)***	—	0.81 (.25)**	—
By phone [1–3]	—	0.82 (.29)**	—	1.87 (.35)***
Familiarity [1–3]	1.38 (.30)***	1.64 (.29)***	0.17 (.33)	0.01 (.37)
Importance [1–3]	0.50 (.27)	0.66 (.26)*	−0.50 (.32)	−0.82 (.34)*
Contact characteristics				
Duration [1–4]	−0.51 (.21)*	−0.53 (.20)*	−0.51 (.28)	−0.5 (.28)
Significance [1–4]	−0.25 (.17)	−0.49 (.16)**	0.22 (.20)	0.26 (.21)
Constants	−5.40 (1.03)***	−4.24 (.86)***	−4.82 (1.06)***	−5.70 (1.00)***
Pseudo R^2	0.362	0.348	0.294	0.384
N	338	338	258	258

Notes: Same as the notes for Table 3.6.
* $p < .05$; ** $p < .01$; *** $p < .001$.

Case 3 displays a somewhat similar pattern of how the informant selects from multiple alters that fit identical positions. In addition to gender homophily, the frequency of contact, familiarity, and the duration of each contact all show significant effects (Models 1 and 2, Table 3.7). When the outlier contacts are dropped, only gender homophily and frequency of contact really matter. However, the length of acquaintanceship also emerges as another meaningful factor that influences the decision (Models 3 and 4). Like Case 1, therefore, only gender homophily and frequency of contact show evident and stable effects when this male informant tries to figure out which alter to list in the position generator. Other factors are either insignificant or unstable, with their effects varying on which index to use in measuring frequency of contact or which contacts (or alters) to include in a model.

In total, demographic homophily, tie strength, and contact situations contribute to about 30–45 percent of the variance that explains why the informants select a specific alter over another. Although the cases are limited, the in-depth information confirms that such a selection of PG alters partly depends on both homophily and tie strength, two important principles of social interaction. Whether the informant is male or female, someone of the same sex or those in frequent contact will come to mind first. The significance of gender homophily coincides with the "gendered social capital," a phenomenon that reflects the social institution of gender (Erickson 2004; cf. Martin 2004). The significance of frequent contact also suggests that people tend to select those who are present constantly in their everyday life, even with a network generator that typically elicits the more peripheral segments of a personal network.

3.6. CONCLUSION

The position generator has served as a powerful instrument in measuring individual social capital by clearly identifying and discerning the positions to which one can get accessed in the occupational hierarchy. With the help of genuine and complete information about active personal networks taken from three contact diaries, this study underlines the obvious advantage of employing position generator. It also clarifies how the informants select their network members into the generator. Although the number of cases is very small, the contact data contain rich information that helps highlight the merit of the methodology.

The study collected separate information about detailed daily contacts and the position generator. The timing of data collection would have rendered different results. By answering the position generator three months after they finished keeping contact diaries, the informants probably avoided an "interview effect" in that the list in the position generator reminded them of someone who had not been in contact for a while. Being more motivated to reactivate these ties, they might make a special effort to contact the specific alters. Likewise, the opposite effect could also be possible had the order of data collection been reversed—the sheer fact that someone appeared in the informants' previous contact diaries would have later led them to enlist that specific alters(s) in the position generator. However, such a scenario inevitably coincides with real life in which all informants or respondents normally use their recent contacts as the frame of reference, whatever instrument is used. The data collection of this study may have thus minimized significant interview effects.

The findings confirm that this unique network generator helps collect information about extensive, diverse, and peripheral network members. By rough counts, the position generator used in this study has elicited about 25–40 percent more positions than that actually recorded contact by contact for three to four months. Further, among the specific acquaintances that the three informants enlisted in the generator, only about 50–70 percent were active network members during that period of time. The remaining 30–50 percent turned out to be distant acquaintances that remained inactive for at least three or four months.

Thus, the position generator can indeed help delineate personal networks well beyond the actual contacts that people encounter in their everyday life. However, when ego needs to choose someone out of multiple alters that occupy the same position, it is those who are of the same gender and those who maintain frequent contacts that come first to ego's mind. These findings should reassure and encourage researchers to feel confident about their studies based on what they learn from the position generator.

4

Social, Cultural, and Economic Capital and Job Attainment: The Position Generator as a Measure of Cultural and Economic Resources

Henk Flap and Beate Völker

4.1. INTRODUCTION

Blau and Duncan's work on status attainment is a milestone in the research on social stratification and mobility in industrialized countries, as a test of the functionalist theory on the growing importance of universalistic achievement values over more particularistic ascription values. That is, education becomes more important as a resource in the occupational attainment process than father's resources or that of the wider family (Blau and Duncan 1967). We start from the classic hypothesis taken from Blau and Duncan's status attainment model. In the pre-industrial era, ascription dominated strongly, that is, father's resources were of overriding importance in his children's attainment; whereas, in modern times, the children's own education is the main resource. Father's resources are still somewhat important, but only in an indirect way in that they lead his children to a better educational achievement (for a review, see Ganzeboom, Treiman and Ultee 1991).

A decade later, Bourdieu (1979) made an impact on stratification research with his theory on compensatory strategies. These strategies are used by the higher social strata to counter measures by social democratic governments to increase social mobility and redistribute wealth. His idea of cultural capital as a compensatory strategy is his best-known theory. Doubting Blau and Duncan's optimistic predictions of a declining importance of class of origin and a growing openness based on an ongoing modernization of Western societies, he suggested that the upper strata have an excess of cultural capital that they will put to use once the pressure from those below grows. Therefore, there will be no increase in social mobility nor a decrease in inequality, and class inequality will be far more enduring over the generations than Blau and Duncan assumed.

Bourdieu's argument that middle- and higher-level occupations can be differentiated according to whether they provide access to cultural or economic resources is less well known. Occupations can be characterized by the amount of cultural and economic resources they require, and by the cultural and economic resources people acquire when working in a particular occupation. Cultural resources include language skills, creative and artistic abilities, and knowledge of art, history, and science. Economic resources include income, wealth, entrepreneurial and commercial skills, and knowledge of trade and economics. Fine examples of high cultural occupations are artists, teachers, and professors. Examples of high economic occupations are managers, accountants, bankers, and owners of businesses. These two kinds of resources correlate imperfectly, especially at the top of the occupational hierarchy. One may also mention two partially independent occupational hierarchies: a cultural and an economic status ladder (De Graaf and Kalmijn 2001). Bourdieu's ideas also imply that children lose resources if they have an occupation outside the sector their father is or was working in. Hansen (1996) studied elite groups in Norway and showed that those who got a job within the same sector as their father earned a significantly better income compared to those who "crossed over" to a job in the other sector. De Graaf and Kalmijn (2001) demonstrate for the whole Dutch work force that the cultural resources of the father indeed significantly contribute to the cultural resources of his son; the same result applies to the father's economic resources and the son's economic resources.

Another innovation in stratification research was made about the same time by Lin, Vaughn, and Ensel (1981*a*). Lin criticized the Blau and Duncan model, pointing out that the modern world is less universalistic than Blau and Duncan portray it to be. Ties to persons with resources are often of great help, even in a modern world. Social resources are actually "second-order resources" (Boissevain 1974); that is, they consist of the resources of the persons within your network, resources that you are allowed to claim contingent on the tie you have to these persons. Adding such social resources to Blau and Duncan's path model learned that these resources have a sizable direct effect on obtained occupational status. In addition, the original effect of a person's education on his attained occupational status has to be attributed at least partially to an indirect effect: a better education helps to create better social resources (Flap 1991). These social resources were first measured by the status of the contact person who helped Ego to get the job (Lin et al. 1981*a*; De Graaf and Flap 1988); later, the position generator was used, which specifies the access a person has to jobs at differing rungs of the occupational prestige ladder. Both types of research demonstrate that the focal person's social resources explain his or her occupational prestige and income (Lin, Fu, and Hsung 2001; see also Lin 1999*b*: 478–80).

In this study, we will combine these two innovations and in that way add to the research literature on social resources as well as that on cultural and economic resources. The research question we address is to what degree the inclusion of cultural and economic resources of the relevant actors, that is, the father, the members in Ego's network as well as Ego, provides a better insight into the occupational attainment process. More specifically, we want to know whether occupational transmission is sector specific or more general (see Flap 2002).

4.2. HYPOTHESES

We contribute to the first research line on social resources and mobility by introducing the cultural and economic resources that one can access via the ties to others who occupy certain occupational positions. We add to the second line of research on the role of cultural and economic resources in the attainment process by focusing on the influence of the social resources, or more precisely the cultural and economic resources in one's network.

The first hypothesis that we test is whether there is still a direct effect of the cultural and economic resources of a person's father on the cultural and economic resources of that person himself or herself. Second, we test whether the cultural and the financial resources of the members of a person's network do indeed explain this person's cultural and financial resources. The third hypothesis that we test is whether this social, cultural, and financial capital in a person's network are a result of one's parent's resources. Fourth, we inquire into the degree to which the (increasing) effect of one's own education has to be attributed to a person's greater social resources; that is, the greater financial or cultural resources embedded in his or her network. Fifth, we analyze whether persons who have a job in the same sector as their father, their friends, and acquaintances, either in the economic or in the cultural sector, fare better with respect to attained occupational prestige and income compared to those who cross over to the other sector.

The latter idea summarizes the crux of our contribution. It was Hansen (1996) who formulated the idea that the cultural resources of the father are important for the children's attained cultural resources, and that the father's economic resources help to attain economic capital. We generalize this idea to the whole network. In fact, a father is just one, though usually a very important, member of a person's network. We specify that the advantages of, for example, a higher occupational prestige or a higher income that accrues to those originating in the upper and middle classes are mainly to be observed among those who found their occupation in the same sector, either cultural or economic, as the members of their social network.

We also have a methodological claim. The position generator as developed by Lin and Dumin (1986), which measures a person's social capital by his or her access to various occupations, can be used to measure that person's cultural and financial resources as well through recoding the job titles according to the financial and cultural resources that a specific job usually accesses. If we succeed in achieving more insight in the transmission of social positions within and between the generations by emphasizing the role of the cultural and economic resources within the focal person's network, we will also come to know whether the position generator is a useful tool to chart the cultural and economic resources embedded in personal networks (see Introduction to this volume by Lin).

To set a benchmark, we start by replicating a simple version of Blau and Duncan's original status attainment model (Blau and Duncan 1967; see also De Graaf and Kalmijn 2001) that includes three variables: father's occupational status, respondent's education, and respondent's occupational status. This model states that the direct effect of father's resources on the occupational attainment of his children will be small, whereas the child's own education will be of great influence. Furthermore, since there (still) is a small direct effect of the father's resources on his children's educational achievements, there will also be a relevant indirect effect of father's resources on the occupational outcomes of his children.

4.3. METHOD, DATA, AND MEASUREMENTS

We test our hypotheses while using data on 1,007 respondents who were included in a representative survey of the Dutch taken in 2000, called SSND (the Survey of the Social Networks of the Dutch). The data includes information on 1,007 individuals between the ages of 18 and 65. The sample had the following stages. First, we sampled 40 municipalities representing the different Dutch provinces and regions and taking into account size differences in municipalities. Subsequently, we randomly sampled four neighborhoods in each municipality. A neighborhood was defined with the help of a zip code. In the Netherlands the zip code system consists of four numbers and two letters for every address. We chose to define a neighborhood as the addresses within a zip code area of identical numbers plus one identical letter. On average, such an area includes 230 addresses. Last, we randomly sampled 25 addresses in every neighborhood. This resulted in a data set consisting of 1,007 individual respondents in 161 neighborhoods. (Since the neighborhoods of one particular municipality were very small, we sampled 5 neighborhoods, thus the number of 161.)

All potential respondents in this sample received a letter telling them about the background of our research and stating that we would call them to make an appointment. If respondents had no telephone, we announced that one of our interviewers would visit them in order to make an appointment for the interview. The interviews took about 1 hrs and 50 mins and were conducted by thoroughly trained interviewers, in most cases at the respondent's home and sometimes at his or her workplace. Most questions in the questionnaire consisted of pre-defined standard answer categories. We oversampled people who were at work because these data were collected for a combination of projects, including one studying the networks of the Dutch labor force and the effects of these networks. The response rate of the survey was 40 percent. In the description of our data, we use the whole sample while imputing the last job for those respondents that were not part of the labor force at the time of the interview.

The occupational status of the occupations is coded according to the ISEI (1992) (see Ganzeboom, De Graaf, and Treiman 1992), an index based on Duncan's socioeconomic status (SES) scale (Duncan 1961).

The respondent's education is measured using a scale with eight categories. The respondent's social resources are measured using a position generator with 30 popular job titles spread along the prestige ladder.

The personal network of the respondent was measured by a version of the position generator (see e.g. Lin and Dumin 1986). Respondents were asked whether they have contact with people in 30 different occupational positions and, if so, whether these were family, friends, or acquaintances. Appendix 1 provides the list of occupational positions that we used. In order to minimize multicollinearity in the analyses, we used only the network of friends and acquaintances. The father of a respondent is considered a member of his or her family network, and we inquired into the effects of father's status separately.

To establish the cultural and economic resources that go with a particular job or to which that job gives access, we use the scales of the cultural and economic capital of jobs that were provided by De Graaf and Kalmijn (2001: 55–8) to recode the respondent's own occupational position as well as that of his or her father and the network members according to their economic and their cultural capital. What De Graaf and Kalmijn actually did is decompose Duncan's original socioeconomic index of occupation (Duncan 1961) into a score for education and for income. Following this logic, education is here considered as the indicator for cultural resources that go with a particular job, and earnings are considered as indicating economic resources that go with a particular job.[1] Ganzeboom, De Graaf, and Kalmijn were pioneers (Ganzeboom, De Graaf, and Kalmijn 1987; Ganzeboom 1989; De Graaf and Kalmijn 2001) in using expert judgments on the cultural, financial, and economic dimensions, respectively, of occupations. Later, De Graaf and Kalmijn (1995) provided a more objective procedure in which they use average earning levels of detailed occupations as measures of the economic resources, and average schooling levels of the detailed occupations as measures of cultural resources (see also Kalmijn 1994). To complete this task, they combined various datasets (dating from 1971 to 1994) to get information on the education and income of more than 52,000 working individuals in the Netherlands. Note that these authors used averages

---

[1] It might be objected that "education" is a poor indicator for someone's cultural resources since these might be richer and more differentiated. The rationale of using a respondent's education as an indicator for cultural resources is not so much that Bourdieu primarily thought of education as being cultural capital. The reason is that since its introduction by (among others) Kalmijn (1994), it has been a common procedure in the existing research literature to decompose SEI-scores, which combine earnings and education, into "education" representing cultural capital and "income" representing economic capital that is accessed by a job. Alternatively, one might also interpret these scores, as Ganzeboom et al. also do, as proxies for the economic and the cultural status of a job.

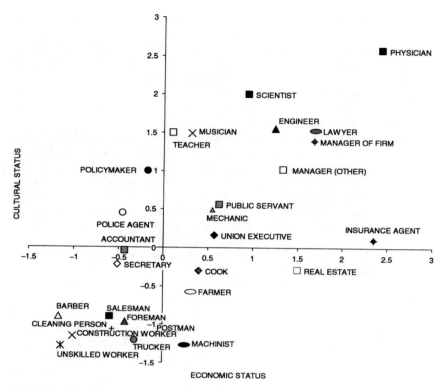

Figure 4.1. The adapted version of the position generator, the cultural and economic resources of 30 occupations in the respondents' network

of schooling and earning per occupational group when they developed the scales.

We employ this second approach. Ideally, we should have amassed more recent data on the incomes of the full range of job titles in a large enough number to make estimates of the average incomes and educational level of these jobs in present day. We use the same scales that were developed by De Graaf and Kalmijn, dating back to 1984. In the meantime, the incomes for the jobs have grown, yet the ranking of these jobs concerning the relative order of earnings have remained rather stable. The scores of the occupation for their educational and financial resources have been recoded such that they range from –2.5 to +2.5.

Furthermore, we controlled in all analyses for a respondents' gender (1 = male, 0 = female) and for his or her age (in years). We have also inquired into possible curvilinear effects of age. Preliminary analyses showed that including age and gender in the analyses does not affect the results.

Figure 4.1 shows a scatterplot of the 30 occupations mentioned in our version of the position generator and their score on the cultural and the economic dimension. These occupations show a spread that is in agreement with Bourdieu's assumptions on the cultural and economic dimensions that pertain to occupations. For example, insurance agents combine a high economic status with a mediocre cultural status, whereas teachers have a high cultural status but only a rather low economic status. These findings give some support to Bourdieu's idea that these dimensions bifurcate much more for the higher than the lower status occupations, showing a "fork structure."

How strongly do these two dimensions in occupations of the network members correlate? This correlation is $r = 0.62$. While comparing 55 broader occupational groups, De Graaf and Kalmijn (2001: 57) found a higher correlation of $r = 0.71$ between the two dimensions.

Lin and Dumin (1986) studied how the access persons depended on the occupational prestige of their fathers. They expected and found the following results: individuals of higher social origin also reached higher via their ties to others, and the average level of the jobs they accessed through these ties was also higher. We found that the ties within a person's network also helped him or her to reach higher in the absolute sense, if the respondent's father had a higher attained occupational position.

4.4. ANALYSIS

In a first model, we analyzed whether the effects of the cultural and economic resources within a person's network relate to his or her own cultural and economic resources. We compared those with above and below the median amount of cultural and economic resources. Table 4.1 presents the average status attained depending on these network resources. As expected, persons who are high on

Table 4.1. Average status attained by network resources (Survey of the Social Networks of the Dutch (SSND), $N = 1,007$)

Network resources		Economic status	Cultural status	Average of both cultural and economic resources
Cultural	High	.31 (1.01)	.40 (1.01)	.35 (.89)
Economic	High			
Cultural	Low	.10 (.97)	.003 (.94)	.07 (.84)
Economic	High			
Cultural	High	.20 (.99)	.38 (1.04)	.29 (.91)
Economic	Low			
Cultural	Low	−.17 (.93)	−.21 (.90)	−.19 (.83)
Economic	Low			
F value (between groups)		11.38**	20.45**	19.47**
F value (within subjects)		10.6**		

** $p < .01$; * $p < .05$.

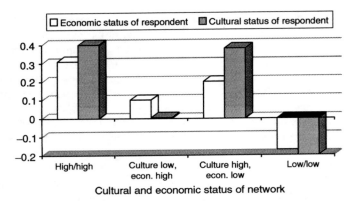

Figure 4.2. Average attained economic and cultural status by cultural and economic status of the network (source: Survey of the Social Networks of the Dutch (SSND), $N = 1,007$)

both dimensions fare best in both respects, and those who do not have cultural and economic resources in their network do most poorly. It is interesting to note that, if the average cultural and economic resources in the network are considered, those who have good cultural resources but fewer economic resources in their network fare better than those who have relatively more economic than cultural resources in their network. Furthermore, if a person has many cultural resources but only a few economic resources in his or her network, his or her own economic resources are comparably higher than the cultural resources attained by a person who scores high in economic network resources but low in cultural resources.

The differences between the different types of network resources are significant, but the differences within economic and cultural resources of an individual (indicated by the significant F value for within subjects) are significant as well. Figure 4.2 summarizes the findings presented in Table 4.1. As can be seen in Figure 4.2, having good cultural resources in one's networks can partially compensate for a lack of economic resources: these persons do well not only culturally but also with respect to their economic status. However, having no cultural resources in the network is clearly detrimental not only to one's cultural but also to one's economic chances, whatever one's economic resources. Our assumption of the specific role of cultural and economic resources seems to bear some truth. To acquire a deeper insight into their relative importance in the transmission of resources over the generations, we performed a number of path analyses. We started with the simple version of the Blau and Duncan model, presented in Figure 4.3. Note that, as already mentioned, all path models are controlled for a respondent's sex and age.

The figure shows that the direct effect of a child's education ($\beta = 0.49$) dominates, yet there still is a direct effect of father's occupational status on that of his children ($\beta = 0.15$), and an even more important indirect effect ($0.31 \times 0.49 = 0.15$) because of the strong effect of father's occupational status

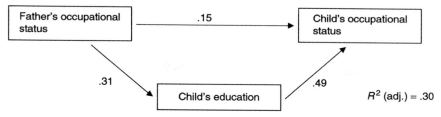

Figure 4.3. Path diagram of regression models of classic attainment model (SSND, N = 1,007). It is controlled for a respondent's sex and age

on the educational achievement of his children (β = 0.31). These results are in line with those found in other data sets for Western industrial countries (see e.g. Ganzeboom, Treiman, and Ultee 1991).

Adding the children's social resources (measured by the occupational status of their network members), as is presented in Figure 4.4, gives a better insight into the inter- and intragenerational transmission process (although the explained variance does not increase much).

The second order resources of the network members have a direct effect on a person's attained status, whereas these social resources themselves largely depend on the person's education and to some extent even on the occupational status of the father. Moreover, the original effects in the simple model remain largely the same.

Next, we analyze whether specifying the effects of fathers' occupational status as consisting of economic and cultural resources improves our understanding of the mobility process. Note that only statistically significant paths are shown in the models.

Figures 4.5 and 4.6 show that there indeed seem to be sector-specific effects of father's economic as well as cultural resources. The effect of father's cultural resources is not so strong; the indirect effect of father's cultural capital on his

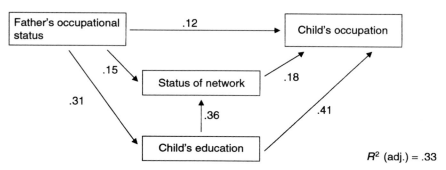

Figure 4.4. Path diagram of regression models of occupational status *including status of network with friends and acquaintances* (SSND, N = 1,007). It is controlled for a respondent's sex and age

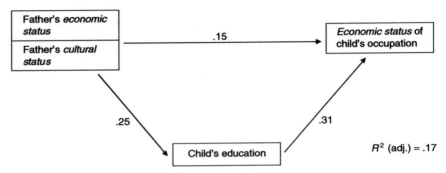

Figure 4.5. Path diagram of regression models of *economic status* (SSND, $N = 1,007$). It is controlled for a respondent's sex and age

children's cultural capital via their education is in fact bigger (0.13) than the direct effect (0.6).

In the following and final step, we introduce into the latter models the cultural and economic resources within the children's networks.

Figures 4.7 and 4.8 show that the cultural and economic resources in children's network have their own, additional effect on the economic and cultural status of the children's occupation. The effects of the cultural and economic status in one's network are completely sector-specific. The same holds for the cultural and economic resources of the father in these last models. The figures show that those who have family in a specific sector are rewarded when they strive for status in the same sector. There is no statistically significant effect of parents' cultural capital on the economic capital of the child, and also no such effect of parents' economic capital on the child's cultural capital. Interestingly, network effects point exactly in the same direction: one benefits only from network resources for achievement if these resources are in the same sector as the resulting occupation. Only the cultural

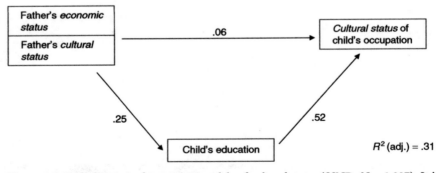

Figure 4.6. Path diagram of regression models of *cultural status* (SSND, $N = 1,007$). It is controlled for a respondent's sex and age

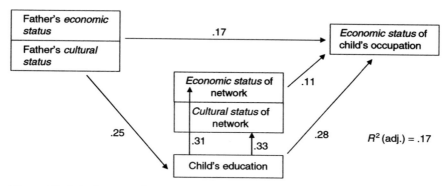

Figure 4.7. Path diagram of regression models of *economic status including status of friends and acquaintances* (SSND, N = 1,007). It is controlled for a respondent's sex and age

resources of the network members contribute to the achievement of cultural status and the economic resources of these network members do not do so, and vice versa.

Last but not least, considering the explained variance of the models depicted in Figures 4.7 and 4.8, it can be seen that the cultural achievement of children can be better explained than their economic achievements.

In a last step, Table 4.2 summarizes the regression models as presented in the Figures 4.5–4.8. The table shows the effects of the inclusion of different types of network resources in the model. The different types of networks that are measured in the position generator do have a different effect. In the previous analyses, we used the network that did not include family members in order to avoid counting father's resources twice. The table presented here inquires whether the different types of networks lead to different outcomes. The first models (M1 and M2) summarize the path models presented in Figures 4.5 and 4.6; the next two

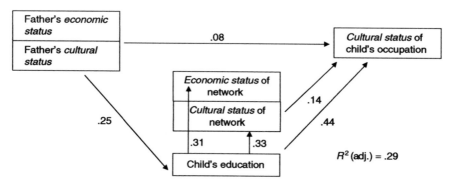

Figure 4.8. Path diagram of regression models of *cultural status including status of friends and acquaintances* (SSND, N = 1,007). It is controlled for a respondent's sex and age

Table 4.2. Regression of child achieved cultural and economic status on status of father, education, and status of network (source, SSND, $N = 1,007$; standardized coefficients)

	Achieved status of respondent							
	Cultural M1	Economic M2	Cultural M3	Economic M4	Cultural M5	Economic M6	Cultural M7	Economic M8
Cultural status of father	.06+	−.01	.08*	−.02	.04	−.05	.06	−.02
Economic status of father	.06	.15**	.05	.17**	.04	.15**	.08+	.16**
Education of child	.52**	.31**	.44**	.28**	.49**	.30**	.44**	.28**
Cultural status of network								
Friends and acquaintances	—	—	.14*	−.01	—	—	—	—
Family	—	—	—	—	.16**	−.05	—	—
All network members	—	—	—	—	—	—	.19**	.03
Economic status of network								
Friends and acquaintances	—	—	−.02	.11*	—	—	—	—
Family	—	—	—	—	−.06	.06	—	—
All network members	—	—	—	—	—	—	−.04	.10+
Control variables								
Sex (1 = male, 0 = female)	.01	.18**	.03	.19**	.02	.18**	−.02	.13**
Age	.09**	.05+	.06*	.03	.07**	.05	.08*	.07*
R^2 (adjusted)	.31	.17	.30	.16	.32	.16	.33	.17

$** \ p < .01; * \ p < .05; + \ p < .10.$

columns (M3 and M4) summarize Figures 4.7 and 4.8. The last four columns show the effects of the family network (M5 and M6) and of the whole network, including family, friends, and acquaintances (M7 and M8). The table shows the following: first, no matter what type of network is added, the effect of a respondent's education decreases. Second, as to the status of the father, the effects of his economic status are far more pronounced than the effects of his cultural status. The latter effects are often nonsignificant or show only weak effects. Third, when including network indicators in the model, effects of father's status remain rather stable. Furthermore, all types of networks show about the same effects with one exception: the effect of a family's economic resources on the economic resources of its offspring is entirely included in the father's economic resources. Therefore, family network resources do not count. Again, the sector-specific effects of social capital are remarkable.

We are aware that the causality of the network effects is open to debate. To a certain extent, one's network is built around an achieved occupation (sometimes a network even comes together with a job). If this is the case, the causal direction is the opposite of the direction that we assumed in this paper. However, personal networks, especially ties and members that have been in place for some time, do not change quickly. Much of the value in a network as measured in our survey probably predates individual outcomes such as occupational attainment (Burt 2000b; Erickson 2004; for a criticism, see Mouw 2003). Most likely, two interacting processes are of importance: networks influence occupational attainment (and of course other things) and in turn, this attainment influences networks. It is a task for future research using longitudinal data to estimate the strength of both effects.[2]

4.5. CONCLUSION

Our analyses produced a number of substantive results and a methodological one. First, the cultural and economic resources of a father directly influence his children's cultural and economic resources. Second, the cultural and economic resources in a person's network help in achieving cultural and economic resources. Third, a person's education not only directly but also indirectly affects the attained cultural and economic status via the cultural and economic resources in the network, whereas there is no such indirect effect of father's cultural and economic resources. Fourth, effects are largely sector specific: people are successful in the sector (cultural or economic) in which they have grown up, and usually their network is confined to the same area as well. Those who want to achieve a high status in a given sector benefit if they have family and friends with a high status in the same sector. In line with this argument, those who cross over from the sector in which they were raised but whose friends and acquaintances remain in the other sector may lose ground compared to those who find a job in the same sector as their father and their friends and acquaintances. We have shown that only those who stay in a sector benefit from the social resources provided by their family and by their network. Fifth, the position generator seems quite capable of tapping the economic and cultural resources in a person's network. Its use is far broader than originally thought. More generally, one can argue that the cultural or economic resources of a person's father as well as the resources in a person's network contribute to the reproduction of inequality over the generations. There is a direct effect of father's economic and cultural resources on the children's resources, and in addition an indirect effect of father's resources through the social resources. This reproduction probably will be less strong if children cross over to another sector; that is, most effects are sector-specific. This means that social capital is goal-specific (Flap 1999).

---

[2] If we assume that the causality works in the other direction, the interpretation would be that the recruitment of network members is highly selective and specific with regard to someone's own occupational sector (see Mouw 2003). We cannot decide that issue here, as much of the relevant information we have is cross-sectional in nature.

To attain cultural capital, one benefits from ties to alters who have many cultural resources, and similarly, if one wants to acquire economic resources. Our analysis of the effects of sector-specific resources provide a better insight into the attainment process, not so much in terms of explained variance but more in terms of a greater understanding of the process of cultural and economic status transmission.

4.6. DISCUSSION

Our present study on the role of the cultural and economic resources in one's networks, including those of one's father in the process of inter- and intragenerational mobility, can be extended in at least four ways. First, Bourdieu's proposal does not only apply to occupational stratification but also to differences in lifestyles. People in a certain occupation are socialized in a particular cultural lifestyle. Ganzeboom (1989) and De Graaf, Ganzeboom, and Kalmijn (1989) demonstrate that cultural and economic dimensions of an occupational status influence a range of lifestyles and values net of the influence of education. High cultural occupational status is associated with participation in high culture, reading of literature and national newspapers, being liberal on moral issues, and an egalitarian division of labor between spouses; high economic occupational status is associated with expensive holidays, consumption of luxury goods, support of free-market ideology, and a traditional orientation to politics, sex roles, and moral issues. Kalmijn (1994) demonstrated that the cultural and economic status influences marriage patterns: cultural and economic status serve as boundaries in the marriage market. There is little intermarriage between high-status economic occupations and high-status cultural occupations. There is a strong degree of assortative marriage by cultural status; assortative marriage by economic status is less important but its importance has grown. Our adapted position generator might thus be used to test whether the cultural and economic resources accessed via one's network will also lead to a specific lifestyle, political attitudes, and marriage behavior.

A second promising extension of this work would be to typify a person's education according to whether it is a cultural or an economic kind of education (Kalmijn and Van der Lippe 1997). One would expect that effects of a certain kind of education are similar to those of a network with certain kinds of resources, or having a father with certain kinds of resources. In earlier research, Hansen (2001) made a distinction between hard and soft types of education, which is quite similar to the distinction between cultural and economic educational training. She showed that those who originate in an economic sector and who have a hard type of education have better economic returns on their educational investments.

Third, it may be worthwhile to differentiate between the effects of cultural and economic resources of the first job, on the one hand, and that of the current or last job, on the other hand. Ascribed cultural or economic resources in one's networks, that is, those of one's father, will have a greater effect on the cultural or economic status of one's first job; whereas the achieved cultural or economic resources in one's network, that is, those of one's friends and acquaintances, are of greater influence on one's current or last job (see Moerbeek 2001 and Moerbeek and Flap 2008, in this volume). We will probably improve our understanding of the role that the cultural and economic resources of one's significant alters have in the reproduction process once we differentiate between the focal person's first and current or last job.

Fourth, it will be interesting to systematically compare our deductive measure of social capital, the cultural and economic resources in a person's social network, derived from Bourdieu's hypotheses on cultural capital and Lin's hypothesis on social capital, with the more inductive measures of social capital obtained by Van der Gaag with respect to their internal and external or predictive validity.[3]

Fifth, a further contribution could be made by inquiring into the effects of sector-specific social capital—the benefits of staying in the same sector as well as the losses of switching sectors—on a person's earnings. Such an analysis would show whether social capital and, above all, sector-specific social capital really pay.

APPENDIX 1

Position Generator of the SSND

Before asking you any more questions about your work and your daily activities, I would like to know about the different kind of occupations you meet and come in contact with in your daily life. I have here a list of some of the different occupations or functions that people can have. Does someone of your family, your friends, or acquaintances have one of these occupations? An acquaintance is considered as somebody to whom you might have a small talk if you meet him/her on the street and whose name is familiar to you.

Interviewer

Begin with family. If Ego doesn't have a family member, ask about friends and lastly ask about acquaintances. If Ego knows someone who is a family member and a friend at the same time he/she should be counted as family.

---

[3] The inductive cumulative scaling analysis by Van der Gaag (2005) (see also Van der Gaag, Snijders, and Flap 2008) of the 30 occupations in our position generator resulted in a number of subscales that only faintly reproduce our deductive results that people have networks with network members with two types of occupations that differ according to whether they provide access primarily to cultural or to economic resources.

	Occupation/function	Family	Friend	Acquaintance	No, n.a.
1	Physician	(1)	(2)	(3)	(0)
2	Cook	(1)	(2)	(3)	(0)
3	Engineer	(1)	(2)	(3)	(0)
4	High ranking civil servant	(1)	(2)	(3)	(0)
5	Construction worker	(1)	(2)	(3)	(0)
6	Manager of a company	(1)	(2)	(3)	(0)
7	Manager (other)	(1)	(2)	(3)	(0)
8	Teacher	(1)	(2)	(3)	(0)
9	Real estate agent	(1)	(2)	(3)	(0)
10	Labor union executive	(1)	(2)	(3)	(0)
11	Lawyer	(1)	(2)	(3)	(0)
12	Mechanic/technician	(1)	(2)	(3)	(0)
13	Accountant/bookkeeper	(1)	(2)	(3)	(0)
14	Scientist	(1)	(2)	(3)	(0)
15	Policy maker	(1)	(2)	(3)	(0)
16	Musician/artist/writer	(1)	(2)	(3)	(0)
17	IT worker	(1)	(2)	(3)	(0)
18	Police agent	(1)	(2)	(3)	(0)
19	Secretary	(1)	(2)	(3)	(0)
20	Insurance agent	(1)	(2)	(3)	(0)
21	Foreman	(1)	(2)	(3)	(0)
22	Nurse	(1)	(2)	(3)	(0)
23	Farmer	(1)	(2)	(3)	(0)
24	Truck driver	(1)	(2)	(3)	(0)
25	Postman	(1)	(2)	(3)	(0)
26	Machine worker	(1)	(2)	(3)	(0)
27	Salesman	(1)	(2)	(3)	(0)
28	Unskilled worker	(1)	(2)	(3)	(0)
29	Cleaner	(1)	(2)	(3)	(0)
30	Barber	(1)	(2)	(3)	(0)

5

The Formation of Social Capital among Chinese Urbanites: Theoretical Explanation and Empirical Evidence[1]

Yanjie Bian

How do individuals form social capital from their networks of social relationships? The view that social capital may be an unintended consequence of interpersonal networking (Arrow 2000) leads us to look at the joint effects of individual attributes and social contexts in which interpersonal networking occurs. The alternative view points to a more conscious process, in which individuals develop social capital by cultivating, maintaining, and utilizing certain social relationships for instrumental or emotional purposes, as is widely found in Chinese society (Liang [1949] 1986; Walder 1986; Hwang 1987; King 1988, 1994; Fei [1949] 1992; Yang 1994; Yan 1996; Bian 1997; Lin 2001c; Gold, Guthrie, and Wank 2002) and elsewhere (Burt 1992, 2001; Erickson 1996b, 2001, 2004; Flap and Volker 2004). This second view urges us to look at the configurations of social and cultural contexts, some of which generate greater pressures on individuals to deliberately develop social networks and social capital than do other contexts (Lin 2000a).

In this chapter, I develop a theoretical model to explain two structural sources of variation in the formation of social capital at interpersonal levels. The first is the extent to which individuals' social class positions constrain them from developing ties of personal relationships with people of certain social class positions, causing variations in structures and resources of personal networks, which, in turn, result in variation of social capital accumulated over time. The second is the extent to which work ties that are conferred by and maintained on a job can be transformed into personal relationships from which to generate social capital. Because some jobs provide greater opportunities for developing

[1] Part of this chapter was presented at the Sunbelt International Conference for Social Network Analysis, Cancun, Mexico, February 12–16, 2003. Funding for the survey analyzed in this chapter was provided by an RGC grant from the Hong Kong Universities Grants Committee (HKUST6052/98H). I thank Xianbi Huang and Yu Li for research assistance, and Bonnie H. Erickson and Nan Lin for their helpful comments on an earlier draft.

networks of social relationships than others do, I argue that occupational life is a source of variation in the formation of social capital among working individuals.

I will begin with an operational definition of social capital, on which I base my theoretical model that will guide a preliminary effort of measuring social capital and testing the model with a 1999 five-city survey of Chinese urbanites.

5.1. DEFINING SOCIAL CAPITAL

Social capital is a heuristic concept, as researchers attach many different meanings to it (see the introductory chapter of this volume). My own definition of social capital begins with a critique of Bourdieu (1986), who advocated many different forms of capital. Bourdieu appeared to be satisfied with recognizing any goal-relevant resource as a distinctive form of capital, as documented in his usage of such terms as material capital, economic capital, human capital, political capital, cultural capital, symbolic capital, social capital, and so on. Readers can easily lose sight of what each of these forms of capital implies for the bigger question about social-structural constrains on individual actions and goal attainments. What is the underlying rule in differentiating one capital form from another? When should we stop naming new forms of capital?

I argue that forms of capital are to be defined and differentiated by the extent to which resources are embodied to human actors. Resources do not transform into capital by themselves; human actors do this. Therefore, without relating resources and capital to human actors, one will lose the central meaning of identifying capital forms. In this actor-centered perspective, three fundamental forms of capital can be identified, and no more than three.

The first is material capital, including various forms of wealth and economic resources. This form of capital is external to human actors, but can be possessed and utilized by them. Material capital may grow, transfer, or be lost in the process of investment and utilization, and in none of these states is it unrelated to human actors by way of ownership and control.

The second form is human capital. It is the productive resource that is internalized into and cannot be detached from human actors. It exists in human actors' physical strength, knowledge, skill, experience, and so forth, thus including what Bourdieu calls symbolic and cultural capitals as well. To any actor, his or her human capital is created, maintained, increased, or decreased in the process of investment and utilization.

Social capital, the third and the last form of capital and one that differs from material capital and human capital, is the resource that is embedded in and can be mobilized from the networks of social relationships among human actors. In network analysis terms, the social capital of any ego is ultimately the material or human resources of his or her alters, such as power, wealth, status, creative knowledge, or value-added information. Actor A's resources are transformed into the social capital of Actor B when B mobilizes them through B's relationship with A. Therefore, social capital cannot be possessed by any single actor alone, nor can it be internalized into actors, simply because it is the relationship that carries and transfers the resources possessed by others with whom one has a relationship. Simply put, social capital necessarily needs a relational bearer.

Not every type of relationship qualifies to be a social capital bearer, however. I argue that to qualify as a social capital bearer, a relationship must be personal, informal, and enduring. A personal relationship, such as kinship and friendship, links the parties through the sharing of human feelings toward each other's personal worlds, the strengthening of affections toward each other, and the exchange of favors, assistances, and materialized resources. By contrast, if linked by a public relationship such as authority–subordinate relationship, the parties would act in well-formalized roles that have no room for the exchange of personal feelings and resources, unless these formal and public relationships are transformed into informal or personal ones. When a personal or informal relationship becomes enduring, it means that the relationship will have a high quality that is characterized by some of the following: mutual trust; psychological interdependency; exchanges of personal feelings, affections, and favors; and sharing of resources and values. When a relationship becomes personal, informal, and enduring, it is the best bearer of social capital. A public, formal, or short-lived relationship is a poor bearer of social capital.

5.2. THE FORMATION OF SOCIAL CAPITAL

5.2.1. From Network Features to Social Capital

All human actors have personal, informal, and enduring relationships with certain others, and the totality of these relationships weaves an egocentric social network. What features of social networks generate social capital? Scholars have pointed out three different features of networks as generating social capital: network ties, network structures, and network resources. The first of these simply equates social capital with network ties. Here network ties are seen as mechanisms through which information flows and resources are mobilized. This leads some researchers to believe that the more network ties an individual has to others, the more information and resources the individual can get from others, and the greater the amount of social capital that the individual can have. Because networks vary in quality of information and resources (Granovetter 1973; Burt 1992), ties to some networks would generate a high level of social capital, others a low level, and still others no social capital at all. One can reasonably believe from these plausible hypothetical situations that the network-tie-as-social-capital view is too simplistic. Despite this obvious weakness, this view implies a highly feasible operationalization in research: an individual's social capital can be measured by counting the number of network ties the individual has to others. This easy-to-operate measure has been widely adopted by many researchers (Portes 1998).

The second feature rejects the tie-as-capital assumption and takes network structures seriously. Density is a composite measure of network structure. But between dense and sparse networks, which kind of network generates more social capital and why? Coleman (1988) argues that dense networks generate more social capital because they help make individuals abide by group norms; encourage cooperation, trust, and solidarity; and provide positive conditions for the creation and acquisition of human capital. Burt (1992), on the other hand, draws attention to arenas of competition, arguing that sparse networks may generate greater social capital because disconnections within sparse networks reduce group constraints, encourage innovations, and present entrepreneurial opportunities for individuals occupying positions of "structural holes" that link otherwise disconnected actors of nonredundant resources. In a more recent effort, Burt (2001) integrates these competing views by looking at the effects of network closure and structural holes on entrepreneurship and innovations. On a methodological note, network density requires information about the entire network for any actor, causing serious measurement difficulties in large-scale studies.

The third view defines social capital as the resources that are embedded in social networks. Lin (2001*b*) is the leading proponent for this approach of network resource as social capital. If capital is a resource that is invested for gains, argues Lin, social capital is the social resource that is accessed and mobilized from the networks of social relationships for gains. The basic forms of social resources are power, wealth, and prestige that are possessed by alters, and these resources become social when egos access and mobilize them through ego's network ties to these alters. As can be seen, social capital as defined by Lin fits the nature of the term: it is network resources that generate gains and produce socioeconomic outcomes. Despite its conceptual sophistication and complexity, however, this view requires information about network connections between ego and alters, alters' possession of resources, and whether these resources can be mobilized for ego's specific actions. These items of information are extremely difficult to collect for any kind of empirical study.

In the context of personal networks, and holding an ego-network perspective, I propose four relational features of a network that best generate social capital. First, assuming personal relations to be bearers of social capital, a large network generates more social capital than does a small network, simply because the former contains more relational bearers of social capital. Second, assuming that such resources as power, wealth, status influence, and information are associated with social positions, and that different social positions bear different kinds of

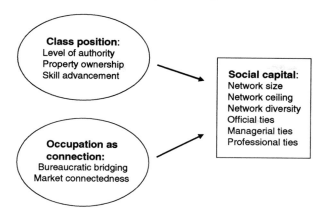

Figure 5.1. A conceptual model explaining the formation of social capital

resources, a high-diversity network that contains alters of many different social positions generates more social capital than does a low-diversity network whose alters occupy a smaller number of different social positions. Third, assuming that social positions form a hierarchy of power, wealth, status, and other types of resources, and that personal networks are hierarchies in which alters vary in power, wealth, status, and other types of resources, a network with a higher ceiling generates more social capital than does a network with a lower ceiling. Finally, assuming that class positions are determined by distinct resources such as property, authority, and skill (Wright 1997), networks with a full combination of distinctive class positions generate more social capital than networks with a less complete class composition.

In summary, my operational definition of social capital requires measures of four relational features of personal networks: network size, network diversity, network ceiling, and network composition. These measurements have face validity for each of the three network views of social capital. Specifically, network size is a measure derived from the network-tie-as-social-capital view; network composition is a measure derived from the network-structure-as-social-capital view; and network ceiling and network diversity are the measures derived from the network-resource-as-social-capital view.

As displayed in Figure 5.1, individuals' social capital comes from the resources embedded in their personal networks, which vary in size, diversity, ceiling, and composition. More specifically, greater social capital is generated by a larger and more diverse network with a higher ceiling and a more complete class composition. What factors influence individuals to form social capital-producing networks? As shown on the left-hand side of Figure 5.1, I propose two structural explanations: a class-as-relational-constraint explanation and an occupation-as-relational-opportunity explanation.

5.2.2. Class as Relational Constraint

Social class is defined here as a position of social distinction. There has long been a debate on whether social class is the same as occupation. Arguing from a realist perspective that modern capitalism has "de-aggregated" the social structure in which "detailed occupations are deeply institutionalized," Grusky, Weeden, and Sørensen (2000: 303) go on to assert that the analyst who ignores fine-grained occupational categories "may be compared to the feudal scholar who eschews the 'surface categories' of serf, lord, and clergy in favor of uncovering latent or subterranean structures that are concealed from ordinary view." From the other side of this debate, Portes (2000: 257) charges that "calling occupations 'classes' leaves no baby after the bath water." In his view, "classes are *theoretical constructs* devised for the structural interpretation of social phenomena and the prediction of major long-term trends" (original emphasis). Portes advocates identifying "the 'real' class structure" prior to empirical analysis in order to apply the class concept subsequently to the analysis of various phenomena. In my analysis below, I take Portes' view by differentiating social class from occupation.

In industrial and postindustrial societies, social class is a major obstacle to voluntary socializing between people. Sociologists have identified property, authority, and skill as resources of distinction that define social class boundaries in contemporary capitalist societies (Wright 1997). In a multicountry sample from America, Sweden, and Norway, Wright and Cho (1992) found that friendship relationships are permitted within class boundaries to a greater extent than those between classes. This is understandable under the homophily principle of social interaction (Laumann 1973): as compared to those of different class positions, people within class boundaries are more likely to have relatively equal resources, status, and lifestyles that confer rich opportunities to socialize with one another, developing interpersonal ties of frequent interaction, intimacy, duration, mutual trust, or relational dependency. Wright and Cho also found that the three class boundaries present unequal degrees of permission for friendships to form between classes. Property presents the most rigid class distinction in forming friendships between owners and nonowners; authority is the next most rigid class distinction in forming friendships between superiors and subordinates, making skill the least rigid class distinction in forming friendships between professionals and nonprofessionals.

In China, where the ownership class is still a minor portion of the population, Bian et al. (2005) found that among Chinese New Year visitors to 400 urban families surveyed, authority is a greater class distinction than is skill. Among those who have political, administrative, and managerial authorities, managers in public and private firms have a greater range of New Year visitors than do government officials. Professionals, too, tend to have advantages in socializing with managers than with government officials during the New Year celebration. While industrial workers were once quasi-middle classes under Mao, they are the most socially marginalized group in the emerging market society. On the whole, while within-class relations can be formed rather easily in any given class, families that have more class resources (authority, skill, and property) are better able to develop between-class relations than do families who have less or no class resources. What causes this pattern to emerge? I identify three underlying mechanisms that are of relevance in China.

The first is the differential resource effect. Persons and families in advantageous classes have greater amounts of resources to engage in social relationships across, as well as within, class positions than do those in disadvantageous classes. This resource effect is especially relevant to the social relationships of enduring nature, which require continuous exchanges of tangible (goods, services, and assets) and intangible (information and influence that are conferred by power, wealth, and prestige) resources between the parties tied by the relationship (Wellman 1979). Since Chinese *guanxi* networks are characterized by enduring ties of favor exchanges between parties of unequal status for both tangible and intangible resources (King 1988, 1994; Yang 1994; Gold, Guthrie, and Wank 2002), the resource effect is expected to be true in China, differentially constraining members of disadvantageous classes from developing between-class connections with members of advantageous classes.

The second mechanism is the relative size effect. In a pyramidal class structure, persons and families in advantageous classes are in smaller numbers than those in disadvantageous classes. Structurally, those in a higher-class position are presented with more opportunities to socialize with those in a lower-class position, but not the other way around. This effect is the basis for Blau's theory of structuralism (Blau 1977), and is evident from the studies of interclass marriages in the United States (Blau, Blum, and Schwartz 1982). It is also evident in New Year visitations among Chinese urbanites: families of elite classes have greater frequency of having New Year visitors from families of nonelite classes than the reverse (Bian et al. 2005).

The third mechanism is the structural mobility effect. In a country with a good pace of industrialization, new positions are created at higher levels of the class hierarchy, causing structural mobility to occur in a manner that sends more persons from lower to higher positions than from higher to lower positions (Featherman and Hauser 1978). At interpersonal levels, this has two relational effects: that premobility "horizontal ties" will transform into postmobility "hierarchical ties" and that more relational transformations of this sort are at higher levels of the class hierarchy. These effects imply that upwardly mobile persons are more likely to maintain between-class connections than do downwardly mobile persons. This implication is of great significance and applicability to China, a country whose economic growth and societal transformations since 1980 have both improved the living standards and created enormous opportunities for upward mobility (Bian 2002).

In sum, while social class distinctions are relational constraints on the formation of social networks among all classes, they present greater constraints for disadvantageous classes than for advantageous classes. Therefore:

HYPOTHESIS 1: *Social class positions alter social interactions in ways such that persons and families in advantageous class positions tend to have larger and more diverse personal networks with a higher ceiling and a more complete composition than those in disadvantageous class positions, resulting in greater social capital for the former than for the latter.*

5.2.3. Occupation as Relational Opportunity

Occupational life provides both a stable communication space and an enduring opportunity for social interaction. In the workplace, people do not just work. Instead, teamworking, apprentice advising, on-the-job training, coffee/tea/lunch breaks, and various face-to-face contacts are a few of the many opportunities for interpersonal networks and informal groups to develop. Indeed, the notion of informal groups is so important in work and occupation that they form the basis of industrial sociology, organizational studies, and management research (Scott 2004). I am less interested in how informal groups develop at work than in the fact that work contacts get translated into personal relationships. If this is true, then occupational life is a relational promoter for people to develop social capital.

There are reasons to believe that two kinds of work contacts do get translated into personal relationships. The first is contacts with colleagues of equal or differential rank. In worldwide observation, work colleagues have proven to be a significant source of discussion networks for matters of personal importance in the United States (Marsden 1987), Europe (Van Der Poel 1993), and China (Ruan 1993, 1998). In Chinese cities, work colleagues account for more than one-fourth of visitations during the Spring Festival, a traditional holiday during which kin and close social contacts pay home visits to each other; the other three-fourths are from relatives, friends, and neighbors (Bian, Davis, and Wang 2007). If one views workplace organization as a bureaucratic structure of vertical and horizontal ties, the jobs that have more of these ties than other jobs are here termed "jobs with higher degrees of bureaucratic bridging." For example, a middle-level manager is one of the jobs with a high degree of bureaucratic bridging, as the manager supervises subordinates, coordinates with other managers of equal rank, and reports to general managers of higher rank. In contrast, an assembly line worker has a job with a lower bureaucratic bridging, for the worker has no other people to supervise and his or her only work contacts are from the team of the same assembly line. Although not all work contacts necessarily get translated into personal relations, the more numerous the work contacts the greater the probability that such translations can be processed. Thus:

HYPOTHESIS 2: *Jobs with higher degrees of bureaucratic bridging provide their occupants with more work contacts from which to develop personal networks and social capital than do jobs with lower degrees of bureaucratic bridging.*

The second kind of work contact is not with colleagues but with clients. To name just a few examples, salespersons make daily contact with purchasing agents, teachers with students, doctors with patients, and managers with other managers of the contracted firms. These "market connections" do not necessarily stay in the marketplace but are sometimes converted into personal spheres. To be sure, some of these will not be instant, impersonal, or transactional contacts; instead, as they connect the parties for an extended period of time, opportunities will arise for the parties to exchange and share human feelings, favors asked and provided, emotional and instrumental exchanges repeated, and personal relationships developed and maintained. Thus jobs with higher degrees of market connections provide opportunities for their occupants to develop personal networks from these connections. This leads to our final hypothesis:

HYPOTHESIS 3: *Jobs with higher degrees of market connection provide their occupants with more market contacts from which to develop personal networks and social capital than do jobs with lower degrees of market connection.*

In summary, jobs with bureaucratic bridging and jobs with market connection provide opportunities for occupants to develop personal networks and social capital. Persons whose jobs have the highest degrees of both bureaucratic bridging and market connection will have the best opportunities to develop personal networks and social capital from their work contacts. Persons whose jobs have a higher degree of either bureaucratic bridging or market connection will have fewer opportunities of doing so. Finally, persons whose jobs have none of these work-contact advantages will have the least opportunities for developing personal networks and social capital.

It is reasonable to believe that occupational connections may help explain some of the effects of social class on social capital. Studies of intergenerational mobility have demonstrated that persons from different class backgrounds are sorted into different job slots, which in return would offer differential opportunities of job-related connections that I describe above. In this study, however, I consider the independent, direct effects of class and occupation, and do not examine the question of how intergenerational mobility within and between class positions would affect opportunities of occupational connections.

5.3. DATA AND MEASURES

To test the three hypotheses just proposed, I analyze data from a 1999 survey I conducted in five Chinese cities: Changchun, Guangzhou, Shanghai, Tianjin, and Xiamen. My primary purpose with the survey was to examine changing efficacies of social networks on job search outcomes in varying labor market contexts, and the selected five cities satisfied this requirement. This research purpose is, however, not relevant for the present analysis. I treat the five Chinese cities in no particular order in this chapter, but use them as a sample of urban China for two reasons. First, the five cities cover a fairly large range of Chinese cities in terms of socioeconomic development, marketization, and regional dispersion. Second, in each city households and respondents were drawn by following a uniform multistage probability sampling procedure. The five-city survey offers a total sample size of 4,752 households and respondents, of whom 82 percent are permanent residents and the rest are temporary residents mainly migrating from rural areas. I describe in length below how I measured four sets of variables of the present analysis: social capital, social class, occupation-as-connection, and other variables.

5.3.1. Measuring Social Capital

As graphed in Figure 5.1, an individual's social capital can be measured by the individual's personal networks in terms of size, diversity, ceiling, and composition. This is rather a difficult job whether in Chinese society or elsewhere. Personal networks are personal and therefore relative: who is included in ego's personal network is subject to ego's evaluation, which varies according to the content of interaction. Alters in ego's "discussion network" are unlikely to be named again in ego's "debit and credit network" or "job search network" in China (Ruan 1998) or Europe (Van Der Poel 1993). Personal networks are also dynamic: close relatives and best friends can lose favor because of interpersonal conflicts and are excluded from the core or entity of ego's personal network. By the same token, increasing interactions or intensifications of emotional and instrumental exchanges can transform acquaintances into close friends, and bad relations into good ones. Still more complicated is the case scenario presented by Chinese sociologist Liang ([1949] 1986), who argues that no real network has a rigid boundary because connections are connected to other connections without a limit. Facing these relational features of personal networks (personal, dynamic, and boundary-relative), how can we still measure the size and other dimensions of egocentric networks in Chinese cities?

The standard network research tool of "name generators" (Laumann 1973; Fischer 1982; Burt 1984; Marsden 1987) may not work. It allows survey and non-survey respondents to name three to five "best friends" or "closest confidants" on matters of personal importance, generating at best the core network of strongest ties for anyone in America (Marsden 1987) or China (Ruan 1998). While the generated discussion networks seem to be quite similar between Americans and Chinese (Blau, Ruan, and Ardelt 1991), these discussion networks may not tell the central story about Chinese *guanxi* networks, whose underlying logic is that of favor exchange (Hwang 1987; King 1988, 1994; Yang 1994; Yan 1996). Favor exchanges are conducted between people with nonredundant resources, and tend to require large and diverse networks in which to generate exchange opportunities (Gold, Guthrie, and Wank 2002). Hence, limiting the number of names to be mentioned by any respondent may unexpectedly distort the very nature of Chinese *guanxi* networks.

Alternatively, "position generators" (Lin and Dumin 1986) make no limit on the number of relational contacts to be named. This approach permits the recording of positions of as many alters as respondents can relate to, from whose characteristics one can measure the structural dimensions of ego's personal networks in terms of positional diversity, status ceiling, and class composition. While this approach has already proven to be a useful network device in Chinese and non-Chinese societies (Lin 2001*b*), one potential weakness is that it makes no reference to the specific events in which networking occurs. Because Chinese *guanxi* networks are favor-exchange networks significant and sensitive to life events, events may be a necessary part of any network-generating device for measuring Chinese *guanxi* networks. Whereas an event of personal importance would allow an ego to socialize with some specific alters, as in the case of "social eating" (Bian 2001), events of common social importance to all residents in a given culture imply that egos are expected to socialize with all significant alters who, sharing the same cultural norm, would have equal desirability to socialize with the egos. If this is true, an important research task is to identify events of cultural significance from which to help generate the maximum size and composition of any ego's personal network.

To meet this challenge, I have developed an event-based position generator approach to measuring personal networks in the Chinese context (Bian and Li 2001; Bian, Davis, and Wang 2007). In my observation, much socializing in Chinese society occurs in relation to events of cultural significance. While birthdays, weddings, and funerals are events for inviting relatives, friends, and other close contacts, traditional holidays such as the Spring Festival (Chinese New Year on the lunar calendar) and Mid-Autumn Festival are occasions for them to visit each other, treat each other to meals, and exchange gifts. To be included in ego's personal network, alters surely socialize with ego at these events. Residents or visitors to China can observe the following in any city, town, or village during the celebration of these festivals: relatives invite each other's families to enjoy big feasts, friends visit each other in person or call to extend good wishes, and other contacts of social or instrumental importance (a part of Chinese *guanxi* network) exchange greetings, gifts, and banquets. On the basis of this observation, in the five-city survey I used a question about the Spring Festival. I asked respondents how many persons (or families) they visited during the celebration of the last Spring Festival. Respondents were then asked to identify the jobs of their visitors from a list of 20 occupations. Table 5.1 presents a summary of the data collected.

The 20 occupations were selected from the classification of 500 plus, three-digit-coded job titles used in the Chinese census. Confined somewhat to the selections by previous researchers (Lin and Xie 1988; Bian and Li 2001), I made sure that the selected 20 occupations covered a wide range of jobs on a scale of occupational prestige. This goal was achieved very well. As shown in Table 5.1, section I, the 20 occupations range from the highest prestige of 95 for scientists to the lowest of 6 for domestic workers (the scores of occupational prestige are taken from a previous study in which respondents rated each of these occupations on a five-point scale; see Bian and Li [2001] for details). Previous studies show that the rated prestige scores are indicative of socioeconomic status or resources each occupation can grant to its occupants in China (Lin and Xie 1988), as in any industrial country (Treiman 1977; Treiman and Yip 1989). These 20 occupations give us a good range of socioeconomic status or resources as contained in the social structure of urban China.

As shown in Table 5.1, section II, respondents had an average of 28.46 visitors, with a standard deviation of 27.89. This is my measure of network size for Chinese urbanites. The smallest network, for a small shop owner, had 2 alters (New Year visitors), and the largest, for a large enterprise manager, 300 alters. Confined to the 20-occupation list, respondents' alters had an average of 6.31 occupations with a standard deviation of 4.43, indicating a large difference in network diversity in terms of alter's job positions. Among all alters of a given respondent's, one alter with the highest prestige can be identified to indicate the "status ceiling" of the respondent's personal network. The mean ceiling is 75.78 with a standard deviation of 22.93, again denoting a large variation among respondents. Finally, network composition takes into account respondents' alters who hold any of the three leading class positions of state officials (61% did, and here "state officials" include the lowest level of cadres working in party, government, and legal offices), managers (45%), or professionals (56%).

Table 5.1, section IV, shows that the network measures are highly correlated with one another. These allow for reaching a one-factor solution from the factor analysis, as shown in section III. With regard to the relative contribution each variable makes to the social capital factor, network diversity ranks highest (a factor loading of 0.866), followed by network ceiling (0.816), ties with professionals (0.762), ties with officials (0.628), network size (0.562), and ties with managers (0.554). This result shows that network diversity may be the best single social capital indicator. From the factor analysis and for this present analysis, the generated factor score is named "Social Capital Volume," which I use as a composite social capital variable for hypothesis testing.

5.3.2. Measuring Social Class

To identify the three underlying dimensions of property, authority, and skill, respondents' current occupations are classified into eight categories as shown in Table 5.2, section I: business owners (0.8%), state officials (8.3%), managers (10.4%), professionals (13.1%), clerks (9.1%), skilled workers (20.5%), unskilled workers (27.5%), and self-employed (10.6%). While this classification is conventional in research of China's social stratification, it is rare to be able to sample

Table 5.1. Dependent variables: social networks and social capital, the 1999 Five-Chinese City Survey ($N = 4{,}521$)

Section I. Position generator: occupations and occupational prestige scores

Scientist	95	Government official	80	Accountant	58	Cook	24
College teacher	91	School teacher	77	Clerk	53	Industrial worker	20
Engineer	86	Party official	73	Police	52	Salesperson	15
Legal staff	86	Manager	71	Nurse	48	Waiter/waitress	11
Physician	86	Business professional	64	Chauffeur	25	Domestic worker	6

Section II. Network measures from the position generator

Variables	Mean/%	SD	Maximum	Minimum
Network size (no. of visitors)	28.46	27.89	300	1
Network ceiling (highest prestige)	75.78	22.93	95	6
Network diversity (no. of occupations)	6.31	4.43	20	1
Network composition				
Ties to officials	61.00		1	0
Ties to managers	45.00		1	0
Ties to professionals	55.70		1	0

Section III. Factor analysis results

Variables	Factor loading	Generated factor (termed "social capital")	
Network diversity	.866	Mean	0
Network ceiling	.816	Standard deviation	1.00
Ties to professionals	.762	Maximum value	2.99
Ties to officials	.628	Minimum value	−2.05
Network size	.562	Sample size	4521
Ties to managers	.554	Resolution	50.23%

Section IV. Correlation matrix for social capital and network measures

	Social capital	Network size	Network ceiling	Network diversity	Ties to officials	Ties to managers	Ties to professional
Social capital	1						
Network size	.562***	1					
Network ceiling	.816***	.281***	1				
Network diversity	.866***	.485***	.575***	1			
Ties to officials	.628***	.255***	.403***	.494***	1		
Ties to managers	.554***	.202***	.385***	.456***	.210***	1	
Ties to professionals	.762***	.277***	.684***	.577***	.325***	.211***	1

*** Correlation is significant at the 0.001 level, 2-tailed.

Table 5.2. Descriptive statistics of independent variables ($N = 4,521$)

Section I. Social-class categories

Officials	8.3%	Skilled workers	20.5%
Managers	10.4%	Nonskilled workers	27.1%
Professionals	13.1%	Business owners	0.8%
Clerks	9.1%	Self-employed	10.6%

Section II. Occupation-as-connection variables

Questionnaire items: In your job, how frequently do you contact people in the following roles? (often = 4, sometimes = 3, rarely = 2, never = 1)		Factors and factor loadings	
	Mean (SD)	Bureaucratic bridging	Market connectedness
Lower-level units	1.88 (1.11)	.805	.196
Upper-level units	2.07 (1.10)	.776	.266
Other work units	2.07 (1.14)	.642	.409
Superiors	2.66 (1.10)	.766	−.017
Subordinates	2.50 (1.32)	.744	−.003
Colleagues of equal rank	3.42 (1.00)	.573	−.297
Clients	2.36 (1.33)	.086	.876
Customers	2.67 (1.34)	−.050	.857
Business visitors	2.37 (1.30)	.174	.844

Generated factors:	Mean (SD)	Maximum	Minimum	Resolution
Bureaucratic bridging	0.00 (1.00)	2.07	2.08	35.2%
Market connectedness	0.00 (1.00)	−1.93	−1.56	28.7%

Section III. Other variables

	% or Mean (SD)	City	%
Gender (male)	51.6%		
Age	38.9 (12.1)	Changchun	19.7
Party membership	14.9%	Guangzhou	17.0
College	20.6%	Shanghai	21.1
Sector (state)	55.7%	Tianjin	21.1
Permanent resident	81.8%	Xiamen	21.1
Household income in 1998 (yuan)	26,940 (99,878)		

owners of sizable private enterprises or high-ranking state officials in any population representative sample. Not surprisingly, the five-city sample has owners of household businesses or small firms and state officials in middle or lower ranks. Despite this weakness, the eight-category classification serves the analytic purpose well, as it covers all three underlying class boundaries: business owners are in the property class, officials and managers in the authority class, professionals in the skill class; other occupational groups are outside one or more of these class boundaries.

5.3.3. Measuring Occupation as Connections

My conceptualization considers occupational life as a social space in which to develop personal networks from two different kinds of job-based connections: (*a*) bureaucratic bridging, which connects ego to alters horizontally and hierarchically within the workplace and (*b*) market connectedness, which connects ego to alters from the marketplace. I describe how each is measured in turn.

Bureaucratic bridging refers to the extent to which some jobs require jobholders to perform and complete their work tasks in connection to others at the workplace. These are the jobs whose incumbents are bridged into the incumbents of next jobs on a chain of information and commands in a technical sense. In this sense I have termed these kinds of jobs as "bureaucratic bridging" jobs. While job titles may provide fairly accurate estimates of the *average* degree of bureaucratic bridging for each job, it is reasonable to believe that the degree of bureaucratic bridging for the same occupation varies across workplaces because of the variations in institutional arrangements, organizational parameters, and management styles of these workplaces. I instead adopted the approach of asking respondents to assess their time allocation on the job.

On the questionnaire, respondents were asked to indicate how frequently ("often" = 4, "sometimes" = 3, "rare" = 2, or "never" = 1) they contacted the following people on a daily basis while performing their jobs: (*a*) supervisors/leaders, (*b*) subordinates, (*c*) other colleagues, (*d*) someone from supervising government offices, (*e*) someone from subordinating organizations, and (*f*) someone from contracted organizations. These six items are assumed to measure a common latent variable—bureaucratic bridging. That is, the more frequently a respondent is in work contact with others identified by each of these six items, the more likely it is for the respondent to be bridged into other jobholders at the workplace, providing him or her with opportunities to develop networks of personal relationships from work colleagues.

Market connectedness, my second occupation-as-connection variable, refers to the extent to which a jobholder performs and completes his or her work tasks in connection to the marketplace. Market connected jobs, as Bian and Logan (1996) note in their study of the dynamics of social stratification in urban China, offer ample market opportunities to earn income, on or off the job, in transitional Chinese economy. In this study, I explore not economic but social returns of market connected jobs: what jobs that are highly market connected would offer ample opportunities of developing networks of personal relationships from job-market connections? While we may again make good guesses about each job's potential to offer these connections, as in Bian and Logan's measurement exercise, in this study I take this one step further by asking respondents to assess their time allocation on the job in connection to the marketplace.

It is conceptually reasonable to define what markets are (although it is difficult to do; see Swedsberg [1990]); on the measurement level, it is a challenge to identify the kinds of connections that are market related and not detached from the workplace. My starting point is to assume that certain roles are highly associated with the notion of market and least connected to the organization at work. For example, both employers and employees may frequently deal with (*a*) customers, (*b*) clients, or (*c*) visitors of all sorts on their jobs, and in doing so their time is spent connecting to the marketplace through contacting people in these roles. Using this assumption, on the questionnaire respondents were asked to assess how frequently (from "often" = 4 to "never" = 1, as in the bureaucratic bridging measures) they contacted people in those three roles while performing their jobs on a daily basis. These three roles are assumed to help measure one common latent variable—market connectedness. That is, the more frequently respondents contact people in any of these roles on the job, the more likely it is that their jobs are market connected.

On the variables of bureaucratic bridging and market connectedness, there are a total of nine items. Although each of these items may be used as an independent variable to denote a specific kind of work connection, the nine items together would blur the theoretical focus of how work connections developed from inside and outside the workplace may contribute to the development of personal networks, and hence the formation of social capital. This concern has led to a factor analysis through which to identify the two latent variables of bureaucratic bridging and market connectedness from the nine items. The exercise of this statistical technique indeed results in a two-factor resolution with a combined 63.9 percent of resolution for the explained variance, confirming the design of the nine items. The result of factor analysis is shown in Table 5.2, section II. Both bureaucratic bridging and market connectedness are standardized variables, with a mean of 0 and a standard deviation of 1. In the analysis that follows, I will use these reconstructed variables, instead of the original items, as predictors of social capital.

5.3.4. Measuring Other Variables

The five-city survey provides a rich profile of respondents, whose characteristics are important parameters for predicting the level of social capital they had developed and maintained at the time of the survey. As shown in Table 5.2, section III, there is a fairly even distribution of respondents across the five cities. Each city's sample was drawn by following the same multistate random sampling procedure, ensuring that intercity variation in social capital, if found, was not due to sampling procedures. Instead, one should interpret this variation in terms of the variations in city contexts. For example, by 1999, the year of the survey, the five cities varied tremendously in the nonstate share of urban jobs (a measure of privatization), direct foreign investments (a measure of economic openness, marketization, and globalization), and indicators of socioeconomic development from highest to lowest: Xiamen, Guangzhou, Shanghai, Tianjin, and Changchun (see Appendix 1).

Of the total respondents, 51.6 percent are males. The average age is about 39. Close to 15 percent are members of the Communist Party. These sample statistics are comparable to those from the city-based samples obtained by previous researchers in the 1980s or early 1990s (Lin and Bian 1991a; Walder 1995; Bian and Logan 1996; Zhou 2000). In all other variables, as compared to these previous samples, the 1999 five-city sample shows that urban China has undergone tremendous changes.

First, the 1999 five-city survey notes a higher percentage of college degree holders, 20.6 percent. This reflects a post-1993 nationwide drive for the expansion of college enrollments that boosted admissions from both high school graduates and on-the-job part-timers.

Second, the 55.7 percent of respondents employed in the state sector is significantly lower than the nearly 80 percent from the 1980s samples, a result of the marketization and privatization of the Chinese economy in the post-1980 reform era. Note that this percentage is higher than the national average of 46 percent in 1999 (Wu 2003: 181, Table 5.1), yet comparable to that of large cities where sizable state-owned enterprises had been protected by a post-1995 national reform directive known as "grab the big, release the small."

Third, an important force contributing to Chinese economy, especially in large cities, has been the migrant labor from the countryside. The five-city survey was able to sample a fairly large number of migrant laborers, 18.2 percent, whereas the great majority, or 81.8 percent, of the sample are respondents with a permanent residence registration in the city.

Finally, the average household income in 1998 (the year proceeding the survey year) was 26,940 yuan, with a standard deviation of 99,878 yuan. Taking the coefficient of variation (SD/mean) as a proxy of inequality index, 3.7, this is several times higher than the index obtained from city-based samples in the 1980s and early 1990s.

These profiles of the respondents indicate both stability and change for the working individuals and their families in the reform era. In this study I do not examine these trends in their own right, but instead use the individual and household variables as controls in the explaining model of social capital formation. Since the formation of social capital at the interpersonal level is apparently attributed in part to, or constrained by, individual and household characteristics, these controls can also be treated as explaining variables in addition to the main explaining variables, social class and occupation-as-connections, in the estimation of social capital formation. Do males develop a higher level of social capital because they are better able to build resource-rich networks in a male-dominated Chinese society? Do older persons have a higher level of social capital as a result of a longer process of network building with age? Do people with a party membership or a college degree have a higher level of social capital because of their stronger political or cultural resources? Do migrant workers have less social capital because they lack connections to residents? And does higher income lead to a higher level of social capital because building a favor-exchange *guanxi* network in China is costly? I shall explore these questions after presenting the results on the effects of the main explaining variables.

5.4. RESULTS

5.4.1. Social Class Effects

Table 5.3 presents regression models estimated to test our three hypotheses. The dependent variable is a logarithm transformation of the social capital factor, so the antilogarithms of regression coefficients in Table 5.3 can be interpreted as percentage difference from the point of comparison. Of the eight class categories, unskilled workers without any class resources (property, authority, or skill) are used as a reference (or "omitted variable"), or the point of comparison. The results show that compared with unskilled workers, officials and managers each have a social capital stock that is 12.7 percent higher ($e^{.12}$), professionals 17.4 percent higher ($e^{.16}$), office clerks 8.3 percent higher ($e^{.08}$), and skilled workers 6.2 percent higher ($e^{.06}$). Business owners and self-employees do not vary from unskilled workers in the volume of social capital. These results lend support to Hypothesis 1 that advantageous class positions lead to greater social capital than do disadvantageous class positions.

Regression results from the models about network size, diversity, ceiling, and composition are suggestive of how class differences in social capital volume are generated by class differences in personal networks. Officials, managers, and professionals all have superior personal networks. For officials as compared to unskilled workers, for example, their networks are 17.4 percent ($e^{.16}$) larger in average size, 15 percent ($e^{.14}$) more diverse in alters' occupational types, 20 percent ($e^{.18}$) higher in alters' occupational status, and have significantly greater probability of being connected to other officials, managers, and professionals. Conversely, the lack of network advantages explains why small business owners and self-employees have relatively less social capital: none of them have advantageous networks as compared to unskilled workers. Most importantly, they are short of ties with officials, managers, and professionals.

The obvious disadvantages in personal networks for business owners deserve further attention. Intuitively, business owners, despite how small their operations are, seem to have wide contacts and economic ties with people in many classes. While this is the impression given by ethnographic studies and day-to-day observations (Wang 2000), the widely accepted scholarly notions of "network capitalism" (Boisot and Child 1996), local state corporatism (Oi 2000), and symbiotic capitalism (Wank 1999) point to the fact that network connections with officials and state managers are the life-blood for private businesses in China.

Table 5.3. Regressions predicting social capital and social networks

Independent variables	Social capital (logarithm) B	Network size (logarithm) B	Network ceiling (logarithm) B	Network diversity (logarithm) B	Ties to officials (1 = yes) Exp(B)	Ties to managers (1 = yes) Exp(B)	Ties to professionals (1 = yes) Exp(B)
Class categories							
Official	0.12***	0.16**	0.18***	0.14***	2.14***	1.10	1.45*
Manager	0.12***	0.14**	0.14***	0.13***	1.79***	1.44**	1.57***
Professional	0.16***	0.19***	0.19***	0.28***	1.42**	1.38**	3.16***
Clerk	0.08***	0.05	0.12***	0.11**	1.44**	1.23	1.28
Skilled worker	0.06***	0.06	0.08***	0.06	1.18	1.10	1.36**
Business owner	0.02	0.28	-0.04	0.11	1.17	0.74	1.09
Self-employed	-0.01	0.06	-0.01	-0.09*	1.08	0.76	0.85
Nonskilled worker (as reference)							
Occupation-as-connection							
Bureaucratic bridging	0.07***	0.15***	0.06***	0.13***	1.30***	1.31***	1.30***
Market connectedness	0.04***	0.05**	0.03**	0.10***	1.19***	1.27***	1.19***
Cities							
Guangzhou	0.11***	0.40***	0.11***	0.34***	1.18	1.04	1.66***
Xiamen	0.09***	0.36***	0.09***	0.19***	1.04	1.24	1.53***
Shanghai	-0.04*	-0.05	0.01	-0.05	0.51***	0.99	0.98
Tianjin	-0.07***	-0.01	0.04	-0.21***	0.44***	1.15	0.67***
Changchun (as reference)							
Gender (male = 1)	0.01	0.06*	-0.01	0.02	1.16*	1.04	0.96
Age	0.00	-0.01*	0.00	-0.01**	0.97	1.03	0.98
Age^2	0.00	0.00	0.00	0.00	1.00	1.00	1.00
Party membership	0.04**	0.09*	0.02	0.09**	1.56***	1.22*	1.16
College	0.10***	0.09*	0.10***	0.17***	1.37***	1.35**	2.48***
Sector (state = 1)	0.00	0.01	-0.01	-0.02	1.16	0.95	0.96
Household income (ln)	0.06***	0.10***	0.07***	0.13***	1.20***	1.33***	1.28***
Permanent resident	0.10***	0.22***	0.11***	0.20***	1.45***	1.81***	1.40**
Constant	0.41***	1.97***	3.40***	0.44***	0.30*	0.01***	0.08***
Adjusted R^2	0.260	0.157	0.155	0.258	0.130#	0.101#	0.158#
N	4,213	4,292	4,213	4,213	4,213	4,213	4,213

Statistical significance in two-tailed test: * p < .05; ** p < .01; *** p < .001.

Cox and Snell R^2.

Why, then, do these connections not get translated into the measures of personal networks and social capital that are based on Chinese New Year visitations? This is not the measurement failure of the survey. Quite the contrary, this demonstrates the novelty and effectiveness of using New Year visitations as an event to collect data on personal networks and social capital. To reiterate, the kinds of network connections that qualify to be translated into social capital are personal, dynamic, and enduring. Business owners' network ties may be wider and more diverse than their New Year visitation networks, but these ties may be business oriented, purpose specific, instant, nonhumanistic, and easily ended, thus not necessarily transferable into personal relationships on emotional and behavioral levels.

5.4.2. Effects of Occupation as Connections

When occupations are constructed as variables of bureaucratic bridging and market connection, both variables produce expected results. In the social capital model, bureaucratic bridging, a continuous variable, has a significant positive coefficient of .07, indicating that a one-point increment in bureaucratic bridging will lead to an increase in social capital volume by 7.3 percent ($e^{.07}$). The variable of bureaucratic bridging is a standardized score, with a range from -3 to $+3$. Given two persons whose jobs are on the opposite extremes on the scale of bureaucratic bridging (resulting in a differential of 6), their social capital difference will be 71.6 percent ($e^{.54}$). This is a huge differential margin as generated by one's job difference in bureaucratic bridging alone, and a strong finding in support of Hypothesis 2: work contacts made on one's job within the workplace will be translated positively and strongly into the accumulation of one's social capital.

Results from the models on network size, diversity, ceiling, and composition help us understand this translation process. A one-point increment in job's bureaucratic bridging will enlarge one's personal network by 16.2 percent ($e^{.15}$), increase network diversity by 13.9 percent ($e^{.13}$), raise network ceiling by 6.2 percent ($e^{.06}$), and provide 35 percent, plus or minus, more chances to develop personal ties with officials ($e^{.30}$), managers ($e^{.31}$), and professionals ($e^{.30}$). Because of the bridging ability of some jobs into other jobs within bureaucratic structures of the workplace, this ability helps the jobholder develop personal networks from work contacts, and because these advantages are meant to develop networks that produce social capital in the interpersonal worlds, jobs with high degrees of bureaucratic bridging are a generator of social capital.

The variable of market connectedness also has a positive coefficient, 0.04, in the social capital equation. This coefficient indicates that a one-point increment in a job's market connectedness will result in an increase of social capital by 4.1 percent ($e^{.04}$). Market connectedness is also a standard score, whose values range from $+3$

to -3. Two persons whose jobs are on the opposite extremes on the scale of market connectedness (resulting in a differential of 6) will have a social capital difference of 35 percent ($e^{.30}$). This considerable difference lends an impressive finding in support of Hypothesis 3: market-connected jobs provide ample opportunities to generate social capital.

The models on the various network variables can clarify how market-connected jobs would generate social capital. A one-point increment in market-connectedness of one's job will enlarge one's personal network by 5.1 percent ($e^{.05}$), increase network diversity by 10.5 percent ($e^{.10}$), slightly raise network ceiling by 3 percent ($e^{.03}$), but substantially boost the chances, by a margin in the range of 21–31 percent, of cultivating and maintaining personal ties to officials ($e^{.19}$), managers ($e^{.27}$), and professionals ($e^{.19}$). Indeed, when the personal networks tend to be larger, more diverse, include more higher-status alters, and have more ties to elite classes, more social resources will be embedded and can be mobilized from them, thus leading to greater social capital volumes.

5.4.3. Effects of Other Variables

I do not have specific hypotheses to test with regard to the effects of the individual, household, and city-dummy variables on social capital. Some of these variables produce interesting results on how social capital formation may be constrained by individual and household characteristics, as well as by city contexts.

On the whole, gender and age do not generate much difference in level of social capital, nor does employment in the state sector. Gender and age appear to make some difference in network building, however. Specifically, men's networks are 6 percent larger ($e^{.06}$) than women's, men are 17 percent better able to cultivate ties to officials ($e^{.16}$) than do women, and older persons have a narrower network as measured by alters' occupational position ($e^{-.01}$). These differences are understandable: two-thirds of officials are men, whose positions generate more New Year visitors for male than for female respondents, and older persons' number of close relatives, friends, and other contacts would decrease after the age of retirement.

Party membership and college education both produce positive and significant coefficients in the social capital model, as well as in social network models. With other variables holding constant, party members' social capital is 4.1 percent ($e^{.04}$) greater than nonparty members', and college graduates' social capital is 10.5 percent ($e^{.10}$) greater than noncollege graduates'. These large advantages in social capital are attributed to the fact that party members and college degree holders have advantageous networks. As compared to nonparty members, party members tend to have larger and more diverse networks, and have significantly more ties to officials and managers (not to professionals, however). College graduates, as compared to lower-educated people, have larger and more diverse networks, have networks in which alters tend to have higher statuses, and have significantly more ties to officials, managers, and professionals. These findings clearly point to the political and cultural components of social capital in the Chinese context.

Residence status and household income make a tremendous difference in the formation of social capital and the development of social networks. First, with other variables being equal, permanent residents maintain a social capital stock that is 10.5 percent ($e^{.10}$) higher than do migrants. This advantage is translated from network advantages: permanent residents tend to have larger and more diverse networks, networks with higher ceilings, and networks with ties to elite classes such as officials, managers, and professionals. Second, respondents will have a 6.2 percent ($e^{.06}$) increase in social capital volume for every increment in household income (in logarithm form). And clearly, higher income households have all the network advantages: their networks are larger, more diverse, with higher ceilings, and with ties to the elite classes of officials, managers, and professionals. Whereas the effects of permanent residence point to the fact that it requires time and opportunities for people to develop, expand, and diversify *local* networks from which to accumulate social capital, the effects of household income testify to the very nature of Chinese *guanxi* networks: networks of favor exchanges can be costly, and financial resources provide a boost.

City differences are found in social capital and network models. With other variables being equal, respondents from Guangzhou and Xiamen show a higher level of social capital than those from Shanghai, Tianjin, and Changchun. Estimates from the network models show similar intercity variations. While these results call for a systematic interpretation, I offer here, as an afterthought that may guide future inquiry, a structural argument about the effect of increased marketization: the greater the marketization, the greater the need to build a diverse network from which to general social capital with multiple sources and possibilities. While Guangzhou and Xiamen certainly have a higher level of marketization than the other cities in the sample (see Appendix 1), the higher network diversity, larger network size, and higher network ceilings for respondents from Guangzhou and Xiamen appear to lend some support for this argument.

5.5. CONCLUSIONS

The empirical analysis has brought out results in support of the hypotheses that are derived from the model displayed in Figure 5.1. I find in the five-city survey that Chinese urbanites vary greatly in structural dimensions of personal networks and the embedded social capital. Although variation in social capital can be explained from diverse perspectives, I have advanced a structural explanation by looking at how this variation is generated by variations in social class and occupational life. With this explanation, I conclude that social class distinctions constrain people from developing personal networks across class boundaries, and the constraint is stronger for those in disadvantageous class positions. In addition, I see occupational life as a social space in which job contacts with colleagues, clients, and customers will get translated into personal networks. I found that jobs with a high degree of bureaucratic bridging (or connections to alters from inside the workplace) and jobs with a high degree of market connectedness (or connections to alters from outside the workplace, or simply put, the marketplace) give jobholders the advantages of converting work contacts into personal ties from which to generate social capital. The three hypotheses—about the effect of class boundary, the effect of job's bureaucratic bridging, and the effect of job's market-connectivity—receive strong support from the five-city survey.

Two findings deserve further discussion. First, the measurement of social capital can require a simple or more sophisticated effort. For network analysts, the latter may prove necessary. This study adopts a multidimensional concept of social capital, which is measured by tapping size, diversity, ceiling, and composition of ego's personal networks. These measures were constructed with data about home visitations during the Chinese New Year celebration. But a non-network researcher may not want to go through this extended effort of measurement. A simpler approach is to use a single network measure as a proxy of social capital. From this study, network diversity, as defined by number of occupations that alters have, seems to be the best of several possibilities. In surveys or field research, this requires only one question: "Roughly how many major occupations do your close relatives and friends work in?" The feasibility and reliability of this question can be confirmed in future studies.

Second, my analysis has made it clear that the quantity and quality of social capital of Chinese urbanites are influenced by their social class positions and their occupations. On the whole, all of my three hypotheses are supported by the five-city survey, but not without intriguing findings. While a job's market-connectedness has all positive effects on network dimensions and embedded social capital, business owners, who should have a broad range of market connections, cannot easily translate these connections into personal networks from which to generate social capital. To explain this finding, I have argued that business owners' connections with others are largely instant, businesslike, and transaction-oriented, therefore it is hard to convert them into enduring and personal networks. This argument awaits further analysis and empirical evidence.

APPENDIX 1: SELECTED INDICATORS OF CITY DEVELOPMENT, 1999

	Unit	Xiamen	Guangzhou	Shanghai	Tianjin	Changchun
% Nonstate-sector workers (including collectives)[a]	%	56.3	53.8	39.7	42.3	31.9
% Private-sector workers (excluding collectives)[a]	%	46.7	32.1	28.7	33.6	14.7
FDI as % of industrial gross product[b]	%	84.0	53.9	50.6	43.2	26.0
FDI[b]	US$ in million	1,342	3,176	5,999	2,745	331
Per capita gross domestic product[b]	Yuan/head	34,221	30,265	30,805	15,976	10,261
Average annual wage of staff and workers[b]	Yuan/head	14,009	16,202	14,147	11,056	8,618
Per capita annual consumption[b]	Yuan/head	7,890	9,751	8,248	5,852	4,571
Internet users as % of total population[b]	%	1.8	1.5	3.2	0.5	0.1
Year-end total population[b]	1,000 persons	1,289 E persons	6,850 persons	13,131 persons	9,101 persons	6,912 persons

Note: FDI, Foreign direct investment.

Sources of Data:

[a] Estimated from the 1999 five-city survey.

[b] Obtained or calculated from official statistics from
Jilin Tongji Nianjian 2000 (*Jilin Statistical Yearbook 2000*). Beijing: China's Statistical Press.
Fujian Tongji Nianjian 2000 (*Fujian Statistical Yearbook 2000*). Beijing: China's Statistical Press.
Shanghai Tongji Nianjian 2000 (*Shanghai Statistical Yearbook 2000*). Beijing: China's Statistical Press.
Tianjin Tongji Nianjian 2000 (*Tianjin Statistical Yearbook 2000*). Beijing: China's Statistical Press.
Xiamen Tongji Nianjian 2000 (*Xiamen Statistical Yearbook 2000*). Beijing: China's Statistical Press.

Section II
Mobilization of Social Capital

6

The Invisible Hand of Social Capital: An Exploratory Study[1]

Nan Lin and Dan Ao

6.1. THE ISSUES

One important line of research contributing to the study of the process of attainment in the labor market examines how social networks and embedded resources affect outcomes. While using personal contacts per se does not necessarily present a competitive edge, finding and using someone who has advantaged resources (i.e. status, class, or power) does help yield better status attainment (Lin 1999*b*; Marsden and Gorman 2001). Thus, if resources of the personal contact used in job search represents mobilized social capital, cumulative and consistent evidence affirming this association has buttressed the argument of returns to mobilizing social capital in instrumental actions.

However, this line of research is currently confronted with certain critical issues. For one, a significant portion of the participants in the job market does not report job search. From one-third to over half of the respondents in surveys conducted in American communities and elsewhere report no search in finding their current jobs (Granovetter 1974; Campbell and Rosenfeld 1985; Hanson and Pratt 1991; McDonald 2002; Yakubovich 2002). Likewise, studies also show that employers do not report the regular use of personal contacts as a recruitment method. The 1991 National Organizational Study showed that between 15 and 20 percent of the US employers reported no "recruitment effort," and slightly more than one-third of the recruitment by firms used personal relations in finding employees, with a somewhat higher figure for the managerial and professional positions (Marsden 1996; Marsden and Gorman 2001). Comparable statistics were found in a survey of employers in the city of Samara, Russia (Yakubovich 2002). The figures go up somewhat when a recruiting firm provides incentives for

[1] Data used in this chapter were drawn from the thematic research project "Social Capital: Its Origins and Consequences," sponsored by Academia Sinica, Taiwan, through its Research Center for Humanities and Social Sciences, and the Institute of Sociology. The principal investigator of the project is Nan Lin. This analysis has been supported in part by a grant from the Chiang Ching-kuo Foundation to Nan Lin.

referrals (see e.g. Fernandez and Weinberg 1997; Fernandez, Castilla, and Moore 2000).[2]

Further, among those who report job search, anywhere from half to about two-thirds of the respondents indicate that they use formal methods or direct applications rather than personal contacts. For example, a 1974 survey supported by the Department of Labor reported that only 54 percent of job seekers used personal contacts. In his study of professional and technical workers in Newton, Massachusetts in the late 1960s, Granovetter found that 56 percent reported the use of personal contacts. Flap and Boxman (2001) reported that the use of personal contacts in job search among Dutch males varied from 34 percent in 1981 to 45 percent in 1991. In Taiwan, the use of personal contacts in job searches was mentioned by about one-third of the job searchers (39% in 1981, 35.8% in 1991, and 32% in 1999; Sun and Wu 2002).

The absence of reported use of job search or personal contacts in job-search data has posed analytic problems in previous studies. One way to get around this issue has been to treat those who do not use job-search or personal contacts as "missing data." Analysis proceeds with those who do use personal contacts while statistically accounting for the selectivity bias resulting from the exclusion of others who claim to have not used personal contacts (Lin, Ensel, and Vaughan 1981; De Graaf and Flap 1988; Marsden and Hurlbert 1988). Yet, it remains puzzling why a significant portion of participants in the job market do not indicate job search or mention the use of personal contacts in job search. Further, some who do not do search for jobs or use personal contacts in job search are not disadvantaged in the labor market (Flap and De Graaf 1986; Marsden and Hurlbert 1988; Mouw 2003). In fact, they may initially be in better socioeconomic positions or end up in better socioeconomic positions than those who do report the use of personal contacts in job searches (Campbell and Rosenfeld 1985; Elliott 2000; McDonald 2002).

These two controversies—that a significant portion of participants in the labor market does not report job search and, when they do, do not use personal contacts—are challenges that need to be addressed if the argument that social capital generates returns in the labor market is to be sustained and advanced. The alternative argument, that social capital is not so important in socioeconomic attainment (Mouw 2003), must be given consideration.

---

[2] A second controversy focuses on those who do use job contacts in job searches. A comparison between those using personal contacts and those who do not does not affirm the relative advantage of personal contacts in better attained statuses. From the social capital perspective, this is not surprising. We have known for decades that it is not the mere use of social ties but rather who the ties are that makes a difference. When contact statuses are employed as an indicator of social capital, the effect on attained status has been strong and consistent. However, a question was recently raised in regard to the actual meaning of contact status. A recent paper (Mouw 2003) suggests that the contact status's effect may be entirely due to homophilous friends' statuses. Mouw demonstrated that when the contacts and egos with same occupations were deleted, the association between contact status and attained status was no longer significant. Due to the length of the present chapter, this controversy will be treated in a separate paper in which we will show that both the argument and empirical demonstration were flawed.

The purpose of this chapter is to argue that those embedded in social networks rich in resources do indeed benefit from such connections. However, the advantage of having such social capital is sometimes more subtle and less visible than responses provided in typical job-search surveys where respondents are asked, among the methods used to find jobs, whether there are any personal contacts or connections. A significant advantage of having such connections is receiving job-related information in routine exchanges. Access to richer and more diverse embedded resources enhances the likelihood of receiving useful information about jobs in the job market in routine exchanges, without asking or actively searching for it. It is a relative advantage beyond and in addition to other assets, including human capital. Such is the power and efficiency of social capital—its invisible hand in the labor market. The remainder of the chapter elaborates on this thesis and subjects the proposed process to an empirical study.

6.2. EXPLANATORY POSSIBILITIES

Before the proposed thesis is introduced and discussed in some detail, it is useful to consider plausible alternative explanations for the absence of reported use of personal contacts in job search. One possible interpretation is the consideration of normative expectations in the formulation of responses to surveys and measurements. In most societies, there is a normative consensus that good jobs go to the best-qualified candidates (Davis and Moore 1945). Thus, when asked in regard to methods used in job search and presented with a checklist of possible methods, usually including direct applications, formal channels, and personal contacts, a respondent may choose the most normatively appropriate response. Such normative responses may result from two cognitive processes. In one way, the norms are subconsciously ingrained so that responses other than those considered "appropriate" are given less cognitive attention and skipped in reporting. These omissions are unconscious or subconscious and unintended. In another way, the omissions are conscious choices. If the normative expectation is that the best-qualified candidate ought to get the best jobs, people may not wish to diminish the impression that their success in the job market is not due to their knowledge and skills—the effect of human capital. Nor would they wish to be viewed as "pulling strings," which may be frowned on socially or even considered illegal in some cases. These responses do not necessarily imply lying. Rather, chances are that multiple methods have been used in a job search; thus, the responses provided are valid, though selective. Normative expectations thus lead to either personal contacts having been used but cognitively "forgotten," or the respondents may cognitively recall such actions but refrain from mentioning the normatively "inappropriate" responses when given alternative choices.

If this explanation of normative choices is valid, then some methodological improvements may reduce but not eliminate the chances of omissions. For example, providing more detailed items and allowing multiple choices may increase the chances of triggering recall about the use of personal contacts. Further probing by directly asking about personal help people use or receive in their job search may further increase such recall or response. These may reduce the errors of unconscious omissions, but will not eliminate conscious decisions to omit. Further, increased responses to the use of personal contacts do not warrant any significant change of the effect of personal contacts on attainment.

Another explanation, especially for the observation that the socioeconomically advantaged are less likely to report the use of personal contacts or even the use of job search, is that they are also the ones with better human capital. Thus, in job searches, signals of their human capital—in the use of formal channels such as placement services, responses to advertised jobs, or direct applications to the firms—can be transmitted (i.e. résumés and supporting documents) and no further credentials or signals, including social capital, are necessary. The empirical fact that human capital, presumably reflected in education and work experience, is significantly associated with socioeconomic attainment seems to lend support to this contention. From the perspective of human capital, therefore, the use of social capital in job searches probably reflects a deficit in human capital. Those less endowed with human capital and less "deserving" would substitute or supplement skills and knowledge with personal connections. The anticipation would be that those with better human capital are less likely to use personal contacts in job searchers.[3]

However, past research has consistently indicated that there is a positive and significant relationship between human capital and any general measurement of access to or capacity of social capital (Lin and Dumin 1986; Marsden and Hurlbert 1988; Flap 1999). The explanation espousing the human capital effect can argue that, in fact, human capital produces social capital: those rich in human capital also tend to become rich in social capital. Once human capital is accounted for, the effect of social capital on attainment will become spurious and no longer significant. In other words, human capital accounts for both social capital and attainment in the labor market. An alternative explanation, espousing social capital, for example, would need to demonstrate that social capital exerts effect on attainment beyond that accounted for by human capital.

6.3. THE INVISIBLE HAND OF SOCIAL CAPITAL: A CONCEPTUALIZATION

The third explanation, espoused here, elaborates the theory of social capital and argues its utility beyond the visible and active job-search process. This theory begins with an account of the nature of social capital. Social capital is defined

---

[3] Still puzzling is why certain employees as well as employers claim no search or recruitment. How are signals of human capital credentials transmitted in these circumstances? A further exploration on the recruitment process by firms deserves research attention, but it is beyond the scope of the present chapter.

as resources embedded in social networks (Lin 2001*b*). It is through the relations in one's social networks[4] that their resources, the embedded resources, may be accessed and mobilized to receive or convey information, influence, or credentials to gain relative advantage in the labor market. It is important to identify and differentiate the two components of social capital: *capacity*—resources of social ties accessible in an actor's social networks; and *mobilization*—social ties and their resources actually used in a particular action (Lin 1982, forthcoming; Lai, Lin, and Leung 1998). Capacity of social capital represents the pool of embedded resources available to an actor (Campbell, Marsden, and Hurlbert 1986; Lin and Dumin 1986; Erickson 1995). Mobilization represents activation of selected ties and resources in particular episodes of action.

While capacity of social capital may be a general measure that can be assessed for every actor, mobilization of social capital inevitably represents only a slice of the capacity of social capital "captured" by research for a particular event (e.g. seeking a job) and time (e.g. for the current and last successful job search). Further, this capturing is usually dictated by a structured instrument in a survey where methods of job search and option choices are set for a respondent's choosing. In the typical job-search studies, when respondents are asked about particular ties (job contacts) and their resources, the operationalization and measurement pertain to one particular incidence of activation of social capital. Depending on the measurement, it may narrowly bring into focus the activated social capital relative to a particular job (first, last, or current); a particular contact (among possibly several approached); and a framing question and wording (e.g. "Did anyone help you in finding this job?" "Did you use any personal contact to find this job?" and so on).

Therefore, the use of a contact in a job-search study is at best a small and partial representation of the capacity of one's social capital (Lai, Lin, and Leung 1998). It does not necessarily represent the optimal possible capacity as other contingent factors come into play (Smith 2005 and her chapter in the present volume). In fact, a direct association between the capacity of social capital and status attainment suggests that much of the capacity is not represented in any studies focusing on job-search events (De Graaf and Flap 1988; Marsden and Hurlbert 1988).

How, then, can capacity of social capital exert influence on attainment without explicit job-seeking or job-recruiting behaviors? There are two plausible ways. First, capacity of social capital carries reputation and prestige by association. Social ties represent the social credentials that an actor carries. The status of the ties symbolically indicates the potential social capital an actor can evoke. When a hiring firm is exposed to such information, this social credential may influence the hiring decision in that social credentials of employees could become possible resources for the firm as well. Exposure to this information may come from close readings of materials provided by the potential employee (her curriculum

---

[4] Social networks consist of direct and indirect ties, so that not all ties in a network are expected to interact or exchange information with one another. However, it is expected that through indirect ties such information can conceivably flow from one tie to another in the networks.

vitae, reference letters, etc.). Thus, awareness of the capacity of social capital of potential employees becomes a factor in hiring decisions, *without* either the potential employees or employers evoking or mobilizing social ties in the labor market.

Second, social capital evokes job information and influences exchanges in an informal way. Consider routine information exchanges among social ties in a social network. In most interactions among friends and acquaintances, even among relatives and strong ties, conversations often flow casually, in a fragmented way and without explicit expectations (Bearman and Parigi 2004; McPherson, Smith-Loving, and Brashears 2006). However, this is not to suggest that such routine flow and exchange of information are always purposeless. In this give-and-take, much potential useful information is embedded and exchanged. Most of the flow may anticipate or generate no specific responses, but such routine flow inevitably triggers interest and response on occasion. When parties become interested in a particular piece of information, however, further pursuit becomes possible and yet remains within the context of informal and routine conversation.

It is entirely reasonable to assume that one type of information routinely exchanged is information about jobs. As many of the ties are either embedded in the labor market and/or connected to others who are in the labor market, they bring information and experiences about jobs to routine conversations and exchanges with others in the networks. The information about work and the job market, as much as that on family, leisure, and other significant social activities and domains, enriches exchanges and stimulates conversation since participants have much to share and contribute. Thus, job information becomes an integrated part of routine social exchanges, rather than a focused market activity—the job search.

What is argued here is precisely the significance of the extent of such information flow and its potential value to the participants in the social exchanges. Routine and repeated exchanges open and expand the scope of one's awareness and knowledge about the labor market—both inside and outside one's company. Because routine exchanges take place among participants in more or less symmetric relations, and job information as a part of routine exchanges may not be specifically intended to solicit or evoke any response, the cost of the information sharing is relatively low. However, repeated exchanges of job information should significantly increase the likelihood of triggering follow-ups and, thus, opportunities in the job market. Further, if one becomes interested in a possibility, the cost of finding out more about it is again relatively low, since social ties by definition assume a certain degree of reciprocity and obligation. Thus, the initial informant or someone else in the network may become useful for obtaining and conveying further information about a job; finding out the likely fit; and, most importantly, providing the bridge to make contact with a firm or employer. All such activities can take place without any party engaging in formal recruitment or search until the near-final phase; by that time, questions have been clarified and answered, and barriers to possible terms eliminated. At that moment, a search-recruitment activity can be staged and formalized, or sometimes completely omitted.

Thus, the flow of social credentials or reputation and the flow of job information and influence in routine exchanges constitute ways that social capital exerts effects on attainment in the labor market, beyond the more visible job-search or job-recruiting behavior. These constitute the invisible hand of social capital. The focus in this chapter is on the job information flow in routine exchanges.

6.4. FURTHER CONCEPTUAL ELABORATION

While job information flows in all networks, the extent and quality of such information exchanged vary. We are proposing that the extent and quality of such information is dictated to a significant extent by the capacity of social capital, or accessible resources in the social networks (Lin 1982, 2001b). That is, a person connected to those with diverse and rich characteristics and backgrounds is more likely to receive more and varied information about the job market. Such routine job information in turn enhances the opportunity to make a connection with a recruiting employer.

Who, then, is more likely to have better capacity of social capital and access better network resources? Social capital theory (Lin 2001b) suggests two possible determinants to account for the endogeneity of social capital capacity: socioeconomic standings and social participation. The sociological principle of exchanges—the principal of homophily—informs us that interactions are more likely to occur among individuals who have similar characteristics and lifestyles (Homans 1950, 1958; Lazarsfeld and Merton 1954; Laumann 1966; Wellman 1979). By extension, we may also expect that social networks tend to be formed among persons of similar characteristics and lifestyles (Lin 1982; Marsden 1988; McPherson, Smith-Loving, and Cook 2001). Thus, there is a general tendency for social networks to form among individuals who have similar socioeconomic characteristics or resources. That is, for a given social network, there should be a tendency toward homophily among the ties. They may come from different sectors of the labor market, but are situated in approximately similar positions in the social hierarchy. In other words, there is a correspondence between a person's own socioeconomic characteristics and others in her or his networks: the higher a person's socioeconomic standing, the higher her or his connections' socioeconomic standings. Further, it is known that those higher up in socioeconomic standings also have greater access to a variety of other positions in the hierarchy (Campbell, Marsden, and Hurlbert 1986; Lin and Dumin 1986). Thus, those higher up in the hierarchy not only have more diverse access to various positions in the hierarchy, but, more importantly, they are even more likely to access diverse resources through their connections (Lin 2000a).

However, socioeconomic standings do not entirely account for social capital capacity. Beyond this expected structural effect, an actor's own activity in social networking and social participation (e.g. participation in voluntary organizations) would add value to his or her social capital. Theory (Lin 2001b) proposes that such action should offer opportunities to extend one's social ties and networks, and they in turn are likely to enhance the variety and richness of resources one may access. Social participation, therefore, is expected to increase the capacity of social capital. Thus, given similar socioeconomic standings, actors who make strategic investment in social participation (e.g. in voluntary organizations) are expected to gain further relative advantage in social capital capacity.[5]

It should be noted that in the social capital literature, participation in voluntary organizations is sometimes considered as social capital (Putnam 1995, 2000). Here, we conceive it as an indication of social participation. Such participation may expand and enhance the capacity of social capital (resources in the networks), but not necessarily always lead to better embedded resources. It is seen as social opportunities which may be facilitating diverse and rich embedded resources in conjunction with one's socioeconomic positions. This differentiation may be verified in two ways: (*a*) the association between such social participation and the capacity of social capital is significant but not overwhelming (not functionally overlapped); and (*b*) the capacity of social capital will largely mediate the effects of social participation on attainment. That is, social participation may enhance social capital that in turn will be a more significant direct contributor to attainment. We will verify these patterns in the present study.

6.5. HYPOTHESES

If these arguments are valid, we should expect that the capacity of social capital (diversity and richness of embedded resources) may indeed be related to the likelihood and richness of such job information flow informally carried out in routine exchanges. That is (*a*) the greater the capacity of social capital (diverse and rich embedded resources in social networks), the more likely routine job information flow is likely to take place; and (*b*) the greater the job information flow, the more the chances of obtaining better jobs increases.

Formally, the two hypotheses of the invisible hand of social capital are (1) that *social capital capacity (network resources) is positively associated with the likelihood of receiving routine job information* (H1); and (2) that *the likelihood of receiving routine job information is positively associated with attainment in the labor market* (H2). Two other hypotheses explicate the endogeneity of social capital capacity: (3) *there is a positive association between social capital capacity and human capital* (H3); and (4) *there is a positive association between social capital capacity and active social participation* (H4).

It should be noted that, even after routine job information is shown to mediate part of the effect of social capital capacity on attainment, it is not expected to account for all of the effects of social capital capacity on attainment. That is, the

---

[5] For similar views on the association between civic engagement and social capital, see the following chapters in the present volume: Bekkers et al. (Chapter 9); Magee (Chapter 14); Hsung and Lin (Chapter 11); Tindall and Cormier (Chapter 13); and Miyata et al. (Chapter 10).

capacity of social capital may still find other paths to impact attainment (e.g. see the reputation and social credential argument in Section 6.3). The capacity of social capital is expected to exert direct effect on attainment beyond its effect mediated by routine job information.

The validity of the theory of the invisible hand of social capital may be demonstrated with the confirmation of the hypotheses discussed above, and with improved measurement of job-search methods, to account for the other alternative explanation. It also needs to take into account other potential exogenous variables, such as gender, race/ethnicity, or regional variations. Empirical work needs to take these factors into account while demonstrating the effects of the invisible hand of social capital. The following will describe a study to examine the invisible hand of social capital. This is a preliminary study, as we have limited guidance from the literature for a refinement of job-contact measurements and the measurement of routine job information flow. If the preliminary results are encouraging, further instrumental refinements would then be warranted.

6.6. DATA

A random-digit dialing telephone survey was conducted, November 2004 to March 2005, among adults (between 21 and 64 years of age) currently or previously employed in the United States. A Computer-Assisted Telephone Interview (CATI) system was utilized.[6] As the survey unfolded it became clear that the response rates from minorities (especially African-Americans and Latinos) were lower than that from whites. To ensure a reasonable representation of minorities in the sample to reflect the census distribution, we imposed an additional sampling criterion—to seek out qualified African-Americans and Latinos to approximate the census distribution. To estimate and control potential bias that such a sampling modification might incur in the data, we created a dummy variable, quota, to distinguish all sampled respondents after the imposition (value = 1) and took it into account in all analyses. As will be seen, the bias was minimal and insignificant.

The final sample consisted of 3,000 respondents. For the present study, only those who were currently working were used, for a study sample size of 2,317.[7] General characteristics of the sample are presented in Table 6.1. As can be seen,

---

[6] The fieldwork was conducted from November 2004 to April 2005. When they were connected by phone, the interviewer asked for the person who fit the screening requirements. If multiple persons were qualified, the person whose birth date was closest to July 1 was sought. If the qualified person was not available, a follow-up call was made. The interview took 34 minutes on average. About 30% of those contacted were qualified and agreed to participate; this was slightly less than but close to the rate obtained in typical telephone community surveys, about 35%. The response rate among those who were qualified and agreed to participate was 43%. Fieldwork was typically conducted from 5:30 to 8:45 p.m., Monday to Friday and Saturdays. On Sundays dialing was conducted from 10 a.m. to 2 p.m. (all local times).

[7] Excluded are unemployed, laid off, retired, in school, keeping house, and those with unspecified responses.

Table 6.1. Sample characteristics

Characteristics	n	Percent ($N = 2{,}317$)
Gender		
Male	1,197	51.7
Female	1,120	48.3
Race/ethnicity		
White (non-Latino)	1,620	69.9
African-American	279	12.0
Latino	291	12.6
Asian	77	3.3
Native American	16	0.7
Other (including multiple)	34	1.5
Marital status		
Married	1,456	62.8
Cohabitation	27	1.2
Divorced	269	11.6
Widowed	28	1.2
Separated	38	1.6
Never married	499	21.5
Education (years of schooling)		
High school or lower	840	36.3
Associate college	490	21.2
College	618	26.7
Master degree and above	367	15.8
Birth place		
Native	2,033	87.7
Foreign	284	12.3
Current occupations		
01 Executive, administrative, managerial	291	12.6
02 Professional	555	24.0
03 Technicians and support	137	5.9
04 Sales	277	12.0
05 Administrative support (including clerical)	265	11.5
06 Private household	17	0.7
07 Protective service	43	1.9
08 Service	228	9.9
09 Precision production, craft, and repair	262	11.3
10 Mechanical operators, assembles, inspectors	81	3.5
11 Transportation and material moving	68	2.9
12 Handlers, equipment cleaners	32	1.4
13 Farming, forestry, and fishing	47	2.0
Supervision		
1 Supervises no one	1,179	50.9
2 Supervises someone	762	32.9
3 Supervises people who supervise	376	16.2
Current annual salary		
$1,000–$1,999	11	0.6
$2,000–$2,999	6	0.3
$3,000–$3,999	9	0.5
$4,000–$4,999	6	0.3
$5,000–$5,999	16	0.8

Table 6.1. *(Continued)*

Characteristics	n	Percent ($N = 2{,}317$)
$6,000–$6,999	9	0.5
$7,000–$7,999	5	0.3
$8,000–$9,999	21	1.1
$10,000–$12,499	72	3.6
$12,500–$14,999	46	2.3
$15,000–$17,499	63	3.2
$17,500–$19,999	54	2.7
$20,000–$22,499	102	5.2
$22,500–$24,999	78	4.0
$25,000–$29,999	154	7.8
$30,000–$34,999	187	9.5
$35,000–$39,999	186	9.4
$40,000–$49,999	314	15.9
$50,000–$59,999	206	10.4
$60,000–$74,999	185	9.4
$75,000–$89,999	117	5.9
$90,000–$109,999	63	3.2
$110,000–$129,999	30	1.5
$130,000–$149,999	6	0.3
$150,000–$169,999	13	0.7
$170,000–$189,999	2	0.1
$190,000 or over	16	0.8

the sample splits evenly between men and women. Slightly more than two-thirds (70%) of the sample are non-Latino white, and about 12 percent are Latinos and African-Americans, respectively. About 12 percent of the respondents are foreign-born. Most of the respondents are either married (63%) or have never been married (22%), while 12 percent are divorced.

Some socioeconomic status characteristics of the sample also appear in Table 6.1. About 64 percent of the respondents have had more than a high-school level of education. The median annual personal salary is about $37,500. About one in eight (12.6%) of them have executive, administrative, or managerial jobs; another 24 percent of the respondents have professional jobs; 11.5 percent hold administrative support or clerical jobs; and another 5.9 percent are technicians. About half of the respondents have some supervising duty and one in six (16%) supervise some people who supervise others.

6.7. MEASUREMENTS

6.7.1. Routine Job Information

As articulated earlier, the critical issue of interest here is whether certain individuals benefit from routine exchanges in which job information is relayed without it pertaining to any particular job, or the individual actively engaging in job search. To measure the extent to which routine exchanges encapsulate information about jobs, a question in the questionnaire asked, "At the time, the year you started your current job, did someone mention job possibilities, openings, or opportunities to you, without your asking, in casual conversations?"[8] Of the 2,317 respondents, 998 or 43 percent answered in the affirmative. Thus, close to half of the respondents received job information through routine exchanges prior to or at the time they started their current job.

The question was framed for the time prior to or at the time of the current job in order to impose a time order prior to current job status, for subsequent causal analyses as implied in Hypothesis 2. However, the questioning could trigger association with the current job search. For those answering this question affirmatively, we ascertained in a follow-up question whether that information pertained to the current job, a job in the company of the current job, or one outside the company. Multiple choices were allowed. More than a half indicated that it was either related to the current job, 32 percent, or to other jobs in the same company, 28 percent. Also, more than half, 58 percent, indicated that this was information about jobs in other companies. Information about the current job or other jobs in the same company may reflect one's relative advantage in the internal networks in the company, whereas information about job opportunities outside the company may indicate the relative advantage in networking in the larger labor market. We will explore the relative efficacy of these networks and information in the analysis.

6.7.2. Capacity of Social Capital

For capacity of social capital, we measured diversity and richness of embedded resources in social networks with the position-generator methodology. The methodology employed a list of sampled socioeconomic positions and assessed the extent to which each person could access occupants of these positions. The assessment could then be used to develop indicators of each person's access to diversity and richness of resources in their social networks, as reflected in the socioeconomic characteristics of the accessed positions. As operationalized in the study, the methodology consisted of a question, "At the time of finding your current/last job, did you know someone who had the following kinds of jobs?" followed by a list of occupations. These occupations represented systematic sampled positions in the socioeconomic hierarchy of the occupations in the United States. A total of 22 positions were sampled from occupations of varying job prestige, based on the Standard International Occupational Prestige Scale (SIOPS) constructed by Ganzeboom, and Treiman (1996).

---

[8] If the response was "yes," a series of questions then ascertained: the quantity of such occasions, the circumstances of the occasions, whether there were any follow-ups on any of the possibilities, and whether the follow-ups led to further discussion, approaches by other contacts, further information, meeting with people who were hiring, visit to the company, job interview, or job offer. For the present study, we will only use the first question to approximate the invisible hand of social capital.

This computation thus allowed us to estimate social capital capacity prior to the current job. Access to these positions is shown in Table 6.2. From these accesses, three summary indexes were computed: (*a*) range—the difference of the highest and lowest prestige scores among the positions that each respondent could access; (*b*) extensity—the number of different positions each respondent could access; and (*c*) upper reachability—the highest score among accessed positions. The means, standard deviations, and range of scores for the indicators are also shown in Table 6.2.

A factor analysis, as shown in Table 6.3 (principal component and varimax rotation), yielded a single factor solution. Thus, a factor score based on the three indexes was constructed for each respondent. We also performed the factor analysis for males and females separately. Since the factor solution and patterns were essentially the same (see Table A.1 in Appendix 1), the same factor scoring procedure was used for all respondents.

6.7.3. Human Capital and Initial Status

We employed education and tenure as measures for human capital. We categorized four groups for education: (1) high school or less, (2) associate program and degree (one or two years in college), (3) college degree (three or four years in college), and (4) master's degree or beyond. In the analysis, they constitute dummy variables and the first category, high school or less, is the reference group. Tenure was measured with the number of years in the current job. We also incorporated additional variables for prior job experiences, with two measures: (*a*) previous job experience (yes or no), and (*b*) previously in executive positions (for those with previous job experience, yes or no). Prior job experiences may or may not reflect human capital. For the sake of the counterargument, we would also consider them to be part of human capital.

6.7.4. Social Participation

In the questionnaire we asked, "Now I would like to know something about the groups or organizations to which individuals belong. Here is a list of various organizations. Could you tell me whether or not you are a member of each type?" A list of 10 types of organizations were listed: political parties; labor unions; religious groups; leisure, sports, or culture groups; professional organizations; charities; neighborhood organizations; school and PTA; ethnic or civil rights organizations; and other voluntary organizations. We also asked how many years they had been a member in each checked organization. From this last item, we reconstructed the voluntary organizations each respondent had participated in at the time of starting their current/last job. A sum of these "prior" voluntary organizations forms the measure of social participation.

Table 6.2. Position generator and social capital capacity indexes

Position (SIOPS)	Respondent accessing (percent, $N = 2{,}317$) Prior to current job
Professor (78)	37.7
Lawyer (73)	52.6
CEO (70)	20.2
Congressman (64)	12.3
Production manager (63)	21.5
Middle school teacher (60)	45.8
Personnel manager (60)	33.5
Writer (58)	20.4
Nurse (54)	61.0
Computer programmer (51)	42.6
Administrative assistant (49)	33.3
Accountant (49)	32.9
Policeman (40)	46.5
Farmer (38)	41.9
Receptionist (38)	46.5
Operator in a factory (34)	29.7
Hair dresser (32)	56.2
Taxi driver (31)	8.6
Security guard (30)	26.5
Housemaid (23)	29.4
Janitor (21)	31.0
Hotel bell boy (20)	3.3
Indexes	
Extensity	
Mean	7.3
SD	4.6
Range of scores	0–22
Range	
Mean	40.1
SD	16.2
Range of scores	0–58
Upper reachability	
Mean	69.3
S.D.	11.2
Range of scores	0–78

Note: SIOPS, Standard International Occupational Prestige Scale.

6.7.5. Attained Status

For attained status, we devised measurements for (*a*) occupational status, (*b*) supervision, (*c*) annual income, and (*d*) high wages (yes or no). For occupational status, we developed an ordered variable of occupational positions. As shown in Table 6.1, there were 13 occupational groups. Because of our interest in developing

Table 6.3. Factor structure of capacity of social
capital prior to current job

Factor	Sample ($N = 2,317$)
I	2.430
II	0.418
III	0.152
Factor loadings on Factor I[a]	
Extensity	0.861
Upper reachability	0.886
Range	0.950
Factor scoring on Factor I[a]	
Extensity	0.354
Upper reachability	0.365
Range	0.391

[a] Principal component analysis and varimax rotation.

an ordered set of categories, we created three "occupational classes": (*a*) executives, (*b*) professional occupations, and (*c*) other occupations.

For supervising, a three-category ordered measure was devised: (*a*) the respondent had no supervising responsibility, (*b*) he or she had supervising responsibility but those they supervised had no supervising responsibility, and (*c*) he or she supervised someone who also supervised others. We tried alternative compositions for these two variables: summing the two variables, or constructing a factor score after a factor analysis (confirming a single factor solution, and using the factor score from a rotated solution). The results from these alternative measurements were nearly identical in all subsequent analyses.

We developed an ordered variable of annual income with 27 categories (see Table 6.1). Those who had an annual wage of more than $60,000 were categorized in the high-wage group.

6.7.6. Control Variables

We also employed a set of control variables in the analyses: (*a*) age and age squared, (*b*) male, and (*c*) quota (for possible sampling bias, see Section 6.6). We also constructed and entered three racial/ethnic categories: African-American, Latinos, and other (non-Latino white was the reference group). In the analyses where social capital capacity and receipt of routine job information were considered as dependent variables, age, marital status, and social participation had been adjusted to their status at the time when she or he was looking for the current job. Table A.2 in Appendix 1 shows the distribution of these variables prior to the present jobs.

6.8. DETERMINANTS OF SOCIAL CAPITAL CAPACITY AND ROUTINE JOB INFORMATION

We begin the analysis with social capital capacity as a dependent variable, to explore factors that contribute to its distribution. As presented in Table 6.4, having college-level education is significant in the ordinary regression analysis for the factor score of social capital capacity. The standardized coefficients for education variables range from 0.12 (for associate degrees) to 0.18 (for college degrees) and 0.24 (for graduate degrees), *confirming Hypothesis 3* about the relationship between human capital and social capital. Social participation is also a strong and significant factor (its partial coefficient is 0.21), *confirming Hypothesis 4*. Age is also positively associated with having a greater social capital capacity. Previous job experience also adds to the capacity of social capital (i.e. not having previous job experience had a negative effect). There is also a modest but significant positive relationship between being African-American and having greater social capital capacity, as compared to whites. We further examined the associations separately for African-American males and females and found a slight advantage of females over males on social capital. But the difference between the zero-order associations (0.03 for males and 0.05 for females) is not significant. Further research is needed to explore the relative advantage of females over males among African-Americans on social capital. There is no evidence that the sampling quota affected the patterns of relationships.

Table 6.4. Regression on social capital capacity

Independent variable	Partial coefficient and significance
Age[a]	.028** (.269)
Age (squared)[a]	−.000 (−.163)
Male	−.067 (−.033)
Native born	.0300 (.009)
Race/ethnicity (reference: non-Latino white)	
African-American	.185*** (.060)
Latino	−.004 (−.001)
Other	−.043 (−.010)
Married[a]	.023 (.012)
Education (base: high school or less)	
Associate college	.287*** (.117)
Bachelor college	.409*** (.182)
Master degree or higher	.645*** (.238)
Previous jobs (base: previous nonexecutive jobs)	
No previous jobs	−.120** (−.048)
Previous executive job	.054 (.016)
Social participation (active in voluntary organizations)[a]	.463*** (.208)
Quota	.003 (.002)
Constant	−1.300***

Note: Normalized β coefficients are in parentheses.

[a] Adjusted to the time (year) of taking on current job.

** Significant at 5%; *** significant at 1%.

Table 6.5. Determination of receipt of routine job information [exp (B): odds ratio]

Variable	Model 1	Model 2
Age[a]	0.996 (.891)	0.961 (.208)
Age (squared)[a]	1.000 (.886)	1.000 (.354)
Male	1.289*** (.004)	1.366*** (.001)
Native born	1.213 (.250)	1.170 (.373)
Race/ethnicity (base: non-Latino white)		
African-American	1.364** (.028)	1.255 (.120)
Latino	1.514** (.013)	1.556** (.012)
Other	0.968 (.875)	1.014 (.947)
Married[a]	0.855* (.086)	0.842* (.070)
Education (base: high school or less)		
Associate college	1.283** (.037)	1.194 (.157)
Bachelor degree	1.556*** (.000)	1.391*** (.005)
Master degree and above	1.822*** (.000)	1.480*** (.005)
Previous jobs (base: previous nonexecutive jobs)		
No previous job	.505*** (.000)	.542*** (.000)
Had a previous executive job	1.305*** (.000)	1.252 (.147)
Social participation (active in voluntary associations)[a]	1.507*** (.000)	1.232** (.049)
Quota	0.876 (.308)	0.904 (.304)
Social capital		1.466*** (.000)
Observations	2,317	2,205

Note: *p* values are in parentheses.
[a] Adjusted to the time (year) of taking on current job.
* Significant at 10%; ** significant at 5%; *** significant at 1%.

Table 6.5 shows the logistic regression models predicting the receipt of job information in routine exchanges. Model 1 incorporates all the control variables and shows that receipt of routine information is significantly associated with being male; being African-American; being Latino; not being married; having a higher education level; having had previous jobs, especially previous executive or professional jobs; and being active in social participation. Model 2 adds the variable of social capital. Social capital becomes a significant contributing factor. While it mediates somewhat the effects of being African-American, having higher education, and social participation (see their reduced coefficients in Model 2 relative to those in Model 1), the effect of social capital is largely independent of the control variables. *This confirms Hypothesis 1.*

6.9. RETURNS TO SOCIAL CAPITAL AND ROUTINE JOB INFORMATION

We next examine models estimating for the relative effect of routine job information on attained status.[9] For routine job information, we created three dummy

---

[9] In analyses of attainment status, current age is centered and experience in the present job is logged to prevent multicollinearity problems.

Table 6.6. Analyses for occupational attainment and supervision

Independent variable	Occupational attainment (multinomial logistic analysis: base: executives)		Supervision (ordered logit estimates)
	Professionals	Other jobs	
Age	−0.030*** (.001)	−0.014 (.086)	−0.010** (.040)
Age (squared)	−0.000 (.902)	−0.000 (.703)	−0.000 (.497)
Tenure	0.098 (.258)	−0.070 (.358)	0.284*** (.000)
Male	−0.717*** (.000)	0.166 (.248)	0.389*** (.000)
Native born	−0.014(.965)	−0.469 (.083)	−0.185 (.264)
Race/ethnicity (base: non-Latino white)			
African-American	−0.058 (.838)	0.243 (.326)	−0.185** (.264)
Latino	−0.924** (.004)	−0.510** (.051)	−0.201 (.155)
Other	−0.295 (.390)	−0.379 (.226)	−0.267 (.118)
Married	0.093 (.579)	0.107 (.473)	0.883 (.329)
Education level (base: high school or less)			
Associate college	0.602** (.028)	−0.437** (.037)	0.179 (.127)
Bachelor degree	0.988*** (.000)	−1.324*** (.000)	0.288*** (.010)
Master degree or above	1.694*** (.000)	−1.980*** (.000)	0.659*** (.000)
Previous job (base: previous nonexecutive job)			
No previous job	0.304 (.173)	0.298 (.151)	−0.172 (.116)
Had a previous executive job	−1.795*** (.000)	−1.181*** (.000)	0.360*** (.015)
Social participation	0.182 (.351)	−0.098 (.557)	0.281*** (.006)
Social capital	−.041 (.659)	−0.114 (.150)	0.259*** (.000)
Routine job information			
About current job	−.222 (.291)	−0.220 (.245)	0.515 (.665)
Other jobs in firm	−.0572** (.012)	−0.192 (.319)	0.302** (.016)
Jobs outside the firm	0.045 (.804)	0.131 (.420)	0.113 (.248)
Quota	0.155 (.365)	0.003 (.985)	−0.127 (.167)
Constant	0.011 (.981)	3.008*** (.000)	
Observations	2,193		2,205
Pseudo R^2	.20		.05

Note: p values are in parentheses.

** Significant at 5%; *** significant at 1%.

variables; for such information about the current job, about other jobs in the same company, and about jobs in other companies. Table 6.6 presents analyses for occupational attainment (having professional or other jobs, relative to being an executive) and having supervisory responsibility.

For comparing three different types of jobs (a professional, executive, or other job), we employed the multinomial logistic analysis, using being an executive as the base. As shown in the first column of Table 6.6, being a professional is significantly different from being an executive on several key variables. Professionals are younger, more likely to be female, white, and have a college education. They are less likely to have been an executive in a previous job and less likely to have received routine job information, especially about other jobs in the same company. In other words, compared to professionals, executives tend to be older, male, a minority (especially a Latino), not as highly educated, have been an executive in a previous job, and have received routine job information, especially about other job opportunities in the company.

Those in other jobs, in comparison with the executives, do not seem to be significantly different on age or gender. They tend to be less educated, less likely to be Latino, and less likely to have been an executive in a previous job. Since the category of "other jobs" consists of many heterogeneous occupations, this comparison does not offer much useful information. Future research, however, may yield some clues by focusing on different groups, especially among native-born Latinos, when the sample size warrants such multigroup analyses.[10]

Supervision, shown in the third column of Table 6.6, shows similar patterns as those found with executives. College degrees and receiving routine job information, especially about other jobs in the same company, both significantly contribute to being a supervisor. Tenure, being male, being white, and having been an executive in a previous job also help. Different from occupational attainment, however, supervision is also associated with being more active in social participation and having a greater capacity of social capital, even when all other factors are taken into account. Being socially involved and having access to greater resources in social networks seem to affect the likelihood of becoming supervisors, independent of human capital, previous job experiences, and other socioeconomic characteristics. We shall return to this topic later in Section 6.11.

Finally, we examined economic returns to routine job information. Economic returns are indicated by two variables: annual income and having a high wage. For annual income, with the 27 categories (see Table 6.1), we used the ordinary least-squaring regression; and for high wage, a dummy variable for those having annual income at or over $60,000, the logistic regression was performed. Table 6.7 presents the results.

Routine job information, especially regarding other jobs in the same company, shows a significant return for annual income. Higher education, tenure, being male, and having previous job experience also contribute to higher income. Again, social capital remains a significant factor while the effect of social participation becomes insignificant; suggesting that the capacity of social capital is not entirely explained by routine job information and that social participation's effect on income may be largely mediated by social capital and routine job information.

---

[10] One puzzle is why Latinos seem to be likely to be executives relative to being professionals or in other jobs. We examined some of their job characteristics (e.g. self-employed or working for family firms), and found no significant distributive differences among the three major race/ethnicity groups (Asians and other groups tend to be working for family firms or self-employed). A significant portion (59%) of the Latinos are foreign born, compared to whites (2.5%) and African-Americans (9%). While foreign-born whites (20%) are more likely to be executives compared to native-born whites (13%), it was the native-born African-Americans (10%) and Latinos (19%) who showed greater likelihood of being executives as compared to their foreign-born counterparts (4% and 8%, respectively). This last result suggests that further analyses should refine native-born Latinos to identify those holding executive jobs.

Table 6.7. Analyses for economic returns (annual income and high wage)

Independent variable	Annual income logged (OLS regression)[a]	High wage (logistic)[b]
Age	0.009 (.022)	1.029*** (.000)
Age (squared)	−0.003*** (−.077)	0.998*** (0.004)
Tenure	0.652*** (.157)	1.296*** (.000)
Male	2.015*** (.239)	3.282*** (.000)
Native born	0.343 (.026)	0.832 (.439)
Race/ethnicity (base: non-Latino white)		
African-American	−0.351 (−.027)	0.869 (.514)
Latino	−0.369 (−.029)	0.691 (1.55)
Other	0.249 (.013)	1.589* (.097)
Married	−0.019 (−.002)	1.155 (.274)
Education level (base: high school or less)		
Associate college	1.274*** (.123)	1.587** (.014)
Bachelor degree	2.224*** (.233)	2.751*** (.000)
Master degree or above	3.29*** (.284)	4.791*** (.000)
Previous job (base: previous nonexecutive job)		
No previous job	−0.515** (−.048)	0.761 (.108)
Previous executive job	0.599* (.041)	1.582 (.018)
Social participation	0.187 (.020)	0.880 (.389)
Social capital	0.330*** (.078)	1.209*** (.008)
Routine job information		
About current job	0.056 (.005)	1.365* (.055)
Other job in firm	0.820** (.064)	1.859*** (.000)
Jobs outside the firm	.003 (.060)	1.123 (.404)
Quota	−0.078 (−.009)	0.776** (.060)
Constant	14.025***	
Adjusted R^2	.213	.159
Observations	1,879	1,879

Note: OLS, ordinary least square.

[a] Normalized coefficients are in parentheses.

[b] p values are in parentheses.

* Significant at 10%; ** significant at 5%; *** significant at 1%.

As shown in the second column of Table 6.7, college education and routine job information are significant contributors for having high wages, as our hypotheses proposed. Tenure and being male also show an advantage. Social capital remains a significant direct contributing factor, while social participation's direct effect becomes insignificant. Two additional factors, however, increase the likelihood of having high wages. Older age becomes significant; it probably reflects the effect of seniority.

Quota, the sampling control variable, shows a borderline significant negative effect, suggesting that those sampled prior to quota sampling for minorities had a greater likelihood of having high wages. Quota may, in fact, reflect deficient returns for minorities, whose presence increased in the latter part of the survey.

We verified this possibility by examining the associations between quota and being African-American or Latino. The zero-order correlation between quota and being African-Americans is 0.20, and between quota and being Latino is 0.25. When we re-ran the equations without quota, both African-Americans and Latinos showed negative coefficients, and the latter was borderline significant (at 0.06 level), confirming the relative disadvantage of being a minority on high-wage returns.

6.10. JOB INFORMATION IN ROUTINE EXCHANGE: FURTHER EXPLORATIONS

Besides the single dichotomous item of job information in routine exchange, much more data were gathered. We asked those who indicated that they received job information through routine job exchanges how many job possibilities, openings, or opportunities were mentioned to him or her on these occasions. About half of the 998 respondents (455) said 1 or 2, nearly one-third (309) said 4 or more, and 1 in 10 (99) indicated 7 or more. Thus, such information repeatedly occurred routinely in exchanges. Furthermore, when asked if the jobs mentioned were in or outside of the company, 32 percent stated that the information was about their current job, 28 percent indicated that the jobs were within the company (organization), and another 58 percent stated that they were outside of the company (organization).

Further, we asked whether the respondent acted on the possibilities, openings, or opportunities she or he received in routine exchanges. Of the 998 respondents, 466 or 46.7 percent of respondents indicated that they did so, reflecting the utility of such routine job exchanges for jobs. As seen from Table 6.8, the follow-ups ranged from further discussions (38.7%), being approached by other contacts (26.2%), having sent for information (15.5%), providing information about oneself (36.9%), further discussions with others who knew about that job or company (35.5%), to meeting with those people who were hiring (38.1%), having had an informal "job interview" (33.7%), visiting the company (35.6%), to having a formal job interview (31.8%), or being offered a job (37.5%). These questions shed further light on how such routine exchanges work.

We conducted a hierarchical cluster analysis on these follow-up items in order to organize them into meaningful structures. Figure 6.1 shows the cluster dendrogram (also called cluster tree).[11] Dendrograms graphically present the information on which kinds of follow-up items are grouped together at various levels of (dis)similarity.

---

[11] The STATA command, *hcavar*, developed by Jean-Benoit Hardouin, realizes a hierarchical analysis on variables. Unfortunately, we cannot obtain the scores for the latent variables associated with each cluster after running this command. Hardouin was programming a new option that generates new variables corresponding to these latent variables (not available at the moment, however).

Table 6.8. Distribution of follow-ups for those who received routine job information

Follow-up	Frequency	Percent ($N = 998$)
Further discussion	386	38.7
Being approached by other contacts	263	26.2
Having sent for information	155	15.5
Providing information about themselves	368	36.9
Further discussions with others knowing about that job or company	354	35.5
Meeting with people hiring	380	38.1
Having an informal "job interview"	336	33.7
Visiting the company	355	35.6
Having a formal job interview	317	31.8
Being offered a job	374	37.5

These analyses suggest that two general clusters of follow-up activities can be discerned. One cluster pertains to general information follow-ups, including items regarding asking for more information about a job or a company, or sending more information about oneself. Another cluster includes items such as visiting the company, meeting with people there, having an informal or formal job interview, and being offered a job—activities associated with more serious job negotiations with a company. We conducted another cluster analysis only for those who received job information that was not about their current job. As can be seen in Figure 6.2, the two main clusters remain the same, with some slight variation (e.g. "providing information about themselves" is now part of the job-negotiation cluster). These follow-up items suggest that routine job information may lead to two kinds of activities: (*a*) further information exchanges and (*b*) job negotiations.

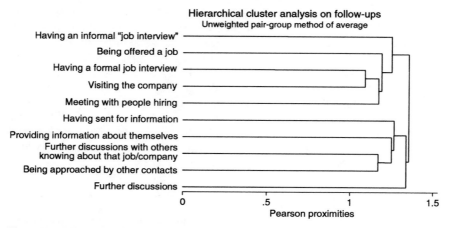

Figure 6.1. Hierarchical cluster analysis on follow-ups

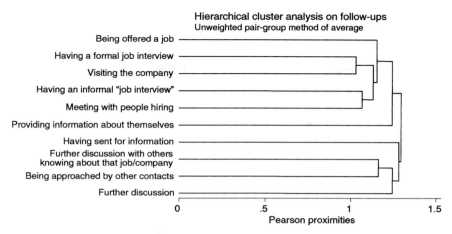

Figure 6.2. Hierarchical cluster analysis on follow-ups for those who received routine job information that was not about their current jobs

These descriptive materials suggest that the dynamics of transitioning from the informal to the formal or the invisible to the visible process of social capital utilization deserves further research attention.

6.11. SUMMARY AND DISCUSSION

In this national survey we tested the informal avenue by which social capital enhances opportunities for job mobility in the labor market—the invisible hand of social capital. Data from a national survey lend strong support to the arguments that social capital capacity increases the likelihood of receiving job information in routine exchanges. Such routine job information is associated with better returns in the labor market in terms of occupation, supervision, and wage. Further, social capital capacity is enhanced by both human capital and social participation.

About one-third of the routine job information received at the time when the interviewees were getting their current job pertains to this current job. However, the remaining interviewees mentioned information about other jobs either in the same company or in a different company. Follow-up probes show two rather distinct types of consequences of receiving such job information in informal exchanges. Some pursued more information about particular jobs or companies, and others followed through with more serious job negotiations. It is clear, therefore, that routine job information occurs regularly in the labor market and it exerts important consequences on job mobility and attainment. Why, then, does job information in routine exchanges assume significance in the labor market? We speculate here on its relative advantages.

The labor market is a field where supply and demand of labor can be seen as exchange relations. These exchanges are seldom symmetric in power. When a person seeks and applies for a job, that person becomes one of several or even many applicants in a pool. A dependence or power-inequality relationship is established (Emerson 1962; Cook 1982), where the employer has multiple choices and the applicant has one. Granted, the same applicant may apply for multiple jobs. Yet, in each application the relationship is asymmetric, where each applicant is obliged to provide all information required by the employer. The employer may provide all applicants some general information in regard to the firm or the position, but she or he is seldom obligated to provide further specific information. On the other hand, each applicant must provide specific information about herself or himself and respond to requests for additional information that the employer deems useful. The employer, in the power position and in the possession of information about the applicants, can determine the process of screening, selecting, and picking the winner. The applicant, on the other hand, in the passive and reactive position and in possession of relatively little information about the employer and the recruitment process, is mostly on the outside and at the mercy of the employer in this exchange.

To change the relatively disadvantaged position in the exchange, an applicant could mobilize personal helpers. But the mere act of mobilizing helpers does not automatically alter the unequal power positions unless the helpers mobilized have an equal or advantaged position relative to the employer (or recruiter), so as to modify the power relationship. The modified relationship provides a chance for the applicant to get "inside information," information not available to other applicants, which may help the applicant in formulating more specific tactics in negotiations, in influencing the decision-making of the recruiter, or in deciding whether to proceed with the application. The evidence is that finding such helpers is not a given; thus, the personal sources for job searchers is generally insignificant.

Routine job information, on the other hand, puts the person and the potential employer in a different exchange relationship. Since the person is "approached" about a job opportunity, the person is not a formal applicant. Further, the approached and the informant are probably symmetric in relations since they are in the same networks. The informant, who passes along the information about the job, is probably also an "insider," someone who is active in the networks involving employers or their agents, or who is connected to someone who is connected to the employers/agents. The informant, who is a disinterested third party (who probably would not have shared the information with the person approached otherwise), engages the employer/agent on an equal footing and assures that the approached is, at the minimum, on an equal-power position relative to the employer. Recipients of routine job information thus gain a relative power advantage over potential employers, depending on their own initial positions and the informant's position.

A further advantage of being a recipient of job information through routine exchanges is that a person does not need to make any commitment as an applicant. Yet at the same time, she or he would be in a position to collect more information about the employer, the position, the criteria of selection, and the expectations of a successful candidate while maintaining control as to how much interest to express and what and how much information to convey to the informant and the employer. In control of information flow, the person can keep probing for the likelihood of success or failure and assess risks and rewards without evoking a commitment as an applicant. Such negotiations can be terminated or allowed to proceed at her or his discretion. Only when the risks for failing have been minimized and rewards optimized to her or his satisfaction does she or he give permission to move the process to the visible and formal stage.

Note that in these equations social capital remains significant in its effect on attained status even when the contributions of routine job information variables have been accounted for. This suggests that the effects of the capacity of social capital on attainment are not exhausted by routine job information, a finding which is not surprising. Social capital capacity enhances job opportunities in multiple ways. It increases the opportunity for the use of personal contacts in job searches and, as shown in this study, it also facilitates receiving job information in routine exchanges. Yet, there remains other latent avenues in which social capital capacity exerts effects on attainment that are unmeasured and therefore undetected in the present study. As shown in the analyses in Tables 6.6 and 6.7, social capital capacity remains significant on attainment, even after the effect of routine job information is accounted for. That is, routine job information only partially accounts for the potential effects of social capital. As discussed earlier, social capital capacity carries reputation and social credentials that may be transmitted informally to hiring firms and such information may carry weight in the hiring decisions. It is also possible that other mobilization avenues have been initiated and have not been detected with the simple instruments used in this and other previous studies. The findings from the present study clearly argue for more research efforts on the link between social capital and attainment in the labor market. Further instrumentation and conceptual articulation may yet identify multiple avenues through which social capital exerts its effects.

6.12. FINAL THOUGHTS

This account of the advantages of the invisible hand of social capital by no means eliminates or discredits formal processes of job search and recruitment in the labor market. Legal, power, and moral considerations may compel employers to engage in formal recruitment processes and to encourage interested individuals to commit themselves as applicants. Further, those who are in disadvantaged social positions and inferior social networks may have limited choices in avoiding formal applications. In these situations, job recruitment and search are necessary. Job search, therefore, should remain pervasive in most labor markets. In this job-search process, finding the "right" connections to overcome the dependence relationship and access inside information and influence would also be useful for an applicant. How the invisible hand and visible hand of social capital jointly operate in the labor market constitutes a topic worthy of immediate research attention, a project we intend to pursue.

APPENDIX 1

Table A.1. Factor structure of access to social capital prior to current job by gender

Factor	Male ($N = 1,197$)	Female ($N = 1,120$)
I	2.444	2.414
II	0.411	0.426
III	0.145	0.159
Factor loadings on Factor I[a]		
Extensity	0.865	0.857
Upper reachability	0.889	0.885
Range	0.952	0.948
Factor scoring on Factor I[a]		
Extensity	0.354	0.355
Upper reachability	0.364	0.366
Range	0.390	0.392

[a] Principal component analysis and varimax rotation.

Table A.2. Summary of sample characteristics prior to the present job (percentage or mean)

	Total (N = 2,317)	Male (n = 1,197)	Female (n = 1,120)	Significance test[a]
Age	34.72	34.37	35.09	0.07
Married	53.78%	52.13%	55.54%	0.10
Active in voluntary associations	71.08%	69.34%	72.95%	0.06

[a] The significance levels for t-tests on the equality of means for males and females.

7

Social Resources and Their Effect on Occupational Attainment through the Life Course[1]

Hester Moerbeek and Henk Flap

7.1. INTRODUCTION

Research on social capital and occupational attainment is often seen as a criticism of stratification research (Lin, Vaughn, and Ensel 1981*a*, 1981*b*). The occupational attainment process, like all of social life, is embedded in social networks. Once differences in social resources are taken into account, the effects of parental resources and of one's own education change. In addition to stressing the importance of social networks on occupational attainment, the research literature shows that the number of people in the social network is not the only factor of importance to one's chances at the labor market, but that the network also has a kind of "quality". It is more profitable to know someone with a relatively high status and a great deal of influence than to know a person of relatively low status. The effects of the parents' occupational prestige as well as the effects of a person's own educational attainment decrease once the effect of social resources, that is, the prestige of contact persons, is taken into account. When these resources are included in the explanation of status attainment, they have their own independent effect on occupational attainment. In addition, part of the effect of education is indirect: having a better education enables someone to mobilize a contact person with better resources (see Lin, Vaughn, and Ensel 1981*a*, 1981*b*; De Graaf and Flap 1988). People with a higher education will have more opportunity to reach people with a high status and thus have access to better social resources.

Much of the research to this point, however, has been concerned with how people find their jobs. If people find their jobs through informal resources (friends, acquaintances, and family) and the status of the contact persons is relatively high, the effect on occupational prestige is significant and positive.

In our contribution to this volume, we want to delve somewhat deeper into a number of ways in which social resources affect one's life chances. First, although

[1] An earlier version of this chapter was presented at the International Sunbelt Social Network Conference XXI, April 25–8, 2001, Budapest, Hungary.

contact persons are an important social resource, we have extensive knowledge primarily about the actual use of social resources because of the way most research was performed until recently. As Lin and Dumin pointed out in 1986, it is also relevant to know what social resources people have access to, regardless of whether they use them or not (Lin and Dumin 1986). Thinking of social resources as social capital points to the importance of having access in addition to the use of social resources. As with money, it is not only important what you actually spend, but also what assets you have, such as savings. In other words, it is important to know what you *can* spend. Instead of the use of social resources, this chapter will mainly focus on people's *access* to social resources. Research has been done on this subject in the United States, China, Taiwan, and former Eastern Germany (German Democratic Republic, GDR), among other countries (Lin and Dumin 1986; Lin and Bian 1991*b*; Lai, Lin, and Leung 1998; Völker and Flap 1999; Lin, Fu, and Hsung 2001). Research on access has become more and more sophisticated, as can be seen in this volume and, for example, in the extensive work of Erickson (2004) in Canada. The inclusion of gender and gendered social capital has proven especially valuable. In this chapter we will look into the effect of access to social resources on people's occupational attainment, learning from these previous studies.

Besides the importance of access to social resources, a second and related issue is that earlier research mainly considered the cases in which the use of social resources was successful in that people did find a job. This makes existing research on social networks and attainment liable to the criticism of standardizing on the dependent variable. Earlier research especially the research by Lin and associates, has been criticized, as selectivity was suspected. Most of the earlier research focused on those people who applied for a job, via either formal or informal resources, and acquired the job. The argument to expect selectivity in this regard is that these people, relative to all the other persons who are able to work, already have more resources and a relatively high occupational status. The "bad" persons are filtered out because they simply do not acquire jobs. A similar reasoning applies to those who are successful in applying informally: Are these the persons who have many resources, including good access to social resources? Similarly, the persons who search through informal channels but do not succeed may have fewer resources or even bad resources.

Furthermore, in this chapter we want to focus on a life-course perspective. Moerbeek (2001) has already proposed a new outlook on the role of social resources during the life course. She specified the role of social resources in a way more congenial to the spirit of modernization theory. The influence of ascribed characteristics, mostly measured by the education and occupational prestige of the father, has diminished over the years, but some influence of social background is still there. Furthermore, the influence of education (achieved characteristics) on a person's labor market position did not increase over time. Moerbeek argues that during a person's life course, the pertaining influence of social background in the beginning of the career converts toward a more substantive effect of one's own education and work experience. Parents' remaining influence on occupational achievement should be seen as influence of parents' social capital rather than that of parents' education and occupational prestige directly. If the argument holds true that a person's social capital is achieved during their education and in the workplace, the same should hold true for their parents. Thus, in this chapter we want to make a distinction between parents' social capital—ascribed (access to) social resources, and a person's own social capital—achieved (access to) social resources. Family as a social resource should then be important to a person's labor market position early on in the career, while friends and acquaintances as social resources should have more influence on a person's later labor market position. We will test whether this argument holds for ascribed and achieved access to social resources.

In this chapter, we will replicate part of the earlier research on access, while focusing on a transition from ascribed to achieved social capital. We will also look at those people who applied for a job with the help of a contact person but failed to get that job. By looking into the so-called "failures", we hope to avoid possible selectivity, as discussed earlier. In the following section we will describe the theoretical background that leads to the hypotheses on the ascribed and achieved access to social resources.

7.2. THEORY AND HYPOTHESES REGARDING ACCESS TO SOCIAL RESOURCES

The study of what kind of resources people have access to, regardless of whether they use them or not, gives a clear picture of the way in which someone's network connects him or her with a multitude of positions. As stated above, using informal resources is only profitable if these resources are of a relatively high quality. And logically, access comes before use. Although Völker and Flap (1999) showed that access does not necessarily lead to use, the causal order can never be the other way around. If we make the logical assumption that access comes before use of social contacts, the same hypotheses that applied to the use of social resources should apply to access. In sociology's search for the reasons why the characteristics of the father continue to have an effect on his children's professional life, even in this day and age of modernization, access cannot be left out as an explanatory factor. In addition to the theoretical importance of access itself, the link between access and use is interesting. One cannot use contacts one has no access to. If one only has access to people with the same or a lower status, then one can logically only make use of these types of contacts.

In order to continue the exploration of the importance of access to social resources, we shall return to some propositions that Lin formulated (Lin 1983). The social-resources proposition states that in seeking a job, an individual who has access to a contact of higher socioeconomic status should find a better job than someone whose contact has a lower status. The strength-of-positions proposition implies that the higher a person's initial position, whether inherited or achieved, the higher the social resources reached through a contact should be.

The strength-of-weak-ties proposition follows directly from Granovetter's work (Granovetter 1973, [1974] 1995), and states that weak ties rather than strong ties permit a wider reach to other parts of the social structure, thus enabling the person who uses weak ties to reach better social resources.

Besides these three propositions, Lin predicted an interaction between the effects of the strength of someone's social position and the strength of ties. The lower the initial position, the more the strength-of-weak-ties proposition will apply. Because of the possibility of a ceiling effect, the strong ties of someone with a high status ought to provide him or her with social resources that are as good as (or better than) the resources available through weak ties. The weak ties of someone with a low status, however, should prove more useful than his or her strong ties.

According to Lin's propositions, certain aspects of the access to social resources appear to be particularly important for status attainment. First, in the social-resources proposition, the (relative) prestige of a contact one has access to is important. In the strength-of-position proposition, initial position is an important factor. Finally, from the strength-of-weak-ties proposition, we learn that the nature of the tie is of importance to the possible effect of access. The first step in the analyses in this chapter is to consider the importance of these three aspects.

The next step in this chapter is to integrate Lin's propositions while applying ideas to ascribed and achieved social capital. One of the implications of this idea is that a person's own education should have a larger effect on the social resources he/she has access to than do the characteristics of the father. We call this the *education hypothesis*. Apart from considering differences in access, it is interesting to look at differences in the effect of access on attained prestige. We hypothesize that inherited access is of greater importance early on in the occupational career, while in later life achieved access gains in importance. This means that social resources accessed through the family are of greater importance to the first job and social resources accessed through friends are of greater importance to later jobs. We call this the *achieved-access hypothesis*.

The interaction between the strength of ties and the achieved social capital is a bit more complex. Granovetter perceived the ties with relatives as strong ones and the ties with friends and acquaintances as weak ones. If we follow him in this, the hypothesis should be that access through relatives has a stronger effect on occupational prestige early on in one's career and access through friends and acquaintances has a stronger effect in later stages. But if we follow Homans's "like me" principle (Homans 1950), then things change. If we do indeed choose our friends because they are alike, then they will most likely have a similar status. Furthermore, because of the alleged transitivity of friendships, our friends will most likely know the same kinds of people we know. This makes the ties with friends strong rather than weak. The ties with relatives are forced upon us. Relatives can be very diverse as to their occupations and the persons they know. Thus ties with relatives can widen the reach to other parts of the social structure. Yet calling ties with relatives weak is intuitively strange. To avoid this problem, we distinguish between relatives, friends, and acquaintances rather than between strong and weak ties.[2] Moreover, we emphasize the *achieved-access hypothesis* that ascribed social capital is more important in the early career and achieved social capital is of more influence in later stages.

The next step is to explore the influence access to social resources has on the actual use of social resources. This step is based mainly on the research Völker and Flap did for the former GDR (Völker and Flap 1999). Völker and Flap found a small positive (though hardly significant) effect of access on use. We will also assume a positive relation between these two factors. In fact, we expect to find a stronger effect. Völker and Flap's research pertained to the communist GDR where there was danger involved in using personal contacts, and especially weak ties (Völker and Flap 2001). For the Netherlands, no such danger can be expected. The *access-leads-to-use hypothesis*, therefore, reads as follows: better access to social resources leads to more intensive use of social resources.

The last addition as compared to earlier research is the promised inclusion of failures. For this, we will make a distinction between those people who ever unsuccessfully applied for a job and those who did not. Furthermore, we will make a distinction between those people who ever unsuccessfully applied for a job with the use of a contact person and those who unsuccessfully applied without a contact person. In fact, this is a test for selectivity. It is very important nonetheless. The research conducted so far on the use of social resources on the labor market has considered only those people who actually found jobs through a contact person. Because the so-called failures were excluded, the effects found may have been biased.[3] In the hope of avoiding the same mistake, we will approach this problem optimistically. In our wish not to discard the findings of earlier research, we hypothesize that there is no selectivity. This means that our *failures hypothesis* reads as follows: people who unsuccessfully apply for a job are not less well educated or of a lower-status background than people who never unsuccessfully apply for a job.

Furthermore, we have to distinguish between people who applied for a job and failed and used informal resources and people who failed and did not use informal resources. The selectivity that might occur here is that perceivably only those with good access to social resources succeed in finding a job via informal channels. Our *failures-via-informal-resources hypothesis* reads as follows: people who unsuccessfully apply for a job via informal resources are not different in education or status background from people who unsuccessfully apply through different resources. We also want to explore factors that lead to unsuccessful applications and the effect of unsuccessful applications further on in the career. For this we will

---

[2] In much of the research into social networks, role-based forms of measurement have been used. In these forms of measurement, colleagues are by definition weak ties (see, for instance, Fischer 1982). We do not agree with this definition of ties with colleagues. In our research, colleagues can be acquaintances, friends, or even relatives.

[3] The bias due to the exclusion of failures pertains only to the models in which the way someone found his or her job was used as an explanatory variable.

turn to background variables that have traditionally been used to explain occupational attainment. This phenomenon will be disentangled in Section 7.5 of this chapter.

Finally, for nearly all analyses we will include controls for age and gender.

7.3. DATA, MEASUREMENTS, AND OPERATIONALIZATIONS

The data used in this chapter stem from the Dutch Telepanel Survey, which was held in 1992 and 1993 on a sample of 3,000 households in the Netherlands. The Telepanel Survey consisted of three waves. The first wave contained all sampled households. The second wave contained about 1,900 households, with approximately 3,500 household members. The background characteristics of these households generally match those of average Dutch households. In Wave 1, life histories (such as educational and occupational career) were researched. In Wave 2, more specialized questions were asked, for example, about social capital. Since it is a panel study, we were able to match data files from both the first and second waves. Thus we have available data about the whole occupational career and the role of several social capital variables therein. Nevertheless, not all respondents were asked all questions. This means that the number of cases may vary between the analyses in this chapter. When such a decision was called for, we have chosen for pairwise deletion of missing cases to use as much of the available information as possible. The response rate for the complete panel is 57 percent. For the Dutch, this is a relatively high response rate. Response rates below 50 percent are no exception in our country. A thorough test of representativeness has been carried out. A complete justification of the total survey can be obtained at the Steinmetz Archive (ESR/Telepanel, Steinmetz Archive).

In order to measure the access people have to other people with a certain occupational prestige, the respondents in the Dutch Telepanel Survey were presented with a position generator of 30 occupations and asked whether they had a friend, relative, or acquaintance with such an occupation. The method of questioning resembles the one Lin and Dumin used, except that Lin and Dumin had only 20 occupations on their list. Völker and Flap used a list with 33 occupations. The beauty of this apparently simple measurement instrument is that it incorporates almost all relevant aspects of social capital that we need for testing our hypotheses.

As a general indicator of access to social resources, we use the number of occupations people have access to, or, in other words, the access network. To measure the "quality" of the access network, we use the highest prestige level reached by the access network. As an indicator of the range of the network, we use the range of prestige (highest minus lowest prestige). For the respondent's initial prestige, we use the prestige of the father as an indicator. For the nature of the tie, we only have to look at the original position generator, which already distinguished between friends, relatives, and acquaintances.

To distinguish between ascribed and achieved access, we make use of a particularly useful set of questions asked in the Dutch Telepanel Survey. In this survey, the respondents were asked to name the occupations of their parents' two best friends when the respondents themselves were young, and the occupations of their own two best friends at the time of the interview. The occupational prestige of the best friends of the parents[4] is used as an indicator for ascribed access to social capital. The occupational prestige of their own best friend is used as an indicator for achieved access to social capital.

For the description of possible differences between people who ever applied for a job and did not get it, we used two questions from the Dutch Telepanel Survey. First, people were asked whether they had ever unsuccessfully applied for a job; and second, they were asked how they learned about this job.

Variables like age[5] and sex were measured straightforwardly. Sex was dichotomized as 1 for female and 0 for male. For the level of education, we used the Standard Educational Index from 1978 (Central Bureau of Statistics 1987): (*a*) primary; (*b*) low vocational, extended primary; (*c*) middle vocational, grammar; (*d*) higher vocational; and (*e*) university. To determine a person's occupational prestige, we applied the occupational prestige scale that was constructed for the Netherlands by Sixma and Ultee (1984). This scale ranges from 13 (garbage collector) to 87 (surgeon). The prestige of the father was reported for the time when the respondent was 12 years old.

In Section 7.4, we will first translate the theory and hypotheses into testable hypotheses.

7.4. PROPOSITIONS AND HYPOTHESES IN TERMS OF VARIABLES

In this section we will translate Lin's propositions and our own hypotheses in terms of variables. The strength-of-position proposition states that the higher someone's initial position is, the higher the quality and the amount of the social resources reached through a contact are. In terms of the variables described in the foregoing section, this leads to the following *strength-of-position hypothesis*: the higher the occupational prestige of someone's father, the higher the lowest prestige accessed, the highest prestige accessed, the range of prestige accessed, and the number of occupations accessed.

---

[4] Although naming two best friends of both the respondents and their parents was requested, we chose to include only the first best friend of the parents (and not the mean of the two) because the prestige of the two friends is not altogether similar. We expect that respondents have answered the question for both parents (i.e. first father's best friend and then mother's, or the reverse). By using the first-mentioned friend, we expect that friends of the family will be included most. We expect the first best friend to have the largest influence on the respondent's daily life. This last line of reasoning also pertains to the respondent's own best friend.

[5] Age was coded according to Dutch Central Bureau of Statistics (CBS) categories: 15–19, 20–24, 25–29, 30–34, 35–39, 40–44, 45–49, 50–54, 55–59, 60–64, 65–69, 70–74, 75–79, 80–84, and 85–older.

The strength-of-weak-ties proposition states that weak ties rather than strong ties permit a wide reach to other parts of the social structure. In terms of variables, this reads as the following *strength-of-weak-ties hypothesis*: contacts with acquaintances give access to more occupations, with higher prestige, and access to a wider range of occupations, as compared to contacts with friends and relatives.

The *education hypothesis* states that one's own education has a larger effect on the social resources accessed than do the characteristics of the father. In terms of variables, this means that one's own education has a larger effect than the father's occupational prestige on the number of occupations accessed, the prestige of the occupations accessed, and the range of the prestige of occupations accessed.

The *achieved-access hypothesis* states that access through relatives has a stronger effect on one's own prestige in the early phase of the occupational career and access through friends has a stronger effect in later stages. In terms of variables, this means that the occupational prestige of the friends of the parents has an effect on the prestige of the respondent's first job. Regarding the occupational prestige of the respondent's job at the time of the interview, the prestige of the respondent's own friends has a larger effect. The foregoing four hypotheses will be tested in Section 7.5.1.

The *access-leads-to-use hypothesis* states very straightforwardly that better access to social resources leads to more intensive use of social resources. We will start by testing this hypothesis in its strictest form. This means that all access variables constructed—number of occupations accessed, access through relatives, access through friends, and access through acquaintances—will be applied to explain the use of informal contacts for the first job, the job before the last, and the current or the last job. This leads to the following hypothesis: a higher number of occupations accessed and wide-ranging access to occupations through relatives, friends, and acquaintances lead to more intensive use of social resources for the first job, the job before the last, and the current or the last job.

This form of the access-leads-to-use hypothesis is, however, a very unrefined one. If we take into account the achieved-access hypothesis, then we expect more influence of relatives on the first job and more influence of friends and acquaintances on the job before the last and the current or the last job. This expectation leads to the following refinement of the access-leads-to-use hypothesis. First, we can refine the general hypothesis into the *higher-number-leads-to-more-use hypothesis*: for all jobs, a higher number of occupations accessed will lead to more use of social resources.

The next refinement is the *achieved-access-leads-to-more-use hypothesis*: for the first job, the access of occupations through relatives leads to more intensive use of social resources, while for the job before the last, and the current or the last job, access through friends and acquaintances leads to more intensive use of social resources.

If we combine the achieved-access-leads-to-more-use hypothesis with the strength-of-weak-ties hypothesis, we reach the even more refined *achieved-access-through-weak-ties-leads-to-more-use hypothesis*: for the job before the last and the current or the last job, access through acquaintances leads to more intensive use of social resources than does access through friends.

Note that we do not include family in this hypothesis. This is done to avoid the discussion about who is considered a weak tie and who is not. We will let the empirical results decide on this matter. All hypotheses regarding the relation between access and use will be tested in Section 7.5.2.

With regard to "failures"—those people who ever unsuccessfully applied for a job, either through informal resources or not—we have formulated two hypotheses. The *failures hypothesis* and the *failures-via-informal-resources hypothesis* need no further operationalization. Since this part of the research is still in a very exploratory phase, we have not formulated hypotheses regarding the analyses of the factors leading to unsuccessful application or the effect of unsuccessful application later on in the career. All analyses regarding unsuccessful applications and failed use of resources will be described in Section 7.5.3.

7.5. ANALYSES

7.5.1. Access to Social Resources

In order to test the hypotheses derived from Lin's propositions, we will first construct two descriptive tables. In Table 7.1, the 30 occupations on the list used in the survey are listed under four main categories: upper white-collar occupations, lower white-collar occupations, upper blue-collar occupations, and lower blue-collar occupations. The percentage of respondents who declared that they knew a person with a certain occupation is listed in the table, as well as the percentage of respondents who declared that they knew someone in one of the four occupational groups.

From Table 7.1, it can be seen that the diversity of access is large. Many respondents seem to know people in a variety of occupations. In general, the access to white-collar occupations seems larger than the access to blue-collar occupations, but this may also be because fewer blue-collar occupations were listed. Lin and Dumin (1986) had a more balanced list of occupations, and they did not find this difference. Völker and Flap (1999) had a list largely similar to ours, and they did find the same difference.[6]

Table 7.2 depicts the means and standard deviations of the number of occupations accessed, the lowest prestige accessed, the average prestige accessed, the highest prestige accessed, and the range of the prestige of occupations accessed.

From Table 7.2, it can be seen that, on average, people state that they have access to eight persons. This seems to be quite a universal number of accessed occupations; the same number was found by Lin and Dumin for Albany (United

---

[6] We chose not to adjust our list to the one Lin and Dumin (1986) used, since we do not want to lose the information on the added occupations.

Table 7.1. Access to occupations through social ties

Occupations accessed, $N = 2,362$		
Upper white collar	85%	—
Direct or public works	—	8%
Real estate agent	—	16%
Computer programmer	—	43%
Lawyer	—	19%
Union official	—	12%
Social scientist	—	22%
Manager of supermarket	—	17%
Musician	—	29%
Building contractor	—	27%
Head of school	—	34%
University professor	—	17%
Director, Industrial organization	—	17%
Reporter	—	18%
Business economist	—	22%
Teacher, elementary school	—	45%
Hotel manager	—	10%
Lower white collar	84%	—
Salesman	—	40%
Secretary	—	50%
Insurance agent	—	31%
Geriatric attendant	—	43%
Telephone operator	—	26%
Nurse	—	58%
Upper blue collar	50%	—
Car mechanic	—	38%
Team boss, construction company	—	14%
Lathe operator	—	21%
Lower blue collar	65%	—
Warehouseman/supply clerk	—	23%
Waiter	—	19%
Garbage collector	—	7%
Shop assistant	—	42%
Dairy farmer	—	27%

Table 7.2. Access to occupations through social ties

	Mean	SD
Number of occupations accessed	8.39	4.98
Lowest prestige	33.50	10.42
Average prestige	52.68	7.98
Highest prestige	72.07	11.74
Range of prestige	38.57	15.81

Table 7.3. Access to occupational categories by father's occupational prestige

	Father's occupational prestige (Ultee–Sixma prestige scores)				
	High (65+) $n = 216$	Medium (45–65) $n = 282$	Low (45–) $n = 574$	Total $N = 1{,}072$	Linearity
Lowest prestige	35.03 (11.36)	33.90 (10.69)	32.61 (9.74)	33.44 (10.37)	**
Highest prestige	75.84 (9.07)	72.86 (11.58)	69.93 (12.09)	71.89 (11.63)	**
Range of prestige	40.81 (14.75)	38.96 (15.67)	37.32 (16.27)	38.45 (15.86)	**
Number of occupations	8.97 (4.84)	8.36 (4.87)	7.90 (4.84)	8.24 (4.86)	**
Between group p	**	**	*	*	—

Note: Standard deviation values are given in parentheses.
* Significant at the 5% level; ** significant at the 1% level.

States) and by Völker and Flap for the GDR. Lin, Fu, and Hsung (2001) found a number of 6.5 occupations accessed for Taiwan while using only 15 different job titles. Although our list of occupations has a lowest prestige score of 23 and a highest prestige score of 85, the mean lowest prestige of occupations accessed is 33. The mean highest prestige is 72. The average level of prestige accessed is about 53, which is more interesting if we compare it to the average level of prestige of the respondents, which is 46. On average, people seem to have access to relatively high-quality social resources.

The descriptive analyses displayed in Tables 7.1 and 7.2 sketch the phenomenon we want to explain. In order to explain differences in occupations accessed, we will first look at the *strength-of-position hypothesis*. In Table 7.3, we have classified the occupational prestige of the respondents' fathers into three categories: high (prestige of 65 and higher), medium (prestige between 45 and 65), and low (prestige lower than 45). The number of occupations accessed, the lowest prestige accessed, the average prestige accessed, the highest prestige accessed, and the range of the prestige of occupations accessed are broken down by the fathers' prestige scores in Table 7.3.

From Table 7.3, we see that the occupation of the father has considerable influence on one's own access to other occupations. The higher the initial position, the higher the mean lowest prestige, the mean highest prestige, the range of occupations accessed, and the number of occupations accessed.

The effect is linear, and the differences between the groups are significant. This means that we can translate the findings into the conclusion that the higher the occupational prestige of the father, the higher the prestige of the occupations his children have access to. Apparently the *strength-of-position hypothesis* is corroborated by the evidence.

In order to test the *strength-of-weak-ties hypothesis*, we have constructed Table 7.4, which depicts the percentages of respondents mentioning relatives, friends, and acquaintances in the four main occupational groups. In the lower panel of Table 7.4, the lowest, average, and highest prestige accessed are again

Table 7.4. Access to occupations through relatives, friends, and acquaintances ($N = 2{,}362$)

Occupational groups	Relatives	Friends	Acquaintances	Any
Percentage of respondents mentioning				
Upper white collar	63	49	70	85
Lower white collar	59	46	65	84
Upper blue collar	26	17	32	50
Lower blue collar	40	27	46	65
Any	85	71	86	—
Mean (SD)				
Lowest prestige	40.20 (13.79)	42.98 (14.22)	37.65 (12.83)	33.50 (10.42)
Average prestige	52.09 (11.09)	52.85 (11.72)	52.85 (9.77)	52.68 (7.98)
Highest prestige	64.78 (14.43)	63.20 (14.81)	67.96 (13.67)	72.07 (11.41)
Range	24.59 (17.87)	20.22 (17.68)	30.30 (18.40)	38.57 (15.81)
Number	3.82 (2.75)	3.42 (2.87)	5.72 (4.31)	8.39 (4.98)

depicted, as well as the range of prestige and the number of occupations accessed. These factors are now broken down by the nature of the tie.

In Table 7.4, we find some support for the *strength-of-weak-ties hypothesis* as Granovetter (1973, 1974) first formulated it. Not only do acquaintances provide wider access to the upper white-collar occupations, but they also provide access to the widest range and the highest number of occupations. The "like me" principle of friendship also finds some support, since friends provide access to the lowest range of occupations, as compared with relatives and acquaintances.

The next step is to incorporate other factors explaining the access to social resources into the analyses in order to test the *education hypothesis*. As we stated in Section 7.2, we expect education to have a higher effect on access than does initial position (i.e. prestige of the father). With regard to the strength-of-weak-ties proposition, our only founded expectation is that acquaintances have a stronger effect on access than do friends or relatives. In the upper panel of Table 7.5 the first expectation is tested, and in the lower panel the second hypothesis is under surveillance.

From Table 7.5, it can be seen that the expectation that education has a relatively large effect on occupational access does not hold. The standardized coefficients in the table show that, in fact, the occupational prestige of the father has a greater influence on all aspects of access. From the lower panel of Table 7.5, it can be seen that access through acquaintances does indeed give the highest maximum occupational prestige accessed. Access through acquaintances also has the largest effect on the range of occupations accessed. Access through friends has no effect on either the maximum or the range of occupations accessed.

However, access through relatives also has a large and positive effect on both aspects of access. This may either mean that the strength-of-weak-ties argument does not hold or that relatives are weaker ties than has been perceived up to this point. Intuitively, we opt for the second explanation.

Table 7.5. Regression of access variables on father's occupational prestige and respondent's education and on strength of ties variables

	Number	Highest prestige	Lowest prestige	Range of prestige
Minimum $N = 1,014$				
Father's prestige	0.511** (0.081)	2.587** (0.178)	1.126** (0.085)	1.504* (0.075)
Education	0.081 (0.026)	0.853** (0.118)	0.262 (0.040)	0.588* (0.059)
Constant	7.365	65.937	31.060	34.815
R^2	0.62%	5.37%	8.33%	8.97%
Minimum $N = 796$				
Father's prestige		2.635** (0.182)		1.238* (0.062)
Friends		−0.001 (0.000)		0.069 (0.012)
Relatives		0.872** (0.209)		1.724** (0.300)
Acquaintances		0.946** (0.355)		1.615** (0.440)
Constant		58.913		20.432
R^2		25.74%		38.86%

Note: Unstandardized and standardized coefficients.
* Significant at the 5% level; ** Significant at the 1% level.

The next and the last step in this section is to test the *achieved-access hypothesis*. In order to do so, we have performed a step-by-step analysis of the status attainment model with the inclusion of the social-capital variables. The results of this analysis are depicted in Table 7.6.

— In Model 1, the original status attainment model for the first job is analyzed. Prestige of the current job is regressed on the same variables. We know that this is a far from perfect model for the current job since important explanatory variables are left out, but we have done this for the sake of comparison. From this model, we can conclude that for the first job, father's occupation and the respondent's education are important explanatory variables. A higher education and a higher initial prestige cause a higher occupational prestige of the first job. The same is true for the current job, but here sex also has a negative effect. Women have significantly lower prestige than men do in their current job. Furthermore, we can see from this model that the prestige of the first job is better explained by these variables than that of the current job.

— In Model 2, the same analysis was carried out, but now the prestige of the parents' best friend was also included. From this model, we see that for the first job the effects of father's occupation and education go down slightly. Furthermore, we see that the prestige of the parents' best friend has a positive effect on the prestige of the first job (although significant only at the 10% level). For the current job, the effects of sex and of father's occupation are no longer significant. The effect of education diminished slightly and the prestige of the parents' best friend also has a positive effect (although, again, significant only at the 10% level). Again, the first job is better explained by the included variables than is the current job. The results from Model 2

Table 7.6. Regression of prestige of first and current job on social background variables and social capital variables

	Model 1, N = 1,382		Model 2, N = 524		Model 3, N = 264	Model 4, N = 264	Model 5, N = 264
	First job	Current job	First job	Current job	Current job	Current job	Current job
Sex	−0.510 (−0.016)	−3.211** (−0.084)	−0.587 (−0.018)	−3.346 (−0.087)	−2.748 (−0.072)	−2.757 (−0.072)	−2.728 (−0.013)
Father's occupation	0.183** (0.225)	0.083** (0.085)	0.151** (0.186)	0.038 (0.039)	0.021 (0.002)	−0.093 (−0.010)	−0.012 (−0.013)
Education	2.371** (0.213)	2.374** (0.176)	2.267*** (0.203)	2.719* (0.162)	1.480*** (0.110)	1.366 (0.101)	1.312 (0.097)
Parents' friend			0.072*** (0.088)	0.123*** (0.125)		0.102 (0.104)	0.100 (0.102)
Own friend					0.280** (0.288)	0.281** (0.289)	0.271** (0.279)
Age						−0.108 (−0.016)	−0.046 (−0.007)
First job						0.060 (0.051)	0.056 (0.048)
Access							0.422*** (0.111)
Intercept	27.509	39.652	25.719	36.232	25.414	24.996	21.533
R^2	12.2%	5.6%	12.8%	6.9%	14.5%	14.7%	16.0%

Note: Unstandardized and standardized coefficients (pairwise deletion of missing values).

* Significant at the 5% level; ** significant at the 1% level; *** significant at the 10% level.

seem to contradict the *achieved-access hypothesis*. Nevertheless, we expect that the effect of the parents' best friends incorporates the effects of other important explanatory variables. Furthermore, the hypothesis is twofold. Not only should the prestige of the parents' best friend help explain the prestige of the first job but also the prestige of the respondent's own best friend should have a larger effect on the prestige of the current job. Therefore, we have continued in our effort to explain the prestige of the current job in Models 3, 4, and 5.

— In Model 3, we have included the prestige of the respondent's best friend as an explanatory variable. From the results, we can see that the effect of education has now almost disappeared. Also, the effect of the parents' best friend is no longer statistically significant. In fact, the only highly significant and positive effect is that of the prestige of the respondent's best friend. This model explains current occupational prestige considerably better than the earlier models. From these results, we conclude that the achieved-access hypothesis should not be refuted.

— In Model 4, the prestige of the first job is also included in the explanation of the prestige of the current job. We have done this to complete the status attainment model and to see whether the effect of the best friend remains significant, even in this stricter test. Again, the prestige of the best friend has a highly significant and positive effect on current prestige. Prestige of the first job has no significant effect in this model, although the explained variance improves slightly.

— In Model 5, general access to occupations is also included. This checks the possibility that the prestige of best friend is a proxy for access. The results in the last column of table 6 show that the effect of the prestige of best friend remains significant and positive. The effect of general access is also positive (although only statistically significant only at the 10% level). Apparently prestige of the best friend has an autonomous effect on current occupational prestige.

From the foregoing, we conclude that the achieved-access hypothesis should not be refuted.

7.5.2. Does Access Lead to Use?

In this section, we will test the general *access-leads-to-use hypothesis*. As described in Section 7.4, this hypothesis can be divided into three more refined hypotheses:

1. The *higher-number-leads-to-more-use hypothesis*, which states that a higher number of occupations accessed will lead to more intensive use of social resources.

2. The *achieved-access-leads-to-more-use hypothesis*, which states that for the first job, access of occupations through relatives leads to more intensive use

of social resources, while for the job before the last and the current or the last job access through friends and acquaintances leads to more intensive use of social resources.

3. The *achieved-access-through-weak-ties-leads-to-more-use hypothesis*, which states that for the job before the last and the current or the last job, access through acquaintances leads to more intensive use of social resources than does access through friends.

In order to test all these hypotheses, we have regressed the way people found their first job, their job before the last, and their current or the last job on the access variables. The three dependent variables are dichotomous. Officially, one cannot use dichotomous variables within ordinary least squares (OLS) regression. This has to do with one of the assumptions of the method, namely, that all variables are measured at interval (or at least ordinal) level. Strictly speaking, the dependent variables in our analysis are measured at a nominal level. However, because the variables are coded 1 if the job was found through personal contact and 0 if it was not, this constitutes no problem. If the coefficients are positive (and significant), then this will still mean that more of the independent variable leads to more of the dependent variable; in this case, it means that more access leads to more intensive use. Because of the clear interpretation of the coefficients in OLS regression, we prefer this method to other methods of analysis that would normally be more appropriate.

The analyses needed to test the *higher-number-leads-to-more-use hypothesis* are reported in Table 7.7.

From Table 7.7, we can conclude that a higher number of occupations accessed indeed leads to a slightly more intensive use of informal resources where the job before the last and the current or the last job are concerned. The intensity of use is, however, only slightly higher, and the effects are significant only at the 10 percent level. This is a similar result to that found by Völker and Flap (1999). The meaning of the results becomes clearer if we put them in regression equations. This leads to

Table 7.7. Regression of the way a job was found on the number of occupations accessed

	Job 1 informal? $N = 1,711$	Job before last informal? $N = 1,300$	Current/last job informal? $N = 2,105$
Number of occupations accessed	0.003 0.028 (0.002)	0.005 0.050 (0.027)***	0.004 0.038 (0.002)***
Intercept	0.434	0.331	0.372
R^2	0.02%	0.17%	0.14%

Note: Unstandardized and standardized regression coefficients (pairwise deletion of missing values, standard errors within parentheses).

* Significant at the 5% level; ** significant at the 1% level; *** significant at the 10% level.

the following two equations:

Job before last informal? = 0.331 + 0.005 × number of occupations accessed.

$$(1)$$

Current or last job informal? = 0.372 + 0.004 × number of occupations accessed.

$$(2)$$

From Table 7.3, we learned that on average people have access to eight different occupations. If we impute this into the equations, then we get the result of 0.371 for the job before the last and 0.404 for the current or the last job. These numbers have to be interpreted on a scale from 0 to 1. The conclusion from these findings has to be that the *higher-number-leads-to-more-use hypothesis* cannot be refuted. The effect of access on use, however, is not strong. Since the effect of access on achieved prestige is relatively strong, we can conclude that social networks are apparently of importance, whether the focal person uses them or not.

The analyses needed to test the *achieved-access-leads-to-more-use hypothesis* and the *achieved-access-through-weak-ties-leads-to-more-use hypothesis* are reported in Table 7.8. With regard to the first hypothesis, we can conclude that access to occupations through relatives indeed leads to more use of informal resources for the first job. Regarding the job before the last and the current or the last job, only access through acquaintances leads to more use. This result does not lead to a rejection of the *achieved-access-leads-to-more-use hypothesis*. However, it is also not a strong confirmation for the hypothesis.

For the *achieved-access-through-weak-ties-leads-to-more-use hypothesis*, we only have to look at the last two columns of Table 7.8. In these columns, we see that

Table 7.8. Regression of the way a job was found on the number of occupations accessed through friends, acquaintances, and relatives, respectively

	Job 1 informal? $N = 1{,}298$	Job before last informal? $N = 994$	Current/last job informal? $N = 1{,}532$
Access through friends	0.000	0.003	−0.000
	0.005	0.021	−0.002
	(0.006)	(0.006)	(0.006)
Access through acquaintances	−0.002	0.009	0.007
	−0.017	0.077	0.065
	(0.004)	(0.004)***	(0.004)*
Access through relatives	0.014	−0.005	0.002
	0.076	−0.031	0.010
	(0.005)*	(0.006)	(0.005)
Intercept	0.414	0.331	0.354
R^2	0.31%	0.40%	0.27%

Note: Unstandardized and standardized regression coefficients (pairwise deletion of missing values, standard errors between parentheses).

* Significant at the 5% level; ** Significant at the 1% level; *** Significant at the 10% level.

the effect of occupations accessed through acquaintances is significant (although only at the 10% level), while the occupations accessed through friends have no effect on the use of informal resources. We thus find no strong confirmation of the hypothesis, but it should not be rejected.

What do the results from the analyses in this section mean for the general *access-leads-to-use hypothesis*? In general, we can conclude that better access leads to more intensive use, but the effects are very small and hardly ever significant above the 10 percent level. "The more, the better" seems to apply to social capital, but not very strongly. A theoretically more interesting conclusion is that social capital is productive in ways other than just through the use of social resources. There seem to be other mechanisms through which social capital has an effect on success on the labor market beyond the process of looking for a job.

7.5.3. Failed Use of Informal Resources

We will now turn to the subject of people who have ever unsuccessfully applied for a job. To tackle this subject, we have made two distinctions. First, we will compare people who have ever unsuccessfully applied for a job with people who have not. Of the 2,362 persons who answered this question, 1,128 (48%) said "no" and 1,234 (52%) said "yes". Second, we will select the people who have ever unsuccessfully applied for a job, and make a comparison between the people who learned about this job through informal resources and the group who learned about it through formal resources. Of the 1,234 persons who ever unsuccessfully applied for a job, 1,131 answered the question about how they learned about this job. Of these, 1,066 (94%) answered "through formal resources." Sixty-five respondents (6%) learned about the job through informal resources.[7] To make the comparison, we have broken the groups down by a few background characteristics: own education, education of the father, prestige of the first job, age, and sex. In Table 7.9, the means of these control variables are shown per selected group. The significance pertains to between-group significance, which shows us whether the groups really differ with respect to the control variables.

From Table 7.9, it can be seen that the people who have unsuccessfully applied for a job are, in general, better educated, had or have a better educated father,[8] and a higher first job prestige. Furthermore, the unsuccessful applicants are

---

[7] This percentage of use of informal resources is low as compared with the percentage of people who did find a job through informal resources. Perhaps the people who unsuccessfully applied for jobs were already in a job at the time. If one has a job and applies for another job, one usually wants as few people as possible to know about this, which would prevent the use of informal resources. It may also be the case that the jobs these generally successful respondents applied for were not really important to them. If one really wants a certain job, one will use all available resources to get it. Consequently, if a job is not that important, one may refrain from using these resources.

[8] In this table, we have included father's education instead of father's occupation. The occupation of the father and use of informal resources combined had too many missing values. Since the number of cases is already very low in this analysis and since father's occupation and education are highly correlated (Pearson's correlation above .50), we chose to include father's education.

Table 7.9. Unsuccessful job applications and the way people learned about the job broken down by education, father's education, prestige of first job, age, and sex

	Education	Father's education	Prestige of first job	Age	Sex
Ever unsuccessfully applied?					
No	1.925 (1,127)	1.842 (499)	39.702 (772)	47.438 (1,127)	0.543 (1,127)
Yes	2.232 (1,234)**	2.026 (564)**	43.523 (889)**	40.179 (1,234)**	0.425 (1,234)**
If yes, how did you learn about the job?					
Formal	2.253 (1,066)	2.034 (503)	44.008 (773)	39.665 (1,066)	0.431 (1,066)
Informal	2.185 (65)	2.154 (26)	40.289 (45)	37.631 (65)	0.369 (65)

Note: Means of control variables per group in cells (number of cases in groups between parentheses).
Between-group significance: ** Significant at the 1% level.

younger. More men than women have unsuccessfully applied (a number closer to 1 indicates more women, a number closer to 0 indicates more men). These results demonstrate that, on average, the people who have ever unsuccessfully applied appear to be more successful in the rest of their lives. In fact, we suggest that the conclusion from the table should be that "better" people have applied unsuccessfully, because they could afford to go and search for another job. A failed application does not mean that one gets fired, but may result in a better job. The results from the upper half of Table 7.9 confirm our failures hypothesis.

We will now look at the bottom half of Table 7.9. Here, the people who unsuccessfully applied for a job are divided into people who learned about this job through formal resources and people who heard about the job through informal resources. From the table, we can clearly see that there are no significant differences between these two groups. Note, however, that the number of people who learned about the job through informal resources is small (65 respondents). Nevertheless, the results in Table 7.9 confirm our *failures-via-informal-resources hypothesis*.

The next step in our analyses is to look into factors explaining unsuccessful applications. In order to do this, we have performed a logistic regression with unsuccessful application as a dependent variable and sex, age, father's occupational prestige, education, and the prestige of the first job as explanatory variables. The choice for these variables is consistent with the choice we made for Table 7.9. We want to check the causal relations between the mentioned variables and unsuccessful applications. The results of the analysis are depicted in Table 7.10.

From Table 7.10, we can see that sex and age have a significant and negative effect on unsuccessful applications. This means that men and younger people have a higher chance to apply unsuccessfully. Father's occupation has no effect. Education has a positive and significant effect. This means that higher-educated people have a higher chance to apply unsuccessfully. Prestige of the first job also has a positive effect (although significant only at the 10% level) on unsuccessful

Table 7.10. Logistic regression of unsuccessful applications on social background and social capital variables

Variables	Unsuccessful application
Sex	−0.408** (0.150)
Age	−0.207** (0.029)
Father's occupation	−0.006 (0.004)
Education	0.366** (0.082)
First job	0.010*** (0.005)
Constant	1.106
Cox and Snell R^2	11.5%

Note: B-coefficients (pairwise deletion of missing values, minimum $N = 861$, standard errors between parentheses).

* Significant at the 5% level; ** significant at the 1% level; *** significant at the 10% level.

application. Our conclusion from this is that the results we found in Table 7.9 can be interpreted causally.

Our final analysis studies the effect unsuccessful applications have on the occupational career. Here, we have included unsuccessful applications in the explanatory model for the prestige of the current occupation. The results of this analysis are depicted in Table 7.11.

We have not included a bivariate regression of current job on unsuccessful applications in Table 7.11. It suffices to say that Pearson's correlation between

Table 7.11. Regression of current job on unsuccessful application, social background variables, and social capital variables

Variables	Current job		
	Model 1, minimum $N = 2,362$	Model 2, minimum $N = 524$	Model 3, minimum $N = 524$
Sex	−2.069* (−0.058)	−1.757 (−0.049)	−1.725 (−0.048)
Father's occupation	0.042 (0.047)	−0.001 (−0.011)	−0.016 (−0.018)
Education	0.878* (0.072)	0.404 (0.033)	0.408 (0.033)
First job	0.313** (0.033)	0.269** (0.244)	0.266** (0.241)
Age	0.555** (0.096)	0.209 (0.036)	0.244 (0.042)
Unsuccessful application	3.260** (0.091)	3.339* (0.093)	3.153* (0.088)
Parents' friend		0.067 (0.074)	0.071*** (0.078)
Own friend		0.221** (0.235)	0.211** (0.225)
Social resources access			0.304* (0.085)
Intercept	23.699	17.188	15.139
R^2	13.4%	19.0%	19.6%

Note: Unstandardized and standardized coefficients (pairwise deletion of missing values).

* Significant at the 5% level; ** significant at the 1% level; *** significant at the 10% level.

the two variables is .12 and significant at the 1% level. In Table 7.11, we have carried out a step-by-step analysis of the status attainment model with inclusion of unsuccessful application and social capital variables.

— In Model 1, the traditional explanatory variables for the prestige of current occupation are included, together with unsuccessful applications. From the results, we see that the effects as we know them from earlier analyses remain significant. The effect of unsuccessful applications is also significant, and it is positive. From this we conclude, although tentatively, that people who apply unsuccessfully are more successful than people who do not.

— In Model 2, we have included the prestige of the parents' best friend and the prestige of the respondent's own best friend. Here, we see that the effects of all variables that have been included in earlier analyses behave the same as before. The effect of unsuccessful applications remains positive and significant.

— In Model 3, the last and the strictest test of the effect of unsuccessful applications on current occupational prestige is carried out. Here also, general access to social resources is included in the analysis. General access turns out to have a positive and significant effect on occupational prestige, next to the positive and significant effect of unsuccessful applications.

From the results in Table 7.11, we can conclude that people who apply unsuccessfully during their career are indeed more successful in the end.

In the last section of this chapter, we will summarize the results of the analyses.

7.6. CONCLUSIONS AND DISCUSSION

In this chapter we have looked at the aspects that influence the access to social resources and at the influence access to social resources has on attained prestige. Regarding the aspects influencing access, we have leaned heavily on Lin and Dumin (1986).

With respect to the aspects that influence access to social resources, the following conclusions can be drawn. First, the diversity of access is large: many respondents seem to know people in all kinds of occupations. Second, on average, people seem to have access to relatively high-quality social resources. Third, we found that the prestige of the father, as an indicator of initial position, has a large effect on the access to social resources, and that this effect is larger than the effect of one's own education. This finding constitutes a rejection of the *education hypothesis*, and it strengthens our conviction that education is not the only important factor explaining access to social resources. The father, or rather one's own social background, remains a factor of great importance for the access to social resources and through that for status attainment, although the effect is, in greater part, indirect. This is a confirmation of the *strength-of-position hypothesis*. This finding justifies the analysis of the influence of ascribed access (past networks) that we performed later on in this chapter. The fourth conclusion to be drawn with respect to aspects influencing the access to social resources is that acquaintances provide the best access, as compared to relatives and friends. Yet relatives also provide rather good access to social resources. In fact, friends give least access to social resources. These findings reject the *strength-of-weak-ties hypothesis*.

With these findings, we can contribute to the discussion on the strength-of-weak-ties argument, started by Granovetter (1973). Relatives have always been perceived as strong ties, but if the argument is started from another point, following Homans's "like me" principle, this does not seem very logical. After having performed the analyses reported in this chapter, we are still convinced that acquaintances provide us with the best access to social resources, because they are the least like us. But we also believe that friends are more like us than relatives. We do not choose our relatives; they are forced upon us. There is no real reason to believe that in general our relatives have a similar occupational reach as we do. One only has to consider the broad meaning of the word "relatives". It incorporates not only our parents and siblings but also our grandparents, uncles, aunts, cousins, nephews, and our own children. In short, based on the findings in this chapter, we are not willing to refute the strength-of-weak-ties argument, but we would like to take a closer look at it in the future.

The analyses of the influence of access to social resources on attained prestige leave us with two conclusions. First, access through relatives (ascribed access to social resources) has a positive effect on the prestige of the first job. Second, access through friends (achieved access) has a strong positive effect on the prestige of the current job, while ascribed access has only a small effect on the prestige of the current job. The latter effect disappears after inclusion of more control variables. Since the *achieved-access hypothesis* about the influence of ascribed and achieved access on attained prestige consists of two elements, namely, that (*a*) ascribed access has more influence early on in the occupational career, while (*b*) achieved access becomes more important in later stages, this hypothesis cannot be refuted. In fact, the findings demonstrate the importance of including ascribed and achieved social capital in the explanation of status attainment. These findings support the expectation that parents' networks, or "past networks," are important in one's own occupational attainment. It would be a valuable contribution to the research of social capital to explore this aspect further. For instance, the work of Erickson (2004) shows the importance of gender and gendered social capital. It would be very interesting to discover whether gender also plays a role in past networks. As we expressed in note 4, we expect it does. There are sometimes large differences between the prestige of the friends of the parents and the respondent's own best friends. People may tend to answer a question about two friends in a sex-indiscriminate manner, thus tending to mention a man and a woman. This could certainly be a subject for further study. Another possibility is that the children work in a different sector of the labor market than their parents (e.g. the parents work in the financial sector, whereas the children try to make a career in the cultural sector) and are therefore somewhat less successful in building their own social capital (see Flap and Völker in this volume).

To answer the question whether access leads to more intensive use of social resources, we formulated one general hypothesis and three more specified hypotheses. The *higher-number-leads-to-more-use hypothesis*, which states that a higher number of occupations accessed leads to more intensive use of social resources, could not be refuted. Although the effects are rather small, a higher number of occupations accessed lead to more intensive use of informal resources when someone is looking for a job.

The *achieved-access-leads-to-more-use hypothesis* stated that with respect to the first job, access to occupations through relatives leads to more intensive use of informal resources, while for the later jobs access through friends and acquaintances is of greater importance. In the analyses we found nothing to contradict this hypothesis, although friends were found to be of no importance for the job before the last and the current or the last job. Access through acquaintances showed an effect on the use of informal resources for the job before the last and the current or the last job. The hypothesis therefore cannot be refuted.

In fact, this last finding points at the importance of including the *achieved-access-through-weak-ties-leads-to-more-use hypothesis*, which claims that for the job before the last and the current or the last job access through acquaintances leads to more intensive use of social resources than access through friends does. Not surprisingly, this hypothesis could not be rejected. Indeed, access through relatives was the only variable that had an effect on the use of informal resources for the first job. Only access through acquaintances had any effect on the use of informal resources for the job before the last and the current or the last job.

The results provide proof for the general *access-leads-to-use hypothesis*. In trying to explain this phenomenon, one needs to be very careful to avoid causality problems. If we try to explain this with the argument of social skills it may, for instance, be the case that people with better social skills know more people (have more access) and are more successful on the labor market. It may also be the case that people who know more people learn more social skills that are important in higher prestige jobs. Another possibility is that persons with a larger social capital are more visible, and they and their qualities are noticed sooner by other employers looking for job candidates and by people who may refer them to an employer (see Flap and Boxman 2001). This is a very interesting problem that deserves to be examined in future research.

Next, we focused on failures in the use of informal resources. For this, we first compared the group of people who have ever unsuccessfully applied for a job with the group of people who have never done this. The conclusion was that, on average, people who have ever unsuccessfully applied for a job have a higher education, a father with a higher education, and a higher first job prestige. Furthermore, this group is on average younger and contains more men than women compared to the group of people who have never unsuccessfully applied for a job. The most straightforward conclusion from this is that "more successful" people more often unsuccessfully apply for a job. As we stated in Section 7.5.3, we find the most logical explanation for this to be that these people could afford to go in search for another job. A failed application does not mean that one gets fired, but it may result in a better job. Those who do not expect to be able to find a better job probably do not continue their job hunt. Whatever the interpretation, the results provide us with strong confirmation of our *failures hypothesis*, that people who unsuccessfully apply for a job are not less well educated or of a lower-status background than people who never unsuccessfully applied for a job. In fact, our conclusions are confirmed by a causal analysis. The everyday notion that people who cannot make it through the formal channels have to rely on informal ways of finding a job does not seem to be true.

Second, of the group of people who ever unsuccessfully applied for a job, we compared the people who learned about the job through informal resources to those who heard about it through formal channels. The conclusion from this comparison was that there is no significant difference between the two groups. From this, we concluded that our *failures-via-informal-resources hypothesis* cannot be rejected. This is a hopeful result for the research into the influence of social capital on the labor market. Since up to this point a lot of the research on this subject has analyzed how people found their jobs, and has excluded those people who used informal resources but did not find a job, there has always been a chance of selectivity. The results in Section 7.5.3 show that this selectivity does not occur, at least not in the Netherlands in 1993.

The last step in the analyses in this chapter was to investigate the effect of unsuccessful applications later on in the career. Here, we found that people who have ever unsuccessfully applied for a job turn out to be more successful. For this, we have several possible explanations. Although, of course, the importance of the issue requires more research and more sophisticated attempts at explaining this phenomenon, our first instinct would be that in order to get ahead during their career people periodically need to apply for better jobs, if only to get a better estimate of their own quality. Of course, the more frequently one applies, the higher the chance of an unsuccessful application. Especially ambitious people may try to get ahead faster than their knowledge and experience allows, whereas those who are somewhat less good at their job may be aware of this and make less effort to get ahead.

8

A Question of Access or Mobilization? Understanding Inefficacious Job Referral Networks among the Black Poor

Sandra Susan Smith

Within the urban poverty literature, conventional wisdom holds that social isolation from mainstream ties and institutions is the basis upon which the black urban poor are presumed to lack social capital that facilitates job finding (Wacquant and Wilson 1989; Briggs 1998; Tigges, Browne, and Green 1998; Rankin and Quane 2000). In *The Truly Disadvantaged*, for instance, William Julius Wilson (1987) argues that because of the exodus of the black middle and working classes from what were once vertically integrated, black urban communities, those left behind have become residents of neighborhoods steeped in poverty. Furthermore, lacking regular and sustained contact with individuals that have strong attachments to mainstream institutions, residents are socially isolated. Relative to the poor who reside in low-poverty neighborhoods, the number of people to whom they are connected is small, and the connections they do have are disadvantaged. Consequently, there are few role models to inform black urban youth about appropriate workplace behavior and to provide links to jobs. Thus, even during strong economic times, members of this group still have great difficulty finding work (Wilson 1987). A structurally based alternative to the culture of poverty theory, Wilson's social isolation thesis is the primary reason behind the widely held beliefs that the black urban poor lack the social capital necessary for labor market entry and upward mobility.

However, this conventional wisdom is now being called into question. Research is increasingly providing convincing evidence that the networks of the black urban poor are larger, more diverse, and wide-ranging, and much less detached from the mainstream than indicated by conventional wisdom (Oliver 1988; Sosin 1991; Hurlbert, Beggs, and Haines 1998; Newman 1999; Jackson 2001). Drawing from these studies, I proposed in prior work that the extent and nature of the black urban poor's isolation from the mainstream had been exaggerated to the point that we could no longer locate their relative inability to find work in limited access to mainstream ties (Smith 2003). In an article recently published in the *American Journal of Sociology*, I provide an alternative explanation (2005). I suggest that what we have come to view as deficiencies in access to social capital among the black urban poor may have more to do with functional deficiencies of their job referral networks. Employing in-depth interviews and survey data of 105 low-income African-Americans, I show that those in possession of job information and influence overwhelmingly approached job-finding assistance with great skepticism and distrust, primarily fearing that their job-seeking relations might negatively affect their reputations with employers. This was especially so among residents of high-poverty neighborhoods. This pervasive distrust, I argued, better explained the inefficacy of the black poor's job referral network in low-wage labor markets where employers rely heavily on job referral networks for recruitment and screening.

However, these two approaches are not necessarily contradictory. Whereas most researchers examining the relationship between social capital and joblessness among the black urban poor assume that mobilization for job-finding will occur contingent on access, and so do not investigate the factors that affect whether mobilization will occur (Wilson 1987, 1996; Wacquant and Wilson 1989; Fernandez and Harris 1992; Rankin and Quane 2000), in my study, I assumed access and set about to better understand the decision-making process that those in possession of job information and influence undertake regarding whether or not to assist. To my knowledge, no study does both. Specifically, to date, no study systematically investigates the relationship between the black poor's access to social capital, their orientation toward providing job-finding assistance when in a position to do so, and neighborhood poverty status. This chapter is an effort to bridge the gaps between these two approaches.

8.1. DEFICIENCIES IN ACCESS?

In the process of status attainment, Lin (2001*b*) differentiates between two types of social capital—accessed and mobilized. Accessed social capital models explain status attainment by pointing to individuals' network structure and composition (Campbell, Marsden, and Hurlbert 1986; Lin and Dumin 1986; Boxman, De Graaf, and Flap 1991; or see Lin 1999*b* for review). This is the tradition within which urban poverty research programs fall, with some moderate adjustments for context (Wacquant and Wilson 1989; Fernandez and Harris 1991; Green, Tigges, and Browne 1995; Hurlbert, Beggs, and Haines 1998; Rankin and Quane 2000).[1] According to Wilson (1987), social isolation from mainstream ties and institutions is the reason the black urban poor lack social capital necessary for job finding. Wilson defines social isolation as "the lack of contact or sustained interaction with individuals and institutions that represent mainstream society" (60).

---

[1] In contrast to accessed social capital models, mobilized social capital models focus on situations in which actors use personal contacts for instrumental action, such as job finding, and these models explain actors' status attainment in terms of the status of the job contact who provided aid (Lin, Ensel, and Vaughn 1981*b*; De Graaf and Flap 1988; Marsden and Hurlbert 1988).

When he speaks of mainstream individuals, he is referring to members of the working and middle classes, specifically individuals who have strong attachments to the labor market. Mainstream institutions are those that the working and middle classes support, such as churches, businesses, schools, social clubs, and community organizations. As the presence of mainstream individuals declines, so too do links to job referral networks that can inform job seekers of employment opportunities and inform them of appropriate workplace behaviors. As a result, in high-to-extreme poverty neighborhoods where relatively few of the working and middle classes reside, the structure and composition of the black poor's personal network of relations do not facilitate job finding in the same way as among black poor residents of low-to-moderate-poverty neighborhoods.

Among the first to empirically examine the relationship between neighborhood poverty and isolation, Wacquant and Wilson (1989) found that when comparing the social capital of low- and extreme-poverty residents, the latter were far less likely to have a current partner or best friend, much less intimates who had completed high school and were steadily employed.[2] As a result, they concluded, "Our data indicate that not only do residents of extreme-poverty areas have fewer social relations but also that they tend to have relations of lesser social worth, as measured by the social position of their partners, parents, siblings, and best friends, for instance. In short, they possess lower volumes of social capital" (1989: 22–3), defining social capital as the "resources [individuals] have access to by virtue of being socially integrated into solidary groups, networks, or organizations" (1989: 22). Introducing various subtleties and distinctions, others followed suit, generally finding as well that residence in high-poverty neighborhoods increases access to relations on public assistance while reducing access to working and educated relations (Fernandez and Harris 1992; Briggs 1998; Tigges, Browne, and Green 1998; Elliott 1999; Rankin and Quane 2000). These results provide support for Wilson's assertion that neighborhood poverty and social isolation are positively correlated among the black urban poor such that residents of high-poverty neighborhoods tend to have access to relations of lesser "social worth," regardless of their socioeconomic status, and that these relations are less likely to facilitate employment.

Findings from a number of studies call the relationship between neighborhood poverty and access to social capital into question, and in so doing problematize the notion that the black poor lack access to contacts that can facilitate job finding. For instance, Melvin Oliver (1988) investigated the network structure and composition of residents in three economically distinct black communities in Los Angeles: Watts (poor), Crenshaw-Baldwin Hills (working class), and Carson (solidly middle). Examining associational, emotional, and material support, he

---

[2] Conducted in 1986 and 1987, this survey employed a multistage stratified probability sample design to study different aspects of family, household, education, employment, and welfare status of black, white, and Latino families living in Chicago's poverty census tracts. The UPFLS is primarily a sample of young parents aged 18–44. Of the 2,490 respondents, all nonblack respondents are parents; the bulk of black respondents are parents as well, but they are also the only racial group represented among nonparents.

found that Watts's residents, the poorest of the three, had no fewer relations than either Crenshaw-Baldwin Hills or Carson residents, and their relations were no more dense. Furthermore, although Watts' social relations were less spatially distributed, fully one-half of their social relations lived in other neighborhoods in Los Angeles or outside of the city. Hurlbert, Beggs, and Haines (1998) used multiple name generators that identified strong ties, regular associates, *and* weak ties, producing a maximum of 15 non-redundant ties for each respondent. They found that residents of the core were no *less* likely to have contact with black middle-class areas than were residents of the outer ring and the middle-class neighborhood. Finally, employing the Urban Poverty and Family Life Survey (UPFLS), Sosin (1991) found that neighborhood poverty concentration had no effect on the number of labor market contacts among the black urban poor. Thus, contrary to expectations consistent with the social isolation thesis, these studies suggest that the networks of the urban poor are larger, more diverse and wide ranging, and much less detached from the mainstream than conventional wisdom indicates and they provide evidence that weakens the link between neighborhood poverty and social isolation.

Why the divergence? It is my contention that deviations from typical name generators may have yielded different accounts of the urban poor's levels of social isolation and its relationship to neighborhood poverty status. Specifically, in most studies of social capital, urban poverty, and joblessness, social support name generators are employed, soliciting information about individuals to whom respondents feel closest or with whom they discuss important matters. Limited to discussing no more than three to five close ties, respondents are then queried about their ties' sociodemographic characteristics. For example, the UPFLS respondents were asked to name up to three friends who were not kin or current partners, up to six people they relied on for everyday favors, and up to six people they could turn to in major crises. Only in reference to friends, however, did researchers gather data on employment, welfare status, and educational attainment.[3] Similarly, the Multi-City Study of Urban Inequality (MCSUI) asked respondents to list no more than three people with whom they spoke about matters important to them. Afterward, investigators gathered information about alters' sex, race and ethnicity, relationship to respondent, employment status, welfare receipt, and educational attainment, from which compositional measures could also be calculated.

Although extensively used, the name generator methodology has major shortcomings. According to Lin (2001*b*), name generator techniques have been critiqued for being content-bound, biased toward the reporting of strong ties, specific to individuals and not the positions in social structure, and generally restrictive—they allow respondents to report access to no more than three to five contacts, regardless of the volume, breadth, or depth of their networks of relations (Lin 2001*b*). First, by employing name generators, researchers tend to

---

[3] This is unfortunate since those providing support during a crisis situation likely have higher social structural standing in terms of employment and education than the respondent or those relied upon for daily support.

elicit information about respondents' closest ties. Among the black urban poor, as with others, the people with whom they discuss important matters are likely to be very similar to themselves, sociostructurally. Thus, if they reside in high-poverty neighborhoods, are unemployed, and support their families on public assistance, there is a high likelihood that their closest associates—those with whom they speak about important matters—are similarly located sociostructurally. These closest ties do not define the extent of the respondent's access to the mainstream, however. Indeed, one might argue that as we move away from the poor's core network of relations, they become more "mainstream." This is what Katherine Newman (1999) finds in her study of Harlem's working poor. Newman writes,

Harlem's working poor travel in two kinds of social circles. The first is a network of like-situated friends working in the same kinds of jobs that Burger Barn workers already possess. The second involves a set of acquaintances and relatives who have or once had better jobs, sometimes significantly better, and who often live outside of the ghetto in suburbs, or working-class enclaves that are largely composed of minorities.   Newman 1999: 161

Thus, by employing name generators, researchers decrease the likelihood that the black urban poor, especially those from high-poverty neighborhoods, would report access to "mainstream" ties.

Second, because name generators identify access to individuals and not positions located within social structure, it is more consistent with a theoretical framework that focuses on individual-level attributes than a framework that provides a decidedly structural perspective on inequality. In other words, if what urban poverty researchers want to know is the extent to which the black urban poor are socially isolated from mainstream contacts, particularly those relations with strong labor market attachments, then a technique that elicits information about individuals as opposed to the positions they hold in social structure is an inefficient way of determining the extent and nature of access to the mainstream. Thus, in the urban poverty context where social isolation is operationalized as having a lack of regular contact and sustained interaction with individuals having strong attachments to the labor market, these constraints inherent to the name generator likely have the effect of overestimating social isolation and exaggerating differences between residents of low- and high-poverty neighborhoods.

The position generator overcomes many of these major shortcomings. Because respondents are asked who among their relatives, friends, and acquaintances hold positions in a sample of occupations, the bias toward strong ties is avoided. Also, because respondents are asked specifically about their access to particular positions in the social structure, we can directly (or indirectly) assess the extent and nature of their access to relations that matter to urban poverty researchers—relations with strong attachments to the labor market. In this chapter, I employ the position generator to better capture the black poor's access to social capital relevant for job finding as well as to determine the extent to which neighborhood poverty has the costs associated with it that much of the research claims.

8.2. A QUESTION OF MOBILIZATION?

In addition to access, the efficacy of job referral networks is contingent on the willingness of the various parties involved to take part in such an exchange. Thus far, the urban poverty literature takes willingness for granted, but it should not. Despite research of the 1970s describing strong obligations of exchange within poor black communities (Ladner 1972; Stack 1974; Aschenbrenner 1975), recent inquiries find that African-Americans' social support networks often lag behind that of other racial and ethnic groups in terms of expressive aid such as advice giving, and instrumental aid such as money lending/giving (Morgan 1982; Hofferth 1984; Eggebeen and Hogan 1990; Parish, Hao, and Hogan 1991; Eggebeen 1992; Green, Hammer, and Tigges 2000). For instance, examining intergenerational support between parents and their adult children, Eggebeen and Hogan (1990) found that African-Americans were consistently less likely than both Mexican-Americans and whites to receive money, advice, assistance, and childcare from parents, less likely to give advice and assistance to parents, and less likely to be highly involved in giving and receiving generally. Given the possibility of multiple interpretations, however, these findings are only suggestive of deteriorating obligations of exchange within poor, black communities.

Less suggestive are findings emerging from research examining the racial differences in job search strategies. In many ways, blacks do not differ dramatically from whites in job search methods used, source of their current or last job, or characteristics of their job contacts (Holzer 1987; Falcon 1995; Green, Tigges, and Diaz 1999; Smith 2000). However, blacks diverge from whites and Latinos in at least one important respect. Research examining racial differences in job search strategies finds that the job contacts of whites and Latinos are far more likely than those of blacks to use proactive matching methods. Green, Tigges, and Diaz (1999) compared the methods of assistance employed by job contacts, identifying three major categories. Job contacts could assist by informing the job seeker about the vacancy, by talking to the employer on the job seeker's behalf, or by hiring the job seeker. They found that roughly 61 percent of blacks reported that their contact told them about the position, the least proactive of informal job-matching methods, whereas only 44 and 41 percent of whites' and Latinos' contacts, respectively, did the same. A significantly higher percentage of whites reported having been hired by their contacts (18% vs. 8%), and a significantly higher percentage of Latinos reported that their contacts talked to the employer on their behalf (37% vs. 25%). Using the same data-set, I find that, net of important controls, the significance of these relationships persists in multivariate analysis (Smith 2002).

Especially in low-wage labor markets where employers rely heavily on job referral networks for recruitment *and* screening, these distinctions are very important. Job seekers with contacts willing to aid by hiring, speaking directly to the employer, or acting as a reference are at a considerable advantage over those without such contacts. Proactive contacts provide employers with information about job seekers at the very least, verifying their reliability and capacity to work well with others. Without brokers to vouch for their reliability, job seekers are less competitive against those whose contacts are willing or able to extend themselves. In this regard, lacking proactivity, job contacts may be no more useful than direct application and walk-in strategies of job search. Indeed, in a study of informal search methods among black and white youth, Holzer (1987) found that roughly one-fifth of the racial difference in the probability of gaining employment could be explained by differences in receiving offers after having searched through friends and relatives. When black youths searched through friends and relatives, they were less likely to be offered employment than were whites. While employers, practicing statistical discrimination, would much prefer to hire the referrals of other racial and ethnic groups (Neckerman and Kirschenman 1991; Waldinger 1997; Newman 1999), it may also be the case that the generally less proactive strategies employed by blacks' job contacts may disadvantage them further.

Qualitative research suggests why this may be the case (Newman 1999; Jackson 2001; Smith 2005). In *No Shame in My Game*, Katherine Newman (1999) notes that among the low-wage workers she studied, personal contacts were vital to the job-matching process, but assistance was not always forthcoming. Fearing that their referrals would prove unreliable and would compromise their reputations with employers, a few of her subjects denied help to their job-seeking relations. Access, therefore, did not guarantee mobilization because those in possession of job information and influence largely distrusted their job-seeking relations.

My work has confirmed this (Smith 2005). I found that potential job contacts overwhelmingly approached job-finding assistance with great skepticism and distrust. Over 80 percent of respondents in my sample expressed a generalized distrust toward job seekers in their networks, proclaiming them too unmotivated to accept assistance, too needy, and/or too irresponsible on the job, thereby jeopardizing the contacts' own reputations in the eyes of employers and negatively affecting their already tenuous labor market prospects. Consequently, they were generally reluctant to provide the type of assistance that best facilitates job acquisition in low-wage labor markets where employers rely heavily on informal referrals for recruitment and screening. When social capital activation did occur, even within the context of pervasive distrust and perceived untrustworthiness, it was contingent on neighborhood poverty and the strength of the relationship between job contacts and job seekers. However, decisions regarding the extent and nature of assistance were most profoundly affected by the interaction between job contacts' own reputations and job seekers' reputations. Overwhelmingly, job contacts were concerned about their job-seeking relations' prior behaviors and actions in the workplace and at home, as these indicated how job seekers might behave once hired. Job seekers whose reputations indicated unreliability and those whose behaviors were characterized as "ghetto" were given little consideration. Both were deemed to be too high a risk to take. Job contacts' decisions to assist also depended a great deal on their own reputations with employers, however. Those held in high regard by employers were generally willing to assist even job seekers of ill-repute, but as their standing with employers declined, contacts' willingness to assist did as well. Thus, findings from this study indicate that inefficacious job referral networks may have less to do with issues of access to mainstream ties than with the disinclination of job contacts to assist when given the opportunity to do so.

8.3. THEORIZING THE RELATIONSHIP BETWEEN ACCESS
AND MOBILIZATION

Because these two approaches are not necessarily contradictory but may be better understood as complementary explanations of the black poor's relatively ineffica-cious job referral network, the question is, what is the relationship between access to social capital and the ability to mobilize that social capital? It could be the case that trust and an open orientation to providing job-finding assistance are more likely to occur within the context of greater access to social capital. One might theorize that as access to social capital increases, one's orientation toward pro-viding assistance would increase as well in ways that implicate trust, an essential mediating factor between access and mobilization (Coleman 1988, 1990; Portes and Sensenbrenner 1993; Paxton 1999; Putnam 2000; Smith 2005). With greater access to social capital, job contacts may perceive less risk to their own reputations or well-being associated with assistance, as their embeddedness may shield them from some of the potentially negative consequences of providing assistance. With less access to social capital, job contacts may perceive greater risk because the resources embedded in their network of relations are less able to buffer them from the potential loss of status or reputation that comes with making a bad match. It may also be the case that greater connection to individuals occupying positions of lower wages, status, and opportunities is indicative of greater connection to individuals struggling to overcome multiple barriers to employment, barriers that make it difficult to find and keep work and that make such job seekers appear untrustworthy.

Thus, in an effort to better understand the relationship between social capital and joblessness among the black poor, I seek to do the following in this chapter. First, using the position generator, I examine the black poor's access to social capital by neighborhood poverty status. Second, because receipt of job-finding assistance is contingent not only on access but also on the willingness of those in possession of job information and influence to assist, I also examine job contact's general orientation toward providing job-finding assistance. I then examine the relationship between access and orientation.

8.4. DATA AND FINDINGS

Between 1999 and 2002, along with a small team of investigators, I gathered data using surveys and in-depth interviews of 105 low-income African-Americans.[4] The primary site for recruitment was one state social service agency ("the Center") located in a "Southeast County," Michigan, which offered a variety of pro-grams designed to aid the transition from unemployment, public assistance, or a

---

[4] Although 105 in-depth interviews were completed, time constraints prohibited two respondents from completing the survey as well. Thus, completed surveys total 103.

current dissatisfying job to labor force participation.[5] These included education, training, and employment programs, including General Educational Development (GED) diploma classes for high school dropouts, childcare referral services, and transportation services. Although the Center claimed to cater to any of the county's residents, the majority of clients were black and low income.

With the assistance of Center staff, we recruited subjects who fit the study criteria—black men and women between the ages of 20 and 40 who resided in Southeast County and who had no more than a high school diploma (or GED).[6] Respondents were surveyed about their family background, networks, employment history, and job-finding methods. They were also questioned in-depth about their childhood (including childhood impressions of work); marriage, relationships, and children; employment history, experiences, and impressions of work; job-referral networks; philosophy of employment; and attitudes and opinions about the extent and nature of job opportunities for low-skilled workers like themselves. Interviews averaged 2 hr.[7]

Displayed in Table 8.1 are mean sample characteristics. At roughly 28 years of age, 78 percent of the sample had never married, and 75 percent had children—2.5 on average. Eighty-four percent were high school graduates (or had gotten a GED), and just over half were employed. On their current or most recent job, respondents' mean wages were $9.30 per hour (median ≈ $8.50). Furthermore, because median tenure was only 11 months—nearly a third had not worked longer than 6 months—most families survived on poverty-level earnings. Indeed, roughly one-third of respondents were receiving public assistance at the time of the interview (14% of men and 47% of women). Nearly half reported having ever received assistance (31% of men and 68% of women). Finally, respondents' addresses were matched with corresponding census tracts to determine the family-level poverty status of their neighborhoods. Employing a variation of the categories of neighborhood poverty concentration typically used in urban poverty studies, I found that 69 percent of respondents lived in census tracts in which rates of family poverty were low to moderate (0–29.9%) and 31 percent resided in neighborhoods characterized by much of the urban underclass literature, with rates of family poverty high to extreme (30+%).[8]

---

[5] Two-thirds of the sample was recruited at the Center. See Appendix for details about all of the recruitment methods employed to complete data collection and the potential impact on results.

[6] Although a few participants did not match one or more of the screening criteria, every respondent can be categorized as economically marginal. Three respondents were below 20 years old; two were over 4 years old. Because the Center served the entire county, the poor from other cities and townships in the immediate area also used the Center. Eighteen respondents reported residences outside the community. Among high school graduates, 54% reported taking one or more courses at the local community college. Two college-educated respondents are also in the sample. However, their inclusion in analyses does not alter results.

[7] All interviewers were African-American.

[8] Not surprisingly, in terms of social and demographic indicators, low-to-moderate-poverty neighborhoods in which respondents resided differed substantially from the neighborhoods in which poverty rates were high to extreme. In the low-to-moderate-poverty neighborhoods in which two-thirds of respondents lived, 31% of residents were black compared with 78% of the residents in

Table 8.1. Summary of sample characteristics ($N = 103$)

	Mean	Range
Age	28.4 (5.9)	17–43
Female	.52	0–1
Never married	.78	0–1
Have children	.75	0–1
Number of children (if parents)	2.5 (1.4)	1–7
High school graduate/GED	.84	0–1
Employed	.52	0–1
Hourly wages ($)	9.30 (3.5)	2.5–23.0
Public assistance		0–1
Currently receiving	.31	—
Women	.47	—
Men	.17	—
Ever received	.46	—
Women	.68	—
Men	.31	—
Neighborhood poverty rate		0–1
Low–moderate	.69	—
High–extreme	.31	—

8.4.1. Access

To determine access to social capital, I employed a position generator to elicit information about respondents' direct connections to labor market contacts. I used a sample of 15 occupations, or structural positions, and asked respondents, "Among your relatives, friends, or acquaintances, are there people who have the following jobs?" The list of positions included, in order of prestige score, physician (86), lawyer (74), registered nurse (66), high school teacher (66), accountant (65), computer programmer (61), police officer (60), social worker (52), electrician (51), secretary (46), nursing aide (41), machine operator (33), cashier (29), child-care worker (29), and taxicab driver/chauffeur (28). Those who reported having a direct tie occupying any one of the 15 listed positions were then queried about the following: whether the association was professional, personal, or both; if the relationship was personal, the nature of the relationship; whether the tie had been mentioned previously as a household member, sibling, or discussion partner (to gauge whether respondents were reporting connection to those already discussed); and frequency of contact. By asking respondents about the extent and nature of their relations to ties within the labor market context, I was able to directly assess

respondents' high-to-extreme poverty neighborhoods, 11% of the former had not completed high school compared with 26% of the latter, 30% were not in the labor force relative to 43% of residents in respondents' high-to-extreme poverty neighborhoods, 13% of individual residents from the former lived in poverty compared with 43% of individuals from the latter, and while just 5% of residents in respondents' low-to-moderate-poverty neighborhoods received public assistance, 23% of residents from respondents' high-to-extreme poverty neighborhoods received assistance.

the black urban poor's connection to mainstream contacts. This would seem to be a more accurate representation of their available job referral networks than previous research has indicated.

With these data, I constructed several position generator measures. These include *extensity*, or the number of positions to which respondents report access; *prestige*, or the average prestige score of the positions to which respondents report access; *upper reachability*, the highest prestige score to which respondents report access; *range of prestige*, measured as the difference between highest and lowest prestige scores; and *accessed positions*, or the percentage of respondents having access to each of the positions listed.

Table 8.2 reports a summary of position generator variables in total and by neighborhood poverty status. Generally speaking, respondents reported access to roughly 8 out of 15 positions. Prestige scores of the 15 occupations ranged from 28 to 86, but the mean prestige score for respondents in this sample was 50, with an upper reachability score of 75.5 and a prestige range of 45.7. The percentage of respondents with access to each of these positions ranged from 34 percent (taxicab driver) to 72 percent (machine operator). Not surprisingly, a greater percentage of respondents reported access to lesser-skilled positions such as machine operators (72%), cashiers (71%), nursing aides (69%), and childcare workers (65%). Also not surprisingly, relatively few respondents reported access to professional positions such as computer programmers (38%), accountants (36%),

Table 8.2. Position generator variables by neighborhood poverty status

	Total	Low-poverty neighborhoods	High-poverty neighborhoods	Significance level
Extensity	8.3	8.2	8.4	.829
Mean prestige	50.2	50.3	50.0	.791
Upper reachability	75.5	75.6	75.3	.905
Range of prestige	45.7	45.7	45.8	.989
Accessed positions				
Physician (86)	.50	.49	.52	.829
Lawyer (74)	.45	.48	.41	.523
Registered nurse (66)	.60	.56	.68	.262
High school teacher (66)	.62	.59	.69	.347
Accountant (65)	.36	.35	.38	.807
Computer programmer (61)	.38	.35	.44	.440
Police officer (60)	.53	.57	.45	.279
Social worker (52)	.67	.66	.68	.878
Electrician (51)	.49	.48	.50	.884
Secretary (46)	.63	**.68**	**.52**	**.119**
Nurse's aide (41)	.69	.68	.71	.792
Machine operator (33)	.72	.68	.81	.211
Cashier (29)	.71	.71	.72	.928
Childcare worker (29)	.65	.62	.72	.340
Taxicab/chauffeur driver (28)	.34	.34	.32	.837

Significant differences, which are differences with a significance level of .15 or below, are highlighted in bold.

and lawyers (45%). In the middle range of access were skilled and professional positions such as physicians (50%), registered nurses (60%), high school teachers (62%), and social workers (67%), to which respondents presumably had access for professional and personal reasons, although the nature of respondents' relations with individuals occupying these positions will be discussed in greater detail later.

Based on the social isolation thesis, we would expect here that residents of low-poverty neighborhoods would report greater access to social capital than would residents of neighborhoods characterized by concentrated disadvantage (Wilson 1987; Wacquant and Wilson 1989; Fernandez and Harris 1991; Rankin and Quane 2000). By employing previous measures of social capital access, which relied on name generators to determine the extent and nature of individuals' access, these expectations have largely been realized. Using the position generator, however, this finding is not borne out by these data. Instead, as compared in columns 2 and 3 in Table 8.2, differences in access between residents of low- and high-poverty neighborhoods largely appear insignificant. Only with reference to one occupation do significant differences emerge.[9] Given prior research, how can this be? Is neighborhood poverty status unrelated to social capital access?

Further analysis reveals that neighborhood poverty status does matter, but only for a subset of residents. As shown in Table 8.3, access to social capital is limited only among *unemployed* residents of neighborhoods characterized by concentrated disadvantage, but it is not so for those who have jobs. Specifically, if we compare employed residents of low- and high-poverty neighborhoods, we find little of significance. Both have access to roughly the same number of positions (8.2 vs. 8.6). Differences in mean prestige (49.4 vs. 51.5), upper reachability (74.4 vs. 76.7), and range of prestige (44.5 vs. 47.0) are also negligible. In some cases, as with access to registered nurses (77% vs. 52%) and high school teachers (78% vs. 56%), employed residents of high-poverty neighborhoods appear to have slightly greater access than their counterparts in low-poverty neighborhoods. To the extent that this is the case, these employed residents probably require greater access to sustain themselves in communities of concentrated disadvantage.

Among the unemployed, however, neighborhood poverty status does appear to matter. Unemployed residents of high-poverty neighborhoods appear disadvantaged from unemployed residents of low-poverty neighborhoods (and the employed generally) in terms of extensity, upper reachability, range, and prestige, although only significantly so with regard to prestige. Whereas unemployed residents of high-poverty neighborhoods have a mean prestige score of 46, those of low-poverty neighborhoods have a significantly higher mean prestige score of 51. Compared to their counterparts in low-poverty neighborhoods, unemployed residents of high-poverty neighborhoods have lower extensity (7.8 vs. 8.4), lower upper reachability scores (72 vs. 77), and access to positions with a narrower range

---

[9] Significant differences, which are differences with a significance level of .15 or below, are highlighted in bold.

Table 8.3. Position generator variables by employment and neighborhood poverty status

	Employed			Unemployed		
	Low poverty	High poverty	Significance	Low poverty	High poverty	Significance
Extensity	8.2	8.6	.685	8.4	7.8	.662
Mean prestige	49.4	51.5	.176	51.0	46.1	**.028**
Upper reachability	74.4	76.7	.487	77.1	71.6	.284
Range of prestige	44.5	47.0	.510	47.5	42.6	.346
Accessed positions						
Physician (86)	.44	.50	.689	.54	.56	.937
Lawyer (74)	.44	.43	.972	.51	.33	.343
Registered nurse (66)	.52	.77	**.075**	.59	.44	.426
High school teacher (66)	**.56**	**.78**	**.106**	.62	.44	.344
Accountant (65)	.20	.35	.259	.46	.44	.937
Computer programmer (61)	.40	.43	.812	.33	.44	.544
Police officer (60)	.64	.59	.737	**.54**	**.11**	**.020**
Social worker (52)	.80	.73	.567	.56	.56	1.0
Electrician (51)	.44	.52	.581	.53	.44	.663
Secretary (46)	.64	.59	.737	**.73**	**.33**	**.025**
Nurse's aide (41)	.56	.64	.604	.76	.89	.400
Machine operator (33)	.72	.73	.957	**.68**	**1.0**	**.048**
Cashier (29)	.68	.74	.661	.51	.67	.623
Childcare worker (29)	.80	.74	.625	.51	.67	.419
Taxicab/chauffeur driver (28)	.36	.27	.532	.34	.44	.582

Significant differences, which are differences with a significance level of .15 or below, are highlighted in bold.

of prestige (43 vs. 48), although these differences are not statistically significant. These are all indicated as well by the significantly greater access that unemployed residents of low-poverty neighborhoods have to lawyers and secretaries, for instance, compared with the greater access that unemployed residents of high-poverty neighborhoods have to machine operators. What these findings indicate is that social isolation is not inherent to residence in high-poverty neighborhoods. Instead, within the context of concentrated disadvantage, access to social capital is strongly associated with employment status, which likely both shapes and is shaped by one's social capital endowment. Furthermore, outside the context of employment, residence in neighborhoods of concentrated disadvantage probably provide fewer opportunities to come into regular and sustained contact with others because of high rates of crime (Anderson 1990, 1999), poorer access to public goods, including grocery stores and other retail establishments, and fewer activities that bring community members together.

It may also be less the case that residents of high-poverty neighborhoods lack access to specific types of positions that might better facilitate job acquisition. For instance, although residents of high-poverty neighborhoods do not have fewer connections generally speaking, they may have fewer connections to the types of positions for which they would be qualified. To determine whether this was the case, I grouped positions into three categories based on skill level. The first category consisted of lesser-skilled workers and included cashiers, childcare workers, nursing aides, machine operators, and taxicab drivers/chauffeurs. The second category consisted of skilled and semiprofessional workers and included electricians, high school teachers, police officers, secretaries, and social workers. The third category consisted of professional workers and included accountants, computer programmers, lawyers, physicians, and registered nurses. I then examined mean differences in extensity by neighborhood poverty status and then again by employment and neighborhood poverty status. However, these analyses revealed no statistically significant differences in access to sets of positions in different skill levels.[10]

8.4.2. Mobilization

As with everyone, the black poor's ability to obtain jobs through personal contacts is not just a function of their access to contacts in possession of job information and influence. It is also contingent on their ability to mobilize these social resources for job-finding assistance. The latter requires that the black poor be embedded in job referral networks that are positively oriented toward providing such assistance. To determine job contacts' general orientation toward job-finding assistance—whether and to what extent they are generally willing to assist—I examine responses to the following set of questions: First, when you hear about job openings at your workplace or elsewhere, what do you do? In other words, do you tell the people you know about them? Second, has anyone ever come to you for help in finding or getting a job? Who has come to you for help and why? What types of jobs did they ask about? How did you help, if at all? Would you help again? Did this/these job seeker(s) get the job(s)? Third, what do you think are the positive aspects of helping others to find work? The negative?

Those who reported that they usually choose not to assist or who limited their assistance were deemed *reluctant contacts*. Comments indicative of reluctance included "I kind of even limit my helping people out to where it won't affect me," or "First of all, I don't know a lot of people that have really looked for employment, and I question the people that I do know. I don't think they would take it as serious, and I don't want to put my name on it." *Open contacts* were those who were willing to help almost anyone who asked. Comments suggestive of openness included "I never turn nobody down" or "If they come to me, of course I will tell them." Based on this coding scheme, 60 percent of respondents were categorized as reluctant, 40 percent as open.

Orientation toward providing job-finding assistance was highly contingent on perceived general trustworthiness of job seekers. Those with job information and influence who generally perceived job seekers as untrustworthy and thus were reluctant to provide the type of job-finding assistance that best facilitates employment gave three reasons for their actions. First, a substantial minority had

---

[10] These findings will be made available upon request.

come to believe that job seekers too often lacked the motivation and determination to follow through on offers of assistance, wasting contacts' time and frustrating them (trustworthiness and the unmotivated job seeker). One-fifth of respondents described situations in which job-seeking relatives, friends, and associates complained about their labor market detachment and would ask for help finding work (see Table 8.4). However, once offered assistance, job seekers would not follow through. Instead, they would either fail to call the contact person or neglect to complete the application. A few days later, the cycle of complaining and requests for assistance would continue. Many, like Leah Arnold, found this cycle of requests and inaction vexing. At the time of the interview, Leah was 25 years old and working full time providing client assistance in a disabled care facility. When asked about the negative aspects of trying to help others to find work, she explained,

It's their enthusiasm. The negative aspects is, you tell them about it, they sound like "Oh, for real!" like that, and then the next thing you know, two weeks later you done told them about five jobs. Two weeks later, "Girl, I still need a job." You're like, okay. Girl, you better look. You better go look cause I done told you, and after so many times, hey. So that's the negative aspect is when they don't have the motivation or the enthusiasm to go out there and get it even after its right there.

However, Leah was not alone. As shown in Table 8.4, while 78 percent of respondents with this concern indicated that they generally limit the extent to which they provide assistance, only 56 percent of respondents without this concern were as reluctant. Although the latter is still a high figure, it is significantly less than the former. In short, the likelihood of engaging in obligations of exchange around job information and influence is reduced because those who have the resources to help have little trust that job seekers are motivated enough to use them.

Second, one-tenth of respondents were concerned that job seekers required too much assistance, expecting contacts to expend too much time and energy finding and helping them to keep their jobs. Some respondents, like Steve Jackson, regarded such responsibility as a source of unwanted stress. Downwardly mobile at 21, Steve earned $7.50 per hour working full time as a delivery truck driver. Both of his parents had earned advanced degrees, and they raised their two children

Table 8.4. Motivation for distrust by reluctance to assist

		Reluctant to assist		
	Respondents reporting (%)	Significance	Expressed distrust (%)	Did not express distrust (%)
Expressed distrust about job seekers	81	**.000**	71	17
Job seekers who are too unmotivated	20	.112	78	56
Job seekers who are too needy	10	.305	80	58
Job seekers who are delinquency-prone	70	**.001**	73	35

Significant differences, which are differences with a significance level of .15 or below, are highlighted in bold.

in middle-class, racially mixed neighborhoods. Although Steve had been working toward a college degree at a major state university, he returned home when he learned that he had impregnated his girlfriend. His plan to work full time to support his child while taking classes at another local university fell through as he became increasingly overwhelmed by his multiple responsibilities and his grades suffered, causing him to drop out. After leaving school, he worked as a sales representative with a telecommunications company, earning $15 per hour. In his next two positions he earned $12 per hour selling cellular phones. Because of conflicts with management, however, he quit. With a downturn in the economy, there were few jobs at his preferred wage rate, and pressed to pay off $2,500 in rising child support arrears, he settled for $7.50 per hour driving a delivery truck.

Given the major stresses in his own life, Steve found the task of helping others emotionally daunting, particularly when close friends were involved. He explained,

It could be a lot of stress, and if you take it seriously to the point where you're really trying to get this person some help, it could be stressful for you. You might meet with them and give them some ideas and that could be extra things to do, and you know, you got your own problems without dealing with someone else's job problems.

This was especially true because the majority of job seekers who had approached Steve had few marketable skills. He now refuses to assist unless job seekers have a resume in hand. To Steve, the resume signals that they will not require more time and emotional energy than he can afford. As shown in Table 8.4, absent trust that job seekers would not overburden them, 80 percent either limited their assistance altogether or extended aid to only those job seekers who demonstrated a willingness to take responsibility for themselves. Only 58 percent of those without this distrust were so reluctant.

Third, many feared that, once hired, those assisted would act inappropriately, compromising their own personal reputation and labor market stability (trust-worthiness and the delinquent job seeker). As shown in Table 8.4, 70 percent of respondents expressed distrust regarding job seekers' use of their names, and thus their reputations, to gain employment at their place of work. They feared that if they personally vouched for referrals, there was no way to ensure that their referrals would show up to work, work beyond the first paycheck, be prompt and regular, be productive on the job, and/or not steal, curse, fight, or disrespect authority. At the very least, contacts experienced embarrassment for having provided a disreputable referral; at most, they lost their jobs as well as future employment opportunities.

Jackie York, a 27-year-old single mother of five children and resident of an extreme-poverty neighborhood, is one such example. Previously, Jackie had a year-long part-time position making $10 per hour supervising a cleaning crew. As supervisor, she could influence hiring, and she described how she helped three friends get jobs. Unfortunately, none worked out. She first assisted her eldest son's granduncle. Although she suspected he had a drug habit, she believed that employment would get him on the track to recovery. At the very least, she reasoned, it would do no harm, as there was nothing on the jobsite that he could steal. Hired on a Tuesday, the uncle worked Wednesday and Thursday, but he did not arrive to work on Friday, nor did he call. Because he had worked so well his first two days, helping the crew to complete their tasks one hour earlier than the norm, Jackie gave him the benefit of the doubt and decided to guarantee his presence by picking him up before work. On Monday and Tuesday, this approach worked; by Wednesday, however, it did not. Within one week of his hire, the uncle was let go and Jackie described herself as "looking a little foolish." In trying to assist the uncle in getting to work on time, she had arrived to work late as well. In the process, she began to lose her employer's trust. She explained, "She's looking at me like you ain't picking up your pieces too well."

Her employer's perception only worsened with Jackie's next two referrals. She then aided the girlfriend of her eldest son's father, reasoning that because their sons were half brothers, the extended family would benefit. However, her ex's girlfriend was also unreliable. She worked the first day, arrived out of uniform the second day (which meant that she could not work), and did not show at all the third day or thereafter. Although Jackie believed her third referral, an ex-boyfriend, was a good worker, her employer found him too slow and fired him without her knowledge, confirming that her employer had lost trust in her.

To get job seekers to acknowledge these consequences, she reminded them of her own poor socioeconomic status and pleaded with them to behave appropriately so as not to harm her reputation. Perceiving this approach as ineffective, however, she changed tactics. "I did get smart. I did get a little bit smart. I said, 'Look, don't tell them you know me. Just go on in there and get the job.' " However, Jackie now declines to partake in obligations of exchange around job finding at all. When asked about the positive aspects of helping others to find work, she explained,

I'm not the right one to ask that question. I would just have to say that that's something you got to do on your own. I don't see anything positive right now. I can't be objective anymore. "No, I ain't heard nothing about no job." You know, I have to say that because if I say, "Well I do know some . . ." "Oh, for real, girl!" "I ain't heard nothing, you know, about your situation."

Self-preservation now dictates that she remove herself from the process.

As shown in Table 8.4, while 73 percent of respondents who distrusted how others would perform in the job took a reluctant approach to providing assistance, just 35 percent of those without this concern were as reluctant. Furthermore, respondents who raised this concern were much more likely to have been burned in the past or to mention others for whom this was a concern. While just 10 percent of respondents without this concern reported having been burned by previous referrals, 33 percent of respondents who expressed concern about how job seekers would behave told stories of prior assists that ended badly. Another 9 percent described the negative experiences of those they knew to explain their distrust. Thus, with little confidence that job seekers would work out, contacts either avoided obligations altogether or provided assistance that did not link them to the applicant in the mind of the employer. For instance, while they may have passed along information about job openings, they often provided the caveat "but don't put my name on it" so that job seekers were clear that they could not use their relationship to vouch for their credibility on the job.

Furthermore, neighborhood poverty status was related to orientation to and concerns about providing job-finding assistance (see Table 8.5). While 53 percent of contacts from low-poverty neighborhoods expressed reluctance to providing job-finding assistance, just 77 percent of contacts from high-poverty neighborhoods did.

What explains this difference in orientation? Compared with those living in low-poverty neighborhoods, a higher percentage of residents of high-poverty neighborhoods had been burned by prior referrals. Indeed, although roughly one-quarter of residents of low-poverty neighborhoods had been negatively affected by providing assistance, almost half of residents from high-poverty neighborhoods had. This is noteworthy because whereas residents of neighborhoods characterized by concentrated disadvantage represented less than one-third of the sample, they comprised almost 43 percent of those who had been burned by prior referrals.

Consistent with concerns of being burned, when asked how they determined whether to assist their job-seeking relations, a higher percentage of contacts from high-poverty neighborhoods made determinations based on job seekers' personal reputation—specifically, whether job seekers were deemed to be "ghetto." Fifty-four percent of those from high-poverty neighborhoods assessed whether they would assist using this criterion, just 36 percent of those from low-poverty neighborhoods did. However, they were no more concerned than were residents of low-poverty neighborhoods about their job-seeking relations' work reputations. Thirty-eight percent of the latter used this criterion to judge their job-seeking relations, whereas 42 percent of the former did.

That residents of neighborhoods of concentrated poverty were far more concerned about "ghetto" behavior is likely attributable less to any inherent differences in how people assess trustworthiness than it is a function of the types of issues that arise for contacts whose sociostructural positions differ. In neighborhoods in which rates of poverty are high to extreme, and in which a significant

Table 8.5. Orientation to providing job-finding assistance, reputational concerns, and history of being burned by neighborhood poverty status

	Total	Low poverty	High poverty	Significance
Reluctant to provide[ing] assistance	61%	53%	77%	.055
Burned by previous referral	33	28	45	.151
Concerned with job seekers' reputations	71	66	83	.135
Concerned with work reputation	40	38	42	.806
Concerned with ghetto reputation	42	36	54	.150

Significant differences, which are differences with a significance level of .15 or below, are highlighted in bold.

minority of residents are unemployed or out of the labor market altogether, ghetto behavior is more prevalent and perceived to be so. And while the majority of residents in such neighborhoods do not act ghetto, residents undoubtedly employ this distinction to ferret out, in various contexts, those who can and cannot be trusted. Indeed, this is what Elijah Anderson's work (Anderson 1990, 1999) shows. Thus, residents of neighborhoods in which rates of poverty were high likely encountered these behaviors to a greater extent, and thus were more likely to employ this criterion to assess whether they would assist. In other words, because they reside in riskier social environments, they were more likely to perceive job-finding assistance as a risky endeavor.

8.4.3. Relating Access and Mobilization

Thus far I have presented evidence that implicates limited access and deficiencies in mobilization capabilities among the black poor. The question is, to what extent are these two related, and how might the relationship be explained? Can mobilization be better understood by taking into consideration its relationship to embeddedness, as measured using position generator variables? To address these questions, I examine the relationship between extensity, prestige, upper reachability, and range, on the one hand, and expressions of (dis)trust and orientation to providing job-finding assistance, on the other. It may be the case that generalized trust and an open orientation to providing job-finding assistance are more likely to take place within the context of greater access to social capital.

Given the literature that sees trust as a form of social capital (Coleman 1988; Portes and Sensenbrenner 1993; Paxton 2000), it is not surprising to find that trust is related to social capital access. In Table 8.6, I display the results from analysis that examines means of position generator variables by trust of job contacts—trusting job contacts were those who did not share concerns about job seekers' lack of motivation, neediness, or delinquency; distrusting contacts mentioned one or more. As shown, trusting job contacts reported significantly greater access to positions than did their distrusting counterparts. Trusting contacts reported connection to 9.3 positions, whereas distrusting contacts reported connection to just 7.7. This is in part because a higher percentage of trusting job contacts reported access to physicians (67% vs. 43%), accountants (56% vs. 27%), police officers (67% vs. 46%), and electricians (71% vs. 43%). Trusting contacts also reported access to positions with higher mean prestige, higher upper reachability, and greater range, but these results were not statistically significant.

The extent and nature of connection to various positions also differed substantially by job contacts' trust. These figures are displayed in Table 8.7. Again, trusting job contacts reported greater access to positions than did distrusting job contacts (9.3 vs. 7.7), but this greater access also extended to personal (8.4 vs. 6.0) and frequent (6.3 vs. 4.7) contact with individuals occupying these positions. That trusting job contacts have greater access overall is in good part due to the

Table 8.6. Position generator variables by (dis)trusting job contacts

	Trusting	Distrusting	Significance
Extensity	**9.3**	**7.7**	**.102**
Mean prestige	50.7	49.7	.501
Upper reachability	77.4	74.2	.341
Range of prestige	47.8	44.8	.378
Accessed positions			
Physician (86)	**.67**	**.43**	**.077**
Lawyer (74)	.44	.43	.904
Registered nurse (66)	.72	.54	.162
High school teacher (66)	.61	.61	.996
Accountant (65)	**.56**	**.27**	**.021**
Computer programmer (61)	.41	.38	.790
Police officer (60)	**.67**	**.46**	**.118**
Social worker (52)	.67	.64	.834
Electrician (51)	**.71**	**.43**	**.039**
Secretary (46)	.61	.62	.955
Nurse's aide (41)	.78	.66	.332
Machine operator (33)	.78	.68	.441
Cashier (29)	.72	.71	.922
Childcare worker (29)	.72	.61	.381
Taxicab/chauffeur driver (28)	.29	.33	.759

Significant differences, which are differences with a significance level of .15 or below, are highlighted in bold.

greater access to skilled and semiprofessional positions. Overall access to relations so categorized was significantly greater (3.3 vs. 2.7), but trusting contacts also reported greater access to individuals occupying skilled and semiprofessional personal positions that were personal (3.1 vs. 2.1) and frequent (2.3 vs. 1.6). Trusting contacts also had significantly greater access to professional workers that were personal (2.2 vs. 1.4) and frequent (1.3 vs. .84), as well as unskilled workers that were personal (3.2 vs. 2.6). These figures suggest that trust is strongly related to access to social capital, that within the context of greater and more diverse connections to positions in social structure trust is greater.

Analysis also reveals a positive relationship between access to social capital and job contacts' orientation to providing job-finding assistance, although relationships appear less strong than those associated with trust. Specifically, as reported in Table 8.8, open job contacts report greater access to positions, access to positions with higher average prestige, and higher reachability. However, none of these differences are statistically significant. That said, open contacts do report significantly greater access to specific positions, such as to registered nurses (68% vs. 51%), high school teachers (77% vs. 53%), and police officers (62% vs. 45%).

Given this, it is not surprising that open job contacts have greater access to skilled and semiprofessional workers. As shown in Table 8.9, open contacts generally have significantly greater access to all positions that are personal (7.3 vs. 6.1) and frequent in contact (5.7 vs. 4.7). But this result is largely driven by their greater

Table 8.7. Position generator skill level by (dis)trusting job contacts

	Trusting job contacts	Distrusting contacts	Significance
Extensity	9.3	7.7	.102
Personal	**8.4**	**6.0**	**.006**
Personal and frequent	**6.3**	**4.7**	**.020**
Skill level			
Unskilled	3.3	3.0	.445
Personal	**3.2**	**2.6**	**.130**
Personal and frequent	2.7	2.3	.219
Skilled	**3.3**	**2.7**	**.080**
Personal	**3.1**	**2.1**	**.011**
Personal and frequent	**2.3**	**1.6**	**.045**
Professional	2.7	2.2	.177
Personal	**2.2**	**1.4**	**.014**
Personal and frequent	**1.3**	**.84**	**.059**

Significant differences, which are differences with a significance level of .15 or below, are highlighted in bold.

Table 8.8. Position generator variables by orientation to providing job-finding assistance

	Open	Reluctant	Significance
Extensity	8.6	7.8	.175
Mean prestige	50.9	49.3	.189
Upper reachability	75.8	74.9	.749
Range of prestige	45.2	45.9	.835
Accessed positions			
Physician (86)	.53	.45	.498
Lawyer (74)	.49	.42	.535
Registered nurse (66)	**.68**	**.51**	**.124**
High school teacher (66)	**.77**	**.53**	**.020**
Accountant (65)	.37	.33	.672
Computer programmer (61)	.41	.38	.782
Police officer (60)	**.62**	**.45**	**.138**
Social worker (52)	.65	.69	.715
Electrician (51)	.59	.44	.168
Secretary (46)	.68	.56	.295
Nurse's aide (41)	.74	.65	.431
Machine operator (33)	.74	.71	.792
Cashier (29)	.69	.72	.715
Childcare worker (29)	.66	.65	.980
Taxicab/chauffeur driver (28)	.42	.30	.228

Significant differences, which are differences with a significance level of .15 or below, are highlighted in bold.

Table 8.9. Position skill level by orientation toward providing assistance

	Open	Reluctant	Significance
Extensity	8.8	7.8	.175
Personal	7.3	6.1	.113
Personal and frequent	5.7	4.7	.076
Skill level			
Unskilled	3.2	3.1	.748
Personal	2.9	2.7	.657
Personal and frequent	2.5	2.4	.571
Skilled	3.1	2.7	.167
Personal	**2.7**	**2.0**	**.032**
Personal and frequent	**2.2**	**1.5**	**.010**
Professional	2.5	2.1	.216
Personal	1.7	1.5	.374
Personal and frequent	1.0	.93	.641

Significant differences, which are differences with a significance level of .15 or below, are highlighted in bold.

access to individuals in skilled positions, access that is both personal (2.7 vs. 2.0) and frequent (2.2 vs. 1.5). In terms of access to unskilled and professional workers, differences between open and reluctant job contacts were negligible.

In sum, compared to job contacts with an open orientation to providing job-finding assistance, reluctant job contacts report fewer personal and frequent connections to different positions, but especially so to skilled/semiprofessional workers. The extent and nature of differences are even more striking when comparing trusting and distrusting job contacts, with the latter reporting substantially fewer and less diverse connections than trusting job contacts. In other words, job contacts are making decisions about the extent and nature of job-finding assistance that they are willing to provide. These are decisions largely driven by reputational concerns, especially ghetto behavior, within particular contexts of network embeddedness, contexts that appear to affect their orientation toward the job-finding process.

8.5. DISCUSSION AND CONCLUSION

There are currently two approaches to understanding inefficacious job referral networks among the black poor. The first approach represents conventional wisdom, which states that residence in neighborhoods characterized by high-to-extreme rates of poverty feeds a social isolation from mainstream ties and institutions that is the basis upon which the black urban poor are presumed to lack social capital that facilitates job finding (Wacquant and Wilson 1989; Briggs 1998; Tigges, Browne, and Green 1998; Rankin and Quane 2000). The second perspective views the relative inefficacy of the black poor's job-referral networks in terms of the willingness of contacts in possession of job information and influence to provide assistance when called upon to do so (Smith 2005). From this perspective, residents of high-poverty neighborhoods are embedded in networks that have pervasive distrust and a greater reluctance toward providing the type of job-finding assistance. These two approaches are not necessarily contradictory, however. Inefficacy can be located both in the relative lack of access to social capital and their relative inability to mobilize the social resources they do have for job finding. Furthermore, these two factors might be related. This chapter was an effort to bridge the gap that exists between these two approaches.

Drawing from in-depth interviews and survey data of 105 low-income African-American men and women, I find that access to social capital, measured using position generator variables, is significantly lower among residents of high-poverty neighborhoods, *but only so among the unemployed.* Employed residents of high-poverty neighborhoods look little different from their counterparts in less poor neighborhoods in terms of access. Indeed, in some cases, they actually appear to have slightly greater access. However, unemployed residents of high-poverty neighborhoods appear disadvantaged from unemployed residents of low-poverty neighborhoods and employed residents of high-poverty neighborhoods. This finding suggests that the relationship between neighborhood poverty status and access to social capital is contingent on the employment of individuals under study. Alone, neighborhood poverty does not appear to depress the social capital of its residents. Within the context of neighborhood poverty, it appears that the ways in which individuals structure their lives—employment versus not, for instance—matter more.

The black poor's relatively inefficacious job referral networks also appear related to pervasive distrust and noncooperation. Not only did I find that distrust toward job seekers was pervasive—80 percent of respondents reported concerns about job seekers' motivation, neediness, and delinquency—and that pervasive distrust was strongly and positively related to respondents' reluctance to assist their job-seeking relations, I found as well that pervasive distrust and noncooperation were greater among residents of high-poverty neighborhoods, who were more likely to report that prior referrals ended badly and that they had major concerns about job seekers' reputations, especially with regard to behavior deemed "ghetto."

However, I also discovered that these two pieces are connected and help to explain a bigger part of the puzzle. Distrusting residents, who, generally speaking, are more reluctant to provide job-finding assistance, also tend to have less access to social capital, especially with regard to their connection to skilled/semiprofessional and professional positions. How do we make sense of this? I suggest the following. Distrusting and reluctant job contacts have individuals employed in lesser-skilled positions, such as cashiers, childcare workers, nursing aides, and the like, as a greater proportion of the positions they are connected to. To the extent that these positions are more likely to be filled by individuals who must overcome multiple barriers to employment, barriers such as safe, reliable, and affordable transportation and childcare, human capital deficiencies, and substance abuse, for instance, workers occupying these positions probably develop problematic work and personal reputations borne from the constraints they face when trying to find and keep work, but have difficulty in doing so. As a result, they are perceived as lacking in motivation, being needy, and delinquent. Consequently, embeddedness in networks so composed might instill in those so embedded the belief that job seekers cannot be trusted and that providing job-finding assistance will put their own reputations at great risk. Given their already tenuous labor market status, this risk is too high to take. This interpretation is consistent with evidence from the qualitative data. However, further research needs to be done to both better theorize and provide empirical evidence linking access and mobilization. This study is only a beginning.

APPENDIX 1: DATA COLLECTION STRATEGIES

As is often the case when studying low-income populations, the principal investigators of this project had great difficulty recruiting participants through random sampling techniques, although great effort was made to do so (Edin and Lein 1997). In the summer of 1999, we contacted GENESYS Sampling Systems, a service that provided us with publicly listed names, addresses, and telephone numbers of 350 randomly selected residents from a poor census tract. Although we had initially thought to restrict the sampling to those aged 25–34 (the 1990 census indicated that there were 379 residents aged 25–34 in this census tract), because there were so few listings for residents in this age group (48 records), we broadened our criteria. From GENESYS, we received the names, addresses, and telephone numbers of 350 residents. We attempted to contact residents with the phone numbers we had been given, but found ourselves facing three major obstacles: many lines were no longer in service, residents had moved, and many households did not have a resident matching our criteria. Thus, from August to December 1999, we had a yield of only nine interviews.

Our next approach involved canvassing the community and recording every address for every housing structure. We then mailed recruitment letters asking respondents to participate and promised a $25 incentive for participation. This method generated only two additional interviews.

Our third strategy involved canvassing the community by going door-to-door and requesting participation. We began canvassing the area's housing projects with the intent of working our way through all of the housing projects in this community. Canvassing usually took place between 10 a.m. and 5 p.m. Although few people who fit the criteria refused to participate when asked, we were presented with some challenges. The projects that housed the most disadvantaged residents were relatively unsafe. Gang activity, including drug dealing, occurred conspicuously. Violent crime was so prevalent that few residents that we spoke with would allow their children to play outside or would venture outside themselves except to leave the neighborhood. Furthermore, residents would often refuse to answer their doors. Many had eviction notices posted on their doors and may have thought that we were bill collectors. We also believed that some did not want interviewers to see their homes. Self-conscious of her dwelling, one respondent requested that we conduct the interview in her barely functioning car.

Because we perceived ourselves to be in some danger, and because many residents clearly had issues of trust where interviewers were concerned, we then decided to recruit residents from social service agencies, where the more semipublic arena would reassure interviewers who feared for their safety, as well as reassure residents who feared for their own well-being. From contacts in the area, we discovered two social services agencies—one catered to residents experiencing various housing issues and provided some employment assistance as well; the other agency (the Center) was most fruitful, yielding the bulk of our 105 interviews conducted (71) between August 2000 and June 2002. In all, 72 percent were recruited at these two social service agencies. During this time, interviewers took up residence at the Center's office during regular business hours. With the assistance of Center staff, they approached prospective subjects who fit the study's criteria and requested their participation. The response rate was fairly high—roughly 80 percent.

There may be some concern that respondents recruited in the early stages of the project differed from those recruited through the social service agencies. Comparing the full sample to Center-recruited respondents, I found minor differences in terms of mean age, number of children, and hourly wages. There were also minor differences in the percentage that had children and received public assistance. However, a lower percentage of the Center-recruited sample was female, ever married, high school graduate, employed, or resident of high-to-extreme poverty neighborhoods. A higher percentage was currently on public assistance, but a lower percentage had ever received assistance. Thus, these different sampling methods yielded individuals from somewhat different populations.

To determine whether this impacted findings, I recalculated the mean percentage of respondents who distrust, by demographic characteristics, for the Center-recruited sample only. However, differences were minor, changing in no substantive way the findings reported in the main text.

Section III

Social Capital, Civil Engagement, Social Participation, and Trust

9

Social Networks of Participants in Voluntary Associations

René Bekkers, Beate Völker, Martin van der Gaag, and Henk Flap

9.1. INTRODUCTION

In the past decade, the study of social capital has gained momentum in sociology and political science. Social capital is assumed to be an important asset for individuals, groups, and communities because it not only increases health and economic growth and decreases crime and suicide rates but also gives access to resources that are important in finding a job, obtaining social support, or achieving political power. While definitions and operationalizations of social capital differ (Coleman 1990; Portes 1998; Putnam 2000; Lin 2001*b*), there is consensus on one issue: social capital inheres in and derives from the networks of people. What is not clear, however, is what element in social networks produces social capital. Which aspects of networks are important for social capital? And how do networks create social capital? Putnam (2000) argues that a high degree of trust, dense social networks, and high degrees of participation in collective action, such as volunteering, philanthropy, or associational membership, all indicate the presence of social capital and that these elements reinforce one another in a virtuous circle: trust, for example, increases participation, which increases trust (Putnam 1993*a*, 2000). However, empirical studies on the relation between characteristics of networks and civic engagement are rare.

We contribute to the debate on social capital by showing which aspects of networks are related to voluntary association membership. We investigate the effects of two groups of network characteristics. The first group consists of characteristics of resources that individuals can access through their ties with others. Through networks, people gain access to the resources of others, which may be helpful for them when they are looking for information, for a job, or for social support (Lin 2001). The second group of network characteristics represents various aspects of social cohesion. Networks also constitute communities that socialize their members to identify with the other members of the community, to contribute to the group, and to impose normative constraints on their actions (Durkheim 1897; Coleman 1990).

Like networks, voluntary associations are also studied from two perspectives: one that emphasizes the value of voluntary associations in the pursuit of group interests and inequality in participation between socioeconomic groups (Nie, Junn, and Stehlik-Barry 1996), and one that emphasizes the value of voluntary associations as a context for socialization of prosocial attitudes and behavior and cohesion and solidarity in communities (Putnam 2000). Knowing which types of network characteristics are related to participation in voluntary associations will also tell us to what extent voluntary associations are places where individuals learn the value of solidarity and produce community, or advance their individual careers or group interests.

9.2. THEORY AND HYPOTHESES

9.2.1. Networks as Sources of Cohesion

Looking at networks from the perspective of cohesion directs our attention to aspects of networks that produce feelings of belonging to a community and norm-conforming behavior that benefits group members. Many social groups have norms that prescribe membership in voluntary associations that serve the interests of the group. Durkheim's theory on social integration predicts that people are more likely to observe social norms in more cohesive groups. This theory is useful in predicting not only suicide (Van Tubergen, Te Grotenhuis, and Ultee, 2004) but also civic engagement (Bekkers 2003). Members of more cohesive groups are more likely to be asked to volunteer (Bryant, Jeon-Slaughter, Kang, and Tax, 2003; Bekkers, 2005a), and if asked they are more likely to say yes, especially if asked by alters with whom they have a close relationship (Bekkers 2004). Durkheim never directly measured the degree of cohesion in social groups, but assumed that more cohesive groups are more likely to produce progroup behavior. We assume that more cohesive groups have denser, more homogeneous social networks, consisting of more durable, intense relationships with a higher degree of trust. We measure these characteristics of networks directly, and hypothesize that they will increase voluntary association membership.

9.2.1.1. Density

Dense social networks are sources of social cohesion: a network made up of individuals who have strong ties to many other individuals is less likely to fall apart than a loosely connected network. There are two mechanisms that link density to progroup behavior. The first has to do with learning, the second with control (Buskens and Raub 2002). In dense social networks information flows faster. This increases the potential for individuals to learn the expectations that others hold regarding their behavior. Dense social networks also facilitate norm enforcement through social control (Coleman 1990). When people share more common friends with others, they are more likely to be punished for norm violations, and they are more likely to be rewarded for norm-conforming behavior. Thus, we hypothesize that network density should be conducive to participation in voluntary associations.

Empirical studies do not always support this hypothesis (see, for instance, Rotolo 2000). Glanville (2004), however, suggests that this null finding may conceal different effects on different types of voluntary associations. Glanville found that density was positively related to membership in local voluntary associations and value-expressive organizations, but found no relationship with membership in national and instrumental voluntary associations. Wilson and Musick (1998) also found that network density was not related to volunteering, but this null finding concealed opposite effects among lower and higher incomes: density was related to more volunteering among high-income people, but to less volunteering among low-income people. Studies of mobilization strategies used by voluntary organizations have shown that members are often recruited through informal strong ties (Booth and Babchuk 1973; Snow, Zurcher, and Ekland-Olson, 1980; Klandermans 1997). However, these studies suffer from a selection bias because they focused only on members. Leaving the organization may be dependent on the strength of ties with (recruiting) members. Recent studies, including members as well as nonmembers, showed that members recruited through weak ties are indeed more likely to leave the association as time goes on (Bekkers 2005*a*, 2005*b*).

9.2.1.2. Heterogeneity

Along with size and density, homogeneity is also a characteristic of cohesive networks that may affect the likelihood of membership in voluntary associations. Theoretically, social norms in homogeneous networks are clearer than in heterogeneous networks. People base their opinions about what is appropriate on the attitudes and behaviors of others in their environment (Latané and Darley 1970). In networks with a greater diversity of attitudes and behaviors it is less clear what is appropriate. Because membership in voluntary associations is evaluated positively in most groups, homogeneous networks should have higher membership rates. Rotolo (2000) did indeed find that persons living in towns with more heterogeneous populations were less likely to be members of voluntary associations. Glanville (2004) and Marsden (1990*b*) report that organizational membership is more common among persons in less heterogeneous networks with respect to religion. We expect that religious and educational heterogeneity decreases membership in voluntary associations.

9.2.1.3. Intensity, Trust, and Duration

The arguments on the role of intensity, trust, and duration of contact in social networks for voluntary association membership are mainly theoretical. Coleman (1990) suggested that dense networks create trust. Theoretically, intensity and duration of contact can also be expected to promote trust. It is unlikely that people invest in intense relations with untrustworthy others. The ties that survive in a social network are more likely to involve trustworthy alters. Putnam (2000) has argued forcefully that trust, in turn, fosters voluntary association membership. However, empirical studies at the microlevel have problems showing a close connection between membership and "general social trust," the agreement with general statements on trust in others (De Hart 1999; Dekker and de Hart 2001; Dekker and de Hart 2002; Delhey and Newton 2003). This is partly because the trust measure commonly used in cross-sectional studies of civic engagement refers to a general attitude toward human nature (Rosenberg 1956), which is part of a cluster of personality characteristics that is relatively stable across the life course (Scheufele and Shah 2000). Therefore, it is not surprising that more sophisticated studies have concluded that the weak relation of generalized trust with civic engagement is probably due mainly to a selection-effect instead of a socialization-effect (Stolle 2001; Wollebæk and Selle 2002). However, measures of trust in network members may be related to participation (Lin 2001).

In sum, from a cohesion perspective we predict that educational and religious heterogeneity are negatively related to membership in voluntary associations, and that network density, trust in network members, and the intensity and duration of ties in the network are positively related to membership.

9.2.2. Networks as Sources of Inequality

Looking at networks from the perspective of social inequality directs our attention to very different aspects of networks. This perspective is often taken in the literature on physical and mental health, social support, social stratification, and social mobility, where networks are studied as resources that individuals can use to their own advantage. Access to resources of alters in the social network is useful for finding a job (Granovetter 1973; Lin and Dumin 1986; De Graaf and Flap, 1988; Bartus 2001; Moerbeek 2001), for social support (Van Leeuwen, Tijhuis, and Flap 1993), for academic achievement (Coleman 1988), and mental and physical health (Lin, Dean, and Ensel 1986; House, Landis, and Umberson 1988). In this chapter, we add civic engagement to this list.

In political science, voluntary associations are viewed as the collective efforts of citizens to be heard in politics (Nie, Junn, and Stehlik-Barry 1996). Citizens organize themselves in groups in order to advocate their collective interests. However, some groups are more able to make their voices heard than others because they have more cognitive, financial, and social resources at their disposal (Verba, Schlozman, and Brady 1995). On the individual level, the hypothesis is that individuals with more resources are more likely to participate in voluntary associations. There are three mechanisms that generate a relation between access to resources and civic engagement. The first mechanism refers to the recruitment activities of voluntary associations (Brady, Schlozman, and Verba 1999). Voluntary associations will try to engage persons with more resources because they are more valuable to the association. Persons with more access to resources are more likely to be asked to participate in voluntary associations (Bekkers 2005*a*). The second mechanism is accessibility. Persons with more access to resources are not only more attractive to voluntary associations but also more accessible for mobilization networks (Klandermans 1997). The third mechanism refers to the role of costs and benefits of participation in the decision to participate. Access to resources also lowers the costs of membership.

The position generator methodology (Lin and Dumin 1986) provides a powerful tool to measure the access to social resources. The position generator produces measures of the number of occupations accessed, the range in accessed prestige, and the highest accessed prestige.

9.2.2.1. Access to Social Resources

People who have access to a network of persons with a higher social status are more likely to be members of social networks because of the recruitment strategies used by voluntary associations. Those who have access to a network of persons with a higher social status are more likely to know people who are members of voluntary associations because participation in voluntary associations is more prevalent among higher status groups. They are therefore more likely to be asked to become members. In addition, individuals with greater access to resources are more attractive as members of voluntary associations. Associations will try to attract and keep members with more social capital. Erickson (2004) showed that members of voluntary associations have more extensive access to resources than do nonmembers.

9.2.2.2. Highest and Range of Prestige Accessed

Persons accessing a higher prestige are more attractive for voluntary associations. They will be the target of recruitment efforts by voluntary associations more frequently. Persons accessing a greater range of resources will be targeted by a greater diversity of voluntary associations. Lin (2000*b*) showed that members of voluntary associations in Taiwan indeed know more prestigious alters than do nonmembers. In the same study, it was shown that the level of trust in these alters has nothing to do with association membership. The effect of highest prestige and the range of prestige accessed will vary between types of voluntary associations (see below).

9.2.2.3. Network Size

People who have a larger network are more likely to know people who are members of voluntary associations because large networks are more likely to contain association members than do small networks. Because the majority of members are recruited through face-to-face interactions with people who are already participating (Booth and Babchuk 1973; Snow et al. 1980; Klandermans 1997; Bekkers

2005*a*), people who are acquainted with association members are more likely to be asked to become a member. In addition, requests to join voluntary associations from members are more effective than requests by nonmembers (Bekkers 2005*a*). Previous research has shown a consistently positive relation between network size and participation in voluntary associations. Fischer (1982) showed that members of voluntary associations have more personal contacts with others, indicating a larger network. A less well-known study from France showed that participation in associations is related to the number of weekly contacts with others (Heran 1988). In the United States, Putnam (2000) and Rotolo (2000) also found that members of voluntary associations have larger networks than do nonmembers. In a study of volunteering, Wilson and Musick (1998) have shown that the number of friends and the frequency of contact with friends are positively related to volunteering activities.

In sum, from the perspective of networks as sources of inequality, we predict that network size, total access to resources through social networks, and the range and highest level of prestige accessed are positively related to membership.

9.2.3. Instrumental versus Expressive Participation

There are good reasons to expect that characteristics of networks have differential effects on instrumental and expressive forms of participation (Gordon and Babchuk 1959). The distinction between instrumental and expressive membership is based on Max Weber's typology of social action (1978). Instrumental participation is a form of instrumentally rational action ("zweckrationalität"), serving purposes beyond the enjoyment of participation itself. Expressive participation is a form of affective or value rational behavior because it constitutes its own reward. Examples of instrumental voluntary associations are interest groups, unions, and political parties. Expressive participation occurs in neighborhood associations, youth and elderly groups, musical groups, church choirs, and sports clubs. The political science perspective on voluntary associations as political interest groups focuses on instrumental participation, and seems to be less relevant when participation generates less group advantages. More generally, Lin (2001) has argued that the distinction between instrumental and expressive action can be used to predict differential effects of networks on behavior. Lin views instrumental action as directed at obtaining new resources, while expressive action is directed at preserving or maintaining resources. For obtaining resources, large, open networks with bridges to dissimilar alters are most useful. Dense, closed networks block access to new resources outside the network, but are also effectively preserving and maintaining existing resources. Such networks contribute to cohesion and solidarity in communities. Because instrumental memberships are more suitable for obtaining resources, they should be more prevalent among people with networks that also serve instrumental purposes. Therefore, we expect instrumental membership to be more strongly related to access to resources than is expressive participation. We expect that a higher range of occupations accessed and a higher prestige accessed increases the likelihood of instrumental participation, but does not increase the likelihood of expressive participation. Expressive participation should be more prevalent among people with networks serving expressive purposes. Therefore, we expect that network characteristics that measure cohesion like trust, intensity, and duration are more strongly related to expressive participation than to instrumental participation. Glanville (2004) and Lin (2000) support these hypotheses. Finally, we hypothesize differential effects of access to resources through different types of ties. Networks that are more strongly oriented toward the local community will more often give access to resources through family ties than through friends and acquaintances, while in more cosmopolitan networks the reverse will be true. Because expressive participation occurs more often in local associations, we expect that access through family ties is more strongly related to expressive participation than to instrumental participation. Access through friends and acquaintances should be more strongly related to instrumental participation.

9.2.4. Human Capital in the Production of Social Capital

One of the most consistent findings in the literature on voluntary associations is that membership increases with education (Babchuk and Edwards 1965; Verba and Nie 1972; Brady, Verba, and Schlozman 1995; Wilson and Musick 1997; Bekkers and De Graaf 2002). The relationship between the level of education and the association membership could be due to higher levels of social capital among the higher educated people (Wilson and Musick 1997; Brown 2002). Research on social networks consistently shows that the higher-educated people are more likely to have the kind of networks that are conducive to participation than are lower-educated people. The higher-educated people have more extensive access to resources through their networks (Lin 2001), which increases their attractiveness for voluntary associations. In addition, the larger networks of the higher-educated people make them more accessible for mobilization attempts. Therefore, it may be expected that access to resources mediate the effect of education on membership. Wilson and Musick (1997) confirmed this expectation. Brown (2002) found evidence for the mediating role of social capital for volunteering.

Not only do we expect that measures of social capital mediate the effect of human capital on participation, but we also expect that financial and human capital moderate the effect of social capital. It takes human capital to take advantage of social capital. People with more cognitive skills probably know how to use a given stock of social resources more effectively. Wilson and Musick (1998) support this hypothesis. They showed that social capital amplifies the role of human capital: network size and density are more strongly correlated with volunteering among the higher-educated people and the higher-income groups. We investigate hypotheses on mediation as well as on moderation of financial and human capital effects by social capital indicators.

9.2.5. Gender Differences in Effects of Networks on Membership

Males and females differ strongly with respect to the extent and nature of participation in voluntary associations. On the whole, males participate in a higher number of associations (Bekkers 2004). Relatively speaking, a higher proportion of women's memberships consists of expressive memberships than those of men (Glanville 2004). Expressive voluntary associations are often locally based. Membership in school boards or youth groups is part of women's traditional role in local community life. Expressive participation, especially by females, has been found to reinforce religious and age homogeneity in the United States (McPherson, Smith-Lovin, and Cook, 2001). It can be concluded from these findings that participation by males expands their networks, while women sustain their disadvantage by their participation patterns. However, Erickson (2004) found no differences between males and females in the relationship of diversity of resources with participation in voluntary associations. Given these inconclusive findings, we have not formulated hypotheses on gender differences in network effects on participation in expressive and instrumental associations, and we will merely explore whether there are any.

9.3. DATA AND METHODS

9.3.1. Sampling Procedure

The data for this study were gathered in 1999–2000, through the program "Creation and Returns of Social Capital." The data-set is called the Social Survey of the Networks of the Dutch 1 (SSND1) (see Völker and Flap 2002, the SSND, first wave; a second wave was completed in 2005). The data include information on 1,007 individuals between the ages 18 and 65, representing the Dutch population. The sample consists of 40 municipalities, representing the different Dutch provinces and regions, and takes size differences in these municipalities into account. As our data are also used for research on neighborhoods, we randomly selected four neighborhoods within each of the 40 municipalities. The Dutch zip code system was used for neighborhood identification.[1] Finally, we randomly sampled 25 addresses in every neighborhood and attempted to interview about 8 of them. Because our observations are clustered within neighborhoods, a cluster correction was applied in order to avoid underestimation of the standard errors using the Huber/White/sandwich estimator of variance.

We realized an overrepresentation of the working population by splitting the sampled addresses within neighborhoods in two, and asking only the individuals

---

[1] The Netherlands has a zip code system consisting of six positions, four numbers and two letters. The complete six-position zip code consists on average of 20 addresses, a five-position zip code (four numbers and one letter) consists of 230 addresses on average, and the four-position code consists of 2,500 addresses.

with paid work in one group and asking all who were selected in the other group. In this way, we realized one sample representing the Dutch active labor force and one that represents the Dutch population. In the final realized sample, 758 respondents are working. The response rate for both samples together was 40 percent. We ended up with a total data-set of 1,007 individual respondents in 161 neighborhoods (since the neighborhoods of one particular municipality were very small, there were 5 neighborhoods sampled, thus the number of 161).

A comparison of sociodemographic characteristics of respondents with statistics on the Dutch population showed that not only persons having paid work but also married and higher-educated persons were overrepresented. In the analyses, we use the whole sample controlling for having paid work, being married, and the level of education. The interviews took on average 1 hrs and 50 mins and were held usually at the respondents' home. In some cases, respondents were interviewed at their workplace because this was more convenient. Before the interviewers started the fieldwork, they were intensively trained and had become familiar with the questionnaire.

9.3.2. Measures

To measure voluntary association membership, we gave the respondents a list of 11 different types of associations: sports clubs, interest groups, and idealistic organizations, unions, professional organizations, political parties, neighborhood organizations, caring groups, dancing clubs, musical clubs, and "another kind of organization." Membership in sports clubs is most common (almost 40%), followed by interest groups and idealistic organizations (34%). Less common are memberships in trade unions, professional organizations, political parties, and other associations. We distinguished between memberships in voluntary associations that mainly serve instrumental goals (interest and idealistic organizations, unions, professional organizations, and political parties) and associations that mainly serve expressive goals (sports clubs, neighborhood organizations, caring groups, dancing clubs, and musical clubs). Memberships in "other organizations" were excluded because it was unclear to which type they belonged. Dichotomous variables reflecting whether the respondents held at least one instrumental membership (58.3% did so) or at least one expressive membership (65.2% did so) served as our dependent variables. We also conducted ordinal logistic regression analyses on the number of instrumental and expressive memberships. These analyses produced qualitatively similar results as the results reported below.

9.3.3. Measures of Network Cohesion

The SSND contains many different types of egocentric network measures using name generators as well as a few position generators. For a detailed description of these measures, we refer to van der Gaag (see Chapter 2 of this volume).

Network density is the degree to which the alters have contact with each other. After the respondents had completed all network delineating questions, a random sample of five network members was taken by the interviewer. The respondents indicated to what extent these alters had contact with each other on a scale from 1 ("they do not know each other") to 3 ("persons know each other quite well and like each other a lot"). The density measure is the total score of contacts among these network members divided by the number of potential contacts in such a network. For example, if 5 persons are mentioned the maximum number of ties is 10. If the respondent stated that 4 of the 5 people have good contact with each other, the density score would be 24 (8 ties with a score of 3), resulting in a density of 24/10 = 2.4. The density variable ranged from 0 to 3, with a mean of 1.16 and a standard deviation of 0.76.

Heterogeneity refers to the index of qualitative variation (IQV) in religion and education, calculated as follows (see Agresti and Agresti 1978):

$$\text{IQV} = \frac{1 - \sum_{i=1}^{k} p_i^2}{1 - 1/k}$$

where k is the number of categories and p_i the fraction of observations (alters and ego) in category i. The respondent (ego) is included in the analysis. The index ranges from 0 to 1 and measures the chance that two randomly selected network members belong to different categories. An index of 1 equals maximal heterogeneity, an index of 0 equals maximal homogeneity. The heterogeneity indxes for religion and education had mean scores of 0.47 and 0.54, with standard deviations of 0.35 and 0.25, respectively. The measure of religious heterogeneity was not normally distributed. A group of respondents had completely heterogeneous networks with respect to religion ($n = 143$, 14.2%), while another group had a completely homogeneous network with respect to religion ($n = 135$, 13.4%). We created two dummies for these groups. The remaining observations were distributed evenly along the continuum from .05 to .96.

Intensity, trust, and duration refer to properties of the relationships with the alters in the core network. For each of the alters mentioned, the respondents indicated how intense their relationship with this person was, how much they trusted this person, how much they liked this person, and for how long they had known each other. Intensity, liking, and trust were measured on a scale from 1 to 5. Mean scores (and standard deviations) were 3.57 (0.63) and 4.30 (0.53), respectively. Duration was measured in the number of years (mean: 16.25; standard deviation 7.57).

In a preliminary analysis, we analyzed bivariate correlations between the various indicators of cohesion in networks (see the upper part of Table 9.1). A cluster of positive correlations (ranging from .197 to .511) was found among density, duration, trust, and intensity, indicating that social relations in dense networks tended to be more durable, with higher levels of intensity and trust. Network heterogeneity with respect to religion and education was not related to density, duration, trust, and intensity. We observe some relationships of network cohesion measures with sociodemographic characteristics (see the bottom part of Table 9.1). Older persons, frequent church attendees, and those who are married tend to have more cohesive networks. In contrast, higher-educated with paid work, and those living in urban areas have less cohesive networks. Participation in expressive and instrumental voluntary associations shows only a few meaningful correlations with measures of network cohesion. These results do not give much support to the predictions made from the perspective of cohesion.

9.3.4. Measures of Access to Resources

Access to resources was measured with a position generator (Lin 2001). (For a detailed exposition of this method we refer to Chapter 1 in this volume.) In the SSND, the respondents received a list of 30 occupations, and were asked to indicate whether they knew someone with this occupation, and if so, their relationship (family, friend, or acquaintance—"someone that you would talk to if you met him or her outside the house"). Respondents were asked to indicate access through family ties first; if they had no access to a given occupation through family ties, the respondents indicated whether they had access to the occupation through ties with friends, and finally, through ties with acquaintances. We computed the number of occupations accessed separately for each type of ties. Thus we obtained three variables: *access through family ties, access through friends*, and *access through acquaintances*. These variables ranged from 0 to 26, 21, and 22, respectively, with means of 6.42, 3.35, and 5.21 (standard deviations of 3.81, 3.25, and 4.44). In additional analyses, we also used the total number of occupations accessed (ranging from 0 to 30, mean: 15.00; standard deviation: 5.63).

Mean prestige accessed indicates the mean prestige of the occupations in the network of the respondent among all types of relationships (family, friends, and acquaintances). Prestige scores from Ganzeboom and Treiman (1996) were used. The mean prestige ranged from 29.86 to 71.15, with a mean of 53.44 and a standard deviation of 6.01. *Range in accessed prestige* indicates the range in social status of all types of the network members of the respondent, obtained by taking the difference between the highest and the lowest prestige accessed. The range measure ranged from 0 to 62, with a mean of 52.17 and a standard deviation of 10.48.

Network size is the total number of persons mentioned in responses to all the network delineating questions included in the survey. Persons whom the respondent met for the first time at an association ($n = 644$, 5.2% of all alters) and foes ($n = 368$, 3.0% of all alters) were excluded. Network size ranged from 1 to 28, with a mean of 11.35 and a standard deviation of 4.06.

In a preliminary analysis, we investigated the correlations of the various measures of access to resources (see the middle-right-hand side of Table 9.1). All correlations among measures of access to occupations exceeded .15 and were

Table 9.1. Correlations among indicators of collective and individual social capital

	A	B	C	D	E	F	G	H	I	J	K	L	M	N	O
A	1.000	—	—	—	—	—	—	—	—	—	—	—	—	—	—
B	.251	1.000	—	—	—	—	—	—	—	—	—	—	—	—	—
C	.215	.262	1.000	—	—	—	—	—	—	—	—	—	—	—	—
D	.197	.258	.511	1.000	—	—	—	—	—	—	—	—	—	—	—
E	.002	−.014	−.025	.002	1.000	—	—	—	—	—	—	—	—	—	—
F	−.011	.033	.074	.068	.008	1.000	—	—	—	—	—	—	—	—	—
G	.056	.084	.022	−.033	−.021	−.542	1.000	—	—	—	—	—	—	—	—
H	.029	.032	.015	.030	.020	.620	−.160	1.000	—	—	—	—	—	—	—
I	−.038	−.109	−.014	−.013	−.029	.001	−.190	−.173	1.000	—	—	—	—	—	—
J	.011	−.034	.059	.003	.038	.009	−.027	−.032	.219	1.000	—	—	—	—	—
K	−.042	−.069	.039	−.067	.006	−.102	−.019	−.142	.123	.076	1.000	—	—	—	—
L	−.001	−.007	.076	.026	.023	−.037	−.029	−.095	.196	.636	.267	1.000	—	—	—
M	.045	.118	.073	.059	.026	.042	−.004	.013	.059	.324	−.009	.193	1.000	—	—
N	−.041	−.232	.005	−.032	−.024	−.055	−.059	−.077	.186	.436	.152	.297	−.292	1.000	—
O	.005	.026	.009	−.023	.043	.016	.012	.004	.090	.672	−.009	.417	−.232	.072	1.000
P	.090	−.085	−.018	−.003	−.054	.013	−.047	−.031	−.010	−.074	.067	−.018	.043	.046	−.165
Q	.119	.612	.146	.093	.049	.037	.037	.007	−.107	−.016	.108	.024	.076	−.193	.056
R	.099	.228	.084	.089	.065	.091	−.008	.028	.012	.084	−.112	.013	.178	−.149	.064
S	−.202	−.275	−.086	−.094	−.075	−.023	−.061	−.060	.312	.172	.068	.073	−.024	.150	.129
T	−.137	−.256	−.031	−.160	−.030	−.068	−.049	−.088	.253	.181	.457	.217	−.077	.246	.116
U	−.067	.024	−.015	−.086	.008	−.042	−.045	−.073	.108	.199	.275	.179	−.043	.139	.187
V	−.052	−.163	−.049	−.041	.032	−.145	.036	−.076	.119	−.007	.154	.056	−.034	.105	−.057
W	.028	.156	.052	.114	.069	.216	−.080	.069	.006	.026	−.037	.022	.132	−.100	−.008
X	−.014	.060	.028	−.035	−.040	−.009	.022	−.004	.081	.182	.133	.116	.053	.123	.096
Y	.063	.100	.022	.016	.038	.028	−.021	−.010	.014	.130	−.081	.061	.072	−.034	.129

A: density; B: duration; C: trust; D: intensity; E: educational heterogeneity; F: religious heterogeneity; G: minimal religious heterogeneity (0–1); H: maximal religious heterogeneity (0–1); I: network size; J: total number of occupations accessed; K: mean prestige accessed; L: range of accessed prestige; M: number of occupations accessed through family ties; N: number of occupations accessed through acquaintances; O: number of occupations accessed through friends; P: gender (1 = female); Q: age; R: married (1 = yes); S: paid work (1 = yes); T: level of education; U: income; V: level of urbanization (1–5); W: church attendance (times per year); X: number of instrumental memberships; Y: number of expressive memberships.

Correlations > .053 p < .10; > .063 p < .05; > .083 p < .01; r > .100 p < .001.

Source: SSND01; n = 1,002.

significant at the $p < .001$ level, except the correlations of mean prestige accessed with the total number of occupations accessed, and access through family ties and acquaintances. Network size was also correlated positively with access measures.

An examination of the correlations of access and cohesion measures (see the middle left-hand side of Table 9.1) shows that they are rather independent of each other. For instance, there are no substantial relationships between density and access to resources, in contrast to a hypothesis formulated by Lin (2001). In line with individual social capital theory, more homogeneous networks with respect to religion confined access to resources, especially through friends. Inspection of correlations of access measures with sociodemographic characteristics and participation variables reveals some interesting findings (see the bottom part of Table 9.1). Males have more extensive access through acquaintances; access through friends decreases with age; and a higher level of education increases total access, especially through ties with friends and acquaintances, the range in accessed prestige, and the mean prestige accessed. The positive correlations of access to resources with the number of instrumental and expressive memberships are promising. As predicted by individual social capital theory, instrumental participation is more strongly related to access to resources than is expressive participation.

9.3.5. Direction of Causality

We have argued above how network structure affects participation in voluntary associations. However, it is very likely that participation in voluntary associations also affects network structure. A large network of persons with a higher status may not only be the cause of association membership but also be the (anticipated) effect: people meet new friends in voluntary associations and gain access to resourceful others. Putnam (2000) assumes that participation in voluntary associations breeds trust in fellow citizens. "Meeting others" is often mentioned as a reason for joining voluntary associations (Clary et al. 1998; Van Daal and Plemper 2003). Voluntary associations constitute an important part of the marriage market (Kalmijn and Flap 2001). Instrumental participation in voluntary associations has been found to increase access to resources in general (Davis, Renzulli, and Aldrich 2006), the likelihood of finding a job among Dutch managers (Boxman, De Graaf, and Flap, 1991), and occupational status among female volunteers in the US (Wilson and Musick 2003). Unfortunately, the data of the SSND do not allow definite conclusions with regard to the causal order of membership and network characteristics. The data contain no information on the timing of membership. However, we do have information on the timing of engaging in relationships with alters in the social network. We know where ego met the alters in the present network for the first time, and whether the relationship is a family relationship, an acquaintance, or a friend. Alters who were first met in an association were excluded from the network measures. This eliminates some of the problems with the causal order. The information on the kind of relationship ego has with the alters in the access network further reduces the problem. Because one does not choose his or her family—or at least not as much as one's friends and acquaintances—we can be more confident on the causal order: it is likely that the social capital accessed through family ties is prior to voluntary association membership. However, with regard to ties with acquaintances and friends, we do not know which came first: the tie or the membership.

9.3.6. Analytical Strategy

In the regression analyses of membership, a first model including sociodemographic characteristics and indicators of human and financial capital serves as a baseline. In the second model, indicators of cohesion in networks are included. The third model introduces indicators of access to social resources. We investigated whether network characteristics mediate the effects of human and financial capital. We expect that differences with regard to income and education will decrease or disappear when access to resources are introduced. In a final model, an interaction of total access with income is added to determine whether social capital amplifies the effects of human capital. To avoid multicollinearity, we decided not to include interactions of access variables for access through family members, friends, and acquaintances separately; nor did we include interactions with education. Our regression models initially included these interactions, but these models violated tolerance statistics for multicollinearity. Separate analyses including interactions of education and income with total access indicated that the interaction with income was driving the results.

Because some of our hypotheses required a comparison of effect sizes, we z-standardized all noncategorical variables.

9.4. RESULTS

The results of our multivariate analyses of membership in expressive and instrumental voluntary associations (see Tables 9.2 and 9.3) support most of the hypotheses based on the inequality perspective, but fail to support almost all hypotheses from the cohesion perspective. They also support the hypothesis that access to resources mediates effects of human capital on membership. In addition, we find some gender differences in network effects (see Table 9.4), but they deviate from findings in the literature on homophily in voluntary associations. We will first summarize the main results from our analyses. We discuss some explanations and implications of our findings below.

9.4.1. Failure to Support the Cohesion Perspective

In flat contrast to hypotheses formulated from the cohesion perspective, membership in voluntary associations is not related to network density, heterogeneity with respect to religion and education, or to trust in network members and intensity

Table 9.2. Logistic regression analysis of instrumental membership

	Model 1	Model 2	Model 3	Model 4
Female	0.95	0.99	0.90	0.87
Age	1.08	0.93	0.93	0.93
Age^2	1.00	0.99	0.98	0.97
Married	1.44*	1.38$^{(*)}$	1.35	1.36
Level of education	1.26**	1.31**	1.18$^{(*)}$	1.19$^{(*)}$
Paid work	1.70**	1.82**	1.68*	1.74*
Income	1.46**	1.46**	1.34*	0.60$^{(*)}$
Level of urbanization	0.96	0.98	0.94	0.94
Church attendance	0.94	0.96	0.95	0.96
Network density		0.99	0.98	0.98
Duration		1.33**	1.36**	1.37**
Trust		1.09	1.05	1.04
Intensity		0.89	0.90	0.91
Educational heterogeneity		0.95	0.94	0.93
Religious heterogeneity		1.03	1.04	1.04
Religious heterogeneity 0		1.29	1.38	1.36
Religious heterogeneity 1		1.14	1.24	1.27
Network size			1.00	0.99
Access through family ties			1.30**	0.94
Access through friends			1.43**	1.08
Access through acquaintances			1.22*	0.82
Mean prestige accessed			1.20*	1.24*
Range of prestige accessed			0.90	0.90
Total access × income				3.14**
Pseudo R^2	.0595	.0687	.0894	.0956
χ^2	64.4***	73.3***	95.8***	95.7***

Note: Entries represent odds ratios for z-standardized independent variables.
*** $p < .001$; ** $p < .01$; * $p < .05$; $^{(*)}$ $p < .10$.

of relations (see Model 2 of Tables 9.2 and 9.3). Instrumental membership does occur more often among those who have more durable relations, but expressive participation does not.

9.4.2. Strong Support for the Inequality Perspective

In line with the hypotheses from the inequality perspective, membership in voluntary associations is consistently related to access to resources (see Model 3 of Tables 9.2 and 9.3). Expressive as well as instrumental memberships are more prevalent among those with more extensive access through family members and acquaintances. Access through friends also increases the likelihood of instrumental membership. As predicted, instrumental participation is more likely among those with access to occupations with a higher prestige. Unexpectedly, a higher prestige of occupations accessed decreases the likelihood of expressive participation. The range of prestige accessed is not related to expressive or instrumental participation.

Table 9.3. Logistic regression analysis of expressive membership

	Model 1	Model 2	Model 3	Model 4
Female	1.08	1.07	1.18	1.22
Age	1.11	1.05	1.10	1.10
Age^2	0.81**	0.81**	0.83*	0.83*
Married	1.37*	1.35*	1.24	1.22
Level of education	1.12$^{(*)}$	1.13$^{(*)}$	1.18*	1.17$^{(*)}$
Paid work	0.61**	0.64*	0.57**	0.56**
Income	0.91	0.91	0.91	1.36
Level of urbanization	0.75***	0.75***	0.76***	0.76***
Church attendance	1.20**	1.21**	1.19**	1.19**
Network density		1.08	1.07	1.08
Duration		1.07	1.04	1.04
Trust		0.98	0.98	0.99
Intensity		0.97	0.97	0.96
Educational heterogeneity		1.07	1.05	1.06
Religious heterogeneity		0.98	0.96	0.96
Religious heterogeneity 0		0.86	0.85	0.86
Religious heterogeneity 1		0.85	0.86	0.85
Network size			1.06	1.07
Access through family ties			1.21*	1.42**
Access through friends			1.08	1.24*
Access through acquaintances			1.37***	1.67***
Mean prestige accessed			0.82*	0.80*
Range of prestige accessed			0.98	0.98
Total access × income				0.61$^{(*)}$
Pseudo R^2	.0471	.0486	.0690	.0711
χ^2	62.5***	68.9***	94.3***	84.2***

Note: Entries represent odds ratios for z-standardized independent variables.

$^{(*)} p < .10; \, ^* p < .05; \, ^{**} p < .01; \, ^{***} p < .001.$

9.4.3. Access to Resources Always Matters

We find mixed support for the hypothesis that access to resources is more strongly related to instrumental participation than to expressive participation. In the regression analyses, the introduction of access to resources, mean prestige, and the range of prestige accessed increases the explained variance with about the same proportion (.206 and .217 for instrumental and expressive participation, respectively). However, if we add up the three access variables into one variable ("extensity" in Erickson 2004), we find that total access has a somewhat larger standardized effect on instrumental membership (1.46, $p < .001$) than on expressive membership (1.36, $p < .001$).

9.4.4. Access Through Family Ties Benefits Both Types of Participation

We reject our hypothesis that access to resources through family ties is more strongly related to expressive participation than to instrumental participation. If anything, the opposite is true. The effect of access through family ties is somewhat larger on instrumental participation (1.30, $p < .01$) than on expressive participation (1.20, $p < .05$). We do observe a stronger effect of access through friends on instrumental participation (1.43, $p < .01$) than on expressive participation (1.08, not significant), but the effect of access through acquaintances is stronger on expressive participation (1.37, $p < .001$) than on instrumental participation (1.22, $p < .01$).

9.4.5. Access to Resources Mediates Effects of Education and Income

In the analysis of instrumental membership, we find strong support for the hypothesis that membership increases with income and education because the networks of persons with higher levels of education and income give access to a more extensive network containing more resources (compare Models 2 and 3 of Table 9.2). Controlling for access to occupations, the effects of income and education decrease substantially, the latter to nonsignificance. Access to resources did not mediate the effects of education and income on expressive membership because income and education were not related to expressive membership in the first place. Unexpectedly, the higher level of expressive participation among married persons and frequent church attendees also seems to be due partly to their more extensive access to resources, especially through family ties.

9.4.6. Effects of Access to Resources Differ by Income

We find support for the hypothesis that access to resources through networks increases income disparities in participation, but only for instrumental memberships (see Model 4 of Table 9.2). Among those with higher incomes, access to resources increases the likelihood of participation more strongly than among those with lower incomes. In the analysis of expressive membership we find the opposite pattern. Access to resources increases the likelihood of expressive membership only among those with lower and median incomes (see Model 4 of Table 9.3).

9.4.7. Few Gender Differences in Network Effects

In contrast to results of studies from the US, we do not find gender differences in the effects of educational and religious heterogeneity on participation (see Table 9.4). We do find that women are more likely to participate in expressive organizations when their networks consist of more women (see the negative effect of gender heterogeneity in the second column of Table 9.4). This result is in line with a role theory of participation: the higher the proportion of women in the networks of women, the more likely they are to participate in organizations that fit in a traditional role for women. We do not find that expressive participation

Table 9.4. Logistic regression analysis of expressive and instrumental membership by gender

	Expressive		Instrumental	
	Males	Females	Males	Females
Age	1.18	1.01	0.84	1.04
Age^2	0.78*	0.88	1.01	0.93
Married	1.58*	1.12	1.30	1.69$^{(*)}$
Level of education	1.29*	1.06	1.20	1.11
Paid work	0.51*	0.73	1.49	2.05*
Income	0.74**	1.21	1.38$^{(*)}$	1.45$^{(*)}$
Level of urbanization	0.67***	0.81$^{(*)}$	0.83	1.08
Church attendance	1.19$^{(*)}$	1.12	1.01	0.87
Network density	1.05	1.08	1.03	0.91
Duration	1.00	1.09	1.46*	1.20
Trust	1.07	0.90	1.18	0.90
Intensity	0.85	1.11	0.68**	1.24$^{(*)}$
Gender heterogeneity	1.03	0.80*	1.05	0.97
Educational heterogeneity	1.06	1.07	0.86	1.04
Religious heterogeneity	0.95	0.98	1.03	1.06
Religious heterogeneity 0	0.60	1.27	1.11	1.53
Religious heterogeneity 1	0.57	1.47	0.96	1.66
Network size	1.04	1.03	0.88	1.09
Access through family ties	1.13	1.35*	1.28$^{(*)}$	1.39*
Access through friends	1.12	1.06	1.58**	1.30
Access through acquaintances	1.30*	1.58***	1.19	1.29
Mean prestige accessed	0.82$^{(*)}$	0.82	1.14	1.32*
Range of prestige accessed	1.04	0.85	0.99	0.77
Pseudo R^2	.0977	.0788	.1071	.1011
χ^2	73.3***	44.7***	60.1***	48.8***

Note: Entries represent odds ratios for z-standardized independent variables.
$^{(*)}p < .10$; $^* p < .05$; $^{**} p < .01$; $^{***} p < .001$.

is more likely among women with less extensive access to resources. Quite the contrary: access to resources through family ties and ties with acquaintances is more strongly related to participation in voluntary associations by women than by men. The effect of extensity (adding up access through all three types of ties) on expressive membership is larger among women than among men (1.53, $p < .002$ vs. 1.32, $p < .029$), while there is no gender difference in the effect of extensity on instrumental membership (1.50, $p < .024$, for males vs. 1.46, $p < .016$ for females).

9.5. DISCUSSION

At several points, the findings we have presented above are at odds with previous research. For instance, we do not find any effects of trust on participation. Putnam (2000) has argued that trust should be related positively to participation. Uslaner

(2002) has found positive relationships of trust with participation in voluntary associations. Brehm and Rahn (1997) show that these relationships are reciprocal. There are two reasons why we do not find a relation between trust and participation. The first is that our data are from the Netherlands, where the relationship of trust with participation seems to be smaller in magnitude than in the US (Uslaner 2002). The second reason is that we measured trust using questions referring to concrete persons in the network, and not using questions on general attitudes toward human nature. The "generalized trust" item was originally formulated by Rosenberg (1956) as part of a "misanthropy scale." Generalized trust is a rather stable trait of individuals throughout the life course (Uslaner 2002). The traditional measure was not included in our data-set. We do have another attitude measure of trust available: (disagreement with) the statement "Before I trust others, I must be certain about their intentions." This (reverse coded) attitude showed a weakly positive correlation with network size ($r = .102$), but did not correlate substantially with the network measure of trust ($r = .067$, $p < .034$) or with the other measures of collective social capital. Introducing this measure in Model 2 of the analyses of membership revealed a significantly positive effect on instrumental participation (z-standardized effect of 1.17, $p < .033$). The effect became weaker and nonsignificant (1.12, $p < .131$) in Model 3 after the introduction of access measures, suggesting that attitudinal trust facilitates the formation of ties to (prestigious) others. The attitudinal trust item was not related to expressive membership.

Another result that deviates from previous research is the nonsignificant effect of network density. Perhaps this is due to the measure. Network density should increase membership as a form of norm-conform behavior because more dense networks will be more likely to reward norm conformity. Sanctioning from strong ties will be more effective than from weak ties. However, to measure density we randomly sampled five network members. Because people tend to have a higher number of weak ties in their networks than strong ties, our measure of density reflects relationships among a majority of persons with whom the respondent has weak ties.

We do not find strong gender differences in effects of network homogeneity, while previous studies have found such differences (Miller McPherson, Smith-Lovin, and Cook, 2001). An explanation for this difference is that the networks of males and females in the Netherlands are more similar than they are in the US. In the SSND1, males and females do not differ with respect to religious and educational homogeneity, nor do they have different association patterns with respect to religion and education within voluntary associations.

The results we have presented should be interpreted with some caution on the issue of which came first: network structure or participation. We have tried to reduce potential concerns about the direction of causality by excluding alters who were met first in voluntary associations in the measures of collective social capital, and by distinguishing resources accessed through family, friends, and acquaintances. Network members who were not met for the first time in a voluntary association but in some other context (work, family, and neighborhood) are less likely to have entered the network because of participation. Resources accessed through family ties are also unlikely to be the result of participation.

Despite these efforts, we could not eliminate our concerns on the causality issue altogether. Alters who were met outside the association may have joined the association together with the respondent, they may have asked the respondent to join, or the respondent may have joined the association in order to meet (a specific type of) alter(s). The desire to broaden the scope of the network may even be a salient motive to join voluntary associations. It is likely that the true causal effects of networks on membership in voluntary associations are smaller than they appear in our tables. It is likely that part of the relation between participation and access to resources through friends and acquaintances is the result of participation rather than the cause. However, access through family ties can only be the result of participation if these family ties still exist because of comembership in the same voluntary associations, and would have been broken without comembership. We believe that this is rather unlikely. Nevertheless, we are eagerly anticipating the completion of the next wave of the SSND in order to discern causes and effects in the relations between social network structure and participation in voluntary associations.

The finding that access to resources through family ties does not have stronger effects on expressive than on instrumental participation requires explanation. We expected that expressive membership would be more strongly related to access to resources through family ties because expressive memberships and access through family ties both indicate a locally oriented network. It could be that this anomaly is due to the efficacy of recruitment through strong ties. Members who are recruited into voluntary associations through family ties are more likely to continue membership. Even those who have locally oriented networks will become members of instrumental associations when recruited by family members, and continue their membership for a longer period.

One may wonder whether measures of cohesion in networks would have more predictive value for examples of civic engagement that require a more substantial investment of time, such as volunteering. Membership in voluntary associations is a low-cost activity that does not require much time (or none at all). Cohesive networks may not be needed to enforce norms prescribing membership as a form of progroup behavior because membership does not cost anything. Selective incentives may be enough to motivate even completely self-interested individuals to become members of voluntary associations (Bekkers and De Graaf 2002). Among members of voluntary associations, however, those who are embedded in more cohesive networks will be more strongly motivated to volunteer and keep the association running. Future research should investigate other examples of civic engagement as well, to test the hypothesis that cohesion in networks is more strongly related to more costly types of civic engagement.

9.6. CONCLUSION

The results of our analyses clearly support the inequality perspective on membership. Persons with more extensive access to resources through their personal networks are more likely to participate in voluntary associations. A lack of access to resources through networks reduces access to voluntary associations. In contrast to hypotheses from the cohesion perspective, participants in voluntary associations do not have higher levels of trust in the people in their network (Olson 1965), they do not have denser networks, and ties in networks of participants are just as intense as the ties in networks of nonparticipants. Social networks of participants in voluntary associations are mainly characterized by their more extensive access to social resources.

Access to large and prestigious networks mediates a part of the effects of education and income on instrumental membership. We found evidence that higher-income households benefit more from access to resources when it comes to instrumental membership. In contrast, lower-income households benefit more from access to resources when it comes to expressive membership. Controlling for income and education, we do not find that women benefit less from access to resources than men.

If we view membership in voluntary associations as an element of social capital, then it is the access to resources embedded in networks that creates social capital, not the closure of the network. This result calls our attention to the inequality in access to resources as a critical factor for participation. Membership in voluntary associations tells us very little about the degree of solidarity and cohesion in networks.

10

The Internet, Social Capital, Civic Engagement, and Gender in Japan

Kakuko Miyata, Ken'ichi Ikeda, and Tetsuro Kobayashi

10.1. INTRODUCTION

Putnam (2000) argues that social capital in the form of diversified networks plays a crucial role in developing civic engagement. People who know a wide variety of others are drawn into civic life directly, because at least some of their diverse contacts are interested in political issues and act as informal political recruiters. People with varied contacts are also encouraged toward civic activity indirectly, because knowing a wide range of others enhances trust in others and an expectation that good deeds will be reciprocated. Trust and the expectation of reciprocity in turn encourage people to work with others on common problems.

This chapter breaks some new ground by exploring Putnam's central argument as it applies to civic engagement in Japan (Putnam focuses mainly on the United States). But this study goes further by adding two important factors neglected in earlier research: the Internet and gender. Putnam (2000) is unsure how the Internet will affect social networks and civic engagement. Other researchers disagree on how the Internet affects social capital, and have had almost nothing to say about how the internet affects civic engagement. This chapter develops a clearer and more nuanced argument about how different kinds of Internet use have different kinds of effects, some (but only some) of which are important positive contributions to social capital and civic engagement.

The Internet, social networks, and political life are all clearly gendered, yet prior work has often neglected gender (see O'Neill and Gidengil, forthcoming). This chapter thus furthers the dissection of gender differences. Men and women use the Internet in different ways, and women have bad social experiences on the net more frequently than men. The result, as we will show, is that the Internet mainly builds ties between men and other men. Thus, the Internet fosters civic engagement by building social capital but only for men, through the diversity of their ties to fellow men. Diverse ties to women also encourage civic engagement, for both men and women, but the Internet does not increase the diversity of ties to women.

10.2. WHAT IS SOCIAL CAPITAL? WHAT IS GENDERED SOCIAL CAPITAL?

Putnam (2000) insists that bridging social capital refers to social networks that bring together different sorts of people, and bonding social capital brings together similar sorts of people. This is an important distinction, because the externalities (in the sense of economics; i.e., effect of the given network onto other group/network) that groups are bridging are likely to be positive, whereas networks that are bonding (limited within particular social niches) are at greater risk of producing externalities that are negative. Of course, bonding social capital offers the kind of assistance and support that comes from affection, willingness to help, and considerable knowledge of one another. By contrast, bridging social capital offers the diverse ties that connect individuals to a wide range of potential resources that facilitate good health (Erickson 2003) and lead to better jobs (Lin 1999*b*). Bridging social capital also enhances civic engagement, and can be the channel through which communities mobilize for the collective good (Putnam 2000).

Thus, since we hypothesize that the variety of people known is the most important form of bridging social capital, we will focus on the diversity of contacts. Our measure clearly measures bridging social capital in Putnam's sense, since it shows the extent to which a person is linked to different kinds of people.

However, some researches insist that there is a gender difference in the diversity of contacts. Studies have shown that males tend to have larger networks than females (Campbell and Rosenfeld 1985), and females tend to have more kin and neighbors in their networks than males (Marsden 1988; Moore 1990). As a result, males tend to have more access to diverse heterogeneous resources than females (Marsden 1988; Moore 1990). This gender difference in network diversity was also found in Taiwan (Lin, Fu, and Hsung 2001). Hence, we examine our hypothesis that:

H1a: Men have more diverse contacts than women.

Moreover, people prefer to have contacts with people more similar to themselves when they have an abundant set of potential contacts. Hence, Erickson (2003) suggests that when contacts are made, homophily leads to further selection, as women are more interested in building ties with the women they meet, and men feel they have more in common with the men they meet. According to this suggestion, we will examine H1b:

H1b: People tend to create more same-gender networks than different-gender networks.

10.3. THE INTERNET AS A PLACE TO MEET PEOPLE

The formation of diversified networks depends partly on the variety of potential network members encountered (Erickson 2003). The Internet is expected to provide a chance to meet heterogeneous people with shared interests. For example, McKenna and Bargh (2000) argue that because communicating via the Internet can reduce the importance of physical appearance and physical distance, heterogeneous people can meet and discuss political issues in online communities. The Pew Internet and American Life Project reported survey results showing that Internet users had wider social networks than people who did not connect to the web (Robinson et al. 2000).

By contrast, critics argue that the Internet pulls people away from other interactions inside and outside of the household (Nie and Erbring 2000) and leads to feelings of alienation (Kraut et al. 1998).

Although the evidence for the strengthening or weakening effects of the Internet on social capital continues to be debated, the impacts of the Internet on social capital are expected to depend on the nature of online activities (DiMaggio et al. 2001). For instance, when the Internet engages people primarily in asocial activities such as web surfing and reading the news, its engrossing nature can turn people away from community, organizational and political involvement, and domestic life (Wellman et al. 2001). By contrast, the connectivity of e-mail adds to the volume of social contact by face-to-face and telephone communication that occurs in relationships such as those among family members and friends (Quan-Haase et al. 2002). E-mail may be useful for maintaining existing ties, because it gives users a low-maintenance and nonintrusive way to maintain social networks. However, it may not create new social networks, nor increase the variety of social networks.

Compared with e-mails, online communities such as mailing lists (listservs), Bulletin Board Systems, and online chat groups in which people discuss shared interests or topics may form new, diverse ties. It is easy for new members to participate in online communities because of the lack of barriers to entry. Anonymity in communication also encourages people, especially marginalized populations, to participate in online communities. Therefore, participants may form diverse social networks through discussion with others who share their interests, but are dissimilar in terms of their basic demographic characteristics, lifestyles, and attitudes.

Hence, it is hypothesized that participation in online communities encourages formation of diverse social networks, while e-mail is predicted to maintain social networks but not facilitate creation of diverse social networks:

H2a: Participation in online communities may be more productive than the exchange of e-mail in facilitating a diversity of networks.

However, we wonder if women create cross-gendered social networks as well as men if they participate in online communities. Norris (2003) has pointed out, from analysis of online group participation data collected by the Pew Internet and American Life Project in 2001, that it is difficult for interaction in online communities to bridge the gap between people who differ by race and socioeconomic status, but not by age. In particular, women are believed to experience more difficulty in creating online social networks as diverse as their male counterparts, since women are much more likely than men to be harassed (usually sexually) online and subjected to negative feedback from men (Kennedy 2000). At times, the special attention that women receive from male participants makes them feel uncomfortable to actively participate (Herring 2000). At times, women are "flamed" (receive hostile messages), and some are so intimidated by such harassment that they withdraw from online discussions (Collins-Jarvis 1993; Winter and Huff 1996). Therefore, it is expected that women are less likely to create diverse social ties with men, even though they participate in online communities:

H2b: Men increase the diversity of both their male and female networks, while women develop solely female networks when they belong to online communities.

10.4. THE CONSEQUENCE OF SOCIAL CAPITAL: TAKING ACTIONS TO SOLVE COLLECTIVE PROBLEMS

Putnam (1993*a*) claims that networks generate norms of reciprocity and trust. He argues that engagement in voluntary associations promotes social capital (social networks and cultural norms), and in turn, social capital is believed to facilitate civic participation and good governance. This assumes a recursive interaction between social capital and civic engagement. He supports this argument by showing that northern Italy, characterized by a higher level of general trust beyond the family or the group, and a stronger civic tradition, has achieved superior economic development and a more efficient democratic system than southern Italy, which is characterized by strong familism.

10.5. DOES THE DIVERSITY OF CONTACT ENHANCE CIVIC ENGAGEMENT?

Norris (2001) suggests civic engagement can be understood to include three distinct dimensions: political knowledge (what people learn about public affairs), political trust (public support for the political system and its actors), and political participation (conventional and unconventional activities designed to influence government and decision-making processes). In this chapter, we focus on the effect of social capital on political participation. We are particularly interested to know if people with diverse networks are likely to discuss social issues in public to resolve social problems such as those related to education and the environment. People who have diverse networks are more likely to be involved in discussion of social issues than people with less diverse networks, because they have more access to information related to social issues and thereby can gain more knowledge on diverse opinions. They also have more chances to be recruited to participate in these discussions. Moreover, they have opportunities to polish their communications and cooperation skills, both of which are fundamental to civic engagement. We therefore hypothesize that the diversity of contacts enhances civic engagement.

By contrast, revealing one's political orientation in the workplace can be a risky thing to do, for it may invite negative sanctions or alienation in Japan (Ikeda 1997; Ikeda and Richey 2005). We thus hypothesize that Japanese are likely to participate in political activities only if they feel they can trust others to accept their political attitude, and/or if they are confident that they can recognize whom they can trust. As talking politics is risky business, it is hypothesized that it is exchanged only among those who have trustworthy relationships.

It is also supposed that expectations of the norm of generalized reciprocity may be nourished by general exchange in horizontal active associations, especially in the situation of diverse individuals, and it may facilitate political participation in order to resolve social problems. Experience of a positive spiral of reciprocal exchanges in associations among equals, through arrangement, compromise, concession, or consensus building from different opinions, is likely to create a positive attitude for discussion among those who have diverse viewpoints, which in turn becomes a cognitive resource that facilitates active orientation toward political participation.

Of course, the reverse can be true, that is, negative reciprocity may develop among those who have different opinions, such as stimulating conflicts or faction formation. But insofar as the members of the given association share their goals or sense of in-group, we assume that the positive spiral prevails over the possibility of negative reciprocity development. Thus, we hypothesize that people who expect the norm of generalized reciprocity are likely to participate in political activities and discuss social problems in public.

10.6. HOW DOES NETWORK DIVERSITY INFLUENCE TRUST AND RECIPROCITY?

Bonding networks that connect similar people sustain particularized reciprocity and particular trust. It is supposed that by repeated interaction, members may reinforce particularized reciprocity in groups and mobilize solidarity. Moreover, when people have repeated interactions in homogeneous groups with close-knit social networks, they are far less likely to shirk or cheat, and are more likely to develop trust with other members in their group. However, bonding social capital, by creating strong in-group loyalty, may also create strong out-group antagonism.

By contrast, bridging networks that connect diverse individuals sustain a sense of generalized reciprocity and general trust. Through social exchanges among diverse members, people tend to obtain a sense of generalized reciprocity.

Generalized reciprocity refers to the normative recognition that if someone helps another person, he or she will be helped by other people (not only by the person who is helped) in the community or society. This reciprocity, in turn, as if following a positive feedback loop, enhances the level of cooperation in a social dilemma and creates "better than rational" results (Lubell and Scholz 2001).

Furthermore, engagement with politically or socially heterogeneous others nurtures general trust. Yamagishi (1998) argues that individuals who are highly trusting are not only more sensitive to information suggesting the trustworthiness of a specific person, but also can predict more accurately whether or not the person will perform trustworthy actions, compared with persons with low levels of trust. Conversely, those who are neither sensitive to informational clues about the trustworthiness of a partner, nor can predict accurately whether or not the partner actually performs trustworthy actions tend to presume, without any premise, that "it's best to regard everyone as a thief," as stated in a widely used Japanese proverb. Yamagishi claims that trusting other people or human nature in general is different from blindly believing that other people are trustworthy. Rather, to trust others is to have mental composure on the bases of improved sensitivity and skills for discerning trustworthy from untrustworthy people, and to assume, until proven otherwise, that people are generally trustworthy. This point of view implies that to foster general trust it is not necessary to preach the importance of the virtue of trust. What is necessary is to provide opportunities for acquiring social intelligence in a broad sense of the term. We infer that open and diverse networks may provide opportunities to nurture general trust as a form of social intelligence. According to Yamagishi's theory, it is expected that people with diverse networks may show higher levels of general trust than those who have less diverse networks.

Consequently, participation in online communities may develop diverse networks, and may cultivate general trust and the norm of generalized reciprocity among people, not only in online communities but also outside online communities. Moreover, it is supposed that this type of social capital may increase civic engagement.

To explore how civic engagement is fostered by the diversity of networks, perceived norms of generalized reciprocity, and general trust, we propose the following hypothesis:

H3: Diversity of contacts, general trust, and the norm of generalized reciprocity foster civic engagement.

Figure 10.1 shows causes and consequence of social capital. The Internet, social capital, and civic engagement have many common causes. For example, educated people use the net more, and have more diversified networks, and are more active in politics. Such common causes could lead to spurious connections. Thus, we will include the major social background variables in every step of our analysis. This will also add to our understanding of the social sources of Internet use, social capital, and civic engagement in Japan.

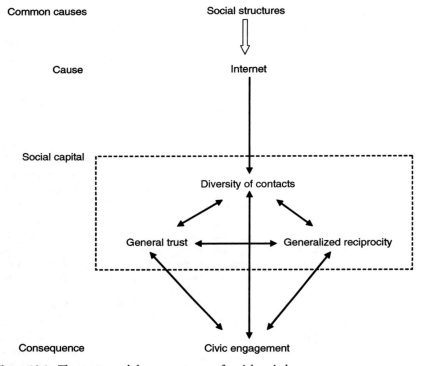

Figure 10.1. The causes and the consequence of social capital

10.7. YAMANASHI STUDY

10.7.1. Method

Our study is based on a random sample survey of 1,320 adults in Yamanashi prefecture in Japan. Yamanashi is a mixed rural and urban area, located in the center of Japan, more than 100 km west of central Tokyo. It is typical of Japan (outside of the Tokyo and Osaka urban agglomerations) in the characteristics of its population and Internet users.

Within Yamanashi prefecture, 40 neighborhoods were randomly selected by postal code. Using the electoral roll, a further random selection of 33 individuals was selected from people aged 20–65 years old within each neighborhood. Paper surveys were delivered and collected in person three weeks later. Three-quarters (75.9%) of the selected individuals completed the survey, giving us a total sample size of 1,002 respondents. This entire process occurred between November and December 2002. The sample consisted of nearly equal numbers of males and females, with a mean period of residence in Yamanashi of 25.44 years. A comparison showed that female respondents were younger, and had received a lower

Table 10.1. Summary of sample characteristics ($N = 1,002$)

Variables	Percentage			Gender difference
	Whole sample	Males	Females	
Gender: males	50.3	—	—	—
Age				
20–29	21.0	20.6	21.3	n.s.
30–39	19.9	19.3	20.5	n.s.
40–49	22.2	24.2	20.1	n.s.
50–59	25.0	24.8	25.1	n.s.
60–65	12.1	11.1	13.1	n.s.
Education				
High school or less	58.0	58.3	57.7	n.s.
Some college	22.3	12.8	31.9	**
Graduate degrees or More	19.7	28.9	10.4	**
Marital status				
Single	23.5	25.0	21.9	n.s.
Married without a child	6.5	6.2	6.8	n.s.
Married with a child who is living	53.1	52.8	53.4	n.s.
Married with a child who is living apart	12.8	11.5	14.1	n.s.
Other type	3.5	3.6	3.4	n.s.
DK/NA	0.7	1.0	0.4	n.s.
Employment status				
Working full time	57.1	80.2	33.7	**
Working part time	13.4	4.0	22.9	**
Student	2.0	1.8	2.2	n.s.
Home maker	14.3	0.0	28.7	n.s.
Other type	8.6	9.7	7.4	n.s.
Unemployed	3.9	4.2	3.6	n.s.
Don't know/No answer	0.8	0.2	1.4	*

$N = 1,002$.
* $p < .05$; ** $p < .01$

education level than males. A summary of respondent characteristics is shown in Table 10.1.

10.7.2. Results

10.7.2.1. Gendered Diversity of Networks

First, we constructed an index from the position-generator items for "diversity of contacts" using different hierarchical positions in Japanese society, to measure the diversity of networks. Respondents were asked to indicate if they had any relatives, friends, or acquaintances in any of 15 categories of diverse occupations for each gender. We used the prestige ratings for Japanese occupations constructed from the Social Stratification and Mobility datasets, which were collected in 1985 and 1995. The sampled positions had prestige scores ranging from 90.1 to 38.1, and

Table 10.2. Summary of position-generated variables in the whole sample

Accessed positions	Prestige		Mean or percent		
	Score[a]	% Female[b]	Diversity of contacts with		
			Anyone	Men	Women
Physician	90.1	19.35%	34.5	32.3	7.5
Owner of large company	87.3	—	12.2	12.1	0.6
Lawyer	87.3	10.40%	3.3	2.9	0.5
Congressperson	74.9	9.00%	7.2	6.9	0.7
Journalist/editor	63.2	27.81%	9.8	8.5	3.0
Teacher (elementary school)	64.6	62.47%	49.8	37.6	31.9
Manager of large company	63.7	2.52%	17.3	17.1	0.9
Nurse	59.7	95.69%	55.5	10.1	52.9
Policeman	57.9	4.12%	33.6	33.3	2.5
Computer programmer	54.6	14.97%	34.2	30.7	8.2
Owner of a shop	51.3	20.02%	56.1	50.4	20.5
Bus driver	48.9	0.50%	16.4	16.1	0.5
Mail carrier	46.2	10.04%	24.4	24.0	0.8
Janitor	39.9	3.48%	10.4	10.2	0.6
Restaurant waiter/waitress	38.1	67.00%	20.1	6.9	17.8

$N = 1,001$.

[a] The data of Social Stratification and Mobility (SSM) surveys that were held in 1995 and 1985.

[b] The data of census in 1995 and wage census in 2001.

can be roughly grouped into three classes: the upper class (high-status professionals such as physicians, lawyers, owners of large companies, and congresspersons); the middle class (middle-level professionals such as elementary school teachers, nurses, and policemen); and the lower class (bus drivers, janitors, and restaurant waiters/waitresses).

We measured the diversity of contacts by counting the number of different occupational categories selected by each respondent, yielding a score from 0 to 15 for each gender, with a higher score indicating greater diversity of contact. As shown in Table 10.2, the respondents accessed almost four sampled positions on average, and they were more likely to access male positions than female positions.

We examined in detail the data of the diversity of contacts, that is, the number of positions accessed. More than half of the respondents (50.4%) answered that they knew a male shop owner. About a third of the respondents had access to a male teacher (37.6%), a male policeman (33.3%), a male physician (32.3%), and a male computer programmer (30.7%). The least accessible positions included a lawyer (2.9%), a politician (6.9%), and a journalist/editor (8.5%). By contrast, for female positions, the respondents had access to nurses (52.9%) and teachers (31.9%).

We explored the differences of social capital between males and females. As shown in Table 10.3, males tend to access more positions, which shows the same tendency as the findings in Taiwan (Lin, Fu, and Hsung 2001). This result suggests

Table 10.3. Means of diversity of contacts by gender of respondents

Respondent gender	Diversity of contacts with				Comparison of male and female
	Anyone	Men	Women	N	
All respondents	3.835	2.978	1.475	1,001	$t = 20.546$**
Female	3.53	2.42	1.68	498	$t = 8.02$**
Male	4.14	3.53	1.24	503	$t = 21.90$**
Comparison of male and female respondents' means*	$t = 3.24$**	$t = 6.57$**	$t = 4.68$**	—	—

Entries are means.

* All t-tests were two tailed.

** $p < .01$.

that the structure of social capital is essentially different for males and females, which supports H1a. Men have higher rates of labor force participation and hence more often have occupations, and further, men are more frequently in the more powerful occupations that lead to many contacts. Hence, Japan shows a great extent of gender segregation and male dominance in social networks.

Table 10.3 also indicates that females are less likely to access male positions, but compared with male respondents they access more female positions. For example, females are more likely to access female teachers, nurses, shop owners, and waitresses. This indicates that while females are generally disadvantaged in accessing many positions, they tend to access female social networks, which are related to the spheres of education, health, and household activities. By contrast, males are less likely to access female positions, but they access more male positions than female respondents. All these results support H1b.

As noted earlier, while there are some superficial similarities, the structure of social capital is essentially different for males and females. Females are generally disadvantaged in terms of the resources embedded in social networks. Social capital, which is useful for achievements in the labor force, is heavily biased toward males. Although females are relatively advantaged in social capital that concerns education for children, health care, and household maintenance, these spheres are limited to private lives. Although the female's advantage in social capital in private lives can be useful for psychological well-being, it cannot lead to advantages for them in more socially expanded areas such as the labor market.

Since social capital is a gendered construct, all subsequent analyses are conducted separately for males and females.

10.7.2.2. The Effect of Internet Use on Diversity of Contacts

In order to verify H2a and H2b, we investigated the factors that affected the diversity of contacts with others using multiple regression analysis. In addition to social structural variables, we included Internet use variables in order to investigate how Internet use influences gendered social capital.

Dependent Variables

Diversity of contacts with males was measured by counting the number of occupations in which the respondent had any male acquaintances. Accordingly, the range of the variable was 0–15.

Diversity of contacts with females was measured by counting the number of occupations in which the respondents had any female acquaintances. Accordingly, the range of the variable was 0–15.

Independent Variables:
Social Structures

The demographic biases in personal social capital have already been noted (Lin Fu, and Hsung 2001; Inglehart and Norris 2003; Erickson 2004). For example, Erickson (2004) shows that work and family life increase cross-gender contacts. However, whether these findings can be applied in Japan has not yet been verified. Using the fundamental demographic variables, we examined the demographic biases in personal social capital in Japan.

Age was measured by an ordered scale. Respondents aged 20–29 were coded as 1, 30–39 as 2, 40–49 as 3, 50–59 as 4, and over 60 as 5. Each of the categories was transformed into categorical variables. The reference category was those aged 20–29(1).

Education was measured using an ordered scale (1: elementary school, 2: junior high school, 3: high school, 4: junior college/technical college/former high school, 5: university, 6: graduate school).

Years of residence: Years of residence in one location was measured directly by asking the respondents how many years they had lived in that area (city).

Full-time employed: A dummy variable was generated to measure if the respondent was employed full time or not (1: employed full time, 2: not employed full time).

Married: Using the items for marital status, a dummy variable was created that indicated respondents' marital status (1: married, 0: single).

Having children: Using the items about marital status, a dummy variable was created to indicate if respondents had children. This variable does not take into account whether respondents live together with their children.

Internet use:

PC e-mails: Whether respondents use e-mail by PC was measured as a dummy variable. Around 36 percent of the respondents used PC e-mail.

Participation in online communities: The number of online communities the respondents participated in was measured by directly asking a number of communities across nine categories shown in Table 10.4. Online communities refer to mailing lists (listservs), Bulletin Board Systems, and chat groups.

While 9 percent of the male respondents participated in online communities, only 5.6 percent of the female respondents participated. Table 10.4 describes

Table 10.4. Percentages of participation in online communities

Types of online communities	Percentage			Chi-squared
	Whole sample	Males	Females	
Fan groups for a particular TV show, entertainer, musical groups	2.30	1.59	3.01	4.583*
Fan groups for particular sport or sports team	1.60	1.79	1.41	0.000
Groups of people who share your life-style	0.80	0.60	1.00	1.176
Support groups, such as for medical condition, child-raising or personal situation	0.70	0.40	1.00	2.230
Groups of people who share information related to your work or study	4.69	6.94	2.41	7.008**
Groups of people who share information related to the region you live in	0.60	0.99	0.20	1.800
Groups of people who share information related to politics and news	0.40	0.60	0.20	0.571
A group for people who share a particular hobby, interest or activity	4.09	4.76	3.41	0.088
Other groups	1.10	1.19	1.00	0.015

$p < .05$; $p < .01$.

participation rates for men and women. Male respondents were more likely to participate in groups of people who shared information related to their work or study than female respondents ($\chi^2 = 7.008$, $p < .01$). By contrast, female respondents participated more in fan clubs for TV shows, popular entertainers, and musical groups than male respondents ($\chi^2 = 4.583$, $p < .05$). Because the summary scale was severely skewed, we broke it down into dummy variables for regression analysis.

Table 10.5 shows the results of multiple regressions predicting the diversity of contacts with others. The four columns on the left side show the results of the male respondents. As can be seen, among the social structural variables, age and education showed consistent effects on the diversity of contacts with others.

Those aged in their 40s, 50s, or 60s significantly enhanced the diversity of contacts. The diversity of contacts for men and women rises to a peak in the 50s and then falls. Those in mid-life are active in many spheres of work, family, and social life, which gives them the greatest range of opportunities to meet a diversity of people (Erickson 2004).

Highly educated men also had more diverse contacts both with males and with females. This is because higher-level educational settings usually include a variety of students and staff.

Years at place of residence had negative effects on the diversity of contacts with females. This means that living for a longer time in the same place makes one's personal network more homogeneous, which decreases cross-gender social ties. Since Japanese women are often housewives, they may tend to make contacts with other women around the neighborhood, and help their husbands to meet people in the neighborhood as well. If they have lived a long time in one area, they are

Table 10.5. Multiple regressions for diversity of contacts

	Coefficient (B)							
	Male respondents				Female respondents			
	Dependent: diversity of contacts with male		Dependent: diversity of contacts with female		Dependent: diversity of contacts with male		Dependent: diversity of contacts with female	
	Model 1	Model 2	Model 1	Model 2	Model 1	Model 2	Model 1	model 2
Age (reference = 20–29)								
30–39	0.72	0.74	0.02	0.03	0.21	0.20	0.18	0.18
40–49	0.95*	1.02*	0.18	0.20	−0.10	−0.13	−0.15	−0.16
50–59	1.71**	1.70**	0.54*	0.56*	0.59	0.55	0.12	0.10
60–65	1.55*	1.56*	0.58+	0.61+	0.19	0.14	0.34	0.33
Education	0.36*	0.36**	0.21**	0.20**	0.68**	0.70**	0.38**	0.39**
Years of residence	−0.01	−0.01	−0.01**	−0.01**	0.01	0.01	0.01	0.01
Full-time employed	0.49	0.47	0.05	0.04	0.76**	0.79**	0.12	0.13
Married without a child	0.29	0.33	−0.25	−0.25	1.06**	1.03**	−0.04	−0.05
Having a child	0.09	0.13	0.26	0.27	−0.38	−0.38	0.03	0.03
PC e-mails	0.30	—	0.02	—	0.07	—	0.03	—
Participation in online communities	—	1.04*	—	0.33	—	−0.52	—	−0.24
Constant	0.67	0.63	0.59+	0.59+	−1.19+	−1.15+	0.14	0.16
Observations	484	484	484	484	481	482	481	482
R^2	0.07	0.08	0.05	0.05	0.10	0.10	0.06	0.06
Adjusted R^2	0.05	0.06	0.03	0.03	0.08	0.09	0.04	0.04

$N = 1,002$.

$+ p < .10$; * $p < .05$; ** $p < .01$.

likely to know everyone they meet (neighbors, shop attendants, and so on). If they move their residence elsewhere, however, they will have new opportunities for local encounters.

Among the Internet use variables, the only significant effect was of participation in online communities on the diversity of contacts with males.

By contrast, the four columns on the right side show some significant results for female respondents. Among social structural variables, education had a consistent effect on the diversity of contacts with others. More highly educated women may meet a greater variety of people at universities, and they may attain higher-level work where they meet not only women but men. This result may also reflect the education system in Japan. We hypothesize that women may have more chances of meeting men during classes in universities, since most universities are coed. On the contrary, it may be difficult for women who attend only junior colleges or high schools to create cross-gendered ties in schools, since many of them are not coed.

Being a full-time employee and being married enhanced the diversity of contacts with males. Females obtained various cross-gender ties through working with males in full-time labor, and also through marriage by incorporating their husbands' same-gender networks (e.g. husbands' male friends or acquaintances) into their own. The Internet use variables did not have any significant effects on the diversity of contacts with others for females.

In sum, the Internet use variable for PC e-mail use did not have a significant effect on diversity of contacts with others among men and women. We think this is because the use of PC e-mail is useful in maintaining established social ties rather than making new ties. Merely using PC e-mail is not enough even for males to gain a diversity of contacts with others. Rather, males can enrich their social capital through collective communication in online communities, such as sharing interests or hobbies and exchanging information. All of these results support H2a and H2b among male respondents.

Why was the participation in online communities insignificant except for diversity of male-to-male contacts?

First, we hypothesize that both sexes have fewer opportunities to meet with women than men in online communities, since fewer females than males participate. Moreover, we hypothesize that female participants may also be less likely to have contacts with men than with other women, since they may fear receiving harassment from men. By contrast, we hypothesize that men may have more chances to have contact with other men, since they are more likely to be recruited within these male-dominated communities.

Second, men participated in online communities that differed from those in which women participated. Table 10.4 shows that men tended to join online communities of people who share information and study, while women tended to participate in online fan clubs for TV shows, popular entertainers, and musical groups. By using a position generator to measure the diversity of contacts, which counted resources structurally embedded within occupational hierarchies, we found that men who participated in online communities related to their work and study had more concern with and chances to develop social networks with people with occupations different from their own. It is expected that male respondents may have fewer opportunities for contact with female participants than male participants, since these online communities are male-dominant.

Third, we hypothesize that women have less diverse contacts, because female participants may be less active in online communities than male participants. When people merely read others' messages and do not post any message in online communities, they are not considered a participant, and other participants cannot provide them with any opportunity for communication. Miyata (2002) showed that participants who did not post any message on a supportive online community over a three-month period received less support from other participants than people who posted a message.

10.8. CIVIC ENGAGEMENT

To verify H3, we conducted multiple regressions predicting civic engagement. In addition to the social structural variables, the Internet use variables and the diversity of contacts with others, general trust, and generalized reciprocity were also included as independent variables.

10.8.1. Dependent Variables

Civic engagement: To measure civic engagement, respondents were asked to select a response on a three-point scale to the question: "Have you ever engaged in activities or formal meetings in order to talk about the following issues in the past five years? (Rarely, about once a month, at least once a week)." We listed five issues: region, community, education, welfare, consumerism, and environment. We summed up these five items to construct a civic engagement variable (Cronbach's $\alpha = 0.85$). Table 10.6 indicates that there was no gender difference in civic engagement.

Table 10.6. Means of civic engagement, general trust, and generalized reciprocity by gender

	Male	Female	t-test
Civic engagement	7.44 (2.80)	7.30 (2.95)	0.76
General trust	2.45 (0.86)	2.36 (0.87)	1.50
Generalized reciprocity	2.18 (0.97)	2.29 (0.92)	−1.93

$N = 1,002$.
* $p < .05$; ** $p < .01$.
Entries are means. ( ) are S.D.

10.8.2. Independent Variables

General trust: General trust off-line was measured by one item, used by most researchers: "Most people are trustworthy." This is very much like the World Values Survey item. This item was measured on a four-point scale: "1: agree, 2: somewhat agree, 3: somewhat disagree, 4: disagree."

Generalized reciprocity: Generalized reciprocity was measured by one item. "If I provide useful help and information to someone, somebody will help me when I need help." The item was measured on a four-point scale similar to that used to measure general trust.

Gender difference of general trust and generalized reciprocity is shown in Table 10.6. We did not find any gender difference in either general trust or generalized reciprocity.

Table 10.7 shows the result of the regression analysis. Age had a significant and strong effect on civic engagement, with people becoming more active as they enter middle age, among both men and women. Younger people may have less concern about issues in their society. Moreover, they may also be too busy to participate in meetings to solve problems in communities because of their work and social activities related to work.

Years of residence had a consistently significant effect on civic engagement among men and women. The longer they live in the same area, the greater their concern for social issues and chances for civic engagement in their communities.

Being highly educated also enhanced civic engagement, except in models 1 and 2 for male respondents. This exception is due to the relatively high correlation between PC e-mail use and education in male respondents ($r = .39$).

Among the Internet use variables, PC e-mail use and participation in online communities had significant direct effects on civic engagement only for male respondents. Controlling the diversity of contacts with men and women, male users of PC e-mail were more likely to engage in civic activities than nonusers. This indicates that male users may keep in touch with other members by e-mail in order to engage in political activities; for example, to arrange meetings.

Participation in online communities also has a significant effect on civic engagement for men once the diversity of contacts was controlled for men. We hypothesize that men who participate in online communities have more interests related to social and political issues. Furthermore, by communicating in online communities, they may be motivated to attend meetings and present their opinions related to these issues. However, for female respondents, the Internet use variables did not have any direct effect on civic engagement. These results suggest that online communities may provide a new arena for those already civically involved to pursue their interests.

Diversity of contacts with others had consistently significant effects on civic engagement for men and women. The more diverse the respondent's personal network, the more they were civically engaged. People with diverse networks develop their interests in various social issues and receive information on social issues through communication with a variety of people. They are also likely to

Table 10.7. Multiple regressions for civic engagement

Dependent: civic engagement

	Coefficient (B)							
	Male respondents				Female respondents			
	Model 1	Model 2	Model 3	Model 4	Model 1	Model 2	Model 3	Model 4
Age (reference = 20–29)								
30–39	-0.17	0.04	-0.20	0.00	0.57	0.56	0.55	0.54
40–49	0.63	0.82*	0.69+	0.90*	1.61**	1.63**	1.57**	1.60**
50–59	1.04*	1.29**	0.88*	1.13**	1.42**	1.48**	1.37**	1.43**
60–65	1.58**	1.75**	1.41*	1.57**	1.80**	1.75**	1.73**	1.69**
Education	0.14	0.13	0.24*	0.24*	0.56**	0.58**	0.59**	0.60**
Years of residence	0.02*	0.02**	0.02*	0.02**	0.03**	0.03**	0.03**	0.03**
Full-time employed	-0.50	-0.40	-0.44	-0.33	-0.34	-0.27	-0.33	-0.25
Married without a child	0.56	0.74+	0.68+	0.87*	0.14	0.31	0.15	0.32
Having a child	0.08	-0.03	0.13	0.04	0.37	0.30	0.38	0.31
PC e-mails	0.88**	0.95**	—	—	0.18	0.19	—	—
Participation in online communities	—	—	0.87*	1.01*	—	—	0.04	0.02
Diversity of contacts with male	0.29**	—	0.28**	—	0.14*	—	0.15*	—
Diversity of contacts with female	—	0.46**	—	0.45**	—	0.23*	—	0.23*
General trust	0.35**	0.43**	0.36**	0.45**	0.05	0.06	0.06	0.07
Generalized reciprocity	0.02	0.05	0.02	0.05	0.10	0.10	0.10	0.10
Constant	-1.46*	-1.81**	-1.67*	-2.03**	-2.49**	-2.71**	-2.53**	-2.76**
Observations	480	480	480	480	471	471	472	472
R^2	0.27	0.24	0.26	0.23	0.14	0.14	0.14	0.14
Adjusted R^2	0.25	0.22	0.24	0.21	0.12	0.11	0.12	0.11

$N = 1,002$.

$^+ p < .10$; $^* p < .05$; $^{**} p < .01$.

be recruited to participate in meetings in which they may be active participants in discussing social issues. Moreover, they may have more chances to develop the necessary communication skills for engaging in political activities.

Among social capital variables, general trust had a consistently significant effect only for male respondents. Men with a higher level of general trust were likely to engage in social and political activities. Japanese men frequently have more important social roles such as full-time employment in higher level jobs where talking politics are risky thing to do as was mentioned previously. Thus, they are politically active only if they feel they can trust others to accept their politics, and/or if they are confident that they can discern who to trust. On the contrary, general trust was not a significant predictor of civic engagement for women. Japanese women may perceive the prospect of publicly discussing their opinions as risky, and hesitate to engage in political activities since, compared with men, they are not trained to engage in these activities. Further, we need to examine the interactive effects between general trust and cognition on the risks of civic engagement for women.

By contrast, generalized reciprocity did not have any significant effect on civic engagement, apart from a few exceptional marginal effects, for both men and women. This is due to the fact that we measured the political activities as civic engagement. People may experience more conflict of opinions when they actively present their opinions. Since people who assume operation of the norm of generalized reciprocity are likely to cooperate and try to resolve social problems (Putnam 2000), we do not expect to see a relationship between generalized reciprocity and social or political activities. Therefore, H3 was supported partially.

10.9. THE RELATIONSHIP BETWEEN THREE FORMS OF SOCIAL CAPITAL

According to Putnam's theory, the diversity of networks fosters both general trust and generalized reciprocity. To explore the relationship between three forms of social capital, we conducted multiple regressions for general trust and generalized reciprocity. Table 10.8 shows that the diversity of contacts with other men was a statistically significant predictor of general trust for men when controlling for social structural variables, while the diversity of contacts with women had no effect on general trust. It implies that men who have more chances for establishing contacts with a variety of other men from diverse occupations will develop general trust as social intelligence. However, the networks with women may not be sufficiently diverse to foster general trust. We infer from our result that highly educated men had higher levels of general trust, and that men may improve sensitivity and skills for discerning trustworthy from untrustworthy people.

Among female respondents, we did not find any effect of diverse contacts on general trust. Since the diversity of contacts for women is less than for men (see

Table 10.8. Multiple regressions for general trust and generalized reciprocity

	Coefficient (B)							
	Male respondents				Female respondents			
	Dependent: general trust		Dependent: generalized reciprocity		Dependent: general trust		Dependent: generalized reciprocity	
	Model 1	Model 2	Model 1	Model 2	Model 1	Model 2	Model 1	Model 2
Age (reference = 20–29)								
30–39	−0.10	−0.08	0.01	0.02	0.12	0.12	0.10	0.11
40–49	−0.05	−0.02	0.05	0.06	0.15	0.15	0.10	0.10
50–59	−0.11	−0.06	0.00	0.02	−0.07	−0.06	−0.06	−0.06
60–65	−0.07	−0.03	0.18	0.21	0.11	0.10	0.14	0.15
Education	0.09*	0.10*	0.04	0.05	0.06	0.06	0.08	0.09
Years of residence	0.00	0.00	0.00	0.00	0.00	0.00	0.00	0.00
Full-time employed	−0.02	−0.01	0.19+	0.20+	0.25**	0.27**	0.19*	0.19*
Married without a child	0.22	0.23	0.10	0.11	0.09	0.13	0.25	0.24
Having a child	0.03	0.03	−0.06	−0.06	0.05	0.04	−0.14	−0.14
Diversity of contacts with male	0.03*	—	0.02	—	0.03	—	0.00	—
Diversity of contacts with female	—	0.01	—	0.00	—	0.04	—	−0.03
Constant	1.94**	1.95**	1.83**	1.84**	1.81**	1.77**	1.75**	1.75**
Observations	483	483	484	484	478	478	477	477
R^2	0.04	0.03	0.02	0.02	0.04	0.04	0.03	0.03
Adjusted R^2	0.02	0.01	0.00	0.00	0.02	0.02	0.01	0.01

$N = 1,002$.

$+ p < .10$; $* p < .05$; $** p < .01$.

Table 10.2), it is suspected that their networks may not be sufficiently diverse to foster general trust.

In contrast to general trust, diversity of contacts with others is not a useful predictor of generalized reciprocity, even when controlling for social structural variables. The norm of generalized reciprocity is expected to be encouraged by general exchange in well-organized horizontal and active associations or communities, which consist of a variety of people (Putnam 2000). However, in this survey the diversity of contacts was measured by the position generator, which counts the number of occupations with different levels of prestige in which the respondent knows someone. Hence, we may not find any effect of diversity of contacts on generalized reciprocity, since the position generator may not be a suitable means for measuring interactivity among diverse people, regardless of their positions.

In Figures 10.2–10.5, we show the relation between participation in online communities, social capital, and civic engagement based on our results.

Figure 10.2 shows that for male respondents, participation in online communities increases the diversity of their ties to men, which in turn facilitates civic engagement and general trust. Through their experiences of social interaction in online communities, they may obtain information and increase their interest related to social issues. At the same time, since they may be sensitive to others in terms of the trustworthiness they gain through their interaction with men who have different positions, they may develop general trust. Accordingly, they are likely to engage in civic activities.

Figure 10.3 indicates, however, that participation in online communities does not have a significant effect on diversity of contacts with women, since they have fewer opportunities to meet women from various occupations in online communities. It also indicates that the diversity of networks that include women fosters civic engagement, not general trust, among male respondents. It suggests that men who have diverse networks that include women may have more chances to be recruited by women to attend meetings to resolve community problems. However, their networks with women may not be sufficiently diverse to nurture general trust as social intelligence, compared with networks that include men. Additionally, an expectation of generalized reciprocity was not developed in social interaction with various people, and it did not nurture civic engagement. Since the norm of generalized reciprocity is assumed to be cultivated in horizontal relationships, connections to people with a different hierarchical position may not contribute for the formation of such norm. This also implies that generalized reciprocity may facilitate cooperation that does not involve political activities, such as presenting opinions in a public forum.

Figures 10.4 and 10.5 indicate that women do not build diverse networks even when they participate in online communities, and participation in online communities does not nourish their civic engagement. This is because women are less likely to participate in online communities that focus on social and political issues. Furthermore, women may have fewer chances to build diverse networks with others, since they may be less active in online communities. These figures also suggest that general trust may not be nourished by social interaction with various

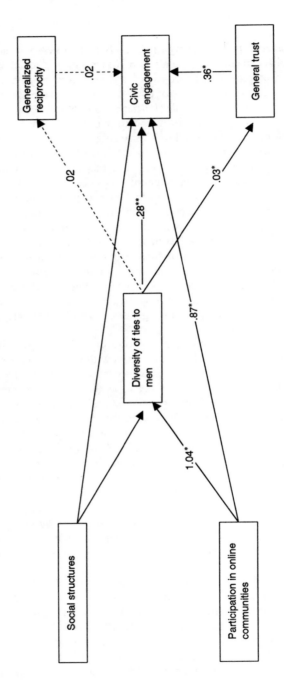

Figure 10.2. Path model between social capital and civic engagement (male respondents)

Note: Solid lines illustrate statistical significance ($p < .05$). Dashed lines indicate that variables are not significantly related. * $p < .05$; ** $p < .01$

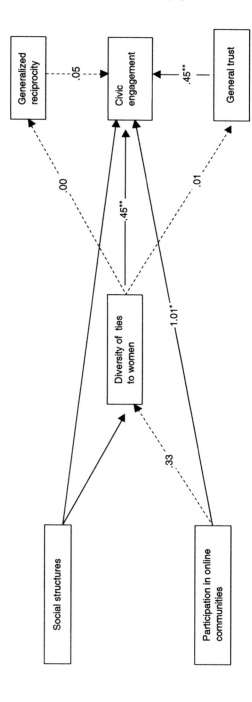

Figure 10.3. Path model between social capital and civic engagement (male respondents)

Note: Solid lines illustrate statistical significance ($p < .05$). Dashed lines indicate that variables are not significantly related. * $p < .05$; ** $p < .01$

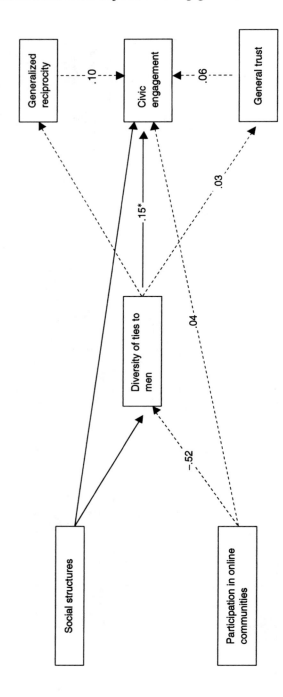

Figure 10.4. Path model between social capital and civic engagement (female respondents)

Note: Solid lines illustrate statistical significance ($p < .05$). Dashed lines indicate that variables are not significantly related. * $p < .05$; ** $p < .01$

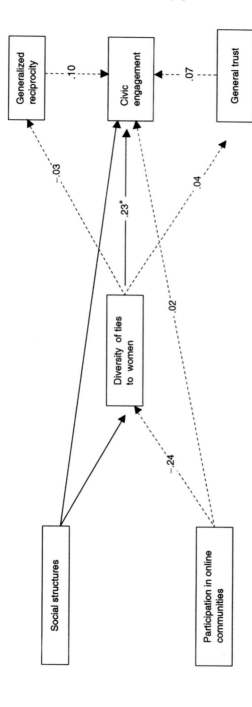

Figure 10.5. Path model between social capital and civic engagement (female respondents)

Note: Solid lines illustrate statistical significance (*p* < .05). Dashed lines indicate that variables are not significantly related. * *p* < .05; ** *p* < .01

people, and it may not impel women to engage in political activities. Therefore, there may be a gender difference in terms of how diversity of contacts enhances civic engagement.

10.10. DISCUSSION

First, our results confirm the notion of gendered social capital in Japan: there are many strong and interesting gender differences.

The results show that people generate more same-gender than cross-gender ties. In other words, men know a greater diversity of men than women do, and women know a greater diversity of women than men do. This is because people encounter those of their own gender more often, and they prefer people of their own gender (Erickson 2004). Our finding also confirms that both men and women know a wider variety of men than women. Men have higher rates of labor force participation, hence more occupational diversity, and further, men are often in the more powerful occupations that entail a greater number of contacts. Consequently, men are overrepresented in the networks of both men and women (Erickson and Miyata 2004).

Second, we found that participation in online communities can develop the diversity of participants' networks. However, the Internet functions differently for women and men. When men participate in online communities, they increase their diversity of contacts with men; however, they do not develop their networks with women. By contrast, online communities do not provide women with the opportunities to form diverse networks not only in a cross-gender sense, but also in a same-gender sense.

It can be assumed that men are more likely to be recruited by these male-dominated communities, since there are more male than female participants. Hence, men tend to increase their opportunities to develop diverse male networks. However, because of the low number of female participants, their female networks do not increase. By contrast, since there are fewer female participants in online communities than males, women have fewer opportunities to form female networks even if they join a community. Moreover, men and women differ in how Internet activity affects them. It is also possible that women who take some part in these communities are less active and less self-confident than men, and that men simply ignore women more than men. Furthermore, since women are less likely to participate in online communities related to work than men, they have fewer chances of making contacts with various people with diverse occupations.

In the future, if women's participation in online communities increases, they may increase the diversity of women's networks. However, it is expected that women may not increase the diversity of their male networks if they continue to be less active in online communities, or if they prefer contact with the same gender online to avoid flaming from men. Investigation is required to see if the prevalence of male-dominated flaming has decreased as Internet use has spread into the general population (Kennedy, Wellman, and Klement 2003).

Third, our findings show that diversity of contacts also facilitates civic engagement for both men and women. People with diverse networks develop interests in various social issues, and receive information on social issues through communication with a variety of people. They are also likely to be recruited to participate in meetings at which they may be active participants in discussing social issues. Moreover, we found indirect paths from a variety of networks to civic engagement through general trust among male respondents. This means that men with diverse networks tend to trust other people and enjoy presenting their opinions and discussing social issues with others. However, we did not find any indirect paths from diversity of contacts to civic engagement through general trust among female respondents. We suspect women do not have enough diverse networks to develop general trust as social intelligence compared with men, and even though they show high levels of general trust, they hesitate to engage in political activities.

In contrast to general trust, the results show that there is no indirect path from diversity of contacts to civic engagement through expectations of the norm of generalized reciprocity. We measured the activities in political participation as civic engagement. People may experience more conflict of opinions when they are active in presenting their opinion. Therefore, even though they expect generalized reciprocity, there are no effects of reciprocity in discussions of social issues.

Fourth, the results controlling for social capital show participants in online communities are more likely than nonparticipants to engage in civic activities, and that the Internet provides a platform for a significant number of additional civic activities. These finding are consistent with previous studies. For example, Hampton and Wellman (2002) revealed that free high-speed Internet access allows people to maintain social ties with physically distant contacts, and suggested that the Internet may facilitate users' commitments to their communities. Katz and Rice (2002) also show that Internet usage is associated with increased community and political involvement. Moreover, Norris (2004) found that use of the Internet was significantly associated with cause-oriented forms of political activism, such as buying or boycotting products for political reasons and signing petitions from the 19-nation European Social Survey. Thus, our results support the utopian vision of the Internet drawing people into civic engagement in a larger capacity. Through the Internet, individuals have a chance to form opinions that are understandable to a broad audience and to polish their skills of coordinating exchanges (Rheingold 2000). These are both fundamental abilities for citizens in affluent social capital communities, especially when traditional communication barriers are likely to melt away. In other words, the Internet is thought to hold promise as a mechanism facilitating alternative channels of civic engagement, thereby revitalizing mass participation in public affairs. It is supposed that the Internet functions like the Agora in supplying social capital as well as a forum for informal and formal voluntary associations. Further, there is a need to explore whether the Internet may provide tools to increase the engagement of those already involved, or encourage civic engagement in users who had previously shown no interest in such matters.

10.11. CONCLUSION

We found that social capital is unequally distributed. We also found that participation in online communities enhances diversity of social networks, while e-mail does not have the same effect. This means that online communities may play a vital role in the production of social capital when they succeed in bridging diverse social differences by integrating people with diverse backgrounds and values. Although we expected that participation in online communities would equally enhance social capital among men and women, online communities had this effect only among male respondents. Furthermore, the more that men participate in online communities, the more their male networks are diversified, and as a result they have an advantage of resources that they can utilize. Since there are such a large number of male participants, this process will continue to grow exponentially.

For female participants, however, their small numbers ensure that their networks will not increase in diversity, even if they join an online community. Although active involvement in associations is said to increase the diversity of contacts regardless of gender (Erickson 2004), online communities seem to facilitate the gender gap for social capital.

In summary, men who are already advantaged in social capital can increase their social capital when they participate in online communities, and the Internet may increase gender difference in social capital. In the future, it will be important to create communities that will increase women's participation, which would in turn increase the variety of women's networks.

In this study, we examined whether participation in online communities had an effect on diversity of contacts and civic engagement. However, we did not examine activities within online communities, since not many of our respondents were participants. It will be necessary to examine how the influence differs depending on the structure of the online community (e.g. the ratio of male/female participants) and its central theme. Norris (2003) argues that the effects of participation in online communities depend on the nature of such communities. She suggests that participation in them has two functions: to strengthen social bonds among those with homogeneous interests and backgrounds and to strengthen social bridges among those with heterogeneous interests and backgrounds. The experience of online contacts among ethnic-cultural groups and groups sharing a similar lifestyle rated highest in both functions, while contact with sports groups was perceived to generate the lowest in both functions.

In our analysis, we cannot establish the direction of causality in these models. With a single cross-sectional survey, it is impossible to disentangle the notion that social capital encourages civic engagement from the notion that prior habit of civic engagement leads to social capital via the Internet. For example, Uslaner (2002) shows that volunteering and giving to charity, both of which link us to people who are different from ourselves, are strongly related to general trust. Thus, our next step should be to undertake a causal analysis using panel data to trace paths of influence consistent with our hypotheses. Using panel data allows us to confirm the causal direction of effect of social capital. If the change of civic engagement, which is measured in the second wave, is predicted by social capital in the first wave, we can more confidently infer the causal direction, which is not possible in this chapter. Further, we have to examine the accumulation of social capital. If some people are continually using the Internet in collective ways, we can expect the social capital of those people to be enhanced in the second wave. We should also check the stability of the measurement of social capital, as the stability of social capital over time is important in ensuring the validity of research.

ACKNOWLEDGMENTS

The authors would like to express their greatest thanks to Professor Bonnie H. Erickson for her major role in creating the questionnaire and offering useful comments. We also thank Professor Nan Lin for his useful comments. Research for this study has been supported by grants from the Japan Society for the Promotion of Science, KAKENHI15330137.

11

Social Capital of Personnel Managers: Causes and Return of Position-Generated Networks and Participation in Voluntary Associations

Ray-May Hsung and Yi-Jr Lin

11.1. INTRODUCTION

Social capital is an individual asset embedded in the resources of personal networks that are accessed and mobilized for purposive actions by individuals (Lin 1999*a*; Lin, Cook, and Burt 2001*a*: 12). It was conceived as an individual asset, mainly because the investment in personal networks was expected to provide the return in career development, such as the return of status attainment and income.

There are different ways of measuring social capital. Position-generated networks (Lin and Dumin 1986; Lin, Fu, and Hsung 2001) have been used more often than name-generated networks as a measurement of social capital (Marsden 1987; Hsung 2001). Because position-generated networks can elicit various contacts (relatives, friends, and acquaintances) and various occupations (the distribution of occupations), the resources of contacts are widely distributed. However, name-generated networks mostly elicit the intimate networks that explain expressive actions better than instrumental actions. Position-generated networks are better predictors of the prestige and income return of current jobs (Lin, Fu, and Hsung 2001). In addition to the personal resources embedded in position-generated networks, voluntary associations are important sources for building social contacts and gaining information and support through participation in work-related clubs and associations. This study includes measurements of participation in voluntary associations as well.

Social capital is more useful for goal attainment by employees at higher levels. Erickson (2001) found that greater network diversity increased the probability of being managers for employees in the security industry. Participation in voluntary associations is also important for managers. The number of memberships of clubs and professional organizations also had an independent effect on income for top managers in the Netherlands (Boxman, De Graaf, and Flap 1991). Diverse social capital is especially advantageous for the performance and return of personnel managers. So, this chapter examines the causes and return of social capital for 126 personnel managers in the export processing zones (EPZs) and one science park (SP) in Taiwan as measured by position-generated networks and participation in voluntary associations.

11.2. SOCIAL CAPITAL: THE FORM OF NETWORK DIVERSITY

Social capital is the function of social networks. The return of network diversity is significant for the instrumental actions of individuals. The investment in social networks can come from the personal networks of daily life and participation in voluntary associations. Position-generated networks have been widely used to elicit the social contacts that people can access from their past social life. Participation in voluntary associations was conceived as social capital in public fields. The diversity of position-generated networks has been widely tested as an effective investment for income return. The variety of civic engagement was conceived as a collective asset (trust) for producing effective democracy. Recently, the instrumental function of participation in voluntary associations has been noted.

11.2.1. Position-Generated Networks

Social capital was conceived as individual assets embedded in the resources of personal networks. Erickson (2004) defined the individual asset as the "array of resources belonging to the person's contacts and potentially available to the person through these contacts." From this definition, social capital includes the array of primary and secondary contacts. Empirical studies have mostly focused on the array of resources of primary contacts. Erickson (2004) suggested that the design of the position generators should consider many dimensions: the variety of positions, the hierarchy or stratification of positions, and the number of strata. As to the average number of accessed positions of primary contacts, Canadians generally accessed 10 outof 15 positions (2/3), whereas Taiwan residents chose 6.5 outof 15 positions (2/5) (Lin, Fu, and Husng 2001). Lin and Dumin's (finding (Lin and Dumin 1986) showed that male residents in Albany (NY) accessed 8.25 outof 20 positions (2/5). The ratio of accessed positions in the United States is quite similar to that for Taiwan.

The resources of position-generated networks include the mobilized resources in purposive actions (Lin, Cook, and Burt 2001a: 12) and the accumulated potential resources. Some of these resources could have been used by an individual in the past and would occasionally have been called for. Social capital measured by position-generated networks has focused on the dimension of diversity (Lin, Fu, and Hsung 2001; Erickson 2001, 2004). Lin, Fu, and Hsung (2001) calculated three indexes: the extensity of accessed positions, the highest prestige of accessed positions, and the range between the highest and the lowest prestige of accessed positions. These three indexes were loaded to the same factor called access to social capital. The range and the highest prestige of accessed positions were loaded more to this factor. Therefore, this factor of access to social capital mainly indicated the dimension of diversity.

Flap's definition of individual social capital was quite similar to Lin's definition, but Flap (2002) added more dimensions of personal networks, such as the status of accessed contacts and the reciprocity of altars. Using more detail, he was more concerned about the preexisting individual social networks and the possibility of mobilizing the altars' resources. Flap's definition of social capital included not only the number and resources of altars but also the availability of resources from altars to the individual. He considered the multidimensional character of the concept of social capital and the reciprocity cost in mobilizing these resources to find a job (Flap and Boxman 2001). Flap and Boxman (2001: 161) specified that "social capital is the result of the size of the network, the structure of the network, the investment in network members, and the resources of these network members." They stressed that stronger reciprocal relationships could reduce the cost of the exchange of information and resources. Völker and Flap (2004) classified social capital into four dimensions: the number of contacts, the resources of these contacts, the degree of help they provide, and the density of the structure of personal networks. The second dimension, the total resources of network contact, can be included in the indexes of position-generated networks. The total resources were measured by summing the human capital of the array of contacts.

Including the total resources of network contacts in the indexes of position-generated networks can enrich the dimensions of social capital. For example, two persons can access the same number of positions. The first person accesses the positions with prestige scores of 70, 60, and 40, respectively. The other person accesses the positions with prestige scores of 70, 50, and 40, respectively. These two persons have the same extensity of accessed positions, the highest prestige of accessed positions, and the range of accessed positions. However, the former has a total prestige score of accessed contacts of 170, and the latter has a total prestige score of accessed contacts of 160.

The greater the variety of contacts distributed among different occupations, industries, or sectors, the better. There was a high correlation between the number of accessed positions and the highest prestige of accessed positions. Those who can access a greater variety of occupational groups have more opportunities to access the highest positions.

11.2.2. Participation in Voluntary Associations

The variety of social resources is greater for those who are active in more voluntary associations that are rich in opportunities to meet others. Participating in more voluntary associations facilitates the extensity of social circles for individuals. Associational activity is a powerful pathway to diversified contacts. People often join voluntary associations because their friends in such groups recruit them. Network diversity and the extent of voluntary association activity may well be reciprocally related. The number of memberships in clubs and associations can be conceived as a kind of social capital (Boxman, De Graaf, and Flap 1991).

Recently, political scientists and sociologists have studied the social capital of civic engagement. Putnam (1995) used general social survey data in the United States to demonstrate the correlation between the decline in participation in civic associations and the decline in general trust. He found that the voting rate had rapidly declined since 1960 because of a similar decline in civic engagement. Participation in voluntary associations facilitated the extensity of social networks, which then produced the norm and trust in communities. Putnam's study conceived civic engagement as collective assets and stressed the function of the aggregating results of civic engagement (Putnam 1995). Paxton (1999) criticized Putnam (1993*a*, 1993*b*) for only noticing the decline of traditional associations and ignoring the rise of some women's and new movement associations. However, both Putnam and Paxton (1999, 2002) still focused on the functions of civic engagement in maintaining healthy democratic institutions.

Lin (2001*d*) used Taiwan Social Change Survey data and found that there was a significant correlation between civic engagement and the material return of the investment in civic engagement. He used the convergent validity method and discriminant validity to test the validity of accessed associations. He also classified civic engagement into different clusters based on the data of participation in six typical community associations and seven general voluntary associations with factor analyses. The six community associations were classified into two clusters: the groups of participation in the village and in school/church. The seven general associations were classified into professional and political groups. Lin used second-order factor analyses to compose an index of civic engagement by the four first-order factor scores. The prestige and income return of the factor score of civic engagement was significant. The general trust was negatively correlated with the material return.

Associations have played important roles in the institutionalization of some industrial sectors. Chung (1996) found that the Association of Edison Illuminating Companies (AEIC) and the National Electric Light Association (NELA) were the dominant governing mechanisms of the electricity industry during the period of 1885–1910 in the United States. The importance of trade associations on industrial development was that they raised the standard of technology, coordinated the different transactional relationships, and were involved in the relationship between the industry and the public. In addition, the leaders in these associations used their preexisting social networks to mobilize collective actions and solve common problems of industry. In most situations, interpersonal networks are intertwined with other governance structures to a significant extent, so associations provided the space or field in which to link the networks from all types of governance structures (Chung 1996).

Granovetter and McGuire (1998) found that trade associations affected the quality of input of labor, capital, and industrial order. The trade associations coordinated with unions and professional groups to create accreditation standards and financial institutions. In addition, the relation between the firm and the electrical engineering profession also played a central role in the institutionalization of technology in the electricity industry. Evans (1996) also pointed out that Taiwan's economic success was due to the cooperation between the state and the associations through dense collaboration between public and nonprofit associations and informal social ties between these two sectors.

11.3. THE CAUSES OF SOCIAL CAPITAL

The causes of social capital, according to previous empirical findings, are gender, human capital, organizational characteristics, and institutional contexts. In Hungary, the extensity of accessed positions was affected by wealth, education, employment, marital status, and being a landowner or self-employed (Angelusz and Tardos 2001). In Taiwan, gender, education, employment, and marital status affected the extensity of accessed positions (Lin, Fu, and Hsung 2001).

Gender significantly affected social capital. Consequently, men tend to have greater diversity of accessed positions (Lin, Fu, and Hsung 2001; Erickson 2004). Men and women access different occupational resources differently. Men are more likely to access positions with higher status, and women tend to access "people"-related occupations, such as nursing and housekeeping (Lin, Fu, and Hsung 2001). Women prefer to build close and similar ties that benefit early promotion, so they access more redundant social circles (Burt 1998). Therefore, women tend to have less diverse networks.

Men and women have different issue interests and also participate in different voluntary associations (McPherson and Smith-Lovin 1987). Men join sports clubs and women join churches. Men tend to belong to larger, more purposive voluntary associations. According to Putnam's findings, men often participated in sports clubs, unions, the credit union of their occupational group, and veterans' groups, whereas women often participated in church, parent and teacher associations, and culture-related associations (Putnam 1995).

Human capital is the major factor that produces social capital. People with higher education tend to access contacts with higher status. According to a national survey (Lin, Fu, and Hsung 2001; Völker and Flap 2004), highly educated people tend to create more social capital. They tend to have better opportunities to access different social circles, and this, in turn, tends to create more social circles. They can also use more advantageous language and knowledge to build up greater social capital.

Organizational and institutional characteristics also affect social capital. The institutional context constrains or provides opportunities to access social capital. Burt (1997) found that managers in the field of sales and service require more social capital than those in the field of production. The characteristics of geographic communities provide constraints on and opportunities for social capital. Erickson (2004) found that residents in the Atlantic region of Canada accessed more positions. She discovered that the reason was not the occupational distribution in this region but the greater proportion of rural residents. These residents have better social support from and more contacts within communities. She also found that people living in rural areas have a higher level of social capital.

11.4. THE RETURN OF SOCIAL CAPITAL

The early studies on the return of social contacts focused on the prestige and income return of weak ties. Granovetter (1973) and Lin, Ensel, and Vaughn (1981*b*) agreed that individuals could extend more diversified social circles and better resources through weaker ties. Lin, Ensel, and Vaughn (1981*b*) found that better contact resources facilitated better status attainment. Bridges and Villemez (1986) found that the earnings advantage of those matched through work-related contacts was substantially diminished when work experience and education were controlled. Generally speaking, the income return of the status of contacts was not consistently significant. In addition, the analysis of the relation between the status of contacts and the prestige and income return missed those cases of jobs found through formal methods. The research on social capital and the return of socioeconomic status or income has focused on how social ties affect status attainment (Lin, Ensel, and Vaughn 1981*b*; Lin 1982; Campbell, Marsden, and Hurlbert 1986; Boxman, De Graaf, and Flap 1991). Lin, Ensel, and Vaughn (1981*b*) found that the social status of contacts significantly affected the attained status. Later findings indicated that the social status of contacts did affect the attained status but did not significantly affect income in different samples and different countries. In addition, using status of contacts as the social capital of finding a job has a limitation. In both Germany and the Netherlands, less than 40 percent of respondents found their jobs through contacts. The status of contacts was not a good predictor of the attained status for all employed respondents.

Later, Lin and Dumin (1986) found that the greater diversification of accessed positions created better return in terms of income and occupational prestige. Lin, Fu, and Hsung (2001) also found that the greater extensity of access to social capital caused greater return of job prestige and income. In their study, males gained access to positions through nonkin ties more and gained more return of occupational prestige and income than females did. Females, in contrast, relied more on human capital (education) to gain job prestige and higher income. Erickson (1996) found that the greater variety of accessed positions facilitated a greater variety of cultural capital. The function of position-generated networks has been widely tested. This measure was used in Europe, North America, and Asia, and also was found to affect the return of job mobility significantly. Erickson (2001) also found that the extensity of accessed positions was beneficial for employees of the security industry trying to attain the position of managers. Evidently, this measure has a considerable degree of validity and reliability.

The effects of social capital on status attainment varied with different institutional contexts and different work sectors (Burt 1992, 1997). Podolny and Baron (1997) found that an individual's large, sparse network of informal ties enhanced his or her mobility in a large high-tech firm. Large, sparse networks can acquire diversified information and resources that are advantageous for work performance and promotion. In particular, diversified social capital created more value for senior managers (Burt 1998; Erickson 2001). As Erickson (2001) pointed out, different jobs required different combinations of human and social capital, and, thus, the return of human and social capital was different.

Participating in more voluntary associations provided better information and social resources, and, in turn, caused better material return. Lin (2001d) found that the higher the score of civic engagement, the better the return of prestige and income.

Social capital is especially important for managers. The greater total human capital of contacts or the diversity of networks is advantageous for the performance and income return of current jobs for managers in the Netherlands (Boxman, De Graaf, and Flap 1991). The researchers used the data from surveys completed by 1,359 top managers to examine the effects of human and social capital on income attainment. In addition, they used external work contacts and association memberships as social capital variables to determine their independent effects on income. They found that human and social capitals interact in the income attainment process. Social capital helps at any level of human capital, but human capital does not make a difference at the highest levels of social capital. This implied that the effects of social capital became more important at the highest-level positions.

Burt (1997) also noticed the contingent value of social capital in different fields and different ranks of managerial positions. The benefits of resources embedded in networks with different degrees of structural holes for different fields of work divisions are different (Burt 1997). Burt (1997) found that the effect of social capital on early promotion worked best for the most-senior managers in sales and service, but did not work as well in the core production sector.

11.5. RESEARCH METHODS

This survey was conducted in the EPZs and in one SP in Taiwan in February 2002. It was an organizational survey on firms, and the representatives interviewed were personnel managers. We firstly stratified the firm population by industry and size. Industries in the EPZs were classified into electronic and nonelectronic industries,

Table 11.1. Summary of sample characteristics ($N = 126$)

Variables	Percentage or mean			Gender significance
	Sample	Males	Females	
Gender		41.3%	58.7%	
Age	37.0	40.7	34.5	***
Education (Years)	15.6	15.8	15.5	
Less than college	6.3%	5.8%	6.8%	
College	31.7%	23.1%	37.8%	
University	43.7%	48.1%	40.5%	
Graduate school	18.3%	23.0%	14.9%	
Marital status				
Single	22.2%	11.5%	29.7%	*
Married	77.8%	88.5%	70.3%	
Area				
EPZs (63)	50.8%	53.1%	46.9%	**
Science Park (61)	49.2%	29.0%	71.0%	
Industry				
Electronic	26.2%	57.6%	42.4%	
Nonelectronic	24.6%	48.4%	51.6%	#
Semiconductor	22.2%	28.6%	71.4%	
Non-semi-conductor	27.0%	29.4%	70.6%	
Size				
≥ 200	41.3%	51.9%	48.1%	*
< 200	58.7%	33.8%	66.2%	
HR size				
1–3	64.3%	32.1%	67.9%	
4–10	25.4%	56.3%	43.8%	**
> 10	10.3%	61.5%	38.5%	

Note: EPZs, export processing zones; HR, human resource.
# $p < .10$; * $p < .05$; ** $p < 0.1$; *** $p < .001$.

and those in the SP were classified into semiconductor and nonsemi-conductor industries. In terms of size, firms were classified into those employing fewer than 200 persons and those employing 200 and above. Originally, we planned to choose 100 firms in each zone, and the selection ratio would have been around 50 percent in the EPZs and 33 percent in the SP. However, only 126 firm representatives or personnel managers in the two zones agreed to be interviewed. Nevertheless, we believe the sample is still quite representative (see Table 11.1). This survey includes information on firm development, human resource institutions (recruiting, training, promotion, wage, and welfare), and e-commerce; it also includes the social networks and mobility experience for individual personnel managers. This chapter focused only on the causes and return of social capital for personnel managers.

The description of the sample distribution of personnel managers is shown in Table 11.1. Of the 126 personnel managers, 58.7 percent were females and 41.3 percent were males. The average age of male personnel managers was significantly older than that of female personnel managers (40.7 vs. 34.5). Their educational levels were similar. The average number of years of education for males was 15.8 and that for females was 15.5 years. Of those managers with graduate degrees, 23.0 percent were males and 14.9 percent were females. A higher percentage (88.5%) of male personnel managers were married compared to female personnel managers (70.3%). The percentage of male personnel managers (53.1%) was higher in the EPZs than that in the SP (29.0%).

Unlike those in the SP, most personnel managers in the EPZs did not have human resource professional backgrounds. In the EPZs, more male personnel managers had worked in the electronic industry (57.6%) and more female personnel managers had worked in the nonelectronic industry (51.6%). However, only around 30 percent of personnel managers were males in both the semiconductor and nonsemi-conductor industries in the SP. On analyzing the data of the in-depth interviews, it was found that the personnel managers in the EPZs stressed the ability to deal with labor conflicts and relations with other unions within the EPZs, but those in the SP stressed professional skills in human resource management. Male personnel managers usually could handle labor disputes better than female personnel managers. A large proportion of firms in the EPZs had unions, but almost none of the firms in the SP did.

Male personnel managers tended to work in large firms, and female personnel managers tended to work in small firms. A greater percentage of male personnel managers worked in firms with more than 200 employees (51.9%), and more female personnel managers worked in firms with less than 200 employees (66.2%). In Taiwan, most firms are small, and over 70 percent of the firms in both the EPZs and the SP had less than 200 employees. Only 10.3 percent of personnel managers worked in human resource divisions with more than 10 employees. A greater proportion of male personnel managers worked in firms with more than 10 employees in the personnel division (61.5%), and a greater proportion of female personnel managers worked in firms with fewer than 3 employees in the personnel division (67.9%).

Before the questionnaire design, we conducted in-depth interviews of personnel managers in the EPZs and the SP. We included the local work-related associations into the array of associations from the information of in-depth interviews. These three work-related associations were the personnel managers' fellowship within the zone, the knowledge management study group, and the human resource management association.

11.6. FINDINGS

11.6.1. The Measurement of Social Capital

The measurement of social capital includes position-generated networks and participation in associations.

11.6.1.1. Position-Generated Networks

The question of position generator was: "Among your relatives, friends, or acquaintances, are there people who have the following jobs? If so, what is his or her relationship to you?" Following these questions were six job positions. These 6 job positions were selected from 15 positions included in the 1997 Taiwan Social Change Survey on Social Networks. Because the personnel managers of this survey had similar educational levels and career development, the most accessible positions in the general population of positions were not suitable for generators. Therefore, to increase the variation of position-generated networks, we chose the six least accessible positions in the 1997 Survey (Lin, Fu, and Hsung 2001: 66). These six jobs were distributed into high (lawyer, owner of large factory or firm, and assemblyman/woman), middle (division head and reporter), and low (housemaid and cleaning worker) categories of occupational prestige (Hwang 2003). We attempted to use these generators to elicit the accessibility of scarce resources for these personnel managers. The following analysis of the position-generated networks will indicate that the six positions were valid and effective measures of social capital.

Table 11.2 presents the percentages of access to the six job positions through relatives, friends, and acquaintances for the total sample of male and female personnel managers. There was a significant difference between male and female personnel managers in terms of access to all six job positions. The most accessible positions were owner of large factory or firm (46.0%), lawyer (42.1%), and housemaid/cleaning worker (40.5%), and the least accessible positions were assemblyman/woman (29.4%), division head (30.2%), and reporter (38.9%). Male personnel managers were more likely to have access to all six job positions than were females. Compared with the findings of Lin, Fu, and Hsung (2001), personnel managers were more likely to have access to these six job positions than were respondents in the national survey. Male personnel managers tended to have significantly higher extensity, upper reachability, and range of prestige than female personnel managers.

Male personnel managers seemed to have a greater variety of access to scarce resources than female personnel managers did. They were also more likely to have access to all six job positions. The gender gap in terms of accessibility to each scarce positional resource seemed to be even stronger than that in the 1997 Taiwan Social Change Survey. The percentages of access to assemblyman/woman, division head, and reporter positions for male personnel managers were two times higher than those for female personnel managers (44.2% vs.18.9%; 42.3% vs. 21.6%; and 55.8% vs. 27.0%, respectively). This implied that the gender inequality of position-generated social capital was stronger in some occupational groups, such as that of the personnel manager.

There are four indexes or dimensions in the position-generated networks: total resources, extensity, upper reachability, and range of accessed positions. The total resources of accessed positions were the sum of the prestige score of the accessed contacts; the extensity index was the total number of positions

Table 11.2. Summary of variables on position-generated networks and participation in voluntary associations

Variables	Mean or percentage			Gender significance
	Sample	Males	Females	
Position-generated networks				
Total resources	130.1	176.7	97.3	***
Extensity	2.3	3.0	1.7	***
Upper reachability	68.6	71.6	65.9	**
Range	32.4	35.6	29.3	*
Lawyer (73)	42.1%	57.7%	31.1%	**
Owner of large factory or firm (70)	46.0%	57.7%	37.8%	*
Assemblyman/woman (69)	29.4%	44.2%	18.9%	**
Division head (55)	30.2%	42.3%	21.6%	**
Reporter (55)	38.9%	55.8%	27.0%	***
Housemaid, cleaning worker (22)	40.5%	44.2%	37.8%	***
Engagement of associations				
Extensity of accessed associations	1.48	1.67	1.35	
Extensity of general associations	.71	.94	.55	*
Clan association	1.6%	3.8%	0.0%	
Occupational association	11.2%	17.3%	6.8%	#
Religious association	12.8	13.5	12.3	
Hometown asociation	2.4	5.8	0.0	#
Recreational association	1.6	1.9	1.4	
Alumni association	11.2	11.5	11.0	
Political association	0.8	1.9	0.0	
Academic association	8.0	13.5	4.1	#
Women's association	4.8	3.8	5.5	
Parents' association	7.2	9.6	5.5	
Personnel managers' fellowship	52.0	61.5	45.2	*
Knowledge management study group	10.4	11.5	9.6	
Human resource management association	29.6	19.2	37.0	*

$\# p < .10; * p < .05; ** p < 0.1; *** p < .001.$

accessed; the upper reachability was the highest prestige position accessed; and the range was the difference between the highest and lowest prestige positions accessed.

11.6.1.2. Participation in Voluntary Associations

Civic engagement was measured by the following question: "In the past year, have you participated in any of the following associations' activities?" We included 17 voluntary associations, but 4 associations had no participants. These four associations were the Lions Club, Rotary Club, Chamber of Commerce, and memorial associations. The other 13 associations were (*a*) clan association, (*b*) occupational association, (*c*) religious association, (*d*) hometown association, (*e*) recreational association, (*f*) alumni association, (*g*) political association, (*h*) academic association, (*i*) women's association, (*j*) parents' association, (*k*) personnel managers' fellowship, (*l*) knowledge management study group, and (*m*) human resource management association. The response for each item was "yes" or "no."

The roles of voluntary associations in the EPZs and the SP have been different to some extent. In the EPZs and the SP, there was a high density of interassociational and interpersonal networks. The KMT (Kuomintang Party) government used the mechanism of associational governance to stabilize the labor conditions of these two zones in order to attract good local and global companies to move to and stay in these two zones. In the EPZs, the KMT government has built stable and integrative networks among trade associations, labor unions, and government agencies since 1966, and the government has played central and integrative roles in different interest groups. However, the role of the government in the SP has been weak, and the market and associations have greater autonomy. The firms in the SP are larger and high-tech and have not supported the formation of unions, so there are almost no labor unions within the SP. Employees tended to engage in professional associations and informal occupational groups, such as personnel managers' fellowships.

Table 11.2 indicates that personnel managers more often participated in professional and work-related associations. The voluntary associations, which were helpful for exchanging work-related information and knowledge, were more popular, such as the personnel managers' fellowship within zones and the human resource association. Male personnel managers participated in the personnel managers' fellowship more than female personnel managers did (61.5% vs. 45.2%). However, female personnel managers participated in the human resource management association more than male personnel managers did (37.0% vs. 19.2%). The personnel managers' fellowship is not an officially registered association but is a well recognized and influential group for personnel managers within the EPZs and the SP. The members of this group were mainly recommended and invited by current members, and they tended to be personnel managers in large companies. However, the human resource management association is an officially registered association which is open to all those who are interested in or engaged in the field of human resource management.

Because of the differential patterns of civic engagement for male and female personnel managers, there was no significant difference in the extensity (number) of associations that men and women participated in. On average, male personnel managers participated in 1.67 associations and female personnel managers participated in 1.35 associations. We used hierarchical analysis to classify these 13 associations into three clusters (Figure 11.1). Then, the proximity or Euclidean distance between two associations of each pair was computed. There are three clusters of associations in terms of the civic engagement of these personnel managers: general associations, human resource management associations, and personnel managers' fellowships. In later analyses, we created three measures on the participation in voluntary associations: the extensity of general associations people participated in, participation in the human resource management association (yes

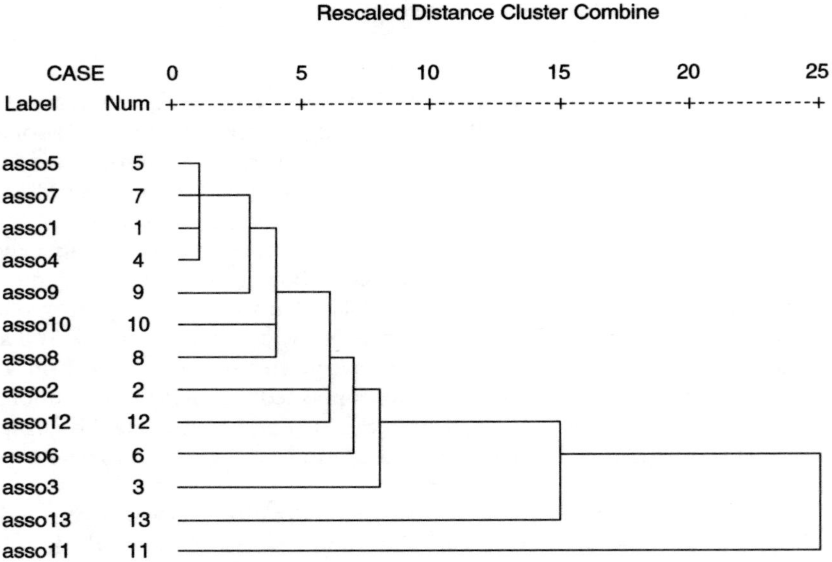

Rescaled Distance Cluster Combine

```
   CASE        0      5      10     15     20     25
  Label   Num  +------+------+------+------+------+

asso5     5  ┐
asso7     7  ┤
asso1     1  ┤
asso4     4  ┘
asso9     9  ┐
asso10   10  ┤
asso8     8  ┤
asso2     2  ┤
asso12   12  ┤
asso6     6  ┘
asso3     3  ┐
asso13   13  ┘
asso11   11  ─────────────────────────────────────┘
```

Figure 11.1. The hierarchical cluster analysis of accessed associations

Note: ASSO1, clan association; ASSO2, occupational association; ASSO3, religious association; ASSO4, hometown association; ASSO5, recreational association; ASSO6, alumni association; ASSO7, political association; ASSO8, academic association; ASSO9, women's association; ASSO10, parents' association; ASSO11, personnel managers' fellowship; ASSO12, knowledge management study group; ASSO13, human resource management association

= 1, no = 0), and participation in the personnel managers' fellowship (yes = 1, no = 0).

11.6.1.3. The Composed Indexes of Position-Generated Networks

We used factor analysis to examine the reliability of measurements on position-generated networks. Table 11.3 indicates that the total resources, the index of extensity, upper reachability, and the range of position-generated networks were loaded to one factor for both male and female personnel managers. The index of extensity had the highest loading coefficient to the factor. Evidently, this factor indicates the diversity of social networks. The composed index was estimated by the following formula: factor score of position-generated networks = total resources × .28 + extensity × .28 + upper reachability × .26 + range × .26. We further compared the pattern of factor-loading coefficients of personnel managers with Lin, Fu, and Hsung's findings from the Taiwan national survey (Lin, Fu, and Hsung 2001). The major difference in our results was that the total resources and the extensity of accessed positions had higher loading coefficients (.97 and .98, respectively) compared with the extensity of accessed positions in Lin, Fu, and

Table 11.3. Factor structures of access to social capital

	Sample	Males	Females
Factor eigenvalues			
I	3.521	3.471	3.536
II	0.279	0.322	0.270
III	0.196	0.203	0.188
IV	0.004	0.004	0.006
Factor loading on Factor I			
Total resources	0.970	0.971	0.969
Extensity	0.981	0.979	0.982
Upper reachability	0.896	0.885	0.899
Range	0.903	0.887	0.908
Factor scoring on Factor I			
Total resources	0.275	0.280	0.274
Extensity	0.279	0.282	0.278
Upper reachability	0.255	0.255	0.254
Range	0.257	0.256	0.257

Hsung's (analyses, which were the lowest (around .80) among three composed indexes (Lin, Fu, and Hsung 2001). The factor score of the composed index was used as the indicator of access to the social capital of position-generated networks in later analyses.

We further examined the accessed positions through kin ties (Table 11.4). Compared with the findings of Lin, Fu, and Hsung (2001), fewer percentages of male and female personnel managers gained access to these six job positions through kin ties. Female personnel managers used more kin ties to have access to the owner of a large factory or firm and assemblyman/woman positions than male managers did. As several studies in Taiwan have shown (Hsung 1994, 2001), females still tend to use more kin ties to access these scarce social resources.

Table 11.4. Access to social capital by kin

Accessed position (prestige score)	Percentage using kin ties			Gender significance
	Sample	Males	Females	
Lawyer (Position 6) (73)	5.7	3.3	8.7	
Owner of large factory or firm (Position 5) (70)	13.8	3.3	25.0	*
Assemblyman/woman (Position 1) (69)	13.5	0.0	35.7	**
Division head (Position 2) (55)	18.4	13.6	25.0	
Reporter (Position 4) (55)	8.2	3.4	15.0	
Housemaid, cleaning worker (Position 3) (22)	3.9	0.0	7.1	

$^*p < .05;\ ^{**}p < .01.$

11.7. THE DETERMINANTS OF SOCIAL CAPITAL

Table 11.5 presents four regression models of social capital. The first regression model attempts to explore the causes of access to social capital, and the other three models attempt to explore the effects of the measurements on participation in voluntary associations. In the first model, gender had a significant effect on access to social capital. Male personnel managers have a greater degree of access to social capital than female personnel do. The greater percentage of positions accessed through kin ties positively affected the access to social capital. This finding is different from the findings of Lin, Fu, and Hsung (2001). Whether kin ties or nonkin ties are more likely to connect with diverse ties is an interesting issue that needs to be examined further.

The second model indicated that the causes of the extensity of general associations that personnel managers engaged in were job tenure and the extensity of accessed positions. In this study, education did not have any significant effect on either the extensity of accessed positions or the extensity of general associations participated in. The major reason was that the variation of education among personnel managers was small. The greater number of years of work experience is more important as an explanation of participation in general associations for

Table 11.5. The determinants of social capital variables

Variables	Accessed capital	TASSO	HRF[a]	HRA
Gender (men = 1)	.61**	.66	.46	−1.84**
Married (=1)	−.13	−.38#	.63	−1.17*
Human capital				
Years of education			−.02	.37*
Categories of education (high school = 0)				
College	−.32	−.52		
University	−.25	−.62		
Graduate school	−.01	.07		
Number of years at previous jobs	.01	.03#	.01	.07#
Tenure of current job	.02	.04**	−.07	.05
Social capital				
Percentage of kin ties among accessed positions	.01*			
Access to social capital		.09*	.17#	.23#
Organizational characteristics				
Log size of HR division	.22	.31	1.80**	2.06**
Zone (SP = 1)	.36	−.14	−.09	.86
Constant	−.47	.66	−.63	−7.88**
Adjusted R^2	.08*	.18***	.15***[b]	.27***
n	123	123	123	123

Note: TASSO, total number of memberships of general associations; HRF, participation in the personnel managers' fellowship; HRA, participation in human resource management association; HR, human resource.
[a] Logistic regression.
[b] Pseudo R^2.
# $p < .10$; * $p < .05$; ** $p < .01$; *** $p < .001$.

these personnel managers, especially the tenure of the current job. Evidently, these personnel managers participated in voluntary associations mainly for their own work interest. In addition, the extensity of accessed positions significantly affected the extensity of general associations. Personnel managers who accessed more diverse resources tended to engage in more general associations.

The personnel managers within both the EPZs and the SP mainly participated in personnel managers' fellowships and human resource management associations. The cluster analysis already indicated that these two associations belonged to two different clusters to some extent (Figure 11.1). Therefore, we used the logistic regression Models 3 and 4 to examine the factors affecting the probability of participation in the personnel managers' fellowship and in the human resource management association. The probability of personnel managers participating in these two associations was significantly affected by the size of the human resource division within the firm. Personnel managers in firms with greater numbers of employees dealing with personnel affairs had a greater probability of participating in the personnel managers' fellowship and the human resource management associations. This result indicated that human resource management has been bureaucratized and professionalized through learning and imitating the personnel institutions of other firms by means of participation in the activities of these two associations.

11.8. THE OUTCOME OF SOCIAL CAPITAL

The prestige and income of the current job were conceptualized as the return or consequences of social capital. Table 11.6 presents two regression models on prestige and three models on the log of income. Comparing Models 1 and 2, we found that the variables in social capital did not increase the explained variance, and R^2 only increased from .27 to .28 after adding the variables in social capital.

In terms of the return of human capital, work experience was more important than education for these personnel managers. Education did not significantly affect the prestige of jobs, but the more years worked in previous jobs increased the prestige of the current job.[1] Most of the younger cohort of personnel managers had a master's degree in human resource management, and the older cohort of personnel managers had built greater work experience in personnel management through career development processes. Table 11.6 shows that the number of years worked in previous jobs and the tenure of current job are the most important variables affecting the increase in job prestige. In the year 2001, most large high-tech firms faced the crisis of the rapid decline of the high-tech industry. Therefore, they tried to restructure their organizational design and transform it into the

---

[1] The personnel managers' distribution in the following occupations and their Treiman's prestige scores were as follows: 39% were managers in other departments (63), 42% were supervisors in a corporation (55), 3.2% were bookkeeper and cashier (41), 2.4% were secretary clerk (31), 8.7% were personnel clerk (38), and 2.4% were unclassified clerk (37).

Table 11.6. The determinants of job prestige and log income

Variables	Prestige Model 1	Prestige Model 2	Log income Model 3	Log income Model 4	Log income Model 5
Gender (men = 1)	3.07#	3.26#	.10***	.10***	4.17***
Married	5.22**	5.49**	.07**	.07**	.08***
Human capital					
Education (high school = 0)					
College	.76	−.60	.08#	.04	.05
University	3.20	1.80	.12**	.08#	.07#
Graduate school	4.22	2.12	.23***	.19***	.172***
Number of years at previous jobs	.38**	.32**	.01***	.01***	.01***
Tenure of current job	.26*	.23#	.01**	.01***	.01**
Social capital					
Access to social capital		−.25		.02#	.02*
No. of general associations		.68		−.004	−.01
Personnel managers' fellowship		2.96#		.07**	.05**
Human resource association		2.12		.05*	.01#
Organizational characteristics					
Size of HR division (log)	4.78**	2.78	.04	−.01	−.02
Zone (high-tech park = 1)	3.46*	3.32*	.03	.01	−.01
Prestige					.01***
Constant	39.56***	39.28***	4.37***	4.38***	4.17***
Adjusted R^2	.27**	.28***	.51***	.58***	.65
n	122	122	123	123	123

Note: HR, human resource.
# $p < .10$; * $p < .05$; ** $p < .01$; *** $p < .001$.

knowledge management structure. The earliest division of transformation is the division of human resource. The most difficult part is how to build the new incentive rules by the criteria of professional education and work experience and force these senior position personnel managers promote their knowledge on human resource knowledge management.

Table 11.6 indicates that married personnel managers had significantly greater prestige than unmarried personnel managers. Married personnel managers used to be perceived as mature enough to deal with the labor disputes between the government labor law and the firm's policy, the union's challenge, and the conflicts among different divisions within the firm. Therefore, married personnel managers performed much better and gained better positions. In the findings of the 1997 national survey of Lin, Fu, and Hsung (2001), marital status did not have a significant effect on prestige. However, the result of our study indicated that marital status seemed to be one of the important characteristics for being a successful personnel manager.

Another interesting phenomenon is that the institutional environments of industrial zones shaped the accessibility of different voluntary associations and the different degrees of return for these personnel managers. The human resource division within the firms in the SP tended to be pressured by its global customers, Intel and Motorola, to restructure itself into a knowledge management division.

Therefore, the division of human resource in the large firms or in the firms within the SP tended to have a more complex division of labor, and, thus, these personnel managers tended to have more opportunities to be promoted into high prestige positions.

The effect of social capital on job prestige was not significant, but participation in the personnel managers' fellowship had a slight effect on the return of job prestige. Part of the reason was that all of our personnel managers were distributed into only five types of occupations, and the variation in occupational prestige was small. In addition, the size of human resource division was the most important determinant of the probability of participation in the personnel managers' fellowship and the human resource management association. After including the size of human resource division into Model 2 of Table 11.6, the effects of participating in the personnel managers' fellowship and the human resource management association on prestige became weaker or disappeared. Obviously, joining the fellowship encouraged the exchange of personnel policy and knowledge of different firms. The faster absorption of information and knowledge on personnel management increased the competitiveness and enhanced the performance of personnel managers.

There are three regression models on the log of income. Model 3 did not include the variables of social capital and prestige, and Model 4 did not include prestige. Model 5 is the full model. The variables of social capital in terms of position-generated networks and participation in associations became significant in the explanation of the log of income. After adding the variables on social capital, R^2 increased from .51 to .58. Similarly, R^2 increased from .58 to .65 after adding the prestige variable.

Social capital was more sensitive to the return of income than to the return of prestige, because the range of income is much larger than that of prestige for personnel managers. Access to social capital and participation in the personnel managers' fellowship and the human resource management association positively affected the log of income. However, the extensity of general associations did not affect the income return. For these personnel managers, participation in the personnel managers' fellowship seemed to be the most effective investment and was more advantageous for the income return. In sum, the diversity of position-generated social capital was still a good capital for personnel managers that significantly benefited the income return as well. Nevertheless, investment in a specific job-related association was more effective than investment in the extensity of non-work-related associations for personnel managers.

The significant effects of participation in the personnel managers' fellowship and the human resource management association on the income return enabled us to pay more attention to the functions of these work-related associations for the individual's good. From the in-depth interviews with the human resource managers of large high-tech firms, we recognized that the social capital accessed through participation in the regular activities of these work-related associations was beneficial not only to the firm but also for personal performance in career development. The function of participating in associations was noted as follows (quoting from the text of an in-depth interview):

The male human resource manager in the largest semiconductor company said, The personnel managers meet once a month in this personnel managers' fellowship. This group is just like a brother/sisterhood. If firm A has some institutions which firm B does not have, firm B can learn from firm A through the exchange of experience in this fellowship meeting. Right? If firm A has disputes about labor conditions or is in a struggle over unionization within the firm, then firm B can learn from the success firm A had in handling such labor disputes. In addition, the function of the personnel managers' fellowship is to exchange the wage information of each firm and maintain the stability of wage levels among firms within zones, and, therefore, keep the labor market within zones more stable.

More than half of the human resource managers in our sample engaged in this kind of personnel managers' fellowship.

The director of the semiconductor occupational association, who was also the manager of the human resource development division in a large semiconductor company, said, I participated in three associations: the semiconductor occupational association in the Science Park, the personnel managers' fellowship, and the human resource management association. The function of the semiconductor occupational association in the Science Park was mainly to negotiate with the government about labor issues and policies in the semiconductor industry. The human resource management association is open to any person who is interested in human resource management. Members of the human resource management association are not necessarily managers from the Science Park, so you seldom know the people there. The attendant overlap rate is around 20% among different events. However, the personnel managers' fellowship is the most supportive group. This group is a closed group, which only allows personnel managers within the zone to join. They meet once a month and discuss many human resource management issues, such as recruitment, training, and wage issues.

A female manager in the training division of the human resource development department in a large Dynamic Random Access Memory (DRAM) company said,

I joined a knowledge management study group. Reading new books on knowledge management is our major activity. We also want to talk with people in the same field. In addition, keeping these *ren-mai* (interpersonal networks or *guanxi* networks in Chinese metaphor) is another purpose. It's easier and faster to get information and resources to deal with knowledge management issues at work through these *guanxi* networks.

From the texts of the in-depth interviews with these personnel managers, we can summarize the functions of joining work-related associations as: learning the institution and system from other companies, exchanging information and resources to deal with work problems, maintaining the order and stability of the labor market, and investing in potential *guanxi* networks.

In addition to the effect of social capital, gender, marital status, and human capital variables still play important roles in the income return. The organizational variables significantly affected the prestige return but did not affect the income return. The large firms in the SP tended to have a larger number of human resource positions and a greater range of prestige among personnel managers, but their wage policy made the income variation smaller. Generally, the large firms had a bonus policy,[2] and a greater percentage of firms in the SP provided stock bonus to their employees annually. The firms also used the policy of stock options as an incentive to motivate their employees. In addition, the firms in both zones tried to standardize the wages at stable levels in order to keep the labor conditions of these two zones as the most appropriate industrial districts for investment.

11.9. DISCUSSION AND CONCLUSIONS

By using the social capital measurements of modified position-generated networks and membership in voluntary associations, we found that the greater access to occupational positions, participation in the personnel managers' fellowship, and participation in the human resource management association significantly improved income return for personnel managers. This study extended the attention to the functions of social capital on work-related voluntary associations. Greater access to position-generated networks created greater extensity of general association memberships and, in turn, greater probability of participating in work-related voluntary associations. The issue of reciprocity between access to position-generated networks and participation in voluntary associations needs to be studied further with longitudinal data.

The findings of this study pointed out some new issues relating to social capital. In previous studies, human capital often significantly affected the extensity of accessed positions, but there was almost no correlation between human capital (educational levels and work experience) and the extensity of accessed positions in the field of personnel managers in our study. Only gender significantly affected the accessed positions, and male personnel managers had greater extensity of the accessed positions. However, the years of education and years of work in previous jobs increased the probability of participating in human resource management associations for these personnel managers. The effect of educational levels on the job prestige return was not significant, but the years of work of previous jobs had a strong effect on the job prestige return. All these findings implied that the interaction effects between human capital and social capital on the status return varied with different occupational groups, and the causes and return of position-generated networks and participation in different types of voluntary associations are different to some extent. Future studies need to clarify the contingent causes and return of different types of social capital.

The item design on position generators and types of voluntary associations also is a methodological issue that deserves further studies. Although we used six generators to indicate the access to the scarce resources of personnel managers, it still effectively predicted the income return. In addition, these six generators match the criteria suggested by Erickson (2004) that the design of the position generators

---

[2] The percentages of firms in the SP and the EPZs offering a stock bonus were 88.7% vs. 48.4%. The percentages of firms in the SP and the EPZs offering stock options were 59.0% vs. 23.4%.

should consider the dimensions of the variety of positions, the hierarchy or stratification of positions, and the number of strata. In our study, the local work-related associations, the personnel managers' fellowship, and the human resource management association are key associations for personnel managers. If we did not do in-depth interview in advance and did not include these two associations into the array of associations, then the social capital from participation in specific work-related associations would not be pointed out. How to design general and specific types of associations would be an important issue for the future studies.

12

It's Not Only Who You Know, It's Also Where They Are: Using the Position Generator to Investigate the Structure of Access to Embedded Resources[1]

Sandra Enns, Todd Malinick, and Ralph Matthews

12.1. INTRODUCTION

The idea that people can benefit from their associations with others is not new. It is a concept that has been immortalized in universal colloquialisms ("It's not what you know, it's who you know"), song ("I get by with a little help from my friends"[2]), and movies ("No one is poor who has friends"[3]). But a more methodological study of the way people can utilize the ties and contacts that they have in their networks for social advantage is a somewhat recent area in sociological research. This rapidly expanding body of research centers around the multidimensional concept of social capital, which incorporates a focus on social networks.

This chapter focuses on the relationship between the social activities and groups in which people are involved and their potential to form ties to resource-rich positions in their social networks. In doing so, we focus particularly on an element aptly described by yet another colloquial saying known to successful realtors and entrepreneurs: "Location, location, location." While most social capital research has focused on the types of ties, whether strong or weak, and the potential resources they represent, comparatively little attention has been given to the impact of location on these ties.

This locational aspect of network composition is especially relevant given that the context of this study is the rural, coastal, resource-based communities of British Columbia (B.C.), Canada. With the exception of the growing urban centers of Vancouver, Victoria, and Nanaimo, coastal B.C. primarily consists of small, rural communities and First Nation (North American Indian) reserves. These are

[1] Funding for this study was provided by the Social Sciences and Humanities Research Council of Canada (SSHRC) through the Strategic Theme Program on "Social Cohesion in a Globalizing Era."
[2] John Lennon and Paul McCartney, *Sgt. Pepper's Lonely Hearts Club Band*, 1978.
[3] *It's A Wonderful Life*, 1947.

mostly located around Vancouver Island and on the many other islands dotting the Pacific Ocean coastline, or sandwiched between the mountains and the ocean on a rugged mainland stretching north to Alaska. Many are inaccessible by road and thus dependent exclusively on air and water transport.

This coastal region of B.C. is, in many respects, in a world of hurt. These communities are, and have been, predominantly resource based, but the resources (i.e. fish, lumber, and minerals) on which they have traditionally relied for financial stability have been depleted through a variety of processes—environmental, political, and global. As a result, many of these communities are experiencing massive unemployment and economic instability leading to extensive out-migration, primarily of the skilled workforce.

Thus, in the context of these somewhat isolated rural communities, we investigate social engagement and the structure of social networks through focusing on ties both inside and between rural communities, and the impact that such bonding and bridging ties have on residents' ability to access potential social resources. In addition, we explore gender differences in civic participation and access to potential resources. Our findings, somewhat contrary to other work on gender and social networks, enable us to show that both the geographical and the social location of network ties are important considerations in understanding the composition and operation of social networks.

12.1.1. The Resilient Communities Project

The data for this analysis were collected through *The Resilient Communities Project* (RCP), which is a multiyear, three-phase research endeavor. The focus of the project is an examination of how B.C.'s rural, coastal communities are responding to the economic downturn. At a conceptual and empirical level, it is directly examining the extent to which community social capital and social network ties within and between communities are able to provide a buffer against the current economic crisis, and also serve as a basis for new avenues of economic development.

In *Phase I* of the project, with the assistance of the government agency B.C. Statistics, we collected data on economic and social indicators available for the past 20 years for each community on the coast. Through this process, we identified 131 coastal communities with a population of over 50 and less than 30,000, including 75 First Nation reserves, 28 unincorporated, and 28 incorporated communities. *Phase II* of the project deals directly with the measurement of social capital within B.C.'s coastal communities. We developed a self-administered questionnaire that we mailed to 4,386 households in 22 communities. The survey was conducted over a period of a year and a half and included several reminder mailings. As a result, we achieved a response rate of 59.9 percent.[4]

---

[4] Though a total response rate of 59.9% was attained, only 1,763 cases are used in the analyses in this paper due to missing data. However, the surveys analyzed in this paper were compared to those with missing data across an array of other survey questions and no noticeable differences were detected.

The questionnaire focuses particularly on indicators of social capital that are operationalized in fixed-choice question format. It is divided into seven distinct sections: demographic measures; employment; community identification and commitment; trust; social activities and networks; media use; and health. Each section is composed of an array of items and constructs, some of which are adapted from past studies and some measures of our own. *Phase III* of the RCP involves extensive interviews in at least six of the communities that formed the sample in *Phase II*. Whereas the data in *Phase II* provide us with information about the *structure of social capital formation* in each community, the questions asked in the interviews are designed to provide more qualitative in-depth information about the *process of social capital utilization*.

In this chapter, we analyze some of the data obtained through the *Phase II* mail-out questionnaire. More specifically, this chapter focuses on data obtained using the position generator, an instrument that examined the extent to which respondents in our 22 communities had access to significant sources of resources through their personal networks. We will discuss our particular formulation of the position generator later in this chapter, and relate our formulation of it to the growing international literature about the use of the position generator in varied sociocultural contexts. Before doing so, we examine the literature on social networks and civic participation that underlie our study and shape our subsequent analysis.

12.2. CONCEPTUAL AND EMPIRICAL BACKGROUND

Social capital theorists have long argued that the essence of social capital *inheres in the structure of relations between persons and among persons* (Coleman 1990: 302). That is, through their involvement in social activities within groups and organizations, people form the ties to others in various positions within the social hierarchy that potentially represent access to beneficial resources. Given this, much consideration has been given to the social character of network social ties, particularly the implications of whether such ties are weak or strong. For example, Granovetter states that the strength of a social tie is a "combination of the amount of time, the emotional intensity, the intimacy and the reciprocal services which characterize the tie" (1973: 1361). Strong ties are generally considered to be ties to those people within an individual's immediate social network, such as family and close friends. Weak ties, on the other hand, are considered to be ties to people who are not within the respondent's immediate social network, such as acquaintances, coworkers, and friends of close friends.

Such strong and weak ties represent different access points to the social capital resources potentially available to the individual. It is the individual's needs, goals, and actions that will determine what type of tie will prove most useful in accessing required resources. Coleman (1990) contends that a closed network made up of strong ties is the best source of social capital, as everyone within the network is provided with useful information quickly and efficiently. The fact that everyone knows everyone else also creates obligations within the network, which in turn increases trust and reduces the chance of free riding or malfeasance (Coleman 1990: 318–19). In addition, such strong ties create norms of reciprocity and a set of effective sanctions that can monitor and guide behavior (Burt 2001: 38). This provides members of the network with access to resources that they would otherwise not be able to access through weak ties, where such norms, obligations, and sanctions would not exist. Research supports this and suggests that, where an individual has the need for social support, security, and reciprocity, strong ties within a dense social network can be an important source of social capital analysis (Tigges, Browne, and Green 1998; Smith 2000).

Strong ties, however, are not without their limitations. Portes warns that those same strong ties that bring benefits to members of a group may also act to bar others from access (1998: 15). While people inside the group may benefit from access to resources provided by mutual strong ties, those outside the group may be unable to gain such access.

Other analysis and research (Granovetter 1973; Lin 1999*b*, 2000*a*, 2001*b*; Smith 2000) suggests that, where individuals are attempting to achieve social mobility or economic stability, making weak ties may be their best strategy for accessing resources that do not exist within their own networks. Weak ties tend to be diffuse and inclusive of a greater number of people. Thus individuals with many weak ties are more likely to have contacts with people who are different from them and are able to gain access to information they could not acquire from their friends. On a more macro level, weak ties play an important role in creating social cohesion. As people establish networks of weak ties and bridges within a community, this allows information and ideas to flow more readily, and trust is created through the ensuing interactions (Granovetter 1973: 1371–3).

12.2.1. Context Matters

As previously noted, a major focus of our analysis here is the effect of location on access to resources through network ties. The predominantly rural character and isolated location of our research communities makes this an important consideration, and this isolation also provides something of an ideal type situation in which to assess the relative impact of internal versus external ties on access to social capital resources.

There is ample empirical evidence (cf. Beggs, Haines, and Hurlbert 1996; Onyx and Bullen 2000; Reimer 2001; Erickson 2003) that the network composition of rural residents differs substantially from those of urban dwellers. As Beggs, Haines, and Hurlbert note, the structure of personal networks is significantly affected by the geographical location of the individual, and they emphasize the importance of taking context into account when analyzing individual behavior (1996: 322). This has significant implications for social capital analysis; if network composition differs, this would suggest that rural and urban residents do not access or utilize social capital in the same way, nor do they necessarily do so for the same purposes.

Beggs, Haines, and Hurlbert found that rural residents' networks were significantly more likely to be composed of long-term relationships, and were also smaller, denser, and lower in diversity than that of their urban counterparts. Similarly, Onyx and Bullen (2000) found that rural communities had higher levels of social capital as well as higher levels of trust, participation, and location connections than urban areas. Their results showed that rural communities generate considerable "bonding social capital," which is characterized by strong mutual support. However, and in support of Portes's caveat regarding the limitations of strong ties, they also found that such support was likely to be limited to insiders and may not be extended to minority groups within the local area or to those outside the area (Onyx and Bullen 2000: 38).

Like Onyx and Bullen, Erickson (2003) found that people living in rural areas have significantly higher levels of social capital than urban residents. However, somewhat in contradiction to Beggs, Haines, and Hurlbert, whose results showed that rural residents had less diverse networks, Erickson found that rural residents' networks were actually *more* diversified than those of urban residents. Her explanation for this is, quite simply, that the smaller size of rural communities means that residents come into contact with persons from all social strata and cannot easily segment themselves into networks of persons with largely similar backgrounds.

A more general analysis of the role of location, this time within and between networks themselves, is found in Burt's (2001) study of persons who occupy the "structural holes" between social networks.[5] Burt argues that holes between social networks create a competitive advantage for a person whose relationships span those holes. He demonstrates that the people whose weak ties locate them at the borders of two networks often act as information brokers between the two groups. These people are also able to control the flow of information and can make the most of opportunities that arise within either group. As well, they represent a potential resource for other people who are looking for such contacts themselves (Burt 2001: 34–7).

Although Burt's analysis is largely about what might be described as social location rather than geographic location, such bridging ties may be particularly relevant to members of rural, resource-based communities, whose geographical isolation and reduced access to goods, services, and resources within their communities may require them to go outside to access necessary social and material resources. The ties they make outside their community may not only help them access material goods and services they could not otherwise get, but also provide a valuable source of social capital through potential contacts to people with information and social resources not otherwise available in their community. These bridging ties may, therefore, represent conduits for information to flow between

---

[5] What Burt (2001) calls structural holes, Granovetter (1973) refers to as "bridges" from one group to another.

communities. There is a downside, however. For many residents of isolated, rural communities, forming such bridging ties to outside communities may be problematic in terms of the expense, time, and effort required to travel outside the community, and may in fact detract from their ability to form strong bonding ties within it. Evidence supporting this theory will become apparent in our data analysis of the relation between the ties located inside and outside our sample communities.

A study by Leonard and Onyx (2003) largely supports Burt's analysis of the importance of bridging ties, and does so in the direct context of social and economic development in rural communities. Their analysis focuses on whether such economic development is better served by strong or weak ties, and on whether such ties serve to bond communities together or bridge them to other communities. In that sense, their analysis closely parallels that presented in this chapter.

The primary issue for Leonard and Onyx is whether bonding social capital in a community, while operating as a defensive strategy against economic instability, serves to hinder positive economic development, which may require a shift to bridging social capital. They relate this to the difference between "getting by" and "getting ahead," and argue that the close, intersecting, multifunctional ties of a strongly bonded community may be detrimental to bridging to a wider arena (Leonard and Onyx 2003: 191). They suggest that, if rural communities want to get ahead, they may need to develop more weak ties outside the community. However, as always, there is a risk involved: "Should a community that is just getting by with high levels of bonding social capital take the risk of decreasing its current social capital for the potential, but less certain economic gains of developing bridging social capital?" (Leonard and Onyx 2003: 193).

In actuality, Leonard and Onyx's research provided only limited support for their proposition, while providing a much more nuanced insight into the way in which network ties operate at a community level. First, their results found that strong ties were very similar to weak ties in many respects. The biggest differences were that strong ties were characterized by long-term relationships and mutual trust, whereas weak ties tended to be with people less well known, and thus not trusted to the same extent. The authors also found that strong ties were used for both bonding (within group) and bridging (between group) connections. In addition, they found that the only weak ties used for bridging were those of people with formal professional status, such as doctors, pastors, teachers, and so on. The authors noted that people were more willing to take risks in bridging to other networks in search of information and resources, when they could work through strong ties to people they trusted and knew well. Leonard and Onyx conclude that these results suggest that rural communities do not need to shift from bonding to bridging social capital to get ahead. Rather, they need to find ways to develop stronger ties *both* within the community and to other communities (Leonard and Onyx 2003: 197–201).

Woolcock (1998) provides support for this conclusion when he states that *both* intracommunity (bonding) and extracommunity (bridging) ties are important to the economic stability and well-being of a community. While he supports Portes's caution about overly strong bonding ties being detrimental to a community's ability to form bridges with the outside, he also argues that too many bridging relationships can likewise be detrimental by reducing levels of trust and cohesion within the community, as the stable collective foundation is eroded by a lack of network integration. Woolcock argues that communities that are able to strike a balance between strong intracommunity ties and high levels of trust, while maintaining supportive networks through weaker ties with outside communities, are in the best position to achieve future economic well-being (Woolcock 1998: 170–3).

In addition to the rural/urban differences just examined, several studies have indicated distinct differences between men and women with regard to access to positions rich in embedded resources. Much of this research suggests that men tend to have greater diversity in their networks, with fewer strong ties and more weak ties to resource-rich positions, while women have less diverse networks, and tend to have a greater number of strong ties to lower positions in the hierarchy (Moore 1990; Smith 2000; Lin 2000a). Recent studies utilizing the position generator (Lin 2001a, 2001b) have shown a similar pattern in which men are more likely to be located in positions within the social hierarchy that give them greater access to resource-rich positions. However, in the sphere of gender differences, Erickson (2003) adds support to our emphasis on the importance of context and/or geographical location. In her research, she found that women living in rural areas have significantly greater diversity in their networks than both men and women living in urban areas, even though urban areas have much more diversified occupational structures (Erickson 2003: 14).[6]

12.2.2. The Contribution of Civic Participation

Research suggests that there is a strong relationship between civic participation and the formulation of beneficial social ties. Putnam, both in his examination of regional economic development in Italy (1993a) as well as in his study of participatory decline in the United States (2000), concluded that civic involvement leads to the development of social networks that facilitate interpersonal trust and ultimately economic cooperation and growth. Granovetter (1973) notes that formal organizations are good sources of ties to others outside of one's own social group, which allows access to resources that might otherwise be inaccessible. A recent study by Erickson concludes that "participation in voluntary associations is by far the most powerful single source of social capital ... because association activity leads to numerous contacts with diversified others" (2003: 46).

Research also suggests that context and/or geographical location is an important contributor to levels of civic participation, with rural residents more likely to be involved in the social and civic life of their communities (Onyx and Bullen

---

[6] Erickson (2003) notes that the social capital advantage of rural life is smaller for men, and is not significant after controls for individual characteristics are included in the analysis.

2000; Erickson 2003). Wall et al. (2003) emphasize that one way to assess the social capital of a rural community is to examine the voluntary sector. They note that: "community organizations provide rich opportunities for people to affirm and reaffirm their common values, to build up trust and obligations, and to establish their attachment to, and identity with, their communities. The voluntary sector has been described as the fabric of rural communities" (Wall et al. 2003: 5). -

Coakes and Bishop provide support for this conclusion when they note that "one of the most salient characteristics of rural communities is the high level of involvement in community affairs" (1998: 250). They state that women, in particular, play a major role in rural community life. In fact, the authors state: "research in metropolitan areas...has shown that few working mothers have the time or energy to join community organizations. If this experience is repeated in rural communities, the impact on the social well-being of rural areas is likely to be considerable, as these areas rely on the voluntary work provided by women" (Coakes and Bishop 1998: 250).

Other related research investigates how gender differences in network composition are related to different *types* of involvement in community activities. McPherson and Smith-Lovin (1982) state that gender differences in network structure are partially due to the fact that men and women participate in organizations and activities with different embedded resources. They note that while women tend to participate in smaller, more peripheral organizations and activities with a focus on domestic or community affairs (i.e. youth, church-related, social, charitable, and neighborhood groups), men tend to participate in large, core organizations that are related to economic institutions (i.e. are business-, professional-, or labor-related), and in nondomestic activities (i.e. sports, politics, and service groups) that expose them to more potential ties and resources. They conclude that men are located in positions within the voluntary network that are much more likely to provide access to information about possible jobs, business opportunities, and chances for professional advancement, whereas women are located in positions more likely to expose them to information about the domestic realm. These authors suggest that such disparity in network composition produces a dramatic difference in the social resources available to men and women through their membership in social organizations and activities (McPherson and Smith-Lovin 1982: 901–2).

These network disparities appear irrespective of urban or rural context, as Beggs, Hurlbert, and Haines obtained similar results in their study on community attachment in a rural setting. They also found gender differences in community participation, with men being more likely than women to belong to community groups (including service, fraternal, political, and sports groups) and interest groups (including labor, farm-related, and veterans groups), but less likely to belong to school and church groups (1996: 421).

In sum, previous analysts have demonstrated that the location of network ties has considerable importance. In particular, they have demonstrated that (*a*) the strength of ties varies considerably between rural and urban areas; (*b*) rural and urban areas generally differ in terms of the extent to which individuals have networks composed of strong versus weak ties; (c) the type of tie appears to be related to its potential social purpose; and (d) there are strong gender differences in social network ties in both rural and urban areas. These findings form the background for our own analysis, using the position generator, of social network relationships in coastal B.C.

12.3. DATA

12.3.1. Measuring the Structure of Access to Embedded Resources: The Position Generator

In order to measure the potential access that respondents had to resource-rich positions in their networks, we employed, with key revisions, a tool designed for such research known as the position generator (Lin and Dumin 1986; Lin, Fu, and Hsung 2001; Lin 2001b). Common to all position generators is the general format, where survey respondents are presented with a sample of socially relevant structural positions (typically occupational) ranging across prestige classes, and asked to indicate whether or not they have any contact with each of the positions. Underlying this approach is the key assumption that various hierarchical positions represent differential resources (Lin and Dumin 1986). Various degrees of wealth, status, and power will be inherent in different positions, and individuals in the social network having access to these positions will likely have access to some of the resources embedded within them as well.

While past position generators typically included a sampling of occupations from some listing, such as US Census data, and assigned some prestige score to each position (see Lin, Fu, and Hsung 2001), this specific approach was deemed unsuitable for this geographic region for two primary reasons. First, in many cases, small, remote, resource-based communities are severely limited in the number and variety of positions present in the region. Second, certain positions quite familiar, influential, and of great interest (i.e. elected or hereditary First Nation Chief; manager or administrative officer of a First Nation band or tribal council; member of a chamber of commerce, town council, or regional district) are not necessarily occupational positions per se (many of these positions are typically unpaid), and are not present on any occupational classification system known to the authors. However, given the flexibility of the position generator, we were able to adapt it to study our research interests within our unique population.

The RCP position generator[7] included a series of 18 different positions, some of which are fairly specific to coastal B.C., while others are relatively common to many regions. These positions covered a range of prestige classifications that we categorized into two broad groups. The group of immediate interest to this study

---

[7] See Appendix 1 for the RCP position generator.

contains the 12 positions shown below that we judged to have relatively greater social prestige and, we assume, a greater amount of embedded resources.

- Aquaculture or fish plant manager
- Elected or hereditary First Nation Chief
- Local health professional
- Police officer
- Manager or administrative officer of a First Nation band or tribal council
- Member of chamber of commerce
- Member of regional district council
- Member of town council
- Mine manager (includes oil and gas)
- Pastor, priest, or other church leader
- Pulp mill, paper mill, or sawmill manager
- Schoolteacher (primary or secondary)

Worth emphasizing here is another distinct difference between the RCP position generator and past tools. Previous position generators have typically been used to develop insightful measures, such as (*a*) *extent*, or number of different structural positions accessed; (*b*) *upper reachability*, or the highest rank accessed; and (*c*) *range* of prestige statuses accessed (see Lin and Dumin 1986; Erickson 1996; Lai, Lin, and Leung 1998; Lin 2001*b*; and Lin, Fu, and Hsung 2001 for examples of the different measures). But our revised tool, instead of assigning individual prestige scores to the positions, dichotomizes the positions into those with relatively greater access to resources and those with relatively less. While still allowing for the calculation of the traditional extent measure, our tool does not allow for the calculation of upper reachability or range. While this does admittedly preclude some comparisons between our tool and previous research, it also points to the flexibility of the position generator in being amenable and adaptable to a wider range of research questions.

A final, but very important, difference between our tool and past position generators is that our tool allows for what we feel is a more insightful exploration of the structure of access to embedded resources. In addition to the traditional extent measure, we inquire about the *total number of ties* to each of the positions. While the extent of access to the positions as a *group*, in terms of the number of positions rich in embedded resources accessed, is of key interest, we suggest that the extent of access to *each* position is also crucial in gaining a better understanding of structure. For example, consider two respondents[8]: the first reveals that they have access to three positions rich in embedded resources (the typical measure of extent)

---

[8] For simplicity of description we ignore the strength or weakness of ties, and also assume that the positions have equivalent prestige scores. Simple extensions to the idea presented can be made by, for example, including some weighted measures of the intensity of tie and prestige score.

and the second reveals they only have access to two. With this information one could only conclude that the former has the access advantage. However, what if we were to discover that even though the latter only has access to two positions, they actually have four separate ties to individuals in each of these positions, while the former has two ties to each position? The second respondent with eight ties in total now has some measure of advantage over the first individual, who only has six ties. Clearly, this information is important and contributes greatly to the mapping of the complex structure of access to embedded resources.

To gain better insight into the structure of these networks, particularly in terms of the type and nature of ties involved as identified by Granovetter (1973) and Burt (2001), the RCP position generator also asked, as in past studies, that respondents differentiate these ties as either acquaintances (weak ties) or close friends (strong ties).[9] Finally, because of the geographic uniqueness of the region with its varying degrees of remoteness and access to other communities, and to obtain a better understanding of the structure of networks *between* communities, we asked that respondents further differentiate these ties as existing with others *inside* or *outside* their community.

12.3.2. Measuring Social Participation

In order to measure the type and extent of social organizations and activities in which respondents were involved, the RCP questionnaire also contained a series of questions asking residents if they participated in 17 types of social activities (and an additional option of including any "other" activities we did not mention).[10] In order to investigate the importance of context and/or geographic location to civic participation, the questionnaire also asked respondents to indicate whether any such activities occurred exclusively inside the community, exclusively outside, or both inside and outside. The activities identified were

- Artistic or craft/hobby group (e.g. pottery guild, crafter's association, quilting club)

- Business (e.g. Chamber of Commerce, Band Economic Development Committee, Community Economic Development Committee)

- Church-related activities (e.g. choir, bible study or care group, coffee or social committee)

- Community Service Group (e.g. Crisis Center, Food Bank or Community Kitchen)

- Cultural or ethnic association (e.g. Heritage Association, First Nations cultural groups)

---

[9] Respondents were also asked about the number of relatives they had inside and outside the community, but due to certain conceptual difficulties with assuming relatives to be strong ties, these were excluded from the current analysis.

[10] See Appendix 1 for the "Social Activities" section of the RCP instrument.

- Educational (e.g. Parent Advisory Council, School Board/Trustee, Curriculum/Language groups)
- Environmental (e.g. resource/conservation/management/action groups)
- Health (e.g. Cancer Society, Health Auxiliary, alternative or traditional healing groups)
- Neighborhood (e.g. Resident's Association, crime prevention groups)
- Political (e.g. political party, band or tribal council, town council)
- Self-help or support
- Service club (e.g. Lions Club, Rotary Club)
- Social club (e.g. card playing, music, book club)
- Spiritual/religious group
- Sports or recreation (e.g. soccer, karate, Little League, Curling Club, weekly pickup games)
- Work-related (e.g. union, cooperative, professional organization)
- Youth (e.g. Girl Guides, Boy Scouts, 4H)
- Any other activities not listed (*Please specify*)

This categorization of activities allows us to develop a measure of social participation for each respondent. Used in conjunction with the measures of network ties derived from the position generator, we are able to explore the extent to which social participation is related to different types of access to resources, which is the fundamental research question underlying our study. Furthermore, we are able to investigate how these relationships between social participation and network ties differ depending on other aspects of the participant's background, namely, their gender, age, educational status, marital status, and employment status.

12.3.3. Other Measures

As noted earlier, previous empirical research indicates significant gender differences in network structure, with men tending to be more active in larger, economic and nondomestic organizations, and women participating in smaller, community-oriented and domestic groups (McPherson and Smith-Lovin 1982). The rural, resource-based communities along B.C.'s coast are, however, distinctive in two important ways that may contribute to contradictory results. First, the number and variety of associations available to residents of an isolated, rural community is also typically much smaller than what is found in larger, more metropolitan areas. Second, people living in rural areas tend to have more diversified networks because, quite simply, they have a smaller pool of people with which they can interact (Erickson 2003). How many people in a large city personally know or interact with the mayor, a council member, or the like? In small, rural communities it is more likely that residents, regardless of gender, have such ties.

A wide range of studies has also shown that differences in network ties tend to be reduced or disappear when other aspects of their social background are taken into account. McPherson and Smith-Lovin's (1982) research showed that disparities in network composition were mitigated by employment status. In addition, they noted that education was one of the strongest predictors of affiliation. Similarly, Moore (1990), in her study of the structural determinants of social networks, found that the majority of network differences between men and women disappeared when variables related to work, age, and family were included as controls. A more recent study by Bekkers et al. (2003), focusing on the relationship between social networks and associations in the Netherlands, showed that male, higher-educated, middle-aged, married, and employed respondents demonstrated the highest levels of civic participation. They too found education to be highly predictive—the higher the level of education, the more likely the respondent would be a member of a voluntary association. Following in this vein, we also included age, marital status, educational attainment,[11] and employment status as controls.

12.4. RESULTS

12.4.1. Univariate Measures

Table 12.1 provides the descriptive statistics and a brief description of each of the variables included in this study. Overall, those who completed the RCP position generator have between 22 and 23 total ties to the resource-rich positions provided.[12] Residents average about 14 weak ties inside the community, and about 5 weak ties outside. As one would predict, the number of strong ties residents have is much less, averaging between two and three inside the community, and between one and two outside.

These results also reveal distinct differences in terms of both tie strength and location. In line with both Granovetter (1973) and Burt (2001), the raw number of weak ties one has to resource-rich positions exceeds the number of strong ties, regardless of the location: ~19 weak ties residents have to individuals holding positions rich in embedded resources greatly exceeds the 4 strong ties

[11] While a common analytic practice is to code educational attainment in a way that differentiates college or university graduates from all others, the decision to code the education variable as differentiating those who attended at least *some* college from others was based on the unique geographic nature of the study area. No major colleges or universities are located in the communities included in this study and opportunities for higher education are relatively limited to those existing outside the community. We decided to code the variable as such because of the desire to control for the fact that those who attended even some college likely did so in a different community, and the ties formed during this period were likely with others outside their community, which is of key interest here.

[12] Note that since, to our knowledge, this is the first time this particular measure of access to positions has been used, we cannot compare these results to other studies and therefore we do not know whether the number of ties is high, low, or unusual in any way.

Table 12.1. Descriptive statistics for relevant response and predictor variables ($N = 1,763$)

Name	Mean	SD	Minimum	Maximum	Description
Response					
WKIN	13.98	21.18	0	237	No. of WEAK TIES INSIDE the community
WKOUT	4.87	16.95	0	Ct	No. of WEAK TIES OUTSIDE the community
STRIN	2.51	5.03	0	62	No. of STRONG TIES INSIDE the community
STROUT	1.37	4.83	0	105	No. of STRONG TIES OUTSIDE the community
TIESTOT	22.73	34.98	0	507	TOTAL no. of TIES
Predictor					
ACTIN	1.92	1.84	0	17	No. of ACTIVITIES—INSIDE
ACTOUT	0.27	0.69	0	6	No. of ACTIVITIES—OUTSIDE
ACTBOTH	0.82	1.23	0	15	No. of ACTIVITIES—BOTH inside and outside
ACTTOT	3.00	2.16	1	17	TOTAL no. of ACTIVITIES
AGE	53.50	14.65	21	104	Age as of May 1, 2003 (in years)
GENDER	0.50	0.50	0	1	0 = 'male'; 1 = 'female'
COUPLE	0.71	0.46	0	1	0 = 'single'; 1 = 'married or live with partner'
FULLEMP	0.44	0.50	0	1	0 = 'not employed full time'; 1 = 'employed full time'
COLLEGE	0.55	0.50	0	1	0 = 'no college'; 1 = 'at least some college'

($t = 22.9$, 1,762 d.f., $p < .001$). Also, as one may expect with isolated communities, the number of ties inside the community far exceeds the number of ties outside the community (on average almost 17 ties inside the community and just over 6 ties outside, regardless of strength; $t = 16.6$, 1,762 d.f., $p < .001$).

Also, from Table 12.1, we see that the average person takes part in about 3 of the 17 total civic activities and/or organizations that were provided in the survey, with activities that are exclusively inside the community being most common (about 2), those functioning exclusively outside the least common (average between .5 and 1.0), and those that operated both inside and outside about 1.

In keeping with past studies, Table 12.1 also provides the extent, or total number of structural positions accessed for each tie type. While noting that significant correlations do exist between our current measure of the total number of ties and the extent measures (weak inside $r = .547$; weak outside $r = .416$; strong inside $r = .731$; strong outside $r = .562$[13]), it is also important to note that they do provide additional useful information. Looking at weak ties inside the community, we observe that the average resident has access to about 3.5 unique positions, but has access to these positions through contacts with ~14 different people. Likewise, for weak ties outside the community, the average resident has access to only one structural position, but is able to access this position through contacts with about

---

[13] Note that all correlations are significant at the .01 level (two-tailed).

Table 12.2. Summary of variables by gender ($N = 1,763$)

Name	Mean or percentage			Significance
	Total	Males	Females	
Weak ties—Inside	13.98	12.83	15.13	0.022
Weak ties—Outside	4.87	4.86	4.87	0.993
Strong ties—Inside	2.51	2.41	2.60	0.420
Strong ties—Outside	1.37	1.19	1.55	0.120
TIES—TOTAL	22.73	21.29	24.15	0.086
Activities—Inside	1.92	1.69	2.14	<0.001
Activities—Outside	0.27	0.27	0.28	0.686
Activities—Both	0.82	0.87	0.77	0.088
ACTIVITIES—TOTAL	3.00	2.82	3.18	<.001
Age	53.50	54.89	51.98	<0.001
Married or with partner	70.6%	75.9%	65.3%	<0.001
Employed full time	44.4%	51.0%	38.0%	<0.001
Attended at least some college	54.9%	50.3%	59.8%	<0.001

five different people. Similar differences are also seen with strong ties inside the community (on average, access to one structural position through contacts with between two and three different people), and strong ties outside the community (access to less than one position on average through just over one contact).

Another important aspect worth noting is the difference between weak ties outside the community and strong ties inside. An analysis looking only at extent would suggest that access to resources through these tie types are essentially the same (mean extent of weak outside = 1.02; mean of strong inside = 1.01). The new information provided by the RCP measure, however, points to a distinct difference: where weak ties to structural positions outside the community are cultivated through almost five different individuals, strong ties to structural positions inside the community are accessed through between two and three different people. Disregarding the functional difference between the strength of the tie and locational nature of it, our measure clearly shows that the two types of ties are not equivalent in terms of access to embedded resources—one who has five ties to a given resource-rich position is surely at an advantage over someone who has only three, as each additional tie increases the chances of knowing someone who is willing to help, and thus a greater probability of receiving assistance.

This is not to say that the traditional extent measure is not useful. On the contrary, it provides very insightful information. An extension of the extent measure is provided in Table 12.2, which shows the mean number of structural positions accessed by tie type, controlling for the total number of positions presented in the RCP position generator.[14]

[14] Note that the mean values were simply derived by taking the raw extent values and dividing each by 12, or the total number of positions presented in the RCP position generator that represented relatively higher levels of embedded resources.

Table 12.3. Civic participation by gender ($N = 1,763$)

Activity	Percentage			Significance
	Total	Males	Females	
Artistic or craft/hobby group	24.3%	17.7%	30.9%	<0.001
Business	12.0%	13.0%	11.1%	0.253
Church-related activities	19.3%	18.0%	20.6%	0.184
Community service group	18.3%	15.0%	21.6%	<0.001
Cultural or ethnic association	7.8%	7.2%	8.4%	0.393
Educational	13.7%	9.7%	17.6%	<0.001
Environmental	15.9%	16.0%	15.7%	0.907
Health	16.1%	11.7%	20.5%	<0.001
Neighborhood	13.4%	14.7%	12.1%	0.130
Political	5.8%	7.2%	4.5%	0.024
Self-help or support	12.8%	10.1%	15.5%	<0.001
Service club	14.0%	18.2%	9.8%	<0.001
Social club	25.0%	21.4%	28.5%	<0.001
Spiritual/religious group	16.9%	13.2%	20.5%	<0.001
Sports or recreation	48.5%	51.8%	45.2%	0.007
Work related	23.8%	25.6%	21.9%	0.081
Youth	7.3%	6.0%	8.6%	0.048
Other	5.5%	5.8%	5.2%	0.655

The mean values given represent the proportion of the total number of structural positions offered in the survey to which residents have access. Clearly, one's access to positions rich in embedded resources varies by tie strength and location. Residents have access to almost a third of all the positions through weak ties inside the community (29%), but less than one-tenth of the positions are accessible through weak ties outside the community (8.5%). Likewise, while 8.4 percent of the positions are accessed through strong ties inside the community, only about half as many (4.1%) are accessible through strong ties outside.

12.4.2. Gender Analysis

Table 12.3 allows us to examine the issue of gender inequality in access to resource-rich positions using the position generator measure. Looking at ties, note that women have significantly more weak ties *inside* the community than men ($p = .022$), contrary to the findings of Moore (1990), Lin (2000a), and Smith (2000), whose results showed that, in general, men have more weak ties to resource-rich positions. In addition, women are involved in significantly more activities *inside* the community than are men ($p < .001$), giving support to Coakes and Bishop's contention (1998) that women play a major role in the associational life of a rural community.

Table 12.4. Relationships between membership/social activities and social ties ($N = 1,763$ for all; all correlations calculated using Kendall's τ-b)

	Weak ties (acquaintances)		Strong ties (close friends)		Total
	Inside	Outside	Inside	Outside	
Activities					
Inside	0.179	−0.008	0.135	0.001	0.139
Significance *(two-tailed)*	(<0.001)	(0.671)	(<0.001)	(.950)	(<0.001)
Outside	−0.072	0.147	−0.037	0.111	0.004
Significance *(two-tailed)*	(<0.001)	(<0.001)	(0.080)	(<0.001)	(0.825)
Both	0.098	0.171	0.110	0.175	0.167
Significance *(two-tailed)*	(<0.001)	(<0.001)	(<0.001)	(<0.001)	(<0.001)
Total	0.200	0.139	0.187	0.136	0.234
Significance *(two-tailed)*	(<0.001)	(<0.001)	(<0.001)	(<0.001)	(<0.001)

Table 12.3 also shows interesting differences in our sample between men and women with regards to whether the respondent is married or with a partner (about 76% of males and 65% of females are married or with partner), employed full time or not (51% of the males and only 38% of the females are employed full time), and whether or not they attended at least some college (50% males and nearly 60% females attended some college).[15]

As can be seen from Table 12.4, the pattern of association found was similar to that found by McPherson and Smith-Lovin (1982) and Beggs, Hurlbert, and Haines (1996). The women in our sample tend to be involved in more domestic and community-centered groups, including artistic, health, and education groups, as well as social clubs and spiritual or religious groups, while the men are more involved in political groups, service clubs, and sports groups. However, we did not find significant differences between their involvement in business and work-related groups. This result may not be entirely surprising given (a) the lower level of full-time employment for the females in our sample and (b) the probability that these types of organizations are not as common in these small, rural communities.

In this region, which provides little opportunity for obtaining employment, only 38 percent of women in our sample were employed full time. This may initially appear to put them at a disadvantage in terms of opportunities to access positions rich in embedded resources. However, a more considered reflection leads us to suggest that this relatively more educated group of women, who are not employed full time, would find community groups, organizations, and social activities a good way to get involved, meet others, and spend their time productively, and in doing so manage to develop useful strong and weak ties.

---

[15] Note $p < .001$ for all tests of proportions mentioned here.

Table 12.5. Model predicting weak ties inside the community ($N = 1,763$)

Name	Estimate	SE	t	$Pr(> |t|)$	Expected % change in DV for inclusion of significant factor	Wald 95% CI lower bound	Wald 95% CI upper bound
INTERCEPT	1.829	0.185	9.863	<0.001	—	—	—
ACTIN	0.106	0.015	7.270	<0.001	11.2	8.3	14.0
ACTOUT	−0.206	0.059	−3.487	<0.001	−18.7	−30.6	−6.7
ACTBOTH	0.112	0.020	5.646	<0.001	11.9	7.9	15.8
AGE	−0.002	0.003	−0.865	0.387	—	—	—
Factor(GENDER) Female	0.157	0.067	2.351	0.019	17.0	3.5	30.5
Factor(COUPLE) married/with partner	0.115	0.071	1.604	0.109	—	—	—
Factor(FULLEMP) employed full time	0.513	0.071	7.221	<0.001	67.0	52.6	81.4
Factor(COLLEGE) some college	0.363	0.069	5.303	<0.001	43.8	29.9	57.7

As for the types of organizations available, McPherson and Smith-Lovin (1982) argued that much of the gender difference they found resulted from the different types of organizations men and women participate in. If this is indeed the case, then the relative lack of diversity of types of activities available in these communities may contribute to our results, but a comparison of the types of activities available in these rural communities, as compared to more urban locales, is beyond the scope of this chapter.

12.4.3. The Structure of Access to Embedded Resources

While the univariate and gender-related analyses are insightful and important, this chapter focuses on the *relationship* between civic participation and access to positions rich in embedded resources. Table 12.5 shows the correlations (Kendall's τ-b) between the number of activities one participates in that are inside the community, outside, and both, against the number of weak and strong ties both inside and outside the community.

Our primary research question asks whether participation in voluntary social activities and organizations is significantly associated with an individual's access to resources embedded in certain structural social positions. In support of Putnam (1993a, 2000), Granovetter (1973), and Erickson (2003), we find that there is in fact a strong relationship between civic participation and the formation of beneficial social ties. At the overall level, the *total* number of activities one participates in is significantly positively correlated with the *total* number of ties that one has to resource-rich positions ($r = .234$; $p < .001$). But, while this resolves this broad question by indicating that civic participation and one's access to embedded resources are not independent of each other, a closer look at the strength and locational aspects is of greater utility.

How does the strength and location of the tie relate to civic participation? Looking at the bottom row of Table 12.5, representing the *total* number of activities one participates in, we note that all types of ties, strong and weak, and inside and outside the community, are significantly associated (all $p < .001$). Initially, this may seem to imply that strength or location does not matter since all are significant, but it is important to keep in mind that we are looking at four *distinctly different forms of access* to resources.

The social resources accessible by an individual differ greatly by the type of tie, weak or strong. If, for example, it is information the individual requires, research suggests that weak ties tend to provide nonredundant information through reaching beyond the bounds of their more immediate social network (Granovetter 1973; Burt 1992, 2001; Lin 2000a, 2001b). However, if the required resource is more economically based, such as a monetary loan, one should expect that strong ties will be more advantageous to the individual (Tigges, Browne, and Green 1998). This represents two very different aspects of access to resources.

In terms of whether the tie is inside or outside the community, here too we can expect distinct differences. As the number and variety of positions accessible to an individual in these rural communities are limited, one should expect that in many instances different positions, and hence different resources, would be accessible outside the community than would be available inside the community. Therefore, we argue that what may seem like a lack of variability between strength and location is more complicated.

As one would expect, the number of social activities one participates in that operate solely inside the community is significantly positively correlated with the number of weak ties one has inside their community ($p < .001$), as well as the number of strong ties inside ($p < .001$). Note that the relationship between participation in activities solely inside the community is not significant against either weak ($p = .671$) or strong ties ($p = .950$) with positions outside the community. Finally, regarding the relationship between participation in activities or groups exclusively outside the community and ties to positions outside the community, our findings show, as one might expect, that these activities are significantly positively related to both weak ($p < .001$) and strong ($p < .001$) ties.

Interestingly, we also find that civic participation outside the community is significantly *negatively* correlated with the number of weak ties inside the community ($p < .001$). This finding offers support for Woolcock's argument (1998) that putting too much emphasis on forming bridging relationships outside the community can be harmful to network integration within the community. Since we cannot determine causation with a correlational analysis, we offer two possible interpretations for this result. First, the time, effort, and expense of traveling to activities and organizations outside the community may detract from the amount of time that one has to formulate weak ties inside the community,

Table 12.6. Model predicting weak ties outside the community ($N = 1,763$)

Name	Estimate	SE	t	Pr(> |t|)	Expected % change in DV for inclusion of significant factor	Wald 95% CI lower bound	Wald 95% CI upper bound
INTERCEPT	0.083	0.423	0.196	0.845	—	—	—
ACTIN	0.027	0.036	0.745	0.456	—	—	—
ACTOUT	0.200	0.073	2.728	0.006	22.1	7.2	37.0
ACTBOTH	0.202	0.029	6.903	<0.001	22.3	16.5	28.2
AGE	0.003	0.006	0.442	0.659	—	—	—
Factor(GENDER) female	0.055	0.144	0.384	0.701	—	—	—
Factor(COUPLE) married/ with partner	0.241	0.158	1.519	0.129	—	—	—
Factor(FULLEMP) employed full time	0.617	0.157	3.933	<0.001	85.4	52.1	118.7
Factor(COLLEGE) some college	0.769	0.160	4.795	<0.001	115.8	81.7	149.9

especially in rural, coastal communities that are fairly isolated. Alternatively, those who have a strong number of weak ties inside their own community may feel little need to go outside their community to participate in activities, while those with strong ties outside the community may have less need to form weak ones internally.

12.4.4. Modeling Access to Embedded Resources

Despite the useful insights provided in the preceding analysis, simple bivariate correlations do not, by themselves, provide adequate insight into the mediating effects of one variable *upon* another, and thus fail to adequately assess how respondents' sociodemographic characteristics and civic involvement affect their variable access to embedded resources. It is worth mentioning here that considerable debate exists regarding the causal direction of the relationship between social ties and civic participation. However, it is our interest to explore how personal attributes as well as voluntary participation in civic activities *affect* one's access to embedded resources, and we therefore chose to model the number of weak and strong ties as *dependent* on the number of social activities one participates in, as well as the sociodemographic variables mentioned previously. Table 12.6 provides the significance of individual coefficient estimates, as well as estimated standard errors, for the models predicting the relation of weak ties to embedded resources inside the community, weak ties outside, strong ties inside, and strong ties outside.[16]

---

[16] Since all of the response variables have the general form of Poisson-distributed counts, typical linear regression procedures are not appropriate as inefficient, inconsistent, and biased estimates can result (Long 1997; Agresti 2002). Also, the overdispersed nature of the data (the variance of the mean

Similar to the correlational results, we see from Table 12.6 that participation in all types of activities are significant in predicting the number of *weak ties* one has *inside* the community (activities inside, $p < .001$; outside, $p < .001$; both, $p < .001$). Also note that the effect of participating in activities that function solely outside the community is again negative, and the estimates imply that, holding all other variables constant, every additional activity outside the community that an individual participates in *decreases*[17] the expected number of weak ties inside the community. Given the geographical considerations of our rural, coastal communities, it is not surprising that time spent socializing outside the community can detract from opportunities to form important ties within the community. Hence, our findings support Leonard and Onyx (2003) and Woolcock (1998), who argue against placing too much emphasis on the formation of weak or bridging ties outside community in favor of more balanced social networks comprised of both strong intracommunity ties and supportive outside ties.

Parallel to our earlier results, and contrary to other studies on gender differences in network diversity (Moore 1990; Smith 2000; Lin 2000a, 2001b), we find that women ($p = .019$) do have a greater number of expected weak ties inside the community. In addition, those who are employed full time ($p < .001$) are expected to have more weak ties than those who are not, and those who have attended at least some college ($p < .001$) are expected to have more weak ties to positions rich in embedded resources than those who have not. Age ($p = .387$) and whether or not the respondent lives with a partner ($p = .109$) were not significant.

Table 12.6 also shows that the number of *weak ties* one has to embedded resources *outside* the community is significantly predicted by the number of voluntary activities and organizations that one participates in exclusively outside the community ($p = .006$), and those that occur both inside and outside ($p < .001$). Holding all other variables constant, both significant relations have a similar effect, where we would expect each additional activity one participates in to increase the expected number of weak ties outside the community. Also as one might expect, the number of activities or organizations one participates in that operate solely inside the community ($p = .456$) is found to have little effect on the number of weak ties to embedded resources one has outside the community.

Whereas gender was a predictor of weak ties inside the community, it is not a significant predictor of the number of weak ties outside the community

---

μ is not equal to the conditional variance σ^2) precluded the use of the simpler Poisson General Linear Model. To confront these difficulties, a *quasilikelihood* GLM in the R statistical software (2003) was used that simultaneously estimates a dispersion parameter, ϕ, along with the coefficients, where this $\phi = 1$ for data fitting the standard Poisson model and some estimated value greater than one for overdispersed data (see Agresti 2002).

[17] Note that in this study we are only focusing on the direction, or sign, of the coefficient estimates instead of the actual values. Those who are interested in mediating the effects of the independent variables should note that with the quasilikelihood GLM the percentage change in the expected count of the dependent variable for a unit change in x_k, holding all other variables in the model constant, is computed as (%change = $100[\exp(\beta_k x \ \delta) - 1]$) (Long 1997).

($p = .701$). Similar to weak ties inside, however, full-time employment is significant ($p < .001$) in predicting the number of weak ties to embedded resources outside the community. Given the nature of resource-based employment in these isolated rural communities which can require extensive traveling to access and transport the resources, this result is likely due to the influence of keeping in touch with coworkers and other business or job-related contacts in other communities.

Additionally, those who have attended at least some college ($p < .001$) have an expected number of weak ties outside the community greater than those who did not. There are two possible, and related, reasons for this. First, those who have attended college or university have likely done so outside their community, and as a result have formed weak ties or friendships which they have currently maintained. Second, as noted by Bekkers et al. (2003) and Moore (1990), the higher-educated are more likely to have ties with individuals in relatively resource-rich positions, which were likely promulgated through their advanced education. Here again, age and whether or not the respondent lives with a partner were not significant.

When predicting *strong ties inside* the community, we again see a pattern similar to the correlations, where participation in activities that function exclusively inside the community ($p < .001$) and those that operate both inside and outside the community ($p < .001$) are highly significant. Here, holding all other variables constant, we see from the positive sign of the coefficient estimates that for every civic activity one participates in exclusively inside the community, the number of strong ties inside the community is expected to increase. Likewise for every additional activity that operates both inside and outside the community, we expect to see an increase in the number of strong ties inside the community.

In terms of measures of variable access to embedded resources as they relate to *strong ties inside* the community, the only sociodemographic variable of significance is the respondent's full-time employment status ($p = .002$), where someone employed full time is expected to have more strong ties inside the community than one not employed full time. While similar to the predictable relations already discussed between full-time employment status and weak ties, this result also seems to point to a not-so-obvious link between employment status and strong ties. Past research (Granovetter 1973; Moore 1990) has implied that employment is an important factor in developing *weak* ties, but little has been said regarding the role of employment in developing *strong* ties. The dynamics and explanation of this relation are not clear or obvious, and future research should explore this phenomenon.

Finally, when predicting *strong ties outside* the community, and somewhat different from the correlational analysis, all activities are found to be significant (activities inside $p = .035$; outside $p < .001$; both $p < .001$). While the correlational analyses failed to show an association between strong ties outside the community and participation in activities solely inside the community, we now see that after controlling for our sociodemographic measures, a significant relation arises. While an explanation for this result is not immediately obvious, it may imply that, after controlling for personal characteristics, people who are involved in more social activities are simply more social in general.

With regard to *strong ties outside* the community, we also see the significant variable effect of full-time employment status ($p = .020$), as those who are employed full time would expect to have more strong ties with individuals outside their community. Again, given the geographical factors existing in B.C.'s rural, coastal communities, it is likely that those who are employed full time would have more opportunity and financial means to go outside the community to participate in social activities with friends. This is also consistent with the finding that those that have attended at least some college ($p = .012$) could expect to have more strong ties, as they would be more likely to have made those strong ties while outside of the community attending college, and would also be more likely to have the ability to maintain them.

Finally, the finding that females ($p = .039$) have more *strong* ties to resource-rich positions *outside* the community than males is consistent with the results on education discussed previously. The women in our sample were more likely to have attended college than the men, and this was likely done outside the community. Thus, they are also more likely to have made strong ties outside the community, and because they are less likely to be employed full time, they have the time and ability to maintain them in the long run.

12.5. CONCLUSION

In this chapter, we have explored the relationship between involvement in social activities and the potential access that this gives to resource-rich positions embedded in the social structure. We have undertaken this analysis using the position generator, an important methodological tool that enabled us to measure the structure of access to social resources by providing vital information on types of ties (weak or strong) and location of ties (inside or outside the community) to resource-rich positions.

The greatest asset of the position generator is its flexibility without losing validity, which allowed us to adapt it to the unique social structural contexts of a remote region of rural Canada dominated by resource-based communities. However, despite its utility and flexibility, the position generator is not without limitations. The insights that it provides are generally limited to a comprehensive overview of the *structure* of people's social networks and the *potential* access to embedded resources located within them. The position generator is not able to explicitly capture the social processes whereby people utilize their network ties for social benefit. That is, the position generator can provide important insight into the extent to which respondents have contact with persons in resource-rich positions and have the potential access to social capital resources that they may be able to call upon. However, access to persons in such positions is a necessary, but not necessarily sufficient, prerequisite to being able to utilize the social resources held by people in those positions. Thus, the next stage in our research will involve an assessment of the *process of utilizing* social capital in these communities.

In this chapter, we have presented results from the revised position generator used in our study of B.C. coastal communities. These results provide support for Putnam (1993*a*, 2000), who argues that civic participation is related to the development of critical networks that are crucial in gaining access to embedded resources and developing social capital, and also provides evidence in support of Granovetter (1973) and Burt (2001) by showing that the *type* of tie is relevant as well.

Granovetter (1973) suggests that going outside one's own social group or community to make weak ties is a way to access new, nonredundant information and resources. Burt (2001) proposes that people who have ties that bridge networks, or communities in this case, have more access to social resources due to their role as "information brokers." While our results show that the majority of ties to potential resource-rich positions were weak ties located inside the community (which is not unexpected, given the geographical isolation of many of these communities), they also show a sizable number of ties to resource-rich positions outside the community as well, and more weak than strong. We can therefore see that coastal B.C. residents are making important ties to positions rich in embedded resources, and that these ties show predictable patterns of significant association with civic participation.

While participation in activities inside these rural, coastal communities is beneficial in making ties inside the community, and participation in activities outside the community is beneficial in making ties outside the community (although they have the ability to detract from making *weak* ties inside the community), participation in activities that bridge or span communities (i.e. located both inside and outside the community) is beneficial for making both strong and weak ties in *both* places. A crucial point worth clarifying is that those activities that take place solely outside the community and those that take place both inside and outside represent what Burt (2001) refers to as structural holes, or conduits; people who participate in them have access to resources in more than one place and thus their ties may expose them to resources they would not be able to access through activities located solely inside or solely outside the community. This finding demonstrates one way for rural residents to form the type of social networks recommended by Leonard and Onyx (2003) and Woolcock (1998), who advocate for balanced networks with no particular emphasis on one type of tie in a given location. Our findings show involvement in groups that span communities leads to both weak and strong ties located both inside and outside the community, and thus allows residents to form diverse, stable networks to resource-rich positions.

In terms of the effects of sociodemographic variables, women have more weak ties inside the community and more strong ties outside the community, despite their lower level of employment. These results may seem to run counter to earlier studies (McPherson and Smith-Lovin 1982; Beggs and Hurlbert 1997; Smith 2000; Lin, Fu, and Hsung 2001; Lin 2001*b*) that have shown a significant difference between men and women in terms of access to embedded resources in general (with men typically having greater access than women, as mentioned earlier). However, the coastal communities in which the RCP study took place provide a distinctive social context and isolated geographical location, both of which produce network patterns different from those often found in more central locations. On the other hand, the very isolation of many of the communities in our study allows us something of an ideal typical situation in which to assess the relationship between ties inside and outside communities in terms of their ability to provide access to social capital resources.

While our findings suggest that full-time employment is a significant predictor of the number and type of ties, regardless of location, education is also quite influential. Even though the women in our sample are less likely to be employed full time, they have a significantly higher level of education, and it is likely that the resulting gender difference in ties favoring women is highly attributable to this educational disparity. Regardless, gender, education, and employment clearly interact in complicated ways in this region, and warrants further research in order to disentangle these effects.

Given these results, we can conclude that, despite being geographically isolated, the residents of rural B.C. are not socially isolated, as they use their participation in social activities to build beneficial social ties *both inside and outside* their communities, therefore gaining potential access to valuable social resources. These results provide strong support for the inclusion of context and/or geographical location in the understanding of the structure of access to potential resources in any community study. In addition, these results also underscore the importance of investigating the influence of sociodemographic factors, such as gender, employment status, and education, on network composition within a given context or geographical location. Our analysis demonstrates that such social variables become highly significant social dimensions that impact how people in rural, coastal B.C. are able to access the social resources potentially available to them through their network ties.

APPENDIX 1 Instruments

RCP Position Generator

69 B. The following are positions that might be held by *other people* in your community. We would like to know whether you know anyone in each of these positions. If you do, please indicate whether these people are *acquaintances, close friends,* or *relatives,* and whether these people live inside or outside of your community by writing how many of these people you know in the boxes below.

For example: If you have **two** acquaintances who are school teachers **inside** your community and **one** friend who is a school teacher **outside** your community, you would fill in the boxes like this:

Type of Position	Number of ACQUAINTANCES		Number of CLOSE FRIENDS		Number of RELATIVES	
	Inside	Outside	Inside	Outside	Inside	Outside
a. School teacher (primary or secondary)	2			1		

Type of Position	Number of ACQUAINTANCES		Number of CLOSE FRIENDS		Number of RELATIVES	
	Inside	Outside	Inside	Outside	Inside	Outside
a. Aquaculture or fish plant manager						
b. Aquaculture related work of any kind (eg, hatchery, grow out, processing, diver, etc.)						
c. Commercial fisherman						
d. Elected or hereditary First Nation Chief						
e. Local health professional (eg, doctor, nurse)						
f. Local police officer						
g. Logger						
h. Manager or administrative officer of a First Nation Band or Tribal Council						
i. Member of the Chamber of Commerce						
j. Member of the Regional District Council						
k. Member of the Town Council						
l. Mine manager (includes oil and gas)						
m. Mine worker (includes oil and gas)						
n. Pastor, priest or other church leader						
o. Pulp mill, paper mill or sawmill manager						
p. Pulp mill, paper mill or saw mill worker						
q. School teacher (primary or secondary)						
r. Union leader or member						

RCP Social Activities Scale

Section E: Your Social Activities

This section asks questions about some of your social activities.

The following question asks about your **current** involvement in various activities and **where** they are located. 62. Are you currently involved with any of the following? (*Please select Yes for ALL that apply.*)	If *Yes*, are these activities located mainly inside your community, outside your community, or both?		
	Yes	**Inside** **Outside** **Both**		
a. Artistic or craft/hobby group (eg, Pottery Guild, crafter's association, quilting club)	○⇨	○ ○ ○		
b. Business (eg, Chamber of Commerce, Band Economic Development Committee, Community Economic Development Committee)	○⇨	○ ○ ○		
c. Church–related activities (eg, choir, bible study or care group, coffee or social committee)	○⇨	○ ○ ○		
d. Community Service Group (eg, Crisis Centre, Food Bank or Community Kitchen)	○⇨	○ ○ ○		
e. Cultural or ethnic associations (eg, Heritage Association, First Nations cultural groups)	○⇨	○ ○ ○		
f. Educational (eg, Parent Advisory Council, School Board/Trustee, Curriculum/Language groups)	○⇨	○ ○ ○		
g. Environmental (eg, resource conservation/management/action groups)	○⇨	○ ○ ○		
h. Health (eg, Cancer Society, Health Auxiliary, alternative or traditional healing groups)	○⇨	○ ○ ○		
i. Neighbourhood (eg, Resident's Association, crime prevention groups)	○⇨	○ ○ ○		
j. Political (eg, political party, Band or Tribal Council, town council)	○⇨	○ ○ ○		
k. Self–help or support	○⇨	○ ○ ○		
l. Service Club (eg, Lions Club, Rotary Club)	○⇨	○ ○ ○		
m. Social club (eg, card playing, music, book club)	○⇨	○ ○ ○		
n. Spiritual/religious group	○⇨	○ ○ ○		
o. Sports or recreation (eg, soccer, karate, Little League, Curling Club, weekly pick–up games)	○⇨	○ ○ ○		
p. Work–related (eg, union, cooperative, professional organization)	○⇨	○ ○ ○		
q. Youth (eg, Girl Guides, Boy Scouts, 4H)	○⇨	○ ○ ○		
r. Any other activities not listed above. (**Please specify** ✎ _____)	○⇨	○ ○ ○		

13

Gender, Network Capital, Social Capital, and Political Capital: The Consequences of Personal Network Diversity for Environmentalists in British Columbia[1]

D. B. Tindall and Jeffrey J. Cormier

13.1. INTRODUCTION

This chapter is an effort to examine the complex relationship that exists between social capital, gender, and political participation. Social capital, understood here as the social resources embedded in networks, can be the property of both individuals *and* communities. The more dense and diverse one's personal network is, measured as ties to a variety of occupations, organizations, and politicians, the greater the amount of social capital resources one has at one's disposal. With this logic, social capital resides largely within the purview of the individual. There are, however, also collective benefits that accrue from these same individuals possessing greater social capital resources. When, as a result of possessing increased social capital resources, individuals are encouraged to participate more fully as citizens, there is an increase in social capital at the aggregate or community level. The link between individual social networks and the ways in which this translates into increased political participation is the starting point for our analysis.

Added to this analysis is the role gender plays in structuring the availability and accessibility of social capital resources. We know that the social networks of women and men are different (Erickson 2004). Does this difference lead to important differences in terms of the types of social capital resources accessible to men and women? More importantly, do these social capital and network differences help explain the differences we observe in terms of women and men's political participation? These are the central questions that motivate our analysis of network structure, social capital, and political participation in the environmental movement in British Columbia.

[1] We thank Bonnie H. Erickson, Barry Wellman, Robert Brym, John Hannigan, Noreen Begoray, Beth Michaela Simpson, and Joanna Robinson for their assistance with this research. This research was supported with funding from the Social Science and Humanities Research Council of Canada.

Our analysis departs somewhat from previous uses of the notions of social capital and networks. Some researchers are interested in how social capital, possessed by individuals, is used to achieve a host of individual instrumental goods, usually related to labor markets (e.g. finding a job, getting a promotion, and hiring for a job). The chapters in Part II of Lin, Cook, and Burt's *Social Capital: Theory and Research* are exemplary examples because they demonstrate the ways in which individuals use social capital to gain purchase on instrumental goals (Lin, Cook, and Burt 2001*a*). Lin reinforces this point in his introduction to the volume: "Research on social-resources theory has verified the proposition that social resources or social capital enhance an individual's attained status, such as occupational status, authority, and placement in certain industries" (Lin 2001*a*: 22). Other work that falls into this tradition include Lin's work on status attainment (Lin 1990, 1999*b*), Burt's research on structural holes (Burt 1992), Granovetter's work on the strength of weak ties (Granovetter 1973, 1974), and Marsden's study of mobility (Marsden 1987).

A second research tradition looks into how social capital, this time conceptualized as in the possession of whole communities, leads to expressive noninstrumental goals. As Hall (1999: 418) points out, "[s]ocial capital is said to facilitate effective participation in politics, the implementation of many kinds of public policy, and generalized support for the political system." One of the fundamental assumptions of this research is that associationalism and cognate forms of sociability generate social capital by the mere fact that people interact face-to-face, irrespective of their primary goals or instrumental interests. Here social capital leads to more expressive outcomes: they include the norms of civility, solidarity, obligation, trust, and so on that result as more and more people associate and participate in political activities. Putnam's work (Putnam 1993*a*) comparing the level of associationalism in regions of Italy is well known, as is his more recent finding that rates of civic engagement are declining in the United States (1995). Peter Hall (1999) has added research on Britain; and Baer, Curtis, and Grabb (2001) provide important cross-national data on 15 nations.

The present analysis departs from these two traditions that tend to assume a link between level of analysis and social capital outcomes. Most analyses of individuals look at the instrumental market-based outcomes of social capital, and most analyses of communities look at expressive politically oriented outcomes. Our interest here is in exploring how individuals, as the unit of analysis, access social capital resources through networks toward broader, expressive, political, and therefore public goals. Methodologically we focus on individuals as possessors of social capital; however, we are most interested in how this type of capital leads to collective public goods such as political participation. Increased political participation by *individuals*, in our estimation, contributes to larger *collective goals*. We analyze secondary data collected from members of the British Columbia environmental movement as a case study of the relationship between social networks, gender, and political participation.

13.1.1. Theoretical Background

13.1.1.1. Networks and Political Participation

Three points about the relationship between networks, gender, and political participation are necessary to begin our analysis. The first has to do with the ways in which social capital, as a resource embedded in networks, acts to facilitate and support participation in a range of political activities, both formal (e.g. voting, political party membership, and participation in a political party) and informal (e.g. membership in a social movement organization, attending a demonstration, and signing a petition). In particular, much has been written about the importance of networks for recruitment into social movements (for a review of this literature, see McAdam 2003). Significantly less has been written, however, on how networks affect more traditional formal norms of political participation (for an exception, see Knoke 1990*b*; Verba, Schlozman, and Brady 1995).

When it comes to the role that networks play in informal political activity, several processes are by now well understood. One is that prior interpersonal ties to friends, relatives, colleagues, or neighbors who are already politically involved facilitate entrance into collective action (McAdam 1986; Klandermans and Oegema 1987; Fernandez and McAdam 1988; Gould 1993, 1995; McAdam and Paulsen 1993; Opp and Gern 1993). Network ties provide potential recruits with much-needed social capital, including information about opportunities for action and solidarity incentives to join in those actions (McAdam 2003). Another is that social movements have a tendency to build on already existent social networks (Della Porta and Diani 1999; Glenn 1999). This happens because the channels of communication essential for mobilizing people to act collectively depend on reciprocal bonds of trust and solidarity. Such bonds reside in those relationships embedded in social networks, which, in turn, facilitate individuals' desire to act collectively. As Diani (2003: 7) points out, "Networks provide opportunities for action through the circulation of information about on-going activities, existing organizations, people to contact, and a reduction of the potential cost attached to participation." In this way, the potential for political action and recruitment is deeply rooted in social networks.

While networks can facilitate political action, they can also inhibit more engaged forms of political participation. For instance, Snow, Zurcher, and Ekland-Olson (1980) demonstrate how interpersonal ties are not in and of themselves enough to account for the differences in recruitment success we see in some social movement activity. They argue that "reasons for participating or not are largely contingent on the extent to which extra-movement networks function as countervailing influences" (Snow et al. 1980: 793). Such countervailing forces include commitments to family (i.e. spouse and children), employer, or even one's reputation (Snow et al. 1980). These alternative extramovement networks demand time, energy, and commitment, personal resources that pull individuals away from committing fully to political activity (McAdam 1986). Some social positions (e.g. student, unmarried, young, and retired) allow for greater "biographical availability," while others (e.g. employed, married, midlife, and primary caregiver) tend to allow for less.

We believe that some of the same network dynamics are at work in the more conventional forms of political participation we are interested in. The question remains as to what extent network effects impact political participation over and above the sometimes countervailing forces of social position. In other words, are the resources that accrue through social networks strong enough to propel individuals into political activity, or is social position— measured in terms of selected demographic variables—a key element for explaining such action? Our analysis will shed light on this question.

13.1.1.2. *Types of Social Networks*

All social networks are not created equal. There are a host of ways to describe and analyze network structure, as well as the type of social tie characteristics that go along with various networks (cf. Burt 1980*a*, 1980*b*). One such way is to look at what has sometimes been referred to as "network range." This particular term has in fact come to take on a variety of meanings in the literature on network structure. Lin, Fu, and Hsung (2001), for instance, use the term "range" to mean differences in prestige ranking between the highest and lowest social tie an individual has to various occupational groups. They use the term "extensity" to refer to the number of occupational positions accessed by individuals. Our own conceptualization follows Burt's definition of range as meaning the diversity of social ties an individual has to other individuals as well as a variety of social groups (Burt 1980*b*). We think that the term "network diversity" better captures the essence of this network property over the more traditional notion of network range.

Previous research reports that network diversity is crucial in providing various social capital resources. Erickson's work (Erickson 1996*b*, 2001, 2003, 2004) on network diversity clearly demonstrates that having acquaintances from a variety of social worlds—in terms of occupation, gender, ethnicity, and so on—expands the types of information and level of social support individuals receive. Her work on the Toronto security industry supports the claim that social capital, here measured as the degree of network diversity, aids in a host of labor market contexts (finding a job, getting a *good* job, mobility, and promotion) as well as related areas of personal health and well-being (Erickson 2003; for social support see Wellman and Wortley 1990). Having a variety of acquaintances, especially those who are very different from oneself, allows individuals more direct access to a variety of information sources. This information is a valuable resource that is put to use at work and at home for both personal and professional advantage.

However, the relationship that exists between network diversity and political participation is less well understood. While it is easy to understand that the more contacts an individual has to others from diverse social class, organizational, and political backgrounds the more likely that individual will be engaged in political debate and discussion, there has been little empirical research into the dynamics of this relationship up to this point. While we can imagine that the exposure to political ideas one gets from having diverse social contacts would lead to some sort of greater engagement politically, this remains to be explored empirically. Our goal here is to begin to look into the connections that exist between network diversity and political participation.

13.1.1.3. Gender and Political Participation

Finally, both social capital and network diversity are heavily mediated by gender. Women and men have different access to social networks and therefore different access to the social capital resources that accrue from these networks (Erickson 2003, 2004). As Helen Russell (1999: 219) points out, ". . . the very building blocks of social networks are gendered." Examining the distribution of these different types of gendered social capital resources within communities, as well as the link between "networks of sociability and patterns of political engagement," are key questions that need to be addressed when looking at the complex relationship between gender, social capital, and political participation (Lowndes 2000: 534).

While it has diminished with time, a gender gap still exists in terms of women and men's interest in and involvement with formal politics. In terms of mass political participation, at least one fact is striking: women participate in politics to a lesser extent than men (Black and McGlen 1979; Kay et al. 1987). With the exception of voting, considered a minimal activity of political involvement, women discuss politics less often, pay less attention to elections, and are less likely to contact politicians about an issue that concerns them (Brodie and Chandler 1991). Brodie and Chandler (1991) found that during the 1980 Canadian federal election, men were more likely to watch the leaders' debate, work for a political party, and discuss politics and political issues with friends, family, and coworkers. Similar findings were revealed during the 2000 federal election: fewer women paid attention to election news, watched the leaders' debate, were members of a political party, or had contacted a parliamentarian (Tremblay and Trimble 2003).

At least part of the explanation for this has to do with women's social role and some of the barriers and limitations that go along with that role (O'Neill 1995; Ollivier and Tremblay 2000). As a result of having heavier domestic responsibilities, especially in terms of childcare (Frederick 1993, 1995), many women have less free time to watch television, read the newspaper, engage in political debate and discuss, or help organize for politics. As with participation in informal politics like social movements, some women lack the biographical availability necessary to participate in extensive political activities.

With regard to voting, already mentioned as the minimal and therefore least onerous activity that counts as political participation, women have managed to all but close the gap (Kay et al. 1987; Maillé 1990). At the elite level of politics, the situation is somewhat more complex. In the Canadian parliament, for instance, women are underrepresented by some 74 percent of their demographic weight (Royal Commission on Electoral Reform and Party Financing 1991). From this it is clear that numerically fewer women are engaged in the highest levels of politics than are men. Further, most of the increase that has taken place in terms of women taking positions as parliamentarians and senators has occurred since the mid-1980s (Trimble and Tremblay 2003). In the 1979 election, for instance, there were only 3.6 percent women in the House of Commons; by 1997, this number had grown to 20.5 percent. These numbers make it clear that barriers still exist to women's full entrance in and access to positions of political power.

The question remains: are the socioeconomic and network resources that elite female politicians possess different from those possessed by either the general female population or their elite male counterparts? While the research record here is mixed, certain trends are clearly evident. The first is that elite female politicians are *very* different from the female population as a whole (Black and Erickson 2000). Recruitment to public office usually means ready access to social, economic, and network resources that far exceed those possessed by the general population. As a result, female politicians tend to have higher educational qualifications, more economic independence, and greater occupational status (Black and Erickson 2000). This sets them apart from the general population as a whole as well as from the majority of women in society, who traditionally have had less access than males have to valuable social, economic, and network resources for political participation.

Second, while female political elites are different from the larger female population, they are in fact closer to their male counterparts in terms of many socioeconomic and network resources (Black and Erickson 2000). One important difference, however, and one especially relevant to our analysis, has to do with types of organizational networks. There is a marked difference in the types of organizations women and men belong to preceding their entrance into politics. Male politicians tend to be much more involved in political and socioeconomically oriented groups and associations. Female politicians, on the other hand, are more involved in cultural, educational, and community-oriented groups (Gingras, Maille, and Tardy 1989; Tardy, Tremblay, and Legault 1997). This general finding is reinforced with Black and Erickson's survey of female and male office seekers to the House of Commons in 1993 (Black and Erickson 2000). Women candidates were much more involved in local interest groups, community service organizations, and women's organizations than were men candidates (Black and Erickson 2000). Clearly, men and women, at least at the elite level of politics, are accessing different types of social capital network resources and from different organizational sources.

We believe that some of the same dynamics at work at the elite level of politics also apply at the level of mass political participation. In other words, people who are more politically active are embedded in more diverse social networks. Further, men and women who are politically active access different types of social networks and belong to different types of organizations. Our task here will be to explore in more detail the impact that network social capital and diversity of network ties have on political participation, particularly as these processes relate to gender differences.

13.2. THEORETICAL MODEL, HYPOTHESES, AND ANALYTICAL STRATEGY

In the literature on social capital, there is sometimes a conflation between social structure as an enabler or predictor of social capital and social structure as a form of social capital (Tindall and Wellman 2001), although Lin (1999*b*) draws a useful distinction between potential access to social capital and utilization of such capital. In the present analysis, we divide the broad category of social capital into three distinct concepts: (*a*) network capital, (*b*) social capital, and (*c*) political capital. First, network capital refers to network structures that provide access to social capital (e.g. personal network ties, Wellman and Frank 2001). In our analyses, we focus on network diversity as a major indicator of network capital.

Second, social capital is thought to be a useful resource in itself (cf. Coleman 1988). We believe that social capital—here understood as resources such as information, social influence, solidarity, and social support—is produced and channeled through the network measures we develop.

In addition, we use the term political capital in a distinct way, measuring it as political participation in conventional forms of political activity (see also Birner and Wittmer 2003). In democracies it is generally assumed that society as a whole benefits from greater aggregate levels of political participation among citizens. We further assume that the greater one's individual political participation, the greater is one's contribution to this type of political capital for the whole community. In principle, then, political capital can be thought of as a special form of social capital. However, we prefer to keep it analytically separate because particular types of social capital, such as information or social support, may facilitate the production of political capital, such as voting or becoming active in a political party. Methodologically, we measure political capital at the individual level, but believe that ultimately it is a collective type of capital.

Figure 13.1 provides a theoretical model that illustrates the interrelationship between key blocks of variables we believe are implicated in the production of political capital. Solid-lined boxes indicate blocks of variables that we have measured, while dashed-lined boxes indicate theoretical unmeasured variables. In the model the main dependent variable is political participation, which we operationalize as an indicator of "political capital." We are interested in building our explanation around network diversity as the main independent variable, which we operationalize as an indicator of "network capital." We see network capital and political capital as linked through the theoretical variable of "social capital."

We also see political capital as influenced by socioeconomic and demographic factors, biographical availability, and political participation values. However, because we want to limit the scope of the present analysis to the relationship between network capital and political capital, and because we lack measures of particular variables (viz biographical availability and social capital), our analysis focuses on the relationships illustrated in Figure 13.2. A series of multiple

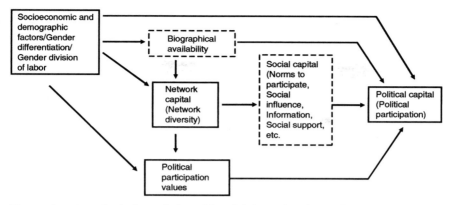

Figure 13.1. A synthetic theoretical model explaining political capital

Note: Solid boxes indicate measured variables, dashed lines indicate theoretical (unmeasured) variables.

regression analyses will be undertaken to examine these latter relationships. Because we do not have direct indicators of social capital, we conjecture that there should be a net association between network capital and political capital.

We analyze three different indicators of network capital: (*a*) diversity of occupational ties, (*b*) diversity of organizational ties, and (*c*) diversity of ties to politicians. Our general guiding hypothesis is that *network diversity is positively associated with level of political participation.* In our regression analyses, we focus upon this relationship and control for the other blocks of variables identified in Figure 13.2.

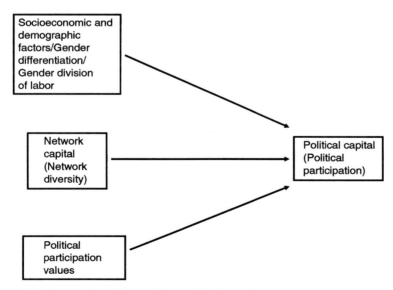

Figure 13.2. Empirical model explaining political capital

Also, because of gender differentiation in both paid and domestic work, and the potential effects of this differentiation, we analyze the relationship between network diversity (for the three different indicators) and level of political participation separately for men and women. Indeed, while we are focusing on networks as social structure, gender itself can be seen as a set of structural relationships. Our guiding hypothesis here is that *the effects of network diversity on level of political participation will differ for men compared with women.* This is a somewhat general conjecture. To be more specific, we assume that men are more likely to be tied to powerful and influential others (because of the gendered division of labor and the principle of homophily), and thus we expect the effect of network diversity on level of political participation to be relatively more important for men than for women. It should also be noted that the separate analyses undertaken for men and women were partly motivated by empirical data. An exploratory zero-order analysis revealed a statistically significant difference between men and women in their levels of political participation: men were relatively more politically active (results not reported here).

13.3. METHODS

The data for the analysis reported in this chapter were obtained from a study that focused on the factors that explain the level of participation among individuals in the environmental movement in British Columbia, Canada. The principal investigator of the study (also the first author) took a catholic approach to data collection, and obtained data on a wide variety of variables to address his central research questions on environmental movement participation (Tindall 1994, 2002, 2004). The present analysis focuses on measures of network capital (network diversity) and political capital (level of political participation). However, because we are conducting secondary analysis on data collected with a different set of research questions in mind, we do not have data on all of the variables that we would optimally have liked to have analyzed for this chapter (e.g. indicators of biographical availability such as hours of free/flexible time), and there are some limitations to the variables that we do have data for. Below, we provide a brief description of the groups that were surveyed, a description of the data collection technique and sample, and a description of the key variables.

13.3.1. Description of Groups

To provide some context for the present analysis, we present a description of the environmental movement and the social movement organizations that compose it. Members of a variety of organizations that are part of the British Columbia Wilderness Preservation Movement were studied (see Tindall and Begoray 1993; Tindall 2002). Members of three formal environmental organizations in Greater Victoria were surveyed. Victoria is the capital of British Columbia (BC) and is situated on Vancouver Island, off Canada's west coast. The province is home to a substantial proportion of the world's remaining old-growth temperate rainforests. These forests are highly valued by a variety of groups, including Aboriginals, nature lovers, and forest industry workers. In recent years, a number of disputes have arisen over the plans of forestry companies to log old-growth rainforests on western Vancouver Island. During the late 1980s and the 1990s, environmental groups lobbied to have a number of these old-growth forests protected as wilderness areas.

The three major organizations that participated in the study—the Sierra Club of Western Canada (SCWC), the Western Canada Wilderness Committee (WCWC), and the Carmanah Forestry Society (CFS)—are all formal environmental social movement organizations, and all are central in the movement to protect and preserve old-growth rainforests in British Columbia (Tindall and Begoray 1993; Wilson 1998). Some of the activities undertaken by these groups include organizing protest rallies on the lawns of the legislature in Victoria; holding public meetings and public slide show presentations; selling movement-related merchandise such as posters of old-growth trees, T-shirts, coffee-table books, and coffee mugs that promote wilderness conservation; lobbying bureaucrats and politicians; producing educational pamphlets and tabloids; and recruiting members and financial resources through door-to-door solicitation.

The individuals studied here are all part of the same movement, and there is substantial overlap between them.[2] This overlap justifies combining members from these three groups into a single sample for the analyses. Statistical analyses are based on an aggregate sample of 381 respondents in order to increase the overall sample size. Our intergroup comparisons reveal no substantial differences, thus offering empirical support for this strategy. It should be noted that, using the nominal definition of group membership, all individuals included in the survey (described later) are movement members. However, it should also be noted that the level of activism of these movement members varied (and, indeed, is normally distributed). Activism ranged from those who were nominal members of an organization but who did not participate in any other way ("checkbook members") to those who participated in a wide variety of activities, such as organizing rallies and demonstrations.

13.3.2. Data Collection and Sample

The primary data-gathering procedure was a self-administered mailed questionnaire.[3] For two of the groups, a systematic random sampling procedure was

---

[2] There is a great deal of collaboration between these organizations and overlap in their memberships. Fifty-five percent of Sierra Club members also belong to the WCWC, and 12% belong to the CFS. Forty percent of WCWC members also belong to the Sierra Club and 13% belong to the CFS. Thirty-one percent of CFS members also belong to the Sierra Club, and 55% belong to the WCWC.

[3] Additional data were also gathered through face-to-face interviews with environmental organization leaders, observations made at movement events, and collection of available documents.

employed. For a third, which is a smaller organization, a census of members was conducted. The response rates for the three groups were as follows: Group A, 35 percent ($n = 146$); Group B, 35 percent ($n = 48$); and Group C, 11 percent ($n = 187$). The response rates for the surveys were relatively low in absolute terms, though not necessarily in comparative terms. For instance, Muller and Opp (1986) obtained a response rate of 32 percent in their study of citizen participation in rebellious political behavior in New York, US and Hamburg, West Germany. Opp (1986) also observed a relatively low response rate for a study of participation in the antinuclear movement in Hamburg, West Germany. With regard to this second study, Opp (1986: 106–7) states: "Since theoretical (and not descriptive) hypotheses were tested, we expect them to hold even for samples that are not necessarily representative" (see also Opp and Gern 1993). These arguments made by Opp and his colleagues regarding response rates also apply to the present analysis. We too focus on the theoretical relationships that exist among variables, not on parameter estimates for particular variables.

The sample varies from the general public in several regards. Members of our sample tend to have higher levels of formal education, to have higher levels of income, and to be more likely to be from upper-middle-class and middle-class white-collar occupations. In terms of the age and gender distribution, the sample reflects the general population quite closely. Because the sampling biases generally reflect the characteristics of the population who participate in elections (e.g. those with higher levels of income and education and those from middle- and upper-class locations are more likely to participate), we do not feel that these biases present a problem for the research questions being examined here. On the other hand, we do not believe that the present sample provides an example of "sampling on the dependent variable." There is substantial variation among respondents in terms of their level of political participation. Some people did nothing or very little (10% either did nothing or at most voted in a single election). A substantial majority did nothing else but vote. But there were also some respondents who were very active (12% had the maximum score for our measure). In sum, we have a sample that varied in terms of their level of political participation, not a sample consisting of primarily highly active respondents. We should caution that our findings are not necessarily empirically generalizable to the general public, as we do not have a sample of the general public. As such, findings should be considered suggestive, rather than descriptive. But they may become theoretically generalizable if future studies find similar patterns under similar conditions.

13.4. MEASUREMENT

Appendix 1 provides details on how each variable was measured. For interval-ratio level variables the table provides means and standard deviations, and for categorical (dummy) variables it provides the percentage of the sample who were members of the category (members of the category = 1; nonmembers = 0).

Univariate statistics are based on the 178 cases with complete data. We briefly describe below the main dependent variable (level of political participation) and the main independent variables (diversity of occupational ties, diversity of organizational ties, and diversity of ties to politicians).

13.4.1. Position Generator

As this volume focuses specifically on the position generator, we briefly describe its use in this study. The position generator (see Lin, Fu, and Hsung 2001) that we used is a modified version of a questionnaire item used by Bonnie H. Erickson in her security industry study (Erickson 1996b). The exact format and content of our instrument is reproduced in Appendix 2. We use this item to measure diversity of occupational ties (described further below). As described above, our overall response rate for the study was somewhat low. This was due to two primary reasons: (a) the questionnaire was relatively lengthy (23 pages in length) and generally took respondents 30–60 mins to complete and (b) because of confidentiality-related provisions maintained by the organizations, the principal investigator was unable to send follow-up reminders or replacement questionnaires in order to boost the response rate.

The item response rate for the completed questionnaires was generally quite good (with the exception of questions regarding postmaterialist values and income). The item response rate for the position generator question was excellent: 98.7 percent overall. Later in this chapter we provide the descriptions of the variables of central analytic concern.

13.4.2. Level of Political Participation

Level of political participation was calculated by summing responses to the following items: (a) Respondent voted in the past provincial election (weight = 0.5); (b) Respondent voted in the past federal election (weight = 0.5); (c) Respondent has a political party membership (weight = 2); and (d) Respondent is an active political party member (weight = 4). The level of political participation index ranges from a minimum of 0 to a maximum of 7.

Because we are dealing with secondary data, there are some limitations to this measure, such as limited number of indicators and somewhat arbitrary weights. However, justification for the creation and use of this index can be provided on both conceptual and empirical grounds. We believe that, similar to level of "social movement activism" (see Tindall 2002), there is a range of activities that can be classified as contributing to an individual's level of "political participation." This involves a variety of activities that vary in terms of cost, effort, and commitment. We give activities that involve less time, effort, and commitment lower weight and activities that involve greater time, effort, and commitment higher weight. It is assumed that the higher the overall score on our political participation index, the more politically active an individual will be. Empirical justification for this measure is based on several grounds: (*a*) There is substantial variation for political participation; (*b*) Each of the indicators is positively and significantly correlated with one another; (*c*) Exploratory factor analysis provides support for a one factor (general political participation) solution (e.g. all indicators loaded at .30 or higher). (*d*) Finally, we believe that the results demonstrate that this index has construct validity (i.e. variables that should logically be associated with it are in fact correlated with it).[4] It should also be noted that the first author has published results using a similar type of weighting scheme (albeit with more indicators) for level of environmental activism (see Tindall 2002).

13.4.3. Network Diversity Measures

1. Diversity of Occupational Ties: Respondents were asked whether they knew of any acquaintances, close friends, or relatives in a series of 40 occupations (see Appendix 2). Responses were coded at the binary level for each occupation: the respondent knew someone in that occupation = 1; the respondent did not know anyone in that occupation = 0. The binarized responses for the 40 occupations were then summed into an index. Values for this variable ranged from 0 to 40.

2. Diversity of Organizational Ties: Respondents were asked about their membership in 19 types of generic voluntary organizations. This measure is a modified version of a questionnaire item used by Edward Laumann (1973). The construction of the index for diversity of organizational ties was similar to that for diversity of occupational ties.[5] A score of 1 was coded if the respondent belonged to a particular generic organization; otherwise, the respondent received a score of 0 for that organization. To create an index for this variable, we calculated the total number of generic organizations that a respondent belonged to. Values for this variable ranged from 0 to 13.

3. Diversity of Ties to Politicians: The ties to occupations questionnaire item included a question asking about ties to politicians. Respondents were asked if they had any acquaintances, friends, or relatives who were (*a*) local (or municipal) politicians; (*b*) provincial politicians; or (*c*) federal politicians. The diversity of ties to politicians index is a sum of these indicators. Because there were only three levels of politicians, in order to maximize variation (unlike the procedure for the other network measures), we did not collapse the responses for acquaintances,

---

[4] For a more extensive discussion of political participation, see Barnes and Kaase (1979).

[5] Abstractly, social networks can be thought of as patterns of relations (ties) linking social units (nodes). Social units can be operationalized as individuals, groups, or higher levels of organization. One can utilize different units in the same analysis. Hence we conceive of diversity of organizational memberships (e.g. ties to different groups) as one indicator of network diversity (see also Tindall 2002, 2004). In this case, the indicator "diversity of organization memberships" becomes an attribute of the individual. People with more diverse organization memberships are potentially exposed to more diverse information, social pressures, and social resources.

friends, and relatives, but rather added them all together for all three levels of politicians. Values for this variable ranged from 0 to 7.

13.5. RESULTS

The analytic strategy we employ is a twofold one: first, we examine separately the effects of different measures of network capital (as indicated by network diversity) on level of political participation for our whole sample; and second, we examine whether there are different effects on level of political participation for men and women.

13.5.1. Network Diversity and Political Participation: Whole Sample

Table 13.1 shows three models predicting political participation in our whole sample. There is a different model for each of the three measures of network capital.[6] Key findings are described below. The nonnetwork effects will be described first.

There is a weak positive association between age and level of political participation in one of the models. Age is probably related to "sense of political efficacy," which, in turn, is related to political participation; it could also be related to biographical availability. We also observe a weak positive association between retirement status and political participation for several of the models. Retired people without work or childrearing responsibilities have more flexible schedules. In addition, there is a weak positive association between "wanting more say at work and in the community" and political participation in all three models, though nonsignificant in one (Note: reverse the sign to interpret this value because it is based on ranking data). This can be considered a very rough measure of political efficacy. The greater the desire to have a say in work and the community, the more politically active people are.

Now we turn to considering the effects of our network capital variables on participation. All of the network diversity measures are positively and significantly

---

[6] In this chapter, we have taken the analytic approach of examining the effects of the different network diversity independent variables separately, in different analyses. Our rationale is twofold: (*a*) because the expected effects are relatively modest, and the sample size is relatively small, including several of these measures together may have "washed out" significant effects; (*b*) several of the measures are strongly intercorrelated (in particular, there is a substantial correlation between diversity of occupational ties and diversity of ties to politicians), and we wanted to avoid potential problems of multicolinearity. Nevertheless, some exploratory analyses were undertaken, including several of the network diversity measures as independent variables in the same model predicting level of political participation. When diversity of organizational ties and diversity of occupational ties are included in the same equation, but diversity of ties to politicians is omitted, then diversity of both organizational and occupational ties have positive significant effects on level of political participation. When diversity of ties to politicians is also included in the model it is significant, diversity of organizational ties remains significant, but diversity of occupational ties becomes nonsignificant.

Table 13.1. Standardized regression coefficients for model predicting *political participation* using *personal network range* variables as an independent variable

Independent variables	Diversity of occupational ties as independent variable	Diversity of organizational ties as independent variable	Diversity of ties to politicians as independent variable
Socioeconomic and demographic variables			
Education	−.07	−.07	−.08
Gender (male = 1)	.13	.09	.12
Age	.20*	.11	.11
Marital status (married = 1)	.05	.05	.02
Full employment (employed full time = 1)	−.02	.00	.06
Parental status (parent = 1)	−.03	−.02	−.02
Retired (retired = 1)	.18*	.22**	.15
Mangers	.00	.02	.00
Social/Cultural specialists	−.03	−.02	−.04
Human service specialists	.13*	.09	.13
Business owners	−.07	−.03	−.06
Technical professionals	.04	.02	.05
Personal income	.11	.12	.10
Political participation values			
More say in government decisions (rank)	−.07	−.05	−.09
More say at work/in community (rank)	−.19**	−.18	−.15*
Network capital			
Diversity of network ties	.16**	.23***	.33***
R^2	.19***	.23***	.26***
Adjusted R^2	.13***	.16***	.20***
n	207	209	207

* $p < .10$; ** $p < .05$; *** $p < .01$.

associated with political participation. The strongest R^2 is for the model with diversity of ties to politicians as an independent variable, followed by diversity of voluntary organization ties (memberships), and diversity of ties to different occupations. In sum, the resulting pattern provides general support for the notion that network diversity is important for explaining level of political participation. As researchers in the social resources tradition have suggested, diversity or range of network ties can serve as a type of social resource that has implications for social and political capital outcomes.

13.5.2. Network Diversity and Political Participation: Women and Men

We now focus on the relationship between network capital, gender, and level of political participation, as this is the relationship of central theoretical interest to the present analysis. In the following tables, as in Table 13.1, we have controlled

Table 13.2. Standardized regression coefficients for model predicting *political participation* using diversity of *occupational ties* as an independent variable to explain political participation: by gender

Independent variables	Men	Women
Socioeconomic and demographic variables		
Education	−.10	.03
Age	.04	.39***
Marital status (married = 1)	−.02	−.17
Full employment (employed full time = 1)	.01	.17
Parental status (parent = 1)	.05	.00
Retired (retired = 1)	.39**	−.05
Mangers	.02	−.05
Social/Cultural specialists	−.07	.03
Human service specialists	.12	.05
Business owners	−.11	.15
Technical professionals	.11	.00
Personal income	.21*	−.16
Political participation values		
More say in government decisions (rank)	−.02	−.16
More say at work/in community (rank)	−.19	−.27**
Network capital		
Diversity of occupational ties	.24**	.04
R^2	.25**	.26**
Adjusted R^2	.12**	.13**
n	105	103

* $p < .10$; ** $p < .05$; *** $p < .01$.

for a variety of other variables that may have an effect on level of political participation. We are not so much interested in developing an exhaustive account of the factors that affect political participation as we are in ruling out the possibility that any observed association between network capital and political participation is spuriously related to a third variable.

13.5.3. Diversity of Occupational Ties and Political Participation

Table 13.2 provides two multiple regression models explaining level of political participation, with *diversity of occupational ties* as a key independent variable and indicator of network capital. There are separate models for men and women. From a theoretical standpoint, the key findings are that diversity of ties to different occupations is positive and significant for men, but there is no effect for women. This provides support for our hypothesis (of different effects for men compared with women) and is likely a result of differential patterns of tie formation in the gendered division of labor.

Table 13.3. Standardized regression coefficients for model predicting *political participation* using diversity of *organizational ties* as an independent variable to explain political participation: by gender

Independent variables	Men	Women
Socioeconomic and demographic variables		
Education	−.07	−.07
Age	−.06	.26*
Marital status (married = 1)	.10	−.09
Employment status (employed full time = 1)	.06	.07
Parental status (parent = 1)	−.01	.00
Retired (retired = 1)	.36***	.07
Mangers	.03	−.05
Social/Cultural specialists	−.04	.02
Human service specialists	.07	.05
Business owners	−.03	.08
Technical professionals	.10	.07
Personal income	.15	−.06
Political participation values		
More say in government decisions (rank)	.03	−.13
More say at work/in community (rank)	−.15	−.25**
Network capital		
Diversity of organizational ties	.22**	.21**
R^2	.24**	.29***
Adjusted R^2	.11**	.17***
n	107	102

* $p < .10$; ** $p < .05$; *** $p < .01$.

For men there were also significant effects for retirement status and income. For women, on the other hand, there were significant effects for age and "having more say at work and in the community."

13.5.4. Diversity of Organizational Ties and Political Participation

Table 13.3 provides two separate multiple regression models explaining level of political participation for men and women, with *diversity of organizational ties* used as a key independent variable and indicator of network capital. The key findings here are that the diversity of voluntary organization memberships is positively and significantly associated with level of political participation for both men and women. This supports the general guiding hypothesis that network diversity is positively associated with level of political participation, but not the hypothesis of different effects for men compared with women.

For men there is also a significant effect for retirement status. Again, for women there were also significant effects for age and for "having more say at work and in the community."

Table 13.4. Standardized regression coefficients for model predicting *political participation* using diversity of *ties to politicians* as an independent variable to explain political participation: by gender

Independent variables	Men	Women
Socioeconomic and demographic variables		
Education	−.12	.03
Age	−.02	.36***
Marital status (married = 1)	−.01	−.16
Employment status (employed full time = 1)	−.02	.17
Parental status (parent = 1)	.03	−.01
Retired (retired = 1)	.24	−.04
Mangers	.03	−.05
Social/Cultural specialists	−.08	.03
Human service specialists	.08	.05
Business owners	−.10	.15
Technical professionals	.12	.00
Personal income	.16	−.15
Political participation values		
More say in government decisions (rank)	.00	−.17
More say at work/in community (rank)	−.10	−.27***
Network capital		
Diversity of ties to politicians	.47***	.05
R^2	.37***	.26**
Adjusted R^2	.27***	.14**
n	105	101

* $p < .10$; ** $p < .05$; *** $p < .01$.

13.5.5. Diversity of Ties to Politicians and Political Participation

Table 13.4 provides two separate multiple regression models explaining level of political participation for men and women, with *diversity of ties to politicians* used as a key independent variable and indicator of network capital. The key findings here are that there is a very strong positive association between diversity of ties to politicians and level of political participation for men. There is a very weak, nonsignificant positive association for women. Again, this pattern of results supports our hypothesis of different effects for men compared with women.

Among women there are also effects for age and for "wanting more say at work/in community."

13.5.6. Summary of Results

In the analyses of the entire sample, network diversity is consistently positively associated with level of political participation. This association is statistically significant in all three of the models. Other factors that had effects on level of political participation include one of the political participation values indicators (wanting more say at work/in the community) and several demographic variables that are likely indicators of the theoretical variable biographical availability (age, retired status).

In the analyses conducted separately for men and women, the general trend was for network diversity to have a positive effect on political participation for men, but not for women. There was an exception to this trend: diversity of organizational ties (memberships) had a positive significant effect for both men and women. Also noteworthy is the relatively large standardized β coefficient for diversity of ties to politicians for men ($\beta = .47$, $p < .01$), while there was no effect for women. This points to substantially different structural contexts experienced by men and women.

In terms of other variables, in the models conducted separately for men and women, retirement status and personal income (in some instances) tended to have effects for men, while age and political participation values tended to have effects for women.

13.6. DISCUSSION

13.6.1. Networks, Social Resources, and Political Participation

There are likely a number of mechanisms responsible for the observed association between network diversity and level of political participation that we found in our whole sample. Our study supports the findings of researchers of political participation and social movements that the better connected one is the more likely one is to be mobilized for a variety of political activities. In previous analyses, the first author found that diversity of ties to others in the environmental movement was positively associated with both level of identification in the movement and general level of participation (Tindall 2002). By contrast, the total number of ties was important for explaining the frequency of communication between individuals, and was also positively correlated with being targeted for recruitment to participate in movement events. Although we do not have detailed measures of communication, recruitment attempts, or level of political identification, it is likely that similar processes are at work.

The resources that one receives through her or his social network (e.g. information, support, and solidarity) increase one's sense of political efficacy, and this, in turn, increases participation. However, there are important feedback loops that underlie this set of relationships. In particular, the more politically active one becomes, the more diverse one's network is likely to become. This is especially true with range of ties to politicians, which partially explains the higher R^2 and β values when diversity of ties to politicians is used to explain level of political participation. People who have greater network range have greater access to diverse and potentially important information. People with larger and more diverse personal networks have potentially greater access to social support as well. Networks serve as conduits through which information and influence flow, and social comparisons are made (Gartrell 1987).

While we have not measured "political efficacy" per se, it seems likely that increased information and social support acquired through network ties increases one's sense of political efficacy (Erickson and Nosanchuk 1990). There are a number of possible explanations for this pattern of findings. For one, the contact that goes on in organizations where one is interacting with a diverse set of others increases awareness of political issues. From here social forces influence the probability that one will, in turn, act politically (Gould 1993). Moreover, continuing participation in large social networks also enhances one's social skills, which can be a useful resource for later political participation. Having a large network, through participation in voluntary organizations or through other means, also adds to a person's name recognition or profile in the community, which may be important for recruitment or running for office. Finally, greater involvement in association activities leads to more numerous contacts with fellow members, which, in turn, increases the odds that one will be recruited into politics directly (Erickson and Nosanchuk 1990). In sum, such interactions enhance the development of political resources such as social skills, a sense of active mastery, and efficacy.

13.6.2. Differences between Men and Women

With the exception of "diversity of organizational memberships," network capital as measured by network diversity appears to be more important for facilitating political participation among men than among women.[7] There are several factors likely at work here, all basically rooted in the gender division of labor that characterizes Canadian (Carroll 1987; Fox and Fox 1987) as well as other Western societies (cf. Charles 1992). While evidence suggests that the level of gender inequality is decreasing, women and men have historically tended to be streamed into gender-typed jobs, with men more likely to end up in higher social class and status positions, and women ending up in lower status positions (Jacobs 1989; Ridgeway 1997; Cohen and Huffman 2003). Also, while patterns of domestic work have changed, women still tend to do the majority of domestic work (Kalleberg and Rosenfeld 1992; Blain 1993; Arai 2000).

---

[7] In fact, one might argue that broadly structural variables such as "retirement status," "personal income," and "network range" are more important for explaining political participation among men, while cognitive variables such as highly valuing "having more say in decision making" are more important for women. Also, age seems to be important for women but not for men. We would conjecture that age is related to a greater sense of "political efficacy" among older women, and also perhaps to greater experience with the political system. We should note that it is possible that part of the reason for a lack of effects related to education and class is the fact that, on average, the people in the sample have higher levels of formal education and income, and are disproportionately from upper-middle-class occupations. Thus we cannot entirely rule out the possibility that there may be insufficient variation on these variables to produce effects within the sample.

This gender division of paid and domestic labor has several implications for the current analysis. First, because of extra constraints, in particular the "double day" (Luxton 1980) or "second shift" (Hochschild 1989) experienced by many working females, women tend to have less "biographical availability" for political participation—that is, they have less time and flexibility for participating in politics and related activities, such as social movement action. Second, because workplaces, as well as other types of institutions and organizations, tend to be organized around gender, men and women form different types of social networks (Erickson 2003, 2004). In particular, men are more likely to have network ties to those in more powerful positions. These twin observations have implications for the present differential results we observe between men and women. Women in our sample have less biographical availability (i.e. less time) and this constrains or limits their political participation. They also tend to have different types of social networks, ones that are usually made up of less powerful and influential people, a handicap when moving in the world of politics where contacts and connections are crucial. For both of these reasons, then, network diversity tends to have a higher payoff for men than it does for women, at least insofar as it affects political participation.

While there are minimal differences in terms of mean network diversity scores between men and women (in results not reported here), as suggested above, men may be better connected to key decision-making and political networks than women are.[8] In analysis of the data not shown here, we found that men had higher network diversity when measured by diversity of acquaintanceship ties, while women had higher diversity when measured by diversity of ties to friends and relatives. This finding has been confirmed in research conducted in Britain. There it was discovered that women had stronger connections to neighborhood networks, friends, and family. While men spent more time in sports-related activities and social clubs, women spent more time visiting with friends and family (Lowndes 2000). It may be the case that the diversity that comes from contacts with many different acquaintances may provide men greater opportunities to engage politically than family and friendship contacts do for women.

Finally, it may be that homophily—the fact that people tend to associate mainly with others who are most like themselves—plays a role, for two reasons. First, men are more likely to have ties with other men and women more likely to share ties with other women. In a larger context where men are more likely to be politicians, men are more likely to know someone who is a politician. In a related way, homogeneity and homophily within organizations may be important. McPherson and Smith-Lovin (1986) looked at the extent to which voluntary organizations were segregated along gender lines. They found that rather than integrating the sexes, many organizations were in fact segregated. In the present study, while men and women belonged to roughly the same total

---

[8] There is a statistically significant difference between men and women regarding ties to politicians, with men having more such ties.

number of voluntary organizations, the organizations they tended to belong to were different—the men's organizations were possibly more important for facilitating political activity than the women's organizations. For example, men in our study belonged to a significantly greater number of "business, professional, or occupational associations" than did women (results not reported here).

The fact that there was some variation in the effects for different indicators of network diversity suggests that more research is needed in this area. Why is diversity of occupations different from diversity of organizations? A more fine-grained analysis focusing on types of ties (weak vs. strong), types of organizations, gender of the ties, degree of homophily, and differential access to powerful positions is needed.

13.7. FUTURE RESEARCH

Our analysis has revealed two gaps that future research may wish to fill: first, studying network capital as a *dependent variable* rather than an independent variable; and second, measuring the mechanisms and intervening variables that lead to the production of network and social capital outcomes. First, because of space limitations we focused our analysis on the direct effects of network capital on political participation. As a result, we did not analyze the many factors that tend to influence the production of network capital. While some work has been done on this, we believe that this is still an underresearched area. In the realm of social movement research, for instance, Mario Diani (1997) has noted that networks have received substantial attention as an independent variable, but relatively little attention as a dependent variable. In particular, he suggests that more attention be paid to the creation of networks and social capital as a result of social movement mobilization. In terms of the gender differences reported here, while there is some research on the differences in social networks among men and women (e.g. Erickson 2003, 2004), more research needs to be done on the mechanisms that may lead women and men to have different types of social networks.

With regard to the second gap, the importance of networks is becoming increasingly recognized in both the social movement and social capital literatures, as illustrated by the observation that the characteristics of people's personal networks is usually correlated with activities like their level of social movement participation (Tindall and Wellman 2001). However, the actual mechanisms underlying such network effects tend to go unmeasured. We know that there is a variety of possible mechanisms that might be responsible for network effects. Tindall and Wellman (2001) propose that such mechanisms may include (*a*) communication, (*b*) recruitment appeals, (*c*) identification, (*d*) social influence, (*e*) incentives and sanctions, (*f*) social support, (*g*) socialization, (*h*) knowledge and information, (*i*) personal efficacy, (*j*) norms, (*k*) subjective interest, (*l*) beliefs about others' willingness to contribute, and (*m*) trust. Many of these mechanisms could be used to also explain the relationship studied here between network capital (network diversity) and political participation. And many of these are implicated as theoretical indicators of social capital. More research on social networks and social capital outcomes needs to be devoted to identifying and measuring the actual mechanisms that underlie the relationship between network properties and outcomes, such as political participation.

Similar arguments can be made about the need to measure the mechanisms that underlie gender effects. One such set of mechanisms is certainly associated with biographical availability. Again, in the context of the social movement literature, scholars such as McAdam (1992) and Mohai (1992) have noted that there are conflicting pressures that affect women's activism. Constraining pressures rooted in the "double day" for women mute much potential political participation for women. McAdam and Mohai have suggested that in order to participate at similar levels women have to be more committed than men, simply because of the additional barriers they face in their domestic situations.

An empirical illustration of this effect of domestic labor is provided by a second survey conducted by the first author using a subsample of participants (*n* = 58) from the original survey. This survey contained questions on hours of housework per week and percentage of the total housework done by the respondent. Consistent with national trends (see Devereaux 1993; Frederick 1993, 1995; Jackson 1996), women in this subsample did an average of 12.83 more hours of housework per week than did men ($p < .05$) and performed 73 percent of the total housework in their households ($p < .001$). This greater burden borne by women provides an explanation for their muted level of environmental movement activism (see Tindall et al. 2003). For women, but not for men, there was a significant negative correlation between the percentage of the housework that they performed and their level of environmental movement activism ($r = -.36$, $p < .05$). In other words, the more housework women did, the less active they were. This supports the assertion that the greater amount of housework done by women constrains their level of environmental movement activism, as highlighted by the theoretical concept of biographical availability. Data were not collected on political participation in this second survey, but we would expect similar results.

More research on these and related issues will certainly improve our understanding of the complex mechanisms involved in the production of political and social capital. Greater emphasis on how social capital resources accessed through networks work to provide individuals with the necessary knowledge, solidarity, identity, and support incentives to act collectively should provide useful information to social network and social movement analysts as well as political scientists in their quest for understanding collective political action. Our analysis here is only a small first step in pushing forward such an agenda.

APPENDIX 1: MEASUREMENT OF VARIABLES*

Variable	Mean/% (SD)	Description
Level of political participation	1.75 (1.85)	This variable is an index created by summing responses to the following items: (*a*) respondent voted in the past provincial election (weight = 0.5); (*b*) respondent voted in the past federal election (weight = 0.5); (*c*) respondent has a political party membership (weight = 2); (*d*) respondent is an active political party member (weight = 4). Values ranged from 0 to 7.
Education	15.76 (2.00)	Years of education. High school degree = 12, Bachelor's degree = 16, etc.
Gender	51%	Dummy variable. Men = 1, Women = 0.
Age	43.61 (13.97)	Chronological age at the time of the survey.
Marital status	59.5%	Dummy variable. Married = 1, Not married = 0.
Full employment	59%	Dummy variable. Employed full time = 1, not employed full time = 0.
Parental status	34.8%	Dummy variable. Parents with children living in the home = 1, others = 0.
Retired	14%	Dummy variable. Retired = 1, nonretired = 0.
Managers	5.6%	Dummy variable. Employed in a managerial position = 1, nonmanagers = 0.
Social/Cultural specialists	7.9%	Dummy variable. Employed in a social/cultural specialist occupation = 1, nonsocial/cultural specialists = 0.
Human Service specialists	15.2%	Dummy variable. Employed in a human service specialist occupation = 1, nonhuman service specialists = 0.
Business owners	9%	Dummy variable. Business owners = 1, nonbusiness owners = 0.
Technical professionals	18%	Dummy variable. Employed in a technical professional occupation = 1, nontechnical professionals = 0.
Personal income	38,089 (24,598)	Total personal income in dollars for the previous year.
More say in government decisions	5.65 (2.86)	Respondents were asked to rank 13 items relating to "materialist" and "postmaterialist" values. The variable is the respondents' rank score for this item.
More say at work/in community	5.65 (2.82)	Respondents were asked to rank 13 items relating to "materialist" and "postmaterialist" values. The variable is the respondents' rank score for this item.
Diversity of occupational ties	17.31 (8.44)	Respondents were asked whether they knew of any acquaintances, close friends, or relatives in a series of 40 occupations. Responses were coded at the binary level for each occupation: the respondent knew someone in that occupation = 1; the respondent did not know anyone in that occupation = 0. The binarized responses for the 40 occupations were then summed into an index. Values ranged from 0 to 40.

(Cont.)

Variable	Mean/% (SD)	Description
Diversity of organizational ties	4.08 (2.38)	Respondents were asked about their membership in 19 types of generic voluntary organizations. Responses were coded yes = 1, no = 0. An index was created by adding the responses together. Values ranged from 0 to 13.
Diversity of ties to politicians	.63 (1.05)	Respondents were asked if they know of any acquaintances, close friends or relatives who were (*a*) local (or municipal politicians); (*b*) provincial politicians; (*c*) federal politicians. The responses were then summed to create an index. Values ranged from 0 to 7.

* Descriptive statistics are based on the 178 cases for which there were complete data. The cases in particular regression models will differ slightly from the cases used to create the descriptive statistics presented here.

APPENDIX 2: POSITION GENERATOR QUESTIONNAIRE ITEM

45. Personal Network: I am interested in whether you know people in certain lines of work in the Greater Victoria Area. If you know anyone in a certain type of work who is an acquaintance (rather than a close friend or relative), tick under "acquaintance"; if you know someone in a certain type of work who is a close friend, tick under "close friend"; if you know someone in a certain type of work who is a relative, tick under "relative." If any of the acquaintances, close friends, or relatives in a given occupation you know also belong to the SCWC, tick under "SCWC Member." As in the example below, you may tick off more than one box per line. For example:

Type of job	Type of relationship			
	Acquaintance	Close friend	Relative	SCWC member
Do you know anyone in the following types of work?				
Example 1: secretary...	X	X		
Example 2: teacher...	X	X		X

Example 1 would indicate that you know at least one acquaintance and one close friend who are secretaries, but you do not know any relatives or SCWC members who are secretaries.

Example 2 would indicate that you know an acquaintance who is a teacher, a close friend who is a teacher, and at least one of these people is also a SCWC member.

Now please complete for the following:

Type of job	Type of relationship			
	Acquaintance	Close friend	Relative	SCWC member

Do you know anyone in the following types of work?

Business owners (outside your own company)...

Business managers who run an establishment (other than your own company)...

Lawyers...

Doctors...

Engineers...

University or college professors...

Primary or secondary school teachers...

Supervisors...

Bankers...

Truck drivers

Secretaries...

Accountants...

Bus drivers...

Gardeners/landscapers

Auto mechanics

Plumbers...

Waiting staff

Police officers...

Loggers...

Mill workers...

Retail sales clerks...

Ministers, priests, or rabbis...

Economists/financial specialists...

Computer/electronics technicians...

Biologists...

Pharmacists...

Chemists...

Social researchers...

Professional painters or sculptors (artists)...

Professional writers...

Architects...

Social workers...

Nurses...

Physiotherapists...

Fishermen/fisherwomen...

Municipal politicians...

Provincial politicians...

Federal politicians...

University or college students...

High school students...

14

Civic Participation and Social Capital: A Social Network Analysis in Two American Counties[1]

Marc Porter Magee

Social capital has emerged over the last decade as a central concept in the social sciences by offering the promise of connecting long-standing research traditions on social integration, norms and values, and civic participation with the traditionally economic focus on investments, production, and returns. As Lin, Cook, and Burt (2001*b*: vii) observed, social capital serves as "an umbrella term that can easily be understood and transported across the disciplines." However, more often than not the promise of this research has exceeded its utility as assumptions and predictions have far outpaced the data and evidence needed to put these ideas to the test. Nowhere is this gap between potential and reality currently wider than at the intersection between the study of social networks and civic participation.

As research into both social networks and civic participation has exploded in the last two decades, there have been a number of attempts to build theoretical connections between these research traditions. In the most prominent of these efforts, Putnam (1995, 2000) has advanced the hypothesis that civic participation is positively and significantly connected to the creation of productive social ties, that declining levels of civic participation in America have led to declining levels of social capital, and that this has led to a wide array of social and economic problems.

While there has been growing empirical evidence to suggest that there are important connections between civic participation and the creation of productive social ties, to date most of this research has failed to take advantage of the recent developments in social network research that could help provide a more complete understanding of this relationship. One of the most important of these developments is the emergence of the position generator methodology (Lin, Fu, and Hsung 2001). This offers a simple, flexible, and reliable survey tool for assessing the degree to which social networks are characterized by the open ties to a variety

[1] This research study was made possible by a grant from the Center for the Study of Voluntarism and Philanthropy at Duke University and a National Science Foundation Dissertation Grant.

of resources that research suggests is the most consistent measure of social capital (Lin 1999*b*; Burt 2001).

In this chapter, an effort is made to strengthen our empirical and conceptual understanding of the connections between civic participation and a network model of social capital through analysis of original survey data employing this position generator instrument.

14.1. EARLIER RESEARCH

Under the moniker of "social capital", research into both social networks and civic participation has exploded in recent years. To some degree, this is due to the interplay between these two concepts in this work but the connections have been tentative and are yet to be more fully developed.

14.1.1. Civic Participation as a Social Resource

Social theorists have long recognized the important role that participation in civil society plays in the lives of individuals and their communities. In the eighteenth century, Adam Ferguson's *On the History of Civil Society* (Ferguson [1767] 1980) laid the groundwork for early scholarship in this area by focusing on the impact of the growing division of labor in the economic world on forms of civic engagement and resulting changes in the social connections between the citizenry. In the nineteenth century, De Tocqueville's *Democracy in America* (De Tocqueville 1975) updated this research tradition with an in-depth examination of the sources of America's rich associational life and its impact on the health of its democratic form of government.

Although civic participation remained an important area of study in the social sciences over the next 150 years, interest in this topic has exploded since the 1980s. This growing interest has led to several important lines of research that have helped to expand our understanding of civic participation as a social resource.

For example, researchers exploring participation in volunteering activities have traditionally focused on improving our understanding of the kinds of characteristics that make individuals more likely to be active participants in civic life (Wilson 2000). More recently, however, this research has shifted to studies that have helped improve our understanding of the way that this participation can act as a resource for the people involved by increasing access to information (Knoke 1990*a*), providing critical organizational skills (Verba et al. 1995), and expanding their social ties in ways that may positively impact both their physical and mental health (House et al. 1988) and their educational and occupation achievement (Johnson et al. 1998). One surprising finding in this line of research is the fact that one in four volunteers report that they were involved in volunteer activities in order to "make new contacts that might help my business or career" (Hodgkinson and Weitzman 1996).

Research into participation in religious organizations has also increased dramatically in recent years, driven in part by the important role that these organizations play in acting as a social resource for individuals and their communities. Researchers have found that in addition to helping to promote a sense of community and shared norms of reciprocity, religious organizations can be particularly effective in helping participants develop social ties that are useful for both collective self-help and upward mobility (Morris 1984; Warner and Wittner 1998; Yang 1998). Perhaps most interestingly, researchers are beginning to document the important role that religious organizations play in promoting an inclination toward "prosocial pursuits" that in turn increases participation in a wide array of civic activities beyond the boundaries of the religious organizations themselves (Ellison 1992; Wilson and Janoski 1995; Greeley 1997).

Finally, researchers have made progress in developing understanding of the relative importance of voluntary organizations in the creation of social ties. This research suggests that voluntary organizations probably are not the source of as many social ties as school and work (Louch 2000), but that they have a critical impact on the characteristics of individuals' social ties because they operate over the entire life course (McPherson and Smith-Lovin 1986). In addition, because participation in voluntary organizations is by definition less constrained than the spheres of family, school, and work, it can be more easily influenced by purposeful change (McPherson et al. 1992).

14.1.2. Putnam's Participation Hypothesis

Much of the last decade of research on civic participation as a social resource has been influenced by the work of political scientist Robert Putnam. Putnam's initial research focused more narrowly on the connection between participation in voluntary associations and the quality of democratic governance (Putnam 1993a). However, beginning with his 1995 article "Bowling Alone" and continuing through the 2000 book of the same name, Putnam advanced a broad research agenda that attempts to connect levels of civic participation in America with levels of social connectedness and trust, which in turn is used to measure the stock of America's social capital, which is finally connected with a wide array of social and political outcomes (Putnam 1995, 2000). Drawing upon a broad collection of historical data, Putnam argues that since the 1960s there has been a steady decline in participation in civic organizations in America, that this decline in civic participation has resulted in a decline in social capital, and that this decline in social capital is a central factor in many of America's most pressing social problems. However, while Putnam and associates have moved quickly from observations about changing rates of civic participation to hypotheses about changing levels of social capital to the public policy implications of this work, our understanding of the way that civic participation affects individuals' levels of social capital remains underdeveloped.

Putnam (2000: 19) himself defines social capital not as civic participation but instead as "connections among individuals—social networks and the norms of reciprocity and trustworthiness that arise from them." In this way, he is in broad agreement with the major sociological researchers in the field who have defined social capital primarily as the characteristics of social networks and the resources embedded in these social ties, including Bourdieu (1986), Coleman (1988), Lin (1982, 1999*b*), Flap (1991), Burt (1992, 2001), and Erickson (1996*b*).

Nevertheless, despite building his model of social capital on a social network foundation, the distinctions between different kinds of social networks so critical in the social network literature is largely missing from *Bowling Alone*. Putnam (2000: 23) states: "I have found no reliable, comprehensive, nationwide measures of social capital that neatly distinguish 'bridgingness' and 'bondingness.' In our empirical account of recent trends in this book, therefore, this distinction is less prominent than I would prefer." Indeed, a review of the empirical account reveals that this critical distinction between bridging (loose, diverse social ties) and bonding (dense, homogeneous social ties) is nonexistent. Instead, national trend data on civic participation is connected directly to the potential effects of social capital without actually measuring the effect of civic participation on social network composition or the effect of social network composition on these outcome variables.

At the same time, more recent evidence has called into question Putnam's original hypotheses on the causes of these changes in civic participation. In his initial work, Putnam (2000) argued that rising television viewership was primarily to blame, with the increasing time pressures created by the rise of two-career families and the geographic isolation of sprawl and suburbanization cited as smaller potential influences. However, more recent evidence collected by Putnam and associates points in the opposite direction toward changes in community characteristics such as rising heterogeneity as the overriding factors, with residents of ethnically and racially diverse communities much less likely to be socially and civically connected to their neighbors than residents in more homogeneous communities (Putnam 2001). This contention that community diversity is a key factor in the decline of social capital finds support in a recent analysis by Costa and Kahn (2003) that suggests that rising levels of socioeconomic, racial, and ethnic heterogeneity in the United States explain 56 percent of the decline in volunteering, 40 percent of the decline in associational membership, and 32 percent of the decline in trust over the last three decades.

If we are to continue to make progress in understanding the impact that the changing nature of civic participation has on America's stock of social capital, we will have to develop a much better understanding of both the connections between civic participation and individuals' social network characteristics, and the connections between these civic and social network characteristics and the characteristics of the communities in which these individuals live. Building on

Erickson's recent position generator research in Canada showing a positive and significant connection between civic participation and social network diversity (Erickson 2004), a greater empirical understanding of the connection between civic participation, community characteristics, and the social network structure of social capital is sought in this chapter through analysis of original survey data in two American counties employing this position generator instrument.

14.2. METHODS

14.2.1. Two-County Telephone Survey

Consistent with recent efforts to understand the connection between civic participation and social capital in the context of different community environments, this study examines these connections within two American counties: one with a population more homogeneous than the US national average, and one with a population more heterogeneous than the national average. Data were collected through a telephone survey that focused on both the respondents' forms of civic participation and their social network characteristics, as well as other important factors such as levels of trust, use of different media and forms of communication, and political and social attitudes.

The first county in our sample is Allegheny, Pennsylvania (PA). Allegheny County is located in the southwestern corner of Pennsylvania. It is 730 square miles in size and contains the city of Pittsburgh and the surrounding suburbs and rural farming communities. Figures from the 2000 US Census show that Allegheny has a population of 1.3 million people, of whom 84 percent are White, 12 percent are Black, and 1 percent is Hispanic (measured as an ethnicity independent of race). Compared with national demographics, Allegheny County has similar percentages of Whites and Blacks, but much lower percentages of Hispanics (1 vs. 13) and residents born outside the United States (4 vs. 11) than the national average. It also has a higher average household income than the national average ($50,573 vs. $42,148).

The second county in our sample is Miami-Dade, Florida (FL). Miami-Dade County is located in southeastern Florida. It is 1,158 square miles in size and contains the city of Miami and the surrounding suburbs and rural areas. Figures from the 2000 US Census show that Miami-Dade County has a population of 2.2 million people, of whom 70 percent are White, 20 percent are Black, and 57 percent are Hispanic. These demographics make Miami-Dade County one of the most ethnically and racially diverse counties in the United States with a lower percentage of Whites (70 vs. 75), a higher percentage of Blacks (20 vs. 12), and a much higher percentage of Hispanics (57 vs. 13) than the national population. In addition to the higher levels of racial and ethnic diversity, Miami-Dade County also has a much higher percentage of residents born outside the United States than the national average (51 vs. 11). The average household income for the

Miami-Dade County is higher than the national average ($49,857 vs. $42,148) and comparable to that of Allegheny County.

Data in these two counties were collected through computer-assisted telephone interviews conducted by National Opinion Research Services (NORS), a respected research, sampling, and interview firm with a specialty in data collection in bilingual populations. The survey was translated from English into Spanish by NORS and all interviewers in the Miami-Data County data collection effort were bilingual. The Miami-Dade interviews were conducted during the first two weeks of July 2001 and the Allegheny interviews were conducted during the first two weeks of June 2001.

For this project, NORS utilized list-assisted random digit dialing, which generated 9,000 calls for Miami-Dade County and resulted in a live residential sample of 3,443 households. Of this group, 700 individuals (20.3% of the live residential sample) met the criteria for and completed the full survey. In Allegheny County, 8,000 calls were generated which resulted in a live residential sample of 3,036 households. Of this group, 709 individuals (24.7% of the live residential sample) met the criteria for and completed the full survey. While these response rates are lower than the average for academic telephone-based surveys of the general population, the divergence of the sample population from the overall population is minimal when comparing the demographic characteristics of the samples with the 2000 US Census figures for each county (see Appendix). The Census and sample nuare closely related in terms of key demographic variables such as gender, race, ethnicity, and household size. However, the samples do contain a slight bias toward high school and college graduates in both counties, and the Miami-Dade sample is skewed toward a lower mean household income.

Thus, some caution is warranted in the discussion about community context giving the slight bias towards the better educated and (in Miami-Dade) higher income families within these counties. In addition, since this is a one-time survey of each county, causal order cannot be as easily determined as in longitudinal studies. Finally, since the survey contains only two counties, the connection between community characteristics and rates of civic participation and social capital is more tentative than large-scale multicommunity studies can provide.

14.3. MEASUREMENT

The survey questionnaire designed for this project utilized 99 questions in four sections: Social Networks, Civic Participation, Neighborhood Characteristics, and Background Characteristics.

14.3.1. Social Networks

The characteristics of respondents' social networks were assessed as a general measure of social capital using the position generator methodology first introduced in Lin and Dumin (1986) and discussed in-depth in Lin, Fu, and Hsung (2001). Respondents were told: "We'd like to ask you some questions about your social ties to different kinds of professions. I'm going to read a list of different professions; just answer yes if there is someone with this profession among your relatives, friends, coworkers and acquaintances." This list contained 12 occupations sampled across the prestige hierarchy (Treiman scale prestige scores in parentheses) that were selected to achieve similar numerical size in the population and overall balance between male and female workers: lawyer (75), college professor (74), registered nurse (66), computer programmer (61), preschool teacher (55), electrician (51), bank teller (43), police officer (42), childcare worker (36), truck driver (30), cashier (29), and janitor (22). The order in which these occupations were read was randomized to minimize bias.

The primary variable calculated from these questions is *network diversity*, which is operationalized as the total number of occupations accessed through an individual's social ties out of a total of 12 occupations.

14.3.2. Civic Participation

The level of civic participation among respondents was measured using a similar question formulation to the measurement of respondents' social networks. Respondents were told: "I'd like to ask you a few questions about different forms of participation. I'm going to read a list of different organizations and activities; just answer yes if you have been involved in the last 12 months." This list was composed of the 12 different forms of civic participation utilized in Putnam's analysis of civic participation trend data (Putnam 2000): church or other religious service; charity or social service activity; professional or academic organization; club meeting; community project; committee for some local organization; public meeting on town affairs; literary, artistic, or discussion group; political party or meeting; labor union; environmental organization; and better government group. The order in which these organizations were read was also randomized to minimize bias.

Two main variables were calculated from these questions. *Civic participation* is a measure of whether an individual has had any level of civic participation in the last 12 months, with responses scored as 0 (involvement in none of the 12 civic organizations) or 1 (participation in one or more of the civic organizations). *Civic diversity* is a measure of the variety of an individual's civic participation, with responses scored as the total number of different civic organizations (of the 12 civic organizations measured) in which an individual was involved in the last 12 months. In addition to these two variables, an individual's participation in each of the 12 organizations was coded as 12 separate variables, with responses scored as 0 (not involved) or 1 (involved in the last 12 months).

For each civic organization in which an individual was involved, a series of nested questions was asked on the importance of traditional values to the group, the familiarity of its members, their level of ethnic and racial diversity, the percentage of members that are female, and the percentage of communication with members that is face-to-face. A four-answer scale was used for each question.

14.3.3. Neighborhood Characteristics

The level of connectedness of the respondents' neighborhood was also assessed through four questions on how familiar people in the neighborhood are to each other, how friendly they are to each other, how supportive they are of one another, and how trusting they are of one another. A four-answer scale was used for each question and responses were coded from 1 to 4 for the variables: *familiarity, friendliness, support,* and *trust.*

14.3.4. Background Characteristics

In addition to basic measures of age, gender, race, ethnicity, marital status, and household size, *employment* was operationalized as working more than 35 hr/week outside the home, *education* was scored from 1 (grade 11 or less) to 7 (graduate or professional degree), and both *personal income* and *household income* were scored from 1 (under $20,000) to 6 (above $100,000).

The way respondents acquire information on a regular basis and how they spend their leisure time was also assessed through four questions on the frequency of their use of newspapers, television, telephone, and email. A five-answer scale was used for each question.

14.4. RESULTS

14.4.1. The Two Counties in Context

Recent research on civic engagement suggests that areas with high levels of socioeconomic, ethnic, and racial diversity are more likely to have low levels of civic engagement and fewer social ties across group boundaries (Putnam 2001; Costa and Kahn 2003). Applying this hypothesis to the two counties in this sample, we would expect to see lower levels of civic participation and network diversity in the community with higher levels of socioeconomic, ethnic, and racial diversity, which is exactly what the results show.

Table 14.1 provides an overview of the level of community diversity and community connectedness for Allegheny County, PA, and Miami-Dade County, FL, based on figures from the 2000 US Census and results from the 2001 survey data. The first section of Table 14.1 presents measures of the two communities

Table 14.1. The community context

	Allegheny, PA	Miami-Dade, FL
Community diversity[a]		
White (%)	84.3	69.7
Black (%)	12.4	20.3
Hispanic (%)	0.9	57.3
Foreign-born (%)	3.5	50.5
Doesn't speak English (%)	2.3	35.2
Income less than $25,000 (%)	32.5	36.7
Income $30,000–$150,000 (%)	62.4	57.8
Income more than $150,000 (%)	4.1	4.7
Less than high school (%)	10.1	25.6
High or college degree (%)	77.1	65.3
Graduate degree (%)	12.5	8.9
Community connectedness		
Very familiar neighbors (%)	30.7	14.7
Very friendly neighbors (%)	40.7	23.9
Very supportive neighbors (%)	35.7	23.1
Very trusting neighbors (%)	52.4	54.5
Civic participation (%)	83.4	70.5
Civic diversity (mean) (%)	2.2	1.6
Network diversity (mean) (%)	6.0	5.2

[a] US Census 2000.

in terms of the distribution of race, ethnicity, place of birth, language, income, and education. Across almost all measures, Miami-Dade has a more heterogeneous population than Allegheny. It has much higher percentages of ethnic and racial minorities, much higher levels of foreign born and non-English speakers, a smaller middle class with larger percentages of both the poor and the wealthy, and a much larger percentage of people who did not finish high school, with a significantly smaller percentage of high school and college graduates.

The second section of Table 14.1 presents basic measures of community connectedness based on the results of our survey. Almost across the board, Allegheny has higher levels of community connectedness than Miami-Dade. It has almost twice the percentage of people who report having very familiar, very friendly, and very supportive neighbors. It has a higher percentage of individuals involved in one or more forms of civic participation, a greater level of civic diversity (the average number of forms of civic participation per person), and a greater level of network diversity (the average number of occupations within a person's social network). One important outlier of this trend in our results is trust. While Miami-Dade has on average one-half the percentage of people who report having very familiar, very friendly, and very supportive neighbors, it actually has a slightly higher percentage of people who report having very trusting neighbors.

Table 14.2. Correlations among social network, civic participation, and neighborhood

	Network diversity	Civic diversity
Allegheny, PA		
Civic diversity	.264**	
Neighborhood		
Familiarity	.178**	.159**
Friendliness	.108**	.085**
Support	120**	.079**
Trust	.052	.066
Miami-Dade, FL		
Civic diversity	.258**	
Neighborhood		
Familiarity	.181**	.271**
Friendliness	.078*	.146**
Support	.061	.137**
Trust	−.087	−.133**

* $p < .05$; ** $p < .01$.

14.4.2. Social Networks, Civic Participation, and Neighborhood Togetherness

While Putnam (2000) uses measures of social networks, civic participation, and neighborhood togetherness interchangeably as measures of social capital, research studies of social networks have pointed toward potential trade-offs between these measures as high levels of group cohesion restrict the diversity of members' social networks (Lin 1999b; Burt 2001). To help understand the connections between these three measures within different community contexts, a correlation matrix was created for network diversity, civic diversity, and the four measures of neighborhood togetherness: familiarity, friendliness, support, and trust. Table 14.2 summarizes these results.

In both Allegheny and Miami-Dade, the connection between network diversity and civic diversity is positive and very significant (<.01). Three of the neighborhood characteristics (familiarity, friendliness, and support) are also positively and significantly (<.01) connected with network diversity and civic diversity in Allegheny. The same three measures are also positively but less significantly connected with network diversity and civic diversity in Miami-Dade. These results lend support not only to the idea that civic participation and network diversity are positively related in different community contexts, but also to the contention that some measures of neighborhood togetherness (familiarity, friendliness, and support) are also important positive influences on civic and social diversity.

However, the big outlier in this correlation matrix is neighborhood trust. In the Allegheny sample, neighborhood trust is not significantly correlated with network diversity, civic participation, or civic diversity. In the Miami-Dade sample, neighborhood trust is not significantly correlated with network diversity and is actually negatively and significantly ($<.01$) correlated with civic diversity. This finding suggests that Putnam's use of trust together with measures of civic participation and social networks should be viewed with caution (Putnam 2000). Indeed, the negative and significant connection between neighborhood trust and civic diversity suggests that high levels of neighborhood trust may in fact restrict the variety of civic organizations in which one participates.

14.4.3. Civic Participation and Social Networks: A Closer Look

While Putnam (1995, 2000) has used trend data on civic participation as a proxy measure for social capital (and therefore, by his own definition, social networks), the relationship between civic participation and network diversity is still not well understood. Previous research (Lazarsfeld and Merton 1954; Fischer et al. 1977; Fischer 1982) on the interplay between civic participation and social ties across group boundaries suggested a complicated picture—with some forms of civic participation helping to encourage more diverse social ties across group boundaries and others to strengthen these boundaries, resulting in a more homogeneous network of friendships and acquaintances. More recently, Erickson (2004), employing a position generator survey instrument, found that overall levels of civic participation were connected with greater network diversity, even when controlling for individual characteristics.

To better understand the relationship between these measures of social and civic connectedness, network diversity was regressed on civic diversity. Controls were used for age, gender, race, ethnicity, martial status, household size, and education. Since both working and nonworking individuals were included in the samples, the *N* was 650 for Allegheny and 592 for Miami-Dade.

As can been seen in Table 14.3, civic diversity is positively and significantly ($p < .001$) related to network diversity in both counties even when controlling for education and other background characteristics. These results lend support to Erickson's finding that civic participation is a reasonable predictor of occupational diversity within an individual's social networks (Erickson 2004). Thus, where it is not possible to collect social network data directly, such as in Putnam's studies of the changes in social capital over the twentieth century, it appears that measures of civic participation may serve as an acceptable proxy.

To explore the relative importance of civic diversity in comparison to a dichotomous measure of civic participation, the average level of network diversity for each additional level form of civic participation was tabulated. As can be seen in Charts 14.1 and 14.2, for every additional form of civic participation, there is on average a corresponding increase by one additional occupation in the diversity of the individual's social network. This positive and linear relationship between civic diversity and network diversity holds true in both counties for up to six forms of participation, after which the average network diversity plateaus in Allegheny and declines more sharply in Miami-Dade.

Table 14.3. Regressions of network diversity on participation, with controls

Independent variables	Allegheny network diversity[a]	Miami-Dade network diversity[a]
Age	−.01 (−.06)	−.01 (−.03)
Gender (female)	.22 (−.04)	.30 (.05)
Race (White)	−1.32 (−.16)***	−.67 (−.10)
Ethnicity (Hispanic)	−1.10 (−.04)	−.16 (−.02)
Marital status (married)	.63 (.10)*	.10 (.02)
Household size[b]	−.11 (−.01)	−.17 (−.01)
Education	.01 (.06)	.17 (.10)*
Civic diversity	.43 (.24)***	.40 (.22)***
Constant	5.91	4.70
R^2	.10	.09
N	650	592

* $p < .05$; *** $p < .001$.

[a] Partial regression estimates with standardized estimates in parentheses.

[b] Household size logged.

These results suggest that while civic participation in general may play an important role in expanding the diversity of one's social network, one of the most important factors may be the number of different kinds of civic organizations in which one participates. The plateau in network diversity in Allegheny after six forms or more of civic participation suggests the possibility that participating in an ever-larger number of different kinds of civic organizations may at some point reduce the time needed to develop meaningful social ties within any one organization. The steeper decline in network diversity after six forms of civic

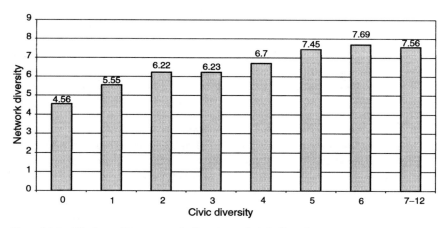

Chart 14.1. Allegheny, PA—network diversity and civic diversity

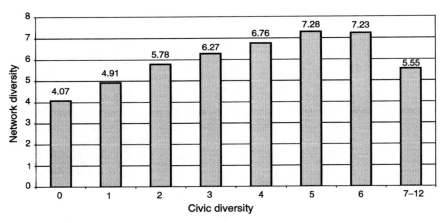

Chart 14.2. Miami-Dade, FL—network diversity and civic diversity

participation in Miami-Dade suggests the possibility that community context may also be a factor in intensifying this trend.

While these results suggest that overall participation in civic institutions is related to greater levels of network diversity and that civic diversity may be a particularly important factor in increasing network diversity, this does not mean that every form of civic participation should be seen as positively and significantly related to network diversity. To test the relative importance of different forms of civic participation, network diversity was regressed on each of the 12 forms of civic participation measured, controlling for the respondent's age, gender, race, ethnicity, marital status, household size, and education, in 12 separate sets of regression equations in each of the two counties. The results from these regression equations are summarized together in Table 14.4.

In Table 14.4, the 12 forms of civic participation are ordered by the percentage of respondents who said they had participated in the last 12 months, with the direction, magnitude, and significance of the association with network diversity placed to the right of these percentages. In every case except for a negative and not significant result for participation in better government groups in Miami-Dade, every form of civic participation was found to be positively, but not always significantly, related to network diversity. This result is somewhat surprising given that studies of civic organizations have consistently demonstrated that the membership of many organizations is more homogeneous than the general population (Laumann 1973; Fisher et al. 1977; Fisher 1982; McPherson and Smith-Lovin 1986; McPherson et al. 1992). One possible explanation is that since most people's social networks are already much more homogeneous than the general population (Marsden 1987, 1988), participation in a civic organization is unlikely to make their social ties any less diverse, and at least offers the possibility that they will interact with a wider range of people than is currently found in their social network.

Table 14.4. Regressions of network diversity on 12 forms of civic participation listed in order of percentage of respondents' involvement[a]

Form of participation	Allegheny, PA		Miami-Dade, FL	
Church or other religious service	54.3	(.15)***	46.0	(.12)***
Charity or social service activity	32.9	(.06)	25.8	(.12)**
Professional or academic organization	22.3	(.09)*	18.1	(.13)**
Club meeting	22.0	(.12)**	12.0	(.06)
Community project	16.8	(.05)	12.9	(.15)***
Committee for some local organization	15.0	(.09)*	7.9	(.01)
Public meeting on town affairs	13.8	(.10)*	10.4	(.10)*
Literary, artistic, or discussion group	12.3	(.11)**	10.9	(.11)**
Political party or meeting	11.7	(.08)*	6.9	(.05)
Labor union	9.0	(.10)*	4.4	(.05)
Environmental organization	5.6	(.07)	5.6	(.06)
Better government group	3.1	(.10)**	2.3	(−.01)

[a] Controlling for respondent's age, gender, race, ethnicity, marital status, household size, and education. Standardized estimates in parentheses.

* $p < .05$; ** $p < .01$; *** $p < .001$.

There was one clear standout among the different forms of civic participation: religious organizations. Participation in religious organizations was positively and very significantly related to the diversity of an individual's social network in both Allegheny and Miami-Dade. In fact, it was the only form of civic participation out of the 12 sampled that was significant at the $p < .001$ level in both counties. This finding lends further support to the growing literature on the important role that participation in religious organizations plays in not only encouraging social connections within a religious setting, but also in promoting a wide array of prosocial behavior that increases social connectedness (Ellison 1992; Wilson and Janoski 1995; Greeley 1997).

In addition to participation in religious organizations, three other forms of civic participation were also found to be positively and significantly related to network diversity in both Allegheny and Miami-Dade counties: participation in public meetings on town affairs; participation in literary, art, or discussion groups; and participation in professional or academic organizations. Finally, five other forms of civic participation (club meeting, local committee, political meeting, labor union, and better government group) were positively and significantly related to network diversity only in Allegheny, two forms of civic participation (social service activity and community project) were positively and significantly related to network diversity only in Miami-Dade, and one form of civic participation (environmental organization) was not significantly related to network diversity in either county.

The fact that more than half of the forms of civic participation measured in this study were found to be significantly related to network diversity in one county but not significantly related to network diversity in the other county lends support to the idea that the significance of this association may be highly dependent on the community context. Since variations in the age, gender, race, ethnicity, marital status, household size, and education were controlled for in the regression equations, the source of this variation is probably not found in traditional demographic variables.

One possible explanation is that the level of significance is simply a reflection of the number of people involved in each civic organization in a given area. While this pattern does fit the data from Miami-Dade, where six of the seven most popular forms of participation are significantly related to network diversity, it does not fit the data from Allegheny, where the significance of different forms of civic participation is evenly distributed throughout the list. In addition, the four forms of participation that are significantly associated with network diversity in both counties show little relation to the rankings by membership percentage in either Allegheny (where they are the first, third, seventh, and eighth most popular) or Miami-Dade (where they are the first, third, fifth, and seventh most popular).

Another possible explanation for the varying levels of significance in the two counties is that different forms of civic participation have different internal characteristics in different communities. Putnam (2000) has suggested that organizations that are better at fostering an environment where everyone is familiar with everyone else are more likely to create lasting social ties among their members. It may be, for example, that club meetings in Allegheny County, PA, are better at fostering familiarity between members than club meetings in Miami-Dade, FL, thus accounting for the greater levels of significance with network diversity in Allegheny.

To explore this possibility, the 12 different forms of civic participation were put in descending order based on the percentage of participants who said they were very familiar with their fellow participants, with the significance of the association with network diversity placed to the right of these percentages. However, as Table 14.5 shows, no clear pattern exists between the level of familiarity between members and the significance of the connection with network diversity. The same lack of pattern was found for other internal measures of the organizations such as the upholding of traditional values, ethnic and racial diversity, gender representation, and the predominance of face-to-face communication. Thus, while not identifying the source of these variations, the results do help rule out some possible explanations, including the demographic characteristics of the participants themselves, their familiarity within one another, and the popularity of the specific form of participation within the community.

14.4.4. Newspapers, Televisions, Telephones, and Email

In Putnam's discussion of the causes of a decline in social capital in America, he identifies rising hours spent in front of the television as the single most important factor in this decline (Putnam 2000). In addition to the damaging effects of

Table 14.5. Regressions of network diversity on 12 forms of civic participation listed in order of percentage of "very familiar" membership[a]

Form of participation	Allegheny, PA	Form of participation	Miami-Dade, FL
Committee	51.9 (.09)*	Club meeting	52.4 (.06)
Club meeting	46.8 (.12)**	Better government	43.8 (−.01)
Labor union	43.8 (.10)*	Community project	42.7 (.15)***
Church	41.0 (.15)***	Committee	39.6 (.01)
Professional	34.8 (.09)*	Church	39.0 (.12)***
Literary or discussion	34.5 (.11)**	Professional	38.4 (.13)**
Community project	35.8 (.05)	Labor union	35.5 (.05)
Charity, social service	33.0 (.06)	Literary or discussion	34.2 (.11)**
Better government	27.3 (.10)**	Public meeting	33.3 (.10)*
Public meeting	16.3 (.10)*	Charity, social service	33.1 (.12)**
Political party	16.3 (.08)*	Environmental	28.9 (.06)
Environmental	15.0 (.07)	Political	27.1 (.05)

[a] Controlling for respondent's age, gender, race, ethnicity, marital status, household size, and education. Standardized estimates in parentheses.
* $p < .05$; ** $p < .01$; *** $p < .001$.

television, he also argues that declining newspaper readership is connected to an overall decline in civic engagement, that rising telephone usage in the twentieth century did not result in greater social connectedness, and that the rise in new forms of communication, such as email, is also unlikely to have a significant impact on social connectedness. By contrast, Lin (2001b) has argued that the increase in Internet-mediated forms of communication like email has led to an increase in network diversity by lowering the boundaries in the creation and maintenance of social ties.

To empirically test these hypotheses, correlations were run between network diversity and civic diversity, and hours spent reading the newspaper, watching television, talking on the telephone, and using email in Miami-Dade and Allegheny counties.

As Table 14.6 shows, newspaper, telephone, and email usage is positively and significantly ($<.01$) correlated with network diversity and civic diversity in both counties. These results suggest that telephone and email usage should not automatically be separated out from newspaper readership as a predictor of social and civic connections. However, consistent with Putnam's thesis, television usage is negatively and significantly correlated with both network diversity and civic diversity in Allegheny and negatively but not significantly correlated with network diversity and civic diversity in Miami-Dade.

To understand whether these correlations represent a real relationship or a spurious one, both network diversity and civic diversity were regressed on newspaper, television, telephone, and email usage, with controls for age, gender, race, ethnicity, marital status, household size, and education.

Table 14.6. Correlations among network diversity, civic diversity, and four means of communication

	Network diversity	Civic diversity
Allegheny, PA		
Newspaper	.08**	.10**
Television	−.09*	−.16**
Telephone	.12**	.09*
Email	.13**	.20**
Miami-Dade, FL		
Newspaper	.12**	.16**
Television	−.02	−.07
Telephone	.12**	.13**
Email	.11**	.26**

$^*p < .05; ^{**}p < .01.$

As can be seen in Table 14.7, once these background characteristics are controlled for, the significance of the relationship between hours of television watched and both network diversity and civic diversity disappears. This suggests that Putnam's thesis that television has caused Americans to "tune out" from their social and civic lives may be more imagined than real. However, some of the significance of the relationship between newspaper, telephone, and email usage and social and civic connectedness remains. For example, in both Allegheny and Miami-Dade, hours spent reading the newspaper is positively and significantly (<.01) related to network diversity. In Allegheny, telephone usage is also positively and significantly (<.05) related to network diversity. Finally, in Miami-Dade email usage is positively and very significantly (<.001) related to civic diversity. Given the increasing use of email in America, these results suggest at least the possibility that "cybernetworks" held together through new forms of electronic communication could play an important role in civic participation in the future (Lin 2001*b*).

14.5. DISCUSSION

The goal of this research project was to expand our empirical understanding of the connection between civic participation, community characteristics, and the social network structure of social capital. The findings above have done so in a way that has answered some important questions, raised additional questions for future study, and shed light on some of the factors at work in the changing nature of America's stock of social capital.

First, the gap between civic participation and social network models of social capital is not really a gap at all. Not only were measures of network diversity

Table 14.7. Regression of network diversity and civic diversity on newspaper, television, telephone, and email, with controls

Independent variables	Allegheny network diversity[a]	Miami-Dade network diversity[a]	Allegheny civic diversity[a]	Miami-Dade civic diversity[a]
Age	−.01 (−.04)	−.00 (−.02)	.00 (.07)	.00 (.72)
Gender (female)	.10 (.02)	.25 (.04)	−.11 (−.81)	.19 (.05)
Race (White)	−1.31 (−.16)***	−.82 (−.11)*	.16 (.04)	−.22 (−.06)
Ethnicity (Hispanic)	−1.12 (−.04)	−.33 (−.05)	−.01 (−.00)	−.19 (−.23)***
Marital status (married)	.52 (.09)	.16 (.03)	−.02 (−.01)	−.03 (−.01)
Household size[b]	−.06 (−.01)	−.40 (− .03)	.07 (.01)	−.27 (.04)
Education	.13 (.08)	.17 (.10)*	.24 (.24)***	.10 (.11)*
Newspaper	.25 (.09)**	.22 (.10)*	.10 (.08)	.02 (.01)
Television	−.23 (−.07)	.04 (.01)	−.14 (.07)	−.05 (−.03)
Telephone	.24 (.09)*	.19 (.07)	.11 (.07)	.07 (.06)
Email	.08 (.05)	.06 (.03)	.09 (.10)	.17 (.18)***
Constant	5.5	4.2	.34	1.2
R^2	.07	.06	.11	.17
N	649	600	650	594

[a] Partial regression estimates with standardized estimates in parentheses.
[b] Household size logged.
* $p < .05$; ** $p < .01$; *** $p < .001$.

and civic diversity found to be positively and significantly related in two very different demographic environments, but this positive relationship remains significant at the $p < .001$ level even when controlling for age, gender, race, ethnicity, marital status, household size, and education. Thus, measures of civic participation, though not as good an indicator as direct measures of social network characteristics, are found to be a reasonable predictor of an individual's, and potentially a community's, stock of social capital. These results add support to Erickson's earlier finding of a significant and positive connection between network diversity and civic participation, and provides empirical credibility to Putnam's argument that declining levels of civic participation in America since the 1960s suggest that there has been a corresponding decline in levels of social capital (Erickson 2004).

Second, there is a great deal of variability in the connection between specific forms of civic participation and social capital that remains to be explained. One of the more surprising findings of this study was the fact that more than half of the forms of civic participation were found to be positively and significantly related to network diversity in one county but not significantly related to network diversity in the other county, even when controlling for age, gender, race, ethnicity, marital status, household size, and education. It appears that the popularity of the form of participation, the familiarity of the members, their values, their ethnic and racial diversity, their gender distribution, and the predominance of face-to-face communication are also not related to this variation. Given the importance that has been placed in public policy discussions on increasing civic participation in an effort to increase social capital (Putnam and Feldstein 2003), uncovering the reasons why different forms of civic participation have varying levels of significance in their connection with network measures of social capital in different communities deserves to be an important area of future research.

Third, any understanding of the connection between civic participation and social capital would be incomplete without a focus on the role of religious organizations. Not only was participation in religious organizations found to be the most popular form of civic participation, but it was also found to have the most significant positive connection with network diversity in both counties, even when controlling for background characteristics. These findings add support to the growing literature on religious organizations as a social resource for individuals and their communities, and suggest that religious organizations should be a key focus of future social network research.

Fourth, in terms of the impact on social networks and civic engagement, email trumps TV. While the initial correlations between television, network diversity, and civic diversity appeared to lend empirical support to Putnam's contention that increasing television viewership is reducing America's stock of social capital, regressions of network diversity and civic diversity on television usage controlling for demographic characteristics suggest that the relationship is most likely spurious. However, the results do show that email usage is positively and very significantly ($<.001$) related to increased civic diversity in one county even when controlling for background characteristics, which offers at least the possibility that rising use of electronic forms of communication could be an increasingly important factor in the interplay between civic participation and social capital.

Finally, when it comes to the creation of social capital, there appears to be a "paradox of diversity." Growing evidence suggests that network diversity is a key indicator of an individual's stock of social capital. Social ties to a wide variety of different skills, knowledge, and perspectives appear to act as a social resource that offers a wide range of benefits for individuals, including economic returns (Lin 2001b). However, while network diversity depends on the existence of a wide variety of skills, knowledge, and perspectives within a community, the evidence in this study and elsewhere suggests that civic participation may be inhibited by the presence of high levels of community diversity. Thus, while increasing community heterogeneity results in rising levels of *potential* social capital, it may reduce the level of *actual* social capital held by individuals within these communities by discouraging one of the main pathways to the creation of diverse social ties. With American society on track to grow even more diverse in the coming decades, and counties like Miami-Dade pointing the way toward this future, uncovering new ways to overcome this paradox of diversity deserves to be a central element of future social network research.

APPENDIX: THE 2000 CENSUS AND THE RESEARCH SAMPLE

Demographics	Allegheny 2000 Census	Allegheny 2001 Survey	Miami-Dade 2000 Census	Miami-Dade 2001 Survey
Female (%)	52.6	54.0	51.7	56.4
White (%)	84.3	83.1	69.7	73.7
Black (%)	12.4	13.5	20.3	19.0
Hispanic (%)	0.9	1.7	57.3	59.6
High school graduate (%)	87.9	95.6	72.1	86.7
College graduate (%)	29.4	34.2	23.6	31.3
Household size (mean)	2.3	2.5	2.9	3.2
Household income (mean)	50,573	50,501	49,857	41,720

Section IV

Social Institutions and Inequality in Social Capital

15

Why Some Occupations Are Better Known Than Others[1]

Bonnie H. Erickson

15.1. INTRODUCTION

Occupations differ greatly in the extent to which they are well represented in the networks of others. For some occupations, almost everyone knows at least one person in that occupation; for others, hardly anyone does. I will call the number of people who know someone in an occupation that occupation's size of *network audience*. This is an important variable, since it indicates the impact of an occupation on the social lives of others. The larger an occupation's network audience, the more other people get to know about the occupation through personal contact, the more people are exposed to flows of information and influence from that occupation, and the larger and more important people will perceive that occupation to be.

The size of an occupation's network audience varies with three things examined in this chapter: the number of people in the occupation, the prestige of the occupation, and the occupation's gender composition.

If people met each other at random, then the sheer number of people in an occupation would determine the size of its network audience. People do not meet at random, but sheer size is one factor contributing to the chances that people in an occupation will become widely known. For more detailed analysis of the many implications of categorical sizes for social relationships, see Blau (1977).

People do not meet at random; those in higher-level social positions have more opportunities to know, and be known by, others. One important form of social position is occupational prestige. Higher occupational prestige goes with greater opportunities to meet people, both on and off the job. On the job, higher-level jobs generally include more work with people and work with a wider range of people. Further, the work with people is more responsible and intense, so that

[1] Data from the 2000 Canadian Election Study funded by the Social Sciences and Humanities Research Council of Canada, Elections Canada, and the Institute for Research on Public Policy; Andre Blais, Elisabeth Gidengil, Neil Nevitte, and Richard Nadeau are the co-investigators for the election study. Elisabeth Gidengil, Stephen Arsenault, and Martin Van der Gaag provided invaluable advice and assistance as I developed the special network item used in this paper.

mere contacts become connections. Some low-prestige jobs, such as that of a waiter or waitress, include abundant contacts but all of a superficial and passing nature. Off the job, those in higher-prestige occupations have still more opportunities to be better known because of their higher levels of education, income, and participation in social settings such as voluntary associations. Thus, the network audiences of higher-prestige occupations are larger than those of lower-prestige occupations with the same number of people in them. More generally, higher-prestige occupations have larger network occupations relative to their population size.

Earlier work by Killworth et al. (1998) indicates that socioeconomic status has a strong effect on networking power, with higher-status people greatly over-represented in networks relative to their group size. Using their data (Killworth et al. 1998: 28), I computed the ratio between the mean number of category representatives that respondents reported knowing and the number of people in the category population. The ratio for those who own a pool is four times the ratio for bowlers, and the ratio for those with family income over $200,000 is over 13 times that of those out of work and looking for a job. However, no prior research tests the impact of occupational prestige on network audience size. This chapter shows that this impact, like the impact of family income, is substantial. Such powerful and important effects deserve special names, and I propose the term *networking power* for the ratio of a category's network audience size to its population size. Networking power is the extent to which members of a social location have the capacity to forge social relationships, and become members of the networks of others, relative to the simple number of people in the social location.

Gender composition could be related to an occupation's networking power in either or both of two ways. First, men and women could be differentially allocated to jobs with different networking opportunities. Second, gender as such could provide men and women with different networking opportunities quite aside from their occupations, and then these gender differences would contribute to the network audiences for occupations mainly composed of men or of women. I return to the second possibility below. For possible differential allocation of men and women to work with different networking opportunities, Ridgeway (1997) offers useful ideas. She argues that gender is so deeply ingrained that we immediately note the gender of any person we meet, and see them through learned expectations of what men and women are like. We then tend to expect men to be good at and suitable for work associated with the masculine stereotype, and expect women to be good at and suitable for work associated with the feminine stereotype. Those who fill jobs or evaluate job performances think in this way, and thus tend to reproduce gender segregation and inequality in work.

Interestingly, this view produces two contradictory predictions about gender composition and occupational networking power. On the one hand, men are widely thought to be better in leadership, assertiveness, decisiveness, and other traits associated with higher-level positions (Holt and Ellis 1998), and hence men are often preferred for more powerful jobs with better chances to meet people. On the other hand, women are thought to be more sympathetic, understanding, and sensitive to the needs of others (Holt and Ellis 1998). Thus, women are widely thought to be better at dealing with other people, and women are often preferred for jobs requiring social skills (Kilbourne et al. 1994). Women may have better access to occupations that include in-depth work with people, so that occupations with a higher proportion of women have greater networking power.

Within occupations, men and women could develop different networking power by two routes, differential assignment to work or gender differences in networking aside from work. For possible gender differences in assignment to work, it is useful to combine Ridgeway's argument with Reskin's (1993). Reskin argues that gender segregation at work grows more and more pronounced as we move to more finely defined kinds of work, from huge census groupings to specific jobs, because men and women are differentially assigned to particular work consistent with their stereotypes and with a queueing process in which men get first crack at more well-rewarded positions. If so, within the "same" broadly defined occupations, men and women will be assigned different jobs with different networking opportunities. Again, the direction of the gender difference is moot: men may get greater networking power along with more powerful and well-paid work within occupations, while women may get greater networking power along with more intensely interpersonal work within occupations.

Quite aside from occupational differences between men and women, gender itself as a social location may bring differences in the networking power of men and women. Here too, opposite predictions seem equally plausible in advance of the evidence. Men may have larger networks because they have higher social status (which makes people more attractive). Men are more active in social locations outside of work in ways that give them more chances to meet people; for example, men may belong to larger voluntary associations (McPherson and Smith-Lovin 1982). But women are seen as more attractive in some ways, since they are thought to be more sociable and pleasant, and they are more socially active outside work in some ways, for example, as the social secretaries for their families as well as for themselves. Ingenious attempts to measure complete networks indicate that people know more men than women (Killworth et al. 1990: 309), suggesting that men have greater networking power overall. However, this difference may reflect gender differences in employment rather than gender as such, much as Moore (1990) found that gender differences in the composition of stronger ties fade after controls for employment and family status. Since this chapter concerns the size of network audiences for men and women in selected occupations, gender differences in employment are in effect controlled, allowing a clearer check on whether gender as such affects networking power.

Results for the networking power of men and women in the same occupations can shed some light on how gender composition is related to an occupation's networking power. If there is no difference between men and women within occupations, the interpretation is clear: any impact of gender composition on occupational networking power is not due to gender differences in networking power, but due to gendered differences in allocation to jobs. If there are gender differences in networking power within occupations, the interpretation is less clear. On the one hand, the gender differences may be due to general gender differences in networking power aside from work. On the other hand, gender differences may be due to differential assignment of men and women to specific jobs within occupations.

15.2. METHODS

The data for this chapter come from the 2000 Canadian Federal Election Study. This study included three surveys of a representative national sample. The first two surveys of this panel were telephone surveys conducted during and just after the November 2000 election; these included over 3,000 respondents. Respondents to the second survey were asked whether they would be willing to receive a mailed questionnaire; those willing were mailed one, and 1,557 people returned a usable questionnaire. Since the last survey was the source of the data used here, the drop in sample size might cause some concern. However, the reduction appears to involve little bias, perhaps because nonresponse occurred rather randomly as the onset of the holiday season slowed the mail and tied up people's time. The mailed survey, compared with the larger earlier surveys, had somewhat fewer young people (22% vs. 29% under 35), fewer low-income people (32% vs. 37% in the lowest categories), and more married people (63% vs. 56%); there were only slight differences in education, sex, employment status, region, and religion (Elisabeth Gidengil, personal communication).

This chapter draws on one question which I developed for the mailed survey (see Figure 15.1). This item is a variation of the popular "position generator" item originally developed by Lin and Dumin (1986). In such questions, we ask people whether they know anyone at all in each of selected occupations. Since this item is generally used to measure social capital, or access to a variety of resources through one's contacts, researchers usually select occupations that vary in prestige because there are different resources at different levels of the occupational prestige hierarchy. Prestige variation is also important for the different purposes of the present chapter, since prestige is a likely predictor of networking power. Occupations selected for this study do vary widely in prestige (see Table 15.1 for prestige scores from Ganzeboom and Treiman 1996). It is essential to add gender, whether studying social capital (because men and women differ in the kinds of resources they control) or networking power (because this may vary by gender or by combinations of gender and occupation). Thus, I asked whether people knew any men in an occupation, and whether they knew any women, instead of just whether they knew anyone at all. Further, I drew on the 1996 Census of Canada for the

Here is a list of occupations. Please put a circle in the appropriate column if you know any men (Column 1) or any women (Column 2) in each of these occupations:

	Men	Women
Lawyer	1	2
Social worker	1	2
Carpenter	1	2
Tailor, dressmaker or furrier	1	2
Computer programmer	1	2
Security guard	1	2
Cashier	1	2
Sales or marketing manager	1	2
Sewing machine operator	1	2
Delivery driver	1	2
Human resources manager	1	2
Janitor or caretaker	1	2
Pharmacist	1	2
Server (waiter or waitress)	1	2
Farmer	1	2

Figure 15.1. The election survey item

Note: This figure gives the English-language version of the questionnaire; a French version was also used in the survey, since Canada is bilingual.

number of people in each occupation and gender composition. I examined several sets of occupations of similar type: higher professionals, middle managers, other professionals, skilled trades, lower-level service workers, semi-skilled trades, and unskilled. Within each set, I chose one of the most male dominated and one of the most female dominated available, to allow study of the possible effects of gender composition. To include rural and agricultural occupations, I added farmers. I also restricted my choices to occupations with at least 20,000 people, since few respondents will know anyone in very rare occupations. I further restricted choice to occupations with clear common-language titles in the census, so that respondents could easily interpret the occupation names yet the census data would be applicable. For size and gender composition of the occupations selected, see Table 15.1.

Using this measure, the network audience for a category is all those people who know at least one person in that category. Underlying this definition is the assumption that the most critical difference is the difference between having any category representatives in one's network and having none at all. Even one contact can be a source of some information or influence that carries the weight of personal experience. For example, if a person knows just one tinker, the person can think: "I know something about tinkers, I know one myself." In this chapter, the important categories are occupations and their gender subcategories, the men and women within these occupations. Anecdotal evidence suggests that people often make inferences about occupations, or about combinations of occupation and gender, from a single known case. For example, in a study of women moving into

Table 15.1. The extent to which occupations are known

Occupation	A	B	C = B/A	D	E
	Population size	Network audience size	Networking power	Prestige	Female (%)
Lawyer	59,965	1,286	.021	73	31
Pharmacist	21,455	1,167	.054	64	56
HR manager	27,685	880	.032	60	47
Sales manager	109,240	937	.009	60	25
Social worker	40,500	1,053	.026	52	76
Computer programmer	74,240	1,200	.016	51	25
Tailor, furrier, dressmaker	27,315	840	.031	40	86
Farmer	238,910	1,131	.005	40	24
Carpenter	123,870	1,255	.010	37	1
Cashier	311,775	1,288	.004	34	86
Delivery driver	104,615	1,072	.010	31	9
Security guard	84,690	992	.012	30	20
Sewing machine operator	78,690	535	.007	25	92
Janitor	305,765	1,126	.004	25	32
Server	249,315	1,190	.005	21	81

Notes: Column A, total number of people in an occupation, and column E, the percentage of female, come from the 1996 Census of Canada.

Column B is the number of respondents who report knowing someone in an occupation, taken from the mailed-back post-election survey following the Canadian Federal Election Survey in 2000; see <http:www.fas.umontreal.ca/pol/ces-eec>.

Column C = B/A.

Column D is occupational prestige; see Ganzeboom and Treiman (1996).

nontraditional work in the security industry (Erickson, Albanese, and Drakulic 2000), a male alarm worker reported that he was confident that a women could be a good installer because he once knew a woman installer and she did the job well. Moreover, respondents can more easily and quickly remember whether they know anyone in an occupation than they can remember just how many they know. Thus, the difference between any network contact and none is both important and practical for research, though it would also be interesting to examine the number of contacts (as in Killworth et al. 1998).

The results from the mailed survey are reported partly in Table 15.1, in which column B gives the number of respondents who reported knowing anyone in an occupation; this could be knowing a man, a woman, or both. This shows the overall network audience size of occupations, as measured through this sample. Table 15.2 gives the proportion who reported knowing a man only, a woman only, or both a man and a woman, among those who reported knowing someone in each occupation. This indicates the networking power of men and women within occupations.

Data analysis consists of a set of correlations and regressions. Since the occupations are chosen theoretically not randomly, the sample size is very large, and the key results are very strong, I do not report significance tests.

Table 15.2. Percentage of knowing men, women, or both in occupations

Occupation	Know a man	Know a woman	Know both
Lawyer	45.7	8.8	45.5
Pharmacist	23.2	24.6	52.1
HR manager	27.1	40.4	32.5
Sales manager	43.9	18.7	37.4
Social worker	12.2	52.8	35.0
Computer programmer	55.3	9.0	35.7
Tailor, furrier, dressmaker	19.1	57.5	23.4
Farmer	55.8	2.8	41.4
Carpenter	88.8	2.5	8.7
Cashier	6.0	56.0	38.0
Delivery driver	68.5	4.2	27.3
Security guard	61.7	7.4	30.9
Sewing machine operator	9.0	77.8	13.1
Janitor	53.1	8.7	38.3
Server	6.7	41.3	52.0

Note: The data come from the mailed-back post-election survey. In each row, entries are the percentage of those who know a man (but not a woman), a woman (but not a man), or both a man and a woman, in that occupation, among those who know anyone at all in that occupation. The N for each row is the same as column B, Network audience size, in Table 15.1.

15.2.1. Results for Occupations

One would expect the network audience for an occupation to grow with the number of people in the occupation, and it does, but quite modestly. The correlation between column A of Table 15.1 (the number of people in an occupation according to the 1996 Census of Canada) and column B (the number of survey respondents who report knowing at least one person in each occupation) is just 0.396. Thus, the sheer number of people that there are to know only explains about 20 percent of the variation in network audience size. The gap between occupation size and audience size is sometimes quite striking; for example, the second largest group (janitors) is 14 times bigger than the smallest (pharmacist), yet the number of survey respondents who knew someone in these occupations is almost the same (1,126 vs. 1,167).

Since I excluded very small occupations in which few respondents would know anyone, it is possible that size and networking power are a little more correlated over the whole range of occupations. Among detailed (four-digit) occupations with descriptive titles, the smallest two are commercial divers ($N = 1,065$ in the 1996 census) and meteorological technicians ($N = 1,040$). Quite possibly, very few people know anyone in these small categories. But at the same time, such tiny occupations are a small component of the workforce, and the occupations observed include most of the full range of sizes for detailed occupations in the census. The full range is from 1,040 for meteorological technicians to 311,775 for retail salespeople, with the latter being the only occupation larger than the largest one (cashiers) included in the election survey. Thus, it is reasonable to conclude that mere population size has a modest correlation with how widely an occupation is known through personal contacts with its members.

Sheer occupation size seems of limited importance because it is overwhelmed by inequalities in the ability of individual members of occupations to build large networks. Earlier I argued that people in higher-prestige occupations should be better known to others because prestige goes with greater ability to build networks on or off the job. My expectations about the gender composition of occupations were less clear: competing arguments predict that a greater proportion of women goes with lesser or with greater networking power. To assess these predictions, I simply computed the ratio between the number of survey respondents who knew someone in the occupation and the number of people in that occupation (column B of Table 15.1 over column A, reported in column C).

As expected, occupational prestige is a strong predictor of networking power, with a correlation of 0.651. The correlation of networking power with proportion female is only 0.175, seemingly suggesting that gender composition does not matter. But closer examination shows an important interaction effect. Networking power is always low when occupational prestige is low; all poor jobs give poor networking opportunities. But when occupational prestige is moderate (say, 40) or more, networking power becomes much more variable, and occupations with more women have more networking power. With some peering, one can see this in Table 15.1, where the four most female occupations (pharmacist, human resources manager, social worker, and tailor/dressmaker/furrier) have higher networking power than other occupations with similar prestige but a higher proportion of men. More formally, I divided the occupations into the seven with highest proportion (0.47 or more) female and the remaining eight, and then computed regressions for prestige and networking power. For more female occupations:

$$\text{Networking power} = 0.00098 \,(\text{prestige}) - 0.0118, r = 0.888$$

For more male occupations:

$$\text{Networking power} = 0.00011 \,(\text{prestige}) - 0.0001, \; r = 0.695$$

Thus, prestige makes a different difference to networking power for men's work and women's work, with networking power rising faster and more strongly with prestige for occupations in which women are more common. Not only does prestige generally bring better networking opportunities, but also women tend to be found in just those kinds of higher-prestige jobs that are especially rich in chances to meet many people.

At this point, we cannot yet be sure whether this interesting finding comes from gender differences in allocation to work or from gender differences in networking. Are women preferred for higher-status jobs which require extensive and intensive work with people? Or, are women generally successful networkers who boost the network audiences for any jobs they are preferred for? The second possibility seems less likely given the lack of impact of gender composition on the networking power of lower-prestige jobs. However, we can see the role of gender as such more clearly by turning to results for knowing men and women in the same occupations (Table 15.2). Results are surprisingly simple: there is no sign of effect of gender as such. The extent to which people know a man, a woman, or both a man and a woman in an occupation simply depends on the occupation's gender composition, in an evenhanded way that shows no bias toward men or women.

If gender as such has no effect, then the chances of knowing only a women will rise with the proportion of women in an occupation, the chances of knowing only a man will rise with the proportion of men in an occupation, and the two trends will be very similar. If gender as such does have an effect, then we will see differences of some kind; for example, if men are better known than women on an average, the trend line for knowing only a man will have a higher intercept. No such effects showed up. The greater the percentage of women in an occupation, the more often respondents report knowing a woman and not a man ($r = 0.939$); the greater the percentage of men in an occupation, the more often respondents report knowing a man and not a woman ($r = 0.957$). Further, the two trend lines are very similar:

$$\% \text{ know woman only} = 0.75 \,(\% \text{ female in occupation}) - 7.0$$

$$\% \text{ know man only} = 0.79 \,(\% \text{ male in occupation}) - 4.4$$

Clearly, these fits could be tidier theoretically (e.g. the intercepts should both be zero and the underlying process should not be strictly linear), but the true process is hard to model and the simple linear approximation works quite well.

If gender as such has no effect, then the chances of knowing both a man and a woman will relate to the percentage of women in an occupation in a strong and simple way. The relationship will be a symmetric inverted U-shaped curve which peaks for occupations with an even gender split. Indeed, the relationship is curvilinear (the R^2 for the quadratic regression is 0.594 compared with the R^2 of only 0.012 for a linear regression), symmetric, and peaks where the proportion female is about 0.5:

$$\% \text{ know a man and a woman} = 1.44X - 0.014X^2 + 10.12$$

$$\text{where } X = \% \text{ female in an occupation.}$$

Thus, gender has a surprising lack of effect on networking power, for men and women in the same occupations. Whatever networking advantages that men may have as men (such as higher status) or that women may have as women (such as a reputation for greater social skills) may cancel each other out. Alternatively, people may be quite unselective in forming ties of weak or modest strength, showing little preference for men or women, because weaker ties have little or no cost.

The lack of detectable gender effects suggests that high-prestige jobs with a higher proportion female have greater networking power because women are preferred for jobs that require meeting many people, not because women as women meet more people. Thus, the networking power of occupations is very much a matter of occupational characteristics: of the number of people there are to know in an occupation, of the occupation's prestige and hence its networking opportunities on and off the job, and of the additional networking opportunities embedded in certain kinds of higher-prestige jobs for which women are differentially selected.

15.2.2. Discussion

People see the world of work through personal knowledge of those in their networks, and what they see is a dramatic distortion. Compared with the real composition of the workforce, people know few people in humble jobs and a great many in higher-prestige occupations. To see the extent of this distortion, consider two pairs of major census groups. Usefully, these two groups have about equal numbers in the workforce reality, are well represented in this study, and are at opposite ends of the prestige ladder. The high-prestige groups are middle managers and professionals, represented in the election survey data by human resources managers, sales and marketing managers, computer programmers, pharmacists, lawyers, and social workers. The low-prestige groups are semiskilled manual workers and "other" (meaning low skill) sales and services, represented here by delivery drivers, sewing machine operators, cashiers, security guards, and janitors. In fact, the census tells us, there are almost exactly equal numbers of people working at these opposite ends of the prestige ladder: 3,359,340 at the top and 3,364,675 at the bottom. But Table 15.1 shows that the ratio between the number who know an occupation member and occupation size has a mean of 0.0263 for occupations from the top groups and a mean of 0.0074 for occupations from the bottom groups. That is, the top group is about 3.5 times better represented in personal networks. From a network point of view, the work world seems to be composed mostly of relatively privileged positions. Networks provide abundant information about such positions and the people in them. Thus, much of the networking power differentials favor transmission of higher-status interests and perspectives.

Among higher-prestige occupations, those with a substantial proportion of women have greater networking power. On average, the three occupations with substantial numbers of women (pharmacists, human resources managers, and social workers) have about 2.5 times the broadcasting power of male-dominated occupations (lawyers, sales and marketing managers, and computer programmers) (Table 15.1). The high-prestige women's occupations considered here all involve work including stereotypically female elements such as nurturance and people skills. So do the other managerial and professional occupations with a large proportion female: these are mostly occupations in health care, teaching, and social services, plus a few in the traditionally female sphere of culture. Thus, women not only get into female-typed work, but this work also has a strong interpersonal orientation which helps the people in such work to meet many people, so that personal networks overrepresent occupations in which women do womanly work. Where networking power is strongest overall, in higher-prestige occupations, much of that networking power favors transmission of information that reinforces gender stereotypes.

The results presented here concern networking power in terms of pure volume of transmission, the sheer size of network audiences for occupations, and the men and women in them. Future work will go beyond questions of network audience size to questions about audience composition and networking impact. One important question concerning audience composition is the extent to which categories have more or less powerful audiences. We have seen that male-dominated occupations have no advantage, indeed, are disadvantaged, in terms of pure networking power. But do male-dominated occupations have smaller audiences of higher-prestige people? For example, human resources managers are known to about as many people as are sales and marketing managers, and human resources managers are more widely known, allowing for their size. But human resources managers work largely with people inside their own firms, providing them with useful services concerning their work, while sales and marketing managers represent the organization to important segments of its environment. Thus, human resources managers may perform their roles before an audience that is just as large as, but less powerful than, the audience for sales and marketing managers.

Future work will ask whether network broadcasts are getting across to their audiences. If people know someone in an occupation, or know a wide variety of men in different occupations, or know a wide variety of women in different occupations, do such contacts have some effect?

Since people tend to know people like themselves, higher-status people probably have higher-status network audiences. Since higher-status people are more influential, they probably have more impact on their audiences. Thus, the overall differences in social impact may favor the privileged even more than this study suggests, based just on the size of network audiences and the volume of networking power.

16

Marriage, Gender, and Social Capital[1]

Gina Lai

16.1. INTRODUCTION

Research literature as well as personal experience informs us that marriage is more than the union of two individuals. It integrates two personal networks (Bott 1971; Milardo 1988; Lin and Westcott 1991; Burger and Milardo 1995; Julien, Chartrand, and Bégin 1999; Milardo and Allan 2000; Kalmijn 2003; Widmer, Kellerhals, and Levy 2004). In the process of network integration, some parts of the two partners' personal networks overlap and others remain separate and connected via the partners. Joint social networks are generally found to foster marital identity, strengthen marital solidarity, enhance family adjustment, and promote individual well-being (Wellman and Wortley 1990; Lin and Westcott 1991; Stein et al. 1992; Burger and Milardo 1995; Julien, Chartrand, and Bégin 1999). Network integration presumably expands and diversifies the pool of resources for couples (Lin and Westcott 1991). Social network analysts (Lin and Dumin 1986; Moore 1990; Lin 2001b) argue that network structure affects the access to social capital. In this light, how individuals structure their marital networks would influence the availability of social capital. However, the existing literature has focused mainly on the impacts of joint networks and overlooked the factors leading to the network structure itself and the implications for couples' access to social capital.

Further, gender differences have been observed in social network characteristics. Compared with married men, married women tend to have denser networks and their networks consist of more kin members. These results are attributed to the family orientation and caring roles of married women (Moore 1990; Lin and Westcott 1991; Munch, McPherson, and Smith-Lovin 1997). Dense networks and networks of predominantly kin ties are viewed as hampering the accumulation of social capital for instrumental use (Moore 1990; Lin 2001b). Two issues thus arise. First, how does gender affect network integration? Second, would network integration generate unequal access to social capital by married men and women? Clarification of these two issues would help illuminate the gendered effects of marriage, and shed light on gender inequality in general.

[1] An earlier version of the paper was presented at the International Sunbelt Network Conference, Cancun, Mexico, February 12–16, 2003. The author wishes to thank the anonymous reviewers of the manuscript as well as students enrolled in SOC2130 in fall 2002 for help with data collection.

The objectives of this chapter are threefold. First, it examines the factors that may affect network integration among married individuals. Second, it tests the relationship between marital network integration and social capital. Third, the gender effect on network integration and its relationship to social capital is analyzed.

16.2. MARRIAGE AND NETWORK INTEGRATION

For many people, marriage is an important life event that brings significant changes to their lives. One such change is the restructuring of social relations. The restructuring process actually begins when two individuals meet and engage in a romantic relationship. Through the coupling process, the two individuals become bridges for two possibly unrelated or minimally related social networks (Lin and Westcott 1991). As the dyadic relationship develops, affective interdependence further encourages the formation of mutual friendship ties (Holland and Leinhardt 1977; Milardo 1982; Surra 1988; Kalmijn 2003). The marital union further formalizes, strengthens, and extends network integration. Through marriage, certain previously indirect ties are transformed into direct ones, such as in-law ties. The network bridging function of the two partners is also strengthened as they enjoy the socially rightful access to resources embedded in each other's networks (Lin and Westcott 1991; Stein et al. 1992). Participation in social activities as married couples further increases mutual friends and, thus, the extent of overlapping ties. In addition, joint social networks may expand as a result of dyadic withdrawal when couples contact their peripheral and demanding social ties less often (Johnson and Leslie 1982; Fischer et al. 1989; Kalmijn 2003).

Previous studies have found that integrated networks constitute a form of capital for married couples. Shared social ties presumably expand and diversify the pool of social resources for instrumental and expressive needs (Lin and Westcott 1991). Bott (1955) suggested that shared social ties impose informal social control on couples, reinforcing norm-conforming behavior and stabilizing marital relations. Marital identity can also be strengthened through association with common friends (Julien, Chartrand, and Bégin 1999). The utility derived from shared social ties further increases marital stability as the exit costs of the marriage would be higher for both spouses (Kalmijn 2003). Married individuals with shared networks report greater marital satisfaction (Milardo and Allan 2000). Spousal networks characterized by shared family ties are associated with better psychological well-being (Stein et al. 1992). However, greater network overlap between the spouses' networks before divorce contributes to poor post-divorce adjustment (Wilcox 1981), possibly because of the break-up of the shared networks cripples each partner's ability to manage the crisis (divorce) and to meet routine life demands (Lin and Westcott 1991). Nevertheless, there may be an optimal point of network integration. Stein et al. (1992) found that compared with spouses who have only separate or joint networks, those with networks characterized by a balanced proportion of joint and separate networks of family and friends report the highest levels of marital satisfaction.

In sum, previous research has shown that penetration into the partner's social network enables ego to capture a diversity of resources, which produces instrumental and expressive outcomes. However, relatively few studies have examined the casual factors for network penetration. In her study of family networks among 20 couples, Bott (1955) found that closed communities and strong economic ties among kin members tend to increase network connectedness, as reflected in network density and overlap between the two partners' personal networks. Kalmijn's study shows that partners with higher education and higher occupational prestige tend to have more separate friendship networks and fewer joint contacts (Kalmijn 2003). The findings were, however, left unexplained. One can speculate that when both partners occupy high-status positions, they may enjoy comparable social capital in their networks as they are equally able to reach resource-rich social ties. Keeping separate networks would be considered a good strategy to fully capture the benefits offered by both networks. Further, employment of both spouses increases joint contacts, particularly for women's shared contacts (Kalmijn 2003). The finding is attributed to occupational homogamy, and shared values and lifestyles in couples intensified by common employment experience.

16.3. GENDER, NETWORK INTEGRATION, AND SOCIAL CAPITAL

As marriage in most societies is largely between a man and a woman, the effect of gender on network integration deserves a closer examination. Lin and Westcott (1991) argue that marital union brings together two personal networks, presumably with different extent of resources. Network integration is a rational process, where couples maximize the utility by shrinking and merging the capital-deficient network into the capital-rich one. However, due to their structural disadvantages (e.g. less likely to have a job and lower job status), women's social networks tend to be less resourceful than men's. Compared to men's, women's social networks tend to be dense, women-centered, kin-oriented, and connected by homophilous ties (Fischer and Oliker 1983; Rosenthal 1985; Marsden 1987; Fischer et al. 1989; Moore 1990; Munch, McPherson, and Smith-Lovin 1997; Lin 2000a). These network characteristics are considered to limit the reach to diverse resources for instrumental purposes (Lin 1982; Moore 1990; Erickson 2004). Network disadvantages pull married women away from their own social ties and into their partners' networks. The women then end up maintaining their partners' social networks and preserving their partners' social capital. This structural perspective thus leads to the expectation that due to women's disadvantaged structural positions, they would report greater access to their husbands' networks than vice versa. Further, women would reap more benefits from access to their partners' social networks than do men.

The feminist approach offers a different explanation for the gender effect on network overlap, although it also predicts gender differences in network integration. Feminist scholars (West and Zimmerman 1987; Ferree 1990; Coltrane 1998; Bielby 1999) argue that gender is a routine and recurring accomplishment. Gendered scripts govern everyday social interactions between men and women. The two gender groups undertake activities that are considered appropriate for their respective sex categories. Gender identities are produced and reproduced through social interactions. In this light, marital relations are highly gendered, and social networking as an everyday routine practice for married couples would follow the gender rules. Because of the social expectation that women should put their family's (husband's and children's) interests ahead of their own, when women face time constraints and conflicting commitments between their personal and partners' networks, it is likely that they would yield to their partners' needs (Lin and Westcott 1991). As a result, women would still be more likely than men to share their partners' social ties, even after controlling for the effect of social positions.

In contrast, Kalmijn (2003) suggests that women may actually be less socially dependent on marriage than men. After taking respondents' socioeconomic characteristics into account, married women are found to have more separate friendship contacts than do married men. Men and women may attach different meanings to friendship. Men are oriented toward doing activities with friends while women tend toward emotional exchange and intimate sharing. That is, the functions of women's friendship ties cannot easily be fulfilled by a husband, and women have to maintain their own networks to meet their emotional needs. The sociopsychological perspective thus predicts that, due to the gendered expectations for friendship ties, women may be less likely than men to be acquainted with their spouses' friends, irrespective of social positions.

16.4. RESEARCH HYPOTHESES

To summarize the above discussion, the following hypotheses are formulated.

1. According to Lin and Westcott (1991), network integration is a rational process where married couples choose to build common ties that give them the most benefits. High social positions presumably enable one to reach more social capital (Lin and Dumin 1986; De Graaf and Flap 1988; Marsden and Hurlbert 1988; Sun and Hsung 1988; Bian and Ang 1997). Thus, compared with their lower status counterparts, individuals in higher social positions would be less likely to enter their partners' social networks. On the other hand, the partner's positional advantage may attract ego to reach his/her social ties.

2. The access to partner's social network would facilitate the reach to social capital. It is due to two factors. First, due to the rationality involved in network integration as outlined in Hypothesis 1, individuals gaining access to their

partners' social ties would presumably be able to enjoy more social capital. Second, being acquainted with one's partner's social ties may expand one's social circle. A large social network would then provide greater opportunity to reach diverse resources.

3. Two competing hypotheses are formulated about gender differences in network integration.

  a. According to the structural and feminist perspectives, women would report greater access to their partners' social networks compared to men.
  b. Informed by the sociopsychological argument, it is expected that women would report lesser access to their partners' social networks than do men.

4. Two competing hypotheses are formulated about the gender effect on network integration.

  a. According to the structural perspective, gender differences in network integration would disappear, after controlling for social positions.
  b. The gender approach predicts that gender differences in network integration would remain, even after holding both partners' social positions, constant.

5. The effect of network overlap on social capital would generally be greater for women than for men.

16.5. DATA

Data for the present analysis were collected in a telephone survey conducted in October 2002. The target population consisted of all Cantonese-speaking adults who were married and residing in Hong Kong at the time of the survey. Telephone numbers were randomly drawn from the Chinese version of the local telephone directory published in 2001.[2] The selected telephone numbers led us to individual households, from each of which one eligible adult was randomly drawn and interviewed. These sampling procedures successfully yielded a sample of 454 respondents. The response rate is 48.76 percent. Table 16.1 displays respondents' demographic characteristics.

The sex distribution of the sample shows more women than men (62.3% women vs. 37.7% men), suggesting an overrepresentation of women in the sample. The survey was conducted between 6:30 p.m. and 10:00 p.m. In 2002, Hong Kong's economy was still at the low point. Layoffs and cutbacks were common. People may have needed to work long hours in order to make ends meet or simply to keep their jobs. As men tend to have a higher labor force participation rate than women (71.9% for men and 51.6% for women in 2001) (Census and Statistics Department 2002), it is thus likely to include more women than men in the

---

[2] Every two years, the major telecommunications company in Hong Kong published and updated the telephone directory in both English and Chinese.

Table 16.1. Sociodemographic characteristics of respondents

Variables	Total ($N = 454$)	Men ($n = 171$)	Women ($n = 283$)
Personal characteristics			
Men (%)	37.7	NA	NA
Age (%)*			
29 or below	3.1	1.8	3.9
30–39	19.4	17.5	20.5
40–49	30.4	26.3	32.9
50–59	27.8	28.1	27.6
60 or above	19.4	26.3	15.2
Education (%)**			
Junior secondary or below	56.5	51.8	59.4
Senior secondary	32.2	30.0	33.6
Post-secondary	11.3	18.2	7.1
Employed (%)***	51.0	72.2	38.3
Personal income[a] (%)***			
No income	32.6	17.5	42.3
HK$9999 or below[b]	28.9	28.3	29.2
HK$10000–19999[b]	21.8	28.9	17.3
HK$20000 or above[b]	16.7	25.3	11.2
Partner's characteristics			
Age (%)**			
29 or below	4.2	7.0	2.5
30–39	18.3	22.8	15.5
40–49	27.8	30.4	26.1
50–59	28.6	25.1	30.7
60 or above	19.8	14.6	25.1
Education (%)			
Junior secondary or below	52.3	54.8	50.7
Senior secondary	34.5	32.7	35.6
Post-secondary	13.2	12.5	13.7
Employed (%)***	62.5	47.1	72.0
Personal income[a] (%)***			
No income	31.1	47.6	20.5
HK$9999 or below	33.3	35.7	31.7
HK$10000–19999	18.3	8.9	24.3
HK$20000 or above	17.3	7.7	23.6
Family characteristics			
Length of marriage (mean)	22.6	21.9	23.1
Presence of children (%)**	90.5	85.4	93.6
Number of children (mean)*	2.0	1.8	2.1
Age of the youngest child (%)[c]			
0–5	11.9	11.9	11.9
6–12	19.9	15.4	22.3
13–17	14.6	17.5	13.1
18 or above	53.6	55.2	52.7

[a] All kinds of income are included.

[b] US$1 = HK$7.8.

[c] Excluding childless respondents.

Gender differences are statistically significant at * $p < .05$; ** $p < .01$; *** $p < .001$.

NA, not applicable.

sample. To control for the gender effect on the zero-order relationship between social position, network integration, and social capital, it will be introduced as a control variable in the relevant analyses.

The sample captures a large proportion of middle-aged individuals. About 60 percent of respondents were between the ages of 40 and 59 at the time of the survey. More than 40 percent of the respondents (43.5%) had attained the educational level of senior secondary school or above. Slightly more than half of the respondents (51%) were employed at the time of survey, and homemakers made up another one-third of the sample (31.9%). The latter is related to the high proportion of female respondents. Because of this prevalence of homemakers, one-third of the respondents (32.6%) reported no income. Among those respondents who had jobs, 28.3 percent reported a monthly income of less than US$10,000, which was the median income from main employment in 2001 (Census and Statistics Department 2002). This suggests that our employed respondents may come from higher income groups.

More than 90 percent of respondents were parents (90.5%) and had, on average, two children. The youngest child of more than half of the parents (53.6%) was age 18 or above. This is largely related to the presence of older respondents in the sample.

16.6. VARIABLES AND MEASUREMENT

Social capital, the dependent variable of the study, has been conceptualized in various ways. It is commonly agreed that social capital as valued resources is embedded in enduring social networks (Lin 1982, 2001*b*; Campbell, Marsden, and Hurlbert 1986; Coleman 1988; Putnam 1993*a*). These resources are not possessed by individuals, but tied to social relations. However, researchers hold different views about what aspects of social networks constitute social capital. Coleman (1988) and Putnam (1993*a*) define social capital as the emergent properties of social networks, such as trust and reciprocity. Such conceptualization views social capital in terms of the outcomes produced by social ties. To avoid the conceptual tautology implied in Coleman's and Putnam's definition, Lin (1982, 2001*b*, 2006) conceptualizes social capital as the configuration of social tie characteristics that reflect the resources valued in a certain society, for example, diversity of occupations of network members. Of the different characteristics, variety of social ties is deemed as important. People with more varied networks are able to tap into various kinds of resources one may need and develop a rich pool of cultural capital (Lin 2001*b*; Erickson 2004). Typically, occupational diversity is used as a measure of social capital in modern capitalist societies because occupation is often a master role for people in these societies (Lin and Dumin 1986; De Graaf and Flap 1988; Marsden and Hurlbert 1988).

To measure occupational variety, the position generator approach is adopted. This approach, first pioneered by Lin and Dumin (1986), samples a number of hierarchically ranked positions in a social structure. These positions are presumably indicative of varying extents of valuable resources in society. Respondents are asked to indicate whether they have contacts in each of the positions. Diversity of resources can be calculated from the responses. This approach is considered superior to the name generator approach, as the former avoids the problems of content specificity and bias toward strong ties, and is able to capture a wide range of relationships (Lin, Fu, and Hsung 2001). Its utility has been demonstrated in previous studies (Lin and Dumin 1986; Erickson 1996*b*).

In the present study, a position generator that situates in the context of Hong Kong society is constructed. As in other Western capitalist societies, occupations largely reflect one's social and economic standing in Hong Kong (Chiu 1994; Bian and Ko 2000). Guided by Chiu's occupational prestige scale (Chiu 1994), 18 occupations are selected to cover the range of resources valued in Hong Kong. Examples are street vendor, cleaning worker, secondary school teacher, police, professor, and medical doctor. The prestige scores of these occupations range from 39.9 (street vendor) to 98.5 (professor). Diversity of social capital is indicated by the number of occupations reached by ego. On average, respondents report a total of 7.77 occupations (Table 16.2).

Network overlap is defined as the extent of acquaintance with the partner's friends. It is indicated by the question, "How many of your partner's friends do you know?" Respondents can choose from one of the five responses provided, ranging from (1) almost none of them to (5) almost all of them. More than 70 percent of respondents (71.7%) know at least half of their partners' friends. About 16 percent of respondents (15.6%) are acquainted with almost all of their partners' friends, and slightly less than 10 percent (9.3%) report no acquaintances at all (Table 16.2). Due to data limitation, the measure of network overlap includes the partner's friends only, who are likely to be strong ties. Previous research suggests that, compared to weak ties, strong ties tend to be more homogenous in social characteristics and not as effective in providing useful resources for instrumental actions (Granovetter 1973; Lin 1982). Thus, the effect of access to partner's social ties on ego's repertoire of social capital may be underestimated. Nonetheless, the result would still serve a good indicative purpose.

Network size is included to examine the intervening effect of network overlap and social capital. Respondents were asked to estimate the number of people they have contact with each day, including face-to-face interactions, telephone calls, exchange of letters, and contact through electronic means. Six answer categories were provided, including (*a*) 0–4 people, (*b*) 5–9 people, (*c*) 10–19 people, (*d*) 20–49 people, (*e*) 50–99 people, and (*f*) 100 people or more. About 40 percent (39.0%) of the respondents have contact with fewer than 10 people each day, whereas 6 percent of respondents have contact with 100 people or more (Table 16.2).

Six variables are constructed to measure ego's social positions. Gender is a dichotomous variable (1 = men, 0 = women). Respondent's age is indicated by 13 age categories, from 19 or below to 75 or above. Education is measured by an 8-point scale, ranging from no formal schooling to graduate school or above.

Table 16.2. Gender comparison of network integration, network size, and social capital

Occupations	Total	Men	Women
Acquaintance with partner's friends (%)			
Hardly know any of them	9.3	5.5	11.6
Know very few of them	19.0	20.0	18.4
Know about half of them	29.0	28.5	29.2
Know most of them	27.1	32.1	24.2
Know almost all of them	15.6	13.9	16.6
Network size (%)*			
0–4 people	21.1	15.0	24.7
5–9 people	17.9	13.8	20.4
10–19 people	22.3	25.0	20.7
20–49 people	22.8	27.5	20.0
50–99 people	9.9	11.9	8.7
100 people or more	6.0	6.9	5.5
Access to occupations (%)			
Government administrator (90.8)[a]	30.5	26.5	33.0
Professor, university lecturer (98.5)	19.2	18.7	19.5
Medical doctor (95.8)	31.5	29.2	32.9
Engineer (96.0)	35.0	39.2	32.5
Functional manager (82.2)	52.3	55.0	50.7
Accountant (91.4)	35.6	34.9	36.0
Nurse (78.1)	48.5	48.5	48.4
Police (73.5)	46.3	48.0	45.2
Secondary school teacher (83.9)	44.5	45.6	43.8
Construction worker (45.0)	43.5	52.9	37.8*
Electrician (60.7)	48.9	59.4	42.6*
Waiter/waitress (47.2)	36.2	37.6	35.3
Salesperson (52.0)	44.6	44.4	44.7
Driver (58.0)	60.1	65.5	56.9
Clerk (60.1)	74.4	77.1	72.8
Cleaning worker (44.1)	46.7	48.0	48.9
Street vendor (39.9)	31.3	30.4	31.8
Watchman (54.0)	49.0	51.5	47.5
Number of occupations reached (mean)	7.77	8.11	7.56

[a] Occupational prestige score (Chiu 1994).

Gender difference is statistically significant at * $p < .05$.

Employment status is a dichotomous variable (1 = employed, 0 = nonemployed). Personal income is the sum of monthly income from all sources. The variable consists of 17 categories, from no income to HK$70,000 (US$8,900) or above. Presence of children is also a dichotomy (1 = yes, 0 = no).

Partner's social position is measured by three variables: education, employment status, and personal income. The three variables are constructed in the same way as those for ego. Due to the high correlations between egos and partner's gender and age, the two characteristics of partner will be removed from the analyses.

Apart from individual traits, the network effects of the relative social position of the couple will also be explored. Two indicators are constructed to compare the education and personal income of the two partners. Each indicator consists of three categories: (*a*) ego's position lower than partner's, (*b*) ego and partner have the same position, and (*c*) ego's position higher than partner's.

16.7. HYPOTHESIS TESTING

16.7.1. The Relationship Between Social Position and Network Integration (Hypothesis 1)

Table 16.3 presents the regression analyses of network overlap on respondent's and partner's socioeconomic characteristics. Three models are estimated and results are displayed in three columns.

The first model (Column 1) estimates the effects of personal traits on network overlap. The second model (Column 2) includes measures of the two partners'

Table 16.3. Regression analyses[a] of network overlap

Independent variables	Column 1	Column 2	Column 3
Personal characteristics			
Men	.03 (.01)	.02 (.01)	.09 (.04)
Age	−.01 (−.01)	−.01 (−.02)	−.03 (−.05)
Education	−.002 (−.003)	−.02 (−.03)	−
Employed	−.34 (−.15)*	−.34 (−.15)*	−.14 (−.06)
Personal income	.04 (.12)	.03 (.10)	−
Presence of children	−.15 (−.04)	−.15 (−.04)	−.23 (−.06)
Partner's characteristics			
Education	.13 (.18)**	.16 (.21)	−
Employed	−.22 (−.09)	−.19 (−.08)	−.06 (−.03)
Personal income	−.01 (−.03)	−.01 (−.02)	−
Relative status of respondent and partner			
Education (reference = same)			
Respondent > partner	−	.02 (.01)	−.11 (−.04)
Respondent < partner	−	−.07 (−.03)	.15 (.06)
Personal income (reference = same)			
Respondent > partner	−	−.07 (−.03)	−.02 (−.01)
Respondent < partner	−	−.17 (−.07)	−.23 (−.09)
Constant	3.18***	3.26***	3.76***
R^2	.06	.07	.02
Adjusted R^2	.04	.03	−.002
N	383	383	427

[a] Values outside the parentheses are unstandardized regression coefficients and values within the parentheses are standardized coefficients.

* $p < .05$; ** $p < .01$; *** $p < .001$.

En-dash (−), variable not in the equation.

relative social position, in addition to personal characteristics. Results show no significant main effect of relative status on network overlap. Further, the addition of the relative measures generally does not change the regression coefficients, except that the effect of partner's education disappears. A further investigation suggests the multicolinearity problem. When respondents have a better-educated partner, their education also tends to be lower than that of their partner ($r = 0.33$, $p < 0.001$). However, no significant zero-order relationship is observed between having a better-educated partner and network overlap ($r = 0.05$, $p = 0.32$). The relative measures remain statistically nonsignificant even when personal characteristics are removed from the equation (Column 3). Even worse, the amount of explained variance drops substantially ($R^2 = 0.02$). Thus, the first model (i.e. the model with only the couple's personal characteristics) shows the best performance in terms of explanatory power and parsimony.

Results show that, controlling for the partner's socioeconomic characteristics, employment significantly reduces the likelihood of reaching the partner's social network ($b = -0.34$). That is, employed individuals tend to report fewer acquaintances with their partners' friends than do their nonemployed counterparts. Employment may facilitate the formation of one's own social ties, which demand time and energy to maintain. The availability of resources from one's personal network may also reduce the need for tapping into the resources embedded in the partner's social network. Ego's other socioeconomic characteristics, however, are not associated with sharing the partner's friends. On the other hand, when ego's socioeconomic characteristics are held constant, the partner's education significantly increases ego's access to their partner's friendship ties ($b = 0.13$). The partner's better social position, as indicated by education, leads to better social capital. The rational calculation suggested by Lin and Westcott (1991) may encourage ego to become more acquainted with the partner's friends.

In sum, the above findings generally support the hypothesis that social position and network overlap are related. To a certain extent, ego's network benefits gained from employment tend to pull him/her away from the partner's network. The partner's positional advantage (i.e. better education), however, attracts ego to connect with his/her social ties.

16.7.2. The Relationship Between Network Integration and Social Capital (Hypothesis 2)

One of the hypothesized pathways through which network integration influences social capital is the expansion of network. Thus, the relationship between network overlap and network size is first examined, and results are displayed in Table 16.4. The first model (Column 1) includes the two partners' personal traits only, whereas the measures of relative position are also entered in the second model (Column 2). Results (Column 2) show that the effects of the partners' relative status on network size are not statistically significant. Further, the addition of the

Table 16.4. Regression analyses[a] of network size

Independent variables	Column 1	Column 2
Personal characteristics		
Men	.25 (.08)	.26 (.09)
Age	−.12 (−.19)**	−.12 (−.19)**
Education	.10 (.10)	.14 (.15)
Employed	.52 (.18)**	.53 (.18)**
Personal income	.06 (.17)*	.06 (.17)*
Presence of children	.20 (.04)	.22 (.05)
Partner's characteristics		
Education	−.07 (−.08)	−.12 (−.13)
Employed	−.35 (−.12)	−.35 (−.12)
Personal income	.07 (.17)*	.07 (.17)*
Relative status of respondent and partner		
Education (reference = same)		
Respondent > partner	–	−.10 (−.03)
Respondent < partner	–	.08 (.03)
Personal income (reference = same)		
Respondent > partner	–	−.01 (−.003)
Respondent < partner	–	−.01 (−.002)
Access to partner's network	.03 (.02)	.03 (.02)
Constant	2.89***	2.87***
R^2	.23	.23
Adjusted R^2	.21	.20
N	370	370

[a] Values outside the parentheses are unstandardized regression coefficients and values within the parentheses are standardized coefficients.

* $p < .05$; ** $p < .01$; *** $p < .001$.

En-dash (–), variable not in the equation.

new variables does not increase the amount of explained variance or change the original estimates. Therefore, the first model is taken as the final result.

Contrary to our expectation, network overlap is not associated with network size ($b = 0.03$) (Column 1). In other words, acquaintance with the partner's friends does not increase the size of one's personal network. It is possible that the addition of new social ties through access to the partner's network might reduce the time and energy input for existing ties. Some of the existing ties may eventually drop out of one's personal network. Withdrawal of social ties (Johnson and Leslie 1982) may then cancel out the effect of network expansion related to network overlap. Unfortunately, the present data does not include measures for network withdrawal. Young age ($b = −0.12$), employment ($b = 0.52$), and high personal income ($b = 0.06$) are associated with a larger network. Having a high-income partner also increases network size ($b = 0.07$).

The main effect of network integration on social capital is examined in Table 16.5. Similar to the previous analyses, the effects of the partners' relative socioeconomic position are assessed in addition to their personal traits (Columns 2 and 4).

Table 16.5. Regression analyses[a] of social capital

Independent variables	Column 1	Column 2
Personal characteristics		
Men	.60 (.06)	.61 (.07)
Age	−.02 (−.01)	−.03 (−.01)
Education	−.17 (−.06)	.25 (.09)
Employed	−.78 (−.09)	−.69 (−.08)
Personal income	.21 (.18)**	.20 (.17)*
Presence of children	.79 (.05)	.92 (.06)
Partner's characteristics		
Education	.40 (.14)*	−.01 (−.003)
Employed	1.54 (.16)*	1.49 (.16)*
Personal income	.03 (.02)	.03 (.02)
Relative status of respondent and partner		
Education (reference = same)		
Respondent > partner	–	−.32 (−.03)
Respondent < partner	–	1.22 (.12)
Personal income (reference = same)		
Respondent > partner	–	−.05 (−.01)
Respondent < partner	–	.08 (.01)
Access to partner's network	.71 (.18)***	.72 (.19)***
Network size	.82 (.26)***	.81 (.26)***
Constant	.09	−.28
R^2	.23	.24
Adjusted R^2	.21	.21
N	370	370

[a] Values outside the parentheses are unstandardized regression coefficients and values within the parentheses are standardized coefficients.

* $p < .05$; ** $p < .01$; *** $p < .001$.

En-dash (–), variable not in the equation.

The addition of the relative measures does not bring significant changes to the original estimates nor increase the amount of explained variance. However, the effect of partner's education on the outcome variable disappears after controlling for relative status. The multicolinearity problem may account for this. As demonstrated before, when respondents have a better-educated partner, their education also tends to be lower than that of their partner. However, the zero-order relationship between relative education and the two outcome variables is nonsignificant ($F = 2.33$, $p = 0.10$). Further, the inclusion of the relative measures does not significantly increase the amount of explained variance. For simplicity's sake, the original model is taken as the final result.

Findings generally lend support to the second hypothesis that greater network overlap is related to better reach to social capital. Respondents with access to the partners' friendship ties tend to report a greater variety of occupations ($b = 0.71$). A larger network increases the likelihood of reaching better social capital ($b = 0.82$). This corroborates the previous findings (Moore 1990; Podolny and Baron 1997; Lin 2000a).

In addition to network access and network size, partner's personal traits also facilitate the access to social capital. A better-educated partner and employed partner help ego to reach diversified occupation ($b = 0.40$ for partner's education and $b = 1.54$ for partner's employment). The independent effects of partner's socioeconomic characteristics on social capital may actually reflect that of ego's social position, as suggested by the status homogamy principle (marrying similar others) (Kalmijn 1994).

16.7.3. The Relationship Between Gender and Network Integration (Hypotheses 3 and 4)

Two sets of competing hypotheses are formulated for the relationship between gender and network integration. The first set of hypotheses deals with gender differences in network integration, whereas the second set tests the independent effect of gender, if gender differences are found. To test these two sets of hypotheses, bivariate analyses are first performed to examine gender differences in social position and network integration. The net effect of gender will be investigated in multivariate analyses.

The set of hypotheses about gender differences in network integration contains two alternative hypotheses. To recap, informed by the structural and feminist perspectives, the first alternative hypothesis expects that compared to men, women would report greater access to their partners' social networks. The second alternative hypothesis, guided by the sociopsychological argument, predicts that women will have lesser access to their partners' social networks than men.

Columns 2 and 3 in Table 16.1 compare the socioeconomic characteristics of male and female respondents. Men are generally older than women. Compared with women, men are significantly better educated, more likely to be employed, and to have higher personal income. More women than men have children. Women also have more children than men.

Partners' socioeconomic characteristics show two marriage patterns. First, men tend to marry younger women, as men's partners are younger than women's. About 40 percent of men's partners (39.7%) are aged 50 or above, whereas more than 55 percent of women's partners (55.8%) are. Second, men tend to marry downward socially and women marry upward. Compared with women's partners, men's partners are less likely to be employed and have lower personal income. Less than half of men (47.1%) report having a working spouse whereas nearly three-fourths of women (72%) do.

Although men are structurally more advantaged than women, no significant gender difference in access to partner's network can be observed (Table 16.2). Both men and women report a similar extent of acquaintance with their partners' friends. Statistical control of respondents' and partners' social positions does not reveal any suppressed effect of gender (Table 16.3). The two sets of hypotheses about gender and network integration are thus not supported. Men and women are equally likely to share the partner's friends. The insignificant gender effect may be due to the way network integration is measured. Respondents were asked to report how many of their partners' friends they know. It is possible that people know about their partners' friends but do not have close contact with them. More precise measures of network integration are needed to detect gender differences.

Further, the bivariate analysis shows that men and women report similar access to social capital, although women report a smaller number of occupations than do men (8.11 for men and 7.56 for women). These findings suggest that married men and women in Hong Kong enjoy comparable social capital, despite their different social positions.

However, men have significantly more daily contacts than do women. About 20 percent of men (18.8%) have contact with an average of 50 or more people a day, whereas 14 percent of women (14.2%) do so. In contrast, one quarter of the female sample (25.1%) have contact with nine or fewer people a day, whereas about 20 percent of men (18.8%) do so. Multivariate analysis (Table 16.4) shows that the gender difference disappears after controlling for men's and women's as well as their partners' social positions. Men are more likely than women to work outside the home and thus may have more opportunities to construct social ties and form larger social networks.

16.7.4. Gendered Effect of Network Integration on Social Capital (Hypothesis 5)

To test the hypothesis that the effect of network overlap on social capital would be greater for women than for men, subgroup analyses are performed on the number of occupations. Results presented in Table 16.6 do not support this hypothesis.

Access to the partner's social network is positively associated with number of occupations among both men ($b = 0.76$) and women ($b = 0.64$). The two unstandardized regression coefficients suggest that the effect for men is slightly greater than that for women. In other words, when personal and partner's characteristics are held constant, husbands are better able than women to reach diversified others if they have access to wives' networks. Married women's family responsibilities may help construct a variety of social ties. To meet the daily demands of the family, married women have to make contact with different kinds of people, for example, kin, neighbors, other parents, menial laborers (plumbers, locksmiths, and electricians), and professional workers (doctors, dentists, and school teachers). Through their wives, men are able to reach people to whom they might otherwise have no access.

The effect of network size also shows a similar gender pattern. Both men and women with larger networks tend to report a greater number of occupations ($b = 0.69$ and $b = 0.91$, respectively). This is consistent with our expectation.

While women do not have particular advantage over men in terms of benefits gained from access to their husbands' social ties, the former are influenced by partner's personal traits to a greater extent than are the latter. Partner's education and employment are positively associated with the variety of occupations among

Table 16.6. Regression analyses[a] of social capital by gender

Independent variables	Men	Women
Personal characteristics		
Age	−.08 (−.05)	−.01 (−.003)
Education	.13 (.05)	.57 (.17)
Employed	−.84 (−.09)	−.73 (−.08)
Personal income	.16 (.17)	.26 (.19)*
Presence of children	.61 (.05)	.76 (.04)
Partner's characteristics		
Education	.12 (.04)	.65 (.22)*
Employed	1.05 (.12)	2.19 (.21)**
Personal income	−.01 (−.01)	.02 (.02)
Access to partner's network	.76 (.19)*	.64 (.17)**
Network size	.69 (.22)*	.91 (.28)***
Constant	2.05	−.27
R^2	.19	.27
Adjusted R^2	.12	.24
N	144	226

[a] Values outside the parentheses are unstandardized regression coefficients and values within the parentheses are standardized coefficients.

* $p < .05$; ** $p < .01$; *** $p < .001$.

women ($b = 0.65$ for partner's education and $b = 2.19$ for partner's employment), but not among men. The effects of partner's traits on women's social capital are even greater than those of personal traits and are independent of network access. The findings suggest that high-status husbands are able to help increase the variety of women's social ties, but this benefit is not provided by men's high-status wives. This may be because social activities among married people tend to be dominated by the husband. As a result, women are more likely than men to participate in their partners' social activities (Erickson 2004) and be able to take advantage of the opportunities to develop social ties of their own. The relative importance of husbands' traits over wives' may also reflect the patriarchal norm that married women should take care of their husbands' welfare, including helping the husbands to build good and useful social relationships. This poses a constraint on women in making use of their own positional advantage to cultivate social capital.

16.8. FURTHER ANALYSES

To further explicate the effect of network overlap on social capital, two related issues are explored. First, would the effect of access to partner's network vary by the length of marriage? The accumulation of social capital is a process that takes time. While access to partner's network would help increase one's social capital, the gain may still be limited when two individuals are married for only a short

Table 16.7. Regression analyses[a] of social capital by length of marriage

Independent variables	10 years or less (Column 1)	11–20 years (Column 2)	21–30 years (Column 3)	Over 30 years (Column 4)
Personal characteristics				
Men	−1.14 (−.14)	−.03 (−.003)	.87 (.09)	.53 (.06)
Education	−.37 (−.14)	.08 (.03)	−.17 (−.05)	−.18 (−.07)
Employed	−.51 (−.05)	−.78 (−.09)	−1.56 (−.16)	1.09 (.09)
Personal income	.43 (.38)*	−.09 (−.09)	.31 (.27)*	.17 (.10)
Presence of children	.79 (.10)	−3.03 (−.16)	−.24 (−.01)	2.56 (.06)
Partner's characteristics				
Education	.28 (.11)	.34 (.11)	.21 (.07)	.71 (.24)
Employed	.12 (.01)	−.49 (−.05)	2.17 (.21)*	1.59 (.17)
Personal income	−.08 (−.08)	.16 (.16)	−.08 (−.06)	.06 (.03)
Access to partner's network	.16 (.05)	.79 (.22)	.78 (.19)*	.79 (.21)*
Network size	.31 (.10)	.71 (.24)	.96 (.29)***	.88 (.28)*
Constant	5.71	5.72	.93	−3.52
R^2	.15	.22	.29	.31
Adjusted R^2	.002	.10	.23	.21
N	70	76	135	81

[a] Values outside the parentheses are unstandardized regression coefficients and values within the parentheses are standardized coefficients.

* $p < .05$; ** $p < .01$; *** $p < .001$.

period. Second, would network overlap strengthen the effect of partner's traits on social capital? When two networks become integrated, it may also imply interdependence of the two partners. Greater social interdependence would presumably increase the couple's influence on each other.

To answer the above two questions, and without sound theoretical guidance, the respondents are divided into four groups according to the length of marriage at 10-year intervals: (*a*) 10 years or less, (*b*) 11–20 years, (*c*) 21–30 years, and (*d*) over 30 years. Subgroup analyses are performed on social capital.

Results of subgroup comparison reveal the interaction effect of network overlap and length of marriage on social capital (Table 16.7). Specifically, the effect of network overlap on the number of occupations tends to be evident among the respondents who have been married for over 10 years. For the partner's network to benefit ego, the network itself has to be resourceful (i.e. containing a variety of social ties). As it takes time for one to establish ties with a variety of people and for the couple to get to know each other's social ties, it is not surprising to find that ego benefits from his/her partner's social network only after being married for an extended period of time. The time factor may also explain the interaction effect of network size and the length of marriage. A large network with heterogeneous ties is often a result of social exposure and life experience, which tends to be age-related as reflected by the length of marriage. The older one gets, the greater one's exposure to various aspects of life, and the greater the variety of social relationships that can be developed.

Table 16.8. Regression analyses[a] of social capital by length of marriage and gender

Independent variables	20 years or less		21 years or longer	
	Men	Women	Men	Women
Personal characteristics				
Education	.73 (.28)	−1.01 (−.34)	.12 (.04)	−.39 (−.10)
Employed	−2.58 (−.14)	−1.32 (−.16)	−.54 (−.06)	−.67 (−.06)
Personal income	−.09 (−.09)	.29 (.27)	.20 (.20)	.30 (.19)*
Presence of children	1.14 (.12)	−.35 (−.03)	−1.60 (−.06)	2.62 (.08)
Partner's characteristics				
Education	−.09 (−.03)	.59 (.22)	.27 (.09)	.59 (.19)
Employed	−.93 (−.11)	.36 (.02)	2.37 (.27)	2.17 (.22)*
Personal income	.38 (.32)	.06 (.06)	−.23 (−.13)	.002 (.002)
Access to partner's network	−.48 (−.12)	.61 (.19)	1.00 (.24)*	.60 (.16)
Network size	−.16 (−.04)	.79 (.28)*	.89 (.30)*	.95 (.28)***
Constant	9.77*	5.05	1.38	−2.54
R^2	.13	.23	.34	.26
Adjusted R^2	−.04	.14	.26	.21
N	57	89	85	131

[a] Values outside the parentheses are unstandardized regression coefficients and values within the parentheses are standardized coefficients.

* $p < .05$; ** $p < .01$; *** $p < .001$.

Because of small sample size, respondents are divided into two groups according to length of marriage (i.e. 20 years or less and 21 years or longer) for gender comparison. Gender differences are found in the interaction effect of network overlap and length of marriage on social capital (Table 16.8). Women tend to gain diversified social resources when they have access to their partner's network, regardless of length of marriage. However, men acquire this benefit only when they have been married for a long time (i.e. over 20 years). Two reasons may account for this finding. First, women may assume greater responsibility than men in maintaining their partner's social network after marriage, in terms of time and effort (Wellman 1985; Coltrane 1998). This facilitates women's access to their husbands' network resources from the early stages of marriage. By contrast, men's less active role in cultivating social relationships may result in a delay before they actually enjoy the benefits offered by their wives' networks. Second, men may be able to construct a resourceful network at a faster speed than do women. As a result, married women are able to capture the resources embedded in their husbands' social networks at the early stage of marriage. Nonetheless, the time variation of the effect of network access awaits future verification with longitudinal data.

Table 16.7 also shows some interaction effect of partner's traits and length of marriage on social capital. Partner's employment tends to increase network diversity among those respondents married for 21–30 years (Column 3). This suggests that partner's characteristics may have an accelerating effect on social capital over time. The effect, however, barely fails to meet the required significance level ($p < 0.05$) in the separate analysis for men and women (Table 16.8), probably

Table 16.9. Regression analyses[a] of social capital by degree of network overlap

Independent variables	Low (Column 1)	Medium (Column 2)	High (Column 3)
Personal characteristics			
Men	−.62 (−.08)	.92 (.10)	1.13 (.13)
Age	.18 (.11)	−.01 (−.01)	−.01 (−.01)
Education	−.01 (−.01)	.25 (.07)	−.17 (−.07)
Employed	.28 (.04)	−1.48 (−.16)	−1.19 (−.13)
Personal income	.41 (.39)***	.28 (.21)	.09 (.09)
Presence of children	1.68 (.11)	1.36 (.10)	.31 (.02)
Partner's characteristics			
Education	.64 (.22)	.32 (.10)	.25 (.10)
Employed	1.99 (.25)*	1.61 (.16)	1.57 (.17)
Personal income	−.16 (−.14)	−.03 (−.02)	.15 (.14)
Network size	.80 (.29)**	1.02 (.31)**	.60 (.20)*
Constant	−3.21	.72	4.76*
R^2	.38	.23	.15
Adjusted R^2	.31	.15	.09
N	101	107	162

[a] Values outside the parentheses are unstandardized regression coefficients and values within the parentheses are standardized coefficients.

* $p < .05$; ** $p < .01$; *** $p < .001$.

due to the small sample size. As a matter of fact, given the number of variables in the equation and the small sample size, existing results of subgroup analyses are indicative only. Validation of results with a larger sample is needed.

The second issue deals with whether access to partner's network would strengthen the partner's influence on social capital. Respondents are grouped according to three levels of network overlap, including low, medium, and high overlap. Subgroup regression analysis of social capital is performed on personal and partner's socioeconomic traits. Network size is included as a control variable.

Results show the interaction effect of network overlap and partner's traits on social capital. Respondents with an employed partner tend to report a greater number of occupations than those without when they limited network access ($b = 1.99$) (Column 1, Table 16.9), particularly among men (Column 1, Table 16.10). Greater access to partner's network would strengthen the effect of partner's employment on women's social capital but not men's (Columns 5 and 6, Table 16.10). This suggests a transfer of social capital accumulated by husbands through employment to wives, when wives have access to husbands' networks. However, wives' employment brings network benefits to men only when men know few of their wives' friends. This finding is unexpected and somewhat counterintuitive. One possible explanation is the measurement problem. While this group of men may not have personal relationships with wives' friends, they may have heard about these people through their wives. Therefore, when asked if they know someone in a certain occupation, they may give a positive answer. In other

Table 16.10. Regression analyses[a] of social capital by degree of network overlap and gender

Independent variables	Low		Medium		High	
	Men (Column 1)	Women (Column 2)	Men (Column 3)	Women (Column 4)	Men (Column 5)	Women (Column 6)
Personal characteristics						
Age	−.33 (−.19)	.20 (.12)	.21 (.13)	−.16 (−.07)	−.24 (−.14)	.23 (.12)
Education	−.11 (−.04)	−.02 (−.01)	.68 (.21)	−.54 (−.13)	.24 (.10)	−.81 (−.28)
Employed	−2.55 (−.28)	.09 (.01)	−.44 (−.04)	−1.82 (−.17)	−2.45 (−.26)	−.80 (−.09)
Personal income	.63 (.59)*	.37 (.33)*	.21 (.20)	.46 (.25)	.07 (.08)	.14 (.12)
Presence of children	4.18 (.31)	.10 (.01)	−.17 (−.02)	2.77 (.15)	.47 (.04)	−.36 (−.02)
Partner's characteristics						
Education	.53 (.15)	.63 (.25)	−.46 (−.16)	1.02 (.29)	.06 (.02)	.43 (.17)
Employed	3.85 (.45)*	.48 (.06)	.33 (.04)	2.38 (.20)	−.26 (−.03)	3.98 (.39)**
Personal income	.001 (.001)	−.15 (−.15)	−.02 (−.02)	−.06 (−.05)	.18 (.14)	.20 (.17)
Network size	.37 (.12)	.93 (.36)**	1.03 (.33)	1.13 (.34)**	.43 (.15)	.76 (.24)*
Constant	−.28	−.92	2.48	−.58	8.80	2.41
R^2	.57	.36	.19	.30	.12	.28
Adjusted R^2	.41	.26	−.03	.19	−.02	.20
N	35	66	42	65	67	95

[a] Values outside the parentheses are unstandardized regression coefficients and values within the parentheses are standardized coefficients.

* $p < .05$; ** $p < .01$; *** $p < .001$.

words, wives' employment may provide these men with an indirect access to social capital. Direct versus indirect access to social capital may have to be delineated in future research. Again, small sample size precludes any definitive conclusion.

16.9. DISCUSSION AND CONCLUSION

This chapter has examined the effect of network integration on the access to social capital. Particular attention is given to the differential effects by gender. Results suggest that access to partner's network facilitates the accumulation of social capital in terms of network variety, particularly among women and respondents married for a long time. Further, despite their better structural locations, men do not differ from women in access to partner's social network or in the availability of social capital. On the contrary, women tend to gain greater network benefits from having a better-positioned partner than do men. Several implications can be drawn from the findings.

First, the present study has demonstrated the social capital effect of marriage. The structural integration of social relations induced by intimate relationships facilitates the access to social capital by marital partners. The social capital effect is particularly obvious among women. While it is documented in previous studies (Hurlbert and Acock 1990; Moore 1990) that marriage tends to constrain women's construction of personal networks, in terms of size and composition, the present study shows no gender difference in variety of social ties. Further, compared to men, women tend to be better able to capitalize on their partners' structural advantage by tapping into resources embedded in their partners' social networks and/or building their own resource-rich ties through participation in their partner's social activities. The partners' social networks may thus compensate women's social capital deficiency caused by structural disadvantages. This suggests that marriage has contradictory effects on women. Marriage puts women in structurally disadvantaged positions, on the one hand, and facilitates women's access to social capital, on the other.

However, whether or not women can activate the pool of social capital for use remains an issue. This is particularly important for the understanding of gender inequality. Previous studies have found that restricted social capital is one of women's major obstacles to advancing in the labor market (Reskin and Hartmann 1986; Lin 2000a). Would access to partner's social capital help women to advance socially and economically? Erickson (2004) argues that ties to men are more instrumental than ties to women in making personal advancement, as men tend to control valuable resources in society. The present study does not identify the gender of social ties in the respondents' networks. Therefore, although women may have access to a variety of social ties, it is not clear whether those ties are actually helpful. Another related issue is how women can mobilize the social capital embedded in their partners' social ties for personal advancement. These issues deserve closer research attention in the future.

Second, the findings corroborate Lin and Westcott's argument about the network effect of marital dissolution. Lin and Westcott (1991) argue that marital dissolution would break up the integrated part of the social network built by marital partners, and the resources embedded within would go with the ties that make up the integrated network. As a result, the partner who contributes most to the integrated network would be able to retain the most social capital. Thus, while women enjoy greater network benefits of marriage than do men, the former may also suffer greater loss of social capital from marital dissolution.

Third, the dependency theory argues that resources could be converted into power (Blood and Wolfe 1960; Cook, Emerson, and Gillmore 1983; Yamagishi, Gillmore, and Cook 1988). Women's dependence on their partners for social capital then implies power imbalance in marital relations. Women may yield to their partners in household and even personal affairs, reinforcing the patriarchal structure in the family. However, the relationship between social capital and power relations between husband and wife awaits future research.

To conclude, the present study has demonstrated the network effect of marriage and the differential effects for men and women. By further exploring the relationship between gender, network integration, and social capital, future research may refine the measurement of network integration by including frequency of contact and feeling of closeness with shared ties by marital partners, separately as well as jointly. Future studies may also probe into the process and underlying principles of network integration of married men and women. Longitudinal investigation would shed light on the changes over the life course, from dating, marital formation, to marital dissolution (widowhood or divorce).

17

Access to Social Capital and Status Attainment in the United States: Racial/Ethnic and Gender Differences

Jennifer L. Moren Cross and Nan Lin

17.1. INTRODUCTION

Over the course of the last three decades, a rich dialogue has developed related to social capital and status attainment. Research on this theme has demonstrated that social capital can have significant effects on status attainment outcomes, over and above personal resources and ascribed status. However, more research is necessary to explore variations in access to and mobilization of social capital, and how this is associated with subsequent status attainment, especially in the context of racial/ethnic and gender differences. Using a national sample of Americans, the present study examines the effects of access to social capital on status attainment outcomes, and how gender and/or racial/ethnic characteristics may condition such effects.

17.2. SOCIAL CAPITAL AND STATUS ATTAINMENT

The pursuit of understanding and explaining variation in status attainment is a cornerstone of the field of sociology. Status attainment can be characterized as "a process by which individuals mobilize and invest in resources for returns in socioeconomic standings" (Lin 1999*b*: 47). The principal model that has been used and built upon for this endeavor, developed by Blau and Duncan (1967), posits that achieved status (i.e. one's educational level and prior occupational status) is the most important factor in explaining status attainment, even after controlling for the direct and indirect effects of one's ascribed status (i.e. parental status). In addition to the personal resources related to one's achieved status, actors can possess and mobilize social resources to increase attained status. While personal resources are possessed by the individual, social resources, or social capital, are accessible through one's social network.

Numerous conceptualizations and definitions of social capital have been advanced in the literature (e.g. Coleman 1990; Putnam 2000; Lin 2001*b*), and there is no consensus that one is universally "correct." As such, we should clarify that our point of departure suggests that "social capital, as an investment in social relations with an expected return in the marketplace, should be defined as *resources embedded in a social structure that are accessed and/or mobilized in purposive actions*" (Lin 2001*b*: 29). This conceptualization is part of a long line of theoretical work pertaining to social resources and status attainment that perhaps began with Mark Granovetter's work. Granovetter's seminal study on how men obtained employment was a significant contribution to the discipline because it introduced a link between social capital and status attainment by proposing a network theory for the flow of information through weak ties (Granovetter 1973). From this, research emerged on the strength of ties and instrumental actions (Lin, Dayton, and Greenwald 1978; Marsden and Campbell 1984; Green, Tigges, and Browne 1995), as well as the composition of ties (e.g. the status of ties and/or their racial/ethnic makeup) and the effects of such characteristics on status attainment outcomes (Tigges, Browne, and Green 1998; Elliott 1999; Johnson, Farrell, and Stoloff 2000; Livingston 2000; Smith 2000; Mouw 2003).

One issue that researchers are beginning to disentangle is the separate processes of access to and mobilization of social capital. Before one can mobilize a tie s/he must have access to it. Social capital theory predicts that having greater access to social capital may enable one to advance status attainment (Lin 2001*b*). More specifically, the quantity and quality of social capital is expected to contribute to its value as a means of social mobility. The quality of people's ties has to do with the height of their status, as it is expected the greater a tie's status, the more valuable the information and influence s/he can provide. Related to quantity, the greater the size of the total network, the greater one's resources may be from which to draw. Measuring such characteristics of one's access to social capital has been accomplished with the name generator methodology and, more recently, the position generator methodology. The name generator methodology generally asked respondents about ties in particular content areas (e.g. employment matters), role relationships (e.g. neighborhood), or intimacy (e.g. confidant), and then obtained information on their resources and demographic characteristics (for examples of studies that used this method, see Campbell, Marsden, and Hurlbert 1986; Boxman, DeGraaf, and Flap 1991; Burt 1992, 1997, 1998). The limitation of this method is that it is biased toward strong ties. The position generator methodology, on the other hand, samples various *positions* in society to which respondents have ties. The methodology is believed to be less biased toward strong ties and less geographically limiting (Lin and Dumin 1986). This method is discussed further in Section 17.5, as this is the methodology used in this study to measure access to social capital.

Because having access to social capital precedes its usage, this study examines a sample's access to social capital and its association with status attainment outcomes. We seek to describe characteristics of the sample's access to social capital, such as whether people's networks predominantly comprise of their own race. We will then test whether access to social capital is associated with status attainment, after taking into account previous status and gender and racial/ethnic characteristics.

17.3. INEQUALITY IN SOCIAL CAPITAL

As with virtually any other resource in a hierarchically ordered society, social capital is unequally distributed among members. Indeed, some individuals are well connected to friends with information and influence, while others have either few connections in general or few connections with influential purchase. It is critically important to observe that, in general, the association between particular people and their quantity and quality of social capital is nonrandom. Certain social groups, by virtue of their race/ethnicity, gender, religion, and other characteristics, are usually systematically more or less advantaged regarding access to social capital compared to other groups. This is important because it can lead to additional inequality across these group's life chances, serving as a mechanism for stratification and social mobility (Lin 2000a).

Unequal access to social capital can be attributed to two fundamental explanations. First, structural processes dictate that some groups tend to largely occupy places higher on the socioeconomic hierarchy relative to others (e.g. white males), while other groups will be clustered among lower positions (e.g. women and most racial/ethnic minorities). These structural processes are shaped by historical and institutional constructions, such as racism, sexism, and other similar forms of discrimination aimed at particular social groups. Coupled with this, the second underlying explanation behind unequal access to social capital is the simple notion of the homophily principle: individuals tend to share sentiments and interact with others who share their own characteristics (Lazarsfeld and Merton 1954; Homans 1958; McPherson, Smith-Lovin, and Cook 2001). Consequently, people usually form networks with others from the same social group.

When these two underlying principles, structural processes and homophily, work in tandem, they produce unequal access to social capital (Lin 2000a). Those occupying lower socioeconomic positions frequently have ties with those who share similar characteristics, and are therefore embedded in resource-poor networks. It is expected that their social capital will have less information related to jobs of higher socioeconomic standing relative to their own, and carry little influence on these higher positions. The opposite is true for those holding higher positions in the socioeconomic hierarchy. They also frequently have networks consisting of others like them, but by virtue of where they are embedded in the network their connections have valuable information and wield influence on social mobility outcomes (Lin 2000a). Of course, some individuals break rank and have ties to people outside their own area on the socioeconomic hierarchy, but this is the exception, not the rule.

Previous research on gender and social networks has shown that, compared to men's, women's networks are disproportionately composed of neighbors and family members rather than organizational coworkers (Marsden 1987, 1988; Campbell 1988; Moore 1990; Hanson and Pratt 1991; Marx and Leicht 1992; Green, Tigges, and Browne 1995; Beggs and Hurlbert 1997; Straits 1998). While family ties do provide contact with a fair number of men, these ties are more qualitatively homogenous regarding resources. That is, women's networks are more limited compared to men's, which have much more heterogeneity in the composition and quality of resources afforded. Related to this, evidence has shown that white men tend to use influential white male contacts to affect status attainment outcomes, which explains a significant portion of the wage gap between genders (Smith 2000). Livingston (2000) also found that men's greater use of male ties explains much of the gender income gap. Such findings lend support to the idea that social capital can serve as a mechanism to reproduce social stratification across societies (Lin 2000*a*).

However, Erickson (2004) employed a position generator that had equal amounts of male- and female-dominated professions with which to identify ties. Using this approach, she found that men and women actually know the same number of ties on average, but the male respondents knew a wider range of positions held by men than by women. She also found that female respondents knew a more diverse range of female ties than did the male respondents. Thus, the amount of social capital people have certainly appears to be a factor of how networks were measured.

In addition to gender differences, scholars have also studied access to and mobilization of social capital by race/ethnicity. The strongest divides in our personal environments are created by racial/ethnic homophily (McPherson, Smith-Lovin, and Cook 2001). Similar to women, African-Americans' networks are disproportionately composed of family (Martineau 1977; Green, Tigges, and Browne 1995) and neighbors (Lee, Campbell, and Miller 1991) compared to whites. The composition of their ties is also generally stronger and more localized as well (Martineau 1977; Green, Tigges, and Browne 1995). Compared to whites and Latinos, African-Americans have smaller networks, measured as the number of people with whom they discussed important matters (Marsden 1988). Compared to their white and Latino counterparts, they are also more likely to be embedded in a network in which at least one strong tie is on welfare or lives in public housing (Johnson, Farrell, and Stoloff 2000).

Consequently, African-Americans' (strong) ties are more homogenous (Marsden 1988), and this may affect status attainment. Wilson (1987) has strongly argued that the black underclass in America is in a particularly dire situation because in addition to being impoverished, it lacks social ties to people who can help provide valuable employment information and influence. Along these lines, research has shown that, compared to nonpoor whites, poor African-Americans have less access to college-educated or employed strong ties (Tigges, Browne, and

Green 1998). Examining a sample of less-educated urban workers, Elliott (1999) found that those who used a nonwhite tie earned significantly lower earnings. In the same vein, Green, Tigges, and Diaz (1999) found an inverse relationship between tie strength and annual income for Latinos. Smith (2000) also found that white males who used male and influential ties achieved wage advantages over Latinos who did not use such ties.

17.4. MODEL AND HYPOTHESES

Guided by social capital theory and the review of literature described above, we have developed a conceptual model with hypotheses to be tested in the present study. Figure 17.1 illustrates our conceptual model, with prior status and social capital regressed on current status, controlling for demographic characteristics. The measurement models and structural equation model are detailed in Section 17.5. The overarching hypothesis depicted in this model is that, even after taking into account demographic characteristics and prior status, access to social capital will be significantly related to current status.

Further, we posit several hypotheses regarding inequality to social capital and status attainment. Drawing from the two processes driving inequality in social capital (i.e. structural processes and the homophily principle working in tandem), we hypothesize that women will have lower prior status and less access to social capital compared to men. As a result, we posit that women will have lower current status relative to men. In addition, using these same processes as a theoretical framework, we hypothesize that African-Americans and Latinos/Hispanics will have lower prior status and less access to social capital compared to whites.[1] We posit that these minority groups will consequently have lower current status relative to whites.

17.5. METHODS

17.5.1. Data

The data for this project are from the Job Search survey, a national telephone survey carried out in 2002. The purpose of the survey was to obtain information related to social networks in job acquisition experiences. The sample of 900 respondents was proportionally recruited from a random digit dialing sampling frame of the 25 largest primary metropolitan statistical areas (PMSA) in the US.

[1] We do not make a hypothesis regarding the "other" racial/ethnic minority category because this category consists of numerous ethnicities, which may or may not be disadvantaged compared with whites. The sample sizes for each of these ethnicities are too small to compare separately with whites. However, they are included as an "other" category to bolster the overall sample size and optimize statistical power.

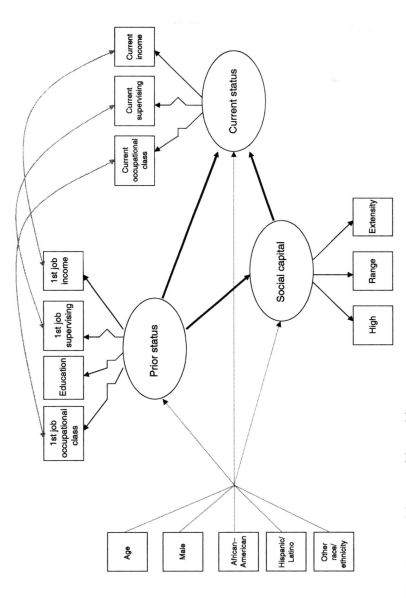

Figure 17.1. Conceptual diagram of the model

Note: Boxes represent observed variables and oblong circles represent latent constructs. The light gray dotted arrow lines represent pathways from each demographic control variable to each latent construct. The medium gray double-arrowed pathways represent correlated error terms. The bold single arrows represent the major pathways between latent constructs. Regular single arrows represent observed variables for latent constructs. Finally, "broken" arrows represent observed variables that are categorical and modeled as such in Mplus.

Eligibility was restricted to people in the age range 21–64 who were currently working or had previously worked. In addition, the respondent had to be English or Spanish speaking. Only one respondent was selected from each household based on a birth date criterion. Fifty-two percent of eligible contacted respondents completed the survey. Interviews lasted approximately 25 minutes each. For this particular study, only those respondents currently working for pay were included, and therefore the sample size was reduced to 689 cases. This sample was further reduced to 557 cases due to listwise deletion of cases with any missing values on variables used in the analysis.[2]

17.5.2. Measurement

17.5.2.1. Social Capital

As demonstrated in Figure 17.1, the latent construct for social capital is measured by three observed variables that were all derived from the position generator methodology. Previous work on social capital utilized a name generator where respondents were asked to name several ties and their respective occupations; however, it was believed that this method was biased toward tapping the respondent's strong ties, but not weak ties (Lin and Dumin 1986). Additionally, as this method samples on occupations, it is believed to be more geographically boundless than the name generator method (Lin 1999*b*). The position generator methodology involves presenting the respondent with a list of a variety of occupational positions relevant to the society under investigation, with various statuses attached to them (e.g. lawyer, teacher, and janitor). Then the respondent is asked whether any of his or her relatives, friends, or acquaintances hold such positions. In the Job Search survey, 14 such occupations were presented to the respondents.[3] The survey also ascertained how long respondents have known each tie they identified in the position generator, as well as how long they have been at their current job. Thus although the survey is cross-sectional, we innovatively used this information on timing of contacts and jobs to calculate whether such ties were known prior to obtaining jobs, a technique we have not previously seen employed in the literature.[4] Using this information, we have included only those

[2] Because the survey included questions on both monthly and annual income, if someone indicated their monthly but not annual income, the former information was extrapolated to the latter to minimize the number of missing income cases. Another technique used to reduce missing information was to use current job's information for missing first job information *if the first job IS the current job* (i.e., the first job the respondent had is the job he or she currently had as well).

[3] The following occupations were included in the Job Search position generator, with their respective NORC/GSS occupational prestige scores in parentheses: elementary school teacher (64), lawyer (75), salesperson (32), waiter/waitress or bartender (28), engineer (71), secretary (46), manager (51), small business owner (59), insurance agent (45), janitor (22), mechanic or repairman (44), laborer (24), foreman (54), and skilled worker (30).

[4] There were no missing data on the 689 respondents regarding whether they knew someone in each of the possible 14 positions. Further, less than 1% of data was missing on how long respondents knew someone in each of the 14 positions.

ties that were reported to be known *prior* to obtaining one's current job. In other words, the respondents' access to social capital was available before they acquired their most recent job. This explains why the paths from social capital to status attainment outcomes are recursive rather than nonrecursive. Obviously, such a measure is subject to some recall bias, but this is nearly unavoidable given the retrospective nature of the data.

Three indicators of social capital are measured. The first social capital indicator derived from this methodology is the highest prestige tie ("high"). It represents the occupational prestige score for the highest occupational status tie identified. For example, if the respondent stated s/he knew an engineer, but did not know anyone occupying any of the higher status positions, then a score of "71" was given, as this corresponds to the NORC/GSS prestige score for an engineer. The second social capital indicator is the range of prestige known by the respondent ("range"). As the name implies, this represents the range of social capital available to the respondent. It is calculated by subtracting the respondent's lowest occupational prestige score identified in his/her network from the highest occupational prestige score identified. It signifies the diversity of social capital available and suggests the network's vertical depth (Campbell, Marsden, and Hurlbert 1986). The third indicator of social capital is extensiveness ("extensity") that represents the size of one's network. It is a sum of the total number of people the respondent identified among the 14 possible.

17.5.2.2. Prior Status

The latent construct corresponding to prior status is measured by four observed variables. First, education is an ordinal variable coded 1 = less than high school, 2 = high school/GED, 3 = associate's degrees, 4 = bachelor's degree, and 5 = master's degree or higher. It corresponds to the highest level of education obtained *prior* to one's current job. Second, the occupational class of one's first job is included. There are four possible ordinal classes: 1 = lower class, made up of private household, service, craft, operator, and handler occupations; 2 = middle class, made up of technician, sales, administrative support, protective service, transportation, and farming occupations; 3 = professional, made up of professional occupations; and 4 = executive, made up of executive occupations. Similar occupational class schemes have been developed elsewhere (Schmidt and Strauss 1975; Filer 1986).

In addition to education and occupational class, prior status is also assessed by how much supervising the respondent did at his/her first job. This is a three-level ordinal variable with 1 = supervised no one; 2 = supervised people, but those people did not supervise anyone; and 3 = supervised people who also supervised others. Finally, a measure of income at the first job is included by asking the respondent what his/her monthly salary was. Twenty-seven ordinal categories were allotted for the response.[5] The logged median of these categories

---

[5] These categories are as follows: under $1,000; $1,000–2,999; $3,000–3,999; $4,000–4,999; $5,000–5,999; $6,000–6,999; $7,000–7,999; $8,000–9,999; $10,000–12,499; $12,500–14,999; $15,000–17,499;

was calculated to reduce the skewed nature of this variable, and adjustments were made with the Consumer Price Index to account for the fact that respondents held their respective first jobs in different years.

17.5.2.3. Current Status

To assess intragenerational status attainment, a latent construct for current status is measured by three observed variables. First, as with prior status, a measure of occupational class is included. The ordinal categories are the same as for prior status (i.e. low, middle, professional, and executive); however, these occupational classes correspond to the respondent's current job. A measure of job supervision is also included; as with prior status, this variable is ordinal and distinguishes whether the respondent supervises anyone, and if so, whether those people also supervise others in the current job. Finally, income of current job is measured. The same 27 ordinal categories are used; however, these categories for current job refer to one's annual, not monthly, salary. The logged median value is calculated, but no Consumer Price Index (CPI) adjustments were needed or made. It should be noted that errors were correlated for first and current job's measures regarding occupational class, supervision, and income because in some cases the current job is the same as the respondent's first job. In addition to these theoretical justifications, model fit was improved when these errors were correlated.

17.5.2.4. Control Variables

To control for other factors that may be associated with status attainment outcomes and their predictors, we control for several sociodemographic variables. Current age is measured in number of years. Gender is coded male = 1. Racial/ethnic groups included are: white, African-American, Hispanic/Latino, and other race. White is the omitted category. Every control variable is regressed on all three latent constructs, as shown in Figure 17.1.

The analyses proceed in several steps. First, we present descriptive statistics to demonstrate distributions of variables in the models. Next, we examine the degree of co-racial/ethnic homophily in the sample, that is, how similar the racial/ethnic makeup is between respondents and their respective networks. This is done because if there is a large degree of co-homophily then racial/ethnic minorities may be disadvantaged regarding their stock of social capital; since whites have historically held more powerful positions and presumably the information and influence to obtain them. Thus, if racial/ethnic minorities have very few whites in their networks then they may not have access to such resources. Finally, structural

---

$17,500–19,999; $20,000–22,499; $22,500–24,999; $25,000–29,999; $30,000–34,999; $35,000–39,999; $40,000–49,999; $50,000–59,999; $60,000–74,999; $75,000–89,999; $90,000–109,999; $110,000–129,999; $130,000–149,999; $150,000–169,999; $170,000–189,999; and $190,000 or over.

equation modeling is used to test whether social capital affects status attainment holding prior status constant, and the effects of gender and race/ethnicity on this process.

17.6. RESULTS

Descriptive statistics on the sample are presented in Table 17.1. They indicate that 49 percent of the sample is male and the mean age is 39 years. Fifty-seven percent of the sample is white, while about 15 percent is African-American, 21 percent is Hispanic/Latino, and nearly 7 percent make up an "other" race/ethnicity.[6] In addition, about 18 percent had less than a high school education, while the highest level of education for 41 percent of the sample was a high school diploma/GED, nearly 6 percent received an associate's degree, 25 percent received a bachelor's degree, and almost 10 percent received graduate degrees. We find a wide observed scope in the sample's highest social capital tie, with this prestige score ranging from 24 to 75, and a mean of 66.43. Similarly, the range of social capital available to the respondents (i.e. lowest tie prestige score subtracted from the highest for each respondent) was diverse, from 0 to 53, with a mean at 33.35. And extensity of social capital has an observed range of 1–13, with a mean of 4.54. Therefore, this sample possessed an array of access to social capital prior to obtaining their current job.

Table 17.2 presents information on co-racial/ethnic homophily in the sample. These figures were derived as follows: the race/ethnicity was identified for every tie known to respondents from the position generator (e.g. after a respondent stated they knew a teacher, we asked about demographic characteristics of the teacher including his/her race/ethnicity). Next, we calculated what proportion of the ties belonged to each racial/ethnic category, and further disaggregated this figure by the race of ego. The findings demonstrate remarkable amounts of co-racial/ethnic homophily. To be sure, nearly 90 percent of the ties identified by white respondents were also white. Similarly, 86 percent of African-American's ties were African-American, and 85 percent of Hispanic/Latino's ties were Hispanic/Latino.

As a basis of comparison for these results, we analyzed the General Social Survey 1985 Topical Module on Social Networks. Participants in this survey were

---

[6] Direct comparisons with Census 2000 data are not possible because the Census allows individuals to identify as multiple races/ethnicities, whereas our survey did not. However, it should be noted that while the overall racial/ethnic distribution in Census 2000 is 69.50% non-Hispanic white, 12.19% non-Hispanic black/African-American, 12.54% Hispanic/Latino, and 5.77% other (calculated from <http://eire.census.gov/popest/data/national/tables/asro/NA-EST2002-ASRO-04.php>), examination of the distributions within the 24 urban areas in our study show that they generally have disproportionately more African-Americans and Latinos/Hispanics and less whites, compared with the overall population. Therefore, we are confident that the racial/ethnic distribution in our sample is relatively representative of those urban areas included. For instance, 10 of the urban areas in our sample have greater than 20% Hispanic/Latino populations, 11 have greater than 15% African-American populations, and 12 have less than 60% white populations (these figures were derived from viewing individual urban areas on <http://mumford1.dyndns.org/cen1000/HispanicPop/HspPopData.htm>).

Table 17.1. Descriptive statistics for variables used in analysis ($N = 557$)

	Mean (or proportion)	S.D.	Observed range
Control variables			
Age	39.29	11.22	21–64
Male	.49	—	0–1
Race/ethnicity			
White	.57	—	0–1
African-American	.15	—	0–1
Hispanic/Latino	.21	—	0–1
Other race/ethnic	.07	—	0–1
Prior status			
First job occupational class			1–4
Lower	.27	—	—
Middle	.44	—	—
Professional	.18	—	—
Executive	.11	—	—
First job supervising			1–3
Supervises no one	.66	—	—
Supervises	.24	—	—
Supervisees supervise	.10	—	—
First job income	6.78	.88	5.27–10.68
Education			1–5
Less than high school	.18	—	—
High school/GED	.41	—	—
Associate's degree	.06	—	—
Bachelor's degree	.25	—	—
Graduate degree	.10	—	—
Social capital			
Highest prestige tie	66.44	12.17	22–75
Range of prestige	33.35	17.34	0–53
Extensity of ties	4.54	2.54	1–13
Current status			
Current job occupational class			1–4
Lower	.17	—	—
Middle	.40	—	—
Professional	.26	—	—
Executive	.16	—	—
Current job supervising			1–3
Supervises no one	.52	—	—
Supervises	.31	—	—
Supervisees supervise	.17	—	—
Current job income	10.08	1.41	6.21–12.25

asked, "From time to time, most people discuss important matters with other people. Looking back over the last six months—who are the people with whom you discussed matters important to you?" Among the 1,534 survey participants asked this question, 1,398 identified at least one tie, and they were permitted to name up to five. As with our own data, we analyzed the racial composition of people's networks. The results, similar to our own, demonstrated that white

Table 17.2. Co-racial/ethnic homophily in access to social capital ($N = 557$)

Race/ethnicity of ego	White ties (%)	African-American ties (%)	Hispanic/Latino ties (%)	"Other" ties (%)
White	89.99	1.93	4.45	3.63
African-American	8.78	86.27	1.65	3.30
Hispanic/Latino	9.95	2.06	85.16	2.83
Other	33.70	5.82	4.69	55.79
Total	57.09	14.64	21.30	6.97

Note: The numerator for the calculation of each percentage is the number of ties of the specified race/ethnicity known prior to obtaining one's current job, and the denominator is the total number of ties known prior to one's current job. The ties are derived from the position generator. For example, if the white respondents knew on average 10 ties total, and on average 7 were white, 1 was black, 1 was Hispanic, and 1 was "other", then the percentages for whites would be 70% white, 10% black, 10% Hispanic/Latino, and 10% "other".

respondents' networks were composed, on average, of 95 percent white people. Also, African-American's networks averaged 86 percent African-Americans, and "other's" networks consisted of, on average, 76 percent "other" racial/ethnic people. Like our own study, this sample is nationally representative of the US. However, unlike the position generator methodology used in our own study to obtain social network information, the General Social Survey question seems to identify the closest ties to the respondents. Regardless, the conclusions are similar: there is an overwhelming amount of racial/ethnic co-homophily in social networks.

To examine the factors associated with intragenerational status attainment, structural equation modeling was employed using Mplus version 2.14. This method was chosen because there are multiple indicators for latent variables in our model, particularly social capital. As mentioned above, and as Figure 17.1 indicates, sociodemographic controls were regressed on all three latent variables. Additionally, errors were correlated for several indicators of prior and current statuses for reasons described above.

Unstandardized measurement model estimates for all three latent variables, controlling for age, gender, and race/ethnicity, are presented in Table 17.3. All of the coefficients in the model are statistically significant at $p < 0.05$. Table 17.3 presents the unstandardized coefficients for the structural equations of the model. Fit indices reveal that the model fits the data reasonably well.

Addressing the principal hypothesis in this chapter, Table 17.4 demonstrates that even after controlling for sociodemographic variables and prior status, access to social capital is significantly ($p < 0.05$) related to current status attainment outcomes. That is, social capital access is positively related to advances in occupational class, supervision, and income. This is consistent with prior evidence examining the effect of access to social capital measured by the position generator on status attainment outcomes in the US (Lin and Dumin 1986) as well as other countries (Hsung and Hwang 1992b; Erickson 1996; Völker and Flap

Table 17.3. Structural equation measurement model estimates controlling for age, gender, and race/ethnicity ($N = 557$)

Latent construct	Observed variable	Unstandardized λ coefficient
Prior status	First job occupational class	1.00[a]
	Education	1.00
	First job supervising	.63
	First job income	.50
Social capital	Highest prestige tie	1.00[a]
	Range of prestige	1.24
	Extensity of prestige	.15
Current status	Current job occupational class	1.00[a]
	Current job supervising	.40
	Current job income	.89

[a] These indicators were fixed at 1.00.

1999). As expected, prior status is also significantly associated with current status ($p < 0.001$). This finding has been a bedrock of status attainment models since Blau and Duncan's decisive work (Blau and Duncan 1967).

Beyond generally demonstrating that social capital affects status attainment, we were also interested in the roles of race/ethnicity and gender. Interestingly, holding age, gender, prior status, and social capital access constant, Hispanic/Latino and "other" racial/ethnic groups have significantly lower status attainment relative to whites ($p < 0.001$ and $p < 0.05$, respectively). African-Americans also have a negative relationship with current status, but it is not statistically significant. *Ceteris paribus*, we do not find a significant relationship between current status and age or gender. Ultimately, nearly 42 percent of the variance in current status is explained by the model.

Race/ethnicity was also predictive of access to social capital. Indeed, both African-American and Hispanic/Latino groups had less access to social capital

Table 17.4. Unstandardized coefficients from the structural equation model ($N = 557$)

	Endogenous variables		
	Prior status	Social capital	Current status
Age	.009* (.004)	−.04	.004 (.004)
Male	−.05 (.08)	−1.36 (1.02)	.08 (.08)
African-American	−.15 (.12)	−3.35* (1.52)	−.17 (.12)
Hispanic/Latino	−.44*** (.10)	−7.28*** (1.30)	−.61*** (.10)
Other race/ethnicity	.26 (.16)	−3.28 (1.97)	−.29* (.14)
Prior status	—	1.49* (.76)	.53*** (.06)
Social capital	—	—	.009* (.004)
R^2	.094	.095	.419

Notes: $\chi^2 = 136,48^{***}$, 38 df; CFI = .89; TLI = .88; RMSEA = .06.

* $p < .05$; ** $p < .01$; *** $p < .001$.

relative to whites ($p < 0.05$ and $p < 0.001$, respectively). The "other" racial/ethnic category was also inversely related to social capital access, but it was not statistically significant. Moreover, gender is not a significant predictor of access to social capital.

As the strength-of-position in social capital theory predicts, our findings demonstrate that those with higher prior status in society will have greater access to social capital ($p < 0.05$) (Lin 2001*b*). This proposition is entirely consistent with the conventional structural theory; it reflects the structural advantage for actors and extends this structural effect to social capital. Ultimately, prior status and sociodemographic variables explained over 9 percent of the variance in access to social capital.

Finally, we find that age and being Hispanic/Latino are significantly predictive of prior status. The older the respondent was, the higher his/her prior status, controlling for gender and race/ethnicity ($p < 0.05$). And, as with access to social capital and current status, Hispanic/Latinos have substantially lower prior status compared to whites ($p < 0.001$). The coefficient for African-Americans is also negative, but it is not statistically significant. Sociodemographic variables accounted for over 9 percent of the variance in prior status.

17.7. DISCUSSION

This study examined the relationship between access to social capital and status attainment. We find that, even after controlling for demographic characteristics, education level, and previous job characteristics, including supervision, occupational class, and income, access to social capital still significantly contributes to current status. "Who you know" adds to status attainment over and above one's prior status. In addition to this general finding, there were several interesting discoveries regarding how gender and race play into this.

To begin our exploration of how race may be involved in the social capital–status attainment relationship, we examined co-racial/ethnic homophily among our respondents. These results confirmed that people mainly associate with others who belong to their same social group, which is a fundamental idea in sociology. They also confirm that racial/ethnic divides are among the strongest in our society (McPherson, Smith-Lovin, and Cook 2001). The problem with this, particularly related to status attainment, is that minorities have historically occupied lower-status positions relative to whites. If minorities are predominantly associated with ties in lower statuses, then their social capital cannot provide them with the information and influence necessary to become upwardly social mobile (Lin 2000*a*).

Indeed, in the next steps of the analyses, we find that African-Americans and Hispanics have less access to social capital compared to their white counterparts. Further, the Hispanics' current status was significantly lower than whites' on average. The Hispanics thus follow a textbook case of what we would expect regarding historical structures, homophily, access to social capital, and status attainment. They start out in significantly worse positions than whites, know mostly other Hispanics, and end up in markedly lower-status positions. African-Americans follow a similar pattern. Their prior status is lower on average (although at nonsignificant levels), they identify mostly other African-Americans in their social network, they have significantly less social capital, and they are slightly disadvantaged in their current status (although at nonsignificant levels). We believe the smaller sample size of African-Americans ($n = 84$) contributed to the fact that these disadvantages did not reach statistical significance. Thus, these findings of disadvantaged racial/ethnic groups regarding social capital and status attainment are generally consistent with theories of inequality in social capital (Lin 2000a).

In the same vein, Smith (2000) found that Latinos' wages were significantly lower compared to white men, partially because the latter mobilized male and influential ties for employment. With the Hispanic/Latino population, now the largest minority population in the US, we need to be aware if they are becoming the new underclass. Furthermore, if social capital plays a significant role in status attainment, as we have found in this study along with others in the past, then groups need to learn how to take advantage of this. Many Hispanic/Latinos may be particularly underprivileged with regard to networking because a significant minority of them cannot speak English.

Inequality in social capital theory predicted that women would have significantly less social capital for similar reasons as with race/ethnicity. That is, they are historically disadvantaged in our society and, based on the homophily principle and prior evidence (that often only examined strong ties), they have less social capital (Marsden 1987, 1988; Campbell 1988; Green, Tigges, and Browne 1995). Using a position generator that in theory captures strong and weak ties, Erickson (2004) found that the size of men's and women's social capital networks were the same when ignoring gender differences in the composition of these networks. Our finding that men and women generally have equal access to social capital (regardless of the gender composition) is consistent with hers. But when Erickson (2004) took the gender composition into account, women knew more women than the men but fewer men than the men, and therefore ultimately had less access to social capital compared to men. Similarly, we conducted a co-gender analysis using our own data (not shown here). Results demonstrated that there is little substantive difference in the proportion of male–female ties by male and female respondents. Indeed, in our sample 63 percent of female respondents' ties are male, while 68 percent of male respondents' ties are male.[7] It appears that females have significantly narrowed any gap in access to social capital with respect to co-gender homophily. In fact, females in this sample seem to have the upper hand in access to social capital the male coefficient for this construct is negative.

---

[7] It is also noteworthy that research (see Chapter 3) demonstrates that when a respondent knows more than one tie in a particular position, they are more likely to identify one with the same gender as the respondent (and the one with whom the respondent interacts more frequently). This may explain some of the reasons men identify more men and women identify more women.

Erickson's analysis did not go a step further in determining whether social capital affected status attainment (Erickson 2004); when we explored this, we found that there were no gender differences in status attainment outcomes.

For further comparisons, we also examined the 1985 GSS Topical Module on Social Networks (described above) for gender differences in networks. We found that, on average, the proportion of men's networks that consisted of men was .58, while the proportion of women's networks comprised by women was .60. These results deviate from our own somewhat, but this is not surprising given that the GSS Module question taps more into strong, closer ties than our own position generator methodology. And both our own sample's results and those from the GSS demonstrate that gender homophily in social networks is nowhere near as strong as racial/ethnic homophily.

Getting back to the Job Search data, why would females have the same access to social capital as males? If social capital theory predicts that in general women hold lower status positions because of historical processes, and will have less social capital because of the homophily principle, what can explain this? As discussed, women barely have more female ties than men in this sample and men have moderately more male ties than do the women, so there is only weak support for a co-gender homophily argument. Second, in our sample, there is no statistically significant difference in prior status between men and women. Perhaps our indicators of status have falsely inflated the status of women relative to men. For instance, our measure of supervision is very crude so that there may be important qualitative differences within supervising that are not captured. Put differently, a male CEO who reports that he supervises people who also supervise others is classified in the same way as a female charge nurse who reports that she supervises people who also supervise others. Future research will have to continue to explore the gendered dynamics concerning access to social capital and status attainment.

In addition to further explorations on the roles of race/ethnicity, gender, and other compositional characteristics, the next step in this line of research needs to connect social capital access to its mobilization. After all, the present study and others like it have only examined whether people have the *potential* in their social resources, not whether it has been exploited. While we have found particular racial/ethnic disadvantages in access to social capital, this does not mean that everyone will use what they have equally. Indeed, it is possible that certain groups do not mobilize what is available to them. At present, there are few studies that have followed the full access to mobilization sequence to examine status attainment outcomes (see Lai, Lin, and Leung 1998).

18

Access to Social Capital and the Structure of Inequality in Ulaanbaatar, Mongolia

Catherine A. Johnson

18.1. INTRODUCTION

Like other resources, social capital is not distributed equally among all members of society. Its distribution is dependent on the constraints and opportunities contained within an individual's social network, which is in turn affected by employment status, income, and level of education. Access to these social resources, or social capital, helps explain individuals' success (or lack thereof) in achieving desired outcomes (Lin 2001*b*). Using the position generator developed by Lin and Dumin (1986), I will investigate the factors that affect how people living in the Mongolian city of Ulaanbaatar gain access to social capital. I will look at two measures of social capital: access to occupations in the position generator and; the diversity of different positions to which people have access. As a poor country still suffering the effects of transition from a communist government to a free market democracy, Mongolia has suffered severe economic and social dislocation over the last 15 years. Access to social capital may help explain who wins and loses in this transition.

18.1.1. Background

With the fall of communism in the early 1990s, Mongolia underwent harsh economic and social dislocation as it adopted free market reforms and adjusted to a democratic form of government. Although the initial instability of the early years of transition has eased, economic self-sufficiency has eluded the people of Mongolia so far. The World Bank states that the Gross National Income (GNI) per capita is at US$480 per year, placing Mongolia in the ranks of the least-developed countries (World Bank 2004). Residents of Ulaanbaatar who lost jobs in state organizations and state-owned factories managed to adjust by working as taxicab drivers, operating small street kiosks, trading small goods in the market, and selling cigarettes and newspapers on the street. In his study of the Ulaanbaatar informal sector, Anderson found that over 60 percent of kiosk owners and taxicab drivers had vocational or higher levels of education (Anderson 1998). Mongolians still have to work hard to make ends meet. Many people have to hold down two or more jobs and rely on their family and friends to help out when crises occur. New small enterprises are plentiful, but with low capital investment they require considerable investment of time and labor by the owners and their relatives to sustain them. On the other hand, a very select few with access to financial capital and influence have been able to start relatively large enterprises and prosper (Rossabi 2005). Despite impressive economic growth and the availability of imported goods and luxury items at the newly revamped State Department Store or the new Korean shopping plaza behind the Chinggis Khan hotel, only a small percentage of Mongolians can afford to shop there. A third of the population still languishes below the poverty level, and inequalities in income have increased substantially during transition. In 1996, the Gini coefficient, which measures the extent to which the distribution of income deviates from a perfectly equal distribution (0 indicates perfect equality and 1 perfect inequality), was 0.31 for Mongolia. By 1998, it was 0.44 compared to 0.33 for Canada in the same year (United Nations Development Programme 2004). The question that this chapter addresses is to what extent does access to social capital reinforce these existing inequalities or provide opportunities for overcoming them.

18.1.2. Methodology

This chapter reports on a study that I conducted in Mongolia in the spring and summer of 2002. The major study investigated the information-seeking behavior of residents of Ulaanbaatar and the influence of social capital on their ability to find information related to their everyday information needs (Johnson 2003). This chapter will discuss the part of the project that used the position generator to measure the social capital of the respondents. Mongolian students from the Cultural College of Ulaanbaatar administered a face-to-face personal network survey to a stratified, random sample of 320 people living in the city and one of the surrounding semiformal or *ger* districts.[1] The survey used both a name generator and a position generator to elicit members of the respondents' social networks.

18.1.3. The Position Generator

The position generator used in this study consisted of a list of occupation categories constructed with the help of local informants and based partially on the occupations chosen by Lin, Fu, and Hsung (2001) in Taiwan. Table 18.1 lists the 17 occupations included in the position generator. Although I was not able to confidently rank occupations in the position generator because prestige rankings

[1] A *ger* is the traditional round felt tent occupied by Mongolian nomads. The *ger* districts consist of both *gers* and small, usually owner-built, wooden houses enclosed in fenced-in family compounds on the edge of the city.

Table 18.1. Occupation categories

Politician
Big business owner
Doctor
Lawyer
Foreign agency worker
Foreign company worker
Government worker
Bank worker
Lama
Teacher
Librarian
Nurse
Small business owner
Taxicab driver
Small kiosk owner
Waiter/waitress
Housecleaner

do not exist for Mongolian occupations, the positions are listed in approximate rank order, with generally equivalent occupations grouped together in the shaded and unshaded areas.

The occupations include those positions that would be particularly useful in the search for information; for example, positions in the health sector, banking, government, education, and law. I also included workers in foreign organizations and foreign companies, since knowing people who work for these organizations may also give respondents access to privileged health, business, or environmental information. Knowing people in these organizations may enhance one's own chances of getting access to these highly desirable jobs or to the resources of these organizations—finding someone to translate an English document, for example. Because Buddhism has been making a steady resurgence and many young people are rediscovering the religion of their ancestors, I also included a lama in the position generator. Although knowing a lama may not increase one's material well-being, it may give one the spiritual resources needed to cope with uncertain and difficult social and economic times. Many people also consult lamas in order to determine the most propitious time for undertaking certain actions or making decisions, and therefore a lama would be a valuable member of one's social network. The benefit of knowing an owner of a big business (employing 20 or more persons) is obvious since they would be the source of jobs, cash, and information about other economic opportunities. Small business owners (those employing fewer than five persons) can be good sources of small loans and information about the marketplace. Working as taxicab drivers and kiosk owners were common strategies in the early years of transition to cope with the massive unemployment and the collapse of the social welfare system. These informal economic activities are still a major source of income for Ulaanbaatar residents, and can result in higher incomes than those earned by people in the more formal state

Table 18.2. Logistic regression analysis on access to occupations as a function of the gender, education, income, and location of respondents ($N = 312$)

	n	Gender[a]	Education[b]	Income[c]	Location[d]
Politician	66	1.27	2.74***	1.39	.33***
Big business owner	97	1.56*	2.01**	1.58*	.62
Doctor	235	.56**	1.42	1.32	.59*
Lawyer	104	1.10	1.74*	1.93**	.83
Foreign agency worker	34	.84	1.27	1.35	1.06
Foreign company worker	31	.54	1.11	2.14*	.28**
Government worker	127	1.15	2.08**	1.90**	.73
Bank worker	87	.94	2.02**	1.31	.52**
Lama	132	.83	1.31	1.10	1.09
Teacher	241	1.29	1.54	2.74***	.49**
Librarian	115	.68	.91	1.71**	1.20
Nurse	141	.51***	1.16	1.05	.52**
Small business owner	141	1.25	1.61	2.00***	.76
Taxicab driver	97	1.53*	1.16	1.05	1.10
Small kiosk owner	183	.56**	.92	1.43	.94
Waiter/waitress	54	1.05	.74	1.28	.52*
Housecleaner	19	.84	.87	.61	1.75

[a] Male = 1.
[b] University education = 1.
[c] Income > 50,000 tugrogs = 1.
[d] Living in *ger* district = 1.
* $p < .10$; ** $p < .05$; *** $p < .01$.

organizations. Housecleaners and waiters, although not prestigious occupations, provide access to information not available elsewhere, and are thus also important members of one's network.

Access to occupations in the position generator indicates both the level and the variety of social capital available to respondents in the study. The figures in Table 18.2 show the effect of gender, education, income, and living in the *ger* district on access to occupations in the position generator. Three hundred and twelve people completed the position generator. The number of respondents reporting that they knew people in each of the positions is indicated in the "n" column. Since most of my data were collected into categorical variables, I recoded them into dummy variables in order to perform regression analyses. Education was dichotomized into either having a university education or not (nearly 20% of my sample had a university education, the same proportion as in the general Ulaanbaatar population). Income is divided between those earning the average monthly income of 50,000 tugrogs (Mongolia National Statistics Office and United Nations Population Fund 2001)[2] and above, and those earning below that amount. In order to ascertain whether where one lives has an effect on access to social capital,

[2] Tugrog is the official currency of Mongolia. In 2002, approximately 1,100 tugrogs was equivalent to $1.

I also included residence location in the analyses, with 1 equal to living in the *ger* district and 0 equal to not living in this district. I performed a separate regression analysis on each occupation as the dependent variable, with all the independent, or predictor variables, entered at the same time.

In 5 of the 17 positions there is a significant relationship between the gender of the respondent and the occupation to which they have access. Women are significantly more likely to know doctors, nurses, and kiosk owners and less likely to know big business owners and taxicab drivers. Homophily may be at work here since doctors, nurses, and kiosk owners are more likely to be women, and big business owners and taxicab drivers are more likely to be men. However, other occupations such as teachers, librarians, and housecleaners are also largely occupied by women, and politicians are much more likely to be men than women— factors that appear to have little bearing on the respondents' access to them. The fact that women generally are more responsible for the healthcare of their families may also explain why women are more likely to know people in the health professions than are men. Their limited access to big business owners and greater access to the limited social capital of kiosk owners reflect the structural inequalities faced by women in Mongolian society.

These findings correspond with the division of labor between men and women in Mongolia. Women are more often found in occupations related to the helping professions, making up the majority of doctors, teachers, and nurses and half the number of lawyers (Anderson 1998; Robinson and Solongo 2000; United Nations Development Fund for Women 2002). In addition, three times as many women as men are classified in the highly educated professions, association professions, technicians, and clerks, suggesting that workers in government, banks, and foreign enterprises may also be predominantly women (Mongolia National Statistics Office and United Nations Population Fund 2001). Overall, however, women are less prevalent than men in decision-making positions in both the public and the private sectors (Robinson and Solongo 2000: 253). According to Robinson and Solongo, women have less influence in policy-making bodies and forums today than they had before transition. Currently, only 5 members of the 76 seat Parliament are women (Women in National Parliaments 2004). The traditional role of men as heads of households and in charge of household assets has also hampered women's access to credit needed to establish businesses in the private sector. As a result, women have concentrated their efforts at generating an income on the informal sector, mainly as owners of small street kiosks, where the requirements to establish small enterprises are considerably less than in the formal sector (Anderson 1998).

Level of education also influences who has access to people in these occupations. Respondents with a university education are more likely to know politicians, big business owners, lawyers, and government and bank workers. People occupying these positions are generally well educated. This may account for the fact that respondents who know people in these positions also have a university education, although this does not appear to be a factor for other occupations that also require a university education, such as doctors and teachers. In the case of these latter occupations, however, people will often have contact with these people through their familial roles, rather than through social ties.

Studies of former communist states have found evidence of growing class distinctions during transition based on wealth (Angelusz and Tardos 2001). Differences in access to occupations on the basis of income could be an indication that a similar process is underway in Ulaanbaatar. Respondents earning more than the average monthly wage in Ulaanbaatar (50,000 tugrogs) are more likely to know people in every occupation in the position generator, except for house-cleaners, than those earning less than this amount. This relationship is statistically significant in the case of knowing lawyers, teachers, librarians, small business owners, and government workers. This indicates a disparity based on income in respondents' access to people in the service professions; that is, lawyers, librarians, and teachers. In Ulaanbaatar, this suggests that poor people cannot afford to go to lawyers to help resolve legal disputes and do not use libraries. It also suggests that poor people have less contact with schools, indicating that they are seriously disadvantaged in their access to education. This supports concerns raised by educators that Mongolian families, especially poor families, are reluctant to send their children to school as they did during communist times. One reason given for this is that poor families are not able to afford the fees that most schools have to charge to make up for the government shortfall in funding schools. Another is the necessity for the children, especially boys, to work to earn money to support the family. As a result, a reverse gender gap has appeared where girls stay in school longer and make up the majority of students in universities (Lhagvasuren 2002). Not knowing owners of small businesses and government workers also indicates restricted access to resources that could help poor people improve their situation.

Perhaps a greater indication of the inequalities that have emerged in Ulaanbaatar society is the effect of living in the informal *ger* districts that surround the city. About 45–50 percent of Ulaanbaatar's residents live in these areas, consisting of people who have recently moved into the city from the countryside and those that have lived there for decades (Bat 2002). Many of the long-term residents wish to move into apartments in the city, but a shortage of available apartments combined with increasing costs has prevented them from making this shift. Disastrous winter storms afflicted Mongolia in 1999 and 2000, killing over three million head of livestock and resulting in many subsistence-level herders losing their entire herds and livelihoods. As a result, herder families moved to the urban centers, particularly Ulaanbaatar, in search of jobs. According to a local consultant, the population of Ulaanbaatar has grown by nearly 40 percent since 2000.[3] Most of these newcomers moved into the *ger* districts with few skills that suit them for urban employment. The *gers* have begun to creep up the low mountains that surround the city, consuming scarce natural resources as residents cut firewood, burn coal, and fetch water from the wells and rivers. While the city attempts to provide some services such as bus routes, electricity, and water, the districts do not have a sewer system, and few schools, banks, and health centers have been established

---

[3] Interview with L. Ariunaa, CEO of Intec Consulting, Ulaanbaatar, Mongolia, June 13, 2005.

to accommodate the large influx. The cost and length of time required to take the bus into the city may also be prohibitive for some. In addition, many are reluctant to leave their homes unattended, fearing that they will be robbed while they are away. People living in the *ger* districts, therefore, are triply disadvantaged—by their poverty, the lack of services and security in their areas, and the distance needed to travel to downtown Ulaanbaatar to access these services.

Living in the *ger* districts also affects access to social capital. The lack of access to politicians may represent the powerlessness of *ger* district residents, as politicians focus their attention on the demands of the wealthier city dwellers. The likelihood of *ger* residents to have no access to doctors, teachers, and bank workers reflects the lack of health, education, and financial services in the districts. Without these services, residents of *ger* districts are left out of the social and economic life of the city. Individuals' social capital will be increasingly restricted as a result, and the opportunities to improve their situations will be severely limited.

18.2. DIVERSITY OF SOCIAL RESOURCES

The position generator also measures diversity of social resources, that is, the number of different occupations to which a respondent has access. The more people one knows in different structural positions, the greater chance one has in acquiring new resources. Erickson's study of the security industry in Toronto demonstrated that people who occupied upper-level positions also had high network diversity (Erickson 2001a). People with diverse networks were able to transcend class divides more easily because of their association with people in different walks of life; they "have more varied cultural repertoires, which help them to build smooth working relationships with a wider variety of other people" (Erickson 154–5). Network diversity, Erickson found, was a prized resource that affected promotion to upper-level positions and also enabled people to associate with others in various structural positions that added to the diversity of their contacts.

In a national survey of social capital conducted in Canada in 2000, Erickson used a position generator that asked respondents to indicate not only who they knew in these occupations but also whether the people they knew were men or women (Erickson 2004). According to Erickson, men and women tend to occupy different positions in society—for example, women seek out occupations requiring more nurturance and people skills. They are also interested in different things—men tend to know more about automobile maintenance while women take more control of health matters. Consequently, ties to men and women may be developed to serve different purposes and therefore have different consequences for people. As Erickson points out, ties to men who have more powerful positions in the workplace may be more useful for getting jobs, while ties to women may have a greater impact on one's health and well-being. The findings from the Canadian study indicate that there are significant differences between the social

Table 18.3. Comparison of means between men and women and diversity of contacts

Respondent gender	Diversity of contacts with			
	Anyone	Men	Women	N
Female	6.75	2.81	3.94	147
Male	6.35	3.29	3.06	153
Significance level	ns	*	**	

Entries are means. Significance levels for comparison of male and female means.
ns = not significant.
* $p < .05$; ** $p < .01$.

networks of men and women. While both men and women tend to form relationships with people of the same gender, opportunities to add opposite sex ties to their networks occur for women when they enter the workforce, and for men when they marry and meet other people who care for children, who are mainly women. Erickson also found that living in the Atlantic region, one of the most economically depressed regions of Canada that has experienced little in-migration over the years, has had a significant effect on people's social capital. People living in this region have significantly higher levels of social capital than those living in other regions of the country. Erickson suggests that because of fewer opportunities for economic advancement they have "both the need and the capacity to build community networks of social support" (Erickson 2004: 40).

I followed a similar methodology to investigate the diversity of contacts of the respondents in my study. The respondents were asked if they knew anyone well enough to talk to in each of the occupations in the position generator and whether this person was a man or a woman. The figures in Table 18.3 represent the overall diversity of male and female respondents.

As Table 18.3 indicates, there was no significant difference in the number of contacts men and women had, with women knowing someone in nearly 7 of the 17 occupations, and men knowing people in just over 6 of the occupations. This is similar to Erickson's Canadian study where there was no significant difference between the social capital of men and women (Erickson 2004: 40), and Angelusz and Tardos' findings for Hungary in 1997 (Angelusz and Tardos 2001), but dissimilar to Taiwan, where men had higher social capital than women (Lin, Fu, and Hsung 2001).

As in the Canadian study, both male and female respondents in the Ulaanbaatar study are more likely to have contact with people of the same sex. Male respondents know a greater diversity of men than female respondents do, and female respondents know a greater diversity of women than male respondents do. However, in contrast to Erickson's study, the gap between the number of men known by both male and female respondents is small, about half an occupation; that is, male and female respondents know almost the same number of men. In Erickson's study, male respondents knew men in almost a whole occupation more than female respondents did. The gap between the number of women known by male and female respondents, however, is much larger in the Mongolian sample than in the Canadian sample. Female respondents know women in nearly one whole occupation more than did male respondents, while the gap is less than half an occupation in the Canadian sample. In comparison to Canadian women, therefore, the addition of same sex contacts adds more to the social capital of Mongolian women than it does for Mongolian men. In Canada, both men and women know a greater variety of men than women, while in Mongolia women know a greater variety of women. That is, while Mongolian men know nearly an equal number of men and women, Mongolian women tend to move in a world occupied largely by other women. The gap between the number of women known by female and male respondents is perhaps reflective of the traditional structure of Mongolian society where the spheres occupied by each gender are more distinct than in Western society. However, with the greater variety of resources available through other women, this is not necessarily a restricted social world.

18.3.   INFLUENCES ON DIVERSITY

I next investigated the factors that influenced access to the social capital of diversity for both male and female respondents. In order to ascertain the effects of life course events on access to social capital, I added age, employment, and marital status to the influence of gender, income, education, and residence location in Table 18.4. As 56 percent of my sample was aged 30 or under (compared to 42% of the Ulaanbaatar population), I made age a dummy variable with 30 and under equal to 1, and over 30 equal to 0. Employment was coded as 1 for employed, and 0 for unemployed, student, and "at home" (either retired or housewife). Marital status is also a dummy variable with married, divorced, separated, or widowed equal to 1, and single equal to 0.[4] Education, income, gender, and location are coded the same as in Table 18.2.

18.3.1.   Age and Marriage

As people age, they tend to be involved in more activities and therefore have the opportunity to meet people in many different spheres of life (Erickson 2004).Younger people who attend the same schools and universities have fewer

---

[4] It must be noted that in Ulaanbaatar very few people live alone. If they are not married they usually live with their family, either with their parents or, when they are older, with their siblings. After marriage, the couple may live with one or the other set of in-laws until they have their own children. A traditional practice for the youngest child is to live with the grandparents. This youngest child, in turn, is expected to look after the grandparents as they age. In my sample, only 5 of 306 respondents said that they lived alone, while in the 2000 Ulaanbaatar census, 5% of the population indicated that they lived alone (Mongolia National Statistics Office and United Nations Population Fund 2001).

Table 18.4. Multiple regressions on effect of age, education, employment, income, marriage, and residence location of respondents on diversity of contacts, by gender of respondents

Predictors	Male respondents: diversity of contacts with			Female respondents: diversity of contacts with		
	Anyone	Men	Women	Anyone	Men	Women
Age	−.31(−.04)	−.12 (−.03)	−.19 (−.05)	−.87 (−.13)	−.43 (−.11)	−.44 (−.11)
Education	1.25* (.15)	.60 (.12)	.64* (.15)	−.005 (−.001)	−.14 (−.03)	.14 (.03)
Employed	.72 (.11)	.39 (.09)	.33 (.09)	−1.08** (−.17)	−.28 (−.07)	−.80** (−.20)
Income >50,000 tugrogs	.89** (.23)	.73*** (.29)	.15 (.07)	1.07**** (.30)	.56*** (.26)	.51*** (.24)
Marital status	−.40 (−.06)	.22 (.56)	−.63^a (−.17)	.53 (.08)	.29 (.07)	.24 (.06)
Location	−1.31** (−.17)	−.46 (−.09)	−.86** (−.21)	−.26 (−.04)	−.06 (−.02)	−.19 (−.04)

Note: Values outside the parentheses are unstandardized multiple regression coefficients and values within the parentheses are standardized regression coefficients.

* $p < .10$; ** $p < .05$; *** $p < .01$; **** $p < .000$.

chances to meet people from outside their usual social circles. Midlife, however, is the most socially active period, when people meet others at work, through their children's schools and friends, and through participation in social and voluntary associations. This is the pattern that Erickson found in her Canadian study, where network diversity reached its peak in the respondents' forties. Work increased women's association with men, and married life and having children increased men's access to women. In Ulaanbaatar, age had no significant effect on diversity of contacts with either men or women. Also, in contrast to the Canadian study, men in Mongolia had a moderate tendency to not meet more women after marriage, but rather tended to have fewer women in their networks after marriage. This reflects the traditional nature of Mongolian society, where men have little involvement in raising children and are not necessarily likely to meet the mothers of their children's friends.

18.3.2. Education

The effects of a university education are slightly different for men and women. For women, this advantage did not affect their likelihood to have more diverse ties to men or other women. For male respondents, however, education had a moderately significant effect on the diversity of their networks with women. While women were able to add diverse contacts to their networks regardless of whether they had a university education, it is an important factor for men who seem to use their education to increase their networking opportunities, particularly for adding women to their networks. In the Canadian sample the situation was reversed, with higher education more significantly affecting women's chances of increasing the diversity of their contacts, while it was not as important a factor for men.

18.3.3. Employment and Income

In Ulaanbaatar, being employed has no significant effect on men's ability to increase their contacts with either men or women. In contrast, employment appears to have a negative impact on women's network diversity, particularly with other women. This finding seems to be counterintuitive—how can being employed reduce the chances of contact with other people? This may be due to the kinds of jobs that women have. In a poor country with inadequate safety nets such as Mongolia, there is little real unemployment. Almost everyone has to work if they want to survive. Many of these jobs are menial, involving long hours and little opportunity to meet others, particularly those in better occupations. The effect of income seems to support this view, since women earning more than the average income are significantly more likely to have larger networks, counteracting the negative impact of employment. That is, women employed in better jobs where they earn higher incomes are just as likely to increase the size of their networks as are men. While increased income improves women's contacts with both men and women, men do not add to the diversity of their contacts with women this way.

18.3.4. Location

In contrast to the Canadian study, where people living in the Atlantic region compensated for their relatively low economic status by building diverse social networks, respondents living in the poor *ger* district of Ulaanbaatar had lower social capital than respondents living in the city. People living close to schools, hospitals, and businesses in central Ulaanbaatar had an advantage for building diverse networks over those living in the peripheral *ger* districts. While it can be assumed that people living in the *ger* districts are generally disadvantaged, both because of the lack of health and educational resources as well as the difficult physical environment and distance from the city center, this is a problem mainly for men. Women, on the other hand, are not affected by location. This may be because women are more willing to travel to make contact with professionals who are important for the welfare of their families, such as doctors, nurses, and teachers. Men, however, may restrict themselves to the people they meet through their occupations and families and have little opportunity to expand their networks. While residence in the *ger* districts has a negative effect on network diversity for men, this is alleviated if they have a higher level of income and education.

18.4. DISCUSSION

When measured as diversity of contacts, men and women in Mongolia have similar levels of social capital. Level of income has the greatest effect on the diversity of contacts for both men and women, but men are additionally affected by where they live. If they live in the *ger* district their social capital overall and their diversity of contacts with women in particular are adversely affected. They are, however, somewhat more likely to include women in their networks if they have a university education. Education is the most important factor for gaining access to the highest status positions in the position generator as well. While level of income does not have a direct effect on access to these top positions, it is apparent in access to service professions such as teachers, librarians, and lawyers; that is, low-income people have less access to people in these positions, indicating a disparity based on income in access to educational and legal resources. Level of income is also important in gaining access to positions that may be helpful in getting started in small enterprises, such as big and small business owners. Employment is not a significant factor affecting the diversity of men's networks, but women have greater difficulty increasing the diversity of their networks when they are employed, particularly in low-paying jobs. Although the size of men's and women's networks is similar, there is a significant difference in the content of these networks—women have more contact with women than men, while men have very nearly the same number of men and women in their networks. Despite the fact that Ulaanbaatar is quickly being transformed into a modern market economy, there are indications from this study that the traditional delineation of men and women into separate spheres of activity persists. Women are more likely to include other women in their networks and men tend not to include women contacts, especially when they are married or live in the *ger* district. Women are also more likely to know people in female-dominated occupations such as doctors, nurses, and kiosk owners, whereas men have a slightly better chance of knowing big business owners and taxicab drivers, occupations generally populated by men.

While men and women seem to move in different spheres in Mongolia, this does not mean that they occupy unequal positions. Women tend to know more women in occupations generally populated by women, but they are not restricted from access to other useful positions as a result of their gender, particularly politicians, workers in foreign and domestic organizations, and small business owners. However, the kind of work that men and women do has a significant impact on their ability to increase their social capital. Women who work in low-paying jobs have a difficult time expanding their network of useful contacts because they are often working in isolation (sitting all day alone in small shops and kiosks, for instance) and have little spare time to get involved in other activities where they might meet people. Men who live in the *ger* district are also disadvantaged in their ability to expand their networks, perhaps for the same reason—working long hours at menial tasks that provide little opportunity to acquire new social resources that might lift them out of their impoverished state.

18.5. CONCLUSION

Despite 15 years of transition since the fall of communism and the adoption of market reform policies, Mongolia is still one of the poorest nations in the world. The percentage of people living below the poverty level has changed little from the 36 percent that was reported in 1994 (Rossabi 2005). Those that started out in an advantageous position have been able to profit from the new regime, but the poor who have neither the social and economic resources nor the opportunity to acquire them remain entrenched in the daily struggle just to survive. From an analysis of access to social capital through the position generator, it is possible to understand some of the constraints on Mongolian society that impede an individual's ability to transcend his or her economic status.

The lack of overlap between the lives of men and women may hamper the ability of both sexes to learn about jobs, since women are more prevalent than men in middle-management jobs and men tend to occupy decision-making positions. Also, despite high levels of education achieved by Mongolian women, the separation of the sexes into different spheres gives women little opportunity to move into top-level positions that are usually occupied by men. Voluntary organizations are still rare in Mongolia for people of low socioeconomic status [only 1% of my sample stated that they met people through social clubs or voluntary organizations (Johnson 2003)], although rotary clubs and a junior chamber of commerce, which tend to cater to the elite and rising professional class, have been established recently. Perhaps in time, with access to the social networking opportunities provided by these organizations, men and women will participate on a more equitable basis in decision-making positions.

The situation for people in lower economic positions, however, shows little possibility of improving without substantial economic progress. With the long working hours required to make a subsistence living, people have few opportunities to acquire new skills that could give them access to better jobs or to meet others in different occupations who could give them new ideas or loans to get started in more profitable enterprises. Residential segregation, which was not highly developed during the communist era, may further exacerbate the isolation of the poor from useful social resources. The increasing number of people moving into the capital city, the majority of whom are locating in the surrounding *ger* districts, also contributes to the entrenchment of poverty in Ulaanbaatar. The general lack of services in these peripheral areas—including indoor plumbing, water, and heating, as well as restricted access to health, educational, and financial services—makes everyday life a struggle. Since many of these newcomers are arriving from the countryside with only a knowledge of herding, there is a great need for training programs to equip them for urban employment.

The question asked at the beginning of this chapter was, to what extent does access to social capital reinforce existing inequalities or provide opportunities for overcoming them? While high levels of social capital at the outset of transition may have contributed to the ability of a few to take advantage of the new economic system and prosper, those who have been left behind have little chance to move beyond their impoverished state. Without training programs to prepare people for better jobs, good-quality services to improve their quality of life, and the availability of voluntary and service organizations that would give people the opportunity to meet and mingle with others in better social and economic positions, there is little hope for improvement in the situation of the poor.

19

Assessing Social Capital and Attainment Dynamics: Position Generator Applications in Hungary, 1987–2003

Róbert Angelusz and Róbert Tardos

19.1. A BRIEF INTRODUCTION

The present study has a double focus. It has the objective, in line with this volume, to present a review of the studies in Hungary applying the position generator approach. While methodologically oriented to a considerable extent, our review will also cover substantive issues related to the utility of social resources in certain aspects of attainment, with special regard to components of social capital most accessible by position generator techniques.

With a network-based conception of social capital, the chosen focus also implies a concentration on certain types of resources. That is, the focus will be on the capital-like character of network ties. This entails an emphasis on instrumental relationships in addition to expressive ones (and therefore emphasizing the choice of heterophilous rather than homophilous ones). It also stresses weak-tie resources above strong ties (extending the focus of study from core networks to wider acquaintanceship, from the micro- to the mesolevel relationships).[1]

---

[1] The distinction of the two dimensions above may not be self-evident. While homophilious + strong (bonding) and heterophilious + weak (linking or bridging) contacts are heavily emphasized in the literature, the less salient heterophilious + strong and homophilous + weak types get less attention. Patronage could be taken as an important example for the first one, manifesting itself through the machinery of interpersonal connections (kinship, local, and organizational ties) bonding people from different grades of the social hierarchy (see in this regard Flap 1991 for a wider range of settings, or Lomnitz and Sheingold 2004 for closer concerns). As to the other type, manifestations of macrogroup identity, class consciousness, and the like are characteristic cases, based on interactions of actors with similar status characteristics, typically related but through a longer chain (as to the important distinction of direct and indirect ties, see White 1992). For a set of dimensions of ties distinguished above, see Granovetter (1974), Blau (1977), Lin (1990), Burt (1992), Woolcock (1998), and Kadushin (2002) as outstanding sources.

The chosen scope of the present study on the "portfolio of ties"[2] is not meant to suggest that heterophilous and weak-type ties are the only significant ones. Methodologically speaking, our special emphasis does not imply that our account of the measurement of social resources, in general, will be restricted to position generator techniques exclusively. Just as in a search for a many-stranded approach, our general approach and multiple studies have used a multiple set of indicators of social capital (including methods closer to the core networks, like various techniques of name generator). Indices deriving from them will also be included in the analyses in order to widen the analytical terrain.

A further narrowing of our substantive focus stems from publishing considerations. While access to social capital gets at least as much focus in our work as its mobilization, findings for the former have been presented in a volume for a wider public of those interested in social network analysis (SNA) issues. This is less true for the latter concern. The present chapter will treat the topic of resource mobilization in more detail, while that of access will only be summarized. Our topic will have to do explicitly with stratification and structural concerns. Matters like inequality in access and use, capital conversion, or the consolidation of various resources will be dealt with throughout.

Our applications have taken place within the framework of research into cultural-interactional stratification in the early phase and political stratification in the recent phase. The moment of dynamics referred to in the title deserves a short mention. The fact that our applications of the position generator embrace a period of nearly two decades permits the implementation of a longitudinal strategy. In certain respects, the presence of a complete replication (as to the set of variables included) has facilitated carrying out dynamic analyses in a stricter sense. With the series of studies prior to and following the change of the system, temporal comparisons may imply particular substantive relevance.

19.2. THE USE OF THE POSITION GENERATOR TECHNIQUE IN HUNGARY[3]

19.2.1. Studies and Versions, 1987–2003

19.2.1.1. The Cultural-Interactional Stratification Project 1987–91

In designing the study of the cultural-interactional stratification of the Hungarian society in the middle of the 1980s, we were led by two ideas as the two

---

[2] To borrow the telling phrase by Wellman (1999).

[3] The studies to be reviewed were implemented under the aegis of our institutes, the Social Science Faculty (earlier Sociological Institute) of Eotvos Lorand University, Budapest; the Institute of Hungarian Public Opinion Research Institute, later the Research Group for Communication Studies of the Hungarian Academy of Sciences at ELTE University, Budapest. Grants from foundations like OKTKT, later OTKA (in the later stages T026033 and T043747) provided the financial support required for carrying out these surveys.

basic pillars: knowledge styles on the one hand and social network affiliations on the other. The latter attributes were built upon ego-centered measures, such as the Fischer–McAllister name generator instrument previously adopted by the German ZUMA (Mannheim) survey from 1986.[4] At the time, this seemed a natural option not the least because of the prevalence of this approach in the studies of the 1970s and early 1980s. Getting acquainted with the innovative position generator technique (Lin and Dumin 1986), which was of interest not only because of the network aspects of the project but because of the knowledge styles as well, occurred in time to permit its inclusion in the first wave of our survey in 1987. While our adoption basically followed the setup of the original instrument, our focus on the concrete occupations of the roster applied to not only the various levels of the social hierarchy but the different types of skills as well set our study apart. In fact, this latter consideration did not require a remarkable divergence from the original setup, as it already contained some diversity.

The second wave in 1988 yielded an opportunity not only for a repetition with some modification (an extension of the roster in the direction followed in later studies as well, plus a follow-up question on "closer" or "casual" acquaintance) but also for an application of the same set of occupations in some further aspects (such as career aspirations for the younger generation, interactive proximity, and perceived social distance). The replication of most items on the list provided a methodological opportunity for reliability estimates as well.

19.2.1.2. Replications in the 1990s

Two Omnibus surveys in 1997 and 1998 offered the opportunity to insert an SNA block with the objective of a replication in the wake of the change of system. The temporal vicinity and overall topical similarity of the two surveys yielded a possibility to merge the data of two national samples (of 1,000 and 800 respondents, respectively) resulting in a pooled sample sizable enough for detailed analyses. While the application of the position generator technique followed the line developed through the earlier Cultural-Interactional Stratification project (with a roster of 24 occupations, including some newer items from the market sphere such as entrepreneur and banker, due to the recent socioeconomic transformations), some new follow-up questions were included as well.

Along with a question on the range of acquaintances concerning specific occupations repeatedly used in our surveys, the 1997 version contained an additional one on the chance of getting support in case of need, while the 1998 version included one on greeting habits relative to the respective partners (the use of first names or some more formal alternative). Our subsequent application in 2000 used this latter version again.

---

[4] See McCallister and Fischer (1978) and Hoffmayer-Zlotnik, Schneid, and Mohler (1987).

19.2.1.3. The Four Village Case Study, 2000

In 2000, our studies on a larger plane were added to by a case study in four low-population villages (with populations below 400 in each). The substantive theme focused on civic participation (electoral and other types of behavior) and the role of contextual and social network influences with special regard to community-level social integration.

The special setting permitted a multilevel approach including, in addition to the regular individual approach, household and community-level indicators as well. Although a wider range of (rural and community-specific) indicators was also inserted, our previous measurement apparatus was again applied for outlining social network resources. Although the limited scope of this paper does not allow us to go into the details of these findings, it should be noted that with regard to our combined index of social resources again applied here, the nexus diversity index derived from the PG instrument had an especially high loading in all of the cases.

19.2.1.4. The Hungarian Political Stratification Project, 2003

A large-scale project on the Hungarian political stratification (based on a 3,000-person national sample compiled by several research institutes and survey organizations) was designed with a primary focus on the block-like segmentation of the political field, and the public at large in particular. The role of network patterns in this context emerged as a clear topic. In mapping the political character (such as the party homophily/heterophily) of interpersonal relationships, the ego-centered ng-technique (with a special subquestion in the block of attribute generators) yielded a solution. The partisan features of wider acquaintanceship presented, in turn, a somewhat more complicated problem, with regard to which a novel application of the position generator method was devised. We will discuss this in Section 19.4 in relation to possible extensions of the approach.

19.2.2. Specific Indicators and Composite Indexes

While it is of crucial importance how specific indicators of pg-instruments are selected in order to provide a fair representation of the positions on the dimension under study (most frequently those along the occupational prestige hierarchy), as a rule the main burden of analytical efficiency lies with composite indexes covering more general network characteristics. The classic apparatus of PG analyses (see Lin and Dumin 1986) highlights three indexes with similar emphasis: (*a*) range of accessibility to different hierarchical positions (to be expressed by the distance between highest and lowest accessed positions), (*b*) extensity of accessibility (as measured by the number of positions accessed), and (c) upper reachability (the prestige of the highest position accessed). Actually, the first two of these features both relate to the range or diversity of social resources. The third has to do with the quality, rather with the quantity, of resources; higher contacts are assumed to be more conducive to positive returns.

All of these measures can be backed by a number of logical arguments and empirical experiences. Our first elaborations of the PG battery applied each component of the three-piece set above. Later, however, only the second is related to extensity. Practical considerations (in particular, the lack of occupational prestige surveys in Hungary from 1988 onward) played a decisive part. But previous experience suggests a similar practice when the extensity indicator is itself presented as the most powerful, integrative component of the composite index, based on several features as outlined above.[5]

As examples from the international literature show, this is not a unique experience. We may refer to the Dutch study as documented in much detail by van der Gaag and Snijders (2003), with a large array of position generator measures even beyond those mentioned above. Out of seven in this order (plus a set of other variables derived from name and resource generator techniques) included in a factor analysis, it was the number of occupations accessed that exhibited the highest loading on the first component. Some distributional features pointed in a similar direction, such as the fairly high variance of this measure along with its good score on skew distribution, which was not quite the case with the other measures. Some of the Taiwanese and urban China findings also fit this pattern, though not in complete accordance (see Lin 2001b and Lin, Fu, and Hsung 2001). In both cases the index of extensity scored high again on the factor loading of various measures, though the range index (distance between highest and lowest status accesses) scored even higher. In the urban China case where the occupational PG measures were complemented by those based on political positions (party functions) of various levels, it was the number of such positions that again had the highest loading on the main component of these measures.

On the whole, one can observe strong relationships between various measures with all cases. Given their logical connectedness, this is no surprise. This stands for not only the relationship of upper reachability (highest prestige) with range (distance between highest and lowest status) but also extensity (total number) with both of them. The sheer multitude of various types of access, with other aspects also involved, is in a sense a guarantee of nexus diversity. While all these considerations may support the practice of reduction to the measure of extensity, we should note that it is not quite identical with the others. Some of our more detailed analyses, as in Section 3.3.2, suggest the relevance of other indices of the qualitative measure of upper reachability.

---

[5] Its loading was .88 on the first component at issue.

Table A.1 permits a closer observation of the particulars of the Hungarian versions of the position generator instrument. Besides specific details of the occupations included in the two main studies (at the end of the 1980s and the 1990s), the factor solutions in both cases help in assessing the consistency of these measures in a synchronic sense and a diachronic sense.[6] Changes between the two points of time, as shown in the left panel of the table, deserve some attention. It may be regarded as a symptom of the transformations that took place in this period that occupations inserted later relating to the market/business sphere contributed to a reorganization of the structural pattern, when they appeared centrally in the zone of highest loadings. The right-hand panel with its standardized solution presents, in turn, a high degree of temporal constancy in spite of all the changes in the workings of society. The rank order of (the remaining) occupations, an expression of their structural centrality, is almost unchanged during the decade. Changes by more than three places rarely occur, just as the concrete loadings stay at more or less the same levels.[7]

A relative homogeneity of the individual indicators/occupations is also found, with most loadings in the zone between .4 and .6. This consistency may be regarded as one more point that supports the composite index of extensity. As indicated by the (.99) correlations in the last row of the left panel, the scores of the first component and the number of positions accessed measure almost the same. When using the latter, we map practically the same latent dimension as expressed by the first components of the occupations included.

Some other characteristics of measurement accuracy could also be calculated, including some based on panel-like replication. The cross-sectional alpha reliability measure (based on the complete sets from 1987 and 1997–8) amounted to .83 in both cases, a quite acceptable level. The replication (with slight modifications) of the 1987 version in the second wave of the CIS project in 1988 yielded an additional opportunity for an intrasubjective reliability assessment. The passage of one year is short, as a rule, for a significant rearrangement of connections. Less than complete correlations may to some degree be ascribed to objective changes; probably a greater part may in fact go to the error component. The item-by-item correlations reached, in a rather homogenous way again, an intermediary level of .4–.5 with most occupations. When taking the composite scores of extensity of accessed position, the correlation already amounted to a solid .62. However, education of the respondents made a significant difference, from the .50 score of those with no high school education to the .68 of those with a college degree. When omitting the less consistent 20 percent of respondents, the overall coefficient grew to a considerable .80. Differences

---

[6] For such a comparison, a type of standardization was also implemented by reducing the two cases to a set of items applied in both cases.

[7] The one case with somewhat greater shift (that of local council employee) is in fact a notable one from a substantive point of view as well (having to do with changes of the political embeddedness of lower-level administration).

in education practically ceased to affect these figures among the remaining population.[8]

For some purposes, like mapping the general features of access to social capital, a composite index was constructed involving different sources of social network resources besides those approached by the position generator instrument. Core network range (through the use of our three-situation name generator), membership in formal or informal associations, along with less usual indicators like the intensity of sending and receiving Christmas cards or one's appearances in the role of best man/bridesmaid in weddings took place among the components. Taking advantage of factor analytic techniques in the procedure of construction, occupational nexus diversity (the PG-based index) came up with a high loading, a leading role in organizing the principal component as the basis for the composite index. Angelusz and Tardos (2001) give more details on this, including issues of the temporal comparability of the combined indexes for the two periods.

19.3. SUBSTANTIVE FINDINGS

19.3.1. Access to Social Resources: Changing Components of Inequality

Our contribution to the volume by Lin, Cook, and Burt (2001a)[9] focused mainly on this problem, with special regard to the shifts of the transformation period in Hungary. This issue will be treated more briefly here, summing up the salient findings of the topic in question.

The analyses on this topic aimed to reveal features of change and stability concerning access to social capital. As the dependent variable in the center of these analyses, the composite variable of social network resources presented above was confronted with several sets of independent variables. The results of a baseline model comprising the three basic variables of education, wealth, and political involvement,[10] which refer to three types of capital— cultural, economic, and political—indicated an unbroken influence of all of these resources in conditioning network resources. This picture of general stability was colored only by the feature of wealth, the effect of which substantially

---

[8] One further problem of validity has to do with self-aggrandizement tendencies on the part of some respondents concerning the skill of nexus formation. This deserves some attention even if we cannot really control for it. While this may somewhat exaggerate the respective figures, this bias is nevertheless mitigated by the circumstance that those very people as a rule tend to possess an above-average skill of networking (see Noelle-Neumann (1987 for the related topic of opinion leadership and the measure of PS-scale,), or in the context of social capital, see Dekker (2004)). Such a relationship between the index of accessed occupations and local opinion leadership has also been found by our Four Village Case Study (2000), and later by the Political Stratification Project (2003) as well.

[9] See Angelusz and Tardos (2001).

[10] Being the basis of a LISREL type g structural equation procedure in the study above.

increased during the decade between the investigations.[11] While cultural and political resources kept their role in shaping social embeddedness, economic resources have joined them in this following the first waves of the transformation process. More than before, access to ties has become a matter of material possession.

Further analyses targeted a more differentiated approach of access to social ties, as permitted by the distinct use of indicators based on the pg- and ng-measures. Besides this bifurcation of the dependent variables, a wider set of independent variables was also involved with regard to inequality, out of the status indicators mentioned above—(urban/rural) locality and the demographic attributes of sex and age, as presented in Table A.2.[12]

This more detailed picture confirms the importance of status variables, education, and wealth in conditioning inequality of network resources. Their influence even grew on the whole in comparison with demographic variables. As an interesting difference between the network resources of the meso and the microlevels, education proved decisive concerning the former, while wealth influenced the latter types. The salience of education with regard to occupational nexus diversity follows to an extent from its direct relationship with one's location in the occupational prestige hierarchy. Job market developments in the decade of economic transformation, however, have added to the role of this status attribute. This has to do with the differential exposure to unemployment or active-age retirement, conditions that badly deteriorate network resources, according to further findings. On the other side, the increased role of wealth with regard to core network resources may look interesting, even surprising—possibly due to the occurrence (and perhaps increasing presence) of instrumental elements in the case of strong ties as well.

Aspects of sex and age are also worthy of attention. While female handicap with regard to nexus diversity has been a repeated finding in the literature (see

---

[11] A note should be made here concerning causality of relationships between the variables involved. While we have introduced wealth in this context as a predictor, in a following section we shall return to the role of social resources in conditioning outcomes like earnings or income. While mutual influences and intertwined mechanisms do actually exist in these respects, it is in order to refer to the distinction between stock and flow components of economic resources. Wealth, belonging to the former ones as a long-range feature going back to family background, may be considered on the whole as one of the antecedent variables. Flow-like components like earnings or income may be located, even if not quite unambiguously, among the outcome variables relative to social resources (which is a common practice in the relevant literature on the status-attainment aspects of social resources).

[12] Similar to subsequent analyses, the categorical regression analysis technique optimal scaling has been applied as a practical way of handling a spectrum of variables with different scale levels, among them nominal ones as well. Besides the usually applied standardized coefficient among others, this procedure also presents "importance" values for a comparison of the role of the variables included. In fact, it is a measure not automatically deducible from the beta-coefficients, but a more complex one based on indirect effects beside direct ones. To assess the role of various indicators one should take account of both measures. As it also occurs with several of the tables to be presented, it is not rare that variables with significant beta-coefficients will turn out with negligible importance values, indicating a virtual element of their effects in the whole set of relationships.

e.g. Lin 2001*b*), Hungarian data have shown the narrowing of this gap. Also, the traditional pattern of age-related patterns has changed. The traditional differences (a greater number of close ties among the youth, more diverse occupational contacts among the older age groups) have diminished; additionally, the sign of relationship has even changed in the latter case. Both tendencies will be illuminated with more detail in later sections concerning the mobilization of social resources.

19.3.2. Mobilization of Social Capital—Material Returns to Social Resources

An early attempt in this direction based on the CIS project (Angelusz and Tardos 1991) focused on the influence of weak and strong ties on some job characteristics and personal earnings in general.[13] Weak-tie related network components presented some relationship with the quality of the workplace, which was not the case with strong-related ones, a fact in accordance with the mainstream literature.[14] However, this could not be heavily emphasized regarding the moderate statistical significance and the restrictions of the design.

Results were more solid with regard to earnings. Matters of synchronicity are less of a problem here, given the fact that pecuniary rewards are influenced by a wider array of factors, among them social resources, often in an indirect way. Our findings, pointing to a similar conclusion, were also statistically more significant in this respect. Based on the inclusion of the later wave from 1997 to 1998, a reanalysis of data was made highlighting the two measures of nexus diversity and core ties range in a temporal comparison. For some analyses, household total income, a material indicator of a different type, was also included in addition to personal earnings. As to the statistical procedures, the optimal scaling regression procedure, which is also able[15] to handle categorical scale attributes, was applied for the set of sociodemographic variables included in our earlier analyses (Table 19.1).

In both respects, an overall change in the setup and size of explanations is accompanied by the growth of (absolute and relative) influence of social resources. The decrease in explanations by the included variables can be attributed in the first place to a decline of demographic (especially gender) effects, which we will return to in more detail with later analyses. While this trend is less emphasized by the

---

[13] The questionnaire of the 1987 survey included quite a detailed set of questions as far as job characteristics were concerned. No questions were directly related to job search at the time of moving to one's position occupied during the survey.

[14] Beginning with Granovetter (1974).

[15] Income data were aggregated into five categories (as additional runnings with more detailed versions proved, overall results are moderately affected by the degree of aggregation. More detailed analyses, those preformed by filtering procedures, for example, are, however, more fragile in case of a highly detailed income clasification. Those not possessing personal income of their own (those with only a symbolic amount) were excluded from these analyses.

Table 19.1. Predictors of material attainment—changes in the relative role of social resources from 1987 to 1998

	Personal earnings				Family income			
	1987		1997–8		1987		1997–8	
	β	Imp.	β	Imp.	β	Imp.	β	Imp.
Nexus diversity (PG access to occupations)	.08	.05	.11	.10	.10	.08	.13	.13
Core ties range (NG-number of persons)	(.03)	.01	.09	.05	.09	.08	.13	.16
Education	.27	.28	.35	.52	.20	.32	.27	.49
Locality (rural: +)	−.17	.09	−.09	.06	−.09	.05	−.06	.03
Sex (female: +)	−.41	.43	−.26	.25	−.04	.02	−.06	.02
Age	−.20	.15	.08	.02	−.28	.45	−.12	.13
R^2	.40		.28		.27		.20	
N	2,471		1,295		2,521		1,504	

Note: Imp.: Importance; NG: Name generator; PG: Position generator. Categorical regression analysis—optimal scaling; β-coefficients and importance values.

Dependent variables: EARNING5 and FAMINC5 (quintiles).

literature on income distribution in Hungary, our results are in line with a general consensus concerning the increased role of education and vertical status components related to it.[16] Even if the growth of inequalities in income[17] is only partially mirrored by the survey data,[18] the increase of the underlying (educational) status effects manifests itself in both regards.

Again, the role of education (and concomitant job) status will be highlighted more sharply by subsequent specific analyses on population segments based on this attribute. These have to do with the role of social resources in an attempt to approach the mechanisms related to their mobilization for material attainments.

Occupational nexus diversity is effective in both respects of material attainment, while the influence of core ties range is more or less restricted to the household (or family) aspect. Change of time was not without implications, however, expressed in a parallel growth of significance of both kinds of ties. This development deserves further attention. The increased significance of broader nexus diversity is easy to interpret in the light of the expansion of markets and the need [of] for up-to-date

[16] See Bukodi, Harcsa, and Vukovich (2004) and Kolosi and Róbert (2004).

[17] See Bukodi, Harcsa, and Vukovich (2004) and Tóth (2004).

[18] The emergence of (partly latent) high-digit incomes has also resulted in an increased difficulty of reaching this higher zone of material attainments by survey facilities. As this practice is more likely with higher-status respondents, this logically reduces explanations concerning status attributes like education or wealth.

information on jobs, as well as goods and capital investments. The growing importance of core ties needs more explanation, however. Even in the respects just mentioned, kinship or local bonds, paternalistic ties may be of help in taking advantage of chances frequently not open to a wider public. "Bonding social capital" could also be of importance, not only in a sense of (family/kinship) shelter but also as an important inside resource of rearranging human and physical assets in coping strategies. This may be the case for a large segment of the population during times of material hardship, such as the peak of unemployment throughout the early and middle 1990s, the hardest years of the transformation period. This should also be taken into account when observing the growing influence of core bonds concerning household income, even though nexus diversity is of significance in this respect as well.

That these distinct types of ties both have their roles is documented when clustering the positions on the two dimensions in a simple fourfold way: high on both; high on nexus diversity (and low on core ties range); high on core bonds (and not high on the other dimension); and last, low on both (see Table A.1 for these clusters and their relationships with earnings and income). While those better off on one or the other dimension turn out with some relative advantage as expected for the given aspects (that is, nexus diversity for personal earnings and core ties range for family income), this lead grows significantly for those scoring high on both dimensions. What is true on the one hand for the resource rich, also stands, with a different sign, for the resource poor: being deprived of both of these social resources implies a considerable lag on both aspects of material attainment.[19]

19.3.3. Approaches to the Differential Utility of Social Resources

19.3.3.1. *Partial Analyses for Certain Groups by Filtered Models*

The mechanisms related to the mobilization of social capital, however, get more transparent when specifying the effects for distinct population segments. It has been a lasting concern in the literature whether the advantages related to social resources in such respects vary among social strata (and if so, how); findings have not been unanimous in this respect. Continuing with our analyses from this specific angle, several filtered models have been run (for education, age, and gender categories) in order to localize the most salient effects for both points of time. Out of the above set of our dependent variables, our analyses were this time restricted to personal earnings as the most direct aspect of material attainment. Among the variables included, the groups of lower and higher educational status (aggregated into two categories for this analysis) come closest to the above considerations.

---

[19] The differences in question remain significant if (by means of an ANOVA-procedure) we control for the effect of the sociodemographic variables included with our regression analyses as well.

Table 19.2. Predictors of personal earnings by distinct educational categories, 1987 and 1997–8

	1987				1997–8			
	Up to vocational school		High school, college		Up to vocational school		High school, college	
	β	Imp.	β	Imp.	β	Imp.	β	Imp.
Nexus diversity (PG)	.07	.04	.11	.06	.09	.09	.20	.24
Core ties range (NG)	.09	.05	.12	.03	.13	.10	.10	.05
Locality (rural: +)	−.18	.06	−.15	.08	−.13	.09	−.10	.05
Sex (female: +)	−.46	.55	−.35	.42	−.34	.70	−.24	.38
Age	−.33	.30	.36	.42	−.05	.03	.22	.28
R^2		.40		.35		.16		.18
N		1,671		890		778		516

Note: Imp.: Importance; NG: Name generator; PG: Position generator. Categorical regression analysis—optimal scaling; β-coefficients and importance values.
Dependent variable: EARNING5 (quintiles).

While the pattern was less clear-cut for the earlier period, it became more transparent for the 1990s. The overall increase in influence of social resources took place in a differentiated way with regard to various educational levels and types of resources. Among the changed circumstances, nexus diversity definitely proves effective for the higher status level, while the utility of core ties range tends to be more salient for those on the lower rungs (Table 19.2). The latter finding is in accordance with the considerations above on the mobilization of family and kinship ties in the framework of coping strategies among those most hard hit by material losses during crisis periods. (We may note that the Hungarian case is similar to the general tendencies with unemployment, but in a broader sense underemployment, being significantly higher for the uneducated strata.) Nexus diversity, on the other hand, is less obviously effective at the higher status level—on a theoretical plane, opposite arguments suggesting the utility of contacts running upward from below may be regarded as just as plausible. That we still have to do with the case as outlined, stands for the benefits of accumulated advantages and the existence of certain social boundaries, to which we will return in a later section (19.3.3.2), with more implications.

Filtered analyses were also carried out for demographic groups. As we can see, results for the population at large indicated some decline in their effects, and it seemed of interest to continue the specification of resource mobilization along these lines. As Table 19.3 shows, males and those from the middle or older (active) age groups formerly exhibited the largest resource effects, more so with regard to nexus diversity. In general, this was in accordance with traditional gender patterns

Table 19.3. Predictors of personal earnings by distinct sex and age categories, 1987 and 1997–8

	Sex								Age							
	1987				1997–8				1987				1997–8			
	Male		Female		Male		Female		Below 44		Above 45		Below 44		Above 45	
	β	Imp.	β	Imp.	β	Imp.	β	Imp.	β	Imp.	β	Imp.	β	Imp.	β	Imp.
Nexus diversity (PG)	.13	.10	.07	.04	.11	.11	.17	.19	(−.02)	.00	.11	.07	.22	.26	−.07	.00
Core ties range (NG)	.08	.07	.08	.05	.10	.08	.13	.10	.07	.03	.12	.07	(.04)	.03	.15	.08
Education	.27	.41	.44	.66	.35	.65	.37	.64	.21	.17	.41	.48	.26	.29	.45	.66
Locality (rural: +)	−.13	.09	−.18	.18	−.13	.09	−.18	.18	−.15	.10	−.16	.09	−.08	.03	−.11	.09
Sex (female: +)	—	—	—	—	—	—	—	—	−.46	.70	−.35	.29	−.32	.40	−.24	.17
Age	−.25	.33	.21	.07	(.04)	.01	.11	.04	—	—	—	—	—	—	—	—
R²	.30		.31		.23		.25		.29		.47		.18		.35	
N	1,189		1,331		636		790		1,356		1,190		596		796	

Note: Imp.: Importance; NG: Name generator; PG: Position generator. Categorical regression analysis—optimal scaling; β-coefficients and importance values.
Dependent variable: EARNING5 (quintiles).

of breadwinner roles and promotion chances on the one hand, and with the social returns on age-related career experiences on the other.

The situation changed significantly with the transition, particularly regarding the influence of nexus diversity (PG). Now the emphasis of gains from resources shifted to females and the younger age group. The latter change may be related to changes of positions in the labor market. In the wake of a large-scale restructuring of workplaces (with a significant downsizing of traditional industrial branches and most of the agricultural production partially compensated by new service jobs), labor market chances drastically narrowed for older age groups, leading to a large portion of males around the age of 50 dropping out of the workforce, mostly through some kind of early retirement. Younger cohorts, especially those entering the job market in the 1990s, could capitalize substantially on new service openings such as the banking sphere, real estate business, tourism, and so on. Again, it was this younger generation in the first place who best matched the labor force preferences of private firms. It was these years of the transformation period that witnessed the conspicuous emergence of a class of "yuppies" in the wake of all this with regard to career and consumption patterns as well. Keeping these developments in mind, it is no wonder that these age groups, as proven by the respective analyses' data, became the most efficient in converting weak-tie social resources to material gains. Taking the term social capital in a stricter sense (with a view to capitalizing on advantageous social contacts), the population segment in question may be regarded as an important case for its increased role in the terrain of attainments.

The case may be somewhat, although not completely, different with regard to sex. The increased resource efficiency revealed among females should be treated from several angles. Classical observations like those by Jahoda, Lazarsfeld, and Zeisel (1975) [1933], or Elder (1974) from the era of the Great Depression pointed out the special difficulties faced by males dropping out of the labor force during crisis periods in accommodating to their changed circumstances, and the tendency to replace their earning capacity by females through rearranging household capacities or taking advantage of new niches in the local job market. While this may have been the case during the years under study in Hungary as well, and the growth of strong-tie resource efficiency among females in the first place proves that in the respective findings, the case is even stronger with regard to nexus diversity, which calls for another line of interpretation. A filter combining sex and age categories (as shown in Table A.4) may take us closer to this, suggesting a tendency not far from the one related to the generation shift. By 1997–8, the group of younger females clearly experienced the largest gain from nexus diversity (a finding with no antecedent whatsoever, according to the earlier data), suggesting again the inclusion of job market considerations introduced above for the younger cohorts in general. The large increase in level of education, especially for the respective female age groups, and the concomitant increase in career aspirations is a further point of relevance, hand in hand with a change in consumption patterns and a new female image cultivated by the global symbolic environment, evidenced by the changes in the media scene in Hungary by the second half of the 1990s.

19.3.3.2. *Specifying the Content of Nexus Diversity by Its Decomposition*

Mapping Social Milieus through the Position Generator

Throughout this study, the indicator nexus diversity based on the extensity of occupational contacts has been in the foreground of our analyses. Among others, an important justification for this practice is the close correlation of the given index with the (unrotated) principal component of the whole roster, accompanied by its good fit with the whole set of basic indicators (the occupations included). That related mechanisms may vary among various populations segments depending on the utility of certain contacts has been suggested by the previous filtering procedures themselves. The character of this difference in efficiency (the effect of nexus diversity being larger among higher than lower strata) calls for further scrutiny.

The procedure of decomposition introduced here follows, to a certain degree, the line of applying the technique of index construction based on principal component analysis. But the focus changes this time, with differentiation of types of contacts moving to the foreground in place of coherence. Outlining various facets of the occupational scale may be conceived as mapping social milieus in their environment (Table 19.4). This approach is in accordance with the notion of diversity having to do with inequality and heterogeneity (or, in terms of the occupational scales, status grades, and horizontal types) at the same time.[20] Turning to the methodological aspect, the procedure in question here includes the rotated solution of factor analysis (as compared to the unrotated one of the previous case).

The target of our first attempt at such an approach (see Angelusz and Tardos 2000) was basically a substantive one having to do with an aspect of cultural-interaction stratification newly raised in our studies. Addressing the problem of changing everyday greeting habits with the use of the first name replacing more formal, traditional alternatives, a relatively simple typology of social milieus proved a plausible option by applying the PG roster of occupational categories. The five types of occupational environments outlined this way could well be interpreted in the light of broader interaction patterns among social strata, and also in accordance with recent research on stratification in Hungary, and perhaps on a larger plane as well.[21]

---

[20] When making reference to the structural parameters by Peter Blau, it should also be noted that in some instances he used this term in a more specific sense, such as status diversity referring to the degree of differentiation of a gradually ordered group-like variable close to inequality and heterogeneity at the same time (see Blau and Schwartz 1984).

[21] The appearance of the horizontal distinction between managers/professionals and cultural intelligentsia on the upper levels is a trait that reminds us of the one outlined by Bourdieu (1979) for the

Table 19.4. Social milieus mapped by patterns of accessed occupations, 1997–8

	Components				
	1	2	3	4	5
	Managers/ professionals	Public sphere/ cultural intelligentsia	Market/ service intermediary	Workers/ urban manual	Rural/ agricultural manual
Engineer	.52				
Entrepreneur	.47			.37	
Manager/director	.47				
High school teacher	.45				
Accountant	.44		.35		
Lawyer	.42				
Actor/actress		.55			
Journalist		.54			
Scientist		.48			
Politician		.47			
Physician		.41			
Banker					
Boutique owner			.56		
Businessman			.54		
Guard			.54		
Waiter/waitress			.37		
Skilled worker				.56	
Factory worker				.52	
Unskilled worker				.49	.45
Driver				.48	
Farmer					.52
Local council employee					.46
Sales person					.39
Railroad worker					
Eigenvalue	6.3	2.1	1.73	1.65	1.41
Explained %	23.6	6.0	22.6	29.5	35.4

Note: Factor analysis, ULS-extraction, equamax rotation; factor loadings included over .35.

It is helpful to devote attention to these types in some detail. The first two correspond to two factions of the (mostly college educated) upper strata. The one with the highest eigenvalue, indicating a kind of positional centrality, which we label "managers/professionals", is a segment at the top of society traditionally linked with high prestige. It includes occupations like engineers, managers/directors, high school teachers, lawyers, and, more recently, a new guard of entrepreneurs.

The next grouping/milieu, called "public sphere/cultural intelligentsia". contains professions related to the social circle of creative cultural production on

French scene on the basis of the distinction of material and cultural (and to a certain degree, social) capitals.

one side and close to the high-profile public arenas on the other. Some of these professions (like actors/actresses, or more generally, artists) embody this double character themselves; others (like scientists, physicians, politicians, or journalists) are closer to this or that side, belonging to either circle of celebrities.

As shown by Table A.5, when the sociodemographic composition of these two groupings is delineated, the first, while somewhat better situated on both status dimensions on the whole, is significantly better off concerning wealth, while the latter is well above the average with regard to education, and much less so concerning material possession. Also, the latter is more of an urban group than the first. In a way, it resembles a "Bohemian" milieu, in contrast with the more "serious" character of the former set.

The third component, "market/service intermediary", is a more heterogeneous grouping. It comprises occupations from various status levels around the middle zone. Businessmen and boutique owners (an emerging domain of small proprietors) belong to it along with the lower situated service positions of waiters and guards (the latter again a recently emerging branch, resulting from security needs of private firms). Although mixed, it exhibits certain coherence in matters of public encounters, interaction, and consumption habits (we refer to the now globally ubiquitous milieu of plazas).

The last two components, those of the "workers/urban manual" and "rural/ agricultural", are simpler in terms of traditional social categories. They constitute the lower middle and lower segments of the ladder. The former, with various industrial and transportation worker categories, embodies an urban (even if not metropolitan) working-class environment, while the latter is marked by farmers and unskilled workers as well as lower level municipal clerks and sales workers, presents itself as a typically rural milieu, strongly confirmed by the outstanding role of locality among the predictors.

While the concrete order of these components as produced by the technique applied may contain some element of chance, practically it corresponds to positions in the social hierarchy. Table 19.5 provides a picture of this hierarchical positioning with scores of broader occupational categories on the various components.

The findings are in accordance with the experiences of the Hungarian social scene that emerged after the change of system. While the picture presented is a general correspondence between hierarchical positions and the extent of nexus, some specific features also stand out as far as involvement in certain milieus is concerned. Among the categories distinguished by the classification applied, it is the higher level executives, whose contacts are the most comprehensive, who embrace practically the entire social range. It is worth noting that they exhibit the highest (relative) score with regard to the milieu of public sphere. In an important development of the last few years, the world of media celebrities has been inhabited more and more, by not only politicians of the highest level but also "stars" of the business world. A conspicuous manifestation of this is the annual Media Boot, which brings together leading representatives of the political and business worlds with media celebrities.

Table 19.5. Mean scores of broad occupational categories on the five components/ connectedness with milieu-types, 1997–8

	Components				
	1	2	3	4	5
	Managers/ professionals	Public sphere/ cultural intelligentsia	Market/ service intermediary Milieus	Workers/ urban manual	Rural/ agricultural manual
Executives (n = 43)	.55	.70	.30	.16	.05
Professionals (nonmanagerial) (n = 112)	.47	.45	.24	−.01	−.06
Nonmanual (with no college) (n = 181)	.40	.11	.36	.02	−.13
Self-employed (n = 93)	.48	.21	.55	.02	.04
Skilled workers (n = 161)	.02	−.17	.18	.36	.01
Unskilled manual (n = 93)	−.24	−.23	.03	.16	.07
Retired (n = 654)	−.21	−.05	−.32	−.18	.02

Note: Factor scores +1 to −1.

Closing with the category of self-employed (that understandably stands out with regard to the market/service intermediary milieu but scores relatively high on the first two as well), the zone of nonmanual and proprietor strata presents some break relative to that comprising the two manual categories. The dense contacts of the latter remain primarily in the frame of the respective zone, apart from some interaction of the skilled with representatives of the intermediary milieu. The asymmetric relationship among this lower grouping also deserves attention, with intensive ties in only one direction (i.e. toward the milieu of urban manuals), while the lower rural milieu remains more or less ignored (even by the unskilled category that is in fact closest to it). This finding suggests the existence of some cultural-interactional closure even among levels within this lower zone.

The last two rows of the table including nonactive categories shed more light on the tendencies related to age and cohorts. Retirement (to a certain degree independently from one's earlier status) entails certain loss of contacts in general. The data related to students, in turn, indicate a growing distance of the emerging young elite from the milieu of lower strata (compared with the corresponding ones related to their "predecessors" in the first two rows of the table).[22]

---

[22] While this model is of interest on its own, it could be extended toward further nuances. Clustering the various dimensions in order to outline more complex configurations would be an obvious line. But it would also be possible to categorize broad occupational categories accordingly, and analyze the interaction patterns between these groupings on the basis of mutual position generator references. In a way, this could yield a plausible way to outline latent "macronetworks" of social interaction.

Table 19.6. Predictors of personal earning—modeling decomposed nexus diversity by total population and broad educational categories, 1997–8

	Total sample		Education			
			Up to vocational school		High school and above	
	β	Imp.	β	Imp.	β	Imp.
Component 1. Connectedness to managers/professionals (PG)	.13	.12	.10	.07	.20	.18
Component 2. Public sphere/cultural intelligentsia (PG)	(.03)	.02	.03	.00	.09	.07
Component 3. Market/service intermediary (PG)	.12	.07	.11	.07	.12	.05
Component 4. Workers/urban manual (PG)	.05	.00	.12	.09	−.13	.02
Component 5. Rural/agricultural manual (PG)	−.09	.02	−.17	.09	.08	.04
Core ties range (NG)	.09	.05	.11	.06	.07	.03
Education	.32	.44	—	—	—	—
Locality (rural: +)	−.05	.03	−.07	.04	−.05	.02
Sex (female: +)	−.27	.24	−.32	.56	−.30	.38
Age	.11	.03	.11	.00	−.20	.22
R^2	.29		.18		.22	
N	1,358		830		528	

Note: Imp.: Importance; NG: Name generator; PG: Position generator. Categorical regression analysis—optimal scaling; β-coefficients and importance values.

Dependent variable: EARNING5 (quintiles).

Differentiation in the Value of Facets of Nexus Diversity

Having made the distinction between the various components, our earlier question can now be answered more fully: Are the gains deriving from contacts with various groupings more or less even or differential, and how does this diverge (or not) with regard to various strata?

By using scores on the various dimensions above and putting them in place of the global count of accessed occupations while keeping other variables unchanged, with personal earnings among them as a dependent variable, then by using broad educational categories as filtering criterion in an extra model, Table 19.6 has been outlined.

The first observation refers to results for the total population, with an eye to the additional information as well. It is the access to the first and third milieus (with more or less economically oriented groupings) that is universally effective in conditioning an instrumental gain like higher earnings. The more detailed models add to this. More educated strata already profit from meeting those from the public/cultural sphere. Lower status earners may also gain from a broader connection with people of the urban working milieu (on the whole, their peers), but much less so (one can even find a negative sign) with regard to representatives of the most traditional social scene (the last component). The higher educated ones profit from contacts of more or less similar levels only, still including the intermediary service milieu (low importance values for both manual components indicate a lack of significance). A substantive implication suggests the "diminishing marginal utility" of nexus diversity depending on the location of the contacted milieus in the social hierarchy.[23] Just as those ranked higher tend to be more efficient, at least in recent Hungary, in making use of nexus resources, access to more prestigious milieus tends to produce more material gain. It is such relationships in the first place, rather than less "convertible" ones, with which resources embedded in network ties tend to work in a capital-like fashion, in a strict sense of the term "social capital".[24]

Other issues of interest (e.g. mental health or esteem) may lead to different results.

19.4. CONCLUSIONS AND A VIEW TO POSSIBLE EXTENSIONS

Focusing on aspects of stratification and resource mobilization concerning substantive topics, our findings suggest a differentiated picture of the relationship of social capital and the extent of inequalities in Hungary during the period of societal transformation. While our previous analyses concerning access to resources pointed to an increased manifestation of the "strength of positions", with a salient appearance of wealth in conditioning the range of contacts along with the

---

[23] One may even speak of a "negative utility" with regard to being attached to some lower-status milieus (see the respective signs with both the upper and the lower educational segments). The nonhomogeneous character of the utility of contacts with various occupational environments may explain that the total explanation of personal earnings increases by the application of the decomposed version with all the three models contained by the table (with the greatest jump from $R^2 = .18$ to $.22$ in the case of the higher educational group exhibiting three significant independent effects out of the five facets). The juncture of the two effects (members of higher status group having access to more prestigious contacts) results even in the further finding, according to the 1997–98 data that included in the model the index of contacts with the managerial/professional milieu alone (and excluding the four more facets). This leads to a higher R^2 (.21) than the application of the basic index of nexus diversity. A methodological lesson for further studies may suggest the increased use of the measure of upper reachability among those distinguished by Lin (2001b) alongside with those of extensity and heterogeneity (a claim also requiring the availability of up-to-date occupational prestige scores, which is not the case with regard to Hungary in the recent decades). Similar recent findings of detailed analysis on a sample of the Dutch population (Van der Gaag and Snijders 2003) by the use of various position generator measures also point to such a line.

[24] The two tendencies certainly have to do with the propositions concerning social capital (as explained in the most exhaustive manner by Lin 2001b), even if the coincidence is not complete. The one concerning higher efficiency by better resources can be regarded as a case of extension of the "Strength-of-Position" Proposition toward the aspect of mobilization besides access to resources, while the one concerning the greater value of more prestigious milieus can be conceived as a case for specifying the domain of the "Social-Capital" Proposition.

continuing influence of cultural and political resources, the newer analyses with regard to the mobilization of resources produce more varied inferences. While the increase in the influence of nexus diversity on the amount of income in itself may imply different implications in the given respect, the results of filtered and decomposed analyses may, again, be regarded as cases for mechanisms of inequality. The greater utility of contacts on the part of those with more accumulated resources on the one hand and the greater value of access to higher milieus on the other (by all probabilities not unrelated to each other) may be considered as further examples of a kind of Mertonian "Matthew effect". This is the case especially in circumstances of rapid change, evaluating up-to-date information, "tips" of new vacancies, promising applications, fruitful investment, and so on (and depreciating "outdated" contacts, ties with less prestigious milieus in the same order). While this may certainly hold, further findings imply some cross-cutting, or even contrary effects. Returning to the results concerning demographic factors, the earnings gain of social capital among the younger generation may be regarded as a development more or less unaffected by traditional lines of social hierarchy (though it may entail some other type of inequality, this time based on the chance of activity).

Should the overall balance tend toward the case of unequal chances, we should keep in mind that by focusing on earnings as our target variable we have picked an explicitly instrumental aspect of the mobilization of social resources. That the outcome may be different with regard to other, more expressive aspects (such as mental health or local prestige) is proven by a number of studies in the literature, and by our newer approaches as well.[25] This statement has relevance from a methodological point of view also. Our analyses have proven the usefulness of the approach of the position generator when focusing on access to social capital with regard to mobilization of resources, and this holds especially true for material aspects during the later phase of our studies after the change of system. For some segments of the population, the variable related to it has proven a particularly influential one in determining earnings. While this has justified the use of filtered and decomposed analyses for specific strata, especially contacts with specific milieus,[26] it is advisable to take note of domains with more and less relevance for aspects of social capital covered by the position generator approach. From an analytical point of view, it proves useful to include variables of social resources only partially (or not) covered by the latter technique, such as those having to do with one's core network concerning even explicitly instrumental aspects.[27] It is

---

[25] Although it deserves attention according to findings of the above-mentioned rural case study, nexus diversity tended to correlate with mental health, while the results for core ties range proved less unanimous in this regard.

[26] As noted above, these analyses, among others, have also pointed to the need for the differentiated use of various measures of social resources depending on specific circumstances, cross-cultural and temporal differences, and so on (see also Lin 2001b for such a consideration).

[27] It should be noted that an important extension of the technique for generating more specific data on concrete persons is the representatives of contacts with certain occupations (an approach

more useful with regard to social resources being closer to expressive aspects such as the examples mentioned above.

However, the approach of the position generator itself implies a considerable potential for further extensions. The first component of the expression, position, has an inherent connotation of structural location/stratification, naturally related to the sphere of occupations, though not necessarily constrained within this framework. One attempt to take advantage of this potential, still remaining with the components of the classical approach, was to outline milieus of social interaction as presented in the previous section. Outside of occupations, however, a whole range of positions may be conceived in the social space as bases for grasping the relationships of individuals and their groupings. An important innovation recently introduced by Bonnie H. Erickson has involved gender as well as occupation, in the position generator technique (see Erickson 2004). The joint application of the two positions may not only shed new light on gender contacts but also enrich the picture of occupational relationships as well.

Still another direction has been tried by the last wave of our research in this field within the framework of the Hungarian Political Stratification Project from the end of 2003. The relevance of political involvement for social capital in Hungary has been repeatedly confirmed by analyses on access to network resources, as briefly recalled in previous sections. Political positions are of interest, however, beyond the degree of participation and its relationship with other resources. Given the large degree of political homophily (in the sense of party or party-block positions) revealed for core networks by respective techniques, the need arose to acquire information about the political character of mesolevel contacts from the sphere of wider acquaintanceship as well. Having adopted the basic design of the PG approach, the roster of occupations was replaced this time by that of the eight parties of relevance in the political life of recent Hungary. As the first findings already reveal,[28] the acquaintanceship data in question indicate a much larger pool of integrative contacts than would be the case if relying on core ties information alone. The occurrence of political heterophily somewhat offsetting the clear predominance of homophily on the microscale is a parallel tendency shown in a simple way by Table A.7. Further elaborations in this direction focus on the value of political nexus diversity in various aspects of individual attainment[29] and its role in social integration on a larger plane.

---

not applied in our previous studies). This may yield relevant information as well. The set of data thus produced, however, may not completely cover the information produced by approaches explicitly targeting core ties (like the various versions of name generator techniques).

[28] See Angelusz and Tardos (2005).

[29] Including, among others, personal earnings as the dependent variable this time as well, political nexus diversity (based on the extent of contacts with supporters of parties from the left and right, the government coalition, and the opposition) proves a significant predictor among the middle-aged/older male population, the group most involved in political affairs.

APPENDIX

Table A.1. Factorial attributes of pg-occupations in 1987 and 1997–8 with complete and overlapping sets

1987		1997–8		1987		1997–8	
Complete set of 20 items	Component 1. Loadings	Complete set of 24 items	Component 1. Loadings	Overlapping 17 items	Component 1. Loadings	Overlapping 17 items	Component 1. Loadings
Manager/director	.64	Manager/director	.65	Manager/director	.66	Manager/director	.68
Engineer	.59	Businessman	.64	Engineer	.60	Engineer	.62
Local council employee	.59	Accountant	.62	Lawyer	.59	Lawyer	.61
Politician	.56	Entrepreneur	.61	Local council employee	.57	Accountant	.60
High school teacher	.56	Boutique owner	.60	High school teacher	.57	Physician	.59
Lawyer	.56	Engineer	.59	Accountant	.55	High school teacher	.55
Accountant	.56	Lawyer	.58	Physician	.53	Politician	.55
Technician	.55	Physician	.54	Journalist	.51	Journalist	.54
Waiter/waitress	.52	High school teacher	.54	Waiter/waitress	.51	Driver	.52
Actor/actress	.50	Guard	.54	Politician	.47	Local council employee	.52
Driver	.50	Driver	.53	Driver	.46	Waiter/waitress	.51
Sales person	.48	Waiter/waitress	.52	Sales person	.45	Railroad worker	.45
Physician	.44	Politician	.51	Railroad worker	.43	Actor/actress	.44
Scientist	.44	Local council employee	.51	Actor/actress	.42	Sales person	.41
Bricklayer	.42	Journalist	.49	Factory worker	.37	Scientist	.40
Factory worker	.40	Skilled worker	.46	Scientist	.35	Factory worker	.37
Journalist	.37	Railroad worker	.44	Unskilled worker	.34	Unskilled worker	.36
Agricultural worker	.33	Sales person	.42				
Unskilled worker	.33	Farmer	.42				
Railroad worker	.31	Banker	.42				
		Actor/actress	.39				
		Factory worker	.38				
		Unskilled worker	.38				
		Scientist	.35				
Explained %	23.9	Explained %	22.7	Explained %	25.3	Explained %	27.1
Correlation with count of accessed occupations[30]	.99	Correlation with count of accessed occupations	.99				

Note: Principal components unrotated factor analysis, order of occupations by size of loadings.

[30] The correlation of the total number of occupations with the count of the 17 occupations also applied in the later 1997–8 survey amounts to .98. In the opposite 1997–8 case, the corresponding correlation of the total number of occupations with the count of the same roster of 17 occupations is at a similar height of .97.

Table A.2. Inequality of various types of social resources in Hungary—changes in the role of conditioning factors from 1987 to 1998)

| | Social nexus diversity (range of useful contacts) PG—number of accessed occupations | | | | Extensity of core bonds (range of ties) NG—number of persons | | | |
| | 1987 | | 1997–8 | | 1987 | | 1997–8 | |
	β	Imp.	β	Imp.	β	Imp.	β	Imp.
Education	.27	.37	.28	.48	.15	.35	.11	.25
Wealth (household assets)	.18	.22	.18	.28	.08	.11	.21	.53
Locality (rural: +)	.25	.18	.18	.07	−.04	.03	−.02	.01
Sex (female: +)	−.17	.16	−.07	.04	.00	.00	.06	.08
Age	.17	.07	−.11	.14	−.22	.51	−.10	.18
R^2	.20		.21		.14		.11	
N	2,652		1,624		2,470		1,557	

Note: Imp.: Importance; NG: Name generator; PG: Position generator. Categorical regression analysis—optimal scaling; β-coefficients and importance values.

Dependent variables: PGDIV5, NGRANGE5 (quintiles).

Table A.3. Material attainment by types of possession of social resources, 1987 and 1997–8

| Types of possession of social resources (clusters) | 1987 | | 1997–8 | |
	Personal earnings	Family income	Personal earnings)	Family income
Resource rich (both +)	+0.54	+0.57	+0.30	+0.64
Nexus diversity (PG) +, core bonds range (NG) −	+0.11	−0.02	+0.14	+0.21
Nexus diversity (PG) −, core bonds range (NG) +	+0.04	+0.24	−0.05	+0.26
Resource poor (both −)	−0.55	−0.51	−0.40	−0.54
η^2	.06	.07	.04	.10
N	2,609	2,960	1,441	1,377

Note: NG: Name generator; PG: Position generator. Quintiles of personal earning and household, deviations of group means from sample means.

Table A.4. Predictors of personal earnings by distinct sex/age categories, 1987 and 1997–8

	1987								1997–8							
	Below 44,				Above 45,				Below 44,				Above 45,			
	male		female		male		female		male		female		male		female	
	β	Imp.	β	Imp.	β	Imp.	β	Imp.	β	Imp.	β	Imp.	β	Imp.	β	Imp.
Nexus diversity (PG)	.13	.14	.09	.06	.14	.09	.13	.08	.17	.20	.29	.48	−.10	.01	.12	.09
Core ties range (NG)	.08	.07	−.10	.00	.16	.13	.11	.07	.11	.08	.11	.10	.14	.10	.15	.12
Education	.35	.78	.26	.47	.42	.61	.49	.70	.30	.51	.28	.42	.46	.79	.43	.72
Locality (rural: +)	(−.02)	.01	−.27	.47	−.20	.17	−.17	.14	−.20	.21	(−.02)	.00	−.13	.12	−.10	.08
R²	.16		.17		.36		.43		.22		.21		.30		.31	
N	647		711		550		620		264		329		373		460	

Note: Imp.: Importance; NG: Name generator; PG: Position generator. Categorical regression analysis—optimal scaling: β-coefficients and importance values.
Dependent variable: EARNING5 (quintiles).
The values in parentheses are not significant (.05).

Table A.5. Predictors of five components/connectedness with milieu-types, 1997–8

	Components									
	1		2		3		4		5	
	Managers/ professionals		Public sphere/cultural intelligentsia		Market/ service intermediary		Workers/ urban manual		Rural/ agricultural manual	
	β	Imp.	β	Imp.	β	Imp.	β	Imp.	β	Imp.
Education	.39	.69	.29	.65	.15	.27	−.14	.12	.07	.00
Wealth	.22	.32	.09	.11	.17	.30	.08	.03	(−.05)	.03
Locality (rural: +)	(−.01)	.00	−.11	.15	(.05)	.00	.20	.30	.37	.89
Sex (female: +)	(.02)	.00	−.06	.03	(.02)	.00	−.21	.31	(−.05)	.02
Age	.06	.00	.13	.07	−.23	.44	−.18	.24	.12	.08
R^2	.27		.15		.18		.18		.15	
N	1,605		1,605		1,605		1,605		1,605	

Note: Imp.: Importance. Categorical regression analysis—optimal scaling; β-coefficients and importance values.

Table A.6. Mean scores of broad occupational categories on the five components/ connectedness with milieu-types 1997–8

	Components				
	1	2	3	4	5
	Managers/ professionals	Public sphere/cultural intelligentsia	Market/ service intermediary	Workers/ urban manual	Rural/ agricultural manual
Executives ($n = 43$)	.55	.70	.30	.16	.05
Professionals (nonmanagerial) ($n = 112$)	.47	.45	.24	−.01	−.06
Nonmanual (with no college) ($n = 181$)	.40	.11	.36	.02	−.13
Self-employed ($n = 93$)	.48	.21	.55	.02	.04
Skilled workers ($n = 161$)	.02	−.17	.18	.36	.01
Unskilled manual ($n = 93$)	−.24	−.23	.03	.16	.07
Retired ($n = 654$)	−.21	−.05	−.32	−.18	.02
Students ($n = 58$)	.36	.08	.15	−.26	−.19

Note: Factor scores +1 to −1.

Table A.7. Political homophily/heterophily among core ties and acquaintance relationships, 2003 (percentage)

	Core ties (NG)	Acquaintanceship (PG)
Homophilious	78	28
Political kin (within-bloc)	8	18
Heterophilious ties	14	54
Total	10	100

Note: NG: Name generator.

References

AGRESTI, A., *Categorical Data Analysis*, 2nd edn. (Hoboken, NJ: Wiley, 2002).
—— and B. AGRESTI, "Statistical Analysis of Qualitative Variation," in K. F. Schuessler (ed.), *Sociological Methodology* (San Francisco, CA: Jossey-Bass, 1978) 204–37.
ANDERSON, E., *Streetwise: Race, Class, and Change in an Urban Community* (Chicago, IL: University of Chicago Press, 1990).
—— *Code of the Street: Decency, Violence, and the Moral Life of the Inner City* (New York: W. W. Norton, 1999).
ANDERSON, J. H., "The Size, Origins, and Character of Mongolia's Informal Sector during the Transition," Policy Research Working Paper 1916, Washington, DC: World Bank, 1998.
ANDERSON, K., "Working Women and Political Participation, 1952–1972," *American Journal of Political Science*, 19(3) (1975), 439–53.
ANGELUSZ, R., and R. TARDOS, "The Strength and Weakness of Weak Ties," *Research Review*, 3 (1991), 7–25.
—— —— "A megszólítási szokások generációs változása: a tegeződés térhódítása" [Generational Changes of Greeting Habits: First Names Gaining Ground], in Z. Spéder and P. P. Tóth (eds.), *Emberi viszonyok [Human Relationships]* (Budapest: Századvég, 2000) 247–70.
—— —— "Change and Stability in Social Network Resources: The Case of Hungary under Transformation," in N. Lin, K. Cook, and R. S. Burt (eds.), *Social Capital: Theory and Research* (New York: Aldine de Gruyter, 2001) 297–323.
—— —— "Választói tömbök rejtett hálózata" [Latent Networks of Electoral Blocks], in R. Angelusz and R. Tardos (eds.), *Törések, hálók, hidak. Választói magatartás és politikai tagolódás Magyarországon [Cleavages, Networks, Bridges, Electoral Behavior and Political Stratification in Hungary]* (Budapest: DKMKA, 2005) 65–160.
ARAI, B., "Self-Employment as a Response to the Double Day for Women and Men in Canada," *Canadian Review of Sociology and Anthropology*, 37(2) (2000), 125–42.
ARROW, K. J., "Observations on Social Capital," in P. Dasguta and I. Serageldin (eds.), *Social Capital: A Multifaceted Perspective* (Washington, DC: World Bank, 2000) 3–5.
ASCHENBRENNER, J., *Lifelines: Black Families in Chicago* (New York: Holt, Rinehart and Winston, 1975).
BABCHUK, N., and J. N. EDWARDS, "Voluntary Associations and the Integration Hypothesis," *Sociological Inquiry*, 35 (1965), 49–62.
BAER, D. E., J. E. CURTIS, and E. G. GRABB, "Has Voluntary Association Activity Declined? Cross-National Analyses for Fifteen Countries," *Canadian Review of Sociology and Anthropology*, 38 (2001), 249–74.
BAKKER, B., I. SIEBEN, P. Nieuwbeerta, and H. GANZEBOOM, "Maten voor prestige, sociaaleconomische status en sociale klasse voor de Standaard Beroepenclassificatie 1992" [Measures for Prestige, Socio-Economic Status and Social Class for the Standard Occupational Classification 1992], *Sociale Wetenschappen*, 40 (1997), 1–22.
BARTUS, T., *Social Capital and Earnings Inequalities. The Role of Informal Job Search in Hungary* (Amsterdam: Thesis, 2001).

BAT, C., "Urban Poverty Profile, Ulaanbaatar City, Mongolia," paper presented at the Learning Workshop on Urban Poverty Reduction in East Asia, Singapore, June 10–11, 2002. Retrieved November 20, 2002, <infocity.org/F2F/poverty/papers2/UB(Mongolia)% Poverty.pdf>

BEARMAN, P., and P. PARIGI, "Cloning Headless Frogs and Other Important Matters: Conversation Topic and Network Structure," *Social Forces*, 83 (2004), 535–57.

BECKER, G. S., *Human Capital* (Chicago: University of Chicago Press, [1964] 1993).

BEGGS, J. J., V. A. HAINES, and J. S. HURLBERT, "Revisiting the Rural–Urban Contrast: Personal Networks in Nonmetropolitan and Metropolitan Settings," *Rural Sociology*, 61 (1996), 306–25.

—— and J. S. HURLBERT, "The Social Context of Men's and Women's Job Search Ties: Membership in Voluntary Organizations, Social Resources, and Job Search Outcomes," *Sociological Perspectives*, 40 (1997), 601–22.

—— —— and V. A. HAINES, "Community Attachment in a Rural Setting: A Refinement and Empirical Test of the Systemic Model," *Rural Sociology*, 61(3) (1996), 407–26.

BEKKERS, R., "De bijdragen der kerckelijken," in T. N. M. Schuyt (ed.), *Geven in Nederland 2003: Giften, legaten, sponsoring en vrijwilligerswerk* (Houten/Mechelen: Bohn Stafleu Van Loghum, 2003) 141–72.

—— "Giving and Volunteering in the Netherlands: Sociological and Psychological Perspectives," Dissertation, Utrecht University, 2004.

—— "Nee heb je, ja kun je krijge," in B. Völker (ed.), *Burgers in de buurt: Samenleven in school, wijk en vereniging* (Amsterdam: Amsterdam University Press, 2005a) 153–74.

—— "Geven van tijd: vrijwilligerswerk," in T. N. M. Schuyt and B. M. Gouwenberg (eds.), *Geven in Nederland 2005: Giften, legaten, sponsoring en vrijwilligerswerk* (Houten/Mechelen: Bohn Stafleu Van Loghum, 2005b) 80–92.

—— and N. D. DE GRAAF, "Verschuivende Achtergronden van Verenigingsparticipatie," *Mens and Maatschappij*, 77 (2002), 338–60.

—— B. VOLKER, H. FLAP, and M. V. D. GAAG, "Social Networks and Associations: The Relation of Cohesive and Instrumental Social Capital to Participation in Voluntary Associations in the Netherlands," work in progress (2008).

BERNARD, H. R., E. C. JOHNSEN, P. D. KILLWORTH, C. McCARTY, G. A. SHELLEY, and S. ROBINSON, "Comparing Four Different Methods for Measuring Personal Social Networks," *Social Networks*, 12 (1990), 179–215.

—— G. A. SHELLEY, and P. D. KILLWORTH, "How Much of a Network Does the GSS and RSW Dredge Up?," *Social Networks*, 9(1) (1987), 49–61.

BIAN, Y., "Bringing Strong Ties Back In: Indirect Connection, Bridges, and Job Searches in Urban China," *American Sociological Review*, 62 (1997), 366–85.

—— "Guanxi Capital and Social Eating: Theoretical Models and Empirical Analyses," in N. Lin, K. Cook, and R. Burt (eds.), *Social Capital: Theory and Research* (New York: Aldine de Gruyter, 2001) 275–95.

—— "Chinese Social Stratification and Social Mobility," *Annual Review of Sociology*, 28 (2002), 91–116.

—— and S. ANG, "Guanxi Networks and Job Mobility in China and Singapore," *Social Forces*, 75 (1997), 981–1005.

—— R. BREIGER, D. DAVIS, and J. GALASKIEWIC, "Class, Occupation, and Social Networks in Urban China," *Social Forces*, 83 (2005), 1443–68.

—— D. DAVIS, and S. WANG, "Family Social Capital: A Social Network Approach," in W. Tang and H. Holzner (eds.), *Social Change in Contemporary China* (Pittsburgh, PA: University of Pittsburgh Press, 2007) 219–32.

BIAN, Y., and K. Y. KO, "Occupational Prestige in the 21st Century Hong Kong: Occupational Ratings among University Students," in S. K. Lau, P. S. Wan, M. K. Lee, and S. L. Wong (eds.), *Market, Class and Politics in Changing Chinese Societies* (in Chinese) (Hong Kong: Institute of Asia-Pacific Studies, The Chinese University of Hong Kong, 2000) 273–96.

—— and Y. LI, "Zhongguo Chengshi Jiating de Shehui Wangluo Ziben" (Social Network Capital of Chinese Urban Families), *Tsinghua Shehuixue Pinglun* (*Tsinghua Sociological Review*), 2 (2001), 1–18.

—— and J. R. LOGAN, "Market Transition and the Persistence of Power: The Changing Stratification System in China," *American Sociological Review*, 61 (1996) 739–58.

BIELBY, D. D., "Gender and Family Relations," in J. S. Chafetz (ed.), *Handbook of the Sociology of Gender* (New York: Kluwer/Plenum, 1999) 391–406.

BIRNER, R., and H. WITTMER, "Using Social Capital to Create Political Capital: How Do Local Communities Gain Political Influence? A Theoretical Approach and Empirical Evidence from Thailand," in N. Dolšak and E. Ostrom (eds.), *The Commons in the New Millennium: Challenges and Adaptations* (Cambridge, MA: MIT Press, 2003) 291–334.

BLACK, J., and L. ERICKSON, "Similarity, Compensation, or Difference? A Comparison of Female and Male Office-Seekers," *Women and Politics*, 21(4) (2000), 1–38.

—— and N. MCGLEN, "Male-Female Political Involvement Differentials in Canada, 1965–1974," *Canadian Journal of Political Science*, 12 (1979), 471–97.

BLAIN, J., "I Can't Come in Today, the Baby Has the Chicken Pox! Gender and Class Processes in How Parents in the Labour Force Deal with the Problem of Sick Children," *Canadian Journal of Sociology*, 18(4) (1993), 405–30.

BLAU, P. M., *Inequality and Heterogeneity* (New York: Free Press, 1977).

—— T. C. BLUM, and J. E. SCHWARTZ, "Heterogeneity and Intermarriage," *American Sociological Review*, 47 (1982), 45–62.

—— and O. D. DUNCAN, *The American Occupational Structure* (New York: Wiley, 1967).

—— D. RUAN, and M. ARDELT, "Interpersonal Choice and Networks," *Social Forces*, 69 (1991), 1037–62.

—— and J. E. SCHWARTZ, *Crosscutting Social Circles* (Orlando, FL: Academic Press, 1984).

BLOOD, R. O., and D. M. WOLFE, "Urban Families: Conjugal Roles and Social Networks," *Human Relations*, 8 (1955), 345–83.

—— —— *Husbands, Wives: The Dynamics of Married Living* (Glencoe: Free Press, 1960).

BOISOT, M., and J. CHILD, "From Fiefs to Clans and Network Capitalism: Explaining China's Emerging Economic Order," *Administrative Science Quarterly*, 41 (1996), 600–24.

BOISSEVAIN, J. F., *Friends of Friends* (Oxford: Blackwell, 1974).

BOOTH, A., and N. BABCHUK, "Personal Influence Networks and Voluntary Association Affiliation," *Sociological Inquiry*, 39 (1973), 179–88.

BOTT, E., *Family and Social Network*, 2nd edn. (New York: Free Press, 1971).

BOURDIEU, P., *Outline of a Theory of Practice* (Cambridge: Cambridge University Press, [1972] 1977).

—— *La Distinction. Critique Social de Jugement* (Paris: Editions de minuit, 1979).

—— "Le Capital Social: Notes Provisoires," *Actes de la Recherche en Sciences Sociales*, 3 (1980), 2–3.

—— "The Forms of Capital," in J. G. Richardson (ed.), *Handbook of Theory and Research for the Sociology of Education* (Westport, CT: Greenwood Press, [1983] 1986) 241–58.

BOURDIEU, P., and J.-C. PASSERON, *Reproduction in Education, Society, Culture* (Beverly Hills, CA: Sage, 1977).

BOXMAN, E., "Contacten en Carriere: Een Empirisch-Theoretisch Onderzoek naar de relatie tussen sociale netwerken en arbeidsmarktposities" [Contacts and Careers: An Empirical-Theoretical Investigation of the Relationship between Social Networks and Labour Market Positions], Ph.D. dissertation, Department of Sociology, University of Utrecht, Utrecht, 1992.

——P. M. DE GRAAF, and H. FLAP, "The Impact of Social and Human Capital on the Income Attainment of Dutch Managers," *Social Networks*, 13 (1991), 51–73.

——H. FLAP, and H. M. WEESIE, "Informeel zoeken op de arbeidsmarkt" [Informal Searching on the Labour Market], in S. Jansen and G. L. H. Van Den Wittenboer (eds.), *Sociale Netwerken en hun Invloed* (Boom: Meppel, 1992) 39–56.

BRADY, H. E., K. L. SCHLOZMAN, and S. VERBA, "Prospecting for Participants: Rational Expectations and the Recruitment of Political Activists," *American Political Science Review*, 93 (1999), 153–69.

——S. VERBA, and K. L. SCHLOZMAN, "Beyond SES: A Resource Model of Political Participation," *American Political Science Review*, 89 (1995), 271–94.

BREHM, J., and W. RAHN, "Individual-Level Evidence for the Causes and Consequences of Social Capital," *American Journal of Political Science*, 41(3) (1997), 999–1023.

BREWER, A., *A Guide to Marx's Capital* (Cambridge: Cambridge University Press, 1984).

BRIDGES, W. P., and W. J. VILLEMEZ, "Informal Hiring and Income in the Labor Market," *American Sociological Review*, 51 (1986), 574–82.

BRIGGS, X., "Brown Kids in White Suburbs: Housing Mobility and the Many Faces of Social Capital," *Housing Policy Debate*, 9(1) (1998), 177–221.

BRODIE, J., and C. CHANDLER, "Women and the Electoral Process in Canada," in K. Megyery (ed.), *Women in Canadian Politics: Toward Equity in Representation* (Research Studies for the Royal Commission on Electoral Reform and Party Financing Volume 6) (Ottawa and Toronto, Canada: RCERPF/Dundurn, 1991) 3–59.

BROWN, E., "Making Philanthropy Work: Social Capital and Human Capital as Predictors of Household Giving," unpublished manuscript, 2002.

BRYANT, W. K., H. J., SLAUGHTER, H. KANG, and A. TAX, "Participating in Philanthropic Activities: Donating Money and Time," *Journal of Consumer Policy*, 26(1) (2003), 43–73.

BUKODI, E., I. HARCSA, and G. Y. VUKOVICH, "Hungary in the Light of Social Indicators," in T. Kolosi, I. Tóth, and G. Vukovich (eds.), *Social Report 2004* (Budapest: Tárki, 2004) 17–46.

BURGER, E., and R. M. MILARDO, "Marital Interdependence and Social Networks," *Journal of Social and Personal Relationships*, 12 (1995), 403–15.

BURT, R., "Autonomy in a Social Topology," *American Journal of Sociology*, 85(4) (1980a), 892–925.

—— "Models of Network Structure," *Annual Review of Sociology*, 6 (1980b), 79–141.

—— "Network Items and the General Social Survey," *Social Networks*, 6 (1984), 293–339.

——*Structural Holes: The Social Structure of Competition* (Cambridge, MA: Harvard University Press, 1992).

—— "The Contingent Value of Social Capital," *Administrative Science Quarterly*, 42 (1997), 339–65.

—— "The Gender of Social Capital," *Rationality and Society*, 10 (1998), 5–46.

—— "The Network Structure of Social Capital," *Research in Organizational Behavior*, 22 (2000a), 345–423.

—— "Decay Functions," *Social Networks*, 22 (2000*b*), 1–28.

—— "Structural Holes Versus Network Closure as Social Capital," in N. Lin, K. Cook, and R. Burt (eds.), *Social Capital: Theory and Research* (New York: Aldine de Gruyter, 2001) 31–56.

BUSKENS, V., and W. RAUB, "Embedded Trust' Central and Learning," in S. R. Thye and E. J. Lawler (eds.), *Group Cohesion, Trust and Solidarity* (Amsterdam: JAI, 2002), 167–202.

CAMPBELL, K. E., "Gender Differences in Job-Related Networks," *Work and Occupations*, 15 (1988), 179–200.

—— and B. A. LEE, "Name Generators in Surveys of Personal Networks," *Social Networks*, 13 (1991), 203–21.

—— P. V. MARSDEN, and J. S. HURLBERT, "Social Resources and Socioeconomic Status," *Social Networks*, 8 (1986), 97–117.

—— and R. A. ROSENFELD, "Job Search and Job Mobility: Sex and Race Differences," *Research in the Sociology of Work*, 3 (1985), 147–74.

CARROLL, S., "Women's Autonomy and the Gender Gap: 1980 and 1982," in C. M. Mueller (ed.), *The Politics of the Gender Gap: The Social Construction of Political Influence* (Newbury Park, CA: Sage, 1988) 236–57.

CARROLL, W. K., "Which Women Are More Proletarianized? Gender, Class and Occupation in Canada," *Canadian Review of Sociology and Anthropology*, 24(4) (1987), 571–85.

CENSUS AND STATISTICS DEPARTMENT, *2001 Population Census: Main Tables* (Hong Kong: Census and Statistics Department, 2002).

CENTRAL BUREAU OF STATISTICS (CBS), *Standaard onderwijsindeling. SOI 1978*. (Voorburg: CBS [Standard Educational Index], 1987).

—— *Standaard beroepenclassificatie 1992 [Standard Occupational Codes for 1992]*. (s-Gravenhage: SDU uitgeverij/CBS-publikaties 's-Gravenhage, 1993).

CHARLES, M., "Cross-National Variation in Occupational Sex Segregation," *American Sociological Review*, 57(4) (1992), 483–502.

CHIU, C. C. H., "Social Image of Stratification in Hong Kong," in S. K. Lau, P. S. Wan, M. K. Lee, and S. L. Wong (eds.), *Inequalities and Development: Social Stratification in Chinese Societies* (Hong Kong: Institute of Asia-Pacific Studies, The Chinese University of Hong Kong, 1994) 123–40.

CHUNG, C. N., "Networks and Governance in Trade Associations: AEIC and NELA in the Development of the American Electricity Industry 1885–1910," *Journal of Sociology and Social Policy*, 17(7/8) (1996), 52–110.

CLARY, G. E., M. SNYDER, R. D. RIDGE, J. COPELAND, A. A. STUKAS, J. HAUGEN, and P. MIENE, "Understanding and Assessing the Motivations of Volunteers: A Functional Approach," *Journal of Personality and Social Psychology*, 74(6) (1998), 1516–30.

COAKES, S. J., and B. J. BISHOP, "Where Do I Fit In? Factors Influencing Women's Participation in Rural Communities," *Community, Work and Family*, 1(3) (1998), 249–71.

COHEN, P., and M. HUFFMAN, "Individuals, Jobs, and Labor Markets: The Devaluation of Women's Work," *American Sociological Review*, 68(3) (2003), 443–63.

COLEMAN, J. S., "Social Capital in the Creation of Human Capital," *American Journal of Sociology*, 94 (1988), S95-S120.

—— *Foundations of Social Theory* (Cambridge, MA: Harvard University Press, 1990).

COLLINS-JARVIS, L. A., "Gender Representation in an Electronic City Hall: Female Adoption of Santa Monica's PEN System," *Journal of Broadcasting and Electronic Media*, 37(2) (1993), 177–96.

Coltrane, S., *Gender and Families* (Thousand Oaks, CA: Pine Forge Press, 1998).

Cook, K. S., "Network Structure from an Exchange Perspective," in P. V. Marsden and N. Lin (eds.), *Social Structure and Network Analysis* (Beverly Hills, CA: Sage, 1982) 177–99.

—— R. M. Emerson, and M. R. Gillmore, "The Distribution of Power in Exchange Networks: Theory and Experimental Results," *American Journal of Sociology*, 89 (1983), 275–305.

Costa, D., and M. Kahn, "Civic Engagement and Community Heterogeneity: An Economist's Perspective," *Perspectives on Politics*, 1 (2003), 103–11.

Cote, R., and B. H. Erickson, "Untangling the Roots of Tolerance: How Networks, Voluntary Associations, and Personal Attributes Shape Attitudes towards Ethnic Minorities and Immigrants," *American Behavioral Scientist*, forthcoming.

Davis, A. E., L. A. Renzulli, and H. E. Aldrich, "Mixing or Matching? The Influence of Voluntary Associations on the Occupational Diversity and Density of Small Business Owners' Networks," *Work and Occupations*, 33 (2006), 42–72.

Davis, K., and W. E. Moore, "Some Principles of Stratification," *American Sociological Review*, 10 (1945), 242–49.

De Graaf, N. D., and H. Flap, "With a Little Help from My Friends: Social Resources as an Explanation of Occupational Status and Income in West Germany, the Netherlands, and the United States," *Social Forces*, 67(2) (1988), 452–72.

De Graaf, P., H. Ganzeboom, and M. Kalmijn, "Cultural and Economic Dimensions of Occupational Status," in W. Jansen, J. Dronkers, and K. Verrips (eds.), *Similar or Different? Continuities in Dutch Research on Social Stratification and Social Mobility* (Amsterdam: Siswo, 1989) 53–74.

—— and M. Kalmijn, "Culturele en Economische Beroepsstatus. Een Evaluatie van Subjectieve en Objectieve Benaderingen" [Cultural and Economic Status of an Occupation. An Evaluation of Subjective and Objective Approaches], *Mens en Maatschappij*, 70 (1995), 152–77.

————— "Trends in the Intergenerational Transmission of Cultural and Economic Status," *Acta Sociologica*, 44 (2001), 51–66.

De Hart, J., "Godsdienst, Maatschappelijke Participatie en Sociaal Kapitaal," in P. Dekker (ed.), *Vrijwilligerswerk Vergeleken* (Den Haag: SCP, 1999) 207–47.

Dekker, P., "Social Capital of Individuals: Relational Asset or Personal Quality?," in S. Prakash and P. Selle (eds.), *Investigating Social Capital: Comparative Perspectives on Civil Society, Participation and Governance* (New Delhi: Sage, 2004) 88–110.

—— and J. De Hart, "Het Sociaal Kapitaal van de Nederlandse Kiezer," in M. Hooghe (ed.), *Sociaal kapitaal en democratie: verenigingsleven, sociaal kapitaal en politieke cultuur* (Leuven, Belgium: Acco, 2001) 83–111.

————— "Het zout der aarde: Een analyse van de samenhang tussen godsdienstigheid en sociaal kapitaal in Nederland," *Sociale Wetenschappen*, 45 (2002), 45–61.

Delhey, J., and K. Newton, "Who Trusts? The Origins of Social Trust in Seven Nations," *European Societies*, 5 (2003), 1–45.

Della Porta, D., and M. Diani, *Social Movements* (Oxford: Blackwell, 1999).

De Sola Pool, I., and M. Kochen, "Contacts and Influence," *Social Networks*, 1 (1978), 5–51.

De Tocqueville, A., "Democracy in America," in J. P. Mayer (ed.), *A New Translation by George Lawrence* (Garden City, NY: Doubleday, 1975).

DEVEREAUX, M. S., "Time Use of Canadians in 1992," *Canadian Social Trends*, 30 (1993), 13–16.

DIANI, M., "Social Movements and Social Capital: A Network Perspective on Movement Outcomes," *Mobilization*, 2(2) (1997), 129–47.

—— "Introduction," in M. Diani and D. McAdam (eds.), *Social Movements and Networks: Relational Approaches to Collective Action* (Oxford: Oxford University Press, 2003) 1–18.

DILLMAN, D. A., *Mail and Telephone Surveys: The Total Design Method* (New York: Wiley-Interscience, 1978).

DIMAGGIO, P., E. HARGITTAI, W. R. NEUMAN, and J. P. ROBINSON, "Social Implications of the Internet," *Annual Review of Sociology*, 27 (2001), 307–36.

DUNCAN, O. D., "A Socio-Economic Index for All Occupations," in A. J. Reiss (ed.), *Occupation and Social Status* (New York: Free Press, 1961) 109–38.

DURKHEIM, E., *Le Suicide: Étude de Sociologie* (Paris: PUF, 1897).

EDIN, K., and L. LEIN, *Making Ends Meet: How Single Mothers Survive Welfare and Low-Wage Work* (New York: Russell Sage Foundation, 1997).

EGGEBEEN, D. J., "From Generation unto Generation: Parent-Child Support in Aging American Families," *Generations*, 16(3) (1992), 45–9.

—— and D. P. HOGAN, "Giving between Generations in American Families," *Human Nature*, 1(2) (1990), 211–32.

ELDER, G., *Children of the Great Depression: Social Change in the Life Experience* (Chicago: Chicago University Press, 1974).

ELLIOTT, J. R., "Social Isolation and Labor Market Insulation: Network and Neighborhood Effects on Less-Educated Urban Workers," *The Sociological Quarterly*, 40 (1999), 199–216.

—— "Class, Race, and Job Matching in Contemporary Urban Labor Markets," *Social Science Quarterly*, 81 (2000), 1036–52.

ELLISON, C. G., "Are Religious People Nice People? Evidence from the National Survey of Black Americans," *Social Forces*, 71(2) (1992), 411–30.

EMERSON, R. M., "Power-Dependence Relations," *American Sociological Review*, 27 (1962), 31–40.

ERICKSON, B. H., "The Relational Basis of Attitudes," in B. Wellman and S. D. Berkowitz (eds.), *Social Structures: A Network Approach* (New York: Cambridge University Press, 1988) 99–121.

—— "Networks, Success, and Class Structure: A Total View," paper presented at the Sunbelt Social Networks Conference, Charleston, SC, February 1995.

—— "A Structural Approach to Network and Cultural Resources," unpublished paper, Department of Sociology, University of Toronto, 1996*a*.

—— "Culture, Class, and Connections," *American Journal of Sociology*, 102 (1996*b*), 217–51.

—— "Social Capital and Its Profits, Local and Global," paper presented at the Sunbelt XVIII and 5th European International Conference on Social Networks, Sitges, Spain, May 28–31, 1998.

—— "Good Networks and Good Jobs: The Value of Social Capital to Employers and Employees," in N. Lin, K. Cook, and R. S. Burt (eds.), *Social Capital: Theory and Research* (New York: Aldine de Gruyter, 2001*a*) 127–58.

—— "Social Networks: The Value of Variety," *Contexts*, 2 (2003), 25–31.

—— "The Distribution of Gendered Social Capital in Canada," in H. Flap and B. Völker (eds.), *Creation and Returns of Social Capital: A New Research Program* (London and New York: Routledge, 2005) 27–50.

ERICKSON, B. H., "Persuasion and Perception: New Models of Network Effects on Gendered Issues," in B. O'Neill and E. Gidengil (eds.), *Gender and Social Capital* (New York and London: Routledge, 2006) 293–322.

—— P. ALBANESE, and S. DRAKULIC, "Gender on a Jagged Edge: The Security Industry, Its Clients, and the Reproduction and Revision of Gender," *Work and Occupations*, 27 (2000), 294–318.

—— and T. A. NOSANCHUK, "How an Apolitical Association Politicizes," *Canadian Review of Sociology and Anthropology*, 27(2) (1990), 206–19.

—— and K. MIYATA, "Macro and Micro Gender Structures: Gender Stratifications and Social Networks in Canada and Japan," paper presented for the 99th Annual Meeting of American Sociological Association, San Francisco, 2004.

ESR/TELEPANEL (formerly SSCW-Telepanel) *Dutch Telepanel Survey* [Data file]. Stichting Economische, Sociaal Culturele en Ruimtelijke Wetenschappen (ESR) van de Nederlandse Organisatie voor Wetenschappelijk Onderzoek (NWO), The Hague. Data Collection: Stichting Telepanel, Amsterdam. Available from: Steinmetz Archive, Amsterdam, 1992.

EVANS, P., "Introduction: Development Strategies Across the Public–Private Divide," *World Development*, 24(6) (1996), 1033–8.

FALCON, L., "Social Networks and Employment for Latinos, Blacks, and Whites," *New England Journal of Public Policy*, 11 (1995), 17–28.

FEATHERMAN, D. L., and R. M. HAUSER, *Opportunity and Change* (New York: Academic Press, 1978).

FEI, X., *From the Soil, the Foundations of Chinese Society* (Berkeley: University of California Press, [1949] 1992).

FERGUSON, A., *An Essay on the History of Civil Society* (New Brunswick, NJ: Transaction Books, [1767] 1980).

—— V. HLEBEC, and T. KOGOVSEK, "Reliability and Validity of Social Network Measurement Instruments," paper for the Amsterdam Colloquium on Creation and Return to Social Capital, 2003.

FERNANDEZ, R. M., E. J. CASTILLA, and P. MOORE, "Social Capital at Work: Networks and Employment at a Phone Center," *American Journal of Sociology*, 105(5) (2000), 1288–356.

—— and D. HARRIS, "Social Isolation and the Underclass," in A. V. Harrell and G. E. Peterson (eds.), *Drugs, Crime, and Social Isolation: Barriers to Urban Opportunity* (Washington, DC: The Urban Institute, 1992) 257–93.

—— and D. MCADAM, "Social Networks and Social Movements: Multiorganizational Fields and Recruitment to Mississippi Freedom Summer," *Sociological Forum*, 3(3) (1988), 357–82.

—— and N. WEINBERG, "Sifting and Sorting: Personal Contacts and Hiring in a Retail Bank," *American Sociological Review*, 62(December) (1997), 883–902.

FERREE, M. M., "Beyond Separate Spheres: Feminism and Family Research," *Journal of Marriage and the Family*, 54 (1990), 866–84.

FILER, R. K., "The Role of Personality and Tastes in Determining Occupational Structure," *Industrial and Labor Relations Review*, 39 (1986), 412–24.

FISCHER, C. S., *To Dwell among Friends: Personal Networks in Town and City* (Chicago: University of Chicago Press, 1982).

—— R. M. JACKSON, C. A. STUEVE, K. GERSON, and L. M. JONES (with M. BALDASSARE), *Networks and Places: Social Relations in the Urban Setting* (New York: Free Press, 1977).

—— and S. J. OLIKER, "A Research Note on Friendship, Gender, and the Life Cycle," *Social Forces*, 52 (1983), 124–33.

——D. L. SOLLIE, G. T. SORELL, and S. K. GREEN, "Marital Status and Career Stage Influences on Social Networks of Young Adults," *Journal of Marriage and the Family*, 51 (1989), 521–34.

FLAP, H., "Patronage: An Institution in Its Own Right," in M. Hechter, K. D. Opp, and R. Wippler (eds.), *Social Institutions: Their Emergence, Maintenance and Effects* (New York: Walter de Gruyter, 1990) 225–44.

—— "Social Capital in the Reproduction of Inequality, a Review," *Comparative Sociology of Family, Health and Education*, 20 (1991), 6179–202.

—— "No Man Is an Island: The Research Program of a Social Capital Theory," paper presented at the World Congress of Sociology, Bielefeld, Germany, July 1994. Also, in pp. 29–59 in O. Favereau and E. Lazega (eds.), *Conventions and Structures in Economic Organization* (Cheltenham, UK: Edward Elgar, 2002, 29–59.

—— "Creation and Returns of Social Capital: A New Research Program," *La Revue Tocqueville*, 20 (1999), 5–26.

—— and E. BOXMAN, "Getting Started: The Influence of Social Capital; on the Start of the Occupational Career," in N. Lin, K. Cook, and R. S. Burt (eds.), *Social Capital: Theory and Research* (New York: Aldine de Gruyter, 2001) 159–81.

—— and N. D. DE GRAAF, "Social Capital and Attained Occupational Status," *Netherlands Journal of Sociology*, 22 (1986), 145–61.

—— and B. VOLKER (eds.), *Creation and Returns of Social Capital* (New York and London: Routledge, 2004).

FOX, B., and J. FOX, "Occupational Gender Segregation of the Canadian Labour Force, 1931–1981," *Canadian Review of Sociology and Anthropology*, 24(3) (1987), 374–97.

FREDERICK, J., "Are You Time Crunched?," *Canadian Social Trends*, 31 (1993), 6–9.

—— "As Time Goes By: Time Use of Canadians," Statistics Canada, Ottawa, 1995.

FREEMAN, L. C., and C. R. THOMPSON, "Estimating Acquaintanceship Volume," in M. K. Norwood (ed.), *The Small World* (New Jersey, NJ: Ablex Pub. Corp., 1989) 147–58.

FU, Y., "Measuring Personal Networks with Daily Contacts: A Single-Item Survey Question and the Contact Diary," *Social Networks*, 27(3) (2005), 169–86.

—— "Contact Diaries: Building Archives of Actual and Comprehensive Personal Networks," *Field Methods*, 19(2) (2007), 194–217 (in press).

GANZEBOOM, H. B. G., *Cultuurdeelname in Nederland* [Cultural Participation in the Netherlands] (Van Gorcum: Assen, 1989).

——P. DE GRAAF, and M. KALMIJN, "De Culturele en Economische Dimensie Van Beroepsstatus" [The Cultural and Economic Dimension of Occupational Status], *Mens en Maatschappij*, 62 (1987), 153–75.

—— —— and D. TREIMAN, "A Standard International Socio-Economic Index of Occupational Status," *Social Science Research*, 21 (1992), 1–56.

—— and D. J. TREIMAN, "Internationally Comparable Measures of Occupational Status for the 1988 International Standard Classification of Occupations," *Social Science Research*, 25 (1996), 201–39.

—— —— "Three Internationally Standardised Measures for Comparative Research on Occupational Status," in J. H. P. Hoffmeyer-Zlotnik and C. Wolf (eds.), *Advances in Cross-National Comparison: A European Working Book for Demographic and Socio-Economic Variables* (New York: Kluwer, 2003) 159–93.

GANZEBOOM, H. B. G., D. J. TREIMAN, and W. ULTEE, "Comparative Intergenerational Stratification Research: Three Generations and Beyond," *Annual Review of Sociology*, 17 (1991), 277–302.

GARTRELL, C. D., "Network Approaches to Social Evaluation," *Annual Review of Sociology*, 3 (1987), 49–66.

GINGRAS, A., C. MAILLE, and E. TARDY, *Sexes et Militantisme* (Montreal, Canada: CIDI-HCA, 1989).

GLANVILLE, J., "Voluntary Associations and Social Network Structure: Why Organizational Location and Type Are Important," *Sociological Forum*, 19 (2004), 465–91.

GLENN, J., "Competing Challengers and Contested Outcome to State Breakdown: The Velvet Revolution in Czechoslovakia," *Social Forces*, 78(1) (1999), 187–211.

GOLD, T., D. GUTHRIE, and D. WANK (eds.), *Social Connections in China: Institutions, Culture, and the Changing Nature of Guanxi* (New York: Cambridge University Press, 2002).

GORDON, C. W., and N. BABCHUK, "A Typology of Voluntary Associations," *American Sociological Review*, 24 (1959), 22–9.

GOULD, R., "Collective Action and Network Structure," *American Sociological Review*, 58(2) (1993), 182–96.

—— *Insurgent Identities: Class, Community and Protest in Paris from 1848 to the Commune* (Chicago: University of Chicago Press, 1995).

—— "Why Do Networks Matter? Rationalist and Structuralist Interpretations," in M. Diani and D. McAdam (eds.), *Social Movements and Networks: Relational Approaches to Collective Action* (Oxford: Oxford University Press, 2003) 233–57.

GRANOVETTER, M., "The Strength of Weak Ties," *American Journal of Sociology*, 78 (1973), 1360–80.

—— *Getting a Job: A Study of Contacts and Careers* (Cambridge, MA: Harvard University Press, 1974).

—— *Getting a Job: A Study of Contacts and Careers*, 2nd edn. (Chicago: University of Chicago Press, 1995).

—— "Economic Action and Social Structure: The Problem of Embeddedness," *American Journal of Sociology*, 91(3) (1985), 481–510.

—— and P. MCGUIRE, "The Making of an Industry: Electricity in the United States," in M. Callon (ed.), *The Law of Markets* (Oxford: Blackwell, 1998) 147–73.

GREELEY, A., "Coleman Revisited: Religious Structures as a Source of Social Capital," *American Behavioral Scientist*, 40 (1997), 587–94.

GREEN, G. P., R. B. HAMMER, and L. M. TIGGES, "Someone to Count On: Informal Support," in D. L. Sjoquist (ed.), *The Atlanta Paradox* (New York: Russell Sage Foundation, 2000) 244–63.

—— L. M. TIGGES, and I. BROWNE, "Social Resources, Job Search, and Poverty in Atlanta," *Research in Community Sociology*, 5 (1995), 161–82.

—— —— and D. DIAZ, "Racial and Ethnic Differences in Job-Search Strategies in Atlanta, Boston, and Los Angeles," *Social Science Quarterly*, 80(2) (1999), 263–78.

GRUSKY, D. B., K. A. WEEDEN, and J. B. SØRENSEN, "The Case for Realism in Class Analysis," in D. E. Davis (ed.), *Political Power and Social Theory* (Greenwich, CT: JAI Press, 2000) 291–305.

HALL, P. A., "Social Capital in Britain," *British Journal of Political Science*, 29(3) (1999), 417–61.

HAMPTON, K. N., and B. WELLMAN, "The Not So Global Village of Netville," in B. Wellman and C. Haythornthwaite (eds.), *The Internet in Everyday Life* (Malden, MA: Blackwell, 2002) 345–71.

HANSEN, M. N., "Earnings in Elite Groups: The Impact of the Social Class Origin," *Acta Sociologica*, 39 (1996), 385–408.

—— "Education and Economic Rewards: Variations by Social-Class Origin and Income Measures," *European Sociological Review*, 17 (2001), 209–31.

HANSON, S., and G. PRATT, "Job Search and the Occupational Segregation of Women," *Annals of the Association of American Geographers*, 81 (1991), 229–53.

HELLIWELL, J. F., "The Role of Government and Stakeholders," International Conference on the Opportunity and Challenge of Diversity: A Role for Social Capital, Canada, November 24–25, 2003.

HERAN, F., "Au Cœur Du Réseau Associatif: Les Multi-Adhérents," *Economie et Statistique*, 208 (1988), 19–25.

HERRING, S. C., "Gender Differences in CMC: Findings and Implications," *Computer Professionals for Social Responsibility Journal*, 18(1)(2000), <http://www.cpsr.org/prevsite/publications/newsletters/issues/2000/Winter2000/herring.html>

HOCHSCHILD, A. (with A. MACHUNG), *The Second Shift: Working Parents and the Revolution at Home* (New York: Viking, 1989).

HODGKINSON, V., and M. WEITZMAN, *Giving and Volunteering in the United States* (Washington, DC: Independent Sector, 1996).

HOFFERTH, S. L., "Kin Networks, Race, and Family Structure," *Journal of Marriage and the Family*, 46 (1984), 791–806.

HOFFMEYER-ZLOTNIK, J. H., M. SCHNEID, and P. P. H. MOHLER, "Egozentrierte Netzwerke in Massen-Umfragen," *ZUMA-Nachrichten*, 20 (1987), 37–56.

HOLLAND, P. W., and S. LEINHARDT, "Transitivity in Structural Models of Small Groups," in S. Leinhardt (ed.), *Social Networks: A Developing Paradigm* (New York: Academic Press, 1977) 49–66.

HOLT, C. L., and J. B. ELLIS, "Assessing the Current Validity of the Bem Sex-Role Inventory," *Sex Roles*, 39 (1998), 929–41.

HOLZER, H. J., "Informal Job Search and Black Youth Unemployment," *American Economic Review*, 77 (1987), 446–52.

HOMANS, G. C., *The Human Group* (New York: Harcourt, Brace, 1950).

—— "Human Behavior as Exchange," *American Journal of Sociology*, 63(6, May) (1958), 597–606.

—— *Social Behavior: Its Elementary Forms* (New York: Harcourt Brace Jovanovich, [1961] 1974).

HOUSE, J. S., K. R. LANDIS, and D. UMBERSON, "Social Relationships and Health," *Science*, 241 (1988), 540–5.

HSUNG, R. M., "Factors Influencing Emotional and Financial Support Networks," *Journal of Humanities and Social Sciences*, 6(2) (1994), 303–33.

—— "Gender, Personal Networks and Social Capital," in Y. J. Bian, E. J. C. Tu, and A. So (eds.), *Survey Research in Chinese Societies: Methods and Findings* (Oxford: Oxford University Press, 2001) 179–216.

—— and Y. J. HWANG, "Job Mobility in Taiwan: Job Search Methods and Contacts Status," paper presented at the Sunbelt XII International Conference on Social Networks, San Diego, United States, February 13–17, 1992*a*.

—— —— "Social Resources and Petit Bourgeois," *Chinese Sociological Quarterly*, 16 (1992*b*) 107–38.

HURLBERT, J. S., and A. S. ACOCK, "The Effects of Marital Status on the Form and Composition of Social Networks," *Social Science Quarterly*, 71 (1990), 163–74.

HURLBERT, J. S., J. J. BEGGS, and V. A. HAINES, "Exploring the Relationship between the Network Structure and Network Resources Dimensions of Social Isolation: What Kinds of Networks Allocate Resources in the Underclass?," paper presented at the Social Capital and Social Network Conference, Duke University, Durham, NC, 1998.

HWANG, K., "Face and Favor: The Chinese Power Game," *American Journal of Sociology*, 92 (1987), 944–74.

HWANG, Y. J., "The Construction and Assessment of the New Occupational Prestige and Socioeconomic Scores for Taiwan: The Indigenization of the Social Science and Sociology of Education Research," *Bulletin of Educational Research*, 49(4) (2003), 1–31.

IKEDA, K., *Changing Reality of Politics* (in Japanese) (Tokyo: Bokutaku-sha, 1997).

——and S. E. RICHEY, "Japanese Network Capital: The Impact of Social Networks on Japanese Political Participation," *Political Behavior*, 27(3) (2005), 239–60.

INGLEHART, R., and P. NORRIS, *Risking Tide: Gender Equality and Cultural Change Around the World* (New York: Cambridge University Press, 2003).

JACKSON, C., "Measuring and Valuing Households' Unpaid Work," *Canadian Social Trends*, 42 (1996), 25–9.

JACKSON, J. L., *Harlem World: Doing Race and Class in Contemporary Black America* (Chicago: University of Chicago Press, 2001).

JACOBS, J., "Long-Term Trends in Occupational Segregation by Sex," *American Journal of Sociology*, 95(1) (1989), 160–73.

JAHODA, M., P. LAZARSFELD, and H. ZEISEL, *Die Arbeitslosen von Marienthal* (Frankfurt, Germany: Suhrkamp, [1933] 1975).

JOHNSON, C. A., "Information Networks: Investigating the Information Behaviour of Mongolia's Urban Residents," unpublished doctoral dissertation, University of Toronto, Toronto, 2003.

JOHNSON, H. G., "The Political Economy of Opulence," *Canadian Journal of Economics and Political Science*, 26 (1960), 552–64.

JOHNSON, J. H., Jr., W. C. FARRELL, Jr., and J. A. STOLOFF, "An Empirical Assessment of Four Perspectives on the Declining Fortunes of the African-American," *Urban Affairs Review*, 35 (2000), 695–716.

JOHNSON, M. P., and L. LESLIE, "Couple Involvement and Network Structure: A Test of the Dyadic Withdrawal Hypothesis," *Social Psychology Quarterly*, 45 (1982), 34–43.

JULIEN, D., E. CHARTRAND, and J. BÉGIN, "Social Networks, Structural Interdependence, and Conjugal Adjustment in Heterosexual, Gay, and Lesbian Couples," *Journal of Marriage and the Family*, 61 (1999), 516–30.

KADUSHIN, C. H., "The Motivational Foundations of Social Networks," *Social Networks*, 24 (2002), 77–91.

KALLEBERG, A. L., and R. A. ROSENFELD, "Work in the Family and in the Labour Market: A Cross-National Reciprocal Analysis," *Journal of Marriage and Family*, 52 (1992), 331–46.

KALMIJN, M., "Assortative Mating by Cultural and Economic Occupational Status," *American Journal of Sociology*, 100 (1994), 422–52.

——"Shared Friendship Networks and the Life Course: An Analysis of Survey Data on Married and Cohabiting Couples," *Social Networks*, 25 (2003), 231–49.

——and T. VAN DER LIPPE, "Types of Schooling and Sex Differences in Earnings in the Netherlands," *European Sociological Review*, 13 (1997), 1–15.

——and H. FLAP, "Assortative Meeting and Mating: Unintended Consequences of Organized Settings for Partner Choices," *Social Forces*, 79(4) (2001), 1289–1312.

KATZ, J. E., and R. E. RICE, "Syntopia: Access, Civic Involvement, and Social Interaction on the Net," in B. Wellman and C. Haythornthwaite (eds.), *The Internet in Everyday Life* (Malden, MA: Blackwell, 2002) 114–38.

KAY, B., R. LAMBERT, S. BROWN, and J. CURTIS, "Gender and Political Activity in Canada, 1965–1984," *Canadian Journal of Political Science*, 20 (1987), 851–63.

KENNEDY, T. "An Exploratory Study of Feminist Experiences in Cyberspace," *Cyber Psychology and Behavior*, 3(5) (2000), 707–19.

—— B. WELLMAN, and K. KLEMENT, "Gendering the Digital Divide," *IT and Society*, 1(5) (2003), 72–96.

KILBOURNE, B. S., P. ENGLAND, G. FARKAS, K. BROWN, and D. WEIR, "Returns to Skill, Compensating Differentials, and Gender Bias: Effects of Occupational Characteristics on the Wages of White Men and Women," *American Journal of Sociology*, 100 (1994), 689–719.

KILLWORTH, P. D., and H. R. BERNARD, "The Reverse Small-World Experiment," *Social Networks*, 1 (1978), 159–92.

—— E. C. JOHNSEN, H. R. BERNARD, G. A. SHELLEY, and C. McCARTY, "Estimating the Size of Personal Networks," *Social Networks*, 12 (1990), 289–312.

—— C. McCARTY, G. A. SHELLEY, and H. R. BERNARD, "A Social Network Approach to Estimating Seroprevalence in the United States," *Social Networks*, 20 (1998), 23–50.

—— —— —— E. C. JOHNSEN, J. DOMINI, and G. A. SHELLEY, "Two Interpretations of Reports of Knowledge of Subpopulation Sizes," *Social Networks*, 25(2) (2003), 141–60.

KING, A., "Human Feelings in Human Relationships," in G. Yang (ed.), *Chinese Psychology* (Taipei: Laureate Book Co., Ltd, 1988) 319–45.

—— "Kuan-Hsi and Network Building: A Sociological Interpretation," in W. Tu (ed.), *The Living Tree: The Changing Meaning of Being Chinese Today* (Stanford, CA: Stanford University Press, 1994) 109–26.

KIRKPATRICK, M., T. BEEBE, M. SNYDER, and T. JEYLAN, "Volunteerism in Adolescence: A Process Perspective," *Journal of Research on Adolescence*, 8 (1998), 301–32.

KLANDERMANS, B., *The Social Psychology of Protest* (Cambridge, MA: Blackwell, 1997).

—— and D. OEGEMA, "Potentials, Networks, Motivations, and Barriers: Steps towards Participation in Social Movements," *American Sociological Review*, 52(4) (1987), 519–31.

KNOKE, D., "Networks of Political Action: Toward Theory Construction," *Social Forces*, 68 (1990*a*), 1041–65.

—— *Political Networks: The Structural Perspective* (Cambridge: Cambridge University Press, 1990*b*).

KOLOSI, T., and P. RÓBERT, "Basic Processes of Structural Transformation and Mobility in the Hungarian Society since the Change of System," in T. Kolosi, I. G. Y. Tóth, and G. Y. Vukovich (eds.), *Social Report 2004* (Budapest: Tárki, 2004) 47–71.

KRAUT, R., M. PATTERSON, V. LUNDMARK, S. KIESLER, T. MUKOPADHYAY, and W. SCHERLIS, "Internet Paradox: A Social Technology That Reduces Social Involvement and Psychological Well-Being?," *American Psychologist*, 53(9) (1998), 1017–31.

KRUIJT, J. P., and W. GODDIJN, "Verzuiling en ontzuiling als sociologisch proces," in A. N. J. Den Hollander, E. W. Hofstee, J. A. A. van Doorn, and E. V. W. Vercruysse (eds.), *Drift en koers: een halve eeuw sociale verandering in Nederland* (Assen: Van Gorcum, 1962) 227–63.

LADNER, J., *Tomorrow's Tomorrow: The Black Woman* (Garden City, NY: Doubleday, 1972).

LAI, G., N. LIN, and S. LEUNG, "Network Resources, Contact Resources, and Status Attainment," *Social Networks*, 20(2, April) (1998), 159–78.

LATANÉ, B., and J. M. DARLEY, *The Unresponsive Bystander: Why Doesn't He Help?* (New York: Meredith, 1970).

LAUMANN, E. O., *Prestige and Association in an Urban Community* (Indianapolis, IN: Bobbs-Merrill, 1966).

—— *Bonds of Pluralism: The Forms and Substance of Urban Social Networks* (New York: Wiley, 1973).

LAZARSFELD, P. F., and R. K. MERTON, "Friendship as Social Process: A Substantive and Methodological Analysis," in P. L. KENDALL (ed.), *The Varied Sociology of Paul F. Lazarsfeld* (New York: Columbia University Press, 1954) 298–348.

LEE, B. A., K. E. CAMPBELL, and O. MILLERE, "Racial Differences in Urban Neighboring," *Sociological Forum*, 6 (1991), 525–50.

LEONARD, R., and J. ONYX, "Networking Through Loose and Strong Ties: An Australian Qualitative Study," *Voluntas: International Journal of Voluntary and Non-Profit Organizations*, 14(2) (2003), 189–203.

LHAGVASUREN, N., "Why Are [sic] the Lion's Share of Mongolian University Graduates Women?," *Transitions Online*, February 2002. Retrieved November 12, 2002, <www.tol.cz>

LIANG, S., *The Essential Meanings of Chinese Culture* (Hong Kong: Zheng Zhong Press, [1949] 1986).

LIN, N., "Social Resources and Instrumental Action," in P. V. Marsden and N. Lin (eds.), *Social Structure and Network Analysis* (Beverly Hills, CA: Sage, 1982) 131–45.

—— "Social Resources and Social Actions: A Progress Report," *Connections*, 6(2) (1983), 10–16.

—— "Social Resources and Social Mobility: A Structural Theory of Status Attainment," in R. L. Breiger (ed.), *Social Mobility and Social Structure* (New York: Cambridge University Press, 1990) 247–71.

—— "Building a Network Theory of Social Capital," *Connections*, 22(1) (1999a), 28–51.

—— "Social Networks and Status Attainment," *Annual Review of Sociology*, 25 (1999b), 467–87.

—— "Inequality in Social Capital," *Contemporary Sociology*, 29(6) (2000a), 785–95.

—— "Social Capital: Social Networks, Civic Engagement, or Trust?," paper prepared for the Workshop on Social Capital, University of Trento, October 2000b.

—— "Building a Network Theory of Social Capital," in N. Lin, K. Cook, and R. S. Burt (eds.), *Social Capital: Theory and Research* (Hawthorn, NY: Aldine de Gruyter, 2001a) 3–29.

—— *Social Capital: A Theory of Structure and Action* (London and New York: Cambridge University Press, 2001b).

—— "Guanxi: A Conceptual Analysis," in A. So, N. Lin, and D. Poston (eds.), *The Chinese Triangle of Mainland, Taiwan, and Hong Kong: Comparative Institutional Analysis* (Westport, CT: Greenwood Press, 2001c) 153–66.

—— "Social Capital: Social Networks, Civic Engagement, or Trust?," The Keynote Address at the Annual Meeting of the Hong Kong Sociological Association, November 25, 2000 (revised version), 2001d.

—— "Social Capital: Social Resources, Civic Engagement, or Trust? An Integration," paper presented at the XXIII International Sunbelt Social Network Conference, Cancun, Mexico, February 12–16, 2003a.

—— "Job Search in Urban China: Gender, Network Chains and Embedded Resources," in H. Flap and B. Volker (eds.), *Creation and Returns of Social Capital: A New Research Program* (New York and London: Routledge, 2005) 145–71.

—— "Social Capital," in J. Beckert and M. Zafirovski (eds.), *International Encyclopedia of Economic Sociology* (London: Routledge Ltd, 2006) 604–12.

—— "Theory, Measurement, and the Research Enterprise on Social Capital", this volume.

—— "A Network Theory of Social Capital," in D. Castiglione, J. V. Deth, and G. Wolleb (eds.), *Handbook on Social Capital* (London: Oxford University Press, forthcoming).

—— and Y. BIAN, "Getting Ahead in Urban China," *American Journal of Sociology*, 97 (1991*a*), 657–88.

—— —— "Social Connections (Guanxi) and Status Attainment in Urban China," paper presented at the Second European Conference on Social Network Analysis, Sorbonne, Paris, June 10–22, 1991*b*.

—— K. COOK, and R. S. BURT (eds.), *Social Capital: Theory and Research* (New York: Aldine de Gruyter, 2001*a*).

—— —— —— "Preface," in N. Lin, K. Cook, and R. S. Burt (eds.), *Social Capital: Theory and Research* (New York: Aldine de Gruyter, 2001*b*).

—— P. DAYTON, and P. GREENWALD, "Analyzing the Instrumental Use of Relations in the Context of Social Structure," *Sociological Methods and Research*, 7 (1978), 149–66.

—— A. DEAN, and W. M. ENSEL, *Social Support, Life Events, and Depression* (New York: Academic Press, 1986).

—— and M. DUMIN, "Access to Occupations Through Social Ties," *Social Networks*, 8 (1986), 365–85.

—— W. M. ENSEL, and J. C. VAUGHN, "Social Resources and Strength of Ties: Structural Factors in Occupational Status Attainment," *American Sociological Review*, 46(4) (1981), 393–405.

—— Y. FU, and R. HSUNG, "The Position Generator: Measurement Techniques for Social Capital," in N. Lin, K. Cook, and R. S. Burt (eds.), *Social Capital: Theory and Research* (New York: Aldine de Gruyter, 2001) 57–81.

—— J. C. VAUGHN, and W. M. ENSEL, "Social Resources and Occupational Status Attainment," *Social Forces*, 59 (1981), 1163–81.

—— and J. WESTCOTT, "Marital Engagement/Disengagement, Social Networks, and Mental Health," in J. Eckenrode (ed.), *The Social Context of Coping* (New York: Plenum Press, 1991) 213–37.

—— and W. XIE, "Occupational Prestige in Urban China," *American Journal of Sociology*, 93 (1988), 793–832.

LINDEMAN, E., *Participatie in Vrijwilligerswerk* (Amsterdam: Thesis, 1995).

LIVINGSTON, G., "Rethinking the Relationship between Social Capital, Gender, and Labor Force Outcomes among Mexican Immigrants", Conference Presentation at the 2000 American Sociological Association, 2000.

LOEVINGER, J., "A Systematic Approach to the Construction and Evaluation of Test of Ability," *Psychological Monographs*, 61(4) (1947), 1–49.

LOMNITZ, L. A., and D. SHEINGOLD, "Trust, Social Networks and the Informal Economy," *Review of Sociology*, 1 (2004), 5–26.

LONG, J. S., *Regression Models for Categorical and Limited Dependent Variables* (Thousand Oaks, CA: Sage, 1997).

LOUCH, H., "Personal Network Integration: Transivity and Homophily in Strong-tie Relations," *Social Networks*, 22 (2000), 45–64.

LOWNDES, V., "Women and Social Capital: A Comment on Hall's 'Social Capital in Britain,'" *British Journal of Political Science*, 30(3) (2000), 533–7.

LUBELL, M., and J. T. SCHOLZ, "Cooperation, Reciprocity, and the Collective-Action Heuristic," *American Journal of Political Science*, 45 (2001), 160–78.

LUXTON, M., *More than a Labour of Love* (Toronto, Canada: Women's Press, 1980).

MAILLÉ, C., *Vers un nouveau pouvoir: les femmes en politique au Canada* (Ottawa: Conseil Consultatif Canadien sur la Situation de la Femme, 1990).

MARSDEN, P. V., "Core Discussion Networks of Americans," *American Sociological Review*, 52 (1987), 122–31.

—— "Homogeneity in Confiding Networks," *Social Networks*, 10 (1988), 57–76.

—— "Network Data and Measurement," *Annual Review of Sociology*, 16 (1990a), 435–63.

—— "Network Diversity, Substructures and Opportunities for Contact," in C. Calhoun, M. Meyer, and R. S. Schott (eds.), *Structures of Power and Constraint: Papers in Honor of Peter Blau* (Cambridge: Cambridge University Press, 1990b) 397–410.

—— "The Staffing Process," in A. L. Kalleberg, D. Knoke, P. V. Marsden, and J. L. Spaeth (eds.), *Organizations in America: Analyzing Their Structure and Human Resource Practices* (New York: Kluwer, 1996) 133–56.

—— "Interviewer Effects in Measuring Network Size Using a Single Name Generator," *Social Networks*, 25 (2003), 1–16.

—— and K. E. CAMPBELL, "Measuring Tie Strength," *Social Forces*, 63 (1984), 482–501.

—— and E. H. GORMAN, "Social Networks, Job Changes, and Recruitment," in I. Berg and A. L. Kalleberg (eds.), *Sourcebook on Labor Markets: Evolving Structures and Processes* (New York: Kluwer/Plenum, 2001) 467–502.

—— and J. S. HURLBERT, "Social Resources and Mobility Outcomes: A Replication and Extension," *Social Forces*, 66(4) (1988), 1038–59.

MARTIN, P. Y., "Gender as Social Institution," *Social Forces*, 82(4) (2004), 1249–73.

MARTINEAU, W. H. "Informal Social Ties among Urban Black Americans: Some New Data and a Review of the Problem," *Journal of Black Studies*, 8 (1977), 83–104.

MARX, J., and K. T. LEICHT, "Formality of Recruitment to 229 Jobs: Variations by Race, Sex and Job Characteristics," *Sociology and Social Research*, 76 (1992), 190–6.

MARX, K., in D. McLellan (ed.), *Capital: An Abridged Edition* (New York and Oxford: Oxford University Press, [1867, 1885, 1894] 1995).

—— *Wage-Labour and Capital* (New York: International Publishers Co., [1849] 1933).

MATTHEWS, R., "Using a Social Capital Perspective to Understand Social and Economic Development," *Horizons*, 6(3) (2003), 25–30.

McADAM, D., "Recruitment to High-Risk Activism: The Case of Freedom Summer," *American Journal of Sociology*, 92(1) (1986), 64–90.

—— "Gender as a Mediator of the Activist Experience: The Case of Freedom Summer," *American Journal of Sociology*, 97(5) (1992), 1211–40.

—— "Beyond Structural Analysis: Toward a More Dynamic Understanding of Social Movements," in M. Diani and D. McAdam (eds.), *Social Movements and Networks: Relational Approaches to Collective Action* (Oxford: Oxford University Press, 2003) 281–98.

—— and R. PAULSEN, "Specifying the Relationship between Social Ties and Activism," *American Journal of Sociology*, 99(3) (1993), 640–67.

McCALLISTER, L., and C. S. FISCHER, "A Procedure for Surveying Personal Networks," *Sociological Methods and Research*, 7 (1978), 131–48.

McCARTY, C., H. R. BERNARD, P. D. KILLWORTH, G. A. SHELLEY, and E. C. JOHNSEN, "Eliciting Representative Samples of Personal Networks," *Social Networks*, 19 (1997), 303–23.

—— P. D. KILLWORTH, H. R. BERNARD, G. A. SHELLEY, and E. C. JOHNSEN, "Comparing Two Methods for Estimating Network Size," *Human Organization*, 60 (2001), 28–39.

McDONALD, S., "Non-Searching for Jobs: Social Capital and the Job Matching Process," presented at the Annual Meeting of the American Sociological Association, Chicago, August 2002.

McKENNA, K. Y. A., and J. A. BARGH, "Plan 9 from Cyberspace: The Implication of the Internet for Personality and Social Psychology," *Personality and Social Psychology Review*, 4 (2000), 57–75.

McPHERSON, M., and L. SMITH-LOVIN, "Women and Weak Ties: Differences by Sex in the Size of Voluntary Organizations," *American Journal of Sociology*, 87 (1982), 883–904.

—— —— "Sex Segregation in Voluntary Associations," *American Sociological Review*, 51 (1986), 61–79.

—— —— "Homophily in Voluntary Associations," *American Sociological Review*, 52 (1987), 370–9.

—— —— and M. E. BRASHEARS, "Social Isolation in America: Changes in Core Discussion Networks over Two Decades," *American Sociological Review*, 71(June) (2006), 353–75.

—— —— and J. COOK, "Birds of a Feather: Homophily in Social Networks," *Annual Review of Sociology*, 27 (2001), 415–44.

—— P. POPIELARZ, and S. DROBNIC, "Social Networks and Organization Dynamics," *American Sociological Review*, 57 (1992), 153–70.

MILARDO, R. M., "Friendship Networks in Developing Relationships: Converging and Diverging Social Environments," *Social Psychology Quarterly*, 45 (1982), 162–72.

—— *Families and Social Networks* (Newbury Park, CA: Sage, 1988).

—— and G. ALLAN, "Social Networks and Marital Relationships," in R. M. Milardo and S. Duck (eds.), *Families as Relationships* (Chichester, UK: Wiley, 2000) 117–33.

MILGRAM, S., "The Small World Problem," *Psychology Today*, 1 (1967), 61–7.

—— "Interdisciplinary Thinking and the Small World Problem," in M. Sherif and C. W. Sherif (eds.), *Interdisciplinary Relationships in the Social Sciences* (Chicago: Aldine Pub. Co., 1969) 103–20.

MIYATA, K., "Social Support for Japanese Mothers Online and Offline," in B. Wellman and C. Haythornthwaite (eds.), *The Internet in Everyday Life* (Malden, MA: Blackwell, 2002) 520–48.

MOERBEEK, H. *Friends and Foes in the Occupational Career—The Influence of Sweet and Sour Social Capital on the Labour Market* (ICS dissertations [73]). (Amsterdam: Thela Thesis Publishers, 2001).

—— and H. FLAP, "Social Resources, Modernization and Occupational Attainment," in N. Lin and B. H. Erickson (eds.), *Social Capital: Theory and Research* (New York: Oxford University Press, 2008).

MOHAI, P., "Men, Women, and the Environment: An Examination of the Gender Gap in Environmental Concern and Activism," *Society and Natural Resources*, 5 (1992), 1–19.

MOKKEN, R. J., "Nonparametric Models for Dichotomous Responses," in W. J. Van der Linden and R. K. Hambleton (eds.), *Handbook of Modern Item Response Theory* (New York: Springer, 1996) 351–67.

MOLENAAR, I., and K. SIJTSMA, *User's Manual MSP5 for Windows: A Program for Mokken Scale Analysis for Polytomous Items* (Groningen, the Netherlands: ProGAMMA, 2000).

MONGOLIA NATIONAL STATISTICS OFFICE and UNITED NATIONS POPULATION FUND, *Population and Housing Census 2000: Statistical Booklet: Ulaanbaatar* (Ulaanbaatar, Mongolia: National Statistical Office, 2001).

MOORE, G., "Structural Determinants of Men's and Women's Personal Networks," *American Sociological Review*, 55 (1990), 726–35.

MORGAN, J. N., "The Redistribution of Income by Families and Institutions and Emergency Help Patterns," in M. S. Hill (ed.), *Five Thousand American Families*, vol. 10 (Ann Arbor, MI: Institute of Social Research, 1982) 1–59.

MORRIS, A. D., *Origins of the Civil Rights Movements* (New York: Free Press, 1984).

MOUW, T., "Social Capital and Finding a Job: Do Contacts Matter?," *American Sociological Review*, 68 (2003), 868–98.

MUELLER, J. H., and K. F. SCHUESSLER, *Statistical Reasoning in Sociology* (Boston: Houghton Mifflin, 1961).

MULLER, E. N., and K. OPP, "Rational Choice and Rebellious Collective Action," *American Political Science Review*, 80 (1986), 471–87.

MUNCH, A., M. McPHERSON, and L. SMITH-LOVIN, "Gender, Children, and Social Contact: The Effects of Childrearing for Men and Women," *American Sociological Review*, 62 (1997), 509–20.

NECKERMAN, K. M., and J. KIRSCHENMAN, "Hiring Strategies, Racial Bias, and Inner-City Workers," *Social Problems*, 38(4) (1991), 433–47.

NEWMAN, K. S., *No Shame in My Game: The Working Poor in the Inner City* (New York: Knopf and Russell Sage Foundation, 1999).

NIE, N. H., and L. ERBRING, *Internet and Society: A Preliminary Report* (Stanford, CA: Stanford Institute for the Quantitative Study of Society, 2000). <www.stanford.edu/group/siqss/Press_Release/Preliminary_Report.pdf>

——— J. JUNN, and K. STEHLIK-BARRY, *Education and Democratic Citizenship in America* (Chicago: University of Chicago Press, 1996).

NOELLE-NEUMANN, E., "Identifying Opinion Leaders," *European Research*, 13 (1987), 18–23.

NORRIS, P., *Digital Divide: Civic Engagement, Information Poverty, and the Internet Worldwide* (Cambridge: Cambridge University Press, 2001).

——— "The Bridging and Bonding Role of Online Communities," in P. Howard and S. Jones (eds.), *Society Online: The Internet in Context* (Thousand Oaks, CA: Sage, 2003).

——— "Civic Engagement and the Knowledge Society", Report for UNESCO World Report "*Building Knowledge Societies*," 2004, <ksghome.harvard.edu/~. pnorris.shorenstein. ksg/Acrobat/UNESCO%20Report%20Knowledge%20Societies.pdf>

OI, L., *Rural China Takes Off: Incentives for Industrialization* (Berkeley, Los Angeles: University of California Press, 2000).

OLIVER, M. L., "The Urban Black Community as Network: Toward a Social Network Perspective," *The Sociological Quarterly*, 29(4) (1988), 623–45.

OLLIVIER, M., and M. TREMBLAY, *Questionnements féminists et méthodologie de la recherché* (Paris: L'Harmattan, 2000).

OLSON, M., *The Logic of Collective Action: Public Goods and the Theory of Groups* (Cambridge, MA: Harvard University Press, 1965).

O'NEILL, B., "The Gender Gap: Re-Evaluating Theory and Method," in S. Burt and L. Code (eds.), *Changing Methods: Feminists Transforming Practice* (Peterborough, ON: Broadview, 1995) 327–56.

——— and E. GIDENGIL, *Gender and Social Capital* (New York: Routledge, 2006).

ONYX, J., and P. BULLEN, "Measuring Social Capital in Five Communities," *The Journal of Applied Behavioural Science*, 36 (2000), 23–42.

OPP, K. D., "Soft Incentives and Collective Action: Participation in the Anti-Nuclear Movement," *British Journal of Political Science*, 16 (1986), 87–112.

——— and C. GERN, "Dissident Groups, Personal Networks, and Spontaneous Cooperation," *American Sociological Review*, 58(5) (1993), 659–80.

PARISH, W., L. HAO, and D. P. HOGAN, "Family Support Networks, Welfare and Work among Young Mothers," *Journal of Marriage and the Family*, 53 (1991), 203–15.

PAXTON, P., "Is Social Capital Declining in the United States? A Multiple Indicator Assessment," *American Journal of Sociology*, 105 (1999), 88–127.

—— "Social Capital and Democracy: An Interdependent Relationship," *American Sociological Review*, 67 (2002), 254–77.

PODOLNY, J. M., and J. N. BARON, "Resources and Relationships: Social Networks and Mobility in the Workplace," *American Sociological Review*, 62 (1997), 673–93.

PORTES, A., "Social Capital: Its Origins and Applications in Modern Sociology," *Annual Review of Sociology*, 22 (1998), 1–24.

—— "The Resilient Importance of Class: A Nominalist Interpretation," in D. E. Davis (ed.), *Political Power and Social Theory* (Greenwich, CT: JAI Press, 2000) 249–84.

—— and J. SENSENBRENNER, "Embeddedness and Immigration: Notes on the Social Determinants of Economic Action," *American Journal of Sociology*, 98(6) (1993), 1320–50.

PUTNAM, R. (with R. LEONARDI and R. Y. NANETTI), *Making Democracy Work: Civic Traditions in Modern Italy* (Princeton, NJ: Princeton University Press, 1993a).

—— "The Prosperous Community: Social Capital and Public Life," *The American Prospect*, 13 (1993b), 35–42.

—— "Bowling Alone: American's Declining Social Capital', *Journal of Democracy*, 6(1) (1995), 65–78.

—— *Bowling Alone: The Collapse and Revival of American Community* (New York: Simon & Schuster, 2000).

—— *Social Capital Community Benchmark Survey* (Cambridge, MA: John F. Kennedy School of Government, 2001).

—— and L. M. FELDSTEIN, *Better Together: Restoring the American Community* (New York: Simon & Schuster, 2003).

QUAN-HAASE, A., B. WELLMAN, J. C. WITTE, and K. HAMPTON, "Capitalizing on the Internet: Network Capital, Participatory Capital, and Sense of Community," in B. Wellman and C. Haythornthwaite (eds.), *The Internet in Everyday Life* (Malden, MA: Blackwell, 2002) 291–324.

R STATISTICAL SOFTWARE (Version 1.8.1), The R Development Core Team, 2003.

RANKIN, B., and J. QUANE, "Neighborhood Poverty and the Social Isolation of Inner-City African American Families," *Social Forces*, 79(1) (2000), 139–64.

REIMER, B., "The Informal Economy in Rural Canada," work in progress, 2001.

RESKIN, B. F., "Sex Segregation in the Workplace," *Annual Review of Sociology*, 19 (1993), 241–70.

—— and H. I. HARTMANN, *Women's Work, Men's Work: Sex Segregation on the Job* (Washington, DC: National Academy Press, 1986).

RHEINGOLD, H., *The Virtual Community*, revised edn. (Cambridge, MA: MIT Press, 2000).

RIDGEWAY, C., "Interaction and the Conservation of Gender Inequality: Considering Employment," *American Sociological Review*, 62(2) (1997), 218–35.

ROBINSON, B., and A. SOLONGO, "The Gender Dimension of Economic Transition in Mongolia," in F. Nixson, B. Suvd, P. Luvsandorj, and B. Walters (eds.), *The Mongolian Economy: A Manual of Applied Economics for a Country in Transition* (Cheltenham, UK: Edward Elgar, 2000) 231–55.

ROBINSON, D. T., and J. W. BALKWELL, "Density, Transitivity, and Diffuse Status in Task-Oriented Groups," *Social Psychology Quarterly*, 58 (1995), 241–55.

ROBINSON, J. P., M. KESTNBAUM, A. NEUSTADTL, and A. ALVAREZ, "Mass Media Use and Social Life among Internet Users," *Social Science Computer Review*, 18 (2000), 490–501.

ROSENBERG, M., "Misanthropy and Political Ideology," *American Sociological Review*, 21 (1956), 690–5.

ROSENTHAL, C. J., "Kinkeeping in the Familial Division of Labor," *Journal of Marriage and the Family*, 47 (1985), 965–74.

ROSSABI, M., *Modern Mongolia: From Khans to Commissars to Capitalists* (Berkeley and Los Angeles: University of California Press, 2005).

ROTOLO, T., "Town Heterogeneity and Affiliation: A Multilevel Analysis of Voluntary Association Membership," *Sociological Perspectives*, 43 (2000), 271–89.

RUAN, D., "Interpersonal Networks and Workplace Controls in Urban China," *Australian Journal of Chinese Affairs*, 29 (1993), 89–105.

—— "The Content of the GSS Discussion Networks: An Exploration of GSS Discussion Name Generator in a Chinese Context," *Social Networks*, 20 (1998), 247–64.

RUSSELL, H., "Friends in Low Places: Gender, Unemployment and Sociability," *Work, Employment and Society*, 13(2) (1999), 205–24.

SCHEUFELE, D. A., and D. V. SHAH, "Personality Strength and Social Capital," *Communication Research*, 27 (2000), 107–31.

SCHMIDT, P., and R. P. STRAUSS, "The Prediction of Occupation Using Multiple Logit Models," *International Economic Review*, 16 (1975), 471–86.

SCHULTZ, T. W., "Investment in Human Capital," *The American Economic Review*, LI(1) (1961), 1–17.

SCOTT, W. R., "Reflections on a Half-Century of Organizational Sociology," *Annual Review of Sociology*, 30 (2004) 1–21.

SIJTSMA, K., and I. W. MOLENAAR, *Introduction to Nonparametric Item Response Theory* (Thousand Oaks, CA: Sage, 2002).

SIXMA, H., and W. C. ULTEE, "An Occupational Prestige Scale for the Netherlands in the 1980s," in B. F. M. Bakker, J. Dronkers, and H. B. G. Ganzeboom (eds.), *Social Stratification and Mobility in the Netherlands* (Amsterdam: Siswo, 1984) 29–39.

SMITH, S. S., "It's Not Just What You Know or Who You Know, It's What Who You Know Can Do for You: Racial and Ethnic Differences in Receipt of Proactive Assistance," unpublished manuscript, 2002.

—— "Social Capital and the Urban Poor: Extending the Scholarly Tradition of William Julius Wilson," *Ethnic and Racial Studies*, 26(6) (2003), 1029–45.

—— " 'Don't Put My Name on It': Social Capital Activation and Job-Finding Assistance among the Black Urban Poor," *American Journal of Sociology*, 111(1) (2005), 1–57.

—— "Mobilizing Social Resources: Race, Ethnic, and Gender Differences in Social Capital and Persisting Wage Inequalities," *The Sociological Quarterly*, 41 (2000), 509–37.

SNIJDERS, T. A. B., "Prologue to the Measurement of Social Capital," *La Revue Tocqueville*, 20 (1999), 27–44.

SNOW, D. A., L. A. ZURCHER, Jr., and S. EKLAND-OLSON, "Social Networks and Social Movements: A Microstructural Approach to Differential Recruitment," *American Sociological Review*, 45 (1980), 787–801.

SOSIN, M., "Concentration of Poverty and Social Isolation of the Inner-City Poor," paper presented at the Chicago Urban Poverty and Family Life Conference, Chicago, IL, October 10–12, 1991.

SPROULL, L., and S. KIESLER, *Connections: New Ways of Working in the Networked Organization* (Cambridge, MA: MIT Press, 1991).

STACK, C., *All Our Kin: Strategies for Survival in a Black Community* (New York: Harper and Row, 1974).

STEIN, C. H., E. G. BUSH, R. R. ROSS, and M. WARD, "Mine, Yours and Ours: A Configural Analysis of the Networks of Married Couples in Relation to Marital Satisfaction and Individual Well-Being," *Journal of Social and Personal Relationships*, 9 (1992), 365–83.

STOLLE, D., "Getting to Trust: An Analysis of the Importance of Institutions, Families, Personal Experiences and Group Membership," in P. Dekker and E. Uslaner (eds.), *Politics in Everyday Life: Social Capital and Participation* (London: Routledge, 2001) 118–33.

STRAITS, B. C., "Occupational Sex Segregation: The Role of Personal Ties," *Journal of Vocational Behavior*, 52 (1998), 191–207.

SUN, C., and R. M. HSUNG, *Social Resources and Social Mobility* (Taiwan: Tunghai University, 1988).

—— and L. WU, "Human Capital and Social Capital in Job Search," Technical Report, Sociology, Tunghai University, 2002.

SURRA, C. A., "The Influence of the Interactive Network on Developing Relationships," in R. M. Milardo (ed.), *Families and Social Networks* (Beverly Hills, CA: Sage, 1988) 48–82.

SWEDSBERG, R., "Markets as Social Structure," in N. J. Smelser and R. Swedberg (eds.), *Handbook of Economic Sociology* (Princeton, NJ, and New York: Princeton University Press and Russell Sage Foundation, 1990) 255–82.

TARDY, E., M. TREMBLAY, and G. LEGAULT, *Maries et mairesses: Les femmes et la politique municipale* (Montreal, Canada: Liber, 1997).

TIGGES, L. M., I. BROWNE, and G. P. GREEN, "Social Isolation of the Urban Poor: Race, Class, and Neighborhood Effects on Social Resources," *The Sociological Quarterly*, 39 (1998), 53–77.

TINDALL, D. B., "Collective Action in the Rainforest: Personal Networks, Identity, and Participation in the Vancouver Island Wilderness Preservation Movement," unpublished doctoral dissertation, University of Toronto, Department of Sociology, 1994.

—— "Social Networks, Identification and Participation in an Environmental Movement: Low-Medium Cost Activism within the British Columbia Wilderness Preservation Movement," *Canadian Review of Sociology and Anthropology*, 39(4) (2002), 413–52.

—— "Social Movement Participation over Time: An Ego-Network Approach to Micro-Mobilization," *Sociological Focus*, 37(2) (2004), 163–84.

—— and N. BEGORAY, "Old Growth Defenders: The Battle for the Carmanah Valley," in S. Lerner (ed.), *Environmental Stewardship: Studies in Active Earthkeeping* (Waterloo, Ontario, Canada: University of Waterloo Geography Series, 1993) 269–322.

—— S. DAVIES, and C. MAUBOULÈS, "Activism and Conservation Behavior in an Environmental Movement: The Contradictory Effects of Gender," *Society and Natural Resources*, 16(10) (2003), 909–32.

—— and B. WELLMAN, "Canada as Social Structure: Social Network Analysis and Canadian Sociology," *Canadian Journal of Sociology*, 26(3) (2001), 265–308.

TÓTH, I., "Composition and Inequality of Incomes 2000–2003," in T. Kolosi, I. G. Y. Tóth, and G. Y. Vukovich (eds.), *Social Report 2004* (Budapest: Tárki, 2004) 72–92.

TREIMAN, D. J., *Occupational Prestige in Comparative Perspective* (New York: Academic Press, 1977).

—— and K. B. YIP, "Educational and Occupational Attainment in 21 Countries," in M. Kohn (ed.), *Cross National Research in Sociology* (Newbury Park, CA: Sage, 1989) 373–94.

TREMBLAY, M., and L. TRIMBLE, "Women and Electoral Politics in Canada: A Survey of the Literature," in M. Tremblay and L. Trimble (eds.), *Women and Electoral Politics in Canada* (Toronto, Canada: Oxford University Press, 2003) 1–20.

TRIMBLE, L., and M. TREMBLAY, "Women Politicians in Canada's Parliament and Legislatures, 1917–2000: A Socio-Demographic Profile," in M. Tremblay and L. Trimble (eds.), *Women and Electoral Politics in Canada* (Toronto, Canada: Oxford University Press, 2003) 37–58.

UNITED NATIONS DEVELOPMENT FUND FOR WOMEN, *Women in Mongolia: Mapping Progress under Transition*, UNIFEM, New York, 2002. Retrieved April 9, 2004, <http://www.unifem.org/index.php?f_page_pid=68>

UNITED NATIONS DEVELOPMENT PROGRAMME, *Human Development Report for 2004*, p. 190. Retrieved May 25, 2005, <http://hdr.undp.org/reports/global/2004/pdf/hdr04_HDI.pdf>

UNITED NATIONS DEVELOPMENT PROGRAMME and GOVERNMENT of MONGOLIA, *Human Development Report—Mongolia—2004: Reorienting the State* (Ulaanbaatar, Mongolia: United Nations Development Programme, 2004).

USLANER, E. M., *The Moral Foundations of Trust* (Cambridge: Cambridge University Press, 2002).

VAN DAAL, H., and E. M. T. PLEMPER, "Geven van tijd: vrijwilligerswerk," in T. N. M. Schuyt (ed.), *Geven in Nederland 2003: giften, legaten, sponsoring en vrijwilligerswerk* (Houten/Mechelen: Bohn Stafleu Van Loghum, 2003) 80–108.

VAN DER GAAG, M. P. J., "Measurement of Individual Social Capital," Ph.D. dissertation, Department of Sociology, Groningen University, Groningen, the Netherlands, 2005.

——and T. A. B. SNIJDERS, "A Comparison of Measures for Individual Social Capital," paper presented at the conference "Creation and Returns of Social Capital," Amsterdam, the Netherlands, October 30–31, 2003.

———— "Proposals for the Measurement of Individual Social Capital," in H. Flap and B. Völker (eds.), *Creation and Returns of Social Capital: A New Research Program* (London: Routledge, 2005a) 199–218.

———— "The Resource Generator: Social Capital Quantification with Concrete Items," *Social Networks*, 27(1) (2005b), 1–29.

———— and H. FLAP, "Position Generator Measures and Their Relation to Other Social Capital Indicators," in N. Lin and B. H. Erickson (eds.), *Social Capital: Theory and Research* (New York: Oxford University Press, 2008).

VAN DER LINDEN, W. J., and R. K. HAMBLETON, *Handbook of Modern Item Response Theory* (New York: Springer, 1997).

VAN LEEUWEN, S., M. A. R. TIJHUIS, and H. FLAP, "Cohesie in de Nederlandse Samenleving. De Relatie Tussen Integratie, Heterogeniteit en Sociale Steun," *Tijdschrift voor Sociale Wetenschappen*, 36 (1993), 23–43.

VAN DER POEL, M. G. M., "Delineating Personal Support Networks," *Social Networks*, 15 (1993), 49–70.

VAN SONDEREN, E., J. ORMEL, E. BRILMAN, and C. H. VAN LINDEN VAN DEN HEUVELL, "A Comparison of the Exchange, Affective, and Role-Relation Approach," in C. P. M. Knipscheer and T. C. Antonucci (eds.), *Social Network Research: Methodological Questions and Substantive Issues* (Lisse, the Netherlands: Swets and Zeitlinger, 1990) 101–20.

VAN TUBERGEN, F., M. TE GROTENHUIS, and W. ULTEE, "Denomination, Religious Context, and Suicide: Neo-Durkheinian Multilevel Explanations Tested with Individual and Contactual Data," *American Journal of Sociology*, 111(3) (2005), 797–823.

VERBA, S., and N. H. NIE, *Participation in America* (New York: Harper and Row, 1972).

—— K. L. SCHLOZMAN, and H. E. BRADY, *Voice and Equality: Civic Voluntarism in American Politics* (Cambridge, MA: Harvard University Press, 1995).

VÖLKER, B., "Should Auld Acquaintance Be Forgot? Institutions of Communism, the Transition to Capitalism and Personal Networks: The Case of East Germany," Ph.D. dissertation, Department of Sociology, University of Utrecht, Utrecht, the Netherlands, 1995.

—— and H. FLAP, "Getting Ahead in the GDR: Social Capital and Status Attainment under Communism," *Acta Sociologica*, 41 (1999), 17–34.

—— —— "Weak Ties as a Liability: The Case of the GDR," *Rationality and Society*, 13 (2001), 397–428.

—— —— *The Social Survey of the Network of the Dutch, First Wave. SSND1, Codebook* (Utrecht, the Netherlands: ICS, 2002).

—— —— "Social Networks and Performance at Work: A Study of the Returns of Social Capital in Doing One's Job," in H. Flap and B. Völker (eds.), *Creation and Returns of Social Capital: A New Research Program* (London: Routledge, 2004) 172–96.

WACQUANT, L. J. D., and W. J. WILSON, "The Cost of Racial and Class Exclusion in the Inner City," *The ANNALS of the American Academy of Political and Social Science*, 501 (1989), 8–25.

WALDER, A. G., *Communist Neo-Traditionalism: Work and Authority in Chinese Industry* (Berkeley, CA: University of California Press, 1986).

—— "Local Governments as Industrial Firms: An Organizational Analysis of China's Transitional Economy," *American Journal of Sociology*, 101 (1995), 263–301.

WALDINGER, R., "Black/Immigrant Competition Re-Assessed: New Evidence from Los Angeles," *Sociological Perspectives*, 40 (1997), 365–86.

WALL, E., D. J. CONNELL, M. TACHIKAWA, and K. YABE, "The Voluntary Sector in Rural Communities: A Comparison of Japan and Canada," work in progress, 2003.

WANG, G., "Cultivating Friendship Through Bowling in Shenzhen," in D. S. Davis (ed.), *The Consumer Revolution in Urban China* (Berkeley: University of California Press, 2000) 250–67.

WANK, D. L., *Commodifying Communism: Business, Trust and Politics in a Chinese City* (Cambridge: University of Cambridge, 1999).

WARNER, R. S., and J. G. WITTNER, *Gatherings in Diaspora: Religious Communities and the New Immigration* (Philadelphia, PA: Temple University Press, 1998).

WEBER, M., *Economy and Society* (Berkeley: University of California Press, [1914] 1978).

WELLMAN, B., "The Community Question: The Intimate Networks of East Yorkers," *American Journal of Sociology*, 84 (1979), 1201–31.

—— "Studying Personal Communities," in P. V. Marsden and N. Lin (eds.), *Social Structure and Network Analysis* (Beverly Hills, CA: Sage, 1982) 61–80.

—— "Domestic Work, Paid Work and Net Work," in S. W. Duck and D. Perlman (eds.), *Understanding Personal Relationships* (London: Sage, 1985) 159–91.

—— "From Little Boxes to Loosely Connected Networks: The Privatization and Domestication of Communities," in J. L. Abu-Lughod (ed.), *Sociology for the Twenty-First Century* (Chicago: University of Chicago Press, 1999) 94–114.

—— and K. FRANK, "Network Capital in a Multilevel World: Getting Support from Personal Communities," in N. Lin, K. Cook, and R. S. Burt (eds.), *Social Capital: Theory and Research* (New York: Aldine de Gruyter, 2001) 233–74.

WELLMAN, B., A. QUAN-HAASE, J. C. WITTE, and K. HAMPTON, "Does the Internet Increase, Decrease, or Supplement Social Capital? Social Networks, Participation, and Community Commitment," *American Behavioral Scientist*, 45(3) (2001), 437–66.

—— and S. WORTLEY, "Different Strokes from Different Folks: Community Ties and Social Support," *American Journal of Sociology*, 96 (1990), 558–88.

WEST, C., and D. H. ZIMMERMAN, "Doing Gender," *Gender and Society*, 1 (1987), 125–51.

WHITE, H. C., *Identity and Control: A Structural Theory of Action* (Princeton, NJ: Princeton University Press, 1992).

WIDMER, E., J. KELLERHALS, and R. LEVY, "Types of Conjugal Networks, Conjugal Conflict and Conjugal Quality," *European Sociological Review*, 20 (2004), 61–77.

WILCOX, B. L., "Social Support in Adjusting to Marital Disruption," in B. H. Gottlieb (ed.), *Social Networks and Social Support* (Beverly Hills, CA: Sage, 1981) 97–115.

WILSON, J., *Talk and Log: Wilderness Politics in British Columbia, 1965–96* (Vancouver, BC: UBC Press, 1998).

—— "Volunteering," *Annual Review of Sociology*, 26 (2000), 215–40.

—— and T. JANOSKI, "The Contribution of Religion to Volunteer Work," *Sociology of Religion*, 56 (1995), 137–52.

—— and M. A. MUSICK, "Who Cares? An Integrated Theory of Volunteer Work," *American Sociological Review*, 62 (1997), 694–713.

—— —— "Social Resources and Volunteering," *Social Science Quarterly*, 79 (1998), 799–814.

—— —— "Doing Well by Doing Good: Volunteering and Occupational Achievement among American Women," *Sociological Quarterly*, 44 (2003), 433–50.

WILSON, W. J., *The Truly Disadvantaged: The Inner City, the Underclass, and Public Policy* (Chicago: University of Chicago Press, 1987).

—— *When Work Disappears: The World of the New Urban Poor* (New York: Alfred A. Knopf, 1996).

WINTER, D., and C. HUFF, "Adapting the Internet: Comments from a Women-Only Electronic Forum," *The American Sociologist*, 27(1) (1996), 30–54.

WOLLEBÆK, D., and P. SELLE, "Does Participation in Voluntary Associations Contribute to Social Capital? The Impact of Intensity, Scope and Type," *Nonprofit and Voluntary Sector Quarterly*, 31 (2002), 32–61.

WOMEN IN NATIONAL PARLIAMENTS WEBSITE. Retrieved May 30, 2005, < http://www.ipu.org/wmn-e/classif.htm>. Data are current to June 2004.

WOOLCOCK, M., "Social Capital and Economic Development: Toward a Theoretical Synthesis and Policy Framework," *Theory and Society*, 27(2) (1998), 151–208.

WORLD BANK, *Mongolia—Country Brief*, 2004. Retrieved May 25, 2005, <www.worldbank.org/Countries/Mongolia>

WRIGHT, E. O., *Classes* (London: Verso Editions, 1985).

—— *Class Counts: Comparative Studies in Class Analysis* (Cambridge and New York: Cambridge University Press, 1997).

—— and D. CHO, "The Relative Permeability of Class Boundaries to Cross-Class Friendships: A Comparative Study of the United States, Canada, Sweden, and Norway," *American Sociological Review*, 57 (1992), 85–102.

WU, J., *Dangdai zhongguo jingji gaige (China's Economic Reform)* (Shanghai: Shanghai Far East Press, 2003).

YAKUBOVICH, V., "Patterns of Inaction: Nonsearch as a Matching Method in the Russian Urban Labor Market," Graduate School of Business, University of Chicago, 2002.

YAMAGISHI, T., *The Structure of Trust: The Evolutionary Game of Mind and Society* (in Japanese) (Tokyo: University of Tokyo Press, 1998).

——— M. R. GILLMORE, and K. S. COOK, "Network Connections and the Distribution of Power in Exchange Networks," *American Journal of Sociology*, 93 (1988), 833–51.

YAN, Y., *The Flow of Gifts: Reciprocity and Social Networks in a Chinese Village* (Stanford, CA: Stanford University Press, 1996).

YANG, F., "Chinese Conversion to Evangelical Christianity: The Importance of Social and Cultural Contexts," *Sociology of Religion*, 59 (1998), 237–59.

YANG, M. M., *Gifts, Favors, and Banquets: The Art of Social Relationships in China* (Ithaca, NY: Cornell University Press, 1994).

ZHOU, X., "Economic Transformation and Income Inequality in Urban China: Evidence from a Panel Data," *American Journal of Sociology*, 105 (2000), 1135–74.

Index

access to social resources and effect on
  occupational attainment 133–56
access-leads-to-more-use hypotheses 140,
  147–50, 155
achieved-access hypothesis 136–7, 140,
  145–7, 154
achieved-access-through-weak-ties-leads-
  to-more-use hypothesis 140–1,
  148
age 139, 151–2
attained prestige 136, 154
barriers to access 258
black poor, job referral networks
  among 158–61, 166–70, 174, 175–8
blue-collar occupations 141
categories of occupation 141
cultural capital 67–8, 171
data 138–9
diversity of access 141, 153
Dutch Telepanel Survey 138–9, 141–53
economic capital 67–8, 71
education 67–8, 71, 133, 134–6, 140,
  145–7, 150–1, 153, 155–6
embedded resources, structure of access
  to 272–4
failed applicants 137–9, 141, 150–6
failures-via-informal resources
  hypothesis 141, 150–3, 156
fathers, occupational prestige of 134, 145,
  151
first job, prestige of 147, 150–1
friends and acquaintances, ties with 136,
  138–41, 143–50, 153–4
gender 139, 145, 151–2, 154–5
higher-number-leads-to-more-use
  hypothesis 140, 147–9, 155
Hungary, application of position generator
  in 400–3, 417
inequality 382–6
informal channels for job searches 134,
  135, 137–8, 140–1, 150–6
intensive use of social resources 140, 155
job searches 120–1, 123–7, 131, 134, 135,
  157–82
life-course, effect on 133–56
location 258
mobilization of social capital 174, 175–8
networks 133
number of persons people have access
  to 141–2

operationalization 138–9, 141
parents, occupational prestige of 133,
  134–6, 145, 151
personal contacts 137
personnel managers in Taiwan, social
  capital of 247
position generators 29
prestige in occupation 133–6, 139, 140–7,
  149, 150–1, 153
propositions and hypotheses in terms of
  variables 139–41
quality of access 138–9
regression of access variables 145–6,
  148–9, 152–3
relatives, ties with 136–8, 140, 143–4,
  147–8, 154
research on access to social
  resources 134–9, 141–53
Resilient Communities Project in British
  Columbia, Canada 258–9, 263–74
returns of social capital 9–10
social skills 155
social ties 142–3
status attainment 145
strength-of-position hypothesis 139, 143,
  153–4
strength-of-weak ties hypotheses 135–6,
  139–41, 143–4, 154
strength of ties 135–41, 143–4, 258,
  267–8
structure of access to embedded
  resources 272–4
Taiwan 247
theory and hypotheses 135–41
Ulaanbaatar, Mongolia, structure of
  inequality in 382–6
use, access leading to 140, 147–50
variables 139–41, 145
voluntary associations 188–91, 195–7,
  199–200, 204–5
weak ties 267–8
white-collar occupations 141
achieved-access hypothesis 136–7, 140,
  145–7, 154
achieved-access-through-weak-ties-leads-to-
  more-use hypothesis 140–1,
  148
acquaintances see friends and acquaintances,
  ties with age
access to social resources 129, 151–2

Chinese urbanites, formation of social
    capital among 101
cultural capital 70, 73
diversity 390
economic capital 70, 73
gender 216, 221, 347, 355, 358
homophily principle 61
Hong Kong, marriage and gender in 348,
    355, 358
Hungary, application of position generator
    in 401–2, 405–7, 411, 418
inequality 388–90
Internet 208–9, 216, 221
Japan, Internet in 216, 221
job searches, effect of social capital
    on 122–3, 126
marriage and gender 347, 355, 358
political participation in, British Columbia,
    Canada 295, 298, 300
position generators 61
occupation 70, 73, 139, 151–2
personnel managers in Taiwan, social
    capital of 241–2
Resilient Communities Project in British
    Columbia, Canada 390
Taiwan 241–2
Ulaanbaatar, Mongolia, structure of
    inequality in 388–90
United States, status attainment in 372,
    373
voluntary associations 192, 195
Allegheny, Pennsylvania, civic participation
    in 22, 312–28
Anderson, Elijah 175
Anderson, JH 380–1
Angelusz, R 6, 8, 10, 16,19, 24, 387
association *see also* voluntary associations
    associationalism 283
    prestige by association 111–12
    sources of social capital 8
attainment *see* access to social resources and
    effect on occupational attainment;
    status attainment
authority-subordinate relationship 83

Baer, DE 283
Bargh, JA 208
Baron, JN 240
Beggs, JJ 160, 258–9, 262, 271
Bekkers, R 8, 21, 267
Bian, Y 5, 13, 19, 95
biographical availability 284–6, 295, 302,
    304
birth, status at 7
Bishop, BJ 262, 270
Black, J 287

black poor, inefficacious job referral networks
    among 157–82
access to social capital 158–61, 166–70,
    174–8
African-Americans 162, 164–78
culture of poverty theory 157
data and findings 164–78
data collection strategies 180–1
direct contacts 166
friends 163
'ghetto' behaviour 174–5, 178–9
Harlem 161
information on jobs 159, 170–1, 179
intergenerational support 162
Los Angeles 159–60
low-wage markets 162–3
mainstream contacts, access to 159, 161,
    163, 167
mobilization of social capital 20–1, 158,
    162–4, 170–8
name generators 160–1, 168
open contacts 170, 176–7
position generator 161, 166–9, 175–9
prestige 167–8
proactive contacts 162–3
professional positions, access to 167–8
referrals 162–4
relatives 163
reluctant contacts 170–4
reputation of contact 163–4, 172–4, 178,
    180
requests for assistance 171
research 163–4
    data and findings 164–78
    data collection strategies 180–1
residence in low-income
    neighbourhoods 157, 159, 165,
    168–70, 174, 179
sample characteristics 165–6
skill levels 169–70, 178
social isolation 157–9, 161, 168
social service agency aiding transition to
    employment 164–78
ties within labour market, access to 166–7
trustworthiness
    contacts, of 175–7, 179
    job seekers, of 170–2, 175
variables 167–8, 176–9
Blau, PM 65, 66, 68, 72, 87, 331, 364, 376
bonding in communities 259–61, 268–9, 279,
    311, 404
Bott, E 343, 344
Bourdieu, P 3, 4, 15–16, 65–6, 71, 78–9, 82,
    311
Boxman, E 33, 36, 108, 236
Brehm, J 203

Bridges, WP 239
bridging ties
  civic participation 311
  diversity 210–11
  Hong Kong, marriage and gender in 343
  Internet, civic engagement and gender in
    Japan 207
  location 259–60
  marriage and gender 343
  Resilient Communities Project in British
    Columbia 259–61, 273–5, 278
  rural communities 258–60
British Columbia, Canada *see* British
  Columbia, Canada, political
  participation in environmental
  organizations in; Resilient
  Communities Project in British
  Columbia, Canada
British Columbia, Canada, political
  participation in environmental
  organizations in 22, 282–307
  activities, types of 291
  age 295, 298, 300
  associationalism 283
  biographical availability 295, 302, 304
  Carmanah Forestry Society (CFS) 291
  collective goals 283
  data collection and sample 291–2
  definition of social capital 288
  description of groups 290–1
  diversity 282–304
  education 292
  domestic work, gender and 301–2,
    304
  friends and acquaintances, ties to 302
  gender 282, 296–9, 301–4
  homogeneity 302
  homophily principle 302
  income 292, 300
  level of political participation 293–4
  networks 282–3, 288–90, 294–5,
    300–1
  occupational ties 294, 297–8
  organizational ties 294
  overlap between movements 291
  political capital 288–9
  politicians, ties to 294–5, 296, 299
  position generator 293, 306–7
  regression analyses 289–90, 297–9
  research
    data collection and sample 291–2
    future research 303–4
    measurement 292–5
    methods 290–2
    results 295–300
    theoretical background 288–97

    theoretical model, hypotheses and
      analytical strategy 288–90
  retired persons 295, 298, 300
  Sierra Club of Western Canada
    (SCWC) 291
  social movements 290–1, 293, 303–4
  social resources 300–1
  use of social capital 288
  variables 288, 290, 292–6, 300, 303,
    305–6
  Victoria 290–1
  voluntary organizations 294, 301–3
  Western Canada Wilderness Committee
    (WCWC) 291
  Wilderness Preservation Society 290–1
Brodie, J 286
Brown, E 191
Bullen, P 259
bulletin boards 208
Burt, S 36, 84, 239, 240, 259–60, 265, 267,
  278, 283, 285, 308, 311, 400
business owners, personal networks
  for 98–100, 103

Campbell, KE 33
Canada *see also* British Columbia, Canada,
  political participation in
  environmental organizations in;
  Resilient Communities Project in
  British Columbia, Canada
  gender stratification 7
  networks 285
  occupational prestige 23
  political participation, gender and 286–7
  sources of social capital 7
  Toronto security industry 285
capacity of social capital 111–15, 118–19,
  121–3
capital, definition of 3
capitalism 98–100
causes of social capital 238–9
  cross-sectional survey 16–17
  education 238
  gender 238
  geographic communities 239
  human capital 238
  Hungary 238
  networks 76–7
  organizational and institutional
    characteristics 239
  position generators 16–17
  rural communities 239
  Taiwan 238
  voluntary associations 197–8, 204
Chandler, C 286
chat groups 208

children
  cultural and economic capital 73, 74–5
  Internet, civic engagement and gender in
    Japan 216
  networks 73, 74–5
  occupation, cultural and economic capital
    and 73, 74–5
Chinese urbanites, formation of social capital
    among 81–104
  age 101
  business owners, personal networks
    for 98–100, 103
  class 81–2, 86–7, 92–4, 98–100, 103
  college education 101–2
  cultural significance, socializing in relation
    to events of 91, 100, 103
  data and measures 89–98
  differential resource effect 87
  discussion networks 90–1
  event-based position generator 91
  favour exchanges 87, 90–1
  gender 101
  guanxi networks 87, 91, 98
  home visits 88
  household income 102
  indicators of city developments,
    selected 104
  interpersonal networking 81–104
  marketization in cities, degree of 102
  measurement of social capital 90–2, 102–3
  migrant labour 97–8, 102
  name generators 90–1
  networks 90–2, 98–103
  occupation 81–2, 88–96, 100–2
  party membership 101–2
  position generators 91
  property ownership 86–7
  regression models 98–9
  relative size effect, class and 87
  residence status 102
  socioeconomic development 96–7
  Spring Festivals, visits during 91–2, 100,
    103
  theoretical model 81–104
  variables
    effect of other 101–2
    measurement of 96–8
Cho, D 86
Chung, CN 237
civic participation 308–28
  Allegheny, Pennsylvania 22, 312–28
  background characteristics 315
  bonding within communities 311
  bridging ties 311
  community connectedness 316
  decline in participation 310–12

democratic institutions, maintenance
  of 237
diversity 209–10, 235, 311, 314,
  317–26
economic development 261
education 267, 315
email, rise in usage of 323–4, 326
ethnic and racial diversity 315, 318, 325
forms of participation 321–2, 325–6
gender 206–33, 267, 270, 318, 325
heterogeneity 311, 316
Hungary, application of position generator
  in 397
income 315
Internet, civic engagement and gender in
  Japan 206–33
Italy 261
Japan 206–33
leisure time 315
location 261–2
Miami-Dade, Florida 22, 312–28
neighbourhood characteristics 315
neighbourhood togetherness 317–18
Netherlands 267
networks 302–28
newspaper reading, decline in 323–4
occupation 315
personnel managers in Taiwan, social
  capital of 237
political knowledge 209
political participation 209–10
political trust 209
position generator 308–9, 313–14, 318
reciprocity 209–10
regression equations 320–2, 325
religious organizations, participation
  in 22, 310, 321–2, 326
research 309–12
  measurement 313–15
  methods 312–13
  results 315–24
  sample 327
Resilient Communities Project in British
  Columbia, Canada 261–3, 268–70,
  272–5, 278
rural communities 261–2
social capital, as 2, 21
social resource, as 309–10
socioeconomic diversity 315–16
Taiwan 237
telephone usage, rise in 323–4
television viewing, rise in 311, 322–4,
  326
time pressures 311
traditional values, importance of 314–15
trust 22, 209, 237, 261, 315, 317–18

civic participation (*cont.*)
  two-county telephone survey 312–13
  United States 237, 261, 310–28
  variables 314
  voluntary associations 188, 237, 261,
      309–10
class
  authority 86
  Chinese urbanites, formation of social
      capital among 81–2, 86–7, 92–4,
      98–100, 103
  cultural capital 65, 89
  definition 86
  differential resource effect 87
  economic capital 89
  ethnicity and race, attitudes to 16
  favour exchanges 90–1
  formation of social capital 86–8
  friendships 86
  homophily principle 86
  hierarchical ties 87
  horizontal ties 87
  immigrants, attitudes to 16
  industrialization 87
  inequality 385
  intergenerational mobility 89
  measurement 92–3
  networks 85, 88, 98, 103
  obstacle to socializing, as 86–8
  occupation 86, 89, 92–4
  position generators 14, 16
  property ownership 86–7
  pyramidal class structure 87
  skill 86
  social mobility 87
  structural mobility effect 87
  structuralism theory 87
  Ulaanbaatar, Mongolia, structure of
      inequality in 385
  United States, status attainment in 371
Coakes, SJ 262, 270
Coleman, JS 1–2, 21, 84, 187–8, 257–8, 311,
      348
communication systems 8 *see also* Internet
community connectedness 316
compensatory strategies theory 65
connections 95–6, 100–1, 332
contact diaries *see* position generators,
      contact diaries and
Cook, J 12, 283, 308, 400
Costa, D 311
Cote, R 16
cultural capital *see also* education; occupation
      and economic (income) and cultural
      capital (education)
  class 65
  compensatory strategies 65

definition of social capital 82
Hungary, application of position generator
      in 400
position generators 16
returns of social capital 6, 16, 66–7
social mobility 65
culture of poverty theory 157
Curtis, JE 283

De Graaf, PM 66, 69–71, 78
De Tocqueville, Alexis 309
definition of capital 3
definition of social capital 1–2, 236
  authority-subordinate relationship 83
  cultural capital 82
  human capital 82
  material capital 82–3
  mobilization of social capital 82–3
  personal relationships, enduring 83
  public relationships 83
  social networks, resources embedded
      in 4
  social participation 21
  social relations, resources embedded in 4
  status attainment 365
  symbolic capital 82
  trust 21
democratic institutions, maintenance
      of 237
density of networks 84, 342
  gender 344
  name generator/interpreter 36, 38
  voluntary associations 186–7, 190, 194,
      203
dependency theory 363
Diani, Mario 284, 303
diaries *see* position generators, contact diaries
      and
Diaz, D 368
discrimination *see* inequality
discussion networks 90–1
dissolution of marriage 363
diversity of resources 85, 92, 285
  access to social resources 141, 153
  age 390
  bridging networks 210–11
  Canada 282–304, 386–8, 390–1
  civic participation 209–10, 235, 311, 314,
      317–26
  community diversity 311
  email 323
  ethnicity and race 16
  gender
    causes of social capital 238
    inequality 286–8, 392
  marriage 344, 348–9,
      359–60

political participation in British
Columbia, Canada 302
Hong Kong, marriage and gender in 344,
348–9, 359–60
Hungary, application of position generator
in 397–8, 403–14
inequality 380, 386–91
instrumental action 235
Internet 208–9
managers 240
marriage and gender 344, 348–9, 359–60
name generator/interpreter 35–6
networks 85, 92, 285
occupation
access to social resources 141, 153
marriage 359–60
political participation in British
Columbia, Canada 294, 297–9
position generators 15–16
returns of social capital 5
paradox of diversity 326
personnel managers in Taiwan, social
capital of 235–8, 249
political participation in British Columbia,
Canada 282–304
politicians, ties to 294–5, 296, 299
position-generated networks 235–6
primary contacts 235
reciprocity 210–12
religious organizations, participation
in 321
residence, years of 217–18
Resilient Communities Project in British
Columbia, Canada 259, 266–7, 272
returns of social capital 4, 5, 240
rural communities 259, 266–7
secondary contacts 235
senior managers 240
Taiwan 235–8, 249
trust 210–12
Ulaanbaatar, Mongolia, structure of
inequality in 380, 386–92
voluntary associations, participation
in 192, 235–7
domestic work, gender and 287, 301–2, 304
Dumin, M 9, 67, 71, 134, 138, 141, 153, 239,
314, 334, 348–9, 380
Duncan, OD 65, 66, 68–9, 72, 364, 376
Durkheim, Emile 186

economic capital *see* occupation and
economic (income) and cultural
capital (education)
economic development 14, 255–6, 260–1
education *see also* cultural capital; occupation
and economic (income) and cultural
capital (education)

causes of social capital 238
Chinese urbanites, formation of social
capital among 101–2
civic participation 216, 219, 221, 267,
315
gender
Internet in Japan 216, 217, 219, 221
Hong Kong, marriage in 348, 349–50,
352, 354–5
inequality 385, 392–3
political participation 287
Resilient Communities Project in British
Columbia, Canada 277, 279
Hong Kong, marriage and gender in 348,
349–50, 352, 354–5
inequality 367–8, 385, 392–3
Internet, civic engagement and gender in
Japan 216, 219, 221
Japan 216, 219, 221
job searches, effect of social capital on 119,
125–6, 144
marriage and gender 348, 349–50, 352,
354–5
personnel managers in Taiwan, social
capital of 242, 243, 248–9, 253
political participation 287, 292
Resilient Communities Project in British
Columbia, Canada 271, 276–7, 279,
390
resources 66, 133, 134–6, 140, 145–7,
150–1, 153, 155–6
sources of social capital 7–8
status attainment 65
Taiwan 242, 243, 248–9, 253
Ulaanbaatar, Mongolia, structure of
inequality in 383–5, 388, 390,
391–3
United States, status attainment in 371
voluntary associations 188, 191, 198–9,
201, 203, 205
weak ties 276
Eggebeen, DJ 162
Ekland-Olsen, S 284
Elder, G 407
Elliott, JR 368
email 208, 323–4, 326
employment *see* occupation
Ensel, WM 66, 239
environment *see* British Columbia, Canada,
political participation in
environmental organizations in
Erickson, Bonnie H 7, 9, 11, 14–16, 23, 40–1,
51, 154, 189, 192, 234, 235, 239–40,
253–4, 259, 261, 272, 285, 293,
311–12, 318, 322, 325, 362, 367,
378–9, 386–8, 390, 415
Erickson, L 287

ethnicity and race *see also* black poor,
    inefficacious job referral networks
    among
  African-Americans 367–8, 373–8
  civic participation 315, 318, 325
  class 16
  diversity of networks 16
  homogeneity 367–8
  homophily 367, 372–3, 375, 377–9
  inequality 23, 367–8
  job searches, effect of social capital on 121,
    122–3, 127
  Latinos/Hispanics 368, 373–8
  mobilization of social capital 367
  position generators 16
  quota sampling 127
  sources of social capital 7
  stratification 14–15
  United States 366–79
exchange relations, supply and demand
    as 130
expressive actions
  name generator/interpreter 234
  position generators 27–8, 44–5
  voluntary associations 190–1, 192, 193,
    198–202

failed job applicants 137–9, 141, 150–6
families *see also* fathers; parents; relatives, ties
    with
  economic resources 76
  voluntary associations 195, 200–1, 203–4
fathers
  cultural capital 65–9, 71–8
  economic capital 65–9, 71–8
  networks 69
  occupational prestige 65–9, 71–3, 76–8,
    134, 145, 151
  returns of social capital, same occupation
    as father and 66
  status attainment model, resources of
    father and 65
favour exchanges 90–1
Ferguson, Adam 309
Fischer, CS 190
Flap, H 4, 5–6, 8, 12–13, 15–16, 18–19, 20,
    21, 33, 41, 108, 135, 137, 138, 143,
    236, 311
Florida, civic participation in
    Miami-Dade 22, 312–28
Fong, Eric 14–15
formation of social capital 83–9
friends and acquaintances, ties with
  access to social resources 136, 138–41,
    143–50, 153–4
  black poor, inefficacious job referral
    networks among 163

class 86
cultural capital 75, 79
duration of acquaintanceship 63
economic capital 75, 79
Hong Kong, marriage and gender
    in 353–6, 360
Hungary, application of position generator
    in 397, 415, 420
job searches 163
marriage and gender 353–6, 360
networks 285
occupation 75, 79
partners friends, acquaintance with 353–6,
    360
political participation in British Columbia,
    Canada 302
position generators 63
prestige in occupation 140, 145–7, 153
voluntary associations 195, 198, 204
Fu, Y 11, 15, 18, 239, 243, 246–7, 250, 285,
    314, 381
full-time employment
  Internet, civic engagement and gender in
    Japan 216, 219
  Resilient Communities Project in British
    Columbia, Canada 271, 276–7, 279
  weak ties 276

Ganzeboom, HBG 78, 118
gender *see also* Hong Kong, marriage and
    gender in
  access to resources 139, 145, 151–2, 154–5
  biographical availability 286, 302, 304
  Canada 7
  causes of social capital 238
  Chinese urbanites, formation of social
    capital among 101
  civic participation 206–33, 267, 270, 318,
    325
  cultural capital 70, 73
  density of networks 344
  diversity, causes of social capital and 238
  domestic work 286, 301–2, 304
  economic capital 70, 73
  education 277, 279, 287, 390
  high-prestige jobs 338–41
  homophily principle 60–1, 63–4, 378–9,
    384
  Hong Kong, marriage and gender in 23
  Hungary, application of position generator
    in 401–2, 405–7, 415, 418
  income 390–1
  inequality 23–4, 367
  Internet 208–9, 206–33
  Japan, Internet in 206–33
  job searches, effect of social capital
    on 122–6, 132

location 391
low-prestige jobs 332–3
marriage 23
mobilization of social capital 367
networks 286–7, 332–4,
   338–41
occupation
   cultural capital 70, 73
   economic capital 70, 73
   high-prestige jobs 338–41
   inequality 390–2
   Resilient Communities Project in British
      Columbia, Canada 271
   size of network audience 332–4, 338–41
outside community, strong ties 277
personnel managers in Taiwan, social
   capital of 241–3, 245, 247–8, 252
political participation 282, 286–7, 296–9,
   301–4
position generators 14, 60–1, 63–4
Resilient Communities Project in British
   Columbia, Canada 261, 262, 266–7,
   270–2, 275–7, 279, 390
returns of social capital 239
rural communities 261, 262, 272
social activities 262, 271
sources of social capital 7, 8
status attainment 367
stereotyping 332–3
stratification 14
strong ties 378
Taiwan 241–3, 245, 247–8, 252
Ulaanbaatar, Mongolia, structure of
   inequality in 23–4, 383–93
voluntary organizations, participation
   in 22–3, 192, 201–2, 203, 237
   causes of social capital 238
   Taiwan 245, 248, 252
voting 286–7
weak ties 270, 275–6, 378
geographic communities 239
Glanville, J 187, 191
Grabb, EG 283
Granovetter, Mark 108, 136, 144, 154, 238,
   239, 257, 261, 265, 267, 272, 278, 283,
   365
Green, GP 368
Grusky, DB 86
guanxi networks 87, 91, 98

Haines, VA 160, 258–9, 262, 271
Hall, PA 283
Hampton, KN 231
Hansen, MN 66, 67, 78
health, physical and mental 188
hierarchy
   class 87

Hong Kong, marriage and gender in 344,
   345
Hungary, application of position generator
   in 410, 413
   inequality 366
   marriage and gender 344, 345
   networks 85
   returns of social capital 5
   voluntary associations, participation
      in 246
higher-number-leads-to-more-use
   hypothesis 140, 147–9, 155
Hogan, DP 162
Holzer, HJ 163
Homan, GC 136
home visits 88
homophily principle
   age 61
   class 86
   demographic homophily 63
   ethnicity and race 367, 372–3, 375,
      377–9
   gender 60–1, 63–4, 378–9
   Hungary, application of position generator
      in 415, 420
   job searches, effect of social capital on 113
   political participation in British Columbia,
      Canada 302
   position generators 15, 52, 60–4
   United States 372–3, 375, 377–9
   voluntary associations 198
Hong Kong, marriage and gender in 342–63
   age 348, 355, 358
   bridging function 343
   dense networks 342, 344
   dependency theory 363
   dissolution of marriage 363
   diversity of resources 344, 348–9,
      359–60
   education 348, 349–50, 352, 354–5
   feminist approach 345, 355
   friends, acquaintance with
      partners' 353–6, 360
   high social positions 344, 345
   high-status occupations, partners in 344
   Hong Kong 346–63
   inequality 23
   integration of networks 342–63
   joint networks 342–3
   length of marriage 358–9
   mobilization of partner's social capital 362
   occupation 344, 346, 348–52, 356–60
   overlap of networks 349, 352–4, 358–61
   personal traits 351–60
   position generator 348–9
   reciprocity 348
   regression analysis 351–4, 356–61

Hong Kong, marriage and gender in (*cont.*)
  research
    data 346–8
    hypotheses 345–6, 351–7
    variables and measurement 348–51
  shared social ties 343
  size of networks 349, 352–3, 356, 358, 360
  social activities 343, 357, 362
  social control 343
  social positions 344, 345, 350–2
  sociodemographic characteristics of
    respondents 347, 352–5
  sources of social capital 8
  trust 348
  variables 349–50, 353–4, 357, 360
  women
    partners' networks, preserving 344–5,
      359
    structural disadvantages 344
Hsung, RM 22, 33, 239, 243, 247–8, 250, 285,
  314, 381
human capital *see also* education
  causes of social capital 238
  definition of social capital 82
  income 240
  job searches, effect of social capital on 110,
    119
  theory of human capital 3
  voluntary associations 191
Hungary, application of position generator
    in 394–420
  access to social resources 400–3, 417
  age 401–2, 405–7, 411, 418
  bonding social capital 404
  causes of social capital 238
  civic participation 397
  composite indexes 397–400
  cultural capital 400
  Cultural-Interactional Stratification
    Project 1987–1991 395–6
  diversity of social resources 397–8,
    403–14
  economic resources 400–1
  education 400–1, 403, 405, 407, 412–13
  filtered models, partial analysis for certain
    groups by 404–8
  Fischer-McAllister name generator 396
  Four Village Case Study 2000 397
  friends and acquaintances, ties with 397,
    415, 420
  gender 401–2, 405–7, 415, 418
  heterophilous ties 395
  higher-status occupations 408–10
  homogeneity 399
  homophily principle 415, 420
  income 402–3, 405–6, 412–14, 418
  inequality 24, 400–2, 417

  instrumental relationships 394, 414–15
  job market 401
  location 415
  managers/professionals 409–10, 411, 412,
    419
  mapping social milieus 408–12
  market/service intermediaries 410, 411,
    412, 419
  media celebrities 410
  mobilization of social capital 395, 402–6,
    413–14
  name generator 396
  networks 397, 415
  occupation 396, 398–9, 402–3, 407–19
  political participation 400, 415, 420
  Political Stratification Project 2003 397,
    415
  predicators of social attainment 403,
    405–6, 412, 418–19
  prestige 398
  public sphere/cultural
    intelligentsia 409–10, 411, 412, 419
  relatives, ties from 404
  research
    filtered models, partial analysis for
      certain groups by 404–8
    substantive findings 400–13
  replications in 1990s 396
  retirement 411
  returns to social resources 402–4
  rural/agricultural 410, 411, 412, 419
  self-employed 411
  social attainment 394, 403, 405–6, 412,
    415–18
  social hierarchy 410, 413
  specific indicators 397–400
  strong tie resources 394, 402
  students 411
  studies and versions 1987–2003 395–7
  use of social resources 404–13
  variables 400–1, 404, 414–15
  weak tie resources 394–5, 402
  wealth 8, 400–1, 413–14
  workers/urban manual 410, 411, 412,
    419
Hurlbert, JS 33, 160, 258–9, 262, 271

Ikeda, K 14, 21
immigrants, attitudes to 16
income *see also* occupation and economic
    (income) and cultural capital
    (education)
  Chinese urbanites, formation of social
    capital among 102
  civic participation 315
  household income 102
  human capital 240

Hungary, application of position generator
in 402–3, 405, 412–14, 418
job searches, effect of social capital on 121
networks 87, 91, 98, 332
personnel managers in Taiwan, social
capital of 250–1
political participation in British Columbia,
Canada 292, 300
professional organizations, membership
of 234–5
size of network audience 332
Taiwan 250–1
Ulaanbaatar, Mongolia, structure of
inequality in 283, 385, 390–1
voluntary associations 201, 205
industrial sectors, institutionalization
of 237–8
industrialization 87
inequality in social capital 366–8 *see also*
Ulaanbaatar, Mongolia, structure of
inequality in
African-Americans 367–8
ethnicity and race 23, 367
gender 23–4, 367
homophily principle 366–7
Hungary, application of position generator
in 24, 400–2, 417
institutional constructions 366
mobilization of social capital 367
occupation, prestige in 23
position generator 23–4
social institutions 23–4
social mobility 366
socioeconomic hierarchy 366
structural processes 366
Ulaanbaatar, Mongolia, social survey
in 23–4
United States 368
voluntary associations 196, 188–90,
199–200
informal resources
economic activities 382–4
failures-via-informal resources
hypothesis 141, 150–3, 156
job searches 134, 135, 137–8, 140–1,
150–6
information
inequality 381–2
inside information 130, 132
job searches, effect of social capital on 109,
112–15, 117–18, 121–31
routine exchanges, information received
in 109, 112–15, 117–18, 121–31
social credentials of job applicants,
information on 111–13
Ulaanbaatar, Mongolia, structure of
inequality in 381–2

instrumental action
diversity 235
Hungary, application of position generator
in 394, 414–15
name generator/interpreter 234
position generators 27–8, 44–5
status attainment 365
voluntary associations 190–2, 193,
197–201
intensity of use of resources 140, 155, 187–8
intergenerational mobility 89, 162, 372, 375
Internet *see also* Internet, civic engagement
and gender in Japan
age 208–9
alienation 208
bulletin boards 208
chat groups 208
diversity of networks 208–9
email 208, 323
gender 208–9
heterogeneity 207–8
mailing lists 208
reciprocity 211
sources of social capital 8
trust 211
Internet, civic engagement and gender in
Japan 206–33
age 216, 221
bridging social capital 207
children, people with 216
diversity of networks 206–7, 213–32
education 216, 217, 219, 221
emails 216, 219, 221
full-time employed 216, 219
married persons 216, 219
method 212–13
occupation 219–20
online communities, participation
in 216–21, 230–2
political involvement 231
position generator 214
reciprocity 221, 223–4
regression analysis 215, 217–18, 221–4
residence, years of 216, 217–18, 221
results 213–20
sources of social capital 7
three forms of social capital, relationship
between 223–30
trust 221, 223–5
types of online communities 217
variables 214, 215–23
voluntary associations 22, 231–2
Yamanashi prefecture, Japan, research
in 21–2, 212–33
invisibility of social capital 110–15, 129,
132
Italy, civic participation in 315

Jahoda, M 407
Japan 210 *see also* Internet, civic engagement and gender in Japan job searches, effect of social capital on 107–32 *see also* black poor, inefficacious job referral networks among
absence of reported use of personal contracts 107–10
access to resources 134, 135
age 122–3, 126
attained status 120–1, 123–7, 131
capacity of social capital 111–15, 118–19, 121–3
Chinese urbanites, formation of social capital among 89–90
cluster analysis 127–9
control variables 121
data from survey 115–17, 129
definition of social capital 110–11
dendrograms 127–9
direct applications 108, 109, 131–2
economic returns, routine job information and 125–6
education 119, 125–6, 144
ethnicity and race 121, 122–3, 127
exchange relations, supply and demand as 130
executive class 121, 125
exploratory study 107–32
failed applicants 137–9, 141, 150–6
follow-ups to receipt of routine job information 127–9
formal methods 108, 109–10, 131–2
gender 122–6, 132
homophily, principle of 113
human capital 110, 119
Hungary, application of position generator in 401
income, ordered variable of annual 121
information
 job applicants, on 130
 jobs, on 109, 112–15, 117–18, 121–31
initial status 119
inside information 130, 132
invisibility of social capital 110–15, 129, 132
missing data 108
mobilization of social capital 19–21, 107, 111–12
Netherlands 108
networks 113
normative expectations 109–10
personal contacts 107–11
position generator 118, 120
prestige by association 111–12
previous experience 122
professional class 121, 124–5

quota sampling 126–7
reciprocity 236
recruitment
 personal contacts, use of 107–8
 social credentials of applicants, information on 111–13
referrals, incentives for 107–8
regression studies 122–3
reputation by association 111–12
returns to social capital, routine job information and 123–7
routine exchanges, information received in 109, 112–15, 117–18, 121–31
sample characteristics 116–17, 132
social exchanges, job information and 112
social participation 113–14, 119–21
socioeconomic attainment 108, 110, 111–15, 120–1, 123–7, 131
socioeconomic standing 113–14
strength of ties 112
supervision 125
survey
 data 115–17
 measurements 117–21
Taiwan 108
tenure in current job 119, 125–6
three categories of occupation 121
United States 108
variables 274
voluntary organizations, participation in 114, 119–20, 188, 264
Johnson, CA 13, 23–4
joint networks 342–3

Kahn, M 311
Kalmijn, M 66, 69–71, 78, 344, 345
Katz, JE 231
Killworth, PD 332

Lai, G 8, 23
Laumann, Edward 294
Lazarsfeld, P 407
leisure time *see* social activities
Leonard, R 260, 278
Liang, S 90
lifestyles, differences in 78
Lin, Nan 5, 9, 14–17, 20, 22–3, 27–8, 30, 66–7, 71, 84, 134, 135–6, 138–9, 141, 153, 158, 160, 189, 190, 236–7, 239, 243, 246–7, 250, 270, 283, 285, 288, 308, 311, 314, 323, 334, 344, 345, 348–9, 363, 380, 381, 400
location *see also* residence; Resilient Communities Project in British Columbia, Canada
access to resources 258

black poor, inefficacious job referral
    networks among bridging ties 259–60
causes of social capital 239
civic participation 261–2
geographic communities 239
Hungary, application of position generator
    in 415
job searches 259–60
networks 258–9
position generators 11–12, 15
Resilient Communities Project in British
    Columbia, Canada 258–63, 266–78,
    391
social activities 255
sources of social capital 7
Ulaanbaatar, Mongolia, structure of
    inequality in 383, 391, 393
Logan, JR 95

mailing lists 208
managers
    diversity 240
    Hungary, application of position generator
        in 409–10, 411, 412, 419
    senior managers 240
    voluntary associations 234–5
marriage and gender *see* Hong Kong,
    marriage and gender in; married
    persons
married persons
    occupation, cultural and economic capital
        and 78
    personnel managers in Taiwan, social
        capital of 242, 250
    Resilient Communities Project in British
        Columbia, Canada 271
    Ulaanbaatar, Mongolia, structure of
        inequality in 388–90
    voluntary associations 195, 197
Marsden, PV 33, 187, 283
Marx, Karl 3
McAdam, D 304
McGuire, P 238
McKenna, KYA 208
McPherson, M 12, 262, 267, 271–2, 302
measurement *see also* name
    generator/interpreter; position
    generators, measurement of social
    capital with
    class 92–3
    Chinese urbanites, formation of social
        capital among 90–2, 102–3
    personnel managers in Taiwan, social
        capital of 242–7
    prestige in occupation 139
    Resilient Communities Project in British
        Columbia, Canada 265–6

resource generator 12–13, 18, 29, 38,
    44
men *see* gender
mental and physical health 188
Miami-Dade, Florida, civic participation
    in 22, 312–28
microconsequences of social capital for
    individuals 4
migrant labour 9708, 102
Miyata, K 7, 14, 21, 220
mobilization of social capital 19–21
    access to resources 174, 175–8
    black poor, inefficacious job referral
        networks among 158, 162–4, 170–8
    definition of social capital 82–3
    embedded resources, mobolization
        of 19–20
    ethnicity and race 367
    gender 362, 367
    Hong Kong, marriage and gender in 362
    Hungary, application of position generator
        in 395, 402–6, 413–14
    inequality 367
    job searches 107, 111–12
        black persons on low-income 20–1, 158,
            162–4, 170–8
        Netherlands 20
        use of personal contacts in 19–20
    marriage and gender 362
    status attainment 364–5, 379
    United States 379
    voluntary associations 187, 189
Moerbeek, H 20, 134
Mohai, P 304
Mokken, RJ 33–4, 45–8
Mongolia *see* Ulaanbaatar, Mongolia,
    structure of inequality in
Moore, G 267, 270, 276, 333
Mueller, JH 35–6
Muller, EN 292
Musick, MA 187, 190, 181

name generator/interpreter 11–12, 18, 35–8,
    42
    black poor, inefficacious job referral
        networks among 160–1, 168
    Chinese urbanites, formation of social
        capital among 90–1
    density measures 36, 38
    exchange-type 29, 30
    expressive actions 234
    Hungary, application of position generator
        in 396
    indicator construction 33
    instrumental actions 234
    job searches 160–1, 168
    networks 11–12, 35–6, 38

name generator/interpreter (*cont.*)
  position generators 11–12, 18, 29–30, 33,
      35–8, 42, 50, 234
  social capital diversity 35–6
  Standardized Index of Qualitative Variation
      (IQV) 35–6
  status attainment 365
  Survey of Social Networks of the Dutch
      (SSND) 37
  types 29
  United States 370
neighbourhood togetherness 317–18
neocapitalist theories 3
Netherlands *see also* Survey of Social
      Networks of the Dutch (SSND)
  access to social resources 138–9, 141–53
  civic participation 267
  job searches, effect of social capital on 108
  managers 240
  mobilization of social capital 20
  returns of social capital 5–6, 66
  voluntary associations 21
networks 1–2 *see also* black poor,
      inefficacious job referral networks
      among; diversity of resources and
      networks; voluntary associations
  access to resources 133
  attained status, effect on members of 73–5,
      77, 79
  biographical availability 284
  business owners 98–100, 103
  capitalism 98–100
  causality of network effects 76–7
  children 73, 74–5
  Chinese urbanites, formation of social
      capital among 87, 90–2, 95, 98–103
  civic participation 302–28
  class 85, 98, 103
  closures 84
  connections through work 332
  cultural capital 71–7, 79, 88–9
  density 36, 38, 84, 342, 344
  dynamic networks 90
  economic capital 71–7, 79, 88–9
  embedded in networks, resources 4
  fathers 69
  features of social capital 83–5
  friends and acquaintances 285
  gender 286–7, 331, 332–41
  guanxi networks 87, 91, 98
  hierarchies 85
  high prestige jobs 331–2, 338, 340
  homophily 113
  Hungary, application of position generator
      in 397, 415
  income 102
  inequality 23

joint networks 342–3
location 258–9
low prestige jobs 332–3, 340
name generator/interpreter 11–12, 35–6,
      38
networking power 332–4, 338–41
occupation 71–7, 79, 88–9, 103
  attainment, effect on 144
  Chinese urbanites, formation of social
      capital among 95
  inequality 23
  position generators 28
  returns of social capital 10
  size of network audience 331–42
political participation 282–3, 285–90,
      294–5, 300–1
political returns 6–7
position generators 11–16, 18, 27–48
reciprocity 258
relational features 84–5
Resilient Communities Project in British
      Columbia, Canada 256–9, 265, 278
resources 4, 83, 84–5
size of network audience 331–42
social movements, ties in 284
strong ties 257–8
structures 83, 84, 103
ties 83–4
Toronto security industry 285
types 285–6
Newman, Katherine 161, 163
newspaper reading, decline in 323–4
Norris, P 208, 209, 231, 232

occupation *see also* access to social resources
      and effect on occupational
      attainment; income; job searches,
      effect of social capital on; occupation
      and economic (income) and cultural
      capital (education)
  bureaucratic building 95–6, 100
  Canada 23
  capital, definition of 3
  Chinese urbanites, formation of social
      capital among 81–2, 88–101
  civic participation 219–20, 315
  class 86, 92–4
  connections 95–6, 100–1, 332
  diversity of networks 15–16, 359–60
  ethnicity and race 16
  fathers' occupational prestige 134, 145,
      151
  first job, prestige of 147, 150–1
  formation of social capital 88–9
  full-time employed 216, 219, 271, 276–7,
      279
  gender 23, 271, 331, 332–41

high-status occupation 331–2, 338–41, 344
home visits 88
Hong Kong, marriage and gender in 344,
    346, 348–52, 356–60
Hungary, application of position generator
    in 396, 398–9, 402–3, 407–19
inequality 23
Internet, civic engagement and gender in
    Japan 219–20
low prestige jobs, size of network audience
    and 332–40
market connections 95–6, 100–1
migrant labour 97–8, 102
networks 23, 28, 95, 103, 332–4, 338–41
number of people in occupation 331, 335,
    338
position generators 9–19, 28, 30–1, 39–41,
    50–1, 53–64, 234
prestige of occupation 9, 23, 28, 30–1,
    39–41, 54, 331
Resilient Communities Project in British
    Columbia, Canada 263, 267, 271,
    276–7, 279
resources 9
returns to social capital 5–6, 9–10, 16,
    66–7, 234–5
self-employed 411
size of network audience 331–41
sources of social capital 8
supervision 125, 371–2
Survey of Social Networks of the Dutch
    (SSND) 30–2
Ulaanbaatar, Mongolia, structure of
    inequality in 380–8, 390–2
United States 370–2
occupation and economic (income) and
    cultural capital (education) 6, 16,
    65–80
    access to occupations 67–8, 71
    age 70, 73
    bureaucratic bridging 88–9, 103
    children's networks 73, 74–5
    class 89
    classic attainment model, regression
        models of 73
    clients, contact with 89
    cultural status, regression models of 75
    economic status, regression models of 74,
        75
    family, economic resources of the 76
    fathers
        cultural resources 73–4, 77
        networks 69
        occupation 65–69, 71–3, 76–8
        prestige 71, 72–3
    friends and acquaintances 75, 79
    gender 70, 73

hypotheses 67–8
informal groups, development of 88
intergenerational mobility 89
lifestyles, differences in 78
market connections 89
marriage 78
networks 71–5, 77, 79, 88–9
parents' resources 67
personal networks 69, 88
personal relationships 88–9
position generator 16, 67–71, 77–80
prestige 71
regression models 73, 74, 75–6
returns of social capital 6, 16, 66–7
sector-specific effect 65–9, 71–3, 76–9
social mobility 73
status attainment 68
Survey of Social Networks of the Dutch
    (SSND) 68–80
occupational returns to social capital 5–6
    access 9–10
    China, state allocation of jobs in 5
    choice of occupations 9
    cultural capital (education) 6, 16, 66–7
    economic capital (income) 6, 16, 66–7
    father's occupation, jobs different
        from 66
    Hungary, introduction of market economy
        into 6
    income 234–5
    Netherlands 5–6, 66
    networks 5, 10
    prestige 5, 9
    processional organizations, membership
        of 234–5
    relative positions, different 13–14
    stratification hierarchies 5
occupations, size of network audience
        of 331–41
    connections 332
    gender 331, 332–41
    high prestige jobs 331–2, 338–41
    income 332
    low prestige jobs 332–3, 340
    networking power 332–4, 338–41
    number of people in occupation 331, 335,
        338
    position generator 334
    prestige of occupation 331
    research
        methods 334–40
        results 337–40
    types of occupation 335–6
Oliver, Melvin 159
online communities, participation
    in 216–21, 230–2
Onyx, J 259, 260, 278

operationalization 27, 28–9, 138–9, 141
Opp, K 292

parents *see also* fathers
 access to resources 133, 134–6, 145,
  151
 economic capital 67
 occupational prestige 133, 134–6, 145,
  151
Passeron, J-C 3
Paxton, P 237
Pennsylvania, civic participation in
  Allegheny 22, 312–28
personnel managers in Taiwan, social capital
  of
 access to social capital, factor structures
  of 247
 age 241–2
 causes of social capital 238
 civic engagement 237
 determinants of social capital 248–9
 diversity of networks 235–8, 249
 education 242, 243, 248–9, 253
 export processing zones 22, 235, 240–54
 gender 241–3, 245, 247–8, 252
 income, determinants of 250–1
 job positions of contacts 243–4
 married persons 242, 250
 measurement of social capital 22, 242–7
 outcome of social capital 249–53
 position-generated networks 235–6,
  243–4, 246–7, 253–4
 prestige 244, 249, 250–3
 professional backgrounds 243
 purposive actions 235–6
 regression models 248, 251
 relatives, ties with 247, 248
 research
  findings 242–7
  methods 240–1
 sample characteristics 241
 science parks 235, 240–54
 size of firms 242, 249
 stock options 253
 tenure 248
 variables 244, 252–3
 voluntary associations, participation
  in 244–6, 248–54
 work experience 248–9, 253
personal relationships, enduring 83
Podolny, JM 240
political capital 294–5, 296, 299
political participation *see also* British
  Columbia, Canada, political
  participation in environmental
  organizations in
 biographical availability 284–6

Canada 286–7
civic participation 209–10, 231
domestic responsibilities 286
education 287
elite level 287
gender 286–7
Hungary, application of position generator
  in 400, 415, 420
informal activity 284
Internet, civic engagement and gender in
  Japan 231
Japan 210, 231
knowledge 209
networks 287
organizational networks 287
social movements, ties in 284
trust 209
voluntary associations 188, 190
voting 286–7
political returns to social capital
 networks 6–7
 power and influence 6–7
 United States, voluntary association
  membership and activity in 6–7
 voluntary association memberships 6–7
Portes, A 86, 258, 260–1
position generators *see* position generators,
  contact diaries and; position
  generators, measurement of social
  capital with position generators,
  contact diaries and 11, 49–64
 acquaintanceship, length of 63
 age homophily 61
 boundaries 56–7
 contact records 50–2
 demographic characteristics 53, 63
 demographic homophily 63
 everyday life, application of position
  generators in context of 50–64
 extensity of accessed positions 54–9
 gender homophily 60–1, 63–4
 homophily principle of networking 52,
  60–4
 identity of alters selected 59–64
 informants, profile of 53
 name generators 50
 networks, size of 60
 occupations 50–1, 53–64
 personal networks, evaluation
  against 49–52
 phone contacts 62
 prestige 54
 resource generators 50
 socioeconomic characteristics 53–4
 strength of ties 52, 54, 60–3
 Taiwan 52–64
 unique situation of contacts 54

position generators, measurement of social capital with 2, 8–19 *see also* Hungary, application of position generator in access 29
adaptation to different social contexts 13–14
available instruments 28–9
black poor, inefficacious job referral networks among 161, 166–9, 175–9
bottom line 15–16
causality 16–17
Chinese urbanites, formation of social capital among 91
civic participation 214, 308–9, 313–14, 318
class 14, 16
close ties 11–12
community and national contexts, examples of 10
community economic development 14
comparison to other network measures 11–14, 27–48
construction of indicators 33–4
cross-sectional reliability 10, 16–17
cultural capital 16, 67–71, 77–80
diversity of networks 235–6
economic capital 16, 67–71, 77–80
distribution characteristics 35
distribution of responses 32
diversity 235–6
ethnic and racial minorities and immigrants, attitudes to 16
ethnic stratification 14–15
event-based position generators 91
expressive actions (maintaining resources) 27–8, 44–5
extensions 15
gender stratification 14
general strategy 8–10
high prestige social capital 34
homophily principle 15
Hong Kong, marriage and gender in 348–9
indicator characteristics 34–5
indicator construction 33–4
inequality 23–4
instrumental actions (gaining resources) 27–8, 44–5
International Social Survey Program 13–14
Internet, civic engagement and gender in Japan 213
Item Response Theory 33
Japan, Internet on 214
job searches, effect of social capital on 118, 120
location 15
longitudinal research 16–17

low prestige social capital 34
marriage 348–9
measurement
    models, comparison of 42
    performance 10–11
Mokken-scaling analyses 33–4, 45–8
multicollinearity problems, solutions to 35–6
name generator/interpreter 11–12, 18, 29–30, 33, 35–8, 42, 234
national samples, examples of 10
networks
    audience, size of network 334
    diversity 15–16, 18, 28, 235–6
other network measures, relationship to 11–14, 27–48
size of 42
occupation 9–11, 13–19, 67–71, 77–80
    distribution of 234
    diversity 15–16
    ethnic and racial minorities and immigrants, attitudes to 16
    network members not associated with occupations 28
    number of occupations 41
    prestige 9, 28, 30–1, 39–41
    resources 9
    size of network audience 334
    subsets 15–16, 19
operationalization 27, 28–9
original data, use of 17
other network measures, relationship to 11–14, 27–48
parsimonious measurement strategy, proposal for 43–4
personnel managers in Taiwan, social capital of 235–6, 243–4, 246–7, 253–4
political effectiveness 14
political participation in British Columbia, Canada 293, 306–7
prestige
    average accessed 33
    high prestige social capital 34, 40, 236
    low prestige social capital 34, 42, 236
    occupation 9, 28, 30–1, 39–41
    total accessed 33, 40–1, 236
proposed strategy 43–5
regional studies, examples of 10
reliability 18–19
research 9–18
Resilient Communities Project in British Columbia, Canada 263–81
resource generator 12–13, 18, 29, 33–4, 38, 44
response rates 10–11
social locations 11–12
social contexts 19

position generators ... (*cont.*)
  stratification 14–15
  subgroups 14
  Survey of Social Networks of the Dutch
      (SSND) 30–9, 45–8, 68–80
  Taiwan 235–6, 243–4, 246–7, 253–4
  Ulaanbaatar, Mongolia, structure of
      inequality in 380, 381–6
  United States 370, 379
  useful measures based on position
      generators 15–16
  validity 18–19
  variation 18–19
  voluntary associations, participation
      in 21–2, 193, 234, 253–4
  World Values Surveys 13
prestige in jobs
  access to social resources 136, 139, 141–5,
      149, 151, 153–4
  association, prestige by 111–12
  average assessed prestige 33
  black poor, inefficacious job referral
      networks among 167–8
  Chinese urbanites, formation of social
      capital among 92
  classification 263–4
  connections 332
  cultural capital 71
  economic capital 71
  fathers 134, 145, 151
  first jobs 147, 150–1
  friends 140, 145–7, 153
  gender 338–41
  high-prestige jobs 4, 34, 236, 338–41
  Hungary, application of position generator
      in 398
  job searches, effect of social capital
      on 111–12
  low-prestige jobs 34, 42, 236, 332–3,
      340
  measurement 139
  occupation 33–4, 40, 42, 236
    cultural and economic capital and 71
    position generators 9, 28, 30–1, 39–41,
      54
    size of network audience 331
  parents 133, 134–6, 145, 151
  personnel managers in Taiwan, social
      capital of 244, 249–53
  position generators 34, 54
  Resilient Communities Project in British
      Columbia, Canada 263–4
  resource generator 38
  returns of social capital 5, 9
  Survey of Social Networks of the Dutch
      (SSND) 42
  Taiwan 244, 249–53

total accessed prestige 33, 40–1, 236
Ulaanbaatar, Mongolia, structure of
    inequality in 381–2
United States 370
voluntary associations, participation
    in 189, 195, 197, 252–3
previous experience 122
proactive contacts 162–3
production of social capital 4
professionals
  black poor, inefficacious job referral
      networks among 167–8
  Hungary, application of position generator
      to 409–10, 411, 412, 419
  job searches, effect of social capital on 121,
      124–5, 167–8
  professional organizations, membership
      of 234–5
  personnel managers in Taiwan, social
      capital of 243
  Ulaanbaatar, Mongolia, structure of
      inequality in 384
  women in professions 384
property ownership 86–7
public relationships 83
Putnam, Robert 1–2, 21, 185, 190, 197,
    202–3, 206–8, 223, 237, 261, 272, 278,
    283, 308, 310–11, 314, 317–18, 322–5,
    348

race *see* black poor, inefficacious job referral
    networks among; ethnicity and race
Rahn, W 203
reciprocity 22, 209–12
  civic participation 209–10, 221, 223–4
  diversity 210–12
  Internet 211, 221, 223–4
  Japan, Internet in 221, 223–4
  job searches, effect of social capital on 236
  networks 10–12, 258
  strong ties 258
  weak ties 258
recruitment
  job searches, effect of social capital
      on 107–8, 111–13
  personal contacts, use of 107–8
  social credentials of applicants,
      information on 111–13
  voluntary associations 188–9
regional studies 10
relatives, ties with *see also* fathers; families
  access to resources 136–8, 140, 143–4,
      147–8, 154
  black poor, inefficacious job referral
      networks among 163
  Hungary, application of position generator
      in 404

personnel managers in Taiwan, social
capital of 247, 248
religious organizations, participation in
civic participation 22, 310, 321–2, 326
diversity 321
voluntary associations 187, 188, 192,
198–9, 203
reluctant contacts 170–4
remuneration *see* income
reputation of contact 111–12, 163–4, 172–4,
178, 180
residence *see also* location
Chinese urbanites, formation of social
capital among 102
duration of residence 216, 217–18, 221
Internet, civic engagement and gender in
Japan 216, 217–18, 221
Resilient Communities Project in British
Columbia, Canada 255–7, 263–81
access to resources 258–9, 263–74
age 390
between communities, networks 265, 268,
277, 279
bonding within communities 259–61,
268–9, 279
bridging ties 259–61, 273–5, 278
civic participation 261–3, 268–70, 272–5,
278
closed networks 257–8
conceptual and empirical
backgrounds 257–63
contacts, access to 258–9, 263–74, 277–8
context 258–61
data 263–5
diversity of networks 259, 266–7, 272,
386–8, 390–1
economic development 255–6, 260
education 276–7, 279, 390
full-time employment 271, 276–7, 279
gender 261, 262, 266–7, 270–2, 275–7, 279,
386–8
inside the community, ties 269–70, 273–7
location 258–63, 266–78, 391
married persons 271
measurement of social participation 265–6
networks 256, 257–9, 265, 278
occupations 263, 267, 271, 276, 279
outside communities, ties outside 268,
273–8
position generator 263–81
prestige classification 263–4
research 256–7, 263–77
data 263–5
results 267–77
results 267–77
rural residents 258–63, 268
bridging ties 258–60

diversity of networks 259, 266–7
full-time employment, travelling to 276
gender 261, 262, 272
social activities 275, 278
strong ties 260
voluntary associations 262, 266–7, 270
weak ties 260, 273–5
social activities 22, 262, 265–6, 271–2,
275–6, 278–81
social cohesion 261
social participation, measuring 265–6
strength of ties 257–60, 267–9, 273, 276–7,
279
strong ties
access to resources 267–8
inside the community 276–7
limits on 259
outside the community 276–7
social activities 274
trust 260–1
structural holes 259, 278
structure of access to embedded
resources 272–4
trust 261
urban residents 258–9, 262–3
use of social capital 278
variables 267–8, 274–6, 279
voluntary associations 262, 266–7, 270–1
weak ties 257, 259, 260, 273–8
access to resources 267–8
education 276
full-time employment, travelling to 276
gender 270, 275–6
inside the community 269–70, 273–5
outside social community to make,
going 277–8
social activities 274
Reskin, BF 333
resource generator 12–13, 18, 38, 44
checklists in interviews, use of 29
civic participation 309–10
contact diaries 50
data 34
indicator construction 33
position generators 12–13, 18, 29, 33–4,
38, 44
prestige 38
social diversity indicator 38
Survey of Social Networks of the Dutch
(SSND) 38, 39
resources *see also* access to social resources
and effect on occupational
attainment; diversity of resources and
networks
education 66
embedded 4, 272–4
networks 4, 83, 84–5

resources...(*cont.*)
  occupation 9
  political participation in British Columbia, Canada 300–1
  voluntary associations 185, 188–92, 195–7, 199–201, 204–5
retired persons 295, 298, 300, 411
returns of social capital 239–40
  access 9–10
  China, state allocation of jobs in 5
  choice of occupations 9
  cultural capital (education) 6, 16, 66–7
  diversity of networks 4, 240
  economic capital (income) 6, 16, 66–7
  father's occupation, jobs different from 66
  gender 239
  Hungary 6, 402–4
  income 234–5, 239
  job searches 123–7
  Netherlands 5–6, 66
  networks 5–7, 10
  occupation 5–6, 9–10, 16, 66–7, 234–5
  political returns 6–7
  position generators 239–40
  power and influence 6–7
  prestige 5, 9, 239–40
  processional organizations, membership of 234–5
  relative positions, different 13–14
  status attainment 239–40
  stratification hierarchies 5
  United States, political returns in 6–7
  voluntary associations, membership of 6–7, 240
  weak ties 239
Rice, RE 231
Ridgeway, C 332–3
rituals and routines, investment in 3
Robinson, B 384
Rosenberg, M 203
Rotolo, T 187, 190
routine exchanges, information received in 109, 112–15, 117–18, 121–31
rural communities
  bridging ties 258–60
  causes of social capital 239
  civic participation 261–2
  diversity of networks 259, 266–7
  full-time employment, travelling to 276
  gender 261, 262, 272
  Resilient Communities Project in British Columbia, Canada 258–63, 266–8, 270, 272, 275–6, 278
  social activities 275, 278
  strong ties 260
  voluntary associations 262, 266–7, 270

  weak ties 260, 273–5
Russell, Helen 286

Schuessler, KF 35–6
self-employed 411
size of networks 85
  audience, size of network 331–41
  Chinese urbanites, formation of social capital among 90, 92
  class 88
  Hong Kong, marriage and gender in 349, 352–3, 356, 358, 360
  name generator/interpreter 35, 38
  position generators 42, 60
  voluntary associations 189–90
Smith, SS 20–1, 270, 368, 378
Smith-Lovin, L 12, 262, 267, 272–3, 302
Snijders, TAB 12–13, 18, 398
Snow, DA 284
social activities *see also* voluntary associations
  categorisation 265–6
  civic participation 315
  class as obstacle to socialization 86–8
  definition of social capital 21
  gender 262, 271
  Hong Kong, marriage and gender in 343, 357, 362
  location 255
  measurement 265–6
  Resilient Communities Project in British Columbia, Canada 22, 262, 265–6, 271–2, 275–6, 278–81
  rural communities 275, 278
  strength of ties 257
  strong ties 274
  weak ties 274
social attainment *see also* access to social resources and effect on occupational attainment; status attainment
social class *see* class
social cohesion
  Resilient Communities Project in British Columbia, Canada 261
  voluntary associations 185, 186–8, 190, 193–5, 197–9, 204
  weak ties 258
social credentials of applicants, information on 111–13
social isolation 157–9, 161, 168
social mobility 63, 65, 73, 87, 258, 366
social movements 284, 290–1, 293, 303–4
social networks *see* networks
social participation *see* social activities
social resources *see* access to social resources and effect on occupational attainment
social skills 155
Solongo, A 384

Sørensen, JB 86
sources of social capital
    associational activities 8
    birth, status at 7
    Canada, gender stratification in 7
    communication systems 8
    education 7–8
    ethnicity or race 7
    gender 7, 8
    Hong Kong, gender in 8
    Internet communities 8
    Japan, gender stratification in 7
    occupation 8
    social location 7
    voluntary associations 8
status attainment
    definition 364
    definition of social capital 365
    education 65
    father's resources 65
    gender 367
    Hungary, application of position generator
        in 394, 403, 405–6, 412, 415–18
    instrumental actions 365
    mobilization of social capital 364–5
    name generator 365
    quality of ties 365
    returns of social capital 239–40
    status attainment model 68
    strength of ties 365
    strong ties 365
    United States 364–79
stereotyping 332–3
stratification hierarchies 5
stratification research 65–6
strength-of-position hypothesis 139, 143,
    153–4
strength of ties *see also* strong ties; weak ties
    barriers to access 258
    job searches, effect of social capital on 112
    position generators 52, 54, 60–3
    Resilient Communities Project in British
        Columbia, Canada 257–60, 267–9,
        273, 276–7, 279
    social activities 257
    status attainment 365
    strength-of-position hypothesis 139, 143,
        153–4
    strength-of-weak ties hypotheses 135–6,
        139–41, 143–4, 154
strength-of-weak ties hypotheses 135–6,
    139–41, 143–4, 154
strong ties
    barriers to access 258
    closed networks 257–8
    definition 257
    economic development 260

gender 378
Hungary, application of position generator
    in 394, 402
long-term relationships 260
reciprocity 258
    Resilient Communities Project in British
        Columbia, Canada 259–61, 267–8,
        274, 276–7
    rural communities 260
    status attainment 365
    trust 260
    United States 378
structural mobility effect 87
structuralism theory 87
students 411
surplus value, capital as 3, 4
Survey of Social Networks of the Dutch
    (SSND) 30–9
    analysis 71–7
    cultural and economic capital of
        occupations 89
    distribution of responses 32
    exchange-type name
        generator/interpreter 30–1, 39,
        45–8
    methods, data and measurements 68–71
    Mokken-scaling analyses 33–4, 45–8
    name generator/interpreter 37
    occupations 30–2, 89
    position generator 30–9, 79–80
    prestige 42
    resource generator 38, 39
    voluntary associations 192–204
symbolic capital 82

Taiwan *see also* personnel managers in
        Taiwan, social capital of
    contact diaries 52–64
    job searches, effect of social capital on 108
    position generators 52–64
Tardos R 6, 8, 10, 16, 19, 24, 386
telephone usage, rise in 323–4
television viewing, rise in 311, 322–4, 326
tenure in job 119, 125–6, 248
theoretical grounding of social capital 3–4
theoretical developments 5–8
Tigges, LM 368
Tindall, DB 10, 22, 303
Toronto security industry 285
trade associations 237
traditional values 314–15
Treiman, DJ 118
trust
    black poor, inefficacious job referral
        networks among 170–2, 175–7, 179
    civic participation 22, 209, 221, 223–5,
        237, 261, 315, 317–18

trust (*cont.*)
  definition of social capital 21
  diversity 210–12
  Hong Kong, marriage and gender in 348
  Internet 211, 221, 223–5
  Japan 221, 223–5
  job seekers 170–2, 175
  marriage and gender 348
  neighbourhood togetherness 317–18
  political trust 209
  Resilient Communities Project in British
    Columbia, Canada 261
  strong ties 260–1
  voluntary associations 187–8, 194, 198,
    203, 205, 262

Ulaanbaatar, Mongolia, structure of
    inequality in 380–93
  access to resources 382–6
  age 388–90
  background 380–1
  class 385
  diversity of social resources 380,
    386–91
  education 383, 384–5, 388, 390, 391–3
  gender 23–4, 383–93
  homophily principle 384
  income 383, 385, 390–1
  informal economic activities 382–4
  information-seeking behaviour 381–2
  lamas, ties with 381
  location 383, 391, 393
  market economy, effects of transition
    to 380–5, 392
  marriage 388–90
  occupations 380, 381–8, 390–2
  position generator 380, 381–6
  prestige 381–2
  professions, women in 384
  regression analysis 383, 389
  research methodology 381
  urban centres, moves to 385–6, 393
  variables 384
  voluntary organizations, participation
    in 392–3
United States, status attainment in
    the 364–79 *see also* black poor,
    inefficacious job referral networks
    among
  African-Americans 367–8, 373–8
  age 372, 373
  Allegheny, Pennsylvania, civic participation
    in 22, 312–28
  civic participation 22, 237, 261, 310–28
  class 371
  control variables 372–3
  current status 372

  education 371
  ethnicity and race 365–6, 368–79
  gender 368, 372, 373, 376–9
  high prestige 370
  homophily principle 372–3, 375, 377–9
  inequality 367–8
  intergenerational attainment 372, 375
  job searches 108, 369–71, 379
  language 378
  Latinos/Hispanics 368, 373–8
  Miami-Dade, Florida, civic participation
    in 22, 312–28
  mobilization of social capital 379
  name generator 370
  occupation 370–2
  political returns 6–7
  position generator 370, 379
  prestige 370
  prior status 370–1, 376
  research
    data 368–70
    measurement 370–3
    methods 368–73
    model and hypothesis 368–9
    results 373–7
  strong ties 378
  supervision in jobs 371–2
  variables 370–4
  voluntary associations, participation
    in 6–7
  weak ties 378
urban areas *see also* Chinese urbanites,
    formation of social capital among
use of resources
  access-leads-to-more-use hypotheses 140,
    147–50, 155
  achieved-access-through-weak-ties-leads-
    to-more-use hypothesis 140–1,
    148
  higher-number-leads-to-more-use
    hypothesis 140, 147–9, 155
  Hungary, application of position generator
    in 404–13
  intensity 40, 155, 187–8
  political participation in British Columbia,
    Canada 288
  Resilient Communities Project in British
    Columbia, Canada 278
Uslaner, EM 232–3

van der Gaag, MPJ 8, 12–13, 18, 21, 79, 398
Vaughn, C 66, 239
Villemez, WJ 239
Völker, B 5–6, 8, 15–16, 19, 21, 41, 135, 137,
    138, 143
voluntary associations
  access 189–90, 195–7

academic achievement 188
age 192, 195
analytical strategy 198
causality, direction of 197–8, 204
civic participation 22, 188, 231–2, 237,
    244–6, 261, 309–10
control 186–7
data and methods 192–8
density of networks 186–7, 190, 194, 203
diversity of networks 192, 235–7, 294
duration of contact 187–8, 194
education 188, 191, 198–9, 201, 203, 205
expressive participation 190–1, 192, 193,
    198–202
family ties 195, 200–1, 203–4
friends and acquaintances, access
    through 195, 198, 204
gender 22–3, 192, 201–2, 203, 237
    causes of social capital 238
    Internet, Japan in 22, 231–2
    political participation in British
        Columbia, Canada 302–3
    Resilient Communities Project in British
        Columbia, Canada 262, 271
group interests 186
heterogeneity 187, 198–9
homophily principle 198
human capital 191
identification with community 185
income 201, 205
industrial sectors, institutionalization
    of 237–8
inequality 186, 188–90, 199–200, 392–3
instrumental participation 190–2, 193,
    197–201
intensity 187–8
Internet, civic engagement and gender in
    Japan 22, 231–2
job searches 114, 119–20, 188, 264
learning 186–7
managers in security industry 234–5
marriage 195, 197
measures
    access to resources 195–7
    network cohesion, of 193–5
mental and physical health 188
mobilization of social capital 187, 189
Netherlands 21
networks 185–205
norm enforcement 186–7
personnel managers in Taiwan, social
    capital of 244–6, 248–54
political participation in British Columbia,
    Canada 294, 301–3
politics 6–7, 188, 190, 294, 301–3
position generator 21, 22, 193, 234
prestige

highest accessed 189
mean prestige accessed 195, 197
range accessed 189
Taiwan 252–3
recruitment 188–9
regression analysis of membership 198,
    199–202
religion 187, 188, 192, 198–9, 203
requests to join 190
Resilient Communities Project in
    British Columbia, Canada 262,
    266–7, 270–1
resources
    access to 188–91, 195–7, 199–200,
        204–5
    characteristics of 185
    diversity 192
    income 201
results of analyses 198–202
returns of social capital 240
rural areas 262, 266–7, 270
sampling procedure 192–3
security industry, managers in 234–5
size of networks 189–90
social cohesion 185, 186–8, 190, 193–5,
    197–9, 204
social control 186–7
social support 188
solidarity 186
sources of social capital 8
Survey of Social Networks of the Dutch
    (SSND) 192–204
Taiwan 244–6, 248–54
theory and hypotheses 186–8
timing of membership 197–8
trade associations 237
trust 187–8, 194, 198, 203, 205, 262
types of associations 193
Ulaanbaatar, Mongolia, structure of
    inequality in 392–3
United States 6–7

Wacquant, LJD 159
wages *see* income
weak ties
    achieved-access-through-weak-ties-leads-
        to-more-use hypothesis 140–1,
        148
    definition 257
    economic development 260
    gender 378
    Hungary, application of position generator
        in 394–5, 402
    reciprocity 258
    Resilient Communities Project in British
        Columbia, Canada 257, 259, 260,
        273–8

weak ties (*cont.*)
  returns of social capital 239
  rural communities 273–5
  social cohesion 258
  social mobility 258
  United States 378
wealth 8, 400–1, 413–14
Weber, Max 190
Weeden, KA 86
Weesie, HM 33
Wellman, B 231, 303
Westcott, J 344, 345, 363
Wilson, J 187, 190, 191

Wilson, William Julius 157, 158
women *see* gender
Woolcock, M 14, 260–1, 273
work *see* occupation
Wright, DO 86

Yamagishi, T 211
Yamanashi prefecture, Japan *see* Internet,
  civic engagement and gender
  in Japan

Zeisel, H 407
Zurcher, LA 284